Correct Writing FIFTH EDITION

Fifth Edition

Correct Writing

Eugenia Butler
University of Georgia

Mary Ann Hickman
Gainesville College

Lalla Overby
Gainesville College

D.C. Heath and Company
Lexington, Massachusetts ▪ Toronto

Acquisitions Editor: Paul Smith
Developmental Editor: Holt Johnson
Production Editor: Renée Mary
Production Coordinator: Lisa Arcese
Text Permissions Editor: Margaret Roll

Cover Design: Hannus Design Associates

Published simultaneously in Canada.

Printed in the United States of America.

International Standard Book Number (Student Edition): 0-669-20474-9.

International Standard Book Number (Instructor's Edition): 0-669-24714-6.

10 9 8 7 6

To the Instructor

College instructors who find it necessary to return to the basics of written Standard English grammar will find *Correct Writing*, Fifth Edition, a versatile and comprehensive aid in teaching grammar, punctuation, mechanics, and diction.

Correct writing is a distinctive combination of the best features of a grammar and composition text, a workbook of exercises, and a convenient reference handbook. The body of grammatical information meets the needs of instructors who must deal with this area before moving on to the teaching of composition and rhetoric. Brief but lucid definitions of terms are provided, along with careful explanations of the principles involved in sentence structure. These definitions and explanations come at the earliest mention of a term, so that instructors need not continue their discussions of a grammatical principle before students have a clear understanding of what they are being told. Another particularly convenient feature of *Correct Writing* is its cross-reference system through which a brief definition refers the reader to lengthier and more detailed discussions of the topic in other chapters.

Several exercises follow each chapter of text, with sentences designed to illustrate the specific point of the chapter, giving students the immediate opportunity to test their knowledge of the material just studied. Whenever possible, the sentences in these exercises are somewhat simplified to make them more obviously illustrative of the grammatical principles involved. Explanation of these principles is presented to the student in the simplest of terms, yet is far more extensive than those in other workbooks. Though discussion of many aspects of grammar is not intended to be exhaustive, it is always sufficiently thorough for a student to grasp and to learn without the instructor's having to spend classroom hours in further explanation.

In this edition the instructor will find enlarged lists of sentence elements that are especially troublesome for students. These include a complete listing of pronouns and their cases; discussions of the problems of tense, voice, and mood of verbs; incorrect modifiers of all kinds; and comprehensive discussions of punctuation and mechanics.

A strong aspect of *Correct Writing* is that rules of punctuation are given in individual chapters and relate to the particular elements of sentence structure under discussion. When students reach Chapter 19, devoted exclusively to punctuation, and Chapter 20, devoted to mechanics, they will already have learned most of the rules in these chapters. Instead of an arbitrary listing of rules to be memorized, these chapters then serve as reinforcement and review.

They also serve as quick references to any given questions on punctuation or mechanics.

An unusually helpful section of *Correct Writing* is the Glossary of Faulty Diction, which appears in Chapter 22. Young people nowadays are constantly exposed, through television and other media, to trite, slangy, and ungrammatical usage. With this fact in mind, the authors make careful distinctions between informal, stale, or incorrect written expressions and those that are acceptable as Standard English. The Glossary has been updated for this edition, with new entries added and outdated terms removed. Arranged in alphabetical order, it is another handy reference.

A recent addition to *Correct Writing* is a complete Glossary of Grammatical Terms, which incorporates simple and understandable examples in sentences that clarify and enhance the definitions. Also added recently is a section of "Paragraph Tests," which has a strongly practical application. These are whole, integrated paragraphs like those students encounter in their everyday reading. Within the paragraphs are grammatical and punctuation errors of all the kinds studied in this book. They provide a realistic method of determining whether a student has learned to be alert to unexpected errors in his everyday reading and writing.

New to this edition is a section of Sentence-Combining exercises. Most college instructors have found a consistent weakness in students' ability to use subordination and to reduce wordiness in order to give texture and variety to their writing, as well as a perspective on the relative importance of several ideas within a single sentence. These exercises will give strong additional practice in this particular area.

One central point which should emerge through a student's careful use of this text is that the study of grammar and sentence elements is a practical means of improving communication and understanding. *Correct Writing* will prove a valuable aid in the instructor's goal to provide that improvement.

The following individuals generously helped us with their suggestions for this edition: Carol Eiten, Carl Sandburg College; Sally Hanson, University of South Dakota; Kaye W. Jeffery, Utah Valley Community College; Thomas A. Mozola, Macomb Community College; Karen K. Reid, Midwestern State University; and Cecilia M. Russo, Saint John's University.

Eugenia Butler
Mary Ann Hickman
Lalla Overby

To the Student

This book is a combination textbook, workbook, and reference handbook. It contains a great deal of information in the various chapters that precede the exercises. It is a workbook in which you will be able to write your answers concerning grammatical principles that you have just studied. When you have worked all the exercises as well as the Review and Achievement Tests, you will still have a convenient reference handbook in which you can check points of grammar, usage, punctuation, and mechanics whenever you need to. The Glossary of Faulty Diction and the Glossary of Grammatical Terms will be of special help to you in questions of usage and in providing familiarity with grammatical terminology that you are likely to encounter.

Working conscientiously through the chapters and exercises of *Correct Writing* will put you well on your way to a mastery of grammar and usage, which in turn will help you to write and speak accurately and effectively.

Contents

Diagnostic Test

In the following sentences identify the part of speech of each *italicized* word by writing one of the following numbers in the space at the right:

1 if it is a *noun*,	**5** if it is an *adverb*,
2 if it is a *pronoun*,	**6** if it is a *preposition*,
3 if it is a *verb*,	**7** if it is a *conjunction*,
4 if it is an *adjective*,	**8** if it is an *interjection*.

1. *Have* you *taken* Anthropology 101 yet?   _____

2. The choir sang *beautifully* today.   _____

3. *None* of the boys brought their sleeping bags.   _____

4. *Either* you go to the grocery store, *or* you cook supper.   _____

5. *Hey*, that is not fair.   _____

6. *Where* is Yosemite National Park?   _____

7. *We* won the homecoming game despite bad weather.   _____

8. The expert's *prediction* did not come true.   _____

9. Once in the house, the curious kitten looked *around* the room.   _____

10. *Both* Matt *and* Jimmy played football in college.   _____

11. Everyone agrees that Kristen is *lovely*.   _____

12. Mary Rose baked *me* a birthday cake.   _____

13. A *college* education opens many doors.   _____

14. I finished my *test* before anyone else.   _____

15. On our way to work *we* passed three car wrecks.   _____

16. *Beyond* the house is the garage.   _____

17. *No!* I really do not want another piece of cake.   _____

18. *Only* three students attended Dr. Ruff's seminar.   _____

19. The itinerary for the summer was mailed *yesterday*.   _____

20. T. S. Eliot's poetry *reflects* the spiritual emptiness of the modern world.   _____

21. Julia Child is best known *for* her French cookbooks.   _____

22. Kay and I *went* rock climbing in the Pisgah National Forest. _____

23. The Blue Ridge Mountains are *part* of the Appalachian Mountain chain. _____

24. His attitude *about* money is shallow and immature. _____

25. Read one of Amanda Cross's *or* Andrew Greeley's mysteries. _____

Each of the following sentences either contains an error in grammar or is correct. Indicate the error or the correctness by writing one of the following numbers in the space at the space at the right:

    1 if the case of the pronoun is incorrect,
    2 if the subject and verb do not agree,
    3 if a pronoun and its antecedent do not agree,
    4 if an adjective or an adverb is used incorrectly,
    5 if the sentence is correct.

26. I know he bought his mother and I a present. _____

27. A few members of the club is coming over tonight. _____

28. Paul's family has always been real nice to us. _____

29. Everyone in the room wore a mask. _____

30. Each of the students waited their turn in the ticket line. _____

31. Me and Jess studied all night for our chemistry final. _____

32. Do you think that she will mind me tagging along? _____

33. Neither the students nor the teacher are attending the rock performance next week. _____

34. The media proved almost unanimous in its support of the prime minister's decision. _____

35. Everybody agrees that Shelby takes his interest in race cars serious. _____

36. I believe that almost everyone except Ellen and I has been to hear the Rolling Stones at some time in her life. _____

37. The class agrees that Mr. Field's frequent use of maps clarify his lectures. _____

38. Stan says that the waves are some higher this afternoon that they were this morning. _____

39. Mr. Hanks as well as his son is interested in UFO's. _____

40. Neither of the children were old enough to change trains alone at Sydney Square. _____

41. Last week each of the chefs in the restaurant prepared their favorite recipe. _____

42. The priest who married he and Kathleen still has family in Ireland. _____

43. Just tell whomever answers the telephone that we will be at least ten minutes late for dinner. _____

44. Dan is one of those collectors who is especially interested in folk art. _____

45. During the first quarter her one aim was to do good enough to keep her scholarship. _____

46. I have heard that everyone taking ceramics must buy their own supplies. _____

47. The data verified by the expert witness is essential to the prosecutor's argument. _____

48. All of us feel badly that Andy is going to have to miss the trip to Six Flags. _____

49. Standing behind Wallace and me on the platform was a large group of Japanese tourists. _____

50. If a person wants to vote in the primary, they must register by Friday. _____

Each of the following sentences either contains an error in sentence structure or is correct. Indicate the error or correctness by writing one of the following numbers in the space at the right:

    1 if the sentence contains a *dangling modifier,*
    2 if the sentence contains a *misplaced modifier,*
    3 if the sentence contains a *faulty reference of a pronoun,*
    4 if the sentence contains *faulty parallelism,*
    5 if the sentence is correct.

51. Driving to work this morning, the fog was very thick. _____

52. Either we need to trade the car or have its transmission repaired. _____

53. I remember that the cat hardly slept anywhere except in its basket by the fireplace. _____

54. We rented a trailer to carry the table to Memphis, which seemed the practical thing to do. _____

55. I didn't wake you when I came in on purpose. _____

56. Although the terrier was wearing a collar, it looked cold, hungry, and it was surely lost. _____

57. To appreciate Susan's wall hangings, there must first be an appreciation of the craft of weaving. _____

58. Pat often shops at the health-food store because she believes that it will lower her cholesterol. _____

59. Oil is an exhaustible resource, which continues to be of deep concern around the world. _____

60. Mr. Miller has promised to at the very first of January prune the hedges. _____

61. Lucy was opposed and appalled by the decorator's suggestion that the ceiling be painted black. _____

62. When reading in bed, it is often hard to stay awake. _____

63. In the play the queen's role is far more significant than her daughter. _____

64. I've nearly seen all the films that Steven Spielberg has directed. _____

65. Rounding the curve, the truck ran almost off the pavement. _____

66. I don't know of another jogger who persists at it as faithfully as Justin. _____

67. Meredith and I were tired, discouraged, and we were very hungry. _____

68. Although we looked everywhere for bread and cheese, we only found half a box of stale crackers. _____

69. While trying to find my sweater, my camera case was lying there in the drawer. _____

70. Anyone who cuts Dr. Haynes's class will find themselves on probation. _____

71. By measuring the distance from our front steps to the sidewalk, it was exactly fifty feet. _____

72. Waiting impatiently in the pouring rain, the bus finally stopped for Suzanne and me. _____

73. I've often thought that it would be a pleasant world if everyone could learn English grammar in your sleep. _____

74. The woman who had vanished suddenly reappeared. _____

75. After my eyes had grown accustomed to the dark, I began to recognize my surroundings and hoping that I could find my way home. _____

Each of the following sentences contains an error in punctuation or mechanics or is correct. Indicate the error or the correctness by writing one of the following numbers in the space at the right:

1 if a comma has been omitted,
2 if a semicolon has been omitted,
3 if an apostrophe has been omitted,
4 if quotation marks have been omitted,
5 if the sentence is correct.

76. Though he was displeased with my behavior Dad let me go with the others to the movie. _____

77. Havent you ever been to San Francisco, Mark? _____

78. We had hoped to drive today to Minneapolis however, because of this snow we had better wait until Tuesday. _____

79. Who's going to keep the baby while you're out of town? _____

80. Henry I have told you three times to go to bed. _____

81. Martha glared at Jack and said, You are going to make me late for church. _____

82. I asked all five boys to come for supper but only three were able to make it. _____

83. I have taken my final exam and am anxiously awaiting news of the outcome. _____

84. Loretta Lynn's concert starts at seven we plan to be there by five. _____

85. When are you planning to give the cat its supper? _____

86. Mr. Thompson I heartily agree with you. _____

87. The angry disconsolate fans were furious with the umpire. _____

88. The name of the song, Don, is Blue Bayou. _____

89. Wheres the key to my locker? _____

90. Edgar Allan Poe's short story The Purloined Letter set the standard for the modern detective story. _____

91. While taking a shower I heard the phone ring, but I could not answer it. _____

92. The Tylers have gone to South Carolina for a visit with their parents. _____

93. Robert Frosts poem "The Road Not Taken" is quite frequently quoted. _____

94. Nathan has found a new way to waste time: hes learning sand sculpture. _____

95. Be sure to be on time tonight, Harry we begin rehearsal promptly at six o'clock. _____

96. Katherine has the feminine lead in *Othello* she will be a good Desdemona. _____

97. Kit's favorite baseball player is Steve Bedrosian, sometimes known as Bedrock. _____

98. But, Dr. Wright, it's not easy to make all *A*s. _____

99. The time has come I'm sure you agree to leave for the airport. _____

100. Maybe we should go in separate cars, said Frank. _____

The Parts of Speech

Our own language is one of the most fascinating subjects that we can investigate, and those of us who speak and write English can find pleasure in seeking to understand its various aspects. The concern of this book is Standard English and its use in contemporary writing. The study and description of Standard English, based on the thoughtful use of language by educated people, provide standards for correct writing. Although the English language is flexible and continually changing, it is possible to follow certain principles and to observe certain characteristics of usage which can make grammar a relatively exact study and one which can widen the scope of the individual in a satisfying way.

An understanding of the accurate and effective use of English is important not only as a means of communication but also as a vital element of creative thought. Because words are used to formulate conscious thought, precise grammatical usage promotes clear thinking and encourages logical and systematic transmission of ideas.

Knowledge of Standard English and its acceptable forms is basic to the education of all college students. Learning grammatical terms is an essential first step toward understanding what is correct and what is incorrect in the writing of English prose. The best place to begin this learning of terms is with the various elements that make up a sentence, elements called **parts of speech.** Many words may function as more than one part of speech, and any word's designation as a particular part of speech depends entirely upon its use within its sentence. (See Section 1i as well as the "Glossary of Grammatical Terms" at the end of this book.) The names of the eight parts of speech are as follows:

noun	verb	conjunction
pronoun	adverb	interjection
adjective	preposition	

■ 1a Noun

A **noun** (from Latin *nomen,* name) is the name of a person, place, thing, or idea. All nouns are either proper nouns or common nouns. A **proper noun** is the name of a particular person, place, or thing and is spelled with a capital letter:

John F. Kennedy	London, England
California	The Washington Monument
The Vatican	O'Keefe Junior High School

A **common noun** is the name of a class of persons, places, things, or ideas and is not capitalized:

girl	park	honesty
teacher	street	disgust
student	dog	friendship
home	automobile	poverty

Nouns may also be classified as **individual** or **collective. Collective** nouns name groups of persons, places, or things that sometimes function as units:

flock	team	the rich
jury	dozen	club

Finally, nouns may be classified as **concrete** or **abstract. The concrete** noun names a person, place, or thing that can be perceived by one of the five senses. It can be seen, felt, smelled, heard, or tasted. Here are some examples of concrete nouns:

door	woman	scream
dress	city	snow
tree	odor	museum

An **abstract** noun is the name of a quality, condition, action, or idea. The following are examples of abstract nouns:

beauty	truth	kindness
fear	loneliness	campaign
dismissal	hatred	courtesy

A noun is said to belong to the **nominative,** the **objective,** or the **possessive case,** depending upon its function within a sentence. Subjects are in the nominative case (The *truck* stopped), objects are in the objective case (He saw the *parade*), and nouns showing possession are in the possessive case (That car is *John's*). As you can see, there is no difference in form between nouns in the nominative and the objective cases. The possessive case, however, changes a noun's form. (See Chapter 11 for a thorough discussion of case.)

A noun may be **singular** or **plural,** forming its plural generally by the addition of *-s* or *-es* to the end of the singular form (*girl, girls; potato, potatoes*).

Nouns, together with pronouns and other words or expressions that function as nouns, are sometimes called **substantives.**

■ 1b Pronoun

A **pronoun** (from Latin *pro*, for, and *nomen*, name) is a word used in place of a noun. A pronoun usually refers to a noun or other substantive already mentioned, which is called its **antecedent** (from Latin *ante*, before, and *cedere*, to go). Most pronouns have antecedents, but some do not.

Pronouns are divided into eight categories:

PERSONAL PRONOUNS: I, you, he, she, it, we, they, and their inflected forms (*See table below.*)

DEMONSTRATIVE PRONOUNS: this, that, these, those

INDEFINITE PRONOUNS: all, any, anyone, anything, each, everyone, everything, either, neither, several, some, someone, something

INTERROGATIVE PRONOUNS: what, which, who, whom, whose

RELATIVE PRONOUNS: which, who, whom, whose, that

REFLEXIVE PRONOUNS: myself, yourself, himself, herself, itself, ourselves, yourselves, themselves

INTENSIVE PRONOUNS: *myself*, you *yourself*, he *himself*, she *herself*, (the dog, the book, the car) *itself*, we *ourselves*, you *yourselves*, they *themselves*

RECIPROCAL PRONOUNS: each other, one another

The personal pronouns have differing forms depending upon whether they are subjects (*I* will help Mr. Curtis) or objects (Gene told *him* the plan) or show possession (The red coat is *hers*). These differences in form, which are seen only in the possessive case of nouns, occur in all three cases (*nominative*, *objective*, and *possessive*) of these pronouns.

Personal pronouns, like nouns, are singular and plural, but their plurals are irregularly formed: I, *we*; he, *they*; she, *they*; it, *they*; etc. The following table shows the various forms of the personal pronouns:

Singular		
	Nominative	Objective	Possessive
1st person	I	me	my, mine
2nd person	you	you	your, yours
3rd person	he, she, it	him, her, it	his, her, hers, its

Plural		
	Nominative	Objective	Possessive
1st person	we	us	our, ours
2nd person	you	you	your, yours
3rd person	they	them	their, theirs

■ 1c Adjective

An **adjective** (from Latin *adjectivum*, something that is added) modifies, describes, limits, or adds to the meaning of a noun or pronoun (*strange, lovely, three, French, those*). In other words, adjectives modify substantives. The articles *the, a,* and *an* are adjectives. Nouns in the possessive case (*Martha's* book, the *cat's* whiskers) and some possessive forms of the personal pronouns are used as adjectives:

my	our
your	your
his, her, its	their

Many demonstrative, indefinite, and interrogative forms may be used as either pronouns or adjectives:

DEMONSTRATIVE: this, that, these, those

INDEFINITE: each, any, either, neither, some, all, both, every, many, most

INTERROGATIVE: which, what, whose

When one of these words appears before a noun or other substantive, describing it or adding to its meaning (*this* cake, *those* gloves, *any* person, *some* food, *which* dress), it is an adjective. When the word stands in the place of a noun (*Those* are pretty roses), it is, of course, a pronoun.

Adjectives formed from proper nouns are called **proper adjectives** and are spelled with a capital letter **(German, Christian, Shakespearean).**

■ 1d Verb

A **verb** (from Latin *verbum*, word) is a word used to state or ask something and usually expresses an action (*spoke, tells, ran, argued, fights*) or a state of being (*is, seemed, existed, appears*). As its Latin origin indicates, the verb is *the* word in the sentence, for every sentence must have a verb, either expressed or understood.

Transitive and Intransitive Verbs

A verb is called **transitive** if its action is directed toward some receiver, which may be the object of the verb or even its subject. (*David flew the plane,* or *The plane was flown by David.* Whether *plane* is the subject or object of the verb, the fact remains that David flew the plane, making *plane* in both sentences the receiver of the verb's action.)

Note: The term *action* should not be misinterpreted as always involving physical activity. The so-called "action" of a verb may not refer to a physical action at all: Mr. Lee *considered* the plan, Amanda *believed* Frank's story, Louise *wants* a new car. The verbs *considered, believed,* and *wants* are transitive verbs; and their objects *plan, story,* and *car* are receivers of their "action," even though there is no physical action involved.

A verb is called **intransitive** if its action is not directed toward some receiver. (*Lightning strikes. Mother is ill.*) Most verbs may be either transitive or intransitive, simply depending on whether or not a receiver of the verb's action is present in the sentence: *Lightning strikes tall trees* (*strikes* is transitive because *trees* is its object). *Lightning strikes suddenly* (*strikes* is intransitive because no receiver of its action is present). The action is complete without an object.

Linking Verbs

There is a special group of intransitive verbs that make a statement not by expressing action but by indicating a state of being or a condition. These verbs are called **linking verbs** because their function is to link the subject of a sentence with a noun, pronoun, or other substantive that identifies it or with an adjective that describes it. A subject and a linking verb cannot function together as a complete sentence without the help of the substantive or adjective needed to complete the thought; for example, in the sentence *Dorothy is my sister* the word *sister* is necessary to complete the sentence, and it identifies *Dorothy*, the subject. In the sentence *Dorothy is vigorous* the word *vigorous* is necessary, and it describes the subject.

The most common linking verb is the verb *to be* in all its forms (see table on pages 8–9), but any verb that expresses a state of being and is followed by a noun or an adjective identifying or describing the subject is a linking verb. Following is a list of some of the most commonly used linking verbs:

appear	look	smell
become	remain	sound
feel	seem	taste*
grow		

You will notice that those verbs referring to states of being perceived through the five senses are included in the list: *look, feel, smell, sound,* and *taste*. (Sally *looks* happy, I *feel* chilly, The coffee *smells* good, The ticking of the clock *sounded* loud, The plum pudding *tastes* spicy.)

Active and Passive Voice

Transitive verbs are said to be in the **active voice** or the **passive voice**. **Voice** is the form of a verb that indicates whether the subject of the sentence performs the action or is the receiver of the action of the verb. If the subject performs the action, the verb is in the *active voice* (*Andy ate soup for lunch today*). If the subject receives the action, the verb is in the *passive voice* (*Soup was eaten by Andy for lunch today*).

Tense

Tense is the form a verb takes in order to express the time of an action or a state of being, as in these examples: *Helen walks* **(present tense);** *Helen walked* **(past tense).** These two tenses, present and past, change the verb's simple form to

---

*These verbs are not exclusively linking verbs; they may also be used in an active sense, possibly having objects, as in the following:

The dog cautiously *smelled* the food in its bowl.
We *looked* everywhere for the lost key.
Sharon *felt* the warmth of the log fire across the room.
Nick *tasted* the chowder and then added salt.

show the time of the verb's action. The other four of the six principal tenses found in English verbs are formed through the use of **auxiliary** (helping) verb forms like the following:

am	was	have
are	were	has
is	will	had

The use of these auxiliary verbs creates **verb phrases** (groups of related words that function as single parts of speech). These verb phrases enable the writer to express time and time relationships far beyond those found in the simple present and past forms: She *has gone* to the office; Maggie *will ride* with me; He *had expected* to win the prize; I *am planning* a trip. Verb phrases are also created by the combination of verbs and words like *must, can,* and *do,* often called modal auxiliaries: I *can walk* to class in five minutes; You *must finish* your dinner; *Do* you *have* the time?

Conjugation of Verbs

Showing all forms of a verb in all its tenses is called **conjugation.** Any verb may be conjugated if its **principal parts** are known. These are (1) the first person singular, present tense, (2) the first person singular, past tense, (3) the past participle. (The **participle** is a verbal form that must always be accompanied by an auxiliary verb when it is used to create one of the verb tenses.)

The principal parts of the verb *to call* are (1) *call,* (2) *called,* (3) *called.* The first two of these provide the basic forms of the simple tenses; the third is used with the auxiliary verbs to form verb phrases for the other tenses. The conjugation in the **indicative mood** (that form used for declarative sentences, which make a statement, or interrogative sentences, which ask a question) of the verb *to call* is given below:

ACTIVE VOICE	
Present tense	
Singular	Plural
1. I call	We call
2. You call	You call
3. He, she, it calls	They call
Past tense	
1. I called	We called
2. You called	You called
3. He, she, it called	They called
Future tense	
1. I will (shall) call	We will (shall) call
2. You will call	You will call
3. He, she, it will call	They will call

Present perfect tense	
1. I have called	We have called
2. You have called	You have called
3. He, she, it has called	They have called

Past perfect tense	
1. I had called	We had called
2. You had called	You had called
3. He, she, it had called	They had called

Future perfect tense	
1. I will (shall) have called	We will (shall) have called
2. You will have called	You will have called
3. He, she, it will have called	They will have called

PASSIVE VOICE

Present tense	
1. I am called	We are called
2. You are called	You are called
3. He, she, it is called	They are called

Past tense	
1. I was called	We were called
2. You were called	You were called
3. He, she, it was called	They were called

Future tense	
1. I will (shall) be called	We will (shall) be called
2. You will be called	You will be called
3. He, she, it will be called	They will be called

Present perfect tense	
1. I have been called	We have been called
2. You have been called	You have been called
3. He, she, it has been called	They have been called

Past perfect tense	
1. I had been called	We had been called
2. You had been called	You had been called
3. He, she, it had been called	They had been called

Future perfect tense	
1. I will (shall) have been called	We will (shall) have been called
2. You will have been called	You will have been called
3. He, she, it will have been called	They will have been called

Note: You have probably noticed that in the future and future perfect tenses the auxiliary verb *shall* is used as an alternate to *will* in the first persons singular and plural. Traditionally, written English has required *shall*, but contemporary grammarians now suggest that the distinction need be made only rarely and that *will* may be used throughout a conjugation. For emphasis, however, *shall* may occasionally be needed, especially to express strong determination or invitation:

> We *shall* overcome!
>
> *Shall* we dance?

Progressive Tenses

To express an action or state in progress either at the time of speaking or at the time spoken of, forms of the auxiliary verb *to be* are combined with the present participle (see Chapter 4, Section C) as follows:

Progressive present tense	
1. I am calling	We are calling
2. You are calling	You are calling
3. He, she, it is calling	They are calling
Progressive past tense	
1. I was calling	We were calling
2. You were calling	You were calling
3. He, she, it was calling	They were calling

This process may be continued through the various tenses of the active voice, as indicated below:

PROGRESSIVE FUTURE TENSE: I will (shall) be calling, etc.

PROGRESSIVE PRESENT PERFECT TENSE: I have been calling, etc.

PROGRESSIVE PAST PERFECT TENSE: I had been calling, etc.

PROGRESSIVE FUTURE PERFECT TENSE: I will (shall) have been calling, etc.

In the passive voice, the progressive is generally used only in the simple present and past tenses:

PROGRESSIVE PRESENT TENSE: I am being called, etc.

PROGRESSIVE PAST TENSE: I was being called, etc.

In the remaining tenses of the passive voice, the progressive forms — though feasible — become awkward (I will be being called, I have been being called, etc.).

Auxiliary Verbs *To Be and To Have*

As you have seen, the verbs *to be* and *to have* are used to form certain tenses of all verbs. Following are the conjugations of these two auxiliary verbs in the indicative mood, active voice:

The principal parts of *to be* are (1) *am*, (2) *was*, and (3) *been*.

Present tense	
Singular	Plural
1. I am	We are
2. You are	You are
3. He, she, it is	They are
Past tense	
1. I was	We were
2. You were	You were
3. He, she, it was	They were
Future tense	
1. I will (shall) be	We will (shall) be
2. You will be	You will be
3. He, she, it will be	They will be
Present perfect tense	
1. I have been	We have been
2. You have been	You have been
3. He, she, it has been	They have been
Past perfect tense	
1. I had been	We had been
2. You had been	You had been
3. He, she, it had been	They had been
Future perfect tense	
1. I will (shall) have been	We will (shall) have been
2. You will have been	You will have been
3. He, she, it will have been	They will have been

The principal parts of the verb *to have* are (1) *have,* (2) *had,* and (3) *had.*

Present tense	
Singular	Plural
1. I have	We have
2. You have	You have
3. He, she, it has	They have
Past tense	
1. I had	We had
2. You had	You had
3. He, she, it had	They had
Future tense	
1. I will (shall) have	We will (shall) have
2. You will have	You will have
3. He, she, it will have	They will have

Present perfect tense	
1. I have had	We have had
2. You have had	You have had
3. He, she, it has had	They have had
Past perfect tense	
1. I had had	We had had
2. You had had	You had had
3. He, she, it had had	They had had
Future perfect tense	
1. I will (shall) have had	We will (shall) have had
2. You will have had	You will have had
3. He, she, it will have had	They will have had

Mood

Mood is the form a verb may take to indicate whether it is intended to make a statement, to give a command, or to express a condition contrary to fact. Besides the **indicative** mood shown in the conjugations above, there are the **imperative** and the **subjunctive** moods.

The **imperative** mood is used in giving commands or making requests, as in *TAKE me out to the ball game.* Here *TAKE* is in the imperative mood. The subject of an imperative sentence is *you,* usually understood, but sometimes expressed for the sake of emphasis, as in *You get out of here!*

The **subjunctive** mood is most often used today to express a wish or a condition contrary to fact. In the sentences *I wish I WERE going* and *If I WERE you, I would not go,* the verbs in capitals are in the subjunctive mood.

■ 1e Adverb

An *adverb* (from Latin *ad,* to or toward, and *verbum,* word) usually modifies or adds to the meaning of a verb, an adjective, or another adverb. Sometimes, however, it may be used to modify or qualify a whole phrase or clause, adding to the meaning of an idea that the sentence expresses. The following sentences illustrate the variety of uses of the adverb:

He ran *fast.* [*Fast* modifies the verb *ran.*]

The judges considered the contestants *unusually* brilliant. [*Unusually* modifies the adjective *brilliant.*]

She sang *very* loudly. [*Very* modifies the adverb *loudly.*]

The doves were flying *just* outside gun range. [*Just* modifies either the preposition *outside* or the whole prepositional phrase *outside gun range.*]

He had driven carefully *ever* since he was injured. [*Ever* modifies either the conjunction *since* or the whole clause *since he was injured.*]

Unfortunately, she has encountered rejection everywhere. [*Unfortunately* modifies the whole idea expressed in the sentence and cannot logically be attached to a single word.]

■ 1f Preposition

A **preposition** (from Latin *prae*, before, and *positum*, placed) is a word placed usually before a substantive, called the *object of the preposition*, to show relationship between that object and some other word in the sentence. The combination of a preposition, its object, and any modifiers of the object is called a **prepositional phrase** (*in the mood, on the porch, of human events, toward the beautiful green lake*). You will see how necessary prepositions are to our language when you realize how often you use most of the ones in the group below, which includes some of the most commonly used prepositions:

about	below	except	through
above	beneath	for	throughout
across	beside	from	to
after	besides	in	toward
against	between	into	under
along	beyond	like	underneath
amid	but (meaning	of	until
among	*except*)	off	up
around	by	on	upon
at	concerning	over	with
before	down	past	within
behind	during	since	without

Ordinarily a preposition precedes its object, as its name indicates. Although a sentence ending with a preposition is frequently unemphatic or clumsy, it is in no way contrary to English usage. *She asked what they were cooked in* is better English than *She asked in what they were cooked*.

■ 1g Conjunction

A **conjunction** (from Latin *conjungere*, to join) is a word used to join words or groups of words. There are two kinds of conjunctions: **coordinating conjunctions** and **subordinating conjunctions.**

Coordinating Conjunctions

Coordinating conjunctions join sentence elements of equal rank. In the sentence *She was poor but honest* the conjunction *but* joins the two adjectives *poor* and *honest*. In *She was poor, but she was honest* the conjunction *but* joins the two independent statements *She was poor* and *she was honest*. The common coordinating conjunctions are the following:

and	or	for
but	nor	

Yet in the sense of *but,* and *so* in the sense of *therefore* are also coordinating conjunctions. **Correlative conjunctions,** which are used in pairs (*either . . . or . . . , neither . . . nor . . .*), are coordinating conjunctions also.

Subordinating Conjunctions

Subordinating conjunctions introduce certain subordinate or dependent elements and join them to the main or independent part of the sentence. In *Jack has gone home because he was tired* the subordinating conjunction *because* subordinates the clause that it is part of and joins it to the main part of the sentence, *Jack has gone home.* There are many subordinating conjunctions. Some common ones are the following:

after	as	if
unless	when	while
although	before	since
until	whether	

Note: Words like *however, therefore, nevertheless, moreover, in fact, consequently, hence,* and *accordingly* are essentially adverbs, not conjunctions; they are sometimes called **conjunctive adverbs.**

■ 1h Interjection

An **interjection** (from Latin *inter,* among or between, and *jectum,* thrown) is an exclamatory word like *oh, ouch, please, why, hey* thrown into a sentence or sometimes used alone. An interjection is always grammatically independent of the rest of the sentence. Adjectives, adverbs, and occasionally other parts of speech become interjections when used as independent exclamations (*good! horrible! fine! what! wait!*).

■ 1i Varying Sentence Functions of Words

The introductory paragraphs in this chapter pointed out that there are many words in the English language that may function as more than one part of speech and that the designation of a word as a particular part of speech is dependent upon its function within its own sentence. It will be helpful for you to see a few examples of this assertion. The word *cause,* for instance, may be a noun, as in the sentence *What was the cause of her distress?* or a transitive verb, as in the sentence *Will the rain cause a delay in the baseball game?* The word *fire* may be a noun, a verb, or an adjective, as shown in the following sentences: *The fire at the warehouse was set by an arsonist; John fired the pistol;* and *We had a fire drill at school yesterday.* The word *near* may be an adverb, an adjective, or a preposition, as in the following sentences: *The end of the year is drawing near; I will make my decision in the near future; Our house is near the campus.*

Exercise 1   Nouns and Pronouns

Write in the first blank at the right any *italicized* word that is a noun and in the second any that is a pronoun.

	Noun	**Pronoun**
Example: *Cliff* spent the weekend with *us*.	*Cliff*	*us*

1. *We* used lanterns to explore the cave's water-falls, *underground* streams, *stalagmites,* and other fasci-nating formations.

2. Jeff bought a *house* and had *it redesigned* and renovated.

3. Computer *science* is the study *of* computers *and* their functions.

4. Amy *invited us* to the *party.*

5. *I* did not understand *that question.*

6. *This* is *not* what *Jeremy* ordered.

7. Karla, *who* has no *confi-dence in* Clyde, will not support him.

8. *Both* of his *children* are *in* the play.

9. Did she enjoy *herself* at the *football games*?

10. I can't believe *that* Mr. Jen-kins approved *this.*

11. *She* is a strong *believer* in *positive* thinking.

	Noun	**Pronoun**
12. *Each* community has more *needs* than *it* can meet.	_____	_____
13. *What* is the *name* of the *College's* mascot?	_____	_____
14. *Nearly everyone* enjoys a good *novel*.	_____	_____
15. *Shelley went* camping with *me* last summer.	_____	_____
16. The library sent *me* the *additional material*.	_____	_____
17. She will go with *us* to *New York*.	_____	_____
18. Her *older brother* is *also* a painter.	_____	_____
19. The weather has been *unseasonably* cool all *summer*.	_____	_____
20. *Do you like* spinach *soufflé*?	_____	_____
21. *We* often *visit* a *museum* and have lunch.	_____	_____
22. Bob hurt *himself* yesterday at *soccer practice*.	_____	_____
23. Is *there anything Sue* can help you do?	_____	_____
24. Aunt Ann enjoys walking *on* the *beach* with *us*.	_____	_____
25. The *innkeeper* led *her down* a long hallway.	_____	_____

Exercise 2   Pronouns

In the sentences below identify the *italicized* pronouns as personal, demonstrative, indefinite, relative, interrogative, intensive, or reflexive by writing **P, D, I, Rel, Inter, Inten,** or **Ref** in the space at the right.

Example: *You* should learn to play bridge.   __*P*__

1. Where did you get *this*?   _____

2. How did you hurt *yourself*?   _____

3. *I* am having battery trouble with my car.   _____

4. The realtor will send *you* pictures of our mountain house.   _____

5. *That* is my sister across the street.   _____

6. *Everyone* will be here by eight o'clock.   _____

7. *She* is a woman of influence.   _____

8. The squirrels ate *all* of the pecans.   _____

9. *Who* will be going on the tour?   _____

10. At first *we* understood what the professor was saying.   _____

11. Did Marie order *these*?   _____

12. Yesterday *she* mailed Bobby a surprise package.   _____

13. Tom is older than *he*.   _____

14. It was I *who* was at fault.   _____

15. *Anyone* who knows anything knows that man cannot fly.   _____

16. I cannot go with you *myself*.   _____

17. *Which* of these blouses looks best on me?   _____

18. He did not want *those*.   _____

19. She *herself* said that she was tired.   _____

20. *Who* is going to the mall with Susan?   _____

21. Can you go to Washington with *us*?   _____

22. She applied for the job *which* was advertised in yesterday's paper.   _____

23. Both *he* and Maurine love skiing.   _____

24. *This* is something you can do quickly. _____

25. I cannot do this report by *myself*. _____

Exercise 3   Adjectives and Adverbs

In the following sentences underline once all the adjectives and words used as adjectives except the articles *a, an,* and *the.* Underline all adverbs twice.

Example: Her hair is <u><u>too</u></u> <u>long</u>.

1. Nick and Laura arrived at the summer house quite early.
2. She was unusually quiet tonight.
3. The professor solved the difficult problem quickly.
4. I have been here nearly three months.
5. The realtor showed us a very level piece of land.
6. A mango is a yellowish red tropical fruit with firm skin and a hard stem.
7. Educational and "how-to" videos are becoming increasingly popular.
8. Naquib Mahfouz may be the best-known Arabic writer in the non-Arabic world.
9. Philip has kept yearly journals for the past ten years.
10. Lobster traps make rather unusual and attractive coffee tables.
11. Cindy Lauper is a strangely popular pop singer.
12. Aftershocks following earthquakes are very alarming and frequently cause damage.
13. Chris is the most popular person in the fraternity.
14. At the party he was extremely rude to everyone.
15. I spotted her bright auburn hair immediately.
16. The class always enjoyed Profesor Mallard's wit.
17. Suddenly the long silence was broken.
18. Does the milk taste sour to you?
19. Our crew works well together.
20. Did you see that she looked angry indeed?

Exercise 4   Verbs

In the first column at the right, write the verbs in the following sentences. In the second column write **A** if the verb is in the active voice, **P** if it is in the passive voice. In the last column write **T** if the verb is transitive, **I** if it is intransitive.

	Verb	A/P	T/I
Example: The lake appeared calm yesterday.	*appeared*	*A*	*I*
1. Female entrepreneurs launch more than half of all new businesses.			
2. I do love the movies.			
3. Storytelling is a rare art.			
4. Angie's sweater was ruined in the washing machine.			
5. Many varieties of flowers had been planted in the back yard.			
6. Magnolia trees have long been cherished for their aromatic flower and their shade.			
7. The student council approved two proposals affecting student appeal procedures.			
8. The homecoming parade will assemble on Foundry Street.			
9. The Treaty of Paris of 1783 ended the American Revolution.			
10. The committee will interview the candidates tomorrow.			

	Verb	**A/P**	**T/I**

11. The rain pelted the roof and windows throughout the night. _____ ____ ____

12. Jamie left early this morning. _____ ____ ____

13. I am having guests this weekend. _____ ____ ____

14. The first American coal mine opened in Virginia in 1750. _____ ____ ____

15. My house was painted last summer by my brother. _____ ____ ____

16. Our class was dismissed early. _____ ____ ____

17. She will meet you at the airport. _____ ____ ____

18. Can you join us for a game of bridge? _____ ____ ____

19. Pam's desserts taste delicious. _____ ____ ____

20. The planning committee meets at 10:00 A.M. _____ ____ ____

21. I am happy to stay with little Tom. _____ ____ ____

22. He won a ticket to the concert. _____ ____ ____

23. Tim's car was hit from behind. _____ ____ ____

24. Our class has been given an extra week to complete term papers. _____ ____ ____

25. The attorney for the state urged the court to reverse its decision. _____ ____ ____

Exercise 5 Prepositions

Write the prepositions in the following sentences in the spaces of the first column to the right. Write the objects of the prepositions in the second column. If a sentence contains no preposition, leave the spaces blank.

	Prep.	Object
Example: Study chapters one and two before your next exam.	*before*	*exam*
1. We ate all the Christmas candy except the peppermint sticks.		
2. In the closet you will find your boots.		
3. You cannot come through the window.		
4. Mario is not serious about his work.		
5. We were on a narrow dirt road when we found the fawn.		
6. I remember my first experience at a haunted house.		
7. Besides Atlanta I think you should visit New Orleans.		
8. Are you going with anyone tomorrow?		
9. Jeff's treehouse is behind the barn.		
10. After the game we went home.		
11. There are three new students in my physics class.		
12. Above the back door you will find the key.		
13. I will be home within the hour.		
14. My best friend has moved across town.		

	Prep.	Object

15. She cannot drive without her glasses.

16. Our hound dog spends the summer under the house.

17. You will find Robyn in the den or upstairs.

18. The old road runs through desolate country.

19. Benjamin Franklin invented bifocal glasses in 1784.

20. For the first time this morning, Lillian left the cabin.

21. What were you doing in Annapolis yesterday?

22. Several current magazines lay on the coffee table.

23. I'll write her a letter after breakfast.

24. Around the corner is Mary's house.

25. Without a word he left the office.

Exercise 6   Conjunctions

In the following sentences there are both coordinating and subordinating conjunctions. Write the conjunction in the space at the right, and after it write **C** if it joins sentence elements of equal rank or **S** if it joins unequal elements.

Example: Before I leave, we will go shopping.   _____*Before, S*_____

1. Alice stayed on campus, but the others are here.   _____

2. My dad wrote me a letter and told me not to write any more checks.   _____

3. While he was climbing in the Alps, Clyde lost his footing and nearly fell.   _____

4. We will take you and your roommate to lunch.   _____

5. When riding in a convertible, one feels strangely free.   _____

6. He lighted the logs and left the room.   _____

7. On Saturday Ferrol Sams will read selections from his latest book and autograph copies.   _____

8. Mr. Bell said that either Ross or I would attend next week's sales meeting.   _____

9. When I go sailing, I watch out for the boom.   _____

10. The movies can be expensive, especially if one buys popcorn, candy, and a drink.   _____

11. Both you and your wife must buy season tickets to the Alliance Theatre.   _____

12. We had just pulled into the driveway when we heard a loud scream.   _____

13. After the ice storm was over, the roads remained dangerous for a week.   _____

14. What will I do if I miss my plane?   _____

15. He agreed to go to the dance, though he doesn't dance.   _____

16. The Smiths moved to Los Angeles because
    Mr. Smith had been transferred.   _____

17. The attorney's advice is not only too late but
    also too expensive.   _____

18. Do you want to "fax" this report to the
    home office or mail it?   _____

19. Although she reads French fluently, she has
    difficulty speaking it.   _____

20. Where did you attend school before you
    transferred to Stanford University?   _____

Exercise 7   Review of Parts of Speech

In the following sentences identify the part of speech of each *italicized* word by writing one of the following abbreviations in the space at the right:

N for noun,   **Adv** for adverb,
V for verb,   **Prep** for preposition,
P for pronoun,   **C** for conjunction,
Adj for adjective,   **I** for interjection.

Example: The cook *snapped* the beans.   _____V_____

1. The rain ruined the *newspaper*.   _____

2. The *main* thing that keeps a bonsai small is careful pruning.   _____

3. *None* in the class understood the assignment.   _____

4. The puppy *eventually* dragged its blanket out of its bed.   _____

5. My family recently visited my nephew *at* the Naval Academy.   _____

6. The first major league *baseball* game played at night took place
   in Cincinnati.   _____

7. The squirrels hid pecans *and* acorns in the flower boxes.   _____

8. The mockingbird woke me early *with* its beautiful song.   _____

9. Libraries maintain many records of our past and present
   civilizations.   _____

10. The car telephone is a time-saving device for *business* people. _____

11. The San Francisco wharf is noted *for* its seafood.   _____

12. *No!* I didn't order a pizza.   _____

13. Please call *us* when you arrive home.   _____

14. Ice hockey is a *very* physical game.   _____

15. The children *believed* that the old, broken-down house was
    haunted.   _____

16. *During* the twilight hours driving can be dangerous.   _____

17. *Miscellaneous* subjects will be discussed at the seminar.   _____

18. According to the National Association for Visually Handi-
    capped, there are 800,000 *legally* blind Americans.   _____

19. *These* are my favorite jeans.   _____

20. *Criticism* is difficult to accept. _____

21. I think that the corporation *will support* the University's research. _____

22. *Because* Steve was late for class, the professor would not let him take the test. _____

23. I'll meet *you* in the morning at the Waffle House. _____

24. Check into the hotel *before* you attend the meetings. _____

25. Jeff talks to *himself* when he is alone. _____

Exercise 8   Review of Parts of Speech

In the following sentences identify the part of speech of each *italicized* word by writing one of the following abbreviations in the space at the right:

N for noun,	**Adv** for adverb,
V for verb,	**Prep** for preposition,
P for pronoun,	**C** for conjunction,
Adj for adjective,	**I** for interjection.

Example: The leaves clogged the *gutters*.   _N_

1. Careers in the military are becoming *more* attractive to young people.   _____

2. Henry nearly collapsed in the locker room *after* a workout.   _____

3. *Many* companies are having difficulty recruiting qualified employees.   _____

4. *That* is a beautiful car.   _____

5. Employees in the business world spend many hours in *company* classrooms.   _____

6. *Oh,* I really love this house.   _____

7. He is in New York *for* a business meeting.   _____

8. Last Saturday my *uncle* made a hole in one.   _____

9. The United States has the *highest* rate of illiteracy of any industrialized country.   _____

10. We walked *and* shopped all day.   _____

11. How many textbooks *did* you *buy* for your history class?   _____

12. The morning train to Boston is *seldom* late.   _____

13. Althea Wilson studied *art* while growing up in Africa.   _____

14. Mary and Paul *are living* in a stilt house on Pawleys Island.   _____

15. Can *you* bring me a quart of milk from the store?   _____

16. Uncle Rainey has retired from the *state* audit department.   _____

17. The rhododendron and mountain laurel were *breathtakingly* beautiful this year.   _____

18. Bertha will be here early *if* she can find a ride.   _____

19. I know *that* I need a comprehensive guide to landscaping.   _____

20. The committee *carefully* analyzed each proposal.   _____

2

Recognizing Subjects, Verbs, and Complements

■ 2a The Sentence

A **sentence** is made up of single parts of speech combined into a pattern that expresses a complete thought. In other words, a sentence is a group of words that expresses a complete thought. When written, it begins with a capital letter and ends with a period, a question mark, or an exclamation mark. In its simplest form this complete statement is an independent clause or a **simple sentence.**

■ 2b Subject and Predicate

Every simple sentence must have two basic elements: (1) the thing we are talking about, and (2) what we say about it. The thing we are talking about is called the **subject,** and what we say about it is called the **predicate.** The subject is a noun, a pronoun, or some other word or group of words used as a noun. The essential part of the predicate is a verb — a word that tells something about the subject. It tells that the subject *does* something or that something *is true* of the subject. A subject and a verb are, therefore, the fundamental parts of every sentence. In fact, it is possible to express meaning with just these two elements:

Pilots fly.

Flowers bloom.

She sings.

Note that in each example the verb says that the subject does something.

■ 2c Finding the Verb

Finding verbs and subjects of verbs in a sentence is the first step in determining whether or not a group of words expresses a complete thought. Look first for the verb, the most important word in the sentence, and then for its subject.

The verb may sometimes be difficult to find. It may come anywhere in the sentence; for instance, it may precede the subject, as in some interrogative sentences (*Where is my pencil?*). It may consist of a single word or a group of two or more words; it may have other words inserted within the verb phrase; it may be combined with the negative *not* or with a contraction of *not*. To find the verb, look for the word or group of words that expresses an action or a state of being. In the following sentences the verbs are in italics:

His friend *stood* at his side. [The verb *stood* follows the subject *friend.*]

At his side *stood* his friend. [The verb *stood* precedes the subject *friend.*]

His friend *was standing* at his side. [The verb *was standing* consists of two words.]

His friend *can*not *stand* at his side. [The verb *can* is combined with the negative adverb *not*, which is not part of the verb.]

Did his friend *stand* at his side? [The two parts of the verb *did stand* are separated by the subject.]

■ 2d Finding the Subject

Sometimes finding the subject may also be difficult, for, as we have just seen, the subject does not always come immediately before the verb. Often it comes after the verb; often it is separated from the verb by a modifying element. Always look for the noun or pronoun about which the verb asserts something and disregard intervening elements:

Many of the children *come* to the clinic. [A prepositional phrase comes between the subject and the verb. The object of a preposition is never a subject.]

There *are flowers* on the table. [The subject comes after the verb. The word *there* is never a subject; in this sentence it is an **expletive,** an idiomatic introductory word.]

In the room *were* a *cot* and a *chair*. [The subjects come after the verb.]

In an imperative sentence, a sentence expressing a command or a request, the subject *you* is usually implied rather than expressed. Occasionally, however, the subject *you* is expressed:

Come in out of the rain.

Shut the door!

You play goalie.

Either the verb or the subject or both may be **compound;** that is, there may be more than one subject and more than one verb:

The *boy* and the *girl* played. [Two subjects.]

The boy *worked* and *played*. [Two verbs.]

The *boy* and the *girl worked* and *played*. [Two subjects and two verbs.]

In the first sentence the compound subject is *boy* and *girl*. In the second sentence there is a compound verb, *worked* and *played*. In the third sentence both the subject and the verb are compound.

■ 2e Complements

Thus far we have discussed two functions of words: that of nouns and pronouns as subjects and that of verbs as predicates.

A third function of words that we must consider is that of completing the verb. Nouns, pronouns, and adjectives are used to complete verbs and are called **complements.** A complement may be a **direct object,** an **indirect object,** a **predicate noun** or **pronoun,** a **predicate adjective,** an **objective complement,** or a **retained object.**

A **direct object** is a noun or noun equivalent that completes the verb and receives the action expressed in the verb:

The pilot flew the plane. [*Plane* is the direct object of *flew.* Just as the subject answers the question *"who?"* or *"what?"* before the verb (Who flew?), so the direct object answers the question *"whom?"* or *"what?"* after the verb (Flew what?).]

An **indirect object** is a word (or words) denoting the person or thing indirectly affected by the action of a transitive verb. It is the person or thing to which something is given or for which something is done. A sentence cannot contain an indirect object without also containing a direct object. Such words as *give, offer, grant, lend, teach,* and the like represent the idea of something done for the indirect object:

We gave *her* the book. [*Her* is the indirect object of *gave.* The indirect object answers the question *"to (for) whom or what?"* after the verb *gave* (Gave to whom?).]

Certain verbs that represent the idea of taking away or withholding something can also have indirect objects:

The judge *denied him* the opportunity to speak in his own defense.

Father *refused Frances* the use of the car.

A **predicate noun** (also called **predicate nominative**) is a noun or its equivalent that renames or identifies the subject and completes such verbs as *be, seem, become,* and *appear* (called linking verbs):

The woman is a *doctor.* [The predicate noun *doctor* completes the intransive verb *is* and renames the subject *woman.*]

My best friends are *she* and her *sister.* [The predicate pronoun *she* and the predicate noun *sister* complete the intransive verb *are* and rename the subject *friends.*]

Mary has become a *surgeon*. [The predicate noun *surgeon* completes the intransitive verb *has become* and renames the subject *Mary*.]

A **predicate adjective** is an adjective that completes a linking verb and describes the subject:

The man seems *angry*. [The predicate adjective *angry* completes the intransitive verb *seems* and describes the subject *man*.]

An **objective complement** is a noun or an adjective that completes the action expressed in the verb and refers to the direct object. If it is a noun, the objective complement is in a sense identical with the direct object; if it is an adjective, it describes or limits the direct object. It occurs commonly after such verbs as *think, call, find, make, consider, choose,* and *believe:*

Jealousy made Othello a *murderer*. [The objective complement *murderer* completes the transitive verb *made* and renames the direct object *Othello*.]

She thought the day *disagreeable*. [The objective complement *disagreeable* is an adjective that describes the direct object *day*.]

A **retained object** is a noun or noun equivalent that remains as the object when a verb having both a direct and an indirect object is put into the passive voice. The other object becomes the subject of such a verb. Although either object may become the subject, the indirect object more commonly takes that position, and the direct object is retained:

The board granted him a year's leave of absence.
He was granted a year's leave of absence.

[In the second sentence the verb has been put into the passive voice, the indirect object of the first sentence has become the subject of the second, and the direct object has been retained.]

The teacher asked the student a difficult question.
A difficult question was asked the student.

[In the second sentence the verb has been put into the passive voice, the direct object of the first sentence has become the subject of the second, and the indirect object has been retained.]

Exercise 9   Subjects and Verbs

In each of the following sentences underline the subject once and the verb twice. Then write the subject in the first column and the verb in the second column at the right.

	Subject	Verb
Example: The <u>kayak</u> is a watertight Eskimo canoe.	*kayak*	*is*
1. Many of the students are staying on campus this weekend.		
2. After the rain the baseball game was resumed.		
3. I can never find my sunglasses.		
4. Halloween was observed with pranks, costumes, and merrymaking.		
5. In 1937 Joe Louis won the heavyweight boxing championship.		
6. What is there in London for the bargain-hunting tourist?		
7. The property is owned by the Russell estate.		
8. There are five new shopping centers in Fort Worth.		
9. After dinner the children gathered to tell ghost stories.		

	Subject	Verb
10. The whole house had been decorated with early American furniture.	_____	_____
11. Everyone except the boys was quiet.	_____	_____
12. In some countries marriages are often arranged.	_____	_____
13. Frequent rains and heavy morning dew keep the rain forests beautiful and green.	_____	_____
14. During the last moments of the game the air was filled with excitement.	_____	_____
15. Some of the fraternity members are building the float.	_____	_____
16. Among her many friends is the president's daughter.	_____	_____
17. Amanda and her brother observed everything in silence.	_____	_____
18. The plumber and the electrician have promised to come today.	_____	_____
19. On her way home Joanna found a little lost kitten hiding in the bushes.	_____	_____
20. I will bring a portable stove and some cooking utensils.	_____	_____

Exercise 10   Subjects and Verbs

In each of the following sentences underline the subject(s) once and its verb(s) twice. Then copy the subject(s) in the first column and the verb(s) in the second column at the right.

	Subject	Verb
Example: Corey, along with his colleagues, designed the house.	*Corey*	*designed*
1. In 1976 Rhodes scholarships were opened to women.		
2. Neither Earl nor his brother was prepared for class.		
3. A group of foreign journalists was visiting the campus last week.		
4. Helen, as well as her sister, will arrive in Rome early for the festival.		
5. Did you return my book to the library?		
6. The team's manager walked to the pitcher's mound.		
7. Robyn washed her clothes and took a nap.		
8. The menu offered a variety of steak and fish dishes.		
9. Jenny has a pleasant voice, and Keith found her company relaxing.		
10. With all due respect, your solutions are somewhat simple.		

	Subject	Verb

11. Our team played flawlessly during the second half of the basketball game.

12. Despite its name buttermilk is very low in fat.

13. In 1954 the first nuclear-powered submarine, the Nautilus, was launched.

14. Jeannette Rankin in 1916 became the first woman elected to the U.S. House of Representatives.

15. There were no introductions or greetings after the invocation.

16. Are you playing golf Saturday?

17. The gentleman by the desk is my boss.

18. Both my brother and his wife are surgeons.

19. One of our students won a scholarship to Notre Dame.

20. Jamie, along with her roommate, is coming home this weekend.

21. The wild boar seldom roams more than five miles from its birthplace.

22. Someone will meet you at the Baltimore-Washington International Airport.

23. In each group of answers there is only one correct response.

24. In the back yard we have a small vegetable garden.

	Subject	Verb
25. John has always had a healthy curiosity.	_____	_____

Exercise 11   Direct Objects and Predicate Nouns

In each of the following sentences underline the complement. Then identify the complement by writing in the space at the right one of the following abbreviations:

DO if it is a direct object,
PN if it is a predicate noun.

Example: French is my favorite <u>subject</u>.   *PN*

1. Aunt Dora's lemon pie won first place.   _____

2. Bill and Dot play excellent tennis.   _____

3. In 1920 Sinclair Lewis published the novel *Main Street*.   _____

4. Will Art become the team's captain?   _____

5. Singing was her whole life.   _____

6. Charles Lindbergh made his solo flight across the Atlantic in
   1927.   _____

7. Mary Lou drove Brenda's car to Florida   _____

8. My neighbor Mr. Franklin is a stockbroker.   _____

9. I can't remember Jane's last name.   _____

10. Bob Hope is one of the great performers of the twentieth
    century.   _____

11. None of us enjoyed his speech.   _____

12. Newman is a born leader.   _____

13. Jim Thorpe won the decathlon and the pentathlon at the 1912
    Olympics.   _____

14. Despite our efforts the Ethics Advisory Committee did not
    complete its research on time.   _____

15. Dr. Harley Rose is a professor of economics at our state
    university.   _____

16. The vice president of the company explained the quarterly
    statement to the board.   _____

17. Martha has always been a delightful woman.   _____

18. Officials at Stanford University closed several buildings after
    the earthquake.   _____

19. Some faculty members opposed the new policy on research
    grants.   _____

20. The mother cat admired her basketful of little kittens.   _____

Exercise 12 — Indirect Objects and Objective Complements

In each of the following sentences identify the *italicized* complement by writing in the space at the right one of the following abbreviations:

IO if it is an indirect object,
OC if it is an objective complement.

Example: In the morning I'll cook *everyone* breakfast.   *IO*

1. Can you paint our house Williamsburg *blue*?   _____

2. The Dean taught *us* physics.   _____

3. Last Saturday the quarterback threw *me* a short, sideline pass.   _____

4. The class voted Charles the *student* most likely to succeed.   _____

5. The class found Professor Wolfe quite *boorish*.   _____

6. Every Saturday night Grandmother told *us* stories of her childhood.   _____

7. The soccer team elected Jason *captain*.   _____

8. Upon reflection Melissa thought Tim's remarks *childish*.   _____

9. On second thought, order our *table* the chef's special.   _____

10. Louise gave *us* tickets to the opera.   _____

11. Pride made Keith *obnoxious*.   _____

12. Senator Jones sent *us* copies of his bill.   _____

13. You should not deny *me* the right to act for myself.   _____

14. The committee wrote *him* a letter about his appeal.   _____

15. Before you go, bring *me* some milk and cookies, please.   _____

16. Why did they paint these walls bright *pink*?   _____

17. The company awarded each *retiree* a month's vacation anywhere in the world.   _____

18. Because of her poor grades we cannot consider her a *candidate* for class president.   _____

19. May I ask *you* a question?   _____

20. Each morning Trix brings *Dad* his paper.   _____

Exercise 13   Complements

A. In each of the following sentences identify the *italicized* word by writing one of the following abbreviations in the space at the right:

    PN if it is a predicate noun,   **IO** if it is an indirect object,
    PA if it is a predicate adjective,   **OC** if it is an objective complement.
    DO if it is a direct object,

Example: Computer languages are *easy* for some students.   ___*PA*___

1. I think that dreams are highly *personal* and symbolic.   _____

2. His attitude toward his class work is *unacceptable*.   _____

3. Because of her excellent record, she became the first woman *president* of the company.   _____

4. Frankly, I have not read that *book*.   _____

5. The University of Colorado offered *him* a full scholarship.   _____

6. Behind the door you will find a red *umbrella*.   _____

7. Paul considered his sister his best *friend*.   _____

8. Attics are often *collections* of old memories.   _____

9. If you can, keep the dinner *simple*.   _____

10. The security guard checks our *building* several times every night.   _____

11. Last spring we conducted a *survey* concerning campus safety.   _____

12. The workshop provided *me* an opportunity to meet other female executives.   _____

13. He dyed his mustache jet *black*.   _____

14. On the way home Shelley bought *us* some hamburgers.   _____

15. Howard's questions seemed quite *straightforward*.   _____

B. Write sixteen sentences, four of which contain direct objects; four, indirect objects; four, predicate nouns; four, predicate adjectives. In the space at the right, write **DO** (direct object), **IO** (indirect object), **PN** (predicate noun), or **PA** (predicate adjective) as the case may be.

1. _____   _____

2. _____ _____

3. _____ _____

4. _____ _____

5. _____ _____

6. _____ _____

7. _____ _____

8. _____ _____

9. _____ _____

10. _____ _____

11. _____ _____

12. _____ _____

13. _____ _____

14. _____ _____

15. _____ _____

16. _____ _____

3

The Sentence Fragment

■ 3a Grammatical Fragments

If you are not careful to have both a subject and a predicate in your sentences and to express a complete thought, you will write sentence fragments instead of complete sentences. Observe, for example, the following:

A tall, distinguished-looking gentleman standing on the corner in a pouring rain.

Standing on the corner in a pouring rain and shielding himself from the deluge with a large umbrella.

The first of these groups of words is no more than the subject of a sentence or the object of a verb or preposition. It may be part of such a sentence, for example, as *We noticed a tall, distinguished-looking gentleman standing on the corner in a pouring rain.* The second group is probably a modifier of some kind, the modifier of a subject, for instance: *Standing on the corner in a pouring rain and shielding himself from the deluge with a large umbrella, a tall, distinguished-looking gentleman was waiting for a cab.*

Another type of fragment is seen in the following illustrations:

Because I had heard all that I wanted to hear and did not intend to be bored any longer.

Who was the outstanding athlete of her class and also the best scholar.

Although he had been well recommended by his former employers.

Each of these groups of words actually has a subject and a predicate, but each is still a fragment because the first word of each is a subordinating element and clearly indicates that the thought is incomplete, that the thought expressed depends upon some other thought. Such fragments are subordinate parts of longer sentences like the following:

> I left the hall because I had heard all that I wanted to hear and did not intend to be bored any longer.

> The valedictorian was Alice Snodgrass, who was the outstanding athlete of her class and also the best scholar.

> He did not get the job although he had been well recommended by his former employers.

◣ 3b Permissible Fragments

A sentence fragment is often the result of ignorance or carelessness and is the sign of an immature writer. On the other hand, much correctly spoken and written English contains perfectly proper fragments of sentences. The adverbs *yes* and *no* may stand alone, as may other words and phrases in dialogue (though our chief concern remains written prose). There is nothing wrong, for example, in such fragments as the following:

> The sooner, the better.

> Anything but that.

> Same as before.

Interjections and exclamatory phrases may also stand alone as independent elements. The following fragments are correct:

> Ouch!

> Tickets, please!

> Not so!

■ 3c Stylistic Fragments

There is another kind of fragment of rather common occurrence in the writing of some of the best authors. It is the phrase used for realistic or impressionistic effect, the piling up of words or phrases without any effort to organize them into sentences: "The blue haze of evening was upon the field. Lines of forest with long purple shadows. One cloud along the western sky partly smothering the red." This kind of writing, if it is to be good, is very difficult. Like free verse it may best be left to the experienced writer. You should learn to recognize a sentence fragment when you see one. You should use this form sparingly in your own writing. And you should remember two things: first, that the legitimacy of the sentence fragment depends upon whether it is used intentionally or not, and second, that *in an elementary course in composition most instructors assume that a sentence fragment is unintended.*

Study carefully the following sentence fragments and the accompanying comments:

A large woman of rather determined attitude who says that she wishes to see you to discuss a matter of great importance. [This is a typical fragment unintended by the writer, who seems to have felt that it is a complete sentence because there are a subject and a predicate in each subordinate clause.]

He finally decided to leave school. Because he was utterly bored with his work and was failing all his courses. [Here the second group of words is an unjustifiable fragment. It is a subordinate clause and should be attached to the main clause without a break of any kind.]

There were books everywhere. Books in the living room, books in the bedroom, books even in the kitchen. [The second group of words is a fragment, but it may be defended on grounds of emphasis. Many writers, however, would have used a colon after *everywhere* and made a single sentence.]

Exercise 14   The Sentence Fragment

Indicate in the space at the right by writing **C** or **F** whether the following groups of words are complete sentences or fragments of sentences. Rewrite any fragment, making it a complete sentence.

Example: If you want to go shopping with Mary and me Saturday morning.   _____F_____

*If you want to go shopping with Mary and me, come early
Saturday morning.*

1. As one enters the building and looks to the left.   _____

2. The psychologist discussed problems faced by everyone.   _____

3. Even though her son attends the Naval Academy.   _____

4. What most students need to develop along with good study
   habits.   _____

5. When planning a ski trip or any other winter outing.   _____

6. Taking the advice of his doctor seriously.   _____

7. Entering the room and looking timidly about.   _____

8. In an effort to provide a more healthful environment for its animals.   _____

9. During the luncheon I sat by the president of the University of Maryland.   _____

10. While John is listening to his hard rock music and trying to study at the same time.   _____

11. A resolution honoring Mr. Rhodes and commemorating his contributions to the Board of Regents.   _____

12. Sea gulls drink both fresh water and sea water.   _____

13. Although he is a college graduate and also has had experience in business.   _____

14. While walking down the street and looking for my lost bracelet. _____

15. That she easily read his handwriting, even the peculiar *g*'s. _____

16. Cutting the ancient trees on federally owned lands. _____

17. After the movie, which was over at eleven. _____

18. Even more mechanical-minded than his mentor, but less patient. _____

19. Throughout his life, speaking to large and sometimes hostile audiences. _____

20. When buying a house, does one get a bank loan approved first? _____

21. Hurrying into the house in order to answer the telephone.   ———

22. The class having ended ten minutes later than usual.   ———

23. Alone and cold, Dean, who had been hiking for hours.   ———

24. Did you ever learn to use WordPerfect 5.1?   ———

25. Because he can never make up his mind about anything.   ———

Exercise 15   The Sentence Fragment

Some of the following groups are fragments. Some are fragments and sentences. Some are complete sentences. Rewrite in such a way as to leave no fragments. If the group of words is already a complete sentence, leave it as it is and mark it **C**.

Example: Maureen the youngest of four children. She wants to
be included in her older sisters' group.   _____F_____

*Maureen, who is the youngest of four children, wants to be
included in her older sisters' group.*

1. In order to see my nephew play football. We drove all night.   _____

2. My favorite bookstore, which has a sandwich shop. I enjoy
browsing there in the evening.   _____

3. Flannery O'Connor, who has been called one of the South's
great writers. She died in 1964.   _____

4. While here, you must follow our rules.   _____

5. *Chronicle of America,* an exhaustive treatment of the United
States and its history.   _____

6. Playing golf, as you know, taking time and patience.   _____

7. It is very important. Being honest with oneself.   _____

8. After failing to salute her senior officer. The soldier was placed on restriction.   _____

9. Her ability to make wise purchases and investments. Jane has a substantial portfolio.   _____

10. Riding a Harley-Davidson is dangerous, frightening, and thrilling.   _____

11. That I cannot be everywhere at once. I know that.   _____

12. We left the house early. Because we were afraid of being caught in traffic.   _____

13. Jake's ability to see the big picture.   _____

14. We did not know his name. Although recognizing the visitor. _____

15. Seeing the cat catch the bird and becoming quite upset. _____

Exercise 16 The Sentence Fragment

Complete or revise the following sentence fragments in such a way as to make complete sentences.

Example: If you need more time to make your decision.

If you need more time to make your decision, I think that the bank will allow you an additional week.

1. Susan and Larry, who are our best friends.

2. Throughout his career as a corporate lawyer, devoting many hours to community service.

3. After spilling milk on the rug and trying to mop up the mess.

4. Professional athletes, who are paid huge sums of money to entertain us.

5. While changing a flat tire on a lonely back road in pouring rain.

6. Tiffany's, which is a famous jewelry store.

7. Being cold-natured and sensitive to sudden drops in temperature.

8. Boxwoods, which are glossy, small-leaf evergreens.

9. After the automobile wreck, which was a terrible experience.

10. When we finish studying and before we go to bed.

4

Verbals

You may sometimes have trouble in recognizing sentence verbs because you may confuse them with certain verb forms that function partly as verbs and partly as other parts of speech. (The *sentence verb* is the verb that states something about the subject, one capable of completing a statement.) These other verb forms are made from verbs but also perform the function of nouns, adjectives, or adverbs. In other words, they constitute a sort of half-verb. They are called **verbals**. The three verbal forms are the **gerund**, the **participle**, and the **infinitive**.

■ 4a Verbals and Sentence Verbs

It is important that you distinguish between the use of a particular verb form as a verbal and its use as a main verb in a sentence. An illustration of the different uses of the verb form *running* will help you to make this distinction:

> *Running* every day is good exercise. [*Running* is a **gerund** and is the subject of the verb *is*.]

> *Running* swiftly, he caught the bandit. [*Running* is a **participle** and modifies the pronoun *he*.]

> The boy *is running* down the street. [*Is running* is the **sentence verb**. It is formed by using the present participle with the auxiliary verb *is*.]

It must be emphasized that *a verbal cannot take the place of a sentence verb* and that *any group of words containing a verbal but no sentence verb is a sentence fragment*:

> The boy *running* [A sentence fragment.]

> *To face* an audience [A sentence fragment.]

59

The boy *running* up the steps is Charles. [A complete sentence.]

To face an audience was a great effort for me. [A complete sentence.]

The following table shows the tenses and voices in which verbals appear:

Gerunds and participles		
Tense	Active voice	Passive voice
Present	doing	being done
Past		done (This form applies only to participles.)
Present perfect	having done	having been done
Progressive present perfect	having been doing	
Infinitives		
Tense	Active voice	Passive voice
Present	to do	to be done
Present perfect	to have done	to have been done
Progressive present	to be doing	
Progressive present perfect	to have been doing	

■ 4b The Gerund

A **gerund** is a verbal used as a noun and in its present tense always ends in *-ing.* Like a noun, a gerund is used as a subject, a complement, an object of a preposition, or an appositive. Do not confuse the gerund with the present participle, which has the same form but is used as an adjective:

Planning the work carefully required a great deal of time. [*Planning* is a gerund used as subject of the sentence.]

She was not to blame for *breaking* the vase. [*Breaking* is a gerund used as object of the preposition *for.*]

I appreciated your *taking* time to help me. [*Taking* is a gerund used as direct object of *appreciated.*]

His unselfish act, *giving* Marty his coat, plainly showed Ed's generosity. [*Giving* is a gerund used as the appositive of *act.*]

In the sentences above, you will note examples of gerunds functioning as nouns but also taking objects as verbs do. In the first sentence the gerund *planning* is used as the subject of the verb *required. Planning* itself, however, is completed by the object *work* and is modified by the adverb *carefully.* This dual functioning of the gerund is apparent in the other three sentences as well.

It is important to remember a rule concerning the modification of gerunds: Always use the possessive form of a noun or pronoun before a gerund. Because gerunds are nouns, their modifiers, other than the adverbial ones just mentioned, must be adjectival; therefore, the possessive form, which has adjectival function, is the correct modifier:

Mr. Bridges was surprised at *Doug's* offering him the motorboat.

NOT

Mr. Bridges was surprised at Doug offering the motorboat.

■ 4c The Participle

A **participle** is a verbal used as an adjective. The present participle is formed by adding *-ing* to the verb: *do — doing*. Again, remember not to confuse the gerund and the present participle, which have the same form but do not function similarly. The past participle is formed in various ways. It may end in *-ed*, *-d*, *-t*, or *-n*: *talk — talked*, *hear — heard*, *feel — felt*, *know — known*. It may also be formed by a change of vowel: *sing — sung*.

The baby, *wailing* pitifully, refused to be comforted. [*Wailing* is a present participle. It modifies *baby*.]

The *broken* doll can be mended. [*Broken* is a past participle, passive voice. It modifies *doll*.]

An old coat, *faded* and *torn*, was her only possession. [*Faded* and *torn* are past participles, passive voice, modifying *coat*.]

Having been warned, the man was sent on his way. [*Having been warned* is the present perfect participle, passive voice. It modifies *man*.]

Like the gerund, the participle may have a complement and adverbial modifiers. In the sentence *Wildly waving a red flag, he ran down the track*, the participle *waving* has the object *flag* and the adverbial modifier *wildly*.

■ 4d The Infinitive

An **infinitive** is a verbal consisting of the simple form of the verb preceded by *to* and used as a noun, an adjective, or an adverb:

To err is human. [*To err* is used as a noun, the subject of *is*.]

He wanted *to go* tomorrow. [*To go* is used as a noun, the object of the verb *wanted*.]

He had few books *to read*. [*To read* is used as an adjective to modify the noun *books*.]

Frank seemed eager *to go*. [*To go* is used as an adverb to modify the adjective *eager*.]

She rode fast *to escape* her pursuers. [*To escape* is used as an adverb to modify the verb *rode*.]

Sometimes the word *to* is omitted:

> Susan helped carry the packages. [*To* is understood before the verb *carry*. *(To) carry* is used as a noun and is the object of *helped*.]

Note: An adverbial infinitive can frequently be identified if the phrase "in order" can be placed before it, as in *Katy paid ten dollars* (in order) *to get good seats for the play.*

Like the gerund and the participle, the infinitive may have a complement and adverbial modifiers:

> He did not want *to cut the grass yesterday*. [The infinitive *to cut* has the object *grass* and the adverbial modifier *yesterday*.]

Exercise 17   Verbs and Verbals

In the following sentences identify each *italicized* expression by writing on the line at the right

    V if it is a verb,   **Part** if it is a participle,
    Ger if it is a gerund,   **Inf** if it is an infinitive.

Example: National Educational Television has informative and *challenging* programs.   ***Part***

1. A world globe is an excellent *teaching* tool for geography class. _____

2. *Collecting* sea shells is fun. _____

3. To rest one's body is *to lift* one's spirits. _____

4. Children *enjoy* learning. _____

5. The *illuminated* dial on the clock kept me awake most of the night. _____

6. Joe has difficulty *solving* word problems. _____

7. The *washing* machine ruined Wright's new sweater. _____

8. *To tell* the truth is not only the best policy but also the right thing to do. _____

9. The children love *to make* ice cream in the crank freezer at their grandparents' home. _____

10. *Bicycling* is one way to increase the efficiency of the heart. _____

11. Most men do not like *to wear* bow ties. _____

12. The greenhouse effect is a *frightening* prospect for the future. _____

13. Canada is a country of vast, beautiful, *undeveloped* areas. _____

14. Josh wants *to be* a polo player. _____

15. *Collecting* old coins can be fun as well as a sound investment. _____

16. The reason he failed German is not difficult *to understand*. _____

17. First-night jitters on *opening* night are common among actors. _____

18. It is too wet *to play* golf today. _____

19. When we go to the mountains, we *enjoy* working jigsaw puzzles. _____

20. Sometimes, *winning* a little league baseball game becomes too important to the players' parents.   _____

21. *Fried* chicken is a Southern specialty.   _____

22. *Being chosen* as an astronaut identifies one as capable and committed.   _____

23. He refused *to observe* the warning lights on his car and subsequently gave out of gas.   _____

24. We have a Christmas tradition of *decorating* with holly and mistletoe.   _____

25. John *likes* to dress up like a vampire and scare his little sister.   _____

Exercise 18 Gerunds

In the following sentences underline each gerund. Copy the gerund in the first column at the right. In the second column write **S** if the gerund is the subject of the verb. **PN** if the gerund is the predicate nominative, **DO** if the gerund is the direct object, **OP** if the gerund is the object of the preposition.

	Gerund	Use
Example: Eating a ripe peach is usually messy.	*Eating*	*S*

1. Marsha's finest characteristic is her sympathetic listening.

2. Injuries from playing sports may cause lifetime disabilities.

3. Singing around a campfire is one of my happiest memories of camp.

4. Tim loves driving his sports car.

5. Having friends is necessary for a fulfilling and rewarding life.

6. I no longer enjoy shopping as I once did.

7. Feeding the hungry is a worldwide challenge.

8. More and more people are finding condominium living comfortable.

9. Did he give you a reason for leaving?

10. Traveling is both educational and strenuous.

11. Lee has a habit of finding fault with every play the coach calls.

12. Visiting my grandparents was a happy experience for my brothers and me.

	Gerund	**Use**
13. Before closing the door, be sure you have your keys.	_____	_____
14. Getting children to brush their teeth is a frustrating chore.	_____	_____
15. Disposing of our nation's garbage is becoming an increasingly difficult task.	_____	_____
16. Fresh fruits, vegetables, and cereals are excellent foods for keeping one healthy.	_____	_____
17. I love hearing the whistle of a train in the night.	_____	_____
18. Paige takes pride in grooming her horse.	_____	_____
19. Bert's favorite pastime is watching dog races.	_____	_____
20. Sign language is essential for communicating with many deaf people.	_____	_____
21. Reading biographies of famous people helps us to understand ourselves.	_____	_____
22. Her parents were proud of her graduating _magna cum laude_.	_____	_____
23. Making jelly and jam is a skill Allison learned from her grandmother.	_____	_____
24. To make amends for being unkind, he surprised his wife with diamond earrings.	_____	_____
25. After changing your clothes, begin your homework.	_____	_____

Exercise 19   Participles

Underline the participle in each of the following sentences, and then write in the space at the right the word that the participle modified.

Example: Surely you aren't using that <u>torn</u> tablecloth?   *tablecloth*

1. The lyceum speaker described the decline of shared knowledge in American education.   _____

2. The answering machine is the modern equivalent of the butler.   _____

3. The psychic made some startling revelations.   _____

4. Nancy's husband gave her a string of pearls bought in Paris.   _____

5. Clutching her teddy bear, the little girl refused to give it up.   _____

6. His friends autographed the cast on his broken leg.   _____

7. Maggie was fascinated with her new camera and spent the day taking pictures.   _____

8. He combed the woods searching for his lost dog.   _____

9. Having been in a hurry to leave, I had left my ticket at home.   _____

10. Hank cut his hand on a piece of barbed wire.   _____

11. The man wearing the red hat is Professor Wimsey.   _____

12. Did you rent a furnished apartment?   _____

13. The cat crossed the street, followed by her kittens.   _____

14. The frightened child hid behind the door.   _____

15. Some fruit salads are made with dried fruits.   _____

16. He spent hours searching for his watch.   _____

17. Our student health center has more practicing physicians than my home town has.   _____

18. Exploring the coral reefs of Biscayne National Park promises breathtaking scenes.   _____

19. Working in the college cafeteria, I met many students.   _____

20. The Board of Trustees unanimously approved the amended policy.   _____

21. Put your soiled shirts in the clothes hamper.   _____

22. Professor Looney has won several teaching awards.   _____

23. The wishing well was filled with coins.   _____

24. When did you get your new racing bike?   _____

25. Weather reports are important when one is planning a backpacking trip.   _____

26. Amy Grant is a popular singer, idolized by many young people.   _____

27. Having been frightened by a dog, the child ran to her mother.   _____

28. There are many attractive vacationing spots along the Florida coast.   _____

29. The cheering crowd was heard all over the campus.   _____

30. Reaching for the milk, I dropped the cereal box.   _____

Exercise 20 Infinitives

Underline the infinitive in each of the following sentences, and in the space at the right indicate its use in the sentence by writing N for noun, Adj for adjective, and Adv for adverb.

Example: To prepare for tomorrow's meeting will take several
hours.   _N_

1. To earn money for his girl friend's Christmas present, he cut grass all summer.   _____

2. To live in a democracy is a priceless heritage.   _____

3. During trying times the human spirit will rise to meet the challenge.   _____

4. Smelling the aroma of brewing coffee is a great way to start the day.   _____

5. To save money is as important as to make money.   _____

6. Eagerness to learn was characteristic of Paul as a child.   _____

7. Fire hoses are used sometimes to disperse a mob.   _____

8. Kirk is anxious to know the score of the game.   _____

9. Do you plan to spend the holidays at home?   _____

10. We want to build an addition onto the house.   _____

11. Study your cards before you play if you want to be a good bridge player.   _____

12. Are you ready to make your speech?   _____

13. It was a pleasure to meet P. D. James, the mystery writer.   _____

14. She attended the University of St. Andrew's to study theology.   _____

15. The Constitution gives Congress the power to tax.   _____

16. His wish was to travel extensively.   _____

17. I think I will lie down to rest for a few hours.   _____

18. His ability to write clearly has improved this semester.   _____

19. Irene tried for years to lose weight.   _____

20. Julia's wish to spend Christmas in New York has come true. _____

21. My sister told me to bring her a sandwich from the deli. _____

22. How much money did you spend to buy that hat? _____

23. To understand economics is important. _____

24. Our plan is to move to Maryland next May. _____

25. If you do not vote, you forfeit your right to vote. _____

26. The committee asked us to reconsider our decision. _____

27. How many countries do you hope to visit while on your tour? _____

28. The company has plans to reorganize the plant operations. _____

29. They expect to arrive in time for dinner. _____

30. Their decision to paint the house was made too quickly. _____

Exercise 21   Verbals

In the following sentences underline each verbal. In the first column at the right identify the *type* of verbal by writing

Ger for gerund,
Part for participle,
Inf for infinitive.

In the second column at the right indicate the *use* of the verbal by writing

Adj for adjective,	**PN** for predicate nominative,
Adv for adverb,	**DO** for direct object,
S for subject,	**OP** for object of a preposition.

	Type	Use
Example: Olympic National Park offers <u>guided</u> tours.	*Part*	*Adj*

1. Helping instructors become better teachers is one function of the Office of Educational Development. _____ _____

2. Next year all students will be required to take a freshman seminar. _____ _____

3. For those interested there is a new course on computers. _____ _____

4. Being part of a large family teaches cooperation. _____ _____

5. To help save lives, trauma and burn centers have been created for emergencies. _____ _____

6. He releases his tensions and gets good exercise by chopping wood. _____ _____

7. Many students take their studying seriously. _____ _____

8. Ray left the party looking ill. _____ _____

9. A popular European sport is cycling. _____ _____

10. Ferrol Sams, author of *Run with the Horsemen,* is a practicing physician. _____ _____

11. The hungry and tired children ate heartily. _____ _____

12. Arguing with the umpire was a waste of time. _____ _____

	Type	Use
13. The outside of the house needs painting.	____	____
14. He enjoyed his class in flower arranging.	____	____
15. To provide you the additional material will require a few extra days.	____	____
16. Open-ended questions are difficult for him.	____	____
17. Some universities have recording studios.	____	____
18. To make a quick decision is often a mistake.	____	____
19. An increasing number of hotels are offering shelter to the homeless.	____	____
20. For me living in Washington is not economically feasible.	____	____
21. It is quite amazing that we seldom see our own faults.	____	____
22. To prepare for my trip, I read several books about Oregon.	____	____
23. Financial security requires establishing priorities.	____	____
24. Having overslept, Dan almost missed his first class.	____	____
25. Her speech was very challenging.	____	____

5

Recognizing Phrases

A **phrase** is a group of related words, generally having neither subject nor predicate and used as though it were a single word. It cannot make a statement and is therefore not a clause.

A knowledge of the phrase and how it is used will suggest to you ways of diversifying and enlivening your sentences. Variety in using sentences will remedy the monotonous "subject first" habit. The use of the participial phrase, for instance, will add life and movement to your style because the participle is an action word, having the strength of its verbal nature in addition to its function as a modifier.

We classify phrases as **gerund, participial, infinitive, absolute, prepositional,** and **appositive.** The following sentences will show how the same idea may be expressed differently by the use of different kinds of phrases:

Sue swam daily. She hoped to improve her backstroke. ["Subject first" sentences.]

By *swimming daily,* Sue hoped to improve her backstroke. [Gerund phrase.]

Swimming daily, Sue hoped to improve her backstroke. [Participial phrase.]

Sue's only hope of improving her backstroke was *to swim daily.* [Infinitive phrase.]

With a daily swim Sue hoped to improve her backstroke. [Prepositional phrase.]

Sue knew of one way to improve her backstroke: *swimming daily.* [Appositive phrase.]

■ 5a The Gerund Phrase

A **gerund phrase** consists of a gerund and any complement or modifiers it may have. The function of the gerund phrase is always that of a noun:

Being late for breakfast is Joe's worst fault. [The gerund phrase is used as the subject of the verb *is*.]

She finally succeeded in *opening the camera*. [The gerund phrase is the object of the preposition *in*.]

Bill hated *driving his golf balls into the lake*. [The gerund phrase is the object of the verb *hated*.]

His hobby, *making furniture*, is enjoyable and useful. [The gerund phrase is an appositive.]

■ 5b The Participial Phrase

A **participial phrase** consists of a participle and any complement or modifiers it may have. It functions as an adjective:

Disappointed by his best friend, Roger refused to speak to him. [The participial phrase modifies the proper noun *Roger*.]

Having written the letter, Julie set out for the Post Office. [The participial phrase modifies the proper noun *Julie*.]

The boy *standing in the doorway* is the one who asked to borrow our rake. [The participial phrase modifies the noun *boy*.]

Punctuation: *Introductory participial phrases are set off by commas. Other participial phrases are also set off by commas unless they are essential to the meaning of the sentence.* (See Chapter 19, Section b.)

■ 5c The Infinitive Phrase

An **infinitive phrase** consists of an infinitive and any complement or modifiers it may have. Infinitives function as adjectives, adverbs, or nouns:

She had a plane *to catch at eight o'clock*. [The infinitive phrase modifies the noun *plane*.]

To be in Mr. Foster's class was *to learn the meaning of discipline*. [The first infinitive phrase is the subject of the verb *was*. The second infinitive phrase is the predicate nominative after the linking verb *was*.]

Millie left early *to avoid the heavy traffic*. [The infinitive phrase modifies the verb *left*.]

After the night outdoors we were happy *to be warm and dry again*. [The infinitive phrase modifies the adjective *happy*.]

Ted has no plans except *to watch television*. [The infinitive phrase is the object of the preposition *except*.]

We decided *to go for a long walk*. [The infinitive phrase is the direct object of the verb *decided*.]

Her fiancé seems *to be very pleasant*. [The infinitive phrase is the predicate adjective after the linking verb *seems*.]

Punctuation: *Introductory infinitive phrases used as modifiers are set off by commas.* (See Chapter 19, Section b.)

■ 5d The Absolute Phrase

A noun followed by a participle may form a construction grammatically independent of the rest of the sentence. This construction is called an **absolute phrase.** It is never a subject, nor does it modify any word in the sentence, but it is used *absolutely* or independently:

The bus having stopped, the tourists filed out.

The theater being nearby, I decided to walk.

I shall do as I please, *all things considered.*

Punctuation: *An absolute phrase is always separated from the rest of the sentence by a comma.* (See Chapter 19, Section b.)

■ 5e The Prepositional Phrase

A **prepositional phrase** consists of a preposition followed by a noun or pronoun used as its object, together with any modifiers the noun or pronoun may have. The prepositional phrase functions usually as an adjective or an adverb:

The plan *of the house* is very simple. [The prepositional phrase modifies the noun *plan.*]

The river runs *through rich farmland.* [The prepositional phrase modifies the verb *runs.*]

Throughout the house there was an aroma of corn beef and cabbage.

Punctuation: *An introductory prepositional phrase, unless unusually long, is not set off by a comma.* (See Chapter 19, Section b.)

■ 5f The Appositive Phrase

An **appositive** is a word or phrase that explains, identifies, or renames the word it follows. An appositive may be a noun phrase (that is, a noun and its modifiers), a gerund phrase, an infinitive phrase, or a prepositional phrase:

This book, *a long novel about politics,* will never be a best seller. [Noun phrase used as an appositive.]

Jean knew a way out of her difficulty: *telling the truth.* [Gerund phrase used as an appositive.]

His greatest ambition, *to make a million dollars,* was doomed from the start. [Infinitive phrase used as an appositive.]

The rustler's hideout, *in the old cave by the river,* was discovered by the posse. [Prepositional phrase used as an appositive.]

An appositive may be **essential** (sometimes called **fused**) or **nonessential;** it is essential if it positively identifies that which it renames, frequently by use of a proper noun. Examples of both essential and nonessential appositives occur in the sentences below:

The Victorian poets *Tennyson and Browning* were outstanding literary spokesmen of their day. [The appositive, *Tennyson and Browning,* identifies *poets* and thus is essential.]

Tennyson and Browning, *two Victorian poets,* were outstanding literary spokesmen of their day. [The appositive, *two Victorian poets,* is nonessential because the poets are already identified by their names.]

Punctuation: *An appositive phrase is enclosed with commas unless it is essential.* (See Chapter 19, Section b.)

Exercise 22   Phrases

In each of the following sentences identify the *italicized* phrase by writing in the space at the right

Prep if it is a prepositional phrase,   **Inf** if it is an infinitive phrase,
Part if it is a participial phrase,   **App** if it is an appositive phrase,
Ger if it is a gerund phrase,   **Abs** if it is an absolute phrase.

Example: The nation's eagle population declined *in the 1960's*.   _**Prep**_

1. He was thrilled *to be making his first solo flight*.   _____

2. Norman is a member *of our study group*.   _____

3. Chicago, *"the windy city,"* has a wonderful restaurant named Cafe 21.   _____

4. Niagara Falls is still a romantic place *for honeymooners*.   _____

5. *Reaching one's goals* will require hard work and dedication.   _____

6. *The house having burned to the ground*, we lost everything.   _____

7. A good way *to begin the day* is to take a ten-minute swim.   _____

8. Lillian Jackson Brau, *a modern mystery writer*, uses Siamese cats to solve her mysteries.   _____

9. *Sitting on the porch*, we listened to the rushing streams.   _____

10. My generation expects *to live longer* than our parents did.   _____

11. *Having studied all day for exams*, Ron was ready for a break.   _____

12. *During the day* I know Jimmy has very little free time.   _____

13. Young people are the future *of our country*.   _____

14. *The rain having stopped*, we hurried to the tennis courts.   _____

15. We never understood *Ben's changing jobs*.   _____

16. James Dickey, *poet and novelist*, may be best known for his novels.   _____

17. *Having waited all afternoon*, I left after Bob finally called.   _____

18. Millions of people enjoy *watching television* by the hour.   _____

19. Arthur Miller was awarded the Pulitzer Prize *in 1948*.   _____

20. The severity of the storm caused many trees *to be uprooted*.   _____

Exercise 23   Phrases

The sentences in the following exercise contain prepositional, verbal, and appositive phrases. Underline each phrase, and in the space at the right of each sentence
show how each phrase is used by writing **Adj** for adjective, **Adv** for adverb, and **N**
for noun.

Example: She enjoys <u>living alone</u>.   _____N_____

1. In the closet you will find a raincoat.   _____

2. We began playing Monopoly early Saturday morning.   _____

3. Horror movies are very popular with teenagers.   _____

4. Some managers seem to understand their employees' motives
   quite well.   _____

5. Steven, an honor student, will graduate this spring.   _____

6. Many critics have tried to explain Robert Frost's symbolism. _____

7. Charles came yesterday to clean my yard.   _____

8. *Gulliver's Travels* is a marvelous satire on human nature. _____

9. Neither Richard nor his lab partner brought his notes to the
   lab.   _____

10. I appreciate your writing me your comments and suggestions. _____

11. My grandfather spent many hours telling us old stories.   _____

12. His main interest in life was playing soccer.   _____

13. Paul understood the problem facing his company.   _____

14. To stop the rumors, the company sent each employee a
    letter.   _____

15. Dr. Canton is looking forward to speaking tomorrow
    morning.   _____

16. Dora and Ed spent several weeks traveling this summer. _____

17. Gary left because he had work to do tonight.   _____

18. Yesterday I registered to win a new truck.   _____

19. Within the hour the concert will surely begin.   _____

20. When I travel, I usually enjoy visiting historical sites.   ———

21. Jan's summer home, a log cabin on top of Sagee Mountain, was built many years ago.   ———

22. To make a snap decision is not wise.   ———

23. Barbara Creswell was a county commissioner for many years.   ———

24. Aunt Jess came a day early to meet some old friends.   ———

25. James Michener has published a novel about the Caribbean Islands.   ———

Exercise 24 Phrases

In each of the following sentences underline the phrase. In the first column at the right identify the type of phrase by writing

Prep for prepositional phrase,   **Inf** for infinitive phrase,
Part for participial phrase,   **App** for appositive phrase.
Ger for gerund phrase,

Then in the second column indicate its use by writing **Adj, Adv,** or **N.**

	Type	Use
Example: Carey, my cousin, attended Baylor University.	*App*	*N*

1. When he was a child, he became fascinated with science. _____ _____

2. Dr. Causey stresses learning mathematical fundamentals. _____ _____

3. Molly Woppie quickly crossed the bridge to escape the giant's wrath. _____ _____

4. Her ambition to be an engineer required many sacrifices. _____ _____

5. Having met last week, the trustees approved a new budget. _____ _____

6. The little boy remained quiet during the sermon. _____ _____

7. I saw Jessica standing alone and tearful. _____ _____

8. Reaching one's potential is very difficult. _____ _____

9. The professor cannot continue to ignore the student's impudence. _____ _____

10. The weather prophets are preparing us for a long, cold winter. _____ _____

11. Studying regularly can improve any student's grades. _____ _____

	Type	Use

12. Neither the players nor the coach has come onto the field. _____ _____

13. Working all day and attending evening classes, Sally is kept quite busy. _____ _____

14. Remember to write legibly. _____ _____

15. Skip seemed happy about his law partner's promotion. _____ _____

16. To get a good seat, we must arrive early. _____ _____

17. Selecting a college is a major decision. _____ _____

18. The Christmas parade and many other activities are planned for the holidays. _____ _____

19. One desire that I have is to become a storyteller. _____ _____

20. Guests will be given free tickets to the Madrigal Dinner. _____ _____

Exercise 25 Phrases

A. Combine the following pairs of sentences, making one sentence a participial phrase. Punctuate each sentence correctly.

Example: Acadia National Park is located in Maine. Last summer we visited Acadia National Park.

Last summer we visited Acadia National Park, located in Maine.

1. Charles Dickens is recognized as a great British novelist. He is buried in Poet's Corner in Westminster Abbey.

2. Laura and John discovered the entrance to an old mine. They were afraid to explore it.

3. The Greek hero Perseus killed the monster Medusa. He saved the life of Andromeda.

4. St. Augustine recorded his spiritual journey in *Confessions*. This book is an exceptional work to guide us through our own journey.

5. The Admissions Committee listened to all of Kyle's explanations. The committee agreed to admit him.

6. Elizabeth I ruled England for forty-five years. Her father was Henry VIII and her mother Anne Boleyn.

7. Chris locked his keys in his car. He became frustrated and disgusted.

8. Reid is an interpreter for the deaf. He has the opportunity to meet many interesting people.

9. Lucy knew the meaning of sacrifice. She was one of seven children.

10. Sister Carol Anne O'Marie wrote *The Missing Madonna*. It is a detective mystery about a missing person.

B. Combine the following pairs of sentences, making one of the sentences an *appositive* phrase.

Example: Nellie Taylor Ross was born in Wyoming. She became the first woman governor in the United States.

Nellie Taylor Ross, the first woman governor in the United States, was born in Wyoming.

1. Umberto Eco is author of *The Name of the Rose*. He has recently published another novel.

2. The San Diego Zoo is one of the largest in the world. It exhibits more than 3,200 animals.

3. There are nine Muses in Greek mythology. They are the daughters of Zeus and Mnemosyne.

4. Paris is one of the most exciting cities in Europe. It is the capital of France.

5. The *Pennsylvania Evening Post* began publication in 1783. It was the first daily newspaper in America.

6. The famous author-critic T. S. Eliot died in London, England. He was seventy-six years old at his death.

7. Dr. Joseph Noth is an ophthalmologist and a humanitarian. He spends several weeks each summer working with the poor in Ethiopia.

8. Louis L'Amour wrote numerous novels about the West. He had experienced many of the situations he chronicled.

9. Elizabeth Blackwell graduated from Geneva College in 1849. She became the first woman physician in the United States.

10. Clyde is our youngest son. He wants to be a concert pianist.

Exercise 26   Punctuation of Phrases

In the following sentences insert all commas required by the rules stated in Chapter 5. In the blanks write the commas with the words that precede them. When the sentence requires no comma, write **C** in the space.

Example: The conference having ended∧Deir-
dre   left   for   New   York.   _____*ended,*_____

1. With   the   rapid   accumulation   of   information   we   will   be   unable   to   master   all
   the   recently   acquired   knowledge.   _____

2. The   new   trend   in   computers   a
   notebook-size   portable   is   extremely
   powerful.   _____

3. By   keeping   the   draperies   closed   she   prevented   her   rugs   from   fading.   _____

4. Having   walked   four   miles   this   morning
   Grace   was   exhausted   before   she   came   to
   work.   _____

5. To   tell   the   truth   I   am   quite   ignorant
   about   computers.   _____

6. The   company's   third-quarter   profits   were
   a   surprise   all   things   considered.   _____

7. Giving   children   responsibility   prepares
   them   for   accepting   responsibility   as
   adults.   _____

8. The   rain   having   fallen   all   day   I
   enjoyed   a   day   of   reading   by   the   fire.   _____

9. Law   enforcement   a   constant   problem   is
   difficult   to   maintain.   _____

10. Learning   to   program   Ada   a   computer
    language   system   is   difficult   and
    confusing.   _____

11. In   1948   the   play   *A   Streetcar   Named
    Desire*   won   the   Pulitzer   Prize   in   drama.   _____

12. Having previously borrowed money from his family Dave was too embarrassed to ask again.   _____

13. Her two brothers Walker and Keith were on the Michigan State swimming team.   _____

14. The young woman sitting in my office has accepted a position with a major brokerage firm.   _____

15. Attracted by the opportunity to expand the board of directors agreed to purchase a telecommunications company.   _____

16. After driving to work on the expressway I am a mess when I get to the office.   _____

17. Francesca, having lived in Europe most of her life says Americans are very wasteful.   _____

18. To be selected to participate in the honors program Judy must make all *A*'s this quarter.   _____

19. Changing of the Guard at Buckingham Palace is a favorite tourist attraction.   _____

20. Working in his father's store he learned the importance of keeping good records.   _____

6

Independent Clauses

■ 6a Independent Clauses

A group of words containing a subject and a verb and expressing a complete thought is called a sentence or an **independent clause.** Some groups of words that contain a subject and a verb, however, do not express a complete thought and therefore cannot stand alone as a sentence. Such word groups are dependent on other sentence elements and are called **dependent clauses.**

Sometimes an independent clause stands alone as a sentence. Sometimes two or more independent clauses are combined into one sentence without a connecting word. Then a semicolon is used to connect the independent clauses:

The day is cold.

The day is cold; the wind is howling.

Sometimes independent clauses are connected by one of the coordinating conjunctions, *and, but, for, or, nor, so,* and *yet.* As these conjunctions do not subordinate, an independent clause beginning with one of them may stand as a complete sentence. Independent clauses joined by a coordinating conjunction are separated by commas. Therefore, to punctuate correctly, you must distinguish between independent clauses and other kinds of sentence elements joined by coordinating conjunctions. In the following examples note that only independent clauses joined by coordinating conjunctions are separated by commas:

The day was *dark* and *dreary.* [The conjunction *and* joins two adjectives, *dark* and *dreary.* No comma permitted.]

The fallen tree *blocked* the highway and *delayed* travel. [The conjunction *and* joins the two verbs. No comma permitted.]

She ran *up the steps* and *into the house.* [The conjunction *and* joins two phrases. No comma permitted.]

Mrs. Brown caught the fish, and *her husband cooked them.* [The conjunction *and* connects two independent clauses, and these are separated by a comma.]

Sometimes two independent clauses are connected by a **conjunctive,** or **transitional, adverb** such as one of the following:

however	moreover	nevertheless	therefore
then	accordingly	otherwise	thus
hence	besides	consequently	

A semicolon is necessary before any of these words beginning a second clause. After the longer *conjunctive adverbs* a comma is generally used:

We drove all day; *then* at sundown we began to look for a place to camp.

It rained during the afternoon; *consequently,* our trip to the mountains had to be postponed.

Note: Conjunctive adverbs can be distinguished from subordinating conjunctions by the fact that the *adverbs* can be shifted to a later position in the sentence, whereas the *conjunctions* cannot:

It rained during the afternoon; our trip to the mountains, *consequently,* had to be postponed.

Summary of punctuation: From the foregoing discussion and examples we can establish the following rules for the punctuation of independent clauses:

1. *Two independent clauses connected by a coordinating conjunction are separated by a comma:*

   Our goat chewed up the morning paper, *and* Father is angry.

   You should call Hank tonight, *for* he is all alone.

2. *Two independent clauses not connected by a coordinating conjunction are separated by a semicolon.* Remember that this rule also holds true when the second clause begins with a conjunctive adverb:

   Philip is quite strong; he is much stronger than I.

   We both wanted to go to the toboggan race; *however,* Mother had asked us to be home by six.

3. *A semicolon is used to separate independent clauses that are joined by a coordinating conjunction but are heavily punctuated with commas internally:*

   Being somewhat excited and, incidentally, terribly tired, Ellen's two children, Mary and Fred, became unruly; but they went quickly to sleep on the trip home.

4. *Short independent clauses, when used in a series with a coordinating conjunction preceding the final clause, may be separated by commas:*

   The audience was seated, the lights were dimmed, and the curtain was raised.

Note: A series consists of at least three elements.

■ 6b The Comma Splice

Use of a comma between two independent clauses not joined by a coordinating conjunction (Rule 2), is a major error called the **comma splice** (This term comes from the idea of splicing or "patching" together two clauses that should be more strongly separated.):

COMMA SPLICE: I enjoyed his company, I do not know that he enjoyed mine.

CORRECTION: I enjoyed his company, but I do not know that he enjoyed mine. (Rule 1)

I enjoyed his company; I do not know that he enjoyed mine. (Rule 2)

OR

I enjoyed his company; however, I do not know that he enjoyed mine. (Rule 2)

■ 6c The Run-together Sentence

The **run-together sentence** results from omitting punctuation between two independent clauses not joined by a conjunction. Basically the error is the same as that of the comma splice: it shows ignorance of sentence structure:

Twilight had fallen it was dark under the old oak tree near the house.

When you read the sentence just given, you have difficulty in getting the meaning at first because the ideas are run together. Now consider the following sentence:

Twilight had fallen, it was dark under the old oak tree near the house.

The insertion of the comma is not a satisfactory remedy, for the sentence now contains a comma splice. There are, however, four reliable devices for correcting the run-together sentence and the comma splice:

1. Connect two independent clauses by a comma and a coordinating conjunction if the two clauses are logically of equal importance:

   Twilight had fallen, and it was dark under the old oak tree near the house.

2. Connect two independent clauses by a semicolon if they are close enough in thought to make one sentence and you want to omit the conjunction:

   Twilight had fallen; it was dark under the old oak tree near the house.

3. Write the two independent clauses as separate sentences if you wish to give them separate emphasis.

   Twilight had fallen. It was dark under the old oak tree near the house.

4. Subordinate one of the independent clauses:

   When twilight had fallen, it was dark under the old oak tree near the house.

Exercise 27   The Comma Splice and the Run-together Sentence

Mark correct sentences **C**, run-together sentences **R**, and sentences containing a comma splice **CS**.

Example: Linemen get very little credit for winning football games, however, they play important roles.   _CS_

1. Beth was the storyteller in her family she remembers making up stories for the younger children.   _____

2. There is a proliferation of "how-to" and "self-help" books on the market, they are frequently on the best-seller list.   _____

3. Curtis is the oldest of five children he is the only one to have graduated from college.   _____

4. Paper towels serve many useful purposes, and they are not very expensive.   _____

5. Ryan's desk was cluttered with computer printouts the mess didn't seem to bother him.   _____

6. She broke the zipper on her evening dress her mother had to cut the dress off.   _____

7. The Director of the Research Center has a top-level managerial position, the director reports directly to the Vice President for Research.   _____

8. Brothers and sisters can be best of friends, they can be worst of enemies.   _____

9. Swimming, running, and bicycling are three parts of a triathlon; it is now an Olympic event.   _____

10. The environmentalists are urging the public to recycle trash however, few people are willing to separate their garbage.   _____

11. If I knew the environmental benefits of various products, I would be a better shopper and environmentalist.   _____

12. All at once she shivered, she began to feel the cold night air.   _____

13. The rain was cold and the wind piercing.   _____

14. In March I often stroll through the woods looking for crocuses, the crocus is a sign that spring is not far away.   _____

15. When our tire blew out, we had to walk three miles to the nearest service station when we got there, the station was closed.   _____

16. The rain forests are essential in keeping the earth healthy, however, developers continue to disregard the role of natural resources in the earth's survival.   _____

17. Ballet requires concentration and self-discipline, it provides great satisfaction to both the dancer and the audience.   _____

18. Journal writing is frequently used in English classes to teach composition; it is also used in weight-loss therapy.   _____

19. On the way to the hospital, the ambulance was involved in an accident, no one was hurt.   _____

20. Ruth Ann devotes many hours of service to charities and the community, she also spends several hours a day writing for the daily newspaper.   _____

Exercise 28   The Comma Splice and the Run-together Sentence

Mark correct sentences **C,** run-together sentences **R,** and sentences containing a comma splice **CS.**

Example: In Hartford, Wisconsin, there is a small Chrysler plant, it
makes outboard motors.   *CS*

1. In 1781 the Revolutionary War ended when General Cornwallis
   surrendered to General Washington at Yorktown.   _____

2. I did not understand that we were to go skiing this weekend, I
   have a book report due on Monday.   _____

3. Ray sold his house he moved to Santa Fe, where he was offered
   a job as a systems analyst.   _____

4. Derrick was not as bright as some of his classmates, however,
   because he worked so diligently, he did better than those who
   had more ability.   _____

5. James Webb, a graduate of the U.S. Naval Academy, is a former
   Secretary of the Navy he has written several books about his
   experiences in the Marines and as a midshipman.   _____

6. Many Russian and French choreographers wrote ballets; some of
   these ballets became popular in America.   _____

7. In 1863 Abraham Lincoln delivered his often-quoted Gettysburg
   Address, he was assassinated two years later in 1865.   _____

8. Once Megan had decided to go back to school, she felt relieved
   that the decision had been made however, she was a little
   apprehensive about attending classes with students so much
   younger than she.   _____

9. Harry hurried into the house; he took his coat off and hung it
   up, then he yelled, "I'm home."   _____

10. The desire to complete a job is frequently the key to completing
    it; someone told me that truth a long time ago.   _____

11. Acid rain is damaging our national forests and polluting our
    lakes it also is ruining the paint on my car.   _____

12. Many homeowners are learning to do their own repairs, some
    are finding the experience rewarding.   _____

13. We ate barbecue at Zeb's last night on the way home I saw a falling star, a sign of good luck.   _____

14. Climbing, hiking, and backpacking are Nicole's favorite pastimes, she is not interested in any indoor sports.   _____

15. The acrid smell of cigarettes may become offensive to non-smokers; it can also be a hazard to their health.   _____

16. Wearing extra large T-shirts and sweat shirts is a current "teeny bopper" fad next year it will be something else.   _____

17. The police were called when the next-door neighbors got into an argument over the boundary line the police persuaded them to discuss the matter calmly.   _____

18. I don't have time to cook a turkey for Christmas, therefore, I ordered one with all the trimmings from The Gourmet Cook.   _____

19. Every year Ed and Helen Phillips have a New Year's Eve celebration at their home this year it is a costume party.   _____

20. Garry, shifting from one foot to another, waited patiently for Amy to finish work he wanted to take her to dinner.   _____

21. Shana was miserably unsuccessful in her first job, however, after she requested a transfer to another department, she moved up rapidly.   _____

22. There are a number of details to be worked out before the contract can be signed the board wants the contract completed by next week.   _____

23. In spite of the many times that Tommy had traveled down this road, he missed the turnoff to Jeff's house.   _____

24. My neighbors get together every Wednesday night for supper, they take turns cooking.   _____

25. *The Old English Peep Show,* written by Peter Dickinson, won the British Crime Writers' Association's Golden Dagger Award.   _____

Exercise 29 Punctuation of Independent Clauses

In the following sentences insert all necessary commas and semicolons. Then in the space at the right write the correct punctuation mark with the word that precedes it. Write **C** if the sentence is correct.

Example: A magazine reported last month that a member of our faculty had been nominated for the Nobel Peace Prize⁄∧the report was in error.   _____*Prize;*_____

1. A young couple has bought the house across the street I think that the new owners are moving here from Fergus Falls, Minnesota.   _____

2. For weeks they had been looking for an apartment in the historic district and this afternoon they finally found one.   _____

3. I was dumfounded by his response yet I suppose that I should have expected it, considering the way that he has been acting.   _____

4. Let's go to a movie tonight a new James Bond is showing at Twin Towers.   _____

5. At the alumnae meeting, President Ross asked that the members become active politically she suggested a letter-writing campaign in support of recycling garbage.   _____

6. The Santa Fe Children's Theatre opens its new season with "The Pied Piper," an adaptation of a German fable this will be the twentieth season for the theatre.   _____

7. Gary Kasparov, the world chess champion, played chess at Harvard University in 1989 against eight opponents simultaneously: seven human beings and one computer he defeated all eight.   _____

8. Before coming to the University as president, Dr. Radford had held several administrative positions and she also had spent ten years teaching history.   _____

9. Jean-Paul Sartre was awarded the Nobel Prize for literature however, he refused to accept it.   _____

10. Connie smiles all the time consequently, some people doubt her sincerity.   _____

11. When President Seeton entered the room, an awkward silence filled the air and then the room was once again alive with chatter.   _____

12. Conrad was thrilled that you came for the presentation of his award your coming made the event complete.   _____

13. Emma and Ronnie are in the den and I will join you as soon as I answer the telephone.   _____

14. Virginia arrived in her faded blue jogging suit and her dirty tennis shoes she was the only one dressed casually.   _____

15. Suffering through another of Professor Zen's dull lectures demands too much energy therefore, I think that I will drop his class before he bores me to death.   _____

16. Some say that the times make the leader but others say that the leader makes the times.   _____

17. Margaret travels several days a week for her company and practically lives out of her suitcase I really wouldn't enjoy her job.   _____

18. Mediation is a process frequently used to settle disputes however, an agreement between the two parties is not always forthcoming.   _____

19. Kalene did not know whether her sister was being complimentary or patronizing so she decided to give her the benefit of the doubt. _____

20. If you visit Salt Lake City, you must attend a performance by the Mormon Tabernacle Choir they sing in the Tabernacle every Sunday. _____

7

Dependent Clauses

As you remember, a dependent clause is one that cannot stand alone as a sentence: although it has both a subject and a verb, it does not express a complete thought. Any clause beginning with a subordinating word like *what, that, who, which, when, since, before, after,* or *if* is a **dependent clause.** Dependent clauses, like phrases, function as grammatical units in a sentence — that is, as nouns, adjectives, and adverbs:

I went to school. ⎫ [Both clauses are independent.]
Too much time had elapsed. ⎭

When I went to school, I studied my lessons. [The first clause is dependent.]

Since too much time had elapsed, she remained at home. [The first clause is dependent.]

In the last two sentences *I studied my lessons* and *she remained at home* are complete statements. But the clauses *When I went to school* and *Since too much time had elapsed* do not express complete thoughts. They depend upon the independent statements to complete their meanings. Both of these dependent clauses function as adverbs.

■ 7a Noun Clauses

A **noun clause** is a dependent clause used as a noun, that is, as a subject, complement, object of a preposition, or appositive. Noun clauses are usually introduced by *that, what, why, whether, who, which,* or *how.* Some of these introductory words can introduce both noun and adjective clauses, since the function of the whole clause in the sentence, and not its introductory word, determines its classification. Most sentences containing noun clauses differ from those containing adjective and adverbial clauses in that, with the clause removed, they are no longer complete sentences.

101

Your *plan* is interesting. [This is a simple sentence, containing no dependent clause. The subject is the noun *plan*. The following example sentences show that dependent noun clauses may be substituted for the word *plan*, and vice versa.]

What you intend to do [your plan] is interesting. [The italicized noun clause is the subject of the verb *is*. Notice that the noun *plan* can be substituted for the clause.]

Tell me *what you intend to do* [your plan]. [The italicized noun clause is the direct object of the verb *tell*.]

That is *what you intend to do* [your plan]. [The italicized noun clause is a predicate nominative.]

I am interested in *what you intend to do* [your plan]. [The italicized noun clause is the object of the preposition *in*.]

The fact *that he had not told the truth* soon became apparent. [The italicized noun clause is in apposition with the noun *fact*.]

Bob's problem, *how he could open the locked door*, seemed insoluble. [The italicized noun clause is in apposition with the noun *problem*.]

Punctuation: *Noun clauses used as nonessential appositives are set off by commas.*

■ 7b Adjective Clauses

An **adjective clause** is a dependent clause that modifies a noun or pronoun. The common connective words used to introduce adjective clauses are the relative pronouns *who* (and its inflected forms *whom* and *whose*), *which*, *that*, and relative adverbs like *where*, *when*, and *why*. (*Where* and *when* can introduce all three kinds of clauses.)

The italicized clauses in the following sentences are all adjective clauses:

She is a woman *who is respected by everyone.*

Mr. Johnson, *whose son attends the University of Oklahoma,* is our minister.

He saw the place *where he was born.*

It was a time *when money did not count.*

I know the reason *why I failed the course.*

Adjective clauses are classified as **essential** (restrictive) and **nonessential** (nonrestrictive).

An *essential* clause, as its name indicates, is necessary in a sentence, for it identifies or points out a particular person or thing; a *nonessential* clause adds information about the word it modifies, but it is not essential in pointing out or identifying a person or thing:

Thomas Jefferson, *who was born on the frontier,* became President. [The name *Thomas Jefferson* has identified the person, and the italicized clause is not essential.]

A person *who loves to read* will never be lonely. [The italicized adjective clause is essential in identifying a particular kind of person.]

My father, *who was a country boy,* has lived in the city for years. [Since a person has only one father, an identifying clause is not essential.]

The girl *by whom I sat in class* is an honor student. [The italicized adjective clause is essential to the identification of *girl*.]

To determine whether an adjective clause is essential, you may apply this test: read the sentence leaving out the adjective clause and see whether the removal omits necessary identification. Try this test on the following sentence:

Jet pilots, *who work under a great deal of stress,* must stay in excellent physical condition.

You will see that the removal of the adjective clause does not change the basic meaning of the sentence. The italicized adjective clause is, therefore, nonessential.

Now read the following sentence, leaving out the italicized adjective clause:

Jet pilots *who are not in excellent physical condition* should not be allowed to fly.

If the adjective clause of this sentence is removed, the statement is not at all what the writer meant to say. The adjective clause is, therefore, essential.

Punctuation: *Nonessential adjective clauses are set off from the rest of the sentence by commas.* (See Chapter 19, Section b.)

■ 7c Adverbial Clauses

An **adverbial clause** is a dependent clause that functions exactly as if it were an adverb. Like an adverb it modifies a verb, an adjective, an adverb, or the whole idea expressed in the sentence's independent clause; for example, *As luck would have it,* we missed his telephone call.

An adverbial clause is used to show *time, place, cause, purpose, result, condition, concession, manner,* or *comparison.* Its first word is a subordinating conjunction. Common subordinating conjunctions and their uses are listed below:

1. Time (*when, before, since, as, while, until, after, whenever*)

   I will stay *until you come.*

   When the whistle blew, the laborer stopped.

2. Place (*where, wherever, whence, whither*)

   He went *where no one had ever set foot before.*

   Wherever you go, I will go also.

3. Cause (*because, since, as*)

   Since I had no classes on Saturday, I went home.

   Because he was afraid of being late, Bob ran all the way.

4. Purpose (*in order that, so that, that*)

   My family made many sacrifices *so that I could have an education.*

   Men work *that they may eat.*

5. Result (*so . . . that, such . . . that*)

   The weather was *so* cold *that I decided not to walk to school.*

6. Condition (*if, unless*)

You will hurt your hand *if you are not careful.*

Unless you apply at once, your name will not be considered.

7. Concession (*though, although*)

Although she had no money, she was determined to go to college.

8. Manner (*as, as if, as though*)

She looked *as though she wanted to laugh.*

Do *as you like,* but take the consequences.

9. Comparison (*as, than*)

He is older *than his brother.*

He is as tall *as his brother.*

Punctuation: *Introductory adverbial clauses are always set off by commas:*

Although he had tests to take and a term paper to write, he went home for the weekend.

While I was eating lunch, I had a phone call from my brother.

■ 7d Kinds of Sentences

For the purpose of varying style and avoiding monotony, you may need to be able to distinguish the four basic types of sentences. According to the number and kind of clauses (phrases do not affect sentence type), sentences may be grouped into four types: **simple, compound, complex,** and **compound-complex.**

1. A **simple** sentence is a single independent clause with one subject and one predicate. The one subject, however, may consist of more than one noun or pronoun, and the one predicate may consist of more than one verb.

Robert has a new car. [Single subject and single predicate.]

Robert and his *brother* have a new car. [There is one verb, *have,* but the subject consists of two nouns.]

Robert *washed* and *polished* his new car on Sunday. [There is one subject, *Robert,* but two verbs.]

Robert and his *brother washed* and *polished* their new car. [The subject consists of two nouns, *Robert* and *brother;* and the predicate consists of two verbs, *washed* and *polished.*]

2. A **compound** sentence contains at least two independent clauses and no dependent clause:

Mary likes the mountains, but Jackie prefers the seashore.

A lamp was lighted in the house, the happy family was talking together, and supper was waiting.

3. A **complex** sentence contains only one independent clause and one or more dependent clauses (the dependent clauses are in italics):

The toy truck *that you gave Molly for her birthday* is broken.

Why he refused to contribute to the fund we do not know.

4. A **compound-complex** sentence has at least two independent clauses and one or more dependent clauses (the independent clauses are in italics):

My friend was offended by my attitude, and *I was sorry* that she was hurt.

We spent the morning looking for the home of the woman who paints landscapes, but *we were unable to find it.*

Exercise 30   Clauses

In the following sentences underline each dependent clause. In the space at the right, write **Adj** if the clause is an adjective clause, **Adv** if it is an adverbial clause, and **N** if it is a noun clause. If the sentence contains no dependent clause, leave the space blank.

Example: Does Kyle know <u>that chocolate contains caffeine?</u>   _____N_____

1. The springs in the sofa broke when the children jumped on it.   _____

2. Everyone listened quietly as the storyteller told of faraway places and kings and princes.   _____

3. Dr. Bliss, who is Dean of the School of Engineering, is an authority on Indian lore.   _____

4. When I try to study in the residence hall, I understand the problem of noise pollution.   _____

5. Gardening is a therapeutic hobby that many people can enjoy.   _____

6. At one time Scott thought that he wanted to be an insurance salesman.   _____

7. Although Jeffrey is known as a practical joker, he cannot take a joke.   _____

8. Since her novels were published, Alice Walker has been in constant demand as a speaker.   _____

9. Lynn's mother, who has a law degree from the University of Chicago, is a practicing attorney.   _____

10. Nelson is not happy living with his parents, even though he has everything done for him.   _____

11. Few American photographers have been as honored and admired as Ansel Adams.   _____

12. Myron is a person whom you may trust.   _____

13. Because he was ashamed, Eric waited a long time to admit that he couldn't read.   _____

14. We were required to take a stress test before we were allowed to begin the exercises.   _____

15. Kim is a more interesting person than her brother.   _____

16. This afternoon we will visit the house where my grandfather was born.   _____

17. Some of the posters that were hanging in the room were amusing to the students' parents.   _____

18. Travis knows that you are coming for his game.   _____

19. What I asked him to do will take only a few minutes.   _____

20. In 1987 van Gogh's *Irises* was sold at auction for 53.9 million dollars, which was the largest amount ever paid for an art item up to that date.   _____

21. Automobile manufacturers make so many different models that Aaron spent three months selecting a car.   _____

22. Astronomy is an old science that every day becomes more important to the earth's survival.   _____

23. I appreciate your being a friend whom I can trust.   _____

24. If the play begins at 8:30 P.M., we must leave the restaurant by eight o'clock.   _____

25. People do unbelievable things when they are under stress.   _____

26. Brian will meet us in Seattle if he can.   _____

27. Pecan growers use machines to shake the trees when the nuts are ready to be gathered.   _____

28. The suggestion that we all ride in the van together makes sense to me.   _____

29. The cost of automobile insurance is usually reduced if the car is equipped with air bags.   _____

30. I did not know that Phil had transferred from the University of Oregon to the University of Arkansas.   _____

Exercise 31 Clauses

Give the function of each of the *italicized* clauses by writing the proper abbreviations in the space at the right:

  S for subject,   **OP** for object of a preposition,
  DO for direct object,   **Adj** for adjective modifier,
  PN for predicate nominative,   **Adv** for adverbial modifier.

Example: *When he arrived at the cabin,* it was nearly ten o'clock.   _Adv_

1. Many educators have concluded *that children spend too many hours watching television.*   _____

2. *If Eric has parked in the hospital lot,* the receptionist will validate his parking ticket.   _____

3. Judge Harkins, *who heard our case,* was recently appointed to the state Supreme Court.   _____

4. *What Rudy submitted as his project* obviously took a great deal of effort.   _____

5. Do I understand *that his office provides the direction for both short-range and long-range financial planning?*   _____

6. I don't like the chandelier in Emily's new house, *which I really don't like anyway.*   _____

7. The speech therapist treated a friend of mine *who had lost her voice in an accident.*   _____

8. The homebuilders *who were developing mountain property* had open house for prospective buyers.   _____

9. Entering the priesthood requires *that a person spend many hours in study and personal reflection.*   _____

10. John Wieland, *who developed our subdivision,* is a personal friend of my father.   _____

11. The sundial in the garden casts long shadows, *which remind us of approaching autumn.*   _____

12. Switching from Daylight Saving Time to Eastern Standard Time upset my son, *who liked to play ball after school.*   _____

13. The artist said *that painting is a creative activity controlled by the right side of the brain.*   _____

14. Eating ice cream late at night is a habit *that I should break.* ———

15. *As soon as Amy finishes her annual report,* she will go to San Francisco for a conference. ———

16. Paul's suggestion is *that we all meet in the hotel lobby.* ———

17. From *what the flight attendant said,* our flight has been delayed. ———

18. The lecture having ended, we rushed to the cafeteria *so that we would beat the crowd.* ———

19. The survey suggests *that the public is aware* of *what many manufacturers are producing.* ———

20. *After she had lit the Christmas tree,* the President's wife returned to the White House. ———

21. The children were interested in *what their grandmother had in the oven.* ———

22. Sweat suits, *which are made in many different colors,* are worn nearly everywhere. ———

23. *Since we left home,* we have had a flat tire, a broken fan belt, and a blown water gasket. ———

24. Shopping the day after Thanksgiving offers many good bargains, *although I don't recommend it.* ———

25. The book *that I recently read* is now on the best-seller list. ———

Exercise 32 Review of Clauses

In the following sentences enclose the dependent clauses in parentheses. In the spaces at the right indicate the number of independent and dependent clauses in each sentence. Be able to tell the function of each of the dependent clauses. (Note that some sentences may not contain a dependent clause.)

	Ind.	Dep.
Example: You do know (that the First Amendment to the Constitution guarantees religious freedom.)	_1_	_1_
1. Although Jan is a grandmother, she still enjoys dancing to beach music.	_____	_____
2. What I want for Christmas is a new car, but what I will get is new tires for my old car.	_____	_____
3. When the children were young, we spent our summers in the country at my grandparents' home.	_____	_____
4. Ivan pretends that he is a mysterious person whose heritage can be traced to royalty, but no one takes him seriously.	_____	_____
5. Although he is no longer young, Frank is stronger than he looks.	_____	_____
6. Whether you buy a new house or one that has been previously occupied, be sure to make a final inspection before you sign the contract.	_____	_____
7. Sam Snead is the only professional golfer to have won twenty-seven official tournaments.	_____	_____
8. Jeffrey is a weight-control physician, yet he is somewhat overweight himself.	_____	_____
9. If Laura has strong ankles, she will be able to dance on point.	_____	_____
10. While she was walking to class, a storm came up and turned her umbrella inside out.	_____	_____

	Ind.	Dep.

11. The poncho that I had at camp came in handy; it kept the dog dry when it rained. ____ ____

12. Pink marble, which comes from a quarry in North Georgia, is beautiful, and it is used all over the world. ____ ____

13. The instructions for assembling the doll house were unclear, and before Jerry had finished, he had spent six hours putting it together. ____ ____

14. Many fast-food restaurants serve giant hamburgers that are three inches high and filled with meat, lettuce, tomatoes, onions, bacon, and pickles. ____ ____

15. Hot chocolate, cappuccino, or a steaming cup of Russian tea is often what we crave on a cold, rainy night. ____ ____

16. Last June, Mary Claire enlisted in the Navy and is now stationed in Iceland, where she is responsible for maintaining the radar equipment. ____ ____

17. If Justin attends the college of his choice, he will go to the University of Arizona to study geology, and when he graduates, he will join his father's firm. ____ ____

18. A knuckleball, which is a difficult pitch to hit, is a batter's nightmare. ____ ____

19. Charlotte, the great-aunt of my brother-in-law, has recently arrived from England; if she finds a teaching position, she wants to stay here permanently. ____ ____

20. During spring break, which comes late this year, several of us will travel south to visit the beaches; we may also go to Disney World if we have the time and money. ____ ____

21. Planning a week-long conference requires mental and physical stamina if it is to be successful. ____ ____

	Ind.	Dep.

22. Where will Shawn go after he leaves college if he decides not to accept the job in Dallas?   ___   ___

23. Charlie, who attended Duke University with my sister, was an instant success in the state legislature; he won high marks from both the Democrats and the Republicans because he was willing to consider an opposing opinion.   ___   ___

24. The long, exhausting week having ended, we had dinner at Nicole's, which is a small, family-owned restaurant.   ___   ___

25. Chuck really wants to teach American literature, but his father insists that he become an attorney.)   ___   ___

Exercise 33 Clauses

Complete each of the sentences below by writing in the spaces an *adjective clause,* an *adverbial clause,* or a *noun clause* as indicated above each space.

(adverbial clause)

Example: *When she entered the contest,* _____ she did not expect to win.

(adjective clause)

1. Roadside stands offer specialties _____

_____

(noun clause)

2. Economists agree _____

(adverbial clause)

3. _____ he   should   be   cautious   about
giving his credit card number.

(adjective clause)

4. The   committee   _____   completed
its report early.

(adjective clause)

5. The World Series and the Super Bowl are games _____

_____

(adverbial clause)

6. _____ perhaps you are watching too much television.

(adverbial clause)

7. Rick was disappointed _____

(adjective clause)

8. The fashion industry, —————————————————

———————— designs many unattractive clothes.

(noun clause)

9. ————————————————— is simply not true.

(adverb clause)

10. A black widow spider's bite may be fatal —————————————

—————————————————————————

Exercise 34 Punctuation of Clauses

In the following sentences supply commas and semicolons where they are needed. In the spaces at the right, write the marks of punctuation with the words that precede them. Write **C** if the sentence is correct.

Example: When I arrived at the beach∧the surf was already up.

_____*beach,*_____

1. The rookie pitcher who had just walked a man was falling behind in the count again.

_____

2. The catcher sensed the young man's growing uneasiness and strode out to the mound for a conference.

_____

3. Deciding how to hang the pictures was no easy job everyone I talked to suggested a different arrangement.

_____

4. Actually hanging them wasn't easy either since I had not measured the space above the couch correctly.

_____

5. The two boys moved down the steep bank gingerly then they discovered that climbing up the slope covered with pine needles was even more difficult.

_____

6. When I arrived at the entrance to Macy's I was annoyed to find that the store had been closed for its annual inventory.

_____

7. What to do about the complex problem of illiteracy was the subject of a recent national conference.

_____

8. Joe says that he doesn't know whom to vote for but I think that there is a clear choice between the two candidates for mayor.

_____

9. One can sit in a hotel in Paris turn to CNN and hear the evening news reported in English.

_____

117

10. My Uncle Ed shoots a great game of pool consequently he has difficulty finding an opponent.   _____

11. A big cup of frozen strawberry yogurt is just what I need on a hot day like this.   _____

12. Although most of us longed for rain the dry weather was what the Versons needed for a good grape harvest.   _____

13. The Tropical Shop which sits on the edge of a vast asphalt parking lot attracts passersby interested in bright green or pink snow cones.   _____

14. In the mornings when the birds appear at the feeder the woodpeckers insist upon eating first.   _____

15. Rick put the alarm clock on his desk so he would have to get up to turn it off he had to be at the track at six o'clock.   _____

16. The shuttle bus that I took from the airport was crowded and I found myself sitting next to the driver who explained in detail why the Pirates were in the cellar.   _____

17. The Hawaii Volcanoes National Park which is located on the largest of the islands offers its visitors opportunities to see an active volcano.   _____

18. The volcano Kilauea spills hot lava into the sea and sends up great clouds of steam.   _____

19. As soon as I saw Professor Rizzo buying books at Oxford's I thought about those crowded bookshelves in his office.   _____

20. A workshop on techniques for survival in the wilderness is being taught by the ranger whom we met last summer.   _____

21. Because newspapers are racing to report results of elections they occasionally publish erroneous information.   _____

22. Mrs. Smoltz feels better since her most experienced chef has told her he has no intention of leaving.   _____

23. One cannot always account for the success of a restaurant however it is safe to say that a good chef is an essential ingredient.   _____

24. If we rent three videos this weekend we can get a fourth one free.   _____

25. I don't think that I have time to look at four tapes between now and Monday morning I have to struggle with my biology assignment today and meet my father for lunch on Sunday.   _____

Exercise 35 Kinds of Sentences

Identify the type of sentence by writing one of the following abbreviations in the space at the right:

S if the sentence is simple, **Cx** if the sentence is complex,
Cp if the sentence is compound, **Cp-Cx** if the sentence is compound-complex.

Example: I do not see Rita very often, but I consider her my
friend.   *Cp*

1. Although Mr. Tran seldom plays golf, he follows the tour as
   if he were a pro.   _____

2. I defy you to find a colder street corner than the one that I
   stood on this morning; furthermore, my bus ran late.   _____

3. A franchise will give Nell an opportunity to try her skills as a
   manager, but it will also give her the security of an established business.   _____

4. The Surfers need a pianist and are going to put an ad in Sunday's *Times*.   _____

5. Mrs. Trumble seems incapable of driving on one side of the
   street; my grandfather says that she "takes her half out of the
   middle."   _____

6. The plane that was to fly me from Kansas City back home
   was grounded because of the snowstorm.   _____

7. While I waited in the airport, I spent most of the time trying
   to guess where the other passengers had come from and
   where they were going.   _____

8. Much to the embarrassment of her older brother, the little girl
   with the red pigtails danced up one aisle and down another
   in the crowded grocery store.   _____

9. Walter despised writing letters; in fact, he could hardly
   remember a letter that he had written since the ones that his
   mother had made him write to his Aunt Sarah.   _____

10. Joe has been a sports reporter for the *Tribune* for several
    years; now his ambition is to have a column of his own.   _____

11. Once upon a time that old house with the boarded-up win-
    dows belonged to Nita's grandparents.   _____

12. Borrow some of Kelly's popcorn, and we will pop it in the microwave oven. _____

13. The man had had no formal instruction, but his paintings with their heavy strokes and bold colors caught the curator's attention. _____

14. Manufacturing plants have been built along this ridge because the railroad runs directly behind it. _____

15. Do you think that one of these small refrigerators would be useful on our hall? _____

16. That we are able to send a probe out of our solar system and into interstellar space is indeed astonishing. _____

17. One morning a few days before Christmas, eight or nine of us met at Maggie's Coffee House, our favorite gathering place, and talked about Mrs. Murdock, the terror of the English Department. _____

18. The golfer needed a birdie on the eighteenth hole to make it to the play-off; nevertheless, she seemed quite relaxed as she addressed the ball. _____

19. It was eleven o'clock, we were hungry, and Max came up with the idea of a pizza. _____

20. We finally decided to place individual orders after none of us could agree on the toppings that we wanted. _____

21. Saturday morning the family gathered on the curb to say good-bye to my sister; she had finally squeezed her belongings into her yellow Camaro and was headed to the city and her first job. _____

22. Old school buses are used to carry everything from bales of hay to crates of chickens to fledgling rock groups. _____

23. The boy who was leaning against the motorcycle looked as if he had pulled off the road to wait for someone. _____

24. The snow, which had lain for days in great gray banks, began to melt; and the streets were wet with small streams of icy water. _____

25. The pine trees, which had been coated with ice, remained bent even after those sharp slivers disappeared in the spring sunshine. _____

8

Agreement of Subject and Verb

The verb in every independent or dependent clause must agree with its subject in person and number. (There are **three persons:** the **first person** is the speaker, the **second person** is the person spoken to, and the **third person** is the person or thing spoken about. There are **two numbers:** the **singular,** denoting one person or thing, and the **plural,** denoting more than one person or thing.) A careful study of the conjugation of the verb in Chapter 1 will show you that a verb can change form not only in *tense* but also in *person* and *number.* If you can recognize the subject and the verb, you should have no trouble making the two agree. Although there is ordinarily no problem in doing so, certain difficulties need special attention.

■ 8a Intervening Expressions

The number of the verb in a sentence is not affected by any modifying phrases or clauses standing between the subject and the verb but is determined entirely by the number of the subject:

> The *evidence* that they submitted to the judges *was* [not *were*] convincing. [*Evidence* is the subject of the verb *was.*]

> The new *library* with its many books and its quiet reading rooms *fills* [not *fill*] a long-felt need. [*Library* is the subject of the verb *fills;* the phrase *with its many books . . .* has nothing to do with the verb.]

> A list of eligible candidates *was* [not *were*] posted on the bulletin board. [*List* is the subject of the verb *was posted.*]

Our big pine tree as well as a small oak *was* [not *were*] damaged by the high winds. [*Tree* is the subject of the verb *was damaged;* the intervening phrase *as well as a small oak* is not a part of the subject.]

The famous golfer along with his many fans *was* [not *were*] heading toward the ninth green. [*Golfer* is the subject of the verb *was heading; along with his many fans* is not a part of the subject.]

My father, together with my two brothers, *is* [not *are*] planning to build a cabin at the lake. [*Father* is the subject of the verb *is planning.* The phrase that comes between the subject and the verb is not a part of the subject.]

■ 8b Verb Preceding the Subject

In some sentences the verb precedes the subject. This reversal of common order frequently leads to error in agreement:

There *is* [not *are*] in many countries much *unrest* today. [*Unrest* is the subject of the verb *is.*]

There *are* [not *is*] a *table,* two *couches,* four *chairs,* and a *desk* in the living room. [*Table, couches, chairs,* and *desk* are the subjects of the verb *are.*]

Where *are* [not *is*] Bob and his *friends going*? [*Bob* and *friends* are subjects of the verb *are going.*]

■ 8c Indefinite Pronouns

The indefinite pronouns or adjectives *either, neither,* and *each;* the adjective *every;* and such compounds as *everybody, anybody, everyone, anyone* are always singular. *None* may be singular or plural. The plural usage is more common:

Each of the plans *has* [not *have*] its advantages.

Everyone who heard the speech *was* [not *were*] impressed by it.

Every bud, stalk, flower, and seed *reveals* [not *reveal*] a workmanship beyond the power of man.

Is [not *Are*] *either* of you ready for a walk?

None of the men *have* brought their wives.

None of the three *is* [*are*] interested.

None — no, not one — *is* prepared.

■ 8d Compound Subjects

Compound subjects joined by *and* normally require a plural verb:

Correctness and *precision* are required in all good writing.

Where *are* the *bracelets* and *beads*?

Note: When nouns joined by *and* are thought of as a unit or actually refer to the same person or thing, the verb is normally singular:

The *sum* and *substance* of the matter *is* [not *are*] hardly worth considering.

My *friend* and *coworker* Mr. Jones *has* [not *have*] gone abroad.

■ 8e Subjects Joined by *Or* and *Nor*

Singular subjects joined by *or* or *nor* take a singular verb. If one subject, however, is singular and one plural, the verb agrees in number and person with the nearer one:

Either the *coach* or the *player was* [not *were*] at fault.

Neither the *cat* nor the *kittens have* been fed. [The plural word *kittens* in the compound subject stands next to the verb *have been fed.*]

Neither the *kittens* nor the *cat has* been fed. [The singular subject *cat* stands next to the verb, which is therefore singular.]

Neither my *brothers* nor *I am* going. [Note that the verb agrees with the nearer subject in person as well as in number.]

■ 8f Nouns Plural in Form

As a general rule use a singular verb with nouns that are plural in form but singular in meaning. The following nouns are usually singular in meaning: *news, economics, ethics, physics, mathematics, gallows, mumps, measles, shambles, whereabouts:*

The *news is* reported at eleven o'clock.

Measles is a contagious disease.

The following nouns are usually plural: *gymnastics, tactics, trousers, scissors, athletics, tidings, acoustics, riches, barracks:*

Athletics attract him.

The *scissors are* sharp.

Riches often *take* wing and *fly* away.

Plural nouns denoting a mass, a quantity, or a number require a singular verb when the subject is regarded as a unit.

Five *dollars is* too much for her to pay.

Fifty *bushels was* all the bin would hold.

Though usage is mixed, phrases involving addition, multiplication, subtraction, and division of numbers preferably take the singular:

Two and two is [are] four.

Two times three is six.

Twelve divided by six is two.

■ 8g Determining Modifiers

In expressions like *some of the pie(s)*, *a percentage of the profit(s)*, *all of the money*, *all of the children*, the number of *some*, *percentage*, and *all* is determined by the number of the noun in the prepositional phrase:

Some of the pie *is* missing.

Some of the pies *are* missing.

Whether to use a singular or plural verb with the word *number* depends on the modifying article. *The number* requires a singular verb; *a number*, a plural one.

The number of students at the art exhibit *was* small.

A small *number* of students *were* at the art exhibit.

■ 8h The Subject of Some Form of *To Be*

When one noun precedes and another follows some form of the verb *to be*, the first noun is the subject, and the verb agrees with it and not with the complement even if the complement is different in number:

The only *fruit* on the market now *is* peaches.

Peaches are the only fruit on the market now. [In the first sentence *fruit* is the subject; in the second, *peaches*.]

■ 8i Relative Pronoun as Subject

When a relative pronoun (*who*, *which*, or *that*) is used as the subject of a clause, the number and person of the verb are determined by the antecedent of the pronoun, the word to which the pronoun refers:

This is the student *who is* to be promoted. [The antecedent of *who* is the singular noun *student*; therefore, *who* is singular.]

These are the students *who are* to be promoted. [The antecedent of *who* is the plural noun *students*.]

Should I, *who am* a stranger, be allowed to enter the contest? [*Who* refers to *I*; *I* is first person, singular number.]

She is one of those irresponsible persons *who are* always late. [The antecedent of *who* is *persons*.]

If sentences such as the last one give you trouble, try beginning the sentence with the "of" phrase, and you will readily see that the antecedent of *who* is *persons* and not *one*:

Of those irresponsible *persons who are* always late she is one.

■ 8j Collective Nouns

Some nouns are singular in form but plural in meaning. They are called **collective nouns** and include such words as *team, class, committee, crowd,* and *crew.* These nouns may take either a singular or a plural verb: if you are thinking of the group as a unit, use a singular verb; if you are thinking of the individual members of the group, use a plural verb:

> The *crew is* striking for higher pay. [The crew is acting as a unit.]

> The *crew are* writing reports of the wreck. [The members of the crew are acting as individuals.]

■ 8k Nouns with Foreign Plurals

Some nouns retain the plural forms peculiar to the languages from which they have been borrowed: *alumni, media, crises.* Still other nouns occur with either their original plural forms or plural forms typical of English: *aquaria* or *aquariums, criteria* or *criterions.* If you are in doubt as to the correct or preferred plural form of a noun, consult a good dictionary.

Note: Be careful not to use a plural form when you refer to a singular idea. For instance, write *He is an alumnus of Harvard,* not *He is an alumni of Harvard.*

Exercise 36   Subject-Verb Agreement

Write the correct form of the *italicized* verb in the space at the right.

Example: Around the corner from the drug store
(*were, was*) a bakery and a supermarket.   _____*were*_____

1. A jury of eight men and four women (*have, has*)
   been impaneled to hear the case involving the cattle rustlers.   _____

2. Neither of the books that I have ordered for Carol's
   birthday (*have, has*) come.   _____

3. A small group of students (*hope, hopes*) to go skiing
   in Quebec over the Christmas holiday.   _____

4. These cinnamon buns, a favorite for breakfast at
   our house, (*are, is*) the best to be found south of
   Philadelphia.   _____

5. In the fall every banner and balloon (*welcome,
   welcomes*) the tourists to the festival sponsored by
   the civic clubs.   _____

6. My nephew Albert can never remember whether
   six times nine (*are, is*) fifty-four or fifty-six. _____

7. The mayor, along with the members of the city
   council, (*have, has*) invited the visitors from Belgium
   to inspect the chocolate factory.   _____

8. Before the game the alumni (*are, is*) meeting in the
   auditorium to hear an address by the president of
   the College.   _____

9. Each of the students maintaining the required average (*are, is*) going to receive a scholarship.   _____

10. Seemingly lost in the depths of her tote bag (*are, is*)
    the parking ticket and the keys to her car.   _____

11. The media (*have, has*) been aggressive in pursuing
    information about the President's decision concern-
    ing the defense budget.   _____

12. Because he had watched Westerns most of his life, he knew that the gallows (*were, was*) not meant for the man in the white hat.   _____

13. Despite the vaccine, measles (*have, has*) reappeared among the kindergarten children.   _____

14. Whenever I read his poetry, I am aware again that E.E. Cummings is one of those poets who (*know, knows*) Americans well.   _____

15. The executive committee (*plan, plans*) to convene immediately after the general meeting.   _____

16. Either her brother or her parents (*have, has*) Leah's address in California.   _____

17. The number of horses running in the Kentucky Derby (*vary, varies*) from year to year.   _____

18. A number of the state's newspapers (*have, has*) already endorsed the governor for re-election.   _____

19. In the middle of the bed (*were, was*) the suitcase along with the clothes I intended to put in it.   _____

20. The long and short of the matter (*are, is*) that the present budget cannot accommodate the scientific research needed for all the space programs.   _____

Exercise 37　Subject-Verb Agreement

Write the correct form of the *italicized* verb in the space at the right.

Example:　A list of the qualifications for membership (*appear,*
appears) in the bylaws.　　　　　　　　　　　　　　　　 *appears*

1. Everybody who (*want, wants*) to go to the Shakespeare festival with Dr. Francisco must sign up today.　　　　　　_____

2. The father and his sons (*were, was*) watching with amusement as I struggled to change my tire.　　　　　　　　_____

3. I am afraid that there (*are, is*) sleet and snow predicted for
the mountains this weekend.　　　　　　　　　　　　_____

4. The problem is that none of us in the camp (*have, has*)
brought clothes warm enough for such weather.　　　　_____

5. The president of the company as well as his administrative
staff (*are, is*) meeting with the insurance commissioner.　_____

6. In the morning paper (*are, is*) a long account of last night's
game and a brief mention of Sam's spectacular run.　　_____

7. Either the director of the play or the designer of the set
(*are, is*) to be congratulated for the elegant backdrop.　_____

8. Now that September has come, the fruit to look for at the
market (*are, is*) pears.　　　　　　　　　　　　　　_____

9. We have reason to be glad that ethics (*are, is*) a growing
concern in every area of our lives.　　　　　　　　　_____

10. Neither the mother bird nor her nestlings (*were, was*) disturbed by our comings and goings along the path to the
barn.　　　　　　　　　　　　　　　　　　　　　　_____

11. Five dollars (*were, was*) entirely too much to pay for the
breakfast that was served the opening morning of the
conference.　　　　　　　　　　　　　　　　　　　_____

12. Norman seems completely oblivious to the fact that his
red-checked trousers (*are, is*) too short.　　　　　　　_____

13. Either you or I (*are, am*) to be responsible for packing up
the equipment after the soccer game.　　　　　　　　_____

14. Every one of the benches along the walk (*were, was*) occupied by old men and women reading the afternoon paper or napping in the sun. _____

15. When we saw the long line at the ticket window, we were certain that every man, woman, and child in Chicago (*were, was*) captivated by the game of baseball. _____

16. During the summer we moved into this house, and the whereabouts of my skates (*are, is*) now anybody's guess. _____

17. There (*are, is*) a grand prize of a trip to Hawaii as well as a VCR and a microwave for the second- and third-place winners. _____

18. Neither the rugged cliffs nor the bottomless chasm (*prove, proves*) indomitable to the Lone Ranger and Tonto and Silver. _____

19. Some of the lights along the expressway (*were, was*) out, and I suddenly realized how dark the afternoon had become. _____

20. Some of the light from the kitchen (*were, was*) shining through the half-closed blinds; I was glad that someone was at home. _____

Exercise 38 Subject-Verb Agreement

Write the correct form of the *italicized* verb in the space at the right.

Example: (*Are, Is*) either of these trains going to Los Angeles?   _____*Is*_____

1. The acoustics in the old gym (*were, was*) hardly suitable for the performance of the Christmas chorale.   _____

2. The high tide along with the strong winds (*were, was*) playing havoc with the dunes in front of the cottage.   _____

3. She was making good time on the narrow back road until she came upon a convoy of trucks that (*were, was*) taking supplies to the ranger camp.   _____

4. I don't know what your favorite dessert may be, but Bananas Foster (*are, is*) mine.   _____

5. Half of the students in my geology class (*have, has*) been given one topic to report on, and the other half another.   _____

6. This half of the class (*have, has*) the more interesting but more difficult assignment.   _____

7. Neither of these routes to San Antonio (*go, goes*) through Forrest City.   _____

8. According to the newspaper article, the Georgia Folklore Archives (*comprise, comprises*) approximately eight thousand tales.   _____

9. *The Storytellers*, containing more than two hundred selections, (*were, was*) a joint venture of a professor and his students.   _____

10. Walking along the fence with the poise of one of the rulers of ancient Arabia (*were, was*) my cat Theo.   _____

11. The scissors that you'll find on Myra's desk (*cut, cuts*) better than this pair.   _____

12. That vase filled with the gorgeous roses from the mayor's garden (*need, needs*) to be moved from that corner and put on this table.   _____

13. The pair of mittens left on the school bus (*belong, belongs*) to either Jo or her younger sister.   _____

14. Bismarck was absolutely right when he said that "politics (*are, is*) not an exact science." _____

15. Inspector Morse is one of those English detectives who (*have, has*) more complex personalities than the reader anticipates. _____

16. You and I have been asked to address the invitations, and some of the others (*are, is*) to decorate the hall. _____

17. Each year a series of concerts (*are, is*) performed by the Lanier Symphony in Pearce Auditorium. _____

18. Neither the boys nor their sister (*have, has*) driven the van that their parents bought last week. _____

19. Why do you think that I, who (*are, am*) the best cook in the family, should listen to Martin's advice about this fruit cake? _____

20. In one of his essays Francis Bacon observed that "riches (*are, is*) a good handmaid but the worst mistress." _____

Exercise 39   Subject-Verb Agreement

Write the correct form of the *italicized* verb in the space at the right.

Example: When (*are, is*) the architect and the designer to meet
with the building committee?   _____*are*_____

1. The sum and substance of the attorney's argument (*were,
   was*) that his clients were ignorant of Boston's traffic laws.   _____

2. Mr. Knowles does not think that the data (*support, supports*)
   the decision to change the flight schedules.   _____

3. Every Tom, Dick, and Lucy (*are, is*) interested in seeing the
   job recruiters who will be on campus next week.   _____

4. A group of congressmen (*have, has*) announced plans to
   attend an international trade conference during the spring
   recess.   _____

5. Neither his charm nor his good looks (*were, was*) sufficient
   to persuade the director that Henry should have the lead
   in the opening production.   _____

6. My former supervisor and long-time friend (*are, is*) organiz-
   ing a camping trip in the Adirondacks.   _____

7. Can you believe that fifty dollars (*are, is*) the price of a
   ticket to the gala?   _____

8. This is a year in which crises (*seem, seems*) to occur in quick
   succession and in every area of the world.   _____

9. Everybody in the stadium (*were, was*) cheering as the
   injured linebacker stood and hobbled to the sidelines.   _____

10. Data Systems (*are, is*) responsible for some of the new
    equipment in the computer lab.   _____

11. Not one of us in the geography class (*were, was*) able to tell
    Mr. Kingsley the current name of the Spice Islands.   _____

12. The phenomena scientifically identified as the aurora
    borealis (*are, is*) often called the northern lights.   _____

13. The economic indices published in Monday's paper (*were,
    was*) sending the usual mixed signals to Wall Street.   _____

14. The guidelines for circulating the large-print books, which are shelved on the first floor, (*were, was*) established by the Library of Congress.   _____

15. Each of the employees at the First National Bank (*own, owns*) shares of its stock.   _____

16. Somebody whose truck is parked in the lower lot (*have, has*) left the headlights on.   _____

17. Athletics (*are, is*) of such importance in our town that every last one of us knows who is on what team.   _____

18. My mother and my best friend (*have, has*) often discussed the possibility of our taking a trip together down the Natchez Trace.   _____

19. It was Karl Gauss, the German mathematician, who said that "mathematics (*are, is*) the queen of the sciences."   _____

20. I dare say that all of us (*do, does*) not agree with Professor Gauss.   _____

Agreement of Pronoun and Antecedent

Pronouns, as you saw in Chapter 1, are words that are used in the place of nouns when repetition of a noun would be awkward. *The dog hurt the dog's foot* is clearly an unnatural expression. Usually a pronoun has a definite, easily recognized *antecedent* (the noun or pronoun to which it refers), with which it agrees in *person, number,* and *gender*. The *case* of a pronoun, however, is not dependent on the case of its antecedent.

■ 9a Certain Singular Antecedents

Use singular pronouns to refer to singular antecedents. The indefinite pronouns *each, either, neither, anyone, anybody, everyone, everybody, someone, somebody, no one, nobody* are singular, and pronouns referring to them should be singular:

> *Each* of the girls has *her* own car.
>
> *Neither* of the boys remembered *his* poncho.
>
> Does *everyone* have *his* or *her* ticket?
>
> Does *everyone* have *his* ticket?

Note: The last two sentences illustrate a current usage dilemma prompted by a limitation of English: the language has no third person singular form of the personal pronoun that refers to persons of either sex. By definition a dilemma has no satisfactory solution; nevertheless, you will need to be aware of and sensitive to the different viewpoints. Some writers use *he or she, his or her,* and *him or her,* although such expressions are awkward. Others use the masculine pronouns (or possessive adjectives) in a universal sense, a practice based on long tradition but one objected to by those who perceive it to be sexist. On many occasions, however, you can avoid the problem by rephrasing the sentence:

Does *everyone* have *a* ticket?

Do *we* all have *our* tickets?

Who doesn't have *a* ticket?

■ 9b Collective Nouns as Antecedents

With *collective nouns* use either a singular or a plural pronoun according to the meaning of the sentence. Since collective nouns may be either singular or plural, their correct usage depends upon (1) a decision as to meaning (see Chapter 8, Section 8i) and (2) consistency:

The *team* has elected Jan as *its* captain. [The team is acting as a unit and therefore requires the singular possessive pronoun *its*.]

The *team* quickly took *their* positions on the field. [Here each member of the team is acting individually.]

Exercise 40 Agreement of Pronoun and Antecedent

From the italicized forms in parentheses choose the correct pronoun for each sentence and write it in the space at the right.

Example: Has either of the cars had (*their, its*) tires rotated
lately?   _____*its*_____

1. I have typed a list of the dancers chosen for the cast of the
musical; now I need to photocopy (*them, it*).   _____

2. The news of the space shuttle's successful landing
appeared in the national press, but (*they, it*) had special
meaning for those reading the captain's hometown
newspaper.   _____

3. The boy, trying the patience of the cashier and other customers alike, slowly counted out pennies, nickels, and
dimes to pay for (*their, his*) model airplane.   _____

4. Every employee attending the time-management seminar
had been given (*their, his*) own packet of information.   _____

5. The criteria for membership in the honor society had
always been listed in the student handbook, but now I
couldn't find (*them, it*).   _____

6. The tactics of the vacuum-cleaner salesman proved successful even though (*they, it*) had been used time and again.   _____

7. The automated indices proved to be like (*their, its*) paper
counterparts in one respect: a subject heading was
essential.   _____

8. Because each of the rides at the county fair had a long line
of people waiting to board (*them, it*), we decided to visit
the exhibit of pickles and jellies.   _____

9. Neither Mrs. Fitzhugh in Room 525 nor the woman across
the hall had received (*their, her*) breakfast tray.   _____

10. Although gymnastics had been offered as a physical education class for a long time, not until recently did (*they, it*)
become a popular choice.   _____

11. It was October, but none of the pecan trees had begun to
lose (*their, its*) leaves.   _____

12. Before we could think of using the old barracks as a meeting place for Troop 10, we had to patch the roof and give (*them, it*) a fresh coat of paint. _____

13. The data had been submitted to the chief executive officer, and he in turn presented (*them, it*) to the board of directors. _____

14. I have heard the glad tidings of Janie's election to the student council, and I am busy spreading (*them, it*) abroad. _____

15. During the morning session Dr. Dobbs lectured on the greenhouse phenomenon; this afternoon Roger and I discussed (*them, it*) over a cup of coffee. _____

16. Even after Carol had cited in her speech the statistics concerning consumption of chocolate, we still had difficulty believing (*them, it*). _____

17. Each of the cats living with Mrs. Fuller had been exceedingly wise in (*their, its*) choice of a home. _____

18. The soccer team played (*their, its*) last game of the season Saturday morning and celebrated with a cookout that night. _____

19. Anyone interested in chess should add (*their, his*) name to the list posted on Mrs. Kennedy's door. _____

20. Every cluster of apartment buildings had (*their, its*) own entrance on Madison Street as well as an exit on Morgan Drive. _____

Exercise 41   Agreement of Pronoun and Antecedent

From the *italicized* forms in parentheses choose the correct pronoun for each sentence and write it in the space at the right.

Example: The director praised the stage crew for (*their, its*)
cooperative spirit.   *its*

1. The alumni had sold most of the tickets to (*their, its*)
dance planned for New Year's Eve.   _____

2. The urban planner listened attentively as the Coalition
of Neighborhood Bikers expressed (*their, its*) dismay at
the closing of the bike trail.   _____

3. Josh's coin collection has grown steadily because of
Dad's interest in (*them, it*).   _____

4. We are certain that either Fran or Emily will have (*their,
her*) key to the dormitory.   _____

5. At one time our high school was so crowded that not
every freshman had (*their, his*) own locker.   _____

6. The meaning of the data is clearer now that you have
generated bar graphs to illustrate (*them, it*).   _____

7. Someone has left (*their, her*) dark glasses by the cash
register in Harden's Video Shop.   _____

8. The crisis resulting from Nina's decision to move into an
apartment of her own took on a life of (*their, its*) own. _____

9. Miraculously, every one of the pitches of the veteran
left-hander found (*their, its*) way across the plate.   _____

10. I can always count on (*them, him*), my grandfather and
faithful ally.   _____

11. Most adults probably remember (*their, his*) childhood as
a mixture of the bitter and the sweet.   _____

12. Once again the United Nations had sent (*their, its*)
peacekeeping force to a troubled part of the world.   _____

13. Nobody crowding into the theater's small foyer seemed
to know where to check (*their, his*) wraps.   _____

14. Our first years in the United States had little meaning for those of us too young to remember (*them, it*). _____

15. As if in one voice the crowd of property owners shouted (*their, its*) approval of the council's new zoning ordinance. _____

16. Pepper's ninety-yard run brought the crowd to (*their, its*) feet. _____

17. On Friday morning the committee concerned with day care at the workplace issued (*their, its*) recommendations to the entire conference. _____

18. Neither of the women had (*their, her*) seatbelt fastened when the car suddenly skidded on the wet pavement. _____

19. The National Association of Business Economists surveyed (*their, its*) members concerning the outlook for the coming fiscal year. _____

20. Either Mrs. Levi or Mrs. Turner can always be counted on to express (*themselves, herself*) at the town meetings. _____

Exercise 42   Agreement of Subject, Verb, and Pronoun

From the *italicized* forms in parentheses choose the correct verb and the correct pronoun or possessive adjective. Write them in the spaces at the right.

Example: Ethics often (*become, becomes*) obvious in (*their, its*) absence.

becomes
    its

1. Each fall all of us look forward to the day when the best fair in all fifty states (*open, opens*) (*their, its*) gates.   _____

2. Neither of the industries (*have, has*) acknowledged (*their, its*) responsibility for the chemicals polluting the river.   _____

3. Everybody who (*want, wants*) to learn to use a word processor must buy (*their, his*) own floppy disc and bring it to the computer lab at four this afternoon.   _____

4. As soon as the season was over, the hockey team said (*their, its*) good-byes and (*were, was*) bound for home.   _____

5. My scissors (*are, is*) not in my desk, and I can't imagine what I did with (*them, it*).   _____

6. Both of the hospitals in this part of the city (*have, has*) (*their, its*) own fully staffed emergency rooms.   _____

7. Although Becky and Christy, the Peterson twins, look very much alike, each of them (*have, has*) (*their, her*) own distinctive personality.   _____

8. Use the data in Table 29: (*they, it*) clearly (*support, supports*) your argument.   _____

9. It's a truism that yesterday's news (*lose, loses*) (*their, its*) significance quickly.   _____

10. No one (*are, is*) always able to do exactly what (*they, he*) would like.   _____

11. The symphony orchestra (*have, has*) generously given of (*their, its*) many talents to the benefit concert.   _____

12. The rolls of carpet, which (*were, was*) stacked haphazardly in the back of the truck, looked as if (*they, it*) would tumble into the street.   _____

13. Although physics (*have, has*) been difficult for me, Ms. West has made (*their, its*) study relatively pleasant.   _____

14. Either the television or the radio (*have, has*) been left on in the kitchen; somebody please turn (*them, it*) off.   _____

15. Everybody in the city auditorium (*were, was*) there to hear (*their, his*) favorite country singer: Willie Nelson.   _____

16. The film explained that every woman in the armored division (*assume, assumes*) (*their, her*) full responsibility.   _____

17. With the prospect of a tropical storm the crew (*were, was*) hurriedly evacuating (*their, its*) oil rig.   _____

18. Either of those houses on Park Lane (*are, is*) well worth (*their, its*) asking price.   _____

19. None of the hollies (*have, has*) lost (*their, its*) berries.   _____

20. I hope that each of you girls coming to see the eclipse (*remember, remembers*) to bring (*their, her*) sweater or jacket.   _____

10

Reference of Pronouns

The word to which a pronoun refers should always be clear to the reader; that is, a **pronoun** and the **antecedent** to which it refers must be instantly identified as belonging together. Even when a pronoun agrees properly with its antecedent in person and number, it may still be confusing or misleading if there is more than one possible antecedent. Therefore, it is sometimes necessary to repeat the antecedent or to reword the whole sentence for the sake of clarity.

■ 10a Ambiguous Reference

Sometimes a sentence contains more than one word to which a pronoun may grammatically refer (the term *ambiguous* means "capable of more than one interpretation"). The sentence should be written in such a way that the reader has no doubt which word is the antecedent:

> Albert told his uncle that his money had been stolen. [The first *his* is clear, but the second *his* could refer to either *Albert* or *uncle*.]

> Albert told his uncle that Albert's money had been stolen. [The meaning is clear, but the sentence is unnatural and awkward.]

To avoid the ambiguous reference of the first sentence and the awkward repetition of the second, reword the sentence:

> Albert said to his uncle, "My money has been stolen."

Another kind of ambiguous reference (sometimes called *divided* or *remote* reference) occurs when a modifying clause is misplaced in a sentence:

> INCORRECT: The colt was almost hit by a car that jumped over the pasture fence.

> CORRECT: The colt that jumped over the pasture fence was almost hit by a car.

Note: A relative pronoun should always be placed as near as possible to its antecedent. (See Chapter 15.)

■ 10b Broad Reference

Usually a pronoun should not refer broadly to the whole idea of the preceding clause:

> She avoided using slang, which greatly improved her speech. [*Which* has no clearly apparent antecedent but refers broadly to the whole idea in the first clause.]
>
> She talked endlessly about her operation, and this was tiresome.

A method often used to improve such sentences is to supply a definite antecedent or to substitute a noun for the pronoun:

> She avoided using slang, a practice that greatly improved her speech.
>
> She talked endlessly about her operation, and this chatter was tiresome.

As you can see, these sentences are awkward, adding unnecessary words. A better method is to get rid of the pronoun and make a concise, informative sentence that says everything in one clause:

> By avoiding slang, she greatly improved her speech.
>
> Her endless talk about her operation was tiresome.

■ 10c Weak Reference

A pronoun should not refer to a word that is merely implied by the context. Nor, as a common practice, should the pronoun refer to a word used as a modifier:

> INCORRECT: My father is a chemist. *This* is a profession I intend to follow. [The antecedent of *This* should be *chemistry*, which is implied in *chemist* but is not actually stated.]
>
> CORRECT: My father is a chemist. Chemistry is the profession I intend to follow.
>
> ALSO CORRECT: My father's profession of chemistry is the one I intend to follow.
>
> INCORRECT: When she thrust a stick into the rat hole, it ran out and bit her. [*Rat* in this sentence is the modifier of *hole*.]
>
> CORRECT: When she thrust a stick into the rat hole, a rat ran out and bit her.

■ 10d Impersonal Use of the Personal Pronoun

Remember that pronouns are frequently used impersonally and when so used do not have antecedents. Notice the correct impersonal use of *it* in statements about *weather, time,* and *distance:*

It looks like rain. [Reference to weather.]

It is now twelve o'clock. [Reference to time.]

How far is *it* to the nearest town? [Reference to distance.]

Avoid the use of *you* and *your* unless you are directing your statement specifically to the reader. Instead, use an impersonal word like *one* or *person*. Also note that the pronoun *you* can never refer to an antecedent in the third person:

INCORRECT: If *you* want to excel in athletics, *you* should watch your diet. [Incorrect when referring to athletes in general.]

CORRECT: If *one* wants to excel in athletics, *he* should watch his diet.

INCORRECT: When a woman marries, *you* take on new responsibilities. [Here *you* refers incorrectly to *woman*, an antecedent in the third person.]

CORRECT: When a woman marries, *she* takes on new responsibilities.

INCORRECT: All those planning to attend the meeting should get *your* registration fees in on time. [Here *your* incorrectly refers to the third person plural antecedent *those*.]

CORRECT: All those planning to attend the meeting should get *their* registration fees in on time.

A rewording of the sentence often produces a clearer and more emphatic sentence while eliminating the problem of the correct pronoun to use:

CORRECT: Those who wish to excel in athletics should watch their diets.

CORRECT: To marry is to take on new responsibilities.

CORRECT: Registration fees must be in on time for those who plan to attend the meeting.

Exercise 43   Reference of Pronouns

Write **R** after each sentence that contains an error in the reference of a pronoun. Then rewrite the sentence correctly. Notice that some sentences may be corrected in more than one way. Write **C** if the sentence is correct.

Example: I'm not surprised that Steve is in medical school; after all, his father was one.   _____R_____

I'm not surprised that Steve is in medical school; after all, his father was a surgeon.

1. With the stereo going full blast in the next room, Herb could not concentrate on *Lord Jim,* which certainly annoyed him.   _____

2. For the second time in as many days the water from the washing machine was streaming across the kitchen floor, which I had bought only a week ago.   _____

3. The radio says that a lumber truck is stalled in one of the southbound lanes on the freeway; that means that Melissa will be late for work.   _____

4. Grandfather told Bernard that he ought to stop watching wrestling on television and do something constructive.   _____

5. Did you realize that Mr. Jacobs, whose photographs are on display in the alumni gallery, has two daughters who are also interested in it?   _____

6. It was so hot and humid that all we could think about was home, an air conditioner, and a tall glass of tea.   _____

7. When anyone learns to read, you have taken the essential step toward acquiring other knowledge.   _____

8. At the half our soccer team was ahead; this was certainly a surprise to those of us who had seen last week's shutout.   _____

9. I could not pull from my memory the name of the man hurrying across the lobby of the bank toward me, which has frozen on more than one occasion.   _____

10. If a person chooses to room alone on the cruise, you will have to pay an additional fee.   _____

11. My rubber boots, which are pile-lined, were ideal for the
long walk from the student center to the biology lab.   _____

12. A girl wearing a black jersey and a pair of purple shorts
has just jogged by the house, which is the second time I've
seen her today.   _____

Exercise 44   Reference of Pronouns

Write **R** after each sentence that contains an error in the reference of a pronoun. Then rewrite the sentence correctly. Notice that some sentences may be corrected in more than one way. Write **C** if the sentence is correct.

Example: After buying pine straw year in and year out, we
finally decided to plant some of our own.   _____R_____

*After buying pine straw year in and year out, we finally
decided to plant some trees of our own.*

1. Although anyone may hold meetings in the clubhouse,
   you do have to check with Miss Bly to be sure that it is
   available.   _____

2. For weeks Mother's car has had something radically wrong
   with it, which probably means that she needs a new one.   _____

3. My brother has sent me a subscription to the *National Geographic* for my birthday ever since I've been away from
   home, which has been five years.   _____

4. Sally, it is at least two miles farther to the lake if you go
   around the mountain rather than over it.   _____

5. I know that Mrs. Kern has been a calligrapher for years, but I don't know what first attracted her to it.   _____

6. We gathered in the kitchen to give Ernie a hand with the dishes; this proved to be more of a hindrance than a help.   _____

7. We lost two starters to injuries at the beginning of the basketball season; we could ill afford to do that.   _____

8. The cheers of the fans interfered with the quarterback's signals, which rose in a great wave from the stands.   _____

9. My Italian grandmother often told us about her childhood, so naturally I want to visit it when I go to Europe this summer.   _____

10. Because Shannon had procrastinated, she had not completed her art project on time; this caused the instructor to lower her final grade.   _____

11. Once you have signaled for a fair catch, the receiver must stick with his decision.   _____

12. I want to find some statistics to support my contention that we have a better understanding of English if we know a second language, and this is proving difficult.   _____

Exercise 45 Reference of Pronouns

Write **R** after each sentence that contains an error in the reference of a pronoun. Then rewrite the sentence correctly. Notice that some sentences may be corrected in more than one way. Write **C** if the sentence is correct.

Example: Ken is a sales representative, and he thrives on it.   _____R_____

Ken is a sales representative, and he thrives on his job.

1. When you have to walk from the subway to your office, a woman needs to wear one pair of shoes and to carry another.   _____

2. I remember when a smokestack belched forth clouds of smoke near my school, which no one considered hazardous.   _____

3. Adam, look at your watch to see whether it is almost time for this lecture to be over.   _____

4. The man in front of me had a mountain of groceries in his cart, which was a clear indication that I wouldn't get home for the six o'clock news.   _____

5. When we read about Jakob and Wilhelm Grimm, who were both philologists, we became interested not only in them but also in it.   _____

6. This jigsaw puzzle must contain a dozen shades of blue, which is a reproduction of a painting by Winslow Homer.   _____

7. If someone decides to order a monogrammed shirt, you should be absolutely sure that it will fit.   _____

8. Some years our muscadine vines are laden with them.   _____

9. More and more of us shop by mail; this saves time, a commodity in short supply.   _____

10. Coach Pankhurst told Gerald that he had to spend more time on the track if he expected to stay in shape.   _____

11. Hazel forgot to bring the nutmeg for the sweet potato custard, and that means that one of us will have to go get some.   _____

12. It was Saturday morning, and the men gathered around
    the restaurant table were discussing last night's game,
    today's weather, and next month's election.   _____

11

Case of Pronouns

Nouns and pronouns have three case functions: the **nominative,** the **objective,** and the **possessive.** Except in the possessive, nouns do not show case by change of form and consequently do not present any problems of case. The chief difficulties are in the correct use of personal and relative pronouns.

■ 11a The Nominative Case

The **nominative case** is used (1) as the subject of a verb (*I* shall come); (2) as the complement after *is, are,* and the other forms of the verb *to be* (It is *I*); or (3) as an appositive of the subject or of the complement after forms of the verb *to be* (Two of us — *he* and *I* — called). Ordinarily the case of a pronoun that comes before a verb presents no difficulties, for we naturally write "I am going," not "Me am going." But all constructions requiring the nominative case are not so simple as this one. Study carefully the following more difficult constructions:

1. A clause of comparison introduced by *as* or *than* is often not written out in full; it is elliptical. The verb is then understood. The subject of this understood verb is in the nominative case:

No one can do the work as well as *he* (can).

He knows more about the subject than *she* (does).

2. After forms of the linking verb *to be,* nouns and pronouns used to identify the subject agree in case with the subject. Nouns and pronouns used in this way

161

are called **predicate nominatives** and are in the nominative case:

> It was *they* [not *them*].
>
> The persons mentioned were *she* and Rob [not *her*].
>
> He answered, "It could not have been *I* [not *me*]."

3. Pronouns are frequently combined with a noun or used in apposition with a noun. If they are thus used in the subject of the sentence or with a predicate nominative, they are in the nominative case:

> *We* boys will be responsible for the equipment.
>
> Two photographers — *you* and *he* — must attend the convention.
>
> My friend and *I* went to town. [Not *Me* and my friend went to town.]

If you read these sentences omitting the nouns, you will see at once the correct form of the pronoun.

4. The position of the relative pronoun *who* often causes confusion, especially if it follows a verb or a preposition. The role of the relative pronoun within the dependent clause determines its case. Thus if *who* is the subject of the verb in the dependent clause, it is in the nominative case:

> You know *who* sent the money. [Since *who* is the subject of the verb *sent* and not the object of *know*, it must be in the nominative case. The whole clause *who sent the money* is the object of *know*.]
>
> Give the praise to *whoever* deserves it. [*Whoever* is the subject of *deserves*. The whole clause *whoever deserves it* is the object of the preposition *to*.]

5. Parenthetical expressions such as *you think, I believe, I suppose,* and *he says* often stand between a verb and the pronoun that is the subject. The pronoun must still be in the nominative case:

> *Who* do you think called me last night? [The expression *do you think* has nothing to do with the case of *who*. Leave it out, or place it elsewhere in the sentence, and you will see that *who* is the subject of *called*.]
>
> The man *who* Jim says will be our next governor is in the room. [Leave out or place elsewhere *Jim says*, and you will see that *who* is the subject of *will be*.]

■ 11b The Objective Case

The **objective case** of a pronoun is used when the pronoun is the direct or indirect object of a verb, the object of a preposition, or an appositive of an object:

1. Compound objects present a special difficulty:

> He wrote a letter to Mary and *me*. [Both words *Mary* and *me* are objects of the preposition *to* and therefore in the objective case. Omit *Mary and* or shift *me* to the position of *Mary*, and the correct form is at once apparent.]

She gave George and *him* the list of names. [*Him* is part of the compound indirect object.]

They invited William and *me* to the barbecue. [*Me* is part of the compound direct object.]

2. You will also have to watch the case of a pronoun, in combination with a noun, that serves as an object or the appositive of an object.

The Dean spoke candidly to *us* boys.

The chairman appointed three of us girls — Mary, Sue, and *me* — to the subcommittee.

Note: In the sentence *The Dean spoke candidly to us boys,* boys is an appositive of *us. Boys* renames *us.* Here both words are substantives. The following sentence may appear similar to this one, but actually its structure is different:

The Dean spoke candidly to *them* boys.

This sentence mistakenly uses a personal pronoun when a demonstrative adjective is needed. First-person speakers do not need to point out themselves; a second person is spoken to directly and needs no pointing out. Only a noun or pronoun in the third person must be pointed out; therefore, use of a demonstrative adjective is called for to modify that noun or pronoun. *Those* is the word needed to modify *boys.* Once the correction is made, you can see that the prepositional phrase in this sentence contains a substantive and a demonstrative adjective, not two substantives.

3. *Whom,* the objective case of *who,* deserves special consideration. Its use, except after a preposition, is declining in colloquial or informal usage (see Chapter 21). Formal usage, however, still requires *whom* whenever the relative pronoun serves as an object:

Whom were you talking to? [To *whom* were you talking?]

He is the boy *whom* we met on the plane. [*Whom* is the object of the verb *met.* The subject of *met* is *we.* Remember that the case of the relative pronoun is determined by its role within the dependent clause.]

Whom do you think we saw last night? [The parenthetical expression does not change the fact that *whom* is the object of *saw.*]

■ 11c Case of Pronouns Used with Infinitives

An infinitive phrase, as you have learned already, can have both an object and adverbial modifiers. In addition, an **infinitive** may have a subject. There are rules governing the case of pronouns when they are subjects or complements of infinitives:

1. When a pronoun is the subject of an infinitive, it will be in the objective case:

We want *him* to be elected.

2. If the infinitive is a form of the verb *to be* and if it has a subject, its complement will also be in the objective case:

She took him to be *me.*

3. If the infinitive *to be* does not have a subject, its complement will be in the nominative case:

The best player was thought to be *he.*

■ 11d The Possessive Case

Personal pronouns and the relative pronoun *who* have **possessive case** forms, which may be used with a noun or a gerund.

1. When the possessive forms *my, our, your, her, his, its,* and *their* modify nouns or gerunds, they are classified as **possessive adjectives:**

My book is on the table. [*My* is a possessive adjective, modifying *book.*]

We appreciate *your* giving to the Community Chest. [Not *you giving.* The object of the verb *appreciate* is the gerund *giving;* therefore, *your* is merely the possessive adjective modifying the gerund.]

2. Personal and relative pronouns form their possessives without the apostrophe:

The boy *whose* car is in the driveway works here.

The dog chewed *its* bone.

Note: Notice the difference between *its,* the possessive form, and *it's,* the contraction of *it is:*

It's time for your car to have *its* oil changed.

Exercise 46   Case of Pronouns

In the following sentences underline each pronoun that is used incorrectly, and then write the correct form in the space at the right. Write **C** if the sentence is correct.

Example: Brian consistently runs the mile faster than <u>me</u>.   _____*I*_____

1. Just call Rick and I if you need help moving the piano.   _____

2. Gilbert and her haven't the vaguest idea of how to install a VCR.   _____

3. The congregation appreciates them arranging the flowers for the morning services.   _____

4. The directions that the state patrol officer gave to we three were easier to follow than our map.   _____

5. No one else in our family enjoys reading science fiction as much as her.   _____

6. I don't know whether she and Allison will have the time or energy to go to both museums.   _____

7. The best mechanic in the family is known to be her.   _____

8. Pete was sure that it was them—the Parker boys—sitting on the gym steps.   _____

9. Between you and I, none of the shoes that I've seen this spring have much pizazz.   _____

10. Who in the world chose he and Margaret to organize the company picnic?   _____

11. Uncle Ernest has agreed to lend you and I his field glasses for Saturday's game.   _____

12. Among us all there should certainly be someone talented enough to design the posters.   _____

13. Us finding a way to finance a trip to Bermuda is nothing short of a miracle.   _____

14. It is easy to see why the children believed Santa Claus to be he.   _____

15. The drop-leaf table that the Bagwells found at the yard sale needs one of it's legs repaired.   _____

16. We were delighted when Jerry "faxed" a letter to the two of us, Liz and I.   _____

17. Instead of you and he, Mr. Comstock should have asked those who were late for practice to pack up the equipment.   _____

18. Her and the Munson twins are over in the park playing on the sliding board.   _____

19. The program committee has asked she and her husband to show the slides of their trip to Australia.   _____

20. Someone in addition to him should be assigned the responsibility of developing a marketing plan.   _____

Exercise 47   Case of Pronouns

In the following sentences underline each pronoun that is used incorrectly, and then write the correct form in the space at the right. Write **C** if the sentence is correct.

Example: I've never known anyone to enjoy a carnival as
much as <u>them</u>.   *they*

1. The Dean and Professor Smithers will sit on the plat-
   form in front of you and I.   _____

2. Us two and the five tellers were told yesterday that the
   bank will begin opening on Saturday mornings.   _____

3. Did you hear about him getting a job with the Forest
   Service?   _____

4. Although both Doug and her were experienced drivers,
   they hesitated to set out across the mountain in the
   snow.   _____

5. Standing behind he and Susie in the long line at the seafood restaurant were their former neighbors.   _____

6. The kindergarten children had not met the new princi-
   pal and thought Carol to be she.   _____

7. Coach is an eternal optimist; he simply will not accept
   us having a losing season.   _____

8. No one but he could have inspired the team to play as it
   has this year.   _____

9. Everybody except him had predicted a miserable record.   _____

10. The dancers in the next scene—Louisa, Rosie, and me—
    have never appeared before so large an audience.   _____

11. Because Alan does not know this section of the city, its
    not unlikely that he missed our exit.   _____

12. No one other than your friend from Saudi Arabia has
    bracelets as handsome as them.   _____

13. In spite of his beard I'm certain that the man in the tele-
    phone booth is him.   _____

14. If it's he, why isn't he wearing a trench coat?   _____

15. Neither Christina nor me heard the thunderstorm dur-
    ing the night.   _____

16. The Chamber of Commerce appreciated you telling the
    visitors from Switzerland about our labor pool.   _____

17. The man sitting between my brother and I on the plane
    offered to exchange seats with either of us.   _____

18. The next chief executive officer of Windsor Mills is
    expected to be him.   _____

19. Sylvia could wear this burnt orange sweater better than
    either you or I.   _____

20. The rock group coming tonight to the College travels in
    it's own van.   _____

Exercise 48   Case of Pronouns

In the space at the right, write the correct form of the pronoun *who* (*whoever*).

Example: (*Who, Whom*) did Beverly come with?   _____Whom_____

1. (*Who, Whom*) does the choir director think is the more talented of the two composers?   _____

2. If this chartreuse umbrella does not belong to Miss Twichell, (*who, whom*) does it belong to?   _____

3. You will have to ask (*whoever, whomever*) is on duty at the gate house how to get to the picnic area.   _____

4. (*Whoever, Whomever*) is running that vacuum cleaner has succeeded in destroying my powers of concentration.   _____

5. Everybody in camp (*who, whom*) had been hoping for a letter arrived at mail call.   _____

6. (*Whose, Who's*) going to call Norman about our plans for the weekend?   _____

7. The afternoon that I met Ann and her bulldog I couldn't decide who was walking (*who, whom*).   _____

8. Neither of us knows (*who, whom*) the woman is in that gorgeous sari.   _____

9. (*Who, Whom*) should we ask for, once we get to the clinic?   _____

10. The names of those (*who, whom*) we have sent season tickets to are posted in the box office.   _____

11. (*Who's, Whose*) glasses are those lying on the beach towel?   _____

12. Tell the Johnsons to ask (*whoever, whomever*) is at the reception desk where the auditorium is.   _____

13. You can be sure that Kim knows (*who, whom*) is responsible for the graffiti on the sidewalk.   _____

14. A computer programmer (*who, whom*) used to work here now works in the Candler Building.   _____

15. The programmer (*who, whom*) Ms. Newsome hired to take his place graduated a year behind us at State.   _____

16. The Russian sailors (*who, whom*) we saw at the Eagle Bar and Grill must be on shore leave.   _____

17. For (*who, whom*) did your friends the Sniggles name their yacht?   _____

18. Ask (*whoever, whomever*) you invite to the Halloween dance to wear a costume.   _____

19. The Congressman is interested in discussing forest preservation with (*whoever, whomever*) will listen.   _____

20. In a small town one speaks to (*whoever, whomever*) one meets in the stores or on the streets.   _____

Exercise 49 Review of Agreement and Case

Underline each word that is incorrectly used. Then write the correct word in the space at the right. Write **C** if the sentence is correct.

Example: Acquaintances often take my sister to be I.   _____*me*_____

1. Raking the leaves in the front and back yards and cleaning out the garage is more than Joel can do in one day.   _____

2. A quick third-down pass gave the team the fresh momentum they needed.   _____

3. We agree with the idea of you flying to San Francisco and then renting a car.   _____

4. The number of bushels of grapes harvested this year are the largest since the vineyard was planted.   _____

5. Sitting in the balcony and across the aisle from we three was a group of students from Nigeria.   _____

6. Each of them were extremely interested in the debate taking place on the House floor.   _____

7. Tom Wolfe is one of those writers who has received both popular and critical acclaim.   _____

8. Could it have been her who left the green cotton sweater on the bench in the courtyard?   _____

9. No one in the advertising department is as well organized as him.   _____

10. At least a dozen of us, including Eleanor and I, are planning to go skiing in Colorado.   _____

11. On the front steps of the church was my mother, talking to two wedding guests whom I did not know.   _____

12. At the convention, space for the electronic media was an important consideration; it depended on more than pencils and paper.   _____

13. Aunt Margie is positive that the prank calls were made by one of two children, either he or Sandy.   _____

14. Because the others need to leave for the road race, us two will have to wash all these dishes.   _____

15. Neither of us wanted to go to the road race, but neither of us enjoy washing dishes either.   _____

16. According to the ad, a mechanic and copilot are needed by the corporation's transportation department.   _____

17. Joyce, Edith, and me plan to rent bikes and tour the island on our own.   _____

18. The data appearing in the *World Almanac* has been gathered from a variety of sources.   _____

19. The waiter whom I think served us the other time we ate lunch here is standing over by the window.   _____

20. The interior decorator along with two buyers is going to the spring furniture market.   _____

21. The idea of us taking a boat down the inland waterway first occurred to us in January.   _____

22. No one is more pleased with the proposed trip than me.   _____

23. Are either of the reporters from the *Gazette* coming to see the exhibit of quilts?   _____

24. On Friday afternoons every highway and byway leading out of town are choked with traffic.   _____

25. Everybody has their own theory of how to beat this traffic.   _____

26. However, neither you nor me often succeed in putting theory into practice.   _____

27. The young woman who you saw going into the state capitol is a representative from the fourth district.   _____

28. Although somewhat taller than Uncle Bert, his son looks like him.   _____

29. Every one of the tools in Dave's furniture shop are carefully maintained.   _____

30. Somebody who drives a yellow Toyota has forgotten to turn off their lights.   _____

31. Do either of you have the nerve to ride the double Ferris wheel at the mountain fair?   _____

32. The English instructor who gives the most horrendous assignments in the department is known to be him.   _____

33. Mrs. Wallingford recounts to whoever will listen the plot of the novel she intends to write.   _____

34. Its a fact that my mother is a better electrician than my father.   _____

35. According to my calculations $35.16 are all I have left in my checking account.   _____

36. Mary Paterno is the person whom everybody says is the best weather prophet on the block.   _____

37. Just between you and I, not everyone enjoys eating a healthful diet all the time.   _____

38. The street that used to be one of the city's main arteries have changed character since the expressway opened.   _____

39. Once the children began eating the gingerbread with lemon sauce, there seemed to be no way for them to stop until it was all gone.   _____

40. On Saturday afternoons a great number of videotapes is usually checked out from the library.   _____

12

Adjectives and Adverbs

Adjectives and adverbs, as you saw in Chapter 1, are words that modify, describe, or add to the meaning of other words in a sentence. It is important to remember the special and differing functions of these two kinds of modifier; *adjectives* modify only nouns and other substantives; *adverbs* modify verbs, adjectives, adverbs, and certain phrases and clauses.

■ 12a Adjective and Adverb Forms

An adverb is frequently formed by adding *-ly* to the adjective form of a word: for example, the adjectives *rapid, sure,* and *considerate* are converted into the adverbs *rapidly, surely,* and *considerately* by this method. But there are numerous exceptions to this general rule. Many common adverbs, like *well, then,* and *quite,* do not end in *-ly;* moreover, there are many *adjectives* that do end in *-ly,* like *manly, stately, lonely,* or *unsightly.*

Sometimes the same form is used for both adjective and adverb: *fast, long,* and *much,* for example. (There are no such words as *fastly, longly,* or *muchly.*) Certain adverbs have two forms, one being the same as the adjective and the other ending in *-ly: slow, slowly; quick, quickly; loud, loudly;* etc. The first form is often employed in short commands, as in the sentences *Drive slow* and *Speak loud.*

■ 12b Predicate Adjectives

In any sentence that follows a "subject-verb-modifier" pattern, you must be careful to determine whether the modifier is describing the subject or the verb:

175

John talks *intelligently.*

John is *intelligent.*

In the first sentence the modifier clearly describes how John talks — that is, it modifies the verb *talks;* consequently, the adverb *intelligently* is needed. But in the second sentence the modifier describes the subject *John;* therefore, an adjective is used. In this construction the adjective following the linking verb *is* is called the **predicate adjective.**

The term **linking verb,** as you learned from Chapter 1, refers to certain intransitive verbs that make a statement not by expressing action but by expressing a condition or state of being. These verbs "link" the subject of the sentence with some other substantive that renames or identifies it or with an adjective that describes it. Any adjective that appears after a subject-linking verb construction is called the **predicate adjective.** The verbs most commonly used as linking verbs are the following:

appear	become	remain	stay
be	grow	seem	feel (as an emotion)

Along with these are the five "sense" verbs, which are usually linking verbs:

look	feel	smell	taste	sound

The following sentences illustrate the use of predicate adjectives:

The little dog was *glad* to be out of his pen. [*Glad,* a predicate adjective, follows the linking verb *was* and describes *dog.*]

Father appeared *eager* to drive his new car.

Laurie became *angry* at being put to bed.

Jackie seems *happy* in her new job.

Remain *quiet,* and I will give you your seat assignments. [*Quiet,* the predicate adjective, describes the subject, *you,* understood.]

The day grew *dark* as the clouds gathered.

Peggy looks *sporty* in her new tennis outfit.

I feel *confident* that Ty will win his case.

That cinnamon bread smells *delicious.*

The rain sounds *dismal* beating on the roof.

Almond toffee ice cream tastes *marvelous.*

This warm robe feels *comfortable.*

A practical test to follow in determining whether to use an adjective or an adverb is to try to substitute some form of the verb *to be* for the verb in the sentence. If the substitution does not substantially change the meaning of the sentence, then the verb should be followed by an adjective. For instance, *She is smart in her new uniform* has essentially the same meaning as *She looks smart in her new uniform;* therefore, the adjective *smart* is the correct modifier.

Occasionally, one of the "sense" verbs is followed by an adverb because the verb is being used not as a *linking* verb but as an *action* verb: *He looked nervously for his keys. Nervously* describes the act of looking, so the adverb is used to express how the looking was done. The substitution test would show immediately that an adjective would be incorrect in the sentence.

■ 12c Misuse of Adjectives

Using an adjective to modify a verb is a common error but a serious one. The sentence *The doctor spoke to the sick child very kind* illustrates this error. *Kind* is an adjective and cannot be used to modify the verb *spoke;* the adverb *kindly* must be used.

Four adjectives that are frequently misused as adverbs are *real, good, sure,* and *some.* When the adverbial form of these words is needed, the correct forms are *really, well, surely,* and *somewhat:*

The mountain laurel is *really* (or *very,* not *real*) colorful.

You did *well* (not *good*) to stop smoking so quickly.

I *surely* (not *sure*) hope to see him before he leaves.

I feel *somewhat* (not *some*) better today.

Note: Remember that *well* can also be an adjective, referring to a state of health, as in *I feel well now, after my long illness.*

■ 12d Comparison of Adjectives and Adverbs

When you wish to indicate to what extent one noun has a certain quality in comparison with that of another noun, change the form of the modifying adjective that describes the quality: My dog is *bigger* than your dog. My dog is the *biggest* dog in town.

Descriptive adverbs, like adjectives, may be compared in the same way:

We awaited the holidays *more eagerly* than our parents did.

The shrimp and the oysters were the foods *most rapidly* eaten at the party.

Adjectives and adverbs show or imply comparison by the use of three forms, called **degrees:** the **positive, comparative,** and **superlative degrees.**

Positive Degree

The **positive degree** of an adjective or adverb is its regular form:

He is a *fine* man.

John took notes *carefully.*

Comparative Degree

The **comparative degree** of an adjective or adverb compares two things, persons, or actions:

He is a *finer* man than his brother.

John took notes *more carefully* than Bob did.

Superlative Degree

The **superlative degree** compares three or more persons, things, or actions:

He is the *finest* man I know.

John took notes *most carefully* of all the boys in his class.

The comparative degree is regularly formed by adding *-er* to the positive form of an adjective or adverb or by using *more* or *less* before the positive form. The superlative degree is formed either by adding *-est* to the positive or by using *most* or *least* before the positive. The number of syllables in the word determines which of these forms must be used:

	Positive	Comparative	Superlative
	strong	stronger	strongest
Adj.	pretty	prettier	prettiest
	difficult	more difficult	most difficult
	quietly	more quietly	most quietly
Adv.	easily	more easily	most easily
	fast	faster	fastest

The comparison of some words is irregular, as of *good* (*good, better, best*) and *bad* (*bad, worse, worst*).

Be careful not to use the superlative form when only two persons, groups, objects, or ideas are involved:

Tom is the *healthier* (not *healthiest*) of the two brothers.

Certain adjectives and adverbs such as *perfect, unique, round, square, dead,* and *exact* cannot logically be used in the comparative or superlative degrees, and most should not be modified by words like *quite* or *very.* These words in their simplest forms are absolute superlatives, incapable of being added to or detracted from:

ILLOGICAL: Samuel is the *most unique* person I know.

LOGICAL: Samuel is a unique person.

ALSO LOGICAL: Samuel is an *almost unique* person.

ILLOGICAL: Beth's engagement diamond is the *most perfect* stone I've seen in years.

LOGICAL: Beth's engagement diamond is a *perfect* stone.

ALSO LOGICAL: Beth's engagement diamond is the *most nearly perfect* stone I've seen in years.

ILLOGICAL: The figures that Ben used in his report are *less exact* than they should be.

LOGICAL: The figures that Ben used in his report are not exact, though they should be.

■ 12e Incomplete Comparisons

When using the comparative degree of an adjective or adverb, be sure that both items being compared are included; for example, do not say, *Using a paint roller is quicker*. Your reader will ask, "Quicker than what?" The unknown answer might even be *Using a paint roller is quicker than daubing paint on with one's fingers*. Always complete a comparison by including both items: *Using a paint roller is quicker than using a brush.*

Exercise 50   Adjectives and Adverbs

Underline the word or words modified by the *italicized* adjective or adverb. Then in the space at the right, write **Adj** if the italicized word is an adjective, **Adv** if it is an adverb.

Example: Barges *regularly* <u>bring</u> iron ore up the waterway.   *Adv*

1. Because of the heavy rain the night before, the pathway was *slippery*.   _____

2. The hikers found that keeping their footing proved *almost* impossible.   _____

3. The student band played loud and *enthusiastically* as the teams ran onto the court.   _____

4. Searching for the sunken ship, the men dived *deep* into the warm waters off the Florida coast.   _____

5. Despite a recent bout with pneumonia, Marcia felt *well* enough to be back at the shop.   _____

6. Are you *ready* to make a practice jump?   _____

7. No, I certainly am not ready to jump, but I do *not* think I have a choice.   _____

8. George wasn't sure that his paisley tie looked exactly *right* with his tweed jacket.   _____

9. To feed the ducks, the children *often* walk to the pond on the other side of the field.   _____

10. In the top of the second inning the first pitch was low and *away*.   _____

11. The gold of the maple leaves seems unusually *bright* this fall.   _____

12. The Labrador retriever loped *along* behind the two boys on their bikes.   _____

13. The pickup truck parked back of the carwash appeared old and *unreliable*.   _____

14. Although Patrick is young to be in this league, he is a *very* enthusiastic player.

     _____

15. Furthermore, he can skate as *skillfully* as any other person on our team.

     _____

16. The children sitting on the front steps waited *impatiently* for the pizza to be delivered.

     _____

17. The Canadian spoke *confidently* about the means we should use to combat acid rain.

     _____

18. Moreover, he remained *confident* as he responded to the questions from the audience.

     _____

19. None of us ever dreamed that Amy would do *well* in her calculus course.

     _____

20. Surprisingly, she felt *good* about her chances of making an *A* from the very beginning of the quarter.

     _____

21. The attic smelled *musty,* just as it had for as long as we could remember.

     _____

22. We knew that Mother had Christmas on her mind because the coffee table was *completely* covered with bright, slick catalogs.

     _____

23. If Charlie runs as *fast* as he can, he will catch the letter carrier.

     _____

24. I first realized that he was *fast* when I saw him run the relay.

     _____

25. Don't you think that the sleeves on your camel jacket are *rather* long?

     _____

26. Up at the ski lodge they were *really* pleased to hear that snow is in the forecast.

     _____

27. The diamonds in her tiara are paste; the *real* ones are in the vault at the bank.

     _____

28. *Never* have I seen as many watermelons as were brought to our block party on the Fourth of July.

     _____

29. Either the CD player was *too* low, or the crowd was too loud.

     _____

30. Once again the detective looked *doggedly* for some clue
    to solve the crime.   _____

Exercise 51　Adjectives and Adverbs

Underline any adjective or adverb that is incorrectly used. Then write the correct form at the right. Write **C** if the sentence is correct.

Example:　You <u>sure</u> do make a good lemon meringue pie.　　_____*surely*_____

1. Jack and Fran painted steady all morning, finishing the deck just before lunch.　　_____

2. My rolls didn't rise, and, to make matters worse, my cheesecake turned out bad.　　_____

3. The train stopped so sudden that her coat and books spilled into the aisle.　　_____

4. Of Joan's two watercolors in the show, this one is surely the best.　　_____

5. His idea of a most perfect morning is to sleep until he wakes up and then have his coffee and the morning paper on the patio.　　_____

6. The child stared uncertain at the clown, who was smiling broadly at the nursery-school audience.　　_____

7. The factory whistle sounded very clearly on that gray Monday afternoon.　　_____

8. My father spoke plain to us children when he disapproved of our behavior.　　_____

9. We always knew when Professor Coldham had arrived in the dining hall: his was a most unique voice.　　_____

10. Thank you very muchly for bringing me the jacket that I left in the golf cart.　　_____

11. Jessica's heart beat rapid when she heard the key turn in the lock.　　_____

12. Once the cloud cover had been burned away, the day grew some warmer.　　_____

13. Uncle Herman feels quite well now that he has given up his steady diet of tamales. _____

14. I'm glad to hear that he feels better: he's felt badly for days. _____

15. The harvest moon is very round tonight. _____

16. The bass tournament scheduled for this weekend is my brother's most favorite of the year. _____

17. Ben certainly drives more careful since having that accident at Birch Corners. _____

18. It seems that Miss Marple proves the innocence of her heroes and heroines as easy as even more experienced sleuths. _____

19. For Agatha Christie's readers the solution to the mystery sometimes proves more difficult. _____

20. Have you noticed that the price of gold has risen regular during the past month? _____

21. Ms. Pinkston says that this just might be the worse day that she has ever had. _____

22. I sympathized with her, agreeing that hers is one of the saddest stories I have ever heard. _____

23. Don't you think that Sharon's black velvet dress is real becoming? _____

24. Edwin's new car runs more smooth than any I've ridden in lately. _____

25. Mrs. Milstein always speaks kind to the old woman selling flowers on the corner. _____

26. Before the highway crew begins repairing a road, it sets up plenty of "Drive Slow" signs. _____

27. Is this computer or that one the most "user friendly"? _____

28. This one really suits me better. _____

29. My neighbor says that the reason my geraniums have done poor is that they need a sunny window. _____

30. The vanilla ice cream sure tasted cold and creamy. _____

Exercise 52   Adjectives and Adverbs

Select the correct form of the word in parentheses, and write it in the space at the right.

Example: The auctioneer speaks too (*rapid, rapidly*) for me to understand him.

_____*rapidly*_____

1. Kim is (*some, somewhat*) better at playing goalie than her cousin.

_____

2. The judges for the debate were relaxed, chatting (*casual, casually*) among themselves.

_____

3. However, those of us on the debate teams huddled (*nervous, nervously*) at the back of the hall.

_____

4. Which of the two lamps looks (*best, better*) on Mom's desk?

_____

5. Nina speaks (*enthusiastic, enthusiastically*) about her sales job at the boutique.

_____

6. In fact, one might say that she has become (*extravagant, extravagantly*) in her praise.

_____

7. Early Christmas morning the children crept (*cautious, cautiously*) into the living room.

_____

8. They (*sure, surely*) didn't know whom or what they would find there.

_____

9. When Marian wears that silk dress, she looks (*more pretty, prettier*) than ever.

_____

10. When one uses the on-line catalog in the library, his spelling has to be (*most exact, exact*).

_____

11. Despite the substitute teacher's growing irritation, he spoke (*even, evenly*) to the children.

_____

12. Although he appeared (*calm, calmly*), his looks belied his feelings.

_____

13. He wished that his rambunctious pupils would read (*quiet, quietly*) at their desks.

_____

14. He wished even more that the final bell would sound (*loud, loudly*) and (*clear, clearly*).

_____

15. The setter, which had been running along the edge of the water, stopped (*sudden, suddenly*).   _____

16. The dog peered (*intent, intently*) at the crab washed up by the tide.   _____

17. This month's weather is the (*worst, worse*) we have had all winter.   _____

18. After Justin took the antibiotic prescribed by his physician, he was as (*good, well*) as he ever had been.   _____

19. The cranberry relish doesn't need more sugar; it tastes (*sweet, sweetly*) enough.   _____

20. Nan believes that it seems even (*sweeter, more sweetly*) than that you made at Thanksgiving.   _____

21. Of all the shoes that I have tried on today, these sneakers feel (*best, better*).   _____

22. They are not things of beauty, but they really fit (*good, well*).   _____

23. The rectangular rug that we saw at the Aladdin Rug Shop is not right for this room; we need one that is (*square, squarer*).   _____

24. Eleanor had grown (*despondent, despondently*) over the prospect of leaving Montreal.   _____

25. Even though few of us at the town meeting agreed with Sam, he stood (*firm, firmly*) in the face of our opposition.   _____

26. The plant manager spoke (*firm, firmly*) to the employees concerning the need for excellence on the job.   _____

27. We were (*real, really*) exasperated with the number of commercials being shown during the movie.   _____

28. Few persons create a painting or a poem or a piece of music that is (*totally unique, unique*).   _____

29. It is surprising how (*well, good*) we can feel at five o'clock on Friday afternoon.   _____

30. It (*sure, surely*) is a different feeling from the one we have on Monday morning.   _____

13

Tense, Voice, Mood

In Chapter 1 you found that a single verb may be classified according to **tense, voice,** and **mood;** therefore, it is not surprising that choosing the appropriate verb form occasionally presents difficulty.

■ 13a Principal Parts of Verbs

There are three **principal parts** of a verb. These are (1) **the first person singular, present indicative;** (2) **the first person singular, past indicative;** (3) **the past participle.** The first two of these provide the basic forms of the present, past, and future tenses; the third is used as the basis for the three perfect tenses:

Principal parts: *begin, began, begun*		
Present:	I begin	
Past:	I began	
Future:	I will (shall) begin ——————	(This form based on present tense *begin*)
Present Perfect:	I have begun	
Past Perfect:	I had begun	(These forms based on past participle *begun*)
Future Perfect:	I will (shall) have begun	

If you know the principal parts of a verb and the way to form the various tenses from them, you should never make a mistake such as the one contained in the following sentence: "The play had already began when I arrived." If the speaker had known that the principal parts of *begin* are *begin, began, begun* and that the past perfect tense is formed by using *had* with the past participle, he would have known that the correct form is *had begun*.

Regular verbs — that is, those verbs that form their past tense and past participle by adding *-d* or *-ed* to the present tense — rarely cause difficulty. It is the **irregular verbs** that are most frequently used incorrectly. When necessary, consult a dictionary for their principal parts. The following list contains the principal parts of certain especially troublesome verbs. Learn these forms:

Present	Past	Past participle	Present	Past	Past participle
ask	asked	asked	know	knew	known
bite	bit	bitten	lead	led	led
blow	blew	blown	ride	rode	ridden
break	broke	broken	ring	rang (rung)	rung
burst	burst	burst	run	ran	run
choose	chose	chosen	see	saw	seen
come	came	come	shake	shook	shaken
dive	dived (dove)	dived	sing	sang (sung)	sung
do	did	done	speak	spoke	spoken
drag	dragged	dragged	steal	stole	stolen
draw	drew	drawn	sting	stung	stung
drink	drank	drunk	suppose	supposed	supposed
drown	drowned	drowned	swim	swam	swum
eat	ate	eaten	swing	swung	swung
fall	fell	fallen	take	took	taken
fly	flew	flown	tear	tore	torn
freeze	froze	frozen	throw	threw	thrown
give	gave	given	use	used	used
go	went	gone	wear	wore	worn
grow	grew	grown	write	wrote	written

Note that the past tense and the past participle of the verbs *ask, suppose,* and *use* are regularly formed by the addition of *-ed* (or *-d*) to the present tense. Possibly because the *d* is not always clearly sounded in the pronunciation of the past tense and the past participle of these verbs, people frequently make the mistake of writing the present-tense form when one of the other forms is required:

I have *asked* (not *ask*) him to go with me.

I was *supposed* (not *suppose*) to do that job.

He *used* (not *use*) to be my best friend.

■ 13b Two Troublesome Pairs of Verbs

Lie and *lay* and *sit* and *set* are frequent stumbling blocks to correct writing. These verbs need not be confusing, however, if the following points are remembered:

1. Each verb has a distinguishing meaning. *Lay* and *set*, for instance, are clearly distinguished from *lie* and *sit* by their meanings: both *lay* and *set* usually mean *place* and are correctly used when the verb *place* can be substituted for them.

2. *Lay* and *set* are always transitive verbs; that is, they require an object to complete their meaning when they are used in the active voice. *Lie* and *sit* are intransitive verbs and hence do not take an object.

3. Although *lay* and *lie* share the form *lay*, they use it in different tenses. The remaining principal parts are clearly distinguishable.

These three points may be graphically shown:

Principal parts			
Intransitive (takes no object)		Transitive (takes an object)	
lie lay lain, *recline, remain in position*		lay laid laid, *place*	
sit sat sat, *be in a sitting position*		set set set, *place*	

Look at a few sentences that illustrate these distinguishing characteristics. Is it correct to say *I set the box on the table* or *I sat the box on the table*? To answer the question, try substituting *placed* for *set* and also see whether a direct object follows the verb. You can see at once that *placed* can be substituted for *set* and that *box* is the direct object of the verb; therefore, the first sentence, employing *set*, is the correct one. But in the sentence *I left the box sitting on the table*, the correct form is *sitting*, not *setting*, since *placing* cannot be substituted for *sitting* and since there is no direct object after *sitting*:

I *laid* (that is, *placed*) the book by the bed and *lay* (past tense of *lie*) down to rest.

Do not fall into the error of thinking that only animate things can stand as subjects of intransitive verbs. Note the following sentences in which inanimate objects are used as subjects of the intransitive verbs:

The book *lies* on the table.

The house *sits* near the road.

■ 13c Tense Sequence

Tense sequence demands that a logical time relationship be shown by the verbs in a sentence. Through force of habit we generally indicate accurate time relationships. A few cautions, however, should be stressed:

1. Use the present tense in the statement of a timeless universal truth or a customary happening:

I wonder who first discovered that the sun *rises* (not *rose*) in the east. [The fact that the sun rises in the east is a universal truth.]

Joe said that the class *begins* (not *began*) at 10:30. [The clause *that the class begins at 10:30* states a customary happening.]

2. Use the present tense of an infinitive or the present participle if the action it expresses occurs at the same time as that of the governing verb:

Yesterday I really wanted *to go.* [Not *to have gone.* The governing verb *wanted* indicates a past time. At that past time I wanted to do something *then* — that is, yesterday — not at a time prior to yesterday.]

Skipping along, she hummed a merry tune. [The skipping and the humming occur at the same time.]

3. When necessary for clarity, indicate time differences by using different tenses:

INCORRECT: I told him that I *finished* the work just an hour before.

CORRECT: I told him that I *had finished* the work just an hour before. [The verb *told* indicates a past time. Since the work was finished before the time indicated by *told,* the past perfect tense *had finished* must be used.]

INCORRECT: *Making* my reservations, I am packing to go to Cape Cod.

CORRECT: *Having made* my reservations, I am packing to go to Cape Cod. [The perfect participle *having made* must be used to denote an action before the time indicated by the governing verb *am packing.*]

■ 13d Voice

Transitive verbs always indicate whether the subject is acting or is being acted upon. When the subject is doing the acting, the verb is said to be in the **active voice:**

I *laid* the book on the table. [*Laid* is in the active voice because the subject *I* is doing the acting.]

When the subject is being acted upon or receiving the action, the verb is in the **passive voice:**

The book *was laid* on the table. [*Was laid* is in the passive voice because the subject *book* is being acted upon.]

Note: The passive voice verb always consists of some form of the verb *to be* plus a past participle: *is seen, was laid, have been taken.*

In general, the active voice is more emphatic than the passive and therefore should normally be used in preference to the passive voice:

WEAK: The automobile *was driven* into the garage.

MORE EMPHATIC: She *drove* the automobile into the garage.

When, however, the receiver of the action should be stressed rather than the doer, or when the doer is unknown, the passive voice is appropriate.

Class officers *will be elected* next Thursday. [The receiver of the action should be stressed.]

The dog *was found* last night. [The doer is unknown.]

Generally speaking, one should not shift from one voice to the other in the same sentence:

AWKWARD: John *is* the best athlete on the team, and the most points *are scored* by him.

BETTER: John *is* the best athlete on the team and also *scores* the most points.

AWKWARD: After Dr. Lovett *was conferred* with, I *understood* the assignment.

BETTER: After I *conferred* with Dr. Lovett (OR After *conferring* with Dr. Lovett), I *understood* the assignment.

■ 13e Mood

In Chapter 1, Section 1d defined the indicative, imperative, and subjunctive moods. Through force of habit we usually select the correct verb forms for the first two moods but sometimes have difficulty choosing the correct forms for the subjunctive mood.

The **subjunctive mood** is most frequently used today to express a wish or to state a condition contrary to fact. In both types of statement the subjunctive *were* is used instead of the indicative *was*. Tenses in the subjunctive do not have the same meaning as they do in the indicative mood. For example, the past subjunctive form points toward the present or future, as seen in the sentence *If I WERE you, I would give his suggestion strong consideration.* The present subjunctive form usually points toward the future with a stronger suggestion of hopefulness than does the past subjunctive. (*I move that John Marshall BE named chairman of our committee.*) The present subjunctive form of the verb *to be* is invariably *be* for all persons, and the past subjunctive form of the verb *to be* is invariably *were.* In all other verbs the subjunctive form varies from the indicative only in that in the present tense the third person singular ending is lost, as in *I suggest that he TAKE the subway to his friend's house.* Note the following examples of verbs in the subjunctive mood:

I wish that I *were* (not *was*) going with you to Hawaii this summer.

If I *were* (not *was*) king, I couldn't be happier.

The subjunctive mood may also be used in the following instances:

If the report *be* true, we will have to modify our plans. [To express a doubt or uncertainty.]

She commanded that the rule *be* enforced. [To express a command.]

Even though he *disagree* with me, I will still admire him. [To express a concession.]

It is necessary that he *see* his parents at once. [To express a necessity.]

I move that the proposal *be* adopted. [To express a parliamentary motion.]

Exercise 53   Tense and Mood

A. In the space at the right, write the correct form of the verb that appears in parentheses.

Example: The prima donna (*sing*) two encores for the
enthusiastic audience.   _____*sang*_____

1. The wind, which had (*blow*) from the east all afternoon, signaled rain by morning.   _____

2. The Webster children have often (*swing*) in the
   swings at Pulaski Park.   _____

3. Yesterday afternoon they (*ride*) a merry-go-round
   that had just been installed.   _____

4. Do you know whether the site for the winter
   Olympics has been (*choose*)?   _____

5. Obviously, Matt was not (*shake*) by the news that
   the desperadoes were waiting for him at the Long
   Branch.   _____

6. Last night we (*steal*) down the basement stairs only
   to discover that the wind was responsible for the
   squeaking door.   _____

7. This is the second pair of shorts that Carlos has
   (*tear*) playing soccer.   _____

8. Aunt Esther's first words always were "My, how
   you've (*grow*)!"   _____

9. The architect has already (*draw*) plans for the syna-
   gogue that is to be built in Trenton Heights.   _____

10. Our hometown hero was a man who (*wear*) his
    fame well.   _____

11. Who has (*drink*) all the eggnog that was in the
    refrigerator?   _____

12. Can you believe that Joe (*throw*) the football almost
    the length of the field?   _____

13. The bags of leaves were too heavy to carry to the
    curb, so we simply (*drag*) them.   _____

14. If Juan had (*see*) the late news, he would know
who won the election.   _____

15. Last night Stephanie wore the onyx earrings that
her fiancé had (*give*) her for her birthday.   _____

B. Underline all verbs in the following sentences. Then write the past tense of the
underlined verbs in the space at the right.

Example: Actually she <u>goes</u> to the grocery store two or
three times a week.   _____*went*_____

1. After supper Alfred comes straight to the room and
writes to Marie.   _____

2. I hear that you know my cousin Sid.   _____

3. The duchess drinks a cup of tea when she grows
tired of writing her memoirs.   _____

4. Marty dives from the dock and swims all the way
to the raft.   _____

5. I suppose that my friend from Cameroun speaks
both French and English.   _____

C. Select the correct form of the verb in parentheses, and write it in the space at
the right.

Example: I wish that I (*were, was*) playing golf this
afternoon.   _____*were*_____

1. It is necessary that this income (*is, be*) reported to
the IRS.   _____

2. (*Cutting, Having cut*) her hair, Della had no use for
the combs that Jim gave her.   _____

3. Valerie told me that the Antique Nook (*opens,
opened*) at ten on Saturdays.   _____

4. According to our minutes it was Mark who moved
that the bylaws (*are, be*) accepted as amended.   _____

5. If I (*were, was*) Mr. Willard, I'd sell that gold-mine
stock today.   _____

Exercise 54 — Tense and Mood

In the space at the right write the correct form of the verb that appears in parentheses.

Example: Who (*lead*) the singing at last year's reunion?   _____*led*_____

1. (*Buying*) their tickets, the two couples visited in the theater lobby until time for the performance.   _____

2. Aloysius thinks that his life would be easier if he (*be*) named "Al."   _____

3. Who knows how many vines Tarzan has (*swing*) from?   _____

4. We were (*suppose*) to leave for Shawnee before lunch, but of course Terence was late.   _____

5. I was (*awaken*) at midnight by the grandfather clock at the end of the hall.   _____

6. Because the small boy had had only a few lessons, he (*blow*) his tuba with more enthusiasm than skill.   _____

7. Last night Ginger hoped to (*finish*) reading *The Glass Menagerie* before going to bed.   _____

8. I remember when my mother (*use*) to call out my spelling words while I was eating breakfast.   _____

9. Jenny has (*begin*) swimming on the weekends at the Y.M.C.A.   _____

10. I am surprised that she has not (*swim*) there before.   _____

11. As they waited to cross the busy street, the small boy (*cling*) to his mother's coat.   _____

12. In the late movie the soldiers (*stand*) at the ship's rail and waved good-bye to the crowd on the dock.   _____

13. It's easy to understand why this stock scene (*use*) to appear regularly in World War II movies.   _____

14. We have (*get*) several cards from Holly since she has been in Mexico City.   _____

15. Everyone else had (*eat*) before Audrey finally came down to breakfast.   _____

16. (*Flying*) often, he felt perfectly at ease in the small commuter plane. _____

17. Every morning the United States flag as well as that of our state is (*raise*) on front campus. _____

18. Billy Budd was (*hang*) from the yardarm, a punishment that is debated by sailors, lawyers, and students. _____

19. Although the blanket was (*wear*), the child continued to consider it essential to life itself. _____

20. The man on first had (*hope*) to steal second. _____

21. He had (*steal*) at least a dozen bases during the season. _____

22. But this time he had (*run*) only halfway down the baseline when the pitcher picked him off. _____

23. Clearly, it is essential that, to steal successfully, a runner (*be*) very fast. _____

24. (*Catching*) the biggest marlin in the tournament, Uncle Leo decided to have it mounted. _____

25. The Wileys are (*accustom*) to having an early dinner and then watching television. _____

26. We had (*drive*) all the way to Greenville before we stopped for gas. _____

27. Although Rufus had (*fall*) from the pecan tree numerous times, he persisted in climbing it. _____

28. Clement Moore's poem tells us that "the stockings were (*hang*) by the chimney with care." _____

29. After the boys had (*ring*) Mrs. Worley's doorbell a half dozen times, they decided that she must be taking her afternoon nap. _____

30. If you had (*take*) the Norman Parkway to the Civic Center, you would have saved ten minutes or more. _____

31. We were told that the ferry (*sail*) for the island every morning, coming back to the mainland before sundown. _____

32. My brother and I (*burst*) into laughter every time we saw Lucy in her candy-factory episode. _____

33. Donna was all but (*freeze*) by the time she walked from the student union building to the bookstore.   _____

34. Mother told me that the clasp on her pearls is (*break*).   _____

35. Jess was (*sting*) by a yellow jacket when he was looking for the shovel in the tool shed.   _____

36. Our class has been (*ask*) to decorate a float for the homecoming parade.   _____

37. Mr. Elliot says that all of the research has been (*do*) for the marketing report.   _____

38. When she called the eight-hundred number, she was told that the train (*leave*) at 8:45 A.M.   _____

39. The White Witch of Narnia commanded that the Lion Aslan (*be*) captured.   _____

40. Have you (*get*) a tax notice from the city?   _____

41. The men (*throw*) their fishing gear into the back of the truck and headed for the lake.   _____

42. The moon had already (*rise*) before they got back to the marina and headed home.   _____

43. Lilly had just (*come*) out on the deck to eat her supper when the mosquitoes found her.   _____

44. Once she was (*bite*), she beat a hasty retreat into the house.   _____

45. If I (*be*) you, I would not wear those sandals when we go to the Metropolitan tomorrow.   _____

46. Zach had (*dive*) off the high board three or four times before he began swimming his daily laps.   _____

47. She told the supervisor that she (*shut*) down the computer system before leaving.   _____

48. After being recognized by the Speaker of the House, the representative moved that the resolution (*be*) adopted.   _____

49. Last year immediately after his graduation he had wanted to (*work*) in the trust department of a bank.   _____

50. The crew that has just (*fly*) in from Chicago will make the return trip tomorrow.   _____

Exercise 55   Two Troublesome Pairs of Verbs

Select the correct form of the verbs in parentheses, and write it in the space at the right.

Example: You shouldn't (*sit, set*) your cacti in the shade.   _____*set*_____

1. The map suggested that the route the fur traders
   needed to follow (*lay, laid*) south of the river.   _____

2. After the kindergarten children had (*sat, set*) in a circle, the teacher began telling the story of "Jack and
   the Beanstalk."   _____

3. Once we had reached the stream, we (*sat, set*) our
   backpacks down and looked for a comfortable spot to
   eat lunch.   _____

4. We had already hiked between four and five miles,
   and the top of the falls (*lies, lays*) at least a mile
   ahead.   _____

5. On that July 4, boats of every conceivable size (*lay,
   laid*) in the New York harbor.   _____

6. Joe is dejected, but most of us would be had we (*sat,
   set*) on the bench for an entire half.   _____

7. The dark clouds, which promised snow, (*lay, laid*)
   heavy on the horizon.   _____

8. My new acquaintance, who had (*sat, set*) by me all
   evening, gave me a picture by picture account of her
   photographic safari.   _____

9. The stonemason selected the pieces of granite one by
   one, carefully (*lying, laying*) each in its proper place.   _____

10. Please (*sit, set*) the plates at this end of the table and
    the glasses at the other.   _____

11. While Dale was in the hardware store, his German
    shepherd (*sat, set*) expectantly in the back of the Jeep.   _____

12. The groundwork for the agreement between union
    and management had been (*lain, laid*) at an early
    morning meeting.   _____

13. We had just (*sat, set*) down for dinner when both the telephone and the doorbell rang. _____

14. She folded the sheets and towels and (*lain, laid*) them in the laundry basket. _____

15. Having (*lain, laid*) back in the recliner, I understood for the first time the furniture saleswoman's definition of "comfortable." _____

16. Of course the cottages that had been (*sat, set*) on the ocean front were the most heavily damaged by the high tides. _____

17. Gayle (*lain, laid*) the receiver on the desk and went to find her mother. _____

18. She found her by the back steps (*sitting, setting*) out a handful of jonquil bulbs. _____

19. The little boy (*sitting, setting*) in the stroller was fast asleep, oblivious of the crowds in the mall. _____

20. Each morning Jeff brings in several logs from the carport and (*lies, lays*) them by the stove. _____

21. After calling the meeting to order, the presiding officer (*lain, laid*) down his gavel. _____

22. When visitors come to Dong and Hanh's house, they (*sit, set*) their shoes by the front door. _____

23. The first step is to (*lie, lay*) all the pieces of the puzzle face up on the table. _____

24. Every day or two someone will come along and (*sit, set*) down to work on it. _____

25. Fortunately, no one minds how long the half-completed puzzle (*lies, lays*) there. _____

26. As soon as Rob had put the groceries in the car, he lifted up the two-year-old and (*sat, set*) her in the carseat. _____

27. (*Lying, Laying*) by the pool, Lydia watched the lifeguard's efforts to stop the game of tag. _____

28. Doc's ten-gallon hat has (*lain, laid*) at the end of the bar for two or three days. _____

29. The baskets of peaches were (*sitting, setting*) in front of the roadside stand. _____

30. Once the peace treaty had been signed, the guerrillas
    (*lain, laid*) down their arms.   _____

Exercise 56   Voice

Revise the following sentences, using verbs in the active voice and eliminating unnecessary verbs.

Example: The position of program analyst has already been filled by the personnel department.

The personnel department has already filled the position of program analyst.

1. An appointment with the dentist was originally made for Friday morning by my roommate.

2. After the tour of the Scandinavian countries had been arranged by the alumnae director, the itinerary was published in the bulletin.

3. All day the picket fence, which had been repaired last week by Dad, was painted by Claire and Dave.

4. First prize was won by Harriet for her one-act play, which was set in New England.

5. The book fair, which is sponsored by the Friends of the Library, is held the first week in October.

6. The child's brown eyes were opened wide when she was spoken to by Santa Claus.

7. After the tent had been pitched by the campers, their sleeping bags and supplies were unloaded from the pickup.

8. The basketball, which was passed from McHale to Bird, was immediately sunk by the latter.

9. The parrot was let out of its cage by Tony, who was promptly chastised by Ms. Quincy, its owner.

10. The music for the classic American opera *Porgy and Bess* was composed by George Gershwin, and the lyrics were written by his brother Ira in collaboration with DuBose Heyward.

11. The referee's warnings had been ignored by both coaches, who were charged with technical fouls in short order.

12. Their books were kept by Joanna, but their tax returns were figured by Chet.

13. The handsome new bank building was designed by an architect who had been selected by the Board of Directors.

14. The film *A Christmas Carol*, which is based on a story which was written by Charles Dickens, was enjoyed by a group of my friends last night.

15. The jewelry which had been given to the Duchess of Windsor by the Duke was sold at auction by Sotheby's.

14

Dangling Modifiers

A **modifier** must always have a word to modify. This fact seems almost too obvious to warrant discussion. And yet we frequently see sentences similar in construction to this one: "Hearing a number of entertaining stories, our visit was thoroughly enjoyable." *Hearing a number of entertaining stories* is a modifying phrase. But where in the sentence is there a word for it to modify? Certainly the phrase cannot logically modify *visit*: it was not our visit that heard a number of entertaining stories. Who did hear the stories? *We* did. Since, however, the word *we* does not appear in the sentence for the phrase to modify, the phrase is said to "dangle." Any modifier dangles, or hangs unattached, when there is no obvious word to which it is clearly and logically related. (Note the similarity of this problem of modifiers and the problem of pronouns and their antecedents.)

■ 14a Recognizing Dangling Modifiers

It is important that you recognize dangling modifiers when you see them. Such modifiers usually appear as two types of constructions — as *verbal phrases* and as *elliptical clauses*. (An elliptical clause, as applicable to this lesson, is a dependent clause in which the subject and/or verb are omitted.)

Hearing a number of entertaining stories, our visit was thoroughly enjoyable. [Dangling participial phrase.]

On entering the room, refreshments were being served. [Dangling gerund phrase.]

To play tennis well, the racket must be held properly. [Dangling infinitive phrase.]

When only three years old, my father took me to a circus. [Dangling elliptical clause.]

209

In each of the examples given above, the dangling modifier stands at the beginning of the sentence. If the modifier were *not* dangling — that is, if it were correctly used — it would be related to the subject of the sentence. In none of these sentences, however, can the introductory modifier logically refer to the subject. If the error is not immediately apparent, try placing the modifier just after the subject. The dangling nature of the modifier becomes easily recognizable because of the illogical meaning that results when you say, "Our visit, *hearing a number of entertaining stories,* . . ." or "Refreshments, *on entering the room,* . . ."

Dangling modifiers frequently appear at the end as well as at the beginning of sentences. The participial phrase dangles in the sentence "The dog had only one eye, *caused by an accident.*"

At this point an exception to the rules governing the recognition of dangling modifiers should be noted: some introductory verbal phrases are general or summarizing expressions and therefore need not refer to the subject that follows:

CORRECT: *Generally speaking,* the boys' themes were more interesting than the girls'.

CORRECT: *To sum up,* our vacation was a disaster from start to finish.

■ 14b Correcting Dangling Modifiers

Sentences containing dangling modifiers are usually corrected in one of two ways. One way is to leave the modifier as it is and to reword the main clause, making the subject a word to which the modifier logically refers. Remember that when modifiers such as those discussed in this lesson stand at the beginning of the sentence, they must always clearly and logically modify or be related to the subject of the sentence:

Hearing a number of entertaining stories, *we* thoroughly enjoyed our visit.

On entering the room, *I* found that refreshments were being served.

To play tennis well, *one* must hold the racket properly.

When only three years old, *I* was taken to a circus by my father.

You may test the correctness of these sentences, as you tested the incorrectness of the others, by placing the modifier just after the subject. Then see whether the sentence reads logically; if it does, the modifier has been correctly used. The following sentence, though awkward, is clear and logical: "We, hearing a number of entertaining stories, thoroughly enjoyed our visit."

The other way to correct sentences containing dangling modifiers is to expand the modifiers into dependent clauses:

Since we heard a number of entertaining stories, our visit was thoroughly enjoyable.

When I entered the room, refreshments were being served.

If one wishes to play tennis well, he must hold the racket properly.

When I was only three years old, my father took me to a circus.

Exercise 57   Dangling Modifiers

Rewrite in correct form all sentences containing dangling modifiers. Write **C** if a sentence is correct.

Example: Diving into the pool, the water was cold.

When he dived into the pool, the water was cold.

1. Before deciding on our condominium, the real estate agent had shown us a townhouse in the same subdivision.

2. Once recommended by the biology department, the science faculty as a whole approved the new botany course.

3. Her number was finally found by looking through almost all the "Browns" in the telephone directory.

4. Having taken the late train to Brookwood, finding seats wasn't a problem for Betty and me.

5. Woven by the Cherokee Indians, we bought a basket to give Mother for her birthday.

6. If actually lost, I'll certainly have to have a new set of keys made.

7. While struggling to complete the inning, Pete was warming up in the bullpen.

8. Having shrunk at least two sizes, I could no longer squeeze into my Shetland sweater.

9. Reading the letter from Abe, a smile slowly spread across Megan's face.

10. To read the morning paper before leaving for his office, Mr. Humphries gets up at six o'clock.

11. After grinding to a halt, the logs on the flat-bed truck shifted significantly.

12. Once papered, the whole atmosphere of the entrance hall changed.

13. Arranged in alphabetical order, she found the latest issue of *Time* immediately.

14. My paper for Dr. Tompkins was finished after sitting up half the night.

15. To decipher his handwriting, a magnifying glass and an active imagination are called for.

16. Never having eaten fried zucchini, I did not know quite what to expect.

17. Freshly squeezed, he drank the orange juice with pleasure.

18. Having fouled out, there was nothing for Oscar to do but to return to the bench.

19. Before looking for a job, careful thought should be given to one's résumé.

20. Generally speaking, Harold prefers a foulard tie to any other kind.

Exercise 58 Introductory Modifiers

Using the following phrases and elliptical clauses as introductory modifiers, write complete sentences.

Example: While wrapping the packages, *Katie watched her favorite soap*

opera. _____

1. After having climbed all the way to the top of the stairs, _____

_____

2. Nodding now and then, _____

_____

3. To challenge her students to think for themselves, _____

_____

4. Encouraged by the applause of the crowd, _____

_____

5. Having played volleyball all winter, _____

_____

6. While screening the applications, _____

_____

7. Before buying a racket, _____

_____

8. To sum up, _____

_____

9. After gaining the lead, _____

_____

10. When writing to his parents, _____

_____

11. Covered with sequins, _____

_____

12. In asking the question, _____

_____

13. Since attending the investment seminar, _____

_____

14. Having been yanked this way and that, _____

_____

15. Not knowing a word of Spanish, _____

_____

16. Upon leaving the freeway, _____

_____

17. To get to the market in Manhattan on time, _____

_____

18. When ten years old, _____

_____

19. Always changing, _____

_____

20. Without once looking back, _____

_____

21. Filled with people, _____

_____

22. Having burned the toast once, _____

_____

23. By using one of the word processors in the library, _____

_____

24. Generally speaking, _____

_____

25. Hurrying down the long, steep stairs, _____

_____

15

Misplaced Modifiers

Modifiers must always be so placed that there will be no uncertainty about the words they modify. A modifier should, in general, stand as close as possible to the word that it modifies. This does not mean, however, that in every sentence there is only one correct position for a modifier. The following sentence, in which the adverb *today* is shifted from one position to another, is equally clear in any one of these three versions:

Today she arrived in Chicago.

She arrived *today* in Chicago.

She arrived in Chicago *today*.

The position of the modifier *today* can be shifted because, no matter where it is placed, it clearly modifies the verb *arrived*.

■ 15a Misplaced Phrases and Clauses

When, however, a modifier can attach itself to two different words in the sentence, the writer must be careful to place it in a position that will indicate the meaning intended:

They argued the subject while I tried to study *at fever pitch*.

This sentence is illogical as long as the phrase *at fever pitch* seems to modify *to study*. The phrase must be placed where it will unmistakably modify *argued*:

CORRECT: They argued the subject *at fever pitch* while I tried to study.

ALSO CORRECT: *At fever pitch* they argued the subject while I tried to study.

A relative clause — that is, a clause introduced by a relative pronoun — should normally follow the word that it modifies:

ILLOGICAL: A piece was played at the concert *that was composed of dissonant chords.*

CORRECT: A piece *that was composed of dissonant chords* was played at the concert.

■ 15b Ambiguous Modifiers

When a modifier is placed between two elements so that it may be taken to modify either element, it is **ambiguous.** These ambiguous modifiers are sometimes called **squinting modifiers:**

The girl who had been dancing *gracefully* entered the room.

Does the speaker mean that the girl had been dancing gracefully or that she entered the room gracefully? Either of these meanings may be expressed with clarity if the adverb *gracefully* is properly placed:

The girl who had been *gracefully* dancing entered the room. [*Gracefully* modifies *had been dancing.*]

The girl who had been dancing entered the room *gracefully*. [Here *gracefully* modifies *entered.*]

■ 15c Misplaced Words Like *Only, Nearly,* and *Almost*

Words such as *only, nearly,* and *almost* are frequently misplaced. Normally these modifying words should immediately precede the word they modify. To understand the importance of properly placing these modifiers, consider in the following sentences the different meanings that result when *only* is shifted:

Only I heard John shouting at the boys. [*Only* modifies *I.* Meaning: I was the only one who heard John shouting.]

I *only* heard John shouting at the boys. [*Only* modifies *heard.* Implied meaning: I heard but didn't see John shouting.]

I heard *only* John shouting at the boys. [*Only* modifies *John.* Meaning: John was the only one whom I heard shouting.]

I heard John *only* shouting at the boys. [*Only* modified *shouting.* Possible implied meaning: I didn't hear John hitting the boys — I heard him only shouting at them.]

I heard John shouting at the boys *only*. [*Only* modifies *boys.* Possible implied meaning: The boys were the ones I heard John shouting at — not the girls.]

Misplacing *only, nearly,* or *almost* will frequently result in an illogical statement:

ILLOGICAL: The baby *only* cried until he was six months old.

CORRECT: The baby cried *only* until he was six months old.

ILLOGICAL: Since his earnings amounted to $97.15, he *nearly* made a hundred dollars.

CORRECT: Since his earnings amounted to $97.15, he made *nearly* a hundred dollars.

ILLOGICAL: At the recent track meet Ralph *almost* jumped six feet.

CORRECT: At the recent track meet Ralph jumped *almost* six feet.

■ 15d Split Infinitives

A **split infinitive** is a construction in which the sign of the infinitive *to* has been separated from the verb with which it is associated. *To vigorously deny* and *to instantly be killed* are split infinitives. Unless emphasis or clarity demands its use, such a construction should be avoided:

AWKWARD: He always tries *to efficiently and promptly do* his work.

CORRECT: He always tries *to do* his work *efficiently and promptly.*

CORRECT: We expect *to more than double* our sales in April. [Placing the modifiers *more than* anywhere else in this sentence would result in ambiguity or changed meaning.]

Exercise 59   Misplaced Modifiers

Place **M** or **C** in the space at the right to indicate whether each sentence contains a misplaced modifier or is correct. Underline the misplaced words and indicate their proper position by means of a caret ($\wedge$). Use additional carets if there is more than one correct position.

Example: We left the museum before we had <u>hardly</u> seen$_\wedge$ half the
exhibits.   *M*

1. They drove the car along the coast to Gulfport with the top
   down.   _____

2. Having sold most of their produce, the Fosters closed their stall
   for the night at the market.   _____

3. Mr. Mendez peered over his glasses at his daughter's date, resting on the end of his nose.   _____

4. The student decided to for the most part follow her adviser's
   suggestions concerning her summer quarter schedule.   _____

5. We have almost seen all the segments of *Power of the Word*, Bill
   Moyers' television series about contemporary poets and their
   work.   _____

6. Marvin took the jacket to the tailor that needed to be fitted.   _____

7. My friend who plays doubles often asked me to be his partner.   _____

8. It was finally determined that Robert Peary did indeed reach the
   North Pole in 1989.   _____

9. She put the sacks of groceries on the kitchen counter that she
   had brought in from the car.   _____

10. Finchley slipped and twisted his ankle on the icy sidewalk.   _____

11. The horse that Horace had bet on lost the lead only in the last
    seconds of the race.   _____

12. Morton saw the production of *Henry V* starring Kenneth
    Branagh along with several of his friends.   _____

13. The recital that Tina heard at Carnegie Hall on Tuesday was
    acclaimed by the critics.   _____

14. The meteorologist reported that tomorrow will be mostly cloudy with a sixty percent chance of rain on the weather channel. _____

15. The coaches discussed the play run by Herschel on the sidelines. _____

16. Mother wants us to without fail call Aunt Flo when we are in Washington. _____

17. The route which the Lowells take to Des Moines occasionally is the one we take. _____

18. For most tourists the Eiffel Tower symbolizes Paris, built in 1889 for the International Exposition. _____

19. The man ducking into the doorway quickly glanced over his shoulder. _____

20. The street should be resurfaced in the spring back of the town hall. _____

Exercise 60 Misplaced Modifiers

Place **M** or **C** in the space at the right to indicate whether each sentence contains a misplaced modifier or is correct. Underline the misplaced words and indicate their proper position with a caret (∧). Use additional carets if there is more than one correct position.

Example: The psychology quiz was short, just taking me∧twenty minutes.   _**M**_

1. I am opposed to eating a hotdog without onions on principle.   _____

2. The balcony is the prime attraction of our apartment, which is accessible from both of these rooms.   _____

3. Eric asked her whenever possible to have lunch with him.   _____

4. I can truthfully say that we enjoyed reading the essays written by George Orwell in freshman English.   _____

5. The chandelier always attracted the attention of visitors that hung in the church sanctuary.   _____

6. Feeling terribly awkward, he finally asked the girl to dance in the white dress.   _____

7. Did you remember to ask Chapman to have breakfast with us last night?   _____

8. Only after a year had passed was it obvious that the city was making real progress restoring the buildings along the waterfront.   _____

9. They are determined to as soon as possible design fresh costumes and a new set for *The Music Man.*   _____

10. She nearly looked all day before finding a sweater to wear with her new corduroy skirt.   _____

11. The sports commentator reporting the news vainly tried to explain "wild-card games."   _____

12. The mural covered the wall of the subway painted by a Canadian artist.   _____

13. My mother especially enjoys Humphrey Bogart, who has always been an ardent movie buff.   _____

14. The director of nursing whom City Hospital employed recently worked at a similar hospital in Lansing.   _____

15. Because of the cold wind, we scarcely walked three blocks before catching a cab.   _____

16. At dinner her diamonds were admired by everyone shimmering in the candlelight.   _____

17. One fine spring day we took the canoe from the boathouse, which had been in storage all winter.   _____

18. We headed down the lake, almost paddling to Thompson Bridge before turning back.   _____

19. Many people who watch late movies regularly get up about noon.   _____

20. The sign read: "Parking in this area by students is prohibited."   _____

16

Parallelism

Frequently in writing and speaking you need to indicate equality of ideas. To show this equality, you should employ **parallel** grammatical constructions. In other words, convey parallel thought in parallel language; and conversely, use parallel language only when you are conveying parallel thoughts.

■ 16a Coordinate Elements

In employing parallelism, balance nouns against nouns, infinitives against infinitives, prepositional phrases against prepositional phrases, adjective clauses against adjective clauses, etc. Never make the mistake of saying, "I have always liked swimming and to fish." Because the object of *have liked* is two parallel ideas, you should say:

I have always liked *swimming* and *fishing*. (*And* joins two gerunds.)

OR

I have always liked *to swim* and *to fish*. (*And* joins two infinitives.)

Parallel prepositional phrases are illustrated in the following sentence. The parallel elements appear immediately after the double bar:

Government ‖ of the people,
‖ by the people,
and ‖ for the people shall not perish from the earth.

Next we see an illustration of parallel noun clauses:

He said ||| that he would remain in the East,
that his wife would travel through the Northwest,
and || that his son would attend summer school in the South.

The following sentence contains parallel independent clauses:

|| I came;
| I saw;
|| I conquered.

Parallel elements are usually joined either by simple coordinating conjunctions or by correlative conjunctions. The most common coordinating conjunctions used with parallel constructions are *and, but, or.* Whenever one of these connectives is used, you must be careful to see that the elements being joined are coordinate or parallel in construction:

FAULTY: Ann is a girl with executive ability and who therefore should be elected class president.

This sentence contains faulty parallelism, since *and* is used to join a phrase (*with executive ability*) and a dependent clause (*who therefore should be elected class president*). To correct the sentence, (1) expand the phrase into a *who* clause, or (2) make an independent clause of the *who* clause:

CORRECT: Ann is a girl || who has executive ability
and || who therefore should be elected class president.

Note: A safe rule to follow is this: *And who* or *and which* should never be used unless preceded by another *who-* or *which-*clause.

ALSO CORRECT: || Ann is a girl with executive ability;
| she therefore should be elected class president.

A common error results from making a construction appear to be parallel when actually it is not:

Mr. Lee is honest, intelligent, and works hard.

The structure of the sentence suggests an *a, b,* and *c* series; yet what we have is not three parallel elements but two adjectives (*honest, intelligent*) and a verb (*works*). The sentence can be corrected in two ways: we can use three adjectives in a series or two independent clauses in parallel construction, thus:

CORRECT: Mr. Lee is || honest,
| intelligent,
and || industrious.
ALSO CORRECT: || Mr. Lee is honest and intelligent,
and || he works hard.

■ 16b Use of Correlative Conjunctions

Correlative conjunctions are used in pairs: *either . . . or . . . ; neither . . . nor . . . ; both . . . and . . . ; not only . . . but also . . . .* When these conjunctions are employed in a sentence, they must be followed by parallel constructions:

INCORRECT: I hope *either* to spend my vacation in Mexico *or* Hawaii. [In this sentence *either* is followed by an infinitive, *or* by a noun.]

CORRECT: I hope to spend my vacation either ‖ in Mexico
 or ‖ in Hawaii.

ALSO CORRECT: I hope to spend my vacation in either ‖ Mexico
 or ‖ Hawaii.

INCORRECT: She knew *not only* what to say, *but also* she knew when to say it.

CORRECT: She knew not only ‖ what to say
 but also ‖ when to say it.

■ 16c Repetition of Certain Words

In order to make parallel constructions clear, you must sometimes repeat an article, a preposition, an auxiliary verb, the sign of the infinitive (*to*), or the introductory word of a dependent clause. Three of these types of necessary repetition are illustrated in the sentences that follow:

OBSCURE: He must counsel all employees who participate in sports and also go on recruiting trips throughout the Southwest.

CLEAR: He must counsel all employees who participate in sports and *must* also go on recruiting trips throughout the Southwest.

OBSCURE: The instructor wants to meet those students who enjoy barber-shop harmony and organize several quartets.

CLEAR: The instructor wants to meet those students who enjoy barber-shop harmony and *to* organize several quartets.

OBSCURE: He thought that economic conditions were improving and the company was planning to increase its dividend rate.

CLEAR: He thought that economic conditions were improving and *that* the company was planning to increase its dividend rate.

■ 16d *Than* and *As* in Parallel Constructions

Than and *as* are frequently used to join parallel constructions. When these two connectives introduce comparisons, you must be sure that the things compared are similar. Don't compare, for instance, a janitor's salary with a teacher. Compare a janitor's salary with a teacher's salary:

INCORRECT: A janitor's salary is frequently larger than a teacher.

CORRECT: || A janitor's salary is frequently larger
than || a teacher's (salary).

■ 16e Incorrect Omission of Necessary Words

A very common kind of faulty parallelism is seen in the following sentence:

I always have and always will *remember* to send my first-grade teacher a Christmas card.

In this sentence *remember* is correctly used after *will*, but after *have* the form needed is *remembered*. Consequently, *remember* cannot serve as the understood participle after *have*:

CORRECT: I || always have *remembered*
and || always will remember   to send my first-grade teacher
a Christmas card.

Other sentences containing similar errors are given below:

INCORRECT: I *was* mildly surprised, but all of my friends gravely shocked. [After *all of my friends* the incorrect verb form *was* seems to be understood.]

CORRECT: I was mildly surprised, but all of my friends *were* gravely shocked.

INCORRECT: He gave me an apple and pear. [Before *pear* the incorrect form *an* seems to be understood.]

CORRECT: He gave me an apple and *a* pear.

INCORRECT: I was interested and astounded *by* the story of his latest adventure.

CORRECT: I was || interested *in*
and || astounded by   the story of his latest adventure

INCORRECT: She is as tall if not taller *than* her sister.

CORRECT: She is as tall *as* her sister, if not taller. [The reader understands *than her sister*.]

ALSO CORRECT: She is as tall *as*, if not taller than, her sister.

■ 16f Correct Use of "Unparallel" Constructions

A caution should be added to this lesson. Parallelism of phraseology is not always possible. When it is not, do not hesitate to use natural, "unparallel" constructions:

CORRECT THOUGH "UNPARALLEL":   He spoke *slowly* and *with dignity.*

Here *slowly* and *with dignity* are parallel in a sense: they are both adverbial modifiers.

Exercise 61 Parallelism

Rewrite in correct form all sentences that contain faulty parallelism. Note that some sentences may be corrected in more than one way. Write **C** if a sentence is correct.

Example: In the picnic basket were three pieces of fruit: an apple, orange, and banana.

In the picnic basket were three pieces of fruit: an apple, an orange, and a banana.

1. The recently published biography of Winston Churchill is interesting, detailed, and it is well written too.

2. The number of apple trees replanted in the orchard this year is greater than last year.

3. The wing chair was upholstered in a linen that had green and white stripes and with red poppies.

4. At six o'clock Thursday morning the telephone rang loudly, persistently, and it woke me up.

5. We not only went horseback riding, but also we took a boat out on the Rio Grande.

6. On New Year's Eve Uncle Brad was both amused and responsive to my request for a small loan.

7. The clap of thunder was as loud, if not louder than, any I had ever heard.

8. October skies seem bluer than any other month.

9. After Janie finally got the bottom drawer open, she found a roll of pink ribbon, an ornament from a Christmas tree, and a dozen or more old photographs.

10. He can either order the cap by mail or by calling a toll-free number.

11. She lives in Puerto Rico, works for a pharmaceutical company, and consequently she speaks Spanish fluently.

12. He always has and probably always will spend his Saturdays working on one or the other of his antique cars.

13. Pat must visit all those hardware stores which sell sporting goods and stop by the specialty shops as well.

14. The car salesmen were impressed with the sleek new model, but the shop foreman somewhat dubious about it.

15. The musical was fast paced, upbeat, and our whole family enjoyed it thoroughly.

16. That commercial was neither accurate nor was it entertaining.

17. Gail hoped to use her frequent-flyer pass to visit Alaska and that she could go in the early fall.

18. The banquet table in the great dining hall was as long, if not longer than, the one at Biltmore House.

19. We assured the visitors from Scotland that the climate in the mountains is cooler than the city.

20. The judge has asked to speak to the defense attorneys whose case is first on the docket and the district attorney as well.

Exercise 62 Parallelism

Complete each of the following sentences by adding a construction that is parallel to the *italicized* construction.

Example: Carl ordered *a hamburger, a small chef's salad,* and <u>*a cup of coffee.*</u>

1. The train was crowded with students *going home to be with their parents during the holidays* or _____

   _____

2. Dad wondered whether he could *see the second half of the game* yet _____

   _____

3. Not only *does the child ask countless questions,* but also _____

   _____

4. The hats and coats were piled everywhere: *on the beds, on the chairs,* and even _____

   _____

5. During our coffee break this morning we had blueberry muffins that were *small* but _____

   _____

6. Reggie will either *have to study after we get back from the show* or _____

   _____

7. *Diggins was an entrepreneur at heart;* nevertheless, _____

   _____

8. The plan was to *cross the English Channel by hydrofoil, rent a car,* and

   then _____

   _____

9. Looking out the window, I saw several boys from the neighborhood

   playing a pickup game of basketball during the morning but _____

   _____

   _____

10. Dennis knew neither *what to say in his letter of application* nor _____

    _____

17

Subordination

Parallelism enables you to indicate equality of ideas. More often, however, your writing will include sentences in which some ideas are more important than others. The main device for showing the difference between major and minor emphasis is **subordination:** reserve the independent clause for the main idea and use dependent clauses, phrases, and single words to convey subordinate ideas:

In our garden there is a birdbath *that is carved from marble.* [Subordinate idea placed in a dependent clause.]

In our garden there is a birdbath *carved from marble.* [Subordinate idea reduced to a participial phrase.]

In our garden there is a *marble* birdbath. [Subordinate idea reduced to a one-word modifier.]

■ 17a Primer Style

It is necessary to understand the principle of subordination, for without subordination you would be unable to indicate the relative importance of ideas or their various shades of emphasis in your thinking. The following group of sentences is both childish and monotonous because six dissimilar ideas have been presented in six simple sentences and thus appear to be of equal importance:

A pep meeting was held last Friday night. Memorial Stadium was the scene of the meeting. The meeting was attended by thousands of students. Over a hundred faculty members were there too. It rained Friday night. There was also some sleet.

As you know, coordinating conjunctions are used to join ideas of equal importance; consequently, the six sentences given above would not be improved if they were joined by such conjunctions. As a matter of fact, a type of sentence that you should avoid is the long, stringy one tied together by *and, but, so,* or *and so.* Instead of using this kind of sentence, weigh the relative importance of your several ideas, and show their importance by the use of main and subordinate sentence elements. Notice how the six ideas can be merged into one clear sentence:

> Despite rain and some sleet the pep meeting held last Friday night at Memorial Stadium was attended by thousands of students and over a hundred faculty members.

In combining the six sentences, the writer has chosen to use the fact about student and faculty attendance as the main idea. Another writer might have chosen otherwise, for there will not always be complete agreement as to which idea can be singled out and considered the most important. You may be sure, however, that if your sentence reads with emphasis and effectiveness you have chosen a correct idea as the main one.

■ 17b Upside-down Subordination

When there are only two ideas of unequal rank to be considered, you should have no difficulty in selecting the more important one:

1. He showed some signs of fatigue.
2. He easily won the National Open Golf Tournament.

Of these two sentences the second is undoubtedly the more important. Hence, when the two sentences are combined, the second should stand as the independent clause, and the first should be reduced to a dependent clause or even a phrase. If you made an independent clause of the first sentence and a subordinate element of the second, your sentence would contain upside-down subordination:

> FAULTY (upside-down subordination): Though he easily won the National Open Golf Tournament, he showed some signs of fatigue.

> CORRECT: Though he showed some signs of fatigue, he easily won the National Open Golf Tournament.

■ 17c Choice of Subordinating Conjunctions

In introducing a subordinate element, be sure that you choose the right subordinating conjunction. The following sentences illustrate the correct use of certain conjunctions:

> I don't know *whether* (or *that;* not *as* or *if*) I can see you tomorrow.

> *Although* (not *while*) she isn't a genius, she has undeniable talent.

> I saw in the autobiography of the actor *that* (not *where*) there is a question about the exact date of his birth.

(See Glossary of Faulty Diction in Chapter 22 for further discussion of accurate word choice.)

Exercise 63　Subordination

Combine the ideas in the following groups of sentences into one effective simple or complex sentence.

Example:　Thursday is the fifth day of the week.
　　　　　　Its name is related to that of a god in Norse mythology.
　　　　　　This god is Thor, the god of thunder.

　　　　　　The name of Thursday, the fifth day of the week, is related to that of Thor, the god of thunder in Norse mythology.

1. Jasper Johns is a world-renowned artist.
   He was born in Georgia.
   He spent his childhood in South Carolina.
   For more than thirty years he has exhibited his work in the United States and abroad.

2. The golf course is located south of Grey Marsh Inlet.
   It was designed by a golf course architect.
   A professional golfer served as the architect's consultant.
   It is a championship golf course.

3. Amelia Earhart was the first woman to fly across the Atlantic.
   The flight was not a solo flight.
   However, today she is remembered for this flight.
   She is also remembered for her last flight, which ended mysteriously.
   She and her copilot failed to reach their destination.

4. Scylla is the name of two characters in Greek mythology.
   One was the daughter of the King of Megara.
   She threw herself from a rock and then turned into a lark.
   The other was a sea monster, who lived in a cave.
   Homer describes this monster as a creature with twelve feet and three heads.

5. "Wild Bill" Hickok was a scout and a marshal in the West of the nineteenth century.
   He was a courageous man.
   Hickok was an inveterate card player.
   Many legends have grown up around his name.

6. The Canary Islands lie off the northwest coast of Africa.
   They are provinces of Spain.
   For centuries they have served as seaports for the trade routes of the Atlantic.
   Now they also serve as a stopover for transatlantic flights.

7. My younger brother read *The Time Machine* by H. G. Wells.
   H. G. Wells was an English writer.
   He is often remembered for his novels that are a mixture of fantasy and science fiction.
   My younger brother spent a great deal of time daydreaming about "time travelling."

8. Ned Rorem is an American.
   He composes music.
   He also is an author.
   In 1976 he was awarded the Pulitzer Prize for *Air Music*.
   Air Music is an orchestral work.
   A brief sketch of his life and a bibliography of his works appear in *The New Grove Dictionary of Music and Musicians*.

9. Gabriel García Márquez is from Colombia.
   He is a noted author.
   Many critics consider his novel *One Hundred Years of Solitude* to be his finest work.
   However, his later novels continue to be acclaimed.

Exercise 64 Subordination

Combine the ideas in each of the following groups of sentences into one effective simple or complex sentence.

Example: There are five Great Lakes.
They lie between the United States and Canada.
Lake Ontario is the smallest lake.
Lake Superior is the largest one.

Of the five Great Lakes, lying between the United State and Canada, Lake Ontario is the smallest and Lake Superior the largest.

1. Jay Hanna Dean was born in Lucas, Arkansas, in 1911.
   In the thirties he became one of baseball's most famous pitchers.
   Today he is much better known as Dizzy Dean.

2. Singapore is the name of a country.
   It is also the name of a great seaport.
   The name is derived from Sanskrit.
   It may be translated "Lion City."
   Sanskrit is an ancient language of India.

3. Marshall McLuhan was a Canadian.
   He taught in universities in Canada and the United States.
   He is often remembered for his problematic observation.
   This observation is that "the medium is the message."

4. There is an exhibit of calligraphy in our local museum.
   Calligraphy is defined as "fair or elegant handwriting."
   It had its origin in China centuries ago.

5. Thyme is a plant that belongs to the mint family.
A line in Shakespeare's *A Midsummer Night's Dream* alludes to it.
The line is spoken by Oberon to Puck.
The line is "I know a bank whereon the wild thyme blows."

6. Helena Rubenstein was born in Poland.
In 1915 she came to the United States to live.
She lived here until her death in 1965.
Her beauty salons made her famous.
These were established in places as far apart as Melbourne, Australia, and Rio de Janeiro, Brazil.

7. The traditional date for the first Olympic contest is 776 B.C.
It consisted of a single event.
It was a race run the length of the stadium in Elis, Greece.
The event was a part of a festival honoring Zeus.

8. Lorraine Hansberry was the author of an award-winning play.
Its name is *A Raisin in the Sun*.
It was the first play by an African-American woman to be produced on Broadway.
The title of this play alludes to a poem entitled "Dream Deferred."
Langston Hughes wrote the poem.

9. The Georges Pompidou Centre is in Paris.
   It is named for a former president of France.
   He was a patron of modern art.
   The building is a cause for much consternation.
   It appears to be a building whose skeleton of pipes and girders has never been covered.
   It also appears to be a building whose scaffolding has never been removed.

Exercise 65   Subordination

The following sentences contain upside-down subordination or too much coordination. Rewrite each sentence to make it an effective simple or complex sentence.

Example: Although the storm uprooted three of our pear trees, it blew over quickly.

Although the storm blew over quickly, it uprooted three of our pear trees.

1. He went to law school, and then he joined a law firm in Miami, and we seldom saw each other anymore.

2. Though the Wildcats' basketball team has the depth necessary to win the tournament, the forwards are small.

3. Racing to the address given by the 911 caller, the ambulance turned on its siren.

4. Olivia enjoys sharing what she bakes, and she baked some apple bread this morning, and she will probably take a loaf to one of her neighbors.

5. Searching for the check that my mother had asked me to deposit in the bank this morning, I frantically retraced my steps.

6. The skies were overcast when I woke up this morning, but I went to the lake, and to my surprise the sun soon came out.

7. Reading her own story in the current issue of *The New Yorker*, the young author experienced a deep sense of satisfaction.

8. The roof began to leak, and several of the stained-glass windows were cracked, and the members of the congregation knew that they must increase the church's maintenance budget for the coming year.

9. Making her debut tonight with the city's new opera company, Octavia has every right to be nervous.

10. Listed in today's want ads under "Business Opportunities" is a desktop-publishing service, and this calls for computer skills, and it is also necessary to have a large dose of imagination.

Exercise 66   Subordination

The following sentences contain upside-down subordination or too much coordination. Rewrite each sentence to make it an effective simple or complex sentence.

Example: He had to go by the dry cleaners, and then he had to pick up his ticket from the travel agent, and he almost missed his flight.

Because he had had to go by the dry cleaners and then pick up his ticket from the travel agent, he almost missed his flight.

1. Miss Lambert was on a diet, and she was hungry, and Mr. Pym offered her a slice of tutti-frutti cake, and she could not resist it.

2. Anticipating his interpretation of Beethoven's *Ninth Symphony*, the audience applauded enthusiastically as the conductor raised his baton.

3. Professor Timrod teaches political science, and he requires outside reading, and his students have to write a research paper, but his lectures are always fresh and stimulating, and his students enjoy them.

4. Clambering out of his truck stalled on the tracks, J. T. heard the whistle of the northbound freight train.

5. We had planned to cook hamburgers on the grill, and we intended to serve supper on the picnic table, and then it rained, and eating outside was impossible.

6. Having been flattened by a defensive lineman twice his size, the place-kicker lay breathless on the ten-yard line.

7. Barreling down the interstate at top speed, the trucker was due in Houston before five o'clock.

8. We turned off the highway exactly three miles north of Brown's Crossing, and we drove another two miles, and then we saw the artist's cabin on the right.

9. Believing briefly that he had invented a perpetual motion machine, the perpetual tinkerer stared in amazement.

10. The rains had been heavy in the spring, and the lake was filling up, and some of my friends were thinking about fishing in the coves, and other friends were thinking about getting out their sailboats.

18

Illogical Comparisons and Mixed Constructions

Correctness and clarity are essential to good writing. To reach these goals, you must know the rules of grammar and punctuation. But further, you must think logically and find the exact words in which to express your thoughts. Nothing is more bothersome to a reader than inexact, illogical, or confusing sentences. Some of the lessons that you have already studied have shown how to avoid errors that produce vagueness or confusion in writing; among these errors are faulty reference of pronouns, dangling or misplaced modifiers, and upside-down subordination. This lesson will consider certain other errors that obstruct clarity of expression.

■ 18a Illogical Comparisons

When you make comparisons, you must be sure not only that the things compared are similar (a matter considered in the lesson on parallelism) but also that all necessary elements of the comparison are included.

Note the following sentence:

Harold is taller than any boy in his class.

Since *Harold*, the first term of the comparison, is included in the classification *any boy in his class*, the comparison is obviously illogical: the sentence might be interpreted to mean *Harold is taller than Harold*. The first term of the comparison must, therefore, be compared with a second term or classification that excludes the first term, thus:

CORRECT: Harold is taller than any *other* boy in his class.

ALSO CORRECT: Harold is taller than any *girl* in his class.

251

When the superlative is followed by *of*, the object of *of* must be plural:

ILLOGICAL: Harold is the tallest of any other boy in his class.

CORRECT: Harold is the tallest of *all the boys* in his class.

ALSO CORRECT: Harold is the *tallest boy* in his class.

Ambiguity results from a comparison like this one:

I helped you more than Jim.

Does the sentence mean *I helped you more than I helped Jim* or *I helped you more than Jim did*? The writer should use one sentence or the other, according to whichever meaning is intended.

The type of incomplete comparison illustrated by the following vague sentences is particularly popular with writers of advertising copy and with careless speakers:

VAGUE: Eastern Rubber Company makes a tire that gives 20 percent more mileage.

CLEAR: Eastern Rubber Company makes a tire that gives 20 percent more mileage *than any tire it made ten years ago.*

ALSO CLEAR: Eastern Rubber Company makes a tire that gives 20 percent more mileage *than any other tire made in the United States.*

VAGUE: Litter is more of a problem in cities.

CLEAR: Litter is more of a problem in cities *than in small towns.*

ALSO CLEAR: Litter is more of a problem in cities *than it used to be.*

■ 18b Mixed or Confused Constructions

Mixed constructions are frequently the result of some sort of shift in a sentence. Through ignorance or forgetfulness the writer starts a sentence with one type of construction and then switches to another. Notice the shift of construction in the following sentence:

She bought an old, dilapidated house, which having it extensively repaired converted it into a comfortable home.

The sentence reads correctly through the relative pronoun *which*. The reader expects *which* to introduce an adjective clause; however, he is unable to find a verb for *which*. Instead, he finds that the sentence is completed by a construction in which a gerund phrase stands as the subject of the verb *converted*. The sentence may be corrected in various ways. Two correct versions follow:

She bought an old, dilapidated house, which after extensive repairs was converted into a comfortable home.

By means of extensive repairs she converted into a comfortable home an old, dilapidated house which she had bought.

Other examples of mixed constructions are given below:

MIXED: Bob realized that during the conference how inattentive he had been. [This sentence is confusing because *that* as used here is a subordinating conjunction and should introduce a noun clause. However, the *that*-construction is left incomplete. Further on, *how* introduces a noun clause. What we find then is only one noun clause but two words, *that* and *how*, used to introduce noun clauses. Obviously, only one such word should introduce the one dependent clause.]

CORRECT: Bob realized that during the conference he had been inattentive.

ALSO CORRECT: Bob realized how inattentive he had been during the conference.

MIXED: Because she had to work in the library kept her from attending the party. [A dependent clause introduced by *because* is always adverbial; hence such a clause can never be used as the subject of a sentence.]

CORRECT: Having to work in the library kept her from attending the party.

ALSO CORRECT: Because she had to work in the library, she could not attend the party.

MIXED: He pulled a leg muscle was why he failed to place in the broad jump. [He *pulled a leg muscle* is an independent clause used here as the subject of *was*. An independent clause, unless it is a quotation, can never be used as the subject of a sentence.]

CORRECT: Because he pulled a leg muscle, he failed to place in the broad jump.

MIXED: By attending the reception as a guest rather than as a butler was a new experience for him. [The preposition *by* introduces a modifying phrase, and a modifying phrase can never be used as the subject of a sentence.]

CORRECT: Attending the reception as a guest rather than as a butler was a new experience for him.

ALSO CORRECT: By attending the reception as a guest rather than as a butler, he enjoyed a new experience.

MIXED: A pronoun is when a word is used in the place of a noun. [Never use *is when* or *is where* in defining a word. Remember that an adverbial *when*- or *where*-clause cannot be used as a predicate nominative.]

CORRECT: A pronoun is a word used in the place of a noun.

MIXED: I was the one about whom she was whispering to my father about. [To correct this sentence, omit either *about*.]

MIXED: We know that if he were interested in our offer that he would come to see us. [To correct this sentence, omit the second *that*. The first *that* introduces the noun clause *that . . . he would come to see us. If he were interested in our offer* is an adverbial clause within the noun clause.]

MIXED: The reason I didn't play well at the recital was because I had sprained my little finger. [This very common error again illustrates the incorrect use of a dependent adverbial clause, introduced by *because*, as a predicate nominative. To correct the mistake, use a noun clause, introduced by *that*.]

CORRECT: The reason I didn't play well at the recital was that I had sprained my little finger.

Exercise 67   Illogical Comparisons and Mixed Constructions

The following sentences contain illogical or ambiguous comparisons and mixed constructions. Rewrite each sentence in a correct form. (Notice that some sentences permit more than one correct interpretation.)

Example: Thomas Wolfe's fiction contains more descriptive passages than Hemingway.

Thomas Wolfe's fiction contains more descriptive passages than Hemingway's.

1. Pollution in Los Angeles is certainly taking a more terrible toll.

2. The lion is reputed to be the bravest of all the other animals.

3. I understand that Maisie's chocolate pound cake was tops among those from which the committee was choosing from.

4. The reason that Maisie's cake is good is because she uses fresh ingredients.

5. By mixing business with pleasure was the way Harry managed to go bankrupt.

6. In baseball a "boot" is when a fielder fails to catch a ground ball.

7. The newspaper reports that the challenger now has sixteen percent more votes in the mayor's race.

8. My classmate Nan Thompson is friendlier than any girl in the class.

9. Stephen, Aunt Martha says that I look more like Roger than you.

10. I had been looking forward to going to the beach with my cousin was why I didn't want to baby-sit with my sister today.

11. Fortunately, by Dad's coming home in time was a lucky break for me.

12. I tried a new route to Richmond, which, taking an unpaved country road, I saved thirty minutes.

13. However, I knew that when I arrived at the Franklins' house how embarrassed I would be about my muddy car.

14. Mimi's voice is louder than any member of our family.

15. Peter Taylor's latest novel is the book about which our professor was telling the class about.

16. Because of a conflict in his schedule was why the senator could not appear at the political rally.

17. The Bettermore Drugstore commercial says that Bettermore gives thirty percent quicker prescription service.

18. Surely, Joanna, you don't think that I like Laura more than you.

19. I have been thinking that if it rains tomorrow, that we may have to cancel our trip.

20. Meg and Susie realized that after the game how hard Dot would be trying to find them.

21. Since I was late for my first class was what made Ted think that I might be ill today.

22. When the bell was ringing was when I came running in, gasping for breath.

23. Just because I can't find my notebook doesn't mean that I am usually a careless person.

24. In lecturing the class about responsibility was how Dr. Pearce got his message across to us.

25. Although they look alike, Marian's car is more powerful than Joe.

19

Punctuation

Punctuation depends largely upon the grammatical structure of a sentence. In order to punctuate correctly, you must therefore understand grammatical elements. For this reason, rules of punctuation in this text have been correlated, whenever applicable, with your study of grammar and sentence structure. You learned, for instance, how to punctuate certain phrases when you studied the phrase as a sentence unit.

In order that this chapter may present a reasonably complete treatment of punctuation, you will find on the pages that follow a summary of the rules already studied, as well as reference by chapter to additional rules. The rules given below have become to a large extent standardized; hence they should be clearly understood and practiced. Following the principle of punctuating "by ear" or of using a comma wherever there is a vocal pause results in an arbitrary and frequently misleading use of punctuation.

■ 19a Terminal Marks

The terminal marks of punctuation — that is, those marks used to end a sentence — are the period, the question mark, and the exclamation mark.

Use a period after a declarative sentence, an imperative sentence, or an indirect question:

DECLARATIVE: John answered the telephone.

IMPERATIVE: Answer the telephone.

INDIRECT QUESTION: She asked whether John had answered the telephone.

259

Note: A request that is stated as a polite question should be followed by a period. Such a request frequently occurs in business correspondence:

Will you please send me your special summer catalog.

Use a period also after most abbreviations:

Mr., Ms., Dr., B.S., Jr., i.e., viz., etc., A.D., B.C., A.M., P.M.

Use three periods to indicate an omission of a word or words within a quoted sentence, three periods plus a terminal mark to indicate an omission at the end of a quoted sentence:

"Fourscore and seven years ago our fathers brought forth . . . a new nation . . . ."

Use a question mark after a direct question:

Did John answer the telephone?

"Have you finished your work?" she asked.

Use an exclamation mark after an expression of strong feeling. This mark of punctuation should be used sparingly:

"Halt!" he shouted.

How disgusting!

There goes the fox!

■ 19b The Comma

1. Use a comma to separate independent clauses when they are joined by the coordinating conjunctions *and, but, or, nor, for, so,* and *yet.* (See Chapter 6.)

The game was over, but the crowd refused to leave the park.

If the clauses are long or are complicated by internal punctuation, use a semicolon instead of a comma. (See 19c, Rule 3.)

2. Use a comma to separate words, phrases, and clauses written as a series of three or more coordinate elements. This rule covers short independent clauses when used in a series, as shown in the third example sentence below.

A trio composed of Marie, Ellen, and Frances sang at the party.

Jack walked into my office, took off his hat, and sat down.

I washed the dishes, I dried them, and I put them away.

3. Use a comma to separate two or more coordinate adjectives that modify the same noun:

The noisy, enthusiastic freshman class assembled in Section F of the stadium. [*Noisy* and *enthusiastic* are coordinate adjectives; therefore they are separated by a comma. But *freshman*, though an adjective, is not coordinate with *noisy* and *enthusiastic*;

actually *noisy* and *enthusiastic* modify not just *class* but the word group *freshman class*. Hence no comma precedes *freshman*.]

To determine whether adjectives are coordinate, you may make two tests: if they are coordinate, you will be able (1) to join them with *and* or (2) to interchange their positions in the sentence. You can certainly say *the noisy and enthusiastic freshman class* or *the enthusiastic, noisy freshman class;* thus *noisy* and *enthusiastic* are clearly coordinate. However, to say *the noisy and freshman class* or *the freshman noisy class* would be absurd; thus *freshman* is not structurally parallel with *noisy:*

a blue wool suit [Adjectives not coordinate.]

an expensive, well-tailored suit [Adjectives coordinate.]

a new tennis court [Adjectives not coordinate.]

a muddy, rough court [Adjectives coordinate.]

4. Use a comma to separate sharply contrasted coordinate elements:

He was merely ignorant, not stupid.

5. Use commas to set off all nonessential modifiers. Do not set off essential modifiers. (See Chapter 5 for a discussion of essential and nonessential phrases; see Chapter 7 for a discussion of essential and nonessential clauses.)

NONESSENTIAL CLAUSE: Sara Sessions, *who is wearing red shorts today,* was voted the most versatile girl in her class.

NONESSENTIAL PHRASE: Sara Sessions, *wearing red shorts today,* was voted the most versatile girl in her class.

ESSENTIAL CLAUSE: The girl *who is wearing red shorts today* is Sara Sessions.

ESSENTIAL PHRASE: The girl *wearing red shorts today* is Sara Sessions.

6. Use a comma after an introductory adverbial clause, verbal phrase, or absolute phrase. (See Chapter 7 for a discussion of dependent clauses, Chapter 5 for a discussion of phrases).

INTRODUCTORY ADVERBIAL CLAUSE: *When he arose to give his speech,* he was greeted with thunderous applause.

INTRODUCTORY PARTICIPIAL PHRASE: *Being in a hurry,* I was able to see him only briefly.

INTRODUCTORY GERUND PHRASE: *On turning the corner,* Tom ran squarely into a police officer.

INTRODUCTORY INFINITIVE PHRASE: *To get a seat,* we have to arrive by 7:30 P.M.

INTRODUCTORY ABSOLUTE PHRASE: *My schedule having been arranged,* I felt like a full-fledged college freshman.

7. Use commas to set off nonessential appositives. (See Chapter 5.)

Tom, *the captain of the team,* was injured in the first game of the season.

Sometimes an appositive is so closely "fused" with its preceding word that it constitutes an essential element in the sentence and thus is not set off by commas:

William *the Conqueror* died in 1087.

The poet *Keats* spent his last days in Italy.

The word *bonfire* has an interesting history.

8. Use commas to set off items in dates, geographical names, and addresses and to set off titles after names:

July 22, 1977, was a momentous day in his life.

Birmingham, Alabama, gets its name from Birmingham, England.

Do you know who lives at 1600 Pennsylvania Avenue, Washington, D.C.?

Alfred E. Timberlake, Ph.D., will be the principal speaker.

9. Use commas to set off words used in direct address:

It is up to you, *Dot*, to push the campaign.

I think, *sir*, that I am correct.

You, *my fellow Americans*, must aid in the fight against inflation.

10. Use a comma after a mild interjection and after *yes* and *no*:

Oh, I suppose you're right.

Yes, I will be glad to go.

11. Use a comma to separate an independent clause from a question dependent on the clause:

You will try to do the work, won't you?

12. Use commas to set off expressions like *he said* or *she replied* when they interrupt a sentence of direct quotation. (But see Rule 1 under The Semicolon, below.)

"I was able," *she replied*, "to build the bookcase in less than an hour."

13. Use commas to set off certain parenthetic elements:

I was, *however*, too tired to make the trip.

My hopes, *to tell the truth*, had fallen to a low ebb.

14. Use a comma to prevent the misreading of a sentence:

Above, the mountains rose like purple shadows.

To John, Harrison had been a sort of idol.

■ 19c The Semicolon

1. Use a semicolon to separate independent clauses when they are not joined by *and, but, or, nor, for, so* or *yet*. (See Chapter 6.)

Wade held the ball for an instant; then he passed it to West.

"He is sick," she said; "therefore, he will not come."

2. Use a semicolon to separate coordinate elements that are joined by a coordinating conjunction but that are internally punctuated:

His tour included concert appearances in Austin, Texas; Little Rock, Arkansas; Tulsa, Oklahoma; and Kansas City, Kansas.

3. Use a semicolon to punctuate independent clauses that are joined by a coordinating conjunction in sentences that are heavily punctuated with commas internally:

Having invited Sara, Susan, and Leon to my party, I began, at long last, to plan the menu; but I could not decide on a dessert.

■ 19d The Colon

1. Use a colon after a clause that introduces a formal list. Do not use a colon unless the words preceding the list form a complete statement:

INCORRECT: The poets I like best are: Housman, Yeats, and Eliot.

CORRECT: The poets I like best are these: Housman, Yeats, and Eliot.

ALSO CORRECT: The poets I like best are Housman, Yeats, and Eliot.

INCORRECT: The basket was filled with: apples, oranges, and bananas.

CORRECT: The basket was filled with the following fruits: apples, oranges, and bananas.

ALSO CORRECT: The basket was filled with apples, oranges, and bananas.

2. Use a colon after a statement that introduces an explanation or amplification of that statement:

One characteristic accounted for his success: complete honesty. [A dash, which is less formal than the colon, may be substituted for the colon in this sentence.]

There was only one way to solve the mystery: we had to find the missing letter.

3. Use a colon after expressions like *he said* when they introduce a long and formal quotation:

The speaker rose to his feet and said: "Students and teachers, I wish to call your attention to . . . ."

4. Use a colon after the formal salutation of a letter, between the hour and minute figures in time designations, between a chapter and verse reference from the Bible, and between a title and subtitle:

Dear Sir:

8:40 P.M.

John 3:16

Victorian England : Portrait of an Age

■ 19e The Dash

1. Use a dash to indicate an abrupt shift or break in the thought of a sentence or to set off an informal or emphatic parenthesis:

Harvey decided to go to — but you wouldn't be interested in that story.

Mary told me — would you believe it? — that she preferred a quiet vacation at home.

At the age of three — such is the power of youth — Mary could stand on her head.

2. Use dashes to set off an appositive or a parenthetic element that is internally punctuated:

Her roommates — Jane, Laura, and Ruth — are spending the weekend with her.

■ 19f Quotation Marks

1. Use quotation marks to enclose direct quotations, but do not use them to enclose indirect quotations:

INCORRECT: He said that "I was old enough to know better."

CORRECT: He said, "You are old enough to know better."

ALSO CORRECT: He said that I was old enough to know better.

If a direct quotation is interrupted by an expression like *he said*, use quotation marks to enclose only the quoted material. This necessitates the use of two sets of quotation marks:

INCORRECT: "It's just possible, Mary responded, that I'll get up before six in the morning."

CORRECT: "It's just possible," Mary responded, "that I'll get up before six in the morning."

If there are two or more consecutive sentences of quoted material, use only one set of quotation marks to enclose all the sentences, not one set for each sentence:

INCORRECT: Ruby shouted, "Wait for me." "I'll be ready in two minutes."

CORRECT: Ruby shouted, "Wait for me. I'll be ready in two minutes."

Use single marks to enclose a quotation within a quotation:

The instructor asked, "Who said, 'Change the name of Arkansas? Never!'?"

Place the comma and the period inside the quotation marks, the semicolon and colon outside. Place the question mark and exclamation mark inside the quotation marks when they apply to the quoted material, outside when they apply to the entire sentence:

"Of course," he replied, "I remember you." [Comma and period inside the quotation marks.]

Her favorite poem was Kipling's "If."

Several times the witness said, "I swear to the truth of my statement"; yet the jury remained unconvinced. [Semicolon outside the quotation marks.]

He asked, "Where are you going?" [The question mark comes within the quotation marks because only the quoted material is a question.]

Did she definitely say, "I accept your invitation"? [The question mark comes outside the quotation marks because the entire sentence is a question.]

2. Use quotation marks to enclose the titles of short works (short stories, short poems, articles, one-act plays, songs, and speeches) and of smaller units of books. (See Rule 3 under Italics, Chapter 20, Section b.)

Benét's story "The Devil and Daniel Webster" was first published in the *Saturday Evening Post*.

The kindergarten children sang "America" for us.

"Who Will Be the New Bishop?" is the title of the first chapter of *Barchester Towers*.

3. Use quotation marks to enclose words taken from special vocabularies or used in a special sense:

All the money he had won on the quiz program was invested in "blue chips."

In certain sections of the United States a man who is both honest and good-natured is known as a "clever man."

■ 19g Parentheses

Use parentheses to enclose certain parenthetic elements. From a study of the preceding marks of punctuation you will remember that commas and dashes are also used to set off parenthetic material. There are no clearly defined rules by which you can always determine which marks to use. In general, however, commas are used to set off a parenthetic element that is fairly closely connected with the thought of the sentence. Dashes are used to set off a loosely connected element such as an abrupt break in the thought of the sentence; they tend to emphasize the element set off. Parentheses are used to enclose (1) material that is supplementary or explanatory and (2) figures repeated to ensure accuracy or used to designate an enumeration. An element enclosed by parentheses is usually even more loosely connected with the sentence than one set off by dashes; and parentheses, unlike dashes, tend to minimize the element set off:

The *Ville de Nantes* (see Plate 5) is a large, semidouble, red and white camellia.

I am enclosing a check for thirty-five dollars ($35.00).

Please write on the card (1) your full name, (2) your home address, and (3) a parent's or guardian's full name.

■ 19h Brackets

Use brackets to enclose any interpolation, or insertion, that you add to material being quoted. (You will note that in this text brackets are used to enclose explanations that follow illustrative sentences.)

In September, 1793, Robert Burns wrote a letter that included this sentence: "So may God ever defend the cause of truth and liberty as he did that day [the day of Bruce's victory over Edward II at Bannockburn]."

If one parenthetical expression falls within another, then brackets replace the inner parentheses:

Thomas Turner, a member of the Class of 1981 (Mr. Turner was his class valedictorian [See Athens *Banner-Herald* story, May 16, 1981] and class president), has been named a Rhodes Scholar.

Exercise 68   The Comma

In the following sentences insert commas wherever they are needed or remove them if they are not needed, replacing them with other marks of punctuation when necessary. If a sentence is correctly punctuated, mark it **C**.

Example: After having been bitten by mosquitoes for two hours ∧ John was ready to go inside.

1. Mary Jo who often runs out of gas says that she wants a car with a large gas tank.

2. While I was trying to think of a name for my puppy I had numerous silly suggestions from my friends and family.

3. Bob Janet and Phyllis asked me to meet them at The Big Chicken for lunch.

4. The girl, whose name is drawn, will present the gift to Mr. Harris, who is retiring.

5. New members of Phi Beta Kappa for this term will be announced on August 20 1991.

6. The Shakespearean critic, A. L. Rowse, has written his auto-biography, *A Cornish Childhood*.

7. Natalie was surprised at Gloria's gloomy appearance for she didn't know that Gloria had a toothache.

8. Ahead of us there was a steep drop-off; behind the savage dogs were closing in fast.

9. Jake is disappointed that he lost in the finals, but he plans to try again next year.

10. Frankly Marjorie I think that you should forget about singing with a rock group.

11. The man, trying to make my car start, is my brother-in-law.

12. The dirty disheveled boy had fallen from his bicycle and hurt himself.

13. My new, green outfit is going to be perfect for fall.

14. Kit and David who will room together at college have known each other since grammar school.

267

15. A man who works as a firefighter must be prepared to face danger.

16. Aunt Miriam says, that learning to use a computer is not as easy as it looks.

17. Against Joe Lawrence has held a lifelong grudge.

18. Underneath the house the old hound dog was hiding trying to stay out of Mother's sight.

19. It was Hank not Kathy who left the cat out all night.

20. Meridian Mississippi is only eighteen miles across the state line from Alabama.

21. Oh I hope that you will be able to go to Harvard, especially since your father went there.

22. "There will be time for that decision in two years " said Tyler.

23. The word *diamond* comes originally from the Greek word *adamas*, meaning hard; the diamond, of course, is the hardest natural substance known.

24. Ashley, knowing that she would be called on next pretended to have a violent coughing spell.

25. Edward, the Confessor, was an early king of England.

26. "Fortunately " said Ruth, "there is enough spaghetti for all the extra guests who showed up."

27. Lapland is a region of northern Europe which includes parts of Norway Sweden Finland and the U.S.S.R.

28. The English poet John Keats died at age thirty-six.

29. When we got home from the Abercorn Cinema Jackie was watching yet another rerun of *Casablanca* on television.

30. "Oh " she sighed, "isn't Bogart wonderful?"

31. To take a cold shower every morning in winter, takes great self-discipline.

32. Trying to avoid perjury the witness took the Fifth Amendment.

33. Don't you realize, Betsy, that Dot is shy not snobbish?

34. On the surface I was able to appear happy; inside my heart was filled with sadness.

35. Adele's fiancé Mark Spratlin is an antique dealer.

Exercise 69   The Comma

In the following sentences insert commas wherever they are needed or remove them if they are not needed. If a sentence is punctuated correctly, mark it **C**.

Example: Honestly ∧Tom∧I didn't expect to see you at this time of night.

1. Hanging from a dogwood tree the silk scarf was twisting in the breeze.

2. We took the path, that the tree overhung, and searched carefully for any further signs of Muriel.

3. Unfortunately we headed east instead of west so we did not find Muriel until several hours later.

4. Sitting on a fallen tree she calmly said, "I knew you would come."

5. Frank W. Young M. D. has announced the opening of his new office in the Medical Arts Building.

6. I have noticed that the French expression *déjà vu* is often mispronounced.

7. The man, who can hold his tongue at the right moment, is often the one who wins the argument.

8. From the top of Mt. Rainier we could see far and wide; below the houses and roads seemed a hundred miles away.

9. Highlands North Carolina has an elevation of over four thousand feet.

10. Father, Mother, and Uncle Tim took us children camping and we saw a black bear not far from our campsite.

11. While learning to water-ski Dave was dumped into the lake more times than he could count.

12. My cousin Fred has recently moved to Missoula Montana, a city unfamiliar to him.

13. Jerry the latest in a long string of Helen's fiancés is a banker from Detroit.

14. She cried she begged she wheedled and she sulked; no one would give in to Mimi's foolish request.

15. Wanting to be a nuclear scientist and actually becoming one are two, entirely different things Peter.

16. Emily told Don that he should jog every morning before breakfast.

17. The full moon was out and its reflection in the lake was brilliant.

18. Lisa wanted to take a moonlit boat ride but could not get the motor started.

19. Thinking that the plate umpire had made a bad call the Mets' catcher moved threateningly toward him.

20. We thought that they would surely have a rhubarb but the pitcher walked over and cooled things off.

21. It was Jonathan Swift who said "There are few wild beasts more to be dreaded than a talking man having nothing to say."

22. Mr. Robinson said that it would be noon before they could begin the climb up Sharp Top Mountain.

23. Please forward all mail to my new address: 225 Macon Street Dallas Texas.

24. Oh Marge, you should have turned left at that last intersection.

25. Last night we went to hear a new rock group called, The Fantastic Saints.

26. Opening the window I peered fearfully out into the darkness.

27. Opening a window is not an easy task when the sash has been painted shut.

28. In his letter to Max Oliver misspelled the word, *psychiatrist* three times.

29. Max as you can imagine was only too quick to correct Oliver's mistake.

30. "How in the world " asked Oliver "was I to know that the word starts with a *p*?"

Exercise 70   The Colon and the Dash

In the following sentences insert colons and dashes wherever they are needed or remove them if they are not needed. If a sentence is correctly punctuated, mark it **C.**

Example: At precisely 8(:)45 P.M. a spectacular lunar eclipse will begin.

1. We have tried very hard to like this girl, but she has one shortcoming stupidity.

2. In his opening speech to the freshman class President McIntosh said that: his office door would always be open to every student.

3. I hear that Jake has been fined three times this month yes, I said three times for overtime parking.

4. The man's briefcase contained a silk tie, a pair of overshoes, a comb, and a cheese sandwich.

5. Finally we could see the town water tower and knew but now I'm repeating myself that we were nearly home.

6. Frances, I would like to borrow your copy of the book that I need Fowler's *Modern English Usage.*

7. Kate's list of necessities for camp includes: three uniforms, two pairs of shoes, soap, a toothbrush, toothpaste, and a flashlight.

8. These are the cooking utensils needed to make a cake: a large mixing bowl, an electric mixer, a cake pan, and a long-handled slotted spoon.

9. I hope that I will do well on the oh, let's talk about something else.

10. The senator's address began as usual "I am here to seek your help in my bid for re-election."

11. Todd, do you mean to tell me that you plan to well, we need not go into what I think of your motorcycle.

12. Looking back over the year just past, I wish that I had done one important thing saved more money.

13. Our plane was scheduled to take off at 4 30; it was almost 7 00, however, when we finally got off the ground.

14. My dog Jep chased a cat up the old pine tree, and the firefighters—oh, they were so angry—spent about an hour getting it down.

15. Give me that hammer, John, and I'll just ouch! I've hit my thumb!

16. The title of his latest mystery book is *Evil Shadows Tales of Wicked Deeds.*

17. That foursome Gene, Harry, Bob, and Don play golf every Friday.

18. There is one thing that will make Fred feign illness on a sunny day his mother's suggestion that he mow the lawn.

19. The following students are eligible for election to the Honors Club Marie Bryan, Joe Rutherford, Tony Barili, Kathy Dykes, and Rob Nolan.

20. At 12:30 we will be starting our tour of Williamsburg and my goodness, Judy, can't you think of anything but lunch?

Exercise 71   Quotation Marks

In the following sentences insert quotation marks wherever they are needed. Remove those not needed and replace them with the proper marks of punctuation or mechanics where necessary. If a sentence is correctly punctuated, mark it **C**.

Example: Does everyone here know the words to that old song ‿You Are My Sunshine‿?

1. I am afraid, said Joan, that I will never be able to wash the new look out of my jeans.

2. An interesting book, titled *"The Story of English,"* lists a variety of slang that the authors call "preppy talk."

3. "You must be tired, said Frank; I know that you got up at six o'clock this morning."

4. Who told Sara "that she was losing too much weight"?

5. Juan and Mario are such good friends that they are known as Pete and Re-peat.

6. Computer operators are sometimes plagued by a problem called "computer virus .

7. "Why did Juliet say, "Wherefore art thou Romeo?"?" asked Jackie.

8. The first chapter in Henry's latest novel is titled "The Mysterious Lake."

9. The police officer at the school crossing calls my little brother Short Stuff.

10. The officer wears one of those glow-in-the-dark caps, so my brother calls her "Mrs. Orange Hat."

11. The dictionary says that the word *"meat"* once referred to any kind of solid food.

12. Carey said, "I think that I will take another nap." "It pays to conserve energy."

13. Anita promised, "I will be on time tomorrow;" she was, however, late, as always.

14. I believe that it was the Scottish poet Robert Burns who wrote "To a Field Mouse".

15. Lucy and I agree with Marge, who says "that we need a stricter dress code at Jefferson High."

16. All the boys agree with Lars, who says, "The dress code is too strict already."

17. Did you really mean it when you said, "I am breaking my engagement?"

18. Many people refer to Wordsworth's famous poem as "The Daffodils;" its correct title, however, is "I Wandered Lonely as a Cloud."

19. Roger came racing in to shout, "Dad has finally said, "You can have the car tonight"!"

20. Tennessee Williams is perhaps best remembered for his play "The Glass Menagerie."

Exercise 72   Review of Punctuation

In the following sentences insert all necessary punctuation marks; remove all unnecessary or incorrect marks, replacing them with the proper ones wherever needed. If a sentence is correctly punctuated, mark it **C.**

Example: "Watch out! "Manuel cried. "Be careful crossing this crowded highway."

1. Nanette Sparks hoping to become the magazine's first woman editor called the publisher every day to ask for an interview.

2. The publisher Jonathan Hatfield finally returned her call, he said that he would review her résumé and see her within a few days.

3. The outcome was a happy one Ms. Nanette Sparks Ph.D. is now managing editor of *Modern Voices,* a monthly publication.

4. David asked Dottie if she planned to wear her new red wool suit to the football game?

5. I believe you will find Mrs. Pomeroy that Rob moved to Enid Oklahoma on August 1 1990.

6. Mr. Tomlinson or may I call you Peter? I agree that Frost's Mending Wall is a splendid poem

7. Dr. Fred Mosconi, who is married to my sister has written an interesting book titled *Your Key to Future Health Vitamin C.*

8. My courses this term are: English 101, Mathematics 200, and Botany 156.

9. The time between 745 P.M. and 230 A.M. is probably the period when the robbery was done.

10. None of the suspects no, not one has an alibi for that crucial period.

11. Joan's letter said, "You may find the book you want at my brother's bookstore in Mineapolis sic ."

12. For Aunt Lucy May sent a box of chocolates and a beautiful book.

13. For our overnight hike bring canned foods, bread, and a camp stove, but you need not bring beverages.

14. Friends gathered from Muncie, Indiana, Louisville, Kentucky, Memphis, Tennessee, and Oxford, Mississippi, for our class reunion.

15. The girl who is getting into that red car is a native of Australia.

16. The front lawn having been mowed to his satisfaction Father next directed his attention or rather mine to pruning the shrubs.

17. Frances Jenkins our class treasurer reports that we have only two dollars in the bank.

18. No, I cannot see you tomorrow nor can I find the time to discuss your plans with you on the telephone.

19. His face grew red he gave an angry snort and he strode quickly from the office.

20. Do you remember this quotation from Keats "Beauty is truth, truth beauty . . . ?

21. Mac said, "Jack is extremely friendly;" Bill, however, questioned Jack's sincerity.

22. I think that I had better try to call Nancy again before oh, there she is now.

23. We have been trying to locate Mrs. Charles Franklin I believe that her maiden name was Douglas in order to inform her of a large legacy.

24. From outside the house looked dark and forbidding; inside the rooms were warm and inviting.

25. Kurt rudely asked Quincy, "What do you think you are doing"?

Exercise 73   Review of Punctuation

In the following sentences insert all necessary punctuation marks; remove all incorrectly used marks, replacing them with the proper ones wherever needed. If a sentence is correctly punctuated, mark it **C.**

Example: Marjorie, you and Ted will be in charge of sending invitations. I will arrange for the refreshments.

1. The little boy trying to hold back tears   told us that he had lost his circus ticket.

2. Lillian immediately took out her wallet, and gave the boy five dollars for she is one of the kindest people I know.

3. Walking briskly down the beach Ken, Laurie, and Sam had gone two miles, before they remembered that Bill was waiting for them at the pier.

4. Walking briskly is good exercise for the heart, dawdling along at a snail's pace doesn't do much for one's circulation.

5. Katherine asked "When did Ralph say   I am ready for a dip in the lake ?"

6. Under no circumstances I repeat no circumstances are you to take the car to Atlanta by yourself, Jane.

7. The traffic on the expressway that's I-85 is nerve-racking for experienced drivers, and you are certainly not experienced.

8. I have started reading a good new mystery novel; the title of the first chapter is "What Did the Cat See"?

9. Once you have attached the back-plate of the lamp to the wall see Figure 1 , secure the brass front of the lamp to the back-plate with brass screws.

10. The quotation "I will wear my heart upon my sleeve" is from Shakespeare's drama " Othello, " and the speaker is the villainous Iago.

11. I hope you will not repeat the news, that I told you yesterday.

12. Charlie, let's finish paring the potatoes have a cold lemonade and go upstairs for a nap.

13. When Holt came to Georgia for a visit, his hosts served him grits, he said that his reaction to the dish was "ambivalent".

14. At lunch Walter announced, "Sue and I will be married in June of next year." "I want you to be my best man."

15. I replied "that I had planned to tour the British Isles next June, but that I would certainly change those plans."

16. Ruth gave Father some gazpacho for lunch; he had never had it before, and he said that he was unimpressed with "iced soup."

17. My flashlight having failed me I stumbled about in the dark growing more frightened with each passing second.

18. The house which had always seemed so pleasant and welcoming began to creak eerily I even imagined that I heard a low moan coming from the next room.

19. My fear however was unfounded as I saw when the lights suddenly came on, and revealed the safe familiar surroundings of my great-grandmother's old home.

20. James Russell Lowell an American poet is the author of the line "And what is so rare as a day in June"?

21. My new manager was intimidating; he said, "Young man, there is one quality that I expect of my employees punctuality."

22. You do understand how to operate this computer don't you Louise?

23. Although I have tried hard to master the thing oh, confound it! I think I'll jog awhile to clear my head.

24. It was Shakespeare who wrote, "When sorrows come, Claudius is the speaker, in *Hamlet* they come not single spies,/But in battalions . . . ."

25. Jenny says that one of her favorite short stories is "The Fall of the House of Usher."

20

Mechanics:
Capital Letters, Italics,
the Apostrophe,
the Hyphen

■ 20a Capital Letters

1. Capitalize the first word of a sentence, of a line of traditional poetry, and of a direct quotation:

All the students attended the meeting.

"Under the spreading chestnut tree / The village smithy stands."

He said, "She does not wish to see you."

2. Capitalize proper nouns, words used as proper nouns, and adjectives derived from proper nouns:

Great Britain, William, the Bible

President, Senator, Captain, University (when these are used with or substituted for the name of a particular president, person of high rank, or university), and similarly

Mother, Grandfather, Uncle (as in *We told Mother to go to bed, We bought Grandfather a bicycle,* and *We buried Uncle in Arlington Cemetery,* but not in *My mother is ill, His grandfather is eighty-two,* and *Our uncle was wounded at Gettysburg*)

British, Shakespearean, Scandinavian

3. Capitalize the names of days, months, and holidays:

Monday, February, Fourth of July, Ash Wednesday, Veterans Day

4. Capitalize the names of historical periods and events:

the Middle Ages, the French Revolution, the Battle of the Bulge, the Reformation

5. Capitalize the first word in the titles of books, chapters, essays, short stories, short poems, songs, and works of art. Capitalize also all other words in these titles except articles, prepositions, and conjunctions:

The Last of the Mohicans, "Without Benefit of Clergy," "Ode to the West Wind," "Only a Bird in a Gilded Cage," El Greco's *View of Toledo*

6. Capitalize names of the Deity, religions, and religious organizations:

Jehovah, God, the Redeemer, Buddhism, Church of England, Society of Jesus, Order of St. Francis.

7. Capitalize the names of governing bodies, political parties, governmental agencies, and civic and social organizations:

The House of Commons, the Senate, the Democratic Party, the Internal Revenue Service, the Chamber of Commerce, Daughters of the American Revolution

8. Capitalize the points of the compass when they refer to a specific region but not when they indicate direction:

He lived in the East all his life.

They traveled west for about a hundred miles and then turned south.

9. Capitalize the names of studies only if they are derived from proper nouns or are the names of specific courses of instruction:

He was studying physics, chemistry, and German.

He failed Mathematics 101 and Human Biology 1.

10. Capitalize personifications:

O wild West Wind, thou breath of Autumn's being.

Daughters of Time, the hypocritic Days.

Be with me, Beauty, for the fire is dying.

■ 20b Italics

1. Italicize words that you wish to emphasize. (In manuscript indicate italics by underlining.)

Do you mean to say that she ate them *all*?

He could hardly have been *the* Robert Frost.

Note: Use this device sparingly. Frequent use of italics for emphasis is a sign of an immature style.

2. Italicize numbers, letters, and words referred to as such:

He made his 7 and his 9 very much alike.

She has never yet learned to pronounce *statistics*.

In his handwriting he uses the old-fashioned *s*.

3. Italicize the names of books, magazines, and newspapers. (Smaller units of books, such as chapters, stories, essays, and poems, are usually set in quotation marks.)

A Tale of Two Cities, the *Atlantic Monthly*, the Atlanta *Journal*

Note: In the names of newspapers or magazines it is not always necessary to italicize the definite article or the name of a city.

4. Italicize the names of ships, trains, and airplanes:

the *Queen Elizabeth*, the *Twentieth-Century Limited*, the *Spirit of St. Louis*

5. Italicize foreign words and phrases in an English context:

The *coup d'état* led to his becoming emperor.

6. Italicize the titles of paintings, statues, and other works of art:

Gainsborough's *Blue Boy*, Rodin's *The Thinker*

■ 20c The Apostrophe

1. Use the apostrophe and *s* to form the possessive case of singular nouns:

the boar's head, Mary's lamb, the boss's orders

Note: Proper names ending in *s* may form the possessive by adding '*s* if the resulting word is not unpleasant or difficult to sound:

Keats's poems, Charles's work, *but* Ulysses' return

2. Use an apostrophe without *s* to form the possessive of plural nouns ending in *s*:

Soldiers' quarters, boys' clothes

3. Use an apostrophe and *s* to form the possessive of plural nouns not ending in *s*:

Men's coats, children's shoes, the alumni's contributions

4. The possessive of words indicating time is formed like the possessive of other nouns:

A week's delay, a day's journey, *but* a two days' visit

5. The apostrophe is frequently omitted in the names of organizations and institutions:

The Farmers Hardware Company, Boys High School, State Teachers College

6. In forming the possessives of compounds, use the apostrophe according to the meaning and the logic of the construction:

Beaumont and Fletcher's plays [Plays written by Beaumont and Fletcher jointly.]

Smith's and Jones's children [The children of Smith and the children of Jones.]

John and Mary's house [The house belonging to John and Mary.]

Somebody else's business [The business of somebody else.]

7. Use an apostrophe to indicate the omission of letters in contractions and of digits in numerals:

Isn't, don't, 'tis

Martha's been sunbathing.

the Class of '23

Note: Be sure that the apostrophe is placed at the exact point where the letter or digit is omitted. Do not write *is'nt, do'nt.*

8. Use an apostrophe and *s* to indicate the plural of letters, numerals, signs, and words used as such:

Dot your *i*'s and cross your *t*'s.

His telephone number contains four *8*'s.

In your next theme omit the *&*'s.

He uses too many *so*'s.

■ 20d The Hyphen

In English, compounds are made in three ways:

(1) by writing the words solid (*bedroom, watchmaker, starlight*),

(2) by writing them separately (*ice cream, motion picture, mountain lion*), or

(3) by separating the words with a hyphen (*name-caller, ne'er-do-well, finger-paint*).

The resulting confusion, like so much confusion in English, lies in the fact that the language is constantly changing. A compound may begin its career as two words; then it may move on to the form with a hyphen; and finally it may end as a solid formation — its destiny accomplished, as it were. So we have *bedroom* (written solid) but *dining room* (two words). We have the noun *bluepoint* to refer to an oyster, but we use the two words *blue point* to describe a Siamese cat. A decision may be *far-reaching,* but a forecaster is *farseeing.* The only solution to this confusing problem is to consult a dictionary. But this authority is not always satisfactory because many compounds are made for the occasion and are not in the dictionary — and dictionaries may disagree. Furthermore, a compound with a hyphen may be correct in one part of a sentence and incorrect in another, or it may be correct as a noun and incorrect as a verb. The stylebook of one publisher says, "If you take hyphens seriously, you will surely go mad." Nevertheless, there is a sort of logic in the use of the hyphen, as well as a kind of common sense; furthermore, one can learn some of the pitfalls to avoid.

Consider the following sentences:

He is a great admirer of Henry Kissinger, the ex-Republican Secretary of State. [Is Mr. Kissinger no longer a Republican? The phrase should read *the former Republican Secretary of State*.]

The parents enjoyed their children's recreation of the first Thanksgiving. [In this sentence *re-creation* is the appropriate word, and the hyphen distinguishes it from *recreation*.]

I would think that your sixteen year old brother could scramble an egg. [In this sentence *sixteen*, *year*, and *old* form a compound modifier and should be hyphenated. The phrase should read *your sixteen-year-old brother*.]

He introduced me to his uncle, an old car enthusiast. [Is his uncle old? Or is his uncle interested in old cars? The phrase is clarified with a hyphen: *an old-car enthusiast*.]

Did you hear the reporter's interview with the singing whale authority? [Did the reporter interview a whale authority who sings or an authority on singing whales? Appropriate hyphenation clears up the confusion; the phrase should read *with the singing-whale authority*.]

The following rules indicate common practice and are fairly reliable:

1. Compound numerals (*twenty-one* through *ninety-nine*) are always written with a hyphen:

twenty-six, forty-eight, fifty-two

2. Fractions are written with a hyphen if they are adjectival:

His speech was one-third fact and two-thirds demagoguery.

But   Three fourths of the apples are rotten.

3. Compounds with *self* are written with a hyphen:

self-styled, self-taught, self-centered

Note the exceptions *selfsame, selfhood, selfless*.

4. The hyphen is used in certain expressions of family relationship:

great-grandfather, great-aunt

5. Most compounds beginning with *ex*, *pre*, and *pro* are written with a hyphen:

ex-president, pre-Christian, pro-British

6. The hyphen is commonly used with compounds with prepositional phrases:

mother-in-law, stick-in-the-mud, heart-to-heart

7. One of the commonest uses of hyphens is to form compound modifiers for nouns and pronouns:

An eight-year-old child, a well-done steak, a blue-green sea

Note: Such compounds are hyphenated when they immediately precede the word they modify, but frequently they are not hyphenated when they are used predicatively:

His well-spoken words pleased the audience [*but* His words were well spoken].

She made a number of off-the-record comments [*but* Her comments were made off the record].

8. Hyphens are used in coined or occasional compounds:

She gave him a kind of you-ought-to-know-better look.

Her bird-on-the-nest hat was sensational.

9. The hyphen is used in compound nouns that name the same person in two different capacities:

Author-publisher, musician-statesman, tycoon-playboy

10. The hyphen is frequently used to avoid confusion between words:

Re-claim [to distinguish from *reclaim*]

Re-cover [to distinguish from *recover*]

11. Hyphens are used to avoid clumsy spellings:

Bull-like, semi-independent, ante-election, pre-empt

Note: *Cooperate* and *coordinate* are common enough to be accepted.

12. The hyphen is used at the end of a line of writing to indicate the division of a word continued on the next line. The division must always come at the end of a syllable. Do not divide words of one syllable:

PROPER DIVISIONS: con-tin-ued, in-di-cate, au-di-ence

IMPROPER DIVISIONS: wo-rd, laugh-ed, comp-ound

Note: If you are uncertain about the division of a word, consult your dictionary.

■ 20e Numbers

1. Numbers that can be expressed in one or two words should be written out: five girls; seventeen giraffes; twenty-five books; four hundred tickets; ten thousand people.

2. Numbers of more than two words should be written as numerals: 9,425; 650; 700,000.

3. Numbers that start a sentence should be written out, even though they would ordinarily be written as numerals: *Four hundred and forty* dollars is a good price for that cashmere coat.

Exercise 74   Capitals

In the following sentences change small letters to capital letters wherever necessary and vice versa. If a sentence is correct as it stands, mark it **C**.

Example: Susan and I will drive ~~g~~randfather [G] over to ~~a~~unt [A]

Miriam's house.

1. As we flew North, I could see snow-covered mountains; the pilot identified them as the adirondacks.

2. *The Call Of The Wild,* by Jack London, has always been a popular book, especially among boys.

3. My mother attended North Carolina State university, where she majored in latin.

4. I have just heard that Ted Fielding has announced his candidacy for a place on the city council.

5. Ted's brother is senator Frank Fielding, so a liking for politics seems to run in the family.

6. A form letter has been mailed to all republicans in town, asking for their support in the upcoming Election.

7. Caroline has done well in College, but she has had to study very hard to pass Trigonometry.

8. Father turned pale when the letter came to him from the internal revenue service; he had paid his tax on time, but even the Government sometimes makes mistakes.

9. "You may go in now," said the doctor's Assistant. "just take a chair, and Dr. Roberts will be with you in a moment."

10. Our English 500 professor says that *King Lear* is, in his opinion, the finest of all the shakespearean plays.

11. Murray asked, "when are you leaving for California?"

12. It was Harry Truman who said, "The buck stops here"; as presidents go, he was quite outspoken.

13. Emily Dickinson's poem about a locomotive begins with the lines "I like to see it lap the miles,/ and lick the valleys up, ..."

14. The Letter Carrier will not be coming today, Phyllis; this is Columbus day.

15. Ken's twin brother, Fred, is a Commander in the U.S. navy.

Exercise 75 Italics

In the following sentences underline all words that should be italicized and remove italics that are incorrectly used, replacing them with other marks if necessary. If a sentence is correct as it stands, mark it **C**.

Example: I believe that he was editor of the Cleveland *Plain Dealer* for a number of years.

1. As a child I loved Stevenson's poem *The Land of Counterpane* from his book *A Child's Garden of Verses*.

2. The Youngs sailed for England last Friday aboard the Queen Elizabeth II.

3. Have you noticed that British spelling includes the letter "u" in such words as honor, vigor, and color?

4. Be careful, Lou; chewing gum in Dr. Sutton's class is strictly verboten.

5. The publishers of The New Yorker boast that theirs is the "best magazine that ever was."

6. Dad says that the single thing he liked best in the Louvre Museum was the statue "Winged Victory."

7. In reference to angels, the plural of the word cherub is cherubim; the plural form cherubs indicates rosy, innocent-looking children.

8. The whole family went to *Porgy and Bess* last night; it is an opera like none other, and we enjoyed it immensely.

9. That pretentious artist likes to call his studio "my little atelier."

10. Our quarterback scored seven—yes, seven—touchdowns in the game against Harvard last Saturday.

11. Mr. Austin, if you are dissatisfied with our product, the company has an ombudsman who will be glad to negotiate with you concerning a possible refund.

12. Terry seems not to be able to spell sophomore correctly; he always leaves out the second o.

13. Did you see van Gogh's "Sunflowers" when you visited the National Gallery in London?

14. In the handwriting of two hundred years ago, an *s* looked very much like our present-day *f*.

15. My grandmother has a full set of the 1911 edition of *Encyclopaedia Britannica*, which I understand is now a collector's item.

16. Although *magazine* originally referred to a storehouse for goods, the word has also been used to mean "a treasury of intellectual wealth" since the sixteenth century.

17. Remember, Harry, that *media* is the plural of *medium* and should be accompanied by plural verbs and pronouns.

18. I know that two of Columbus's ships were the *Nina* and the *Pinta*, but I never can remember the name of the third one.

19. Patricia's dream was at last coming true: to travel aboard the *Orient Express* from Paris to Istanbul.

20. No, Ellen, you misunderstood me—I said that Jane is *not* naive!

Exercise 76   The Apostrophe

In the following sentences underline all words that should have apostrophes and all those that have apostrophes incorrectly used; then write the word(s) correctly in the space at the right. If a sentence is correct, mark it **C**.

Example: <u>Arent</u> you going to have breakfast before
leaving for school?   *Aren't*

1. Since it's raining, why do'nt you get Margaret to
   drive you to class today?   _____

2. The Bryan's were in Charleston during Hurricane
   Hugo in 1989.   _____

3. Whose going to help me with this tremendous sack
   of groceries that Linda brought home?   _____

4. That green notebook on the dining room table
   must be Marvins.   _____

5. Back in the 1930s the Great Depression caused a
   great deal of unemployment.   _____

6. Your going to need a heavy overcoat when you
   move to Oregon, Max.   _____

7. The girls basketball team has won the championship for the fifth year in a row.   _____

8. I hurried through the rain to my eleven oclock
   class, but it had been canceled because Dr. Raines
   was ill.   _____

9. Everyone likes Frances new boyfriend; he's both
   handsome and well-mannered.   _____

10. I've been trying to reach you for three days; why
    haven't you returned my calls?   _____

11. That's a beautiful mohair jacket in the closet; is it
    your's, Marian?   _____

12. Aunt Grace's and Uncle Jack's cottage at the lake is
    roomy and comfortable.   _____

13. The cottage is enjoyable for many reasons, but per-
    haps especially for it's peace and quiet.   _____

14. Tillie's chatter was loaded with a large number of
    <u>I</u> s and <u>me</u> s.   _____

15. The twin's identical dress became ridiculous after
    theyd reached their teens.   _____

16. I'll be glad when Sam comes home; this weeks
    laundry is piling up.   _____

17. In Mr. Loring's speech to the Jaycee's he spoke elo-
    quently of the importance of using one's potential.   _____

18. Eric and Marie's children are all going to summer
    camp this July.   _____

19. Gladys long, boring tale about the alligator made
    my eyelids grow heavier with each moments
    passing.   _____

20. The Hudson's new van is much more comfortable
    than our's.   _____

Exercise 77 The Hyphen

In the following sentences underline the incorrect compounds and write the correct forms at the right. If a sentence is correct, mark it **C**. Some sentences contain more than one error. If you are doubtful about whether a term should be hyphenated, consult a dictionary for guidance.

Example: A <u>three month</u> trip around the
world on a freighter is not my idea
of a good time, Florence. _____*three-month*_____

1. Tom thinks that he will have an up in the
   air feeling until his college plans are finally
   definite. _____

2. The self styled "authoress" is fond of giving readings of her work at literary teas. _____

3. I wonder whether a half gallon of ice cream
   will be enough for the six of us at dinner
   tonight. _____

4. We will need a heavy duty vacuum cleaner
   to remove these muddy foot-prints on the
   carpet. _____

5. I was able to give a blow by blow account
   of the set-to between the two men, for I
   was an interested onlooker. _____

6. Henry enjoys reading Japanese *haiku*; they
   are three line, unrhymed verse forms containing five, seven, and five syllables
   respectively. _____

7. The two former antagonists met face to face
   for the first time since their heated political
   battle and gave each-other half-hearted
   smiles. _____

8. His hairraising story about being in a storm at sea has been upheld by the first-hand account of another crew member. _____

9. My great grandmother has a one of a kind silver bowl, reputedly made by Paul Revere. _____

10. Some people find Alice's lighthearted approach to life rather annoying; I find it endearing. _____

11. Judy's sister-in-law goes deep sea fishing every chance she gets. _____

12. My art professor is a French Impressionism enthusiast. _____

13. Philip dislikes the designated hitter option employed by baseball teams in the American League. _____

14. Shakespeare was born in a half-timbered house typical of those built in sixteenth century England. _____

15. I want to thank-you, Sally, for the delicious sandwiches that you made for the picnic. _____

16. That six year old dictionary may be out of date for your purpose, Joanna. _____

17. His remarks were well meant, but Pat took offense for some reason. _____

18. When I finally found my dog-eared old copy of _Heidi_ in the attic, I was over-joyed. _____

19. My little niece, who is four years old, loves to play hide and seek with her older brothers and sisters. _____

20. Marge was tired of the orange slipcover on her wing chair, so she recovered the chair in a pretty green fabric. _____

Exercise 78 Review of Mechanics

Underline the errors in the following sentences and then write the correct forms in the spaces at the right. If a sentence is correct, mark it **C**.

Example: After living in the <u>east</u> from early
childhood, I found the Pacific <u>north-</u>
<u>west</u> almost like another country.

East
_____*Northwest*_____

1. Bobs trying to persuade Marilyn to let us
use her cabin over the week-end.

_____

2. Did you like the PBS dramatization of *A
Tale Of Two Cities*?

_____

3. The color photograph of Mrs. Roosevelt
(see page 59) was taken when she was
twenty one.

_____

4. Hal told Bud in a know it all way, "You
cant make it to Miami before dark."

_____

5. At eight oclock I was sleepy; now, at midnight, I am wide awake.

_____

6. I would like to re-imburse you for all the
pains-taking work that you did while you
filled in for me at the office.

_____

7. Our heating bill for last january was two
hundred and forty-seven dollars.

_____

8. The lecturer said, "Thomas Stearns Eliot,
the American born poet critic, died in
1965."

_____

9. Mother was aghast when she heard
Tommy tell Mrs. Mayfield, "you should try
the new ten day diet."

_____

10. Mary Sue is struggling this Semester with
Calculus and Quantitative Analysis.

_____

11. One of Irving Berlins best-loved songs is
    "God Bless America."   _____

12. The mens' section of that big department
    store carries very good woolen sweaters
    and other sports-wear.   _____

13. The little forward-slanting mark often
    found over the e in French words is called
    accent aigu.   _____

14. My father considers The Christian Science
    Monitor an all-around fine newspaper.   _____

15. The Freemans are a large family, and
    their's is a very happy household.   _____

16. I certainly did'nt expect to run out of gas;
    my tank was one third full when I left
    home.   _____

17. The four-year-old boy recited, " 'Little Jack
    Horner/ sat in a corner/ eating a Christmas
    pie'— Ive forgotten the rest."   _____

18. When the Class of 70 had it's twentieth
    reunion, three hundred and forty alumni
    attended.   _____

19. Masterpiece Theater's popular serial
    Upstairs, Downstairs has always been
    greatly loved by the American public.   _____

20. After two months anxious waiting for my
    order to arrive, I was disgusted and wrote
    the mail-order company a red hot letter.   _____

21

Use of the Dictionary

A convenient and valuable source of linguistic information is a standard dictionary. It is easy to use, and, if used intelligently, very informative. Many people do not realize that a dictionary contains important facts far beyond simple definitions and guides to pronunciation and spelling. One of the best investments that you can make is the purchase of a standard collegiate dictionary. Your frequent use of a good dictionary, besides being a necessary step toward the development of an effective vocabulary, is essential for understanding the material you encounter daily. In any college course, in the newspapers, and in regular communication with others, you will read and hear unfamiliar words. Your desire to learn the meaning, spelling, and pronunciation of a new word should lead you to a dictionary providing this information along with other features such as the derivation of the word and its level of usage. It may also discuss the word's synonyms and frequently an antonym to illuminate still further its precise shade of meaning.

The best dictionaries have taken years of preparation by hundreds of workers directed by the finest scholars of the time. Unabridged dictionaries are comprehensive in their explanations and descriptions of words, containing thousands more entries than the more commonly used desk dictionary. In the United States perhaps the best-known unabridged dictionary is *Webster's Third New International Dictionary of the English Language*, often called simply *Webster's Third*. It was published by the G. & C. Merriam Company of Springfield, Massachusetts, in 1961; there have been several subsequent printings and supplements. This work, though it is too bulky to be used as a casual desk dictionary (and for most purposes unnecessary), may be found in a college library.

Any one of several extremely reliable collegiate dictionaries is the best choice for you. Severely abridged paperback editions of these dictionaries are a poor substitute, as they do not contain the detailed information that you may find necessary for specialized assignments in your college courses. Most language authorities recommend the latest editions of the following standard college dictionaries: *Webster's New Collegiate Dictionary*, published by G. & C. Merriam Co., Springfield, Massachusetts; *Webster's New World Dictionary of the American Language*, Simon and Schuster, New York; *The American Heritage Dictionary of the English Language*, The American Heritage Publishing Co., Inc., and Houghton Mifflin Co., Boston; *The Random House Dictionary of the English Language*, Random House, New York; *Funk and Wagnall's Standard Collegiate Dictionary*, Harcourt, Brace and World, Inc., New York.

Select one of these dictionaries and buy it as soon as you get to college; then follow the list of suggestions given below in order to familiarize yourself with the dictionary and the ways in which you can get the maximum use from this very handy and easy-to-use reference work.

1. Read all the introductory material in the front of the dictionary because this explains what information the book has to offer. If some of it seems too scholarly for you to understand, read on, and at least find out what it is mainly concerned with and what you can expect to find in its entries.

2. Study carefully the key to pronunciation, and check it with words that you know so that you will be sure of understanding it. A need for guidance in pronunciation is one of the most common reasons for consulting a dictionary.

3. Refer often to the table of abbreviations, which is most likely to be found inside the front cover of your dictionary. To save space, dictionaries necessarily use many abbreviations, and these are explained in the table. Become familiar with these abbreviations so that no piece of information escapes your notice.

4. Examine the appendixes to learn what information is given in them. Some dictionaries list biographical and geographic information in their appendixes; others list them in the main entries in the book. Other information often found in the appendixes of a dictionary includes tables of interpretations of various specialized symbols, like those connected with mathematics, chemistry, music, chess, medicine, and pharmacy; a directory of colleges and universities; a table of weights and measures; a dictionary of English given names, and so on.

One of the most important things a dictionary can tell you is the *level of usage* of a given term. The English language, ever-changing and full of colorful informality, functions on many levels. Young people may use the expression *laid back* to describe a person who has a relaxed, uncomplicated approach to life. Politicians and reporters use the term *bottom line* to mean the end result of something. An educated adult may in conversation refer to *lots of trouble*. And an editor of a magazine may write of the *dichotomy between work and leisure classes* or, in a book review, of an *involuted search for self*. Each of these expressions is in a sense proper in its own context. Judgment of a term as "good English" is usually determined by the level on which it is used. The magazine editor would not in a formal article use the term *laid back*; the youth of today would hardly think or write using terms like *dichotomy*. Your dictionary will tell you whether the use of

in brackets gives the derivation or origin of the word. It tells that *burden* is a variant form of the older word *burthen*, which is derived from the Old English form *byrthen*, and that the word is linguistically akin to the word *bear* as described in the first *bear* entry elsewhere in the dictionary. Finally we learn that the synonyms of *burden*[1] are discussed under the entry *load*. The second entry, *burden*[2], is arranged on the same principles.

Consider now the following entry from *Webster's New World Dictionary of the American Language*:*

> **drunk** (druŋk) *vt., vi.* [ME *dronke* < *dronken*, DRUNKEN] *pp. & archaic pt. of* DRINK —*adj.* 1 overcome by alcoholic liquor to the point of losing control over one's faculties; intoxicated 2 overcome by any powerful emotion [*drunk* with joy] 3 [Colloq.] DRUNKEN (sense 2) Usually used in the predicate —*n.* 1 [Colloq.] a drunken person 2 [Slang] a drinking spree
> **SYN.**—*drunk* is the simple, direct word, usually used in the predicate, for one who is overcome by alcoholic liquor [he is *drunk*]; *drunken*, usually used attributively, is equivalent to *drunk* but sometimes implies habitual, intemperate drinking of liquor [a *drunken* bum]; *intoxicated* and *inebriated* are euphemisms; there are many euphemistic and slang terms in English expressing varying degrees of drunkenness: e.g., *tipsy* (slight), *tight* (moderate, but without great loss of muscular coordination), *blind drunk* (great), *blotto* (to the point of unconsciousness), etc. —*ANT.* sober

Here we learn that the adjective *drunk*, with the specific meanings that follow, is the past participle and was formerly a past tense of the verb *to drink*. Two definitions are given: the first of these is the common one; the second is often used figuratively. The discussion of synonyms gives us the fine shades of distinction among a group of words that mean essentially the same thing. In addition, one antonym, or word of opposite meaning, is given. The final part of the entry, defining *drunk* as a noun, explains that when the word is used as a noun, meaning a person in a drunken condition or a period of heavy drinking, the word is slang.

The kind of knowledge that a good dictionary can give you far exceeds what has been discussed here. Most good dictionaries, for instance, pay special attention to biography and geography. One can learn when Beethoven died and the name of the capital of Peru. One can find the height of Mount Everest and the approximate number of islands in the Philippines. Literature, mythology, and particularly science are well covered in the modern dictionary. Finally, special appendixes sometimes include such miscellaneous information as the meanings of common Christian names, foreign words and phrases, abbreviations, and the symbols used in the preparation of copy for the printer and in proofreading. Some books even contain a dictionary of rhymes. The following exercises illustrate the variety of information one may obtain from a good dictionary.

---

*By permission. From *Webster's New World Dictionary of the American Language*, Third College Edition. Copyright © 1988 by Simon and Schuster, Inc.

a word in a particular sense is slang, informal (colloquial), dialectal, archaic, obsolete, or none of these, i.e., Standard English.

Slang is the term used to describe the spontaneous, vivid, and sometimes racy inventions used frequently in the speech and writings of groups like teenagers, gangsters, popular musicians, soldiers, and sports writers — not that these groups necessarily have anything else in common. The life of a slang expression is usually short, but sometimes, if it is striking enough and colorful enough, it may gain universal usage and become at least an informal part of the national vocabulary.

The term *informal* or *colloquial* is applied to words or expressions that are acceptable in the speech of the educated but not in formal writing. It is all right to say, "He's going to have *lots of trouble* explaining his whereabouts on the night of June third," but it is not Standard English to write this statement formally.

Dialect, another usage label, means that a word or expression is common to the speech of a particular group or geographical region. *Archaic* means that the word or term is rarely used today, except in certain contexts like church ritual, but that it may be found fairly frequently in early writings. *Obsolete* means that the term is no longer used but may be found in early writings. In addition, as a part of its usage discussion, a dictionary will inform you if a word or term is commonly considered obscene, vulgar, or profane.

To see how a dictionary presents its information, consider now the following entry from *The Random House Dictionary of the English Language:**

bur·den[1] (bûr/dᵊn), *n.* **1.** that which is carried; load: *a horse's burden of rider and pack.* **2.** that which is borne with difficulty; obligation or trouble: *the burden of leadership.* **3.** *Naut.* **a.** the weight of a ship's cargo. **b.** the carrying capacity of a ship: *a ship of a hundred-tons burden.* **4.** *Mining.* the earth or rock to be moved by a charge of explosives. **5.** *Accounting.* overhead (def. 6). —*v.t.* **6.** to load heavily. **7.** to load oppressively; trouble. [ME, var. of *burthen.* OE *byrthen;* akin to G *Bürde,* Goth *baurthei;* see BEAR[1]] —**bur/den·er,** *n.* —**bur/den·less,** *adj.* —**Syn. 1.** See **load. 2.** weight, encumbrance, impediment.

Here we are given the correct spelling of the word *burden* and its proper division into syllables. The small numeral[1] after the entry word indicates that this is the first of two or more words with the same spelling but differing radically in meaning and derivation and therefore listed separately. Next, the proper pronunciation is given. It becomes clear immediately that you need to learn the significance of the signs, called diacritical marks, that indicate pronunciation. In this entry the first five numbered definitions are preceded by *n* (for *noun*) and the last two by *v.t.* (for *verb, transitive*). After 3, *Naut.* (*Nautical*) means that the definitions given under 3 are special technical senses of the word as used in shipping. The same interpretation is true of definitions 4 and 5. The information

Exercise 79   Word Origins

After each of the following words indicate in the first column at the right the first systematically recorded language from which the word is derived, and in the second column the meaning of the source word.

	Language	**Meaning**
Example:		
cemetery	*Greek*	*sleeping place*
1. bait	_____	_____
2. bamboo	_____	_____
3. blush	_____	_____
4. butter	_____	_____
5. caterpillar	_____	_____
6. chutney	_____	_____
7. daisy	_____	_____
8. decent	_____	_____
9. drink	_____	_____
10. foreign	_____	_____
11. glory	_____	_____
12. grasp	_____	_____
13. green	_____	_____
14. horizon	_____	_____
15. jungle	_____	_____
16. league	_____	_____
17. malady	_____	_____
18. monument	_____	_____
19. neglect	_____	_____
20. nerve	_____	_____
21. perfume	_____	_____
22. sherbet	_____	_____

	Language	**Meaning**
23. skin	_____	_____
24. trek	_____	_____
25. vehicle	_____	_____

Exercise 80 British and American Usage

The following words illustrate the differences between British and American usage. Write the equivalents of these British terms:

Example: bounder _____*ill-mannered fellow*_____

1. biscuit _____

2. bonnet _____

3. bowler _____

4. carriageway _____

5. chemist _____

6. corn (n.) _____

7. draper _____

8. draughts _____

9. dustman _____

10. fell (n.) _____

11. football _____

12. gaol _____

13. geyser _____

14. holiday _____

15. ironmonger _____

16. kerb _____

17. lift (n.) _____

18. lorry _____

19. mate _____

20. nappy _____

21. nought _____

22. paraffin _____

23. pasty (n.) _____

24. pavement _____

25. petrol   _____

26. pillarbox   _____

27. post (v.)   _____

28. pub   _____

29. public school _____

30. queue (n.)   _____

31. rates   _____

32. removal   _____

33. roundabout (n.) _____

34. rubbish   _____

35. runners   _____

36. sieve (v.)   _____

37. spanner   _____

38. sultanas   _____

39. sweet (n.)   _____

40. tin (n.)   _____

41. tipping (n.) _____

42. torch   _____

43. trolley   _____

44. underground, tube (n.) _____

45. verge   _____

Exercise 81   Plurals

Write the plural form of each of the following nouns:

Example: ruby   *rubies*

1. ability   _____

2. alibi   _____

3. alumnus   _____

4. analysis   _____

5. banjo   _____

6. belief   _____

7. chimney   _____

8. church   _____

9. country   _____

10. court-martial   _____

11. crisis   _____

12. datum   _____

13. deer   _____

14. genius   _____

15. goose   _____

16. half   _____

17. handkerchief   _____

18. hero   _____

19. layman   _____

20. lens   _____

21. maid-of-honor   _____

22. match   _____

23. mouse   _____

24. mouthful   _____

25. ox   _____

26. passerby   _____

27. path   _____

28. penny   _____

29. radio   _____

30. radius   _____

31. series   _____

32. thesis   _____

33. tomato   _____

34. turkey   _____

35. wolf   _____

Exercise 82   Levels of Usage

After each of the following sentences indicate the level of usage of the italicized words or expressions, using these abbreviations:

A for archaic,   **I** for informal (colloquial),
D for dialectal,   **S** for slang.

Note: Most standard collegiate dictionaries agree in their classifications of these words and expressions. Other dictionaries may differ in their classifications (or show none at all), so use a reliable collegiate dictionary whenever you need information about the level of usage of an expression.

Dictionary used for this exercise: _____

Example: Was it Polonius who said, "to *thine* own self be true"?   _A_

1. The *guy* in the plaid slacks is a champion golfer.   _____

2. The little town where my cousins live is out in the *boonies*, but they seem to enjoy life there.   _____

3. That restaurant is too expensive; I paid a *fiver* for a sandwich and a cup of coffee there yesterday.   _____

4. Can that little *dogie* keep up with the rest of the herd when it's feeding time?   _____

5. I would like to go to the movie with you, but I am *broke*.   _____

6. The catcher on our home baseball team is never without his *chaw* of tobacco; doesn't he know that tobacco is hazardous to his health?   _____

7. *Methinks* I saw a dark shadow outside the window; I hope a thief isn't out there.   _____

8. Don't worry about your child's safety, Mrs. Robbins; baby-sitting is a *piece of cake* for me.   _____

9. The *kine* in the pasture are huddling together, sensing that a thunderstorm is coming.   _____

10. We searched everywhere for the lost windbreaker, but it was *nowheres* to be found.   _____

11. Although everyone tried to tell Harriet that Egbert is a *loser*, she married him anyway.   _____

12. Jerome says that he would as *lief* jump into boiling oil as face his father after getting that speeding ticket. _____

13. Getting on his *cayuse*, the old cowhand rode off into the proverbial sunset. _____

14. For one who has much to be humble about, Mrs. Gladstone is a *proudful* woman. _____

15. We all thought that Mark's treatment of Susan was really *crummy*. _____

16. Use your *nut*, Jerry, and decipher these instructions on how to make a birdhouse. _____

17. Bonnie thought that Don sounded silly when he said, "You are *mine* own true love." _____

18. When she saw Ben's new red convertible, Margot *flipped*. _____

19. I knew that Ted had *pulled a boner* when he mentioned Tim's date with Louise. _____

20. Honestly, Jake, you *slay me* with all the practical jokes that you play on your sister. _____

21. Let's all go back to my *pad* and play my video of *Friday the Thirteenth*. _____

22. The *reavers* stole my mother's jewelry and her sterling silver too. _____

23. After Macbeth had killed Duncan, he said to Lady Macbeth, "I have done the deed/*Didst* thou not hear a noise?" _____

24. Uncle Percy says that it *blows his mind* to think of the U.S. trade deficit. _____

25. The Cubs' pitcher *fanned* the first two batters who came up in the fourth inning. _____

Exercise 83 General Information

Refer to your dictionary for the information you will need to fill in the blanks below.

Example: Date of the completion of the Erie
Canal: _____*1825*_____

1. Genus and family name of the jack-in-the-
   pulpit: _____

2. Continent which the Bantu peoples occupy: _____

3. Family of musical instruments to which the
   mandolin belongs: _____

4. Island for which the Manx cat is named: _____

5. Coloring of the magpie: _____

6. Length of the Nile River: _____

7. Another name for Holland: _____

8. Height of Mount St. Helens: _____

9. Definition of *triskaidekaphobia*:   _____

10. Country where the obi sash originated: _____

11. Insignia worn by a lieutenant general: _____

12. Author of a tragic drama titled *Othello*:   _____

13. Location of the Parthenon: _____

14. Equatorial diameter (in miles) of the planet
    Jupiter: _____

15. Names of the city and the country where
    Limoges porcelain is made: _____

16. Symbol for the chemical element iron: _____

17. Birth and death years of Albert Einstein: _____

18. Nationality of the poet Robert Burns: _____

19. Abductor of Helen of Troy: _____

20. Location of Vanderbilt Unversity: _____

Exercise 84   Borrowed Foreign Expressions

The following words and expressions occur frequently in our everyday speech and writing. They have been borrowed in their original forms from languages other than English and have in most instances become integral parts of our language. After consulting your dictionary, write the meaning of each expression and the language from which it was borrowed.

Example: coleslaw   *salad made of shredded cabbage, often mixed with* _____

salad dressing and seasoning (Dutch)

1. aloha   _____

_____

2. alumna, alumnus   _____

_____

3. amen   _____

_____

4. banzai   _____

_____

5. carpe diem   _____

_____

6. chaise longue   _____

_____

7. charisma   _____

_____

8. crochet   _____

_____

9. croissant   _____

_____

10. debut   _____

_____

11. en masse _____

12. gratis _____

13. in absentia _____

14. loco _____

15. née _____

16. non sequitur _____

17. pied-à-terre _____

18. pizza _____

19. sauerkraut _____

20. ski (n.) _____

22

Diction

Diction is one's choice of words in the expression of ideas. Because one speaks and writes on various levels of usage, the same expression may be appropriate to one level but not to another. The diction, for instance, of formal writing seems overprecise in informal conversation, and the acceptable diction of everyday speech seems out of place in serious, formal composition. But on all levels of speech and writing, faulty diction appears — in wordiness, in trite expressions, and in faulty idiom.

■ 22a Wordiness

Wordiness is the use of too many words — more words, that is, than are necessary to express an idea correctly and clearly. Many sentences written by college students may be greatly improved by reducing the number of words. The following kind of sentence is common in student themes:

WORDY: There is a man in our neighborhood, and he has written three novels.

BETTER: A man in our neighborhood has written three novels.

A neighbor of ours has written three novels.

What is called **excessive predication** is responsible for a common type of wordiness. Usually this fault results from the too frequent use of *and* and *but*. It may usually be remedied by proper subordination:

WORDY: The test was hard, and the students were resentful, and their instructor was irritated.

BETTER: Because the students resented the hard test, their instructor was irritated.

Another kind of wordiness originates in the desire to impress but ends in pretentious nonsense. It is the language of those persons who refer to bad weather as the "inclemency of the elements," who speak of "blessed events" and "passing away" instead of birth and death. Following are further examples of this kind of wordiness:

Our horse Hap has gone to the big round-up in the sky.

Our horse Hap has died.

Due to the fact that he was enamored of Angela, Thomas comported himself in such a way as to appear ridiculous.

Because he was in love with Angela, Thomas behaved foolishly.

I regret extremely the necessity of your departure.

I am sorry you must go.

Sometimes, of course, expressions like these are used facetiously. But do not make a habit of such usage.

Jargon is also a kind of wordiness, popular among people of specialized occupations. It has now spread to much everyday writing and speaking, probably because it is believed to make its users sound and appear knowledgeable. It is the jargon of government officials, social workers, educators on all levels, and others. Its basic principles seem to be these: Never use one word where two or more will do the work. Never use a concrete expression if it is possible to use an abstract one. Never be plain if you can be fancy. The clear sign of this kind of writing and speaking is the repeated use of such phrases as *frame of reference, in terms of, point in time,* and compounds formed with the suffix *-wise.* The writers of this new jargon never simply look at the budget; they "consider the status budget-wise." They don't study crime among the young; they "examine social conditions in terms of juvenile delinquency." They "critique," they "utilize," they "expedite," and they "finalize." They speak of the "culturally deprived," the "classroom learning situation," "meaningful experiences," "togetherness," and "lifestyle." All these expressions reflect a desire to be a part of the "in-group" (another example of this jargon) by picking up catchwords that seem to show a certain sophistication; what they really show is a failure to use precise language and a lack of judgment.

Redundancy, or unnecessary repetition, is another common type of wordiness, due to carelessness or ignorance of the meanings of certain words. Note the following examples of redundancy:

Repeat that again, please. [Why *again*?]

His solution was equally as good as hers. [Why *equally*?]

The consensus of opinion of the group was that Mrs. Jacobs will make a good mayor. [Use either *consensus of the group* or *the opinion of the group*.]

This location is more preferable to that one. [The word *preferable* means "more desirable"; therefore, the word *more* is unnecessary. The sentence should read *This location is preferable to that one.*]

The union continues to remain at odds with factory management. [*Continues* and *remain* mean essentially the same thing. Say, *The union continues at odds with factory management* or *The union remains at odds with factory management.*]

It was a dog large in size and brown in color. [*It was a large brown dog.*]

Mrs. Frost rarely ever wears her fur coat. [*Mrs. Frost rarely wears her fur coat.*]

■ 22b Vagueness

A general impression of vague thinking is given by the too frequent use of abstract words instead of concrete words. Note especially the vagueness of such common words as *asset, factor, phase, case, nature, character, line,* and *field.* All these have basic meanings and should be used cautiously in any other sense. The following examples show that the best way to treat these words is to get rid of them:

In cases where a person receives a ticket for speeding, he must pay a fine of fifty dollars. [*In cases where* can be replaced with the single word *if.*]

Industry and intelligence are important assets in business success. [Omit *assets* and the sense remains the same.]

The course is of a very difficult nature. [*The course is very difficult.*]

Jerry was aware of the fact that he was risking his savings. [*Jerry was aware that he was risking his savings.*]

Whenever you are tempted to use such words, stop and ask yourself just what you are trying to say. Then find the exact words to say it, cutting out all the "deadwood."

■ 22c Triteness

Trite means worn. Certain phrases have been used so often that they have lost their original freshness. Oratory, sermons, newspaper headlines and captions, and pretentious writing in general are frequently marred by such diction. Expressions of this kind are often called **clichés.** The following list is merely illustrative; you can probably think of numerous ones to add to these:

upset the applecart	proud possessor
an ace up his sleeve	nipped in the bud
dull thud	few and far between
one fell swoop	on pins and needles
up on Cloud Nine	make one's blood boil
grim reaper	eat one's heart out
last but not least	having a ball
face the music	as luck would have it
as straight as a die	quick as a wink
bitter end	gung ho

Avoid also quotation of trite phrases from literature and proverbs. Expressions like the following have already served their purpose:

a lean and hungry look	the best laid plans of mice and men
a sadder but wiser man	where angels fear to tread
a rolling stone	love never faileth
those who live in glass houses	to be or not to be

■ 22d Euphemisms

Euphemisms are expressions used to avoid the outright statement of disagreeable ideas or to give dignity to something essentially lowly or undignified. The Victorians were notoriously euphemistic: they called their legs "limbs," and instead of the accurate and descriptive terms *sweat* and *spit*, they substituted the vague but more delicate words "perspire" and "expectorate." Unfortunately, the Victorians were not the last to use euphemisms. While we cannot admire or condone some of today's obscenely explicit language, there is little justification for the fuzzy-minded delicacy of euphemisms. There is a decided difference between choosing an expression that offers a tactful, rather than hurtful, connotation and choosing an expression that is deliberately misleading. Pregnancy is euphemistically referred to as "expecting"; a garbage collector is a "sanitation engineer"; a janitor is a "superintendent," etc. *Death*, of course, has numerous euphemistic substitutes such as "passing on," "going to his reward," and many others.

Again, it should be emphasized that the laudable wish to spare the feelings of others is not to be confused with the sort of prudery or false sense of gentility that most often produces euphemisms. Unless your use of a euphemism is inspired by the necessity to soften a blow or to avoid offensiveness, use the more factual term. Ordinarily, avoid euphemisms — or change the subject.

■ 22e Idiom

Construction characteristic of a language is called **idiom.** The established usage of a language, the special way in which a thing is said or a phrase is formed, must be observed if writing is to be properly idiomatic. In English the normal sentence pattern has the subject first, then the verb, and then the direct object. In French, if the direct object is a pronoun, it usually (except in the imperative) precedes the verb. In English an adjective that directly modifies a noun usually precedes it. In French the adjective usually follows the noun. In English we say, "It is hot." The French say, "It makes hot." Such differences make learning a foreign language difficult.

Another meaning of the word *idiom* is somewhat contrary to this one. The word is also used for all those expressions that seem to defy logical grammatical practice, expressions that cannot be translated literally into another language.

"Many is the day" and "You had better" are good examples. Fortunately, idioms of this sort cause little trouble to native speakers.

In English, as in most modern European languages, one of the greatest difficulties lies in the idiomatic use of prepositions after certain nouns, adjectives, and verbs. Oddly enough, one agrees *with* a person but *to* a proposal, and several persons may agree *upon* a plan. One may have a desire *for* something but be desirous *of* it. One is angry *at* or *about* an act but *with* a person. These uses of prepositions may seem strange and perverse, but they are part of the idiomatic structure of English and must be learned. Good dictionaries frequently indicate correct usage in questions of this kind. Do not look up the preposition but rather the word with which it is used. The definition of this word will usually indicate the correct preposition to use with it.

■ 22f Connotation

In selecting words that will express their thoughts accurately, careful writers pay attention to the **connotations** of certain expressions. *Connotation* is the associative meaning, or what the word suggests beyond its literal definition.

Through popular usage certain terms convey favorable or unfavorable impressions beyond their literal meanings; they frequently have emotional or evaluative qualities that are not part of their straightforward definitions. Careless use of a word with strong connotations may cause faulty communication of your ideas. On the other hand, skillful use of connotation can greatly enrich your ability to communicate accurately. For example, you would not refer to a public figure whom you admire and respect as a "politician," a term that suggests such qualities as insincerity and conniving for personal gain. The word *childish* is inappropriate when you mean "childlike." The adjective *thin* suggests something scanty or somehow not full enough (especially when describing a person's figure); but *slim* and *slender*, two words close to *thin* in literal meaning, imply grace and good proportion.

Again, your dictionary can provide these shades of meaning that will keep you from writing something far different from your intention and will help you develop a vocabulary you can use accurately.

■ 22g Slang

Slang is, as you know, one of the usage labels given in a dictionary to define extremely informal language, frequently earthy but often vividly expressive. It usually has no true equivalent in Standard English and has the advantage of being forceful and dynamic. Although many slang terms, because of these qualities, eventually become acceptable as colloquial English, many more remain current for only a year or two; then, like all overused expressions, they gradually lose their force. Old slang expressions are constantly being abandoned, while new ones are constantly coming into use. There is no need to list slang expressions here, as they so quickly become dated. Be aware, however, that they are easily recognizable and that you must avoid them in all but the most informal written contexts.

Glossary of Faulty Diction

The following glossary should help you rid your speech and writing of many errors. The term **colloquial** means that an expression is characteristic of everyday speech. **Dialectal** means that an expression is peculiar to a particular place or class.

Note: Remember that colloquialisms, the language we use in our everyday conversations with friends and associates, are perfectly acceptable in informal writing and speech. The purpose of this Glossary of Faulty Diction is to point out expressions that should be avoided in formal writing of any kind.

About, Around. *About* means *rather close to,* usually referring to time or number (*about a year, about forty*). *Around* is concerned with spatial arrangement (*They sat around the table*) and is colloquial when used to mean *about.*

Above. Avoid the use of *above* as a modifier in such phrases as *the **above** reference, the **above** names.* An exception to this rule is that the word is proper in legal documents.

Accept, Except. *To accept* is *to receive; to except* is *to make an exception of, to omit. Except* (as a preposition) means *with the exception of.*

Accidently. There is no such word. The correct form is *accidentally,* based on the adjective *accidental.*

A.D. This is an abbreviation of *Anno Domini* (in the year of our Lord). Strictly considered, it should be used only with a date: *A.D. 1492.* But it has recently come to mean *of the Christian era,* and expressions like *the fifth century A.D.* have become common. Here logic has bowed to usage.

Adapt, Adopt. *To adapt* is *to make suitable;* to adjust. *Adopt* is *to accept* or *to take as one's own.* (*He adapted to his environment; They adopted a child.*)

Administrate. There is no such word. The verb is *administer;* the noun formed from it is *administration.*

Adverse, Averse. *Adverse* means *unfavorable* (*The weatherman forecast **adverse** conditions for the yacht race*). *Averse* means *opposed to* (*Mother was **averse** to our plans for ice skating at midnight*).

Affect, Effect. In common usage *affect* is a verb meaning *to influence, to have an effect upon* or *to like to have or use* (*He **affects** a gold-headed cane*) or *to pretend* (*She **affects** helplessness*). *Effect* is both verb and noun. *To effect* is *to produce, to bring about.* The noun *effect* is a *result,* a *consequence.*

Aggravate. Colloquial when used to mean *provoke* or *irritate. Aggravate* means to make *worse* (*The rainy weather **aggravated** his rheumatism*).

Agree to, Agree with, Agree upon or **on.** One agrees *to* a proposal, *with* a person, and *upon* or *on* a settlement (*We **agreed to** his suggestion that we go, The boy did not **agree with** his father, The two factions could not **agree upon** a settlement*).

Ain't. This form is occasionally defended as a contraction of *am not*, but even those who defend it do not use it in writing.

Alibi. Colloquial for *excuse*. In formal usage *alibi* has legal significance only and means a confirmation of one's absence from the scene of a crime at the time the crime was committed.

All ready, Already. *All ready* means simply that all are ready (*The players were all ready*). *Already* means *previously* or *before now* (*He has already gone*).

All together, Altogether. *All together* means all of a number taken or considered together (*She invited them all together*). *Altogether* means *entirely, completely* (*He was altogether wrong*).

Allusion, Illusion. An *allusion* is a casual or indirect reference to something, usually without naming the thing itself (*The quotation in her speech was an allusion to Shakespeare's* Macbeth). An *illusion* is a false or unreal impression of reality (*After his unkind treatment of the puppy Mildred lost her illusions about Arthur*).

Alright. This is not an acceptable alternate spelling for the words *all right*.

Alumnus, Alumna. *Alumnus* is masculine and has the plural *alumni*. *Alumna* is feminine and has the plural *alumnae*.

Among, Between. The common practice is to use *between* with two persons or objects (*between a rock and a hard place*) and *among* with more than two (*The crew quarreled among themselves*). Exception: *The plane traveled between New York, Chicago, and Miami.* Here *among* would be absurd.

Amount, Number. *Amount* is a total mass or body, considered as one entity (*He spent a large amount of money*). *Number* refers to a group of things made up of individual parts that can be separated and counted (*A number of errors appeared in his essay*).

Anxious, Eager. *Anxious* means *fearful; worried*. *Eager* means *showing keen desire; ardent*. (*Jane was eager* [not *anxious*] *to go to summer camp*.)

Anyone, Any one. *Anyone*, the indefinite pronoun, is one word. *Any one*, meaning any single person or any single thing, should be written as two words (*Any one of your friends will be glad to help you*).

Any place, No place. Dialectal corruptions of *anywhere* and *nowhere*.

Apt, Liable, Likely. *Apt* means *suitable, appropriate, tending to*, or *inclined to* (*an apt phrase, a man apt to succeed*). *Liable* means *exposed to something undesirable* (*liable to be injured, liable for damages*). *Likely* means *credible, probable, probably* (*He had a likely excuse*). It can also overlap to some extent with *apt* in its sense of probability (*It is likely — or apt — to rain today*).

As far as. This expression is frequently misused when it is not followed by words that would complete a clause (*As far as her ability she is perfectly able to do the work*). This expression should always function as a subordinating conjunction, introducing both a subject and a verb (*As far as her ability is concerned, she is perfectly able to do the work*).

Asset. In its essential meaning this word is used in law and accounting (*His assets exceeded his liabilities*). But it seems to have established itself in the meaning of *something useful or desirable*. When used in this sense, it is frequently redundant.

Attend, Tend.   *Attend* means *to be present at.* When meaning *to take care of,* it is followed by *to* (He **attends to** his own business). *Tend* without a preposition also means *to take care of* (He **tends** his own garden). *Tend to* means *to have a tendency to* (She **tends to** become nervous when her children are noisy).

Audience, Spectators.   *Audience,* interpreted literally, means *a group of listeners; spectators* are *a group of viewers.* The distinction need not be rigid, but it is better not to say "The **spectators** applauded loudly at the end of the concert," or "The **audience** booed the rude tennis player."

Author, Host, Chair, Position.   These nouns and many others like them are frequently misused as verbs (She has **authored** three best sellers, The Joneses plan to **host** a party for their friends, The woman who **chairs** the committee is a lawyer, Please **position** the chairs around the table). In these four sentences there are perfectly adequate verbs that should be used: *written, give, is chairman of,* and *place.*

Awful, Awfully.   Either of these is colloquial when used to mean *very.*

Awhile, A while.   *Awhile* is used as an adverb (They stayed **awhile** at their friend's house). When used after the preposition *for, while* is a noun, the object of the preposition (I thought for **a while** that you were going to miss the plane). The adverb is written as one word; the object of the preposition and its article are written as two.

Bad, Badly.   *Bad* is an adjective, *badly* an adverb. Say *I feel* **bad,** not *I feel* **badly,** if you mean *I am ill* or *I am sorry.*

Balance.   Except in accounting, the use of *balance* for *difference, remainder, the rest* is colloquial.

Being as.   Dialectal for *since* or *because.*

Beside, Besides.   *Beside* is a preposition meaning *by the side of* (Along came a spider and sat down **beside** her). *Besides* is a preposition meaning *except* (He had nothing **besides** his good name) and an adverb meaning *in addition, moreover* (He received a medal and fifty dollars **besides**).

Blame on.   Correct idiom calls for the use of *to blame* with *for,* not *on.* (They **blamed** the driver **for** the accident, not They **blamed** the accident **on** the driver.) *Blame on* is colloquial.

Boyfriend, Girlfriend.   These two terms are colloquial, meaning *a favored male or female friend, a sweetheart.* If no other term seems appropriate, write them as two words: *boy friend, girl friend.*

Burst, Bursted, Bust.   The principal parts of the verb *burst* are *burst, burst,* and *burst.* The use of *bursted* or *busted* for the past tense is incorrect. *Bust* is either sculpture or a part of the human body. Used for *failure* or as a verb for *burst* or *break,* it is slang.

But.   When *but* is used to mean *only,* it should not be used with a negative verb (I **haven't but** one dollar in my wallet). The correct form is *I* **have but** *one dollar in my wallet.* Of course, the more natural expression is *I have only one dollar in my wallet.*

But what.   Use *that* or *but that* instead of *but what* (They had no doubt **that** help would come).

Calvary, Cavalry.   Mistakes here are chiefly a matter of spelling, but it is important to be aware of the difference: *Calvary* is the name of the hill where Jesus was crucified; *cavalry* refers to troops trained to fight on horseback, or more recently in armored vehicles.

Cannot.   This word is the negative form of *can*. It is written as one word.

Cannot help but.   This is a mixed construction. *Cannot help* and *cannot but* are separate expressions, either of which is correct (*He **cannot but** attempt it*, or *He **cannot help** attempting it*).

Capital, Capitol.   *Capital* is a city; *capitol* is a building. *Capital* is also an adjective, usually meaning *chief, excellent*.

Case.   This is a vague and unnecessary word in many of its common uses today. Avoid *case* and seek the exact word.

Chairperson.   Use the terms *chairman* and *chairwoman* in preference to *chairperson*, which should be used only if it is an official title in an organization or if you are quoting directly someone who has used the term.

Chaise lounge.   The second word in this term is *longue*, not *lounge*. It is a French expression meaning "long chair," and the word *longue* is pronounced the same as the English *long*. Many people simply misread the similar spelling and think that the word is our English word *lounge*.

Childish, Childlike.   *Childish* strongly implies the lack of maturity or of reasonable attitude characteristic of childhood (*She behaved **childishly** in refusing to eat*). *Childlike* has the connotation of innocence, faith, or trust (*He has a **childlike** faith in the power of good*).

Cite, Site.   *Cite* means *to quote*, or *to summon officially to appear in court* (*Thomas **cited** Einstein as his authority, George was **cited** by the police for drunken driving*). *Site* is the position or area on which anything is, has been, or will be located (*We visited the **site** where our new home will be built*).

Claim.   Do not use simply to mean *say*. In the correct use of *claim* some disputed right is involved (*He **claims** to be the heir of a very wealthy man*).

Clear.   When *clear* is used to mean *all the way* (*The ball rolled **clear** across the road*), it is colloquial.

Complement, Compliment.   In its usual sense *complement* means *something that completes* (*Her navy blue shoes and bag were a **complement** for her gray suit*). A *compliment* is an expression of courtesy or praise (*My **compliments** to the chef*).

Connotate.   There is no such verb as *connotate*; the verb is *connote*, and its noun form is *connotation*.

Consensus of Opinion.   The word *consensus* alone means *general agreement*. The phrase *of opinion* is redundant.

Considerable.   This word is an adjective meaning *worthy of consideration, important* (*The idea is at least **considerable***). When used to denote a great deal or a great many, *considerable* is colloquial or informal.

Contact.   Colloquial and sometimes vague when used for *see, meet, communicate with*, as in *I must **contact** my agent*.

Continual, Continuous.   *Continual* means *repeated often* (*The interruptions were **continual***). *Continuous* means *going on without interruption* (*For two days the pain was **continuous***).

Convince, Persuade.   Do not use *convince* for *persuade* as in *I* **convinced** *him to wash the dishes*. *Convince* means *to overcome doubt* (*I* **convinced** *him of the soundness of my plan*). *Persuade* means *to win over by argument or entreaty* (*I* **persuaded** *him to wash the dishes*).

Couple.   This word, followed by *of*, is informal for *two* or *a few*.

Credible, Creditable.   *Credible* means *believable* (*His evidence was not* **credible**). *Creditable* means *deserving esteem or admiration* (*The acting of the male lead was a* **creditable** *performance*).

Critique.   This word is a noun, not a verb; it means a critical review or comment dealing with an artistic work. The correct verb is *evaluate* or *review*.

Cupfuls, Cupsful.   The plural of cupful is *cupfuls*, not *cupsful*.

Data.   *Data* is the plural of *datum, something given or known*. It usually refers to a body of facts or figures. It normally takes a plural verb (*These* **data** *are important*). At times, however, *data* may be considered a collective noun and used with a singular verb.

Definitely.   This is frequently used to mean *very* or *quite*. A trite expression, it should be avoided for this reason as well as for its lack of accuracy.

Desert, Dessert.   The noun *desert(s)* means *a deserved reward or punishment* (*to receive one's just deserts*). Do not confuse this word with *dessert*, which is *the sweet course served at the end of a meal*.

Different than.   Most good writers use *different from*, not *different than*.

Disburse, Disperse.   *Disburse* means *to pay out; spend* (**disbursement** *of funds*). *Disperse*, which is sometimes confused with *disburse*, means *to scatter* (*The crowd* **dispersed** *quickly*).

Disinterested.   Often confused with *uninterested*. *Disinterested* means *unbiased, impartial; uninterested* means *lacking interest in*.

Don't.   A contraction of *do not*. Do not write *he, she,* or *it don't*.

Drapes.   Incorrect when used as a noun to mean *curtains*. *Drape* is the verb; *draperies* is the correct noun form.

Due to.   Do not use *due to* for *because of* as in **Due to** *a lengthy illness, he left college*. *Due to* is correctly used after a noun or linking verb (*His failure,* **due to** *laziness, was not surprising. The accident was* **due to** *carelessness*).

Dyeing, Dying.   *Dyeing* refers to the coloring of materials with dye. Do not omit the *e*, which would confuse the word with *dying*, meaning *expiring*.

Each other, One another.   *Each other* is used to denote two people (*Nancy and John like* **each other**); *one another* involves more than two people (*All human beings should try to be kind to* **one another**).

Emigrant, Immigrant.   A person who moves from one place to another is both an *emigrant* and an *immigrant,* but he emigrates *from* one place and immigrates *to* the other.

Enormity.   This word means *great wickedness; a monstrous or outrageous act*. It should not be used to mean great size or vastness (*The* **enormity** *of his crime was shocking*, not *The* **enormity** *of his generosity is wonderful*).

Enthuse, Enthused.   These words are colloquial and always unacceptable in writing.

Equally as.   Do not use these two words together; omit either *equally* or *as*. Do not write *Water is* **equally as** *necessary as air*; write *Water is* **as** *necessary as air* or

Water and air are equally necessary.

Etc.   An abbreviation of Latin *et* (*and*) and *cetera* (*other things*). It should not be preceded by *and*, nor should it be used as a catch-all expression to avoid a clear and exact ending of an idea or a sentence.

Everyday, Every day.   When written as one word (*everyday*), this expression is an adjective (*Mother's everyday china is ironstone*). When used adverbially to indicate how often something happens, it is written as two words (*Every day at noon I eat an apple and drink a glass of milk*).

Exam.   A colloquial abbreviation for *examination*. Compare *gym, dorm, lab,* and *prof*.

Expect.   This word means *to look forward to* or *foresee*. Do not use it to mean *suspect* or *suppose*.

Fact that.   This is an example of wordiness, usually amounting to redundancy. Most sentences can omit the phrase *the fact that* without changing the sense of what is said (*The fact that he wanted a new bicycle was the reason why he stole the money* may be effectively reduced to *He stole the money because he wanted a new bicycle*). Whenever you are tempted to use this expression, try rewording the sentence without it; you will have a more concise and a clearer statement.

Farther, Further.   The two words are often confused. *Farther* means *at or to a more distant point in space or time; further* means *to a greater extent, in addition*. One says *It is farther to Minneapolis from Chicago than from here,* but *We will talk further about this tomorrow*.

Faze.   Colloquial for *to disturb* or *to agitate*. Most commonly used in the negative (*Mother's angry looks didn't faze Jimmy*).

Feel.   *Feel* means to perceive through the physical senses or through the emotions. This word should not be used as a careless equivalent of *think* or *believe*, both of which refer to mental activity.

Fellow.   Colloquial when used to mean a *person*.

Fewer, Less.   Use *fewer* to refer to a number, *less* to refer to amount (*Where there are fewer persons, there is less noise*).

Fine.   Colloquial when used as a term of general approval.

Fix.   *Fix* is a verb, meaning *to make firm or stable*. Used as a noun meaning *a bad condition,* it is colloquial.

Flaunt, Flout.   *Flaunt* means *to exhibit ostentatiously, to show off* (*She flaunted her new mink coat before her friends*). *Flout* means to show *contempt for, to scorn* (*Margaret often flouts the rules of good sportsmanship*).

Forego, Forgo.   *Forego* means to *precede* or *go before* (*The foregoing data were gathered two years ago*. *Forgo* means *to give up, relinquish* (*I am afraid I must forgo the pleasure of meeting your friends today*).

Formally, Formerly.   *Formally* means *in a formal manner* (*He was formally initiated into his fraternity last night*). *Formerly* means *at a former time* (*They formerly lived in Ohio*).

Gentleman, Lady.   Do not use these words as synonyms for *man* and *woman*.

Got.   This is a correct past participle of the verb *to get* (*He had got three traffic tickets in two days*). *Gotten* is an alternative past participle of *to get*.

Guess.   Colloquial when used for *suppose* or *believe*.

Guy.   Slang when used for *boy* or *man*.

Hanged, Hung.   *Hanged* is the correct past tense or past participle of *hang* when capital punishment is meant (*The cattle rustlers were **hanged** at daybreak*). *Hung* is the past tense and past participle in every other sense of the term (*We **hung** popcorn and cranberries on the Christmas tree*).

Hardly, Scarcely.   Do not use with a negative. *I can't hardly see it* borders on the illiterate. Write *I can **hardly** see it* or (if you cannot see it at all) *I **can't** see it*.

Healthful, Healthy.   Places are *healthful* if persons may be *healthy* living in them.

Hopefully.   This word means *in a hopeful manner* (*She **hopefully** began getting ready for her blind date*). Do not use this modifier to mean *it is hoped* or *let us hope* (***Hopefully**, the new rail system for Atlanta will be completed within five years*).

Human.   *Human* is an adjective, preferably not used alone as a noun. *Human being* is the correct term.

If, Whether.   In careful writing do not use *if* for *whether*. *Let me know **if** you are coming* does not mean exactly the same thing as *Let me know **whether** you are coming*. The latter leaves no doubt that a reply is expected.

Impact, Conference, Author, Host, Position, Defense, and many other nouns are frequently misused as verbs (*She has **authored** many best sellers, The Joneses will **host** a party for their friends, New taxes will **impact** modest wage earners, The Bears **defensed** poorly in the second half of the game*). In these four sentences perfectly adequate verbs are available and should be used.

Imply, Infer.   *Imply* means *to suggest, to express indirectly*. *Infer* means *to conclude*, as on the basis of suggestion or implication. A writer *implies* to a reader; a reader *infers* from a writer.

Incidently.   There is no such word. The correct form is *incidentally*, based on the adjective *incidental*.

Into, In to.   *Into* is a preposition meaning *toward the inside* and is followed by an object of the preposition. Do not use the one-word form of this expression when the object of the preposition is the object of *to* only and *in* is an adverbial modifier. Say *He went **into** the building* but *The men handed their application forms **in to** the personnel manager*.

Irregardless.   No such word exists. *Regardless* is the correct word.

Its, It's.   The form *its* is possessive (*Every dog has **its** day*). *It's* is a contraction of *it is* (***It's** a pity she's a bore*).

It's me.   Formal English requires *It is I*. *It's me* is informal or colloquial, perfectly acceptable in conversation but not proper for written English. Compare the French idiom *C'est moi*.

Kid.   Used to mean a child or young person or as a verb meaning *to tease or jest, kid* is slang.

Kind, Sort.   These are singular forms and should be modified accordingly (*this kind, that sort*). *Kinds* and *sorts* are plural, and they, of course, have plural modifiers.

Kind of, Sort of.   Do not use these to mean *rather* as in *He was **kind of** (or **sort of**) lazy*.

Last, Latest. *Last* implies that there will be no more. *Latest* does not prevent the possibility of another appearance later. The proper sense of both is seen in the sentence *After seeing his **latest** play, we hope that it is his **last**.*

Lay, Lie. *Lay* is a transitive verb, always taking an object and meaning *to make something lie; to set or place* (*Please **lay** the cards on the table*). *Lie*, an intransitive verb, means *to be at rest* (*I will **lie** down for a nap*), not *I will **lay** down for a nap*).

Lend, Loan. The use of *loan* as a verb is incorrect. *Loan* is a noun. The distinction between the two words may be seen in the sentence *If you will **lend** me ten dollars until Friday, I will appreciate the **loan**.*

Less, Fewer. These are comparatives. *Less* refers to amount as an inseparable mass or body (*My car weighs **less** than Harry's*). *Fewer* refers to number, things that can be counted (*I had **fewer** colds this winter than last*).

Like, As. Confusion in the use of these two words results from using *like* as a conjunction. The preposition *like* should be followed by an object (*He ran **like** an antelope*). The conjunction *as* is followed by a clause (*He did **as** he wished, He talked **as** though he were crazy*). The incorrect use of *as* as a preposition is a kind of reaction against the use of *like* as a conjunction. Consider the sentence: *Many species of oaks, **as** the red oak, the white oak, the water oak, are found in the Southeast.* Here the correct word is *like*, not *as*.

Literally. The word means *faithfully, to the letter, letter for letter, exactly*. Do not use in the sense of *completely*, or *in effect*. A sentence may be copied *literally*; but one never, except under extraordinary circumstances, **literally** *devours a book*. Frequently, the word *virtually*, meaning *in effect or essence, though not in fact*, is the correct word.

Lot, Lots. Colloquial or informal when used to mean *many* or *much*.

Mad. The essential meaning of *mad* is *insane*. When used to mean *angry*, it is informal.

Masterful, Masterly. *Masterful* carries the suggestion of being forceful or even domineering (*He is a **masterful** dean of the college*). *Masterly* indicates expertness and skill (*John did a **masterly** job of editing the magazine*).

May Be, Maybe. *May be* is a verb phrase (*It **may be** that you are right*). *Maybe* used as an adverb means *perhaps* (***Maybe** you are right*).

Mean. Used for disagreeable or cruel (*He had a **mean** disposition, She is **mean** to me*), the word is informal or colloquial.

Media. *Media* is the plural of *medium, a means, agency*, or *instrumentality*. It is often incorrectly used in the plural as though it were singular, as in *The **media** is playing an important role in political races this year.*

Midnight, Noon. Neither of these words needs the word *twelve* before it. They themselves refer to specific times, so *twelve* is redundant.

Most, Almost. *Most* is colloquial when used to mean *almost; nearly* (***Most** all my friends are at the beach*). *Almost* is the correct expression (***Almost** all the work was finished on time*).

Muchly. There is no such word as *muchly*. *Much* is both adjective and adverb (***Much** water has flowed over the dam. Thank you very **much***).

Mutual. The use of *mutual* for *common* is usually avoided by careful writers.

Common knowledge, *common* property, *common* dislikes are things shared by two or more persons. *Mutual* admiration means *admiration of each for the other.*

Myself. Colloquial when used as a substitute for *I* or *me*, as in *He and **myself** were there.* It is correctly used intensively (*I **myself** will do it*) and reflexively (*I blame only **myself***).

Nauseated, Nauseous. These two words are frequently confused. *Nauseated* means "feeling a sickness at the stomach; a sensation of impending vomiting" (*I was **nauseated** because of having eaten my lunch too fast*). *Nauseous* means "sickening, disgusting; loathsome" (*The **nauseous** odor of the gas was affecting everyone in the building*).

Nice. *Nice* is a catch-all word that has lost its force because it has no clearcut, specific meaning as a modifier. When writing in praise of something, select an adjective that conveys more specific information than *nice* does.

Noted, Notorious. *Noted* means *distinguished; renowned; eminent* (*He was **noted** for his skill as a surgeon*). *Notorious* refers to something or someone widely but unfavorably known and discussed (*He was **notorious** for his unethical business dealings*).

Of. Unnecessary after such prepositions as *off, inside, outside* (not *He fell **off of** the cliff* but *He fell **off** the cliff*).

On account of. Do not use as a conjunction; the phrase should be followed by an object of the preposition *of* (**on account of** *his illness*). *He was absent **on account of** he was sick* is incorrect.

Oral, Verbal, Written. Use *oral* to refer to spoken words (*An **oral** examination is sometimes nerve-wracking for a student*); use *verbal* to contrast a communication in words to some other kind of communication (*His scowl told me more than any **verbal** message could*); use *written* when referring to anything put on paper.

Orientate. There is no such word. The verb is *orient*, meaning *to cause to become familiar with or adjusted to facts or a situation* (*He **oriented** himself by finding the North Star*). The noun is *orientation*.

Over with. The *with* is unnecessary in such expressions as *The game was **over with** by five o'clock.*

Party. Colloquial when used to mean *a person.* Properly used in legal documents (***party** of the first part*).

Peeve. Either as a verb or noun, *peeve* is informal diction.

Persecute, Prosecute. *Persecute* means *to harass persistently*, usually in order to injure for adherence to principle or religious belief (*Oliver Cromwell **persecuted** Englishmen who were loyal to the Crown*). *Prosecute* means *to institute legal proceedings against a person* (*The man has been indicted, and his case will be **prosecuted** in April*).

Personally. This word is often redundant and is a hackneyed, sometimes irritating expression, as in ***Personally,** I think you are making a big mistake.*

Plan on. Omit *on*. In standard practice idiom calls for an infinitive or a direct object after *plan*. *They **planned** to go* or *They **planned** a reception* are both correct usage.

Plenty. This word is a noun, not an adverb. Do not write *He was **plenty** worried.*

Pore, Pour. *Pore,* meaning *to meditate* or *to study intently and with steady application,* is a verb used with the preposition *over* (*She* **pored over** *her chemistry assignment for several hours*). It should not be confused with *pour,* meaning *to set a liquid flowing or falling* (*They* **poured** *the tea into fragile china cups*).

Principal, Principle. *Principal* is both adjective and noun (**principal** *parts,* **principal** *of the school,* **principal** *and interest*). *Principle* is a noun only (**principles** *of philosophy, a man of* **principle**).

Pupil, Student. Schoolchildren in the elementary grades are called *pupils;* in grades nine through twelve *student* or *pupil* is correct; for college the term must always be *student.*

Quote, Quotation. *Quote* is a verb and should not be used as a noun, as in *The* **quote** *you gave is from Shakespeare, not the Bible. Quotation* is the noun.

Real. Do not use for *really. Real* is an adjective; *really* is an adverb (*The* **real** *gems are* **really** *beautiful*).

Reason is because. This is not idiomatic English. The subject-linking verb construction calls for a predicate nominative, but *because* is a subordinating conjunction that introduces an adverbial clause. Write *The* **reason** *I was late* **is that** *I had an accident,* not *The* **reason** *I was late* **is because** *I had an accident.*

Regrettable, Regretful. *Regrettable* means that something is to be regretted (*It was a* **regrettable** *error*). *Regretful* describes a person who is sorry or rueful about something (*I am* **regretful** *about my error*).

Rein, Reign. *Rein* is a narrow strap of leather used by a rider to control a horse; it is frequently used figuratively to indicate control (*He took up the* **reins** *of government*); it should not be confused with *reign,* having to do with royal power (*Queen Victoria's* **reign** *lasted sixty-four years*).

Respectfully, Respectively. *Respectfully* means *with respect,* as in *The young used to act* **respectfully** *toward their elders. Respectively* is a word seldom needed; it means *in the order designated,* as in *The men and women took their seats on the right and left* **respectively.**

Reverend. This word, like *Honorable,* is not a noun, but an honorific adjective. It is not a title like *doctor* or *president.* It is properly used preceding *Mr.* or the given name or initials, as in *the* **Reverend** *Mr. Gilbreath, the* **Reverend** *Earl Gilbreath, the* **Reverend** *J. E. Gilbreath.* To use the word as a title as in *Reverend, will you lead us in prayer?* or *Is there a* **Reverend** *in the house?* is incorrect. *Reverend Gilbreath* instead of *the* **Reverend** *Mr. Gilbreath* is almost as bad.

Right. In the sense of *very* or *extremely, right* is colloquial or dialectal. Do not write (or say) *I'm* **right** *glad to know you.*

Same. The word is an adjective, not a pronoun. Do not use it as in *We received your order and will give* **same** *immediate attention.* Substitute *it* for *same.*

Savings. This word is frequently misused in the plural when the singular is the correct form. It is particularly puzzling that many people use this plural with a singular article, as in *The 10 percent discount gives you a* **savings** *of nine dollars. A saving* is the proper usage here. Another common error occurs with *Daylight* **Saving** *Time;* the right form again is *Saving,* not *Savings.*

Shape. In formal writing do not use *shape* for *condition* as in *He played badly because he was in poor* **shape.** In this sense *shape* is informal.

Should of, would of.   Do not use these terms for *should have, would have*.

Situation.   This is another catch-all term, frequently used redundantly, as in *It was a fourth down* **situation**. Fourth down *is* a situation, so the word itself is repetitious. This vague term can usually be omitted or replaced with a more specific word.

So.   Avoid the use of *so* for *very*, as in *Thank you* **so** *much*. *So* used as an adverb means *thus* or *like this*.

Some.   Do not use for *somewhat*, as in *She is* **some** *better after her illness*.

Species.   This word is both singular and plural. One may speak of *one species* or *three species*. The word usually refers to a kind of plant or animal.

Sprightly, Spritely.   *Sprightly* means *animated, vivacious, lively*. There is no such word as *spritely*, but many people use this term, probably because it suggests the word *sprite*, an *elf* or *fairy*. Do not write *Her* **spritely** *conversation was fascinating*.

Stationary, Stationery.   *Stationary* means *fixed, not moving*. Remember that *stationery*, which is paper for writing letters, is sold by a *stationer*.

Statue, Stature, Statute.   A *statue* is a piece of sculpture. *Stature* is bodily height, often used figuratively to mean *level of achievement, status,* or *importance*. A *statute* is a law or regulation.

Strata.   This is the plural of the Latin *stratum*. One speaks of *a stratum* of rock but of *several strata*.

Super, Fantastic, Awesome, Terrific, Incredible.   When used to describe something exciting or marvelous, these overworked words actually add little to our everyday conversation because they have lost their original force through constant repetition. They should never be a part of written English because they are both slangy and trite.

Suppose, Supposed.   Many people incorrectly use the first form *suppose* before an infinitive when the second form *supposed* is needed, as in *Am I* **suppose** *to meet you at five o'clock?* The past participle *supposed* must go along with the auxiliary verb *am* to form the passive voice. This error almost certainly arises from an inability to hear the final *d* when it precedes the *t* in the *to* of the infinitive. The correct form is *Am I* **supposed** *to meet you at five o'clock?*

Sure, Surely.   Do not use the adjective *sure* for the adverb *surely*. *I am* **sure** *that you are right* and *I am* **surely** *glad to be here* are correct.

Thusly.   *Thus* is an adverb. The *-ly* ending is not needed (*Baste the seam* **thus**, not *Baste the seam* **thusly**).

Trustee, Trusty.   The word *trustee* means *a person elected or appointed to direct funds or policy* for a person or an institution, as in *Mr. Higginbotham is a* **trustee** *on the bank's board of directors*. A *trusty*, on the other hand, is a prisoner granted special privileges because he is believed trustworthy, as in *Although he was a* **trusty**, *Harris escaped from prison early today*.

Too.   *Too* means *in addition,* or *excessively*. It is incorrect to use the word to mean *very* or *very much*, as in *I was not* **too** *impressed with her latest book* or *I'm afraid I don't know him* **too** *well*.

Try and.   Use *try to*, not *try and*, in such expressions as **Try to** *get here on time* (not **Try and** *get here on time*).

Type.   Colloquial in expressions like *this type book;* write *this type of book.*

Undoubtably, Undoubtedly.   There is no such word as *undoubtably.* The correct word is *undoubtedly.*

Unique.   If referring to something as the only one of its kind, you may correctly use *unique.* (*The Grand Canyon is a unique geological formation.*) The word does not mean *rare, strange,* or *remarkable,* and there are no degrees of *uniqueness;* to say that something is *the most unique thing one has ever seen* is faulty diction.

Use (Used) to could.   Do not use for *once could* or *used to be able to.*

Very.   Do not use as a modifier of a past participle, as in *very broken.* English idiom calls for *badly broken or very badly broken.*

Wait for, Wait on.   *To wait for* means *to look forward to, to expect* (*For two hours I have waited for you*). *To wait on* means *to serve* (*The butler and two maids waited on the guests at dinner*).

Wangle, Wrangle.   *Wangle* is a colloquial expression meaning *to bring about by persuasion or adroit manipulation* (*I managed to wangle permission from Mother to go to the game*). *Wrangle* means *to quarrel noisily and contentiously* (*I am tired of the children's constant wrangling*). Do not confuse the two words.

Want in, Want off, Want out.   These forms are dialectal. Do not use them for *want to come in, want to get off, want to get out.*

Way.   Colloquial when used for *away* as in *Way down upon the Swanee River.*

Ways.   Colloquial when used for *way* as in *a long ways to go.*

Where . . . at, Where . . . to.   The word *where* is an adverb meaning *in or at what place.* The addition of *at* or *to* is redundant.

Where, That.   *Where* is incorrect when used to mean *that* (*I see in the paper where the president will visit Europe next week*). Use *that* instead of *where* in the foregoing sentence.

Whose, Who's.   The possessive form is *whose* (*Whose book is this?*). *Who's* is a contraction of *who is* (*Who's at the door?*). The use of *whose* as a neuter possessive is confirmed by the history of the word and the practice of good writers. *The house whose roof is leaking* is more natural and less clumsy than *the house the roof of which is leaking.*

-Wise.   This suffix has become a cliché, attached indiscriminately to many nouns (*healthwise, budgetwise, fashionwise, ecologywise*). Try not to use this catch-all suffix habitually.

Wrest, Wrestle.   *Wrest* means *to twist violently in order to pull away by force* (*Bob wrested the pistol from the burglar*). *Wrestle* means *to struggle bodily with an opponent to force him down* (*The two men wrestled until Hugh threw Roger to the mat*). The two words are not interchangeable.

Your, You're.   The possessive form is *your* (*Tell me your name*). *You're* is a contraction of *you are.*

Exercise 85   Diction

Rewrite the following sentences, reducing wordiness. Be careful that your reduction does not lead to a series of short, choppy sentences, sometimes called "primer style." At the same time, be sure also not to omit any information essential to the overall sense of the sentence.

Example: Every now and then I occasionally think about my schoolmates who were my friends when we were children and who went to grammar school with me, and I wonder what has happened to them in their later lives in the years since then.

Occasionally I think of the friends I had in grammar school and wonder what has happened to them.

1. Todd says that in his opinion he believes that there will eventually come a time in the future when it will be the case that every man, woman, and child will be traveling only by air in planes and helicopters.

2. I am absolutely sure, with complete certainty, that my pickup truck is equally as good as that blue one of Kirk's that he has been boasting about.

3. Please repeat again what you said to us about Mr. Johnson's having been the very first originator of the universally adopted plan that all colleges are now using in reference to the awarding of athletic scholarships.

4. If you could return back to the point in time five years ago, when you determined on a course of pursuing a journalistic career, would you still continue in the exact same decision?

5. Truthfully, Jack, I can honestly say that I sincerely believe that in taking this course of action, you are making the most of a unique opportunity that is a once-in-a-lifetime chance.

6. Considering the nature of your request and the fact that the request is a difficult one to comply with, I have come to the conclusion that I must decline to grant you your wish.

7. Walter trudged along slowly on foot for about two miles, again trying anew to find the path that would lead him back again to the cabin.

8. In my reading of Sir Horace Fothergill's autobiography of his life story, I was able to ascertain that he was a man who had an arrogant and crotchety nature.

9. Betsy is a girl who is attractive in personality, but she wears clothes that are too small in size and makeup that is too bright in color.

10. In a talk with my parents I told my father and mother that I am ready to test the abilities that I have and to venture alone into the business world on my own.

Exercise 86 Diction

Rewrite the following sentences, reducing wordiness and/or needless repetition. Be careful that your reduction does not lead to a series of short, choppy sentences, sometimes called "primer style." At the same time, be sure also not to omit any information essential to the overall meaning of the sentence.

Example: In reference to the possibility of your chances of getting the job that you seek to hold, I would say as a guess that in most cases of individuals of your limited experience the chances are poor and unfavorable.

I believe that for one of your limited experience the chances of getting the job you want are poor.

1. Eric went to the opening of the new department store, optimistically hoping that he would be a recipient of one of the complimentary free gifts being offered during the promotion.

2. Frances came to the decision that she absolutely must have the sweater that she had seen in the window of Marshall's, because of the fact that its purple color would go well with her new skirt, which was gray.

3. There is a family that lives next door, and each member of the family has his own car and drives too fast, and that even includes the eighty-year-old grandfather, who used to be a race-car driver.

4. The fact of the matter is that Geraldine has broken her engagement to Clarence, and he is no longer her fiancé.

5. The Athletic Club held a meeting to settle the question as to whether the Johnson City Road Race will become an annual event, to be held once a year.

6. Thomas is a man who is a delightful individual, and he is universally popular because he is liked and admired by everyone.

7. Although her admirers are many in number, Janet continues undecided as to whom she will marry and remains in a state of indecision.

8. Qualitywise, this unique product stands out above all others in its superiority, and this fact should be strongly considered in the selection process because of its importance in the question of durability.

9. In the final analysis, each and every one of us should personally take an interest in protecting the environment, both now and in the foreseeable future.

10. Frankly, it is my personal opinion that Vivian's smile, which is beautiful, and her manner, which is sincere, are valuable assets in her campaign for the class presidency.

Exercise 87   Diction

The following sentences contain one or more trite expressions or euphemisms. Underline the trite and euphemistic phrases, and for each one write either **T** or **E** in the space at the right.

Example: Joyce is <u>walking on air</u> because she is now <u>the proud possessor</u> of a little white poodle that is <u>as cute as a button.</u>   _T, T, T_

1. Pat's father is in his golden years, but I understand that as a young man he was a big shot.   _____

2. My cat is growing by leaps and bounds, and it will come as no surprise if she one day reigns supreme over the dogs in the neighborhood.   _____

3. I don't want to be a wet blanket, but it stands to reason that we can expect at least six contributions of baked beans for our covered-dish supper.   _____

4. Slowly but surely the mercury was dropping, and we were down in the dumps for fear that the weather would ruin our well-laid plans.   _____

5. Mr. Featherstone's principles are as American as Mom and apple pie; he is as honest as the day is long, all wool and a yard wide.   _____

6. Amy has been in the depths of despair since she was asked to resign from her job in the candy shop.   _____

7. "You're beautiful when you're angry," murmured David to Marcia, "with your flashing eyes and your pouting ruby lips."   _____

8. The Ryans are expecting a blessed event any day now; they are hoping against hope for a girl this time.   _____

9. Joe has asked me to tide him over until his next payday; he says that he has had an uneven cash flow for the past few weeks.   _____

10. Mrs. Smith has learned that her nephew has a chemical dependency and that he and his parents will have counseling for this serious problem.   _____

11. After her shopping trip this afternoon Judy came home as happy as a lark with blouses, skirts, slacks, and last but not least, a beautiful coat that made us all green with envy.   _____

12. After the boat flipped over, Rodney, cool as a cucumber, swam quick as a flash to Marie, holding her head above water until they were rescued.   _____

13. In a towering rage over the loss of her jewels in the burglary, Mrs. Larkins complained that the building engineer should have stopped the thieves.   _____

14. Although she had a terrible pain in her tummy, Mimi refused to give up the trip to Seattle, and to make a long story short, she was fit as a fiddle the next day.   _____

15. The young man has had a somewhat checkered career, but he grew up in a depressed area, and his parents were as poor as Job's turkey.   _____

16. Hannah's great-grandfather passed away last night; he was a senior citizen who had led a full and happy life.   _____

17. In this modern world of today many people view with alarm the actions of the powers that be, but it is as plain as the nose on your face that there will always be naysayers.   _____

18. Mr. Martin always refers to Mrs. Martin as his better half and frequently tells her that she is as pretty as a picture.   _____

19. Placing my groceries in the trunk of my car, the bag boy turned to me and said, "Have a nice day!"   _____

20. Now don't repeat what I am going to tell you because it's a deep, dark secret, but I hear that the stork is going to pay a visit to the Davises.   _____

Exercise 88 Diction

The following sentences contain unidiomatic uses of prepositions. Underline each preposition that is incorrectly used or omitted and write the correct form at the right.

Example: The hurricane dashed the ship <u>on</u> the rocky

shore. _____*onto*_____

1. The teacher's opinion regarding Ted's efforts differed with that of the boy's mother. _____

2. Where are the Jacksons living at, now that they have left Texas? _____

3. When Roger and I take bicycle trips, we like to ride off of the beaten track. _____

4. When we got home yesterday, we were so tired that for about an hour, we lay onto the floor besides the fire. _____

5. Heather, you should give more attention and take better care of your new boots. _____

6. Dorothy is quite gifted with playing the guitar; she is popular and admired by her friends for her talent. _____

7. After waiting almost an hour on Frank, Genevieve finally left the hotel and took a taxi toward the airport. _____

8. I was sitting in the den listening at a Beethoven symphony when suddenly I heard the loud noise of rock music coming out from an upstairs bedroom. _____

9. Francis rushed in the house, shouting that he had won fifty dollars for an essay he had written about his dog. _____

10. There is trouble brewing among the twin sisters; Sara wants to continue dressing identically, but Julia does not. _____

11. Ten boys out of our class say that they have definitely decided to continue at their education after high school. _____

12. Jess reminded Sue that he would agree with the proposition only through certain conditions. _____

13. Medical tests revealed that the woman's illness was caused from a viral infection. _____

14. Dad is angry at Louise for failing to hand her work into her teacher on time. _____

15. Between the three of us we didn't have above thirty cents left after paying for our lunch. _____

Exercise 89 Diction

The following exercises (89–92) are based on the Glossary of Faulty Diction in Chapter 22. Underline all errors, colloquialisms (informal expressions), and slang and write the correct or preferred forms at the right.

Example: I hear that your father is an <u>alumni</u> of the
college where you are teaching now.   _____*alumnus*_____

1. Daisy put four cupsful of flour in the cake batter instead of three, so the cake couldn't help but be heavy.   _____

2. Incidently, Bill, that quote is not from a Shakespearean play but from one of the sonnets.   _____

3. It took me a couple of hours to convince Tina to drive to Burlington with us.   _____

4. The news announcer said that police have finally arrested the gentleman who robbed the First National Bank last month.   _____

5. Martha claims that she made all *A*'s last term; I can't hardly believe that.   _____

6. We all feel that the legislature should pass a medical care bill, irregardless of the governor's speech last night.   _____

7. I expect that the seedy-looking individual is a guy who is apt to cause trouble.   _____

8. Suzy felt awful bad this morning; hopefully she will be able to play in the basketball game tonight.   _____

9. The four executives conferenced all afternoon; no one knows if they reached a consensus of opinion.   _____

10. Our team has to play without it's star forward on account of he has a broken toe.   _____

11. Personally, I believe that Pierce has done a master-ful job on his last novel, and the reason is because he has such a vivid imagination.   _____

12. Keith now holds the reigns of city government; I never would of believed that he could be elected mayor.   _____

13. These kind of apples are not too good for making pies, so try and remember to get the tart ones next time.   _____

14. Don't you know that your suppose to place the garment on the hanger thusly?   _____

15. June can't understand why Alice is enthused about Simon; I think that June use to be engaged to him.   _____

Exercise 90 Diction

Underline all errors, colloquialisms, and slang expressions in the following sentences and write the correct or preferred forms at the right.

Example: Jan and Edgar agree with me that the <u>affect</u>
of Denise's change in hair color is less than
pleasing.   *effect*

1. Assisted by our teacher, the principle marched us
   in the Capital building, where we were met by
   Congressman Banks.   _____

2. Hoping to be a matchmaker, Aunt Flora was thoroughly frustrated when the two young people
   seemed disinterested in each other.   _____

3. Due to his attack of bronchitis in early December,
   Bryan decided to forego his plans to try out for the
   track team.   _____

4. Todd and myself were virtually asleep on our feet,
   but Todd kept saying that the Rogers' house was
   only a little further.   _____

5. The defeated candidate, muchly disappointed in
   the election results, blamed the outcome on the
   media.   _____

6. There were sure far less people at the Harpers' dinner party than I had expected.   _____

7. Despite the obvious restlessness of the congregation and the clock's steady progress toward the
   dinner hour, Reverend Highgate droned on,
   undoubtably ready to preach for another half-hour.   _____

8. I guess that it don't matter that you burned
   the beans, Juanita, because Harry don't like beans
   anyways.   _____

9. As far as his published works, I don't doubt but what Harrison's finest novel is *The Lonely Man*. _____

10. Liana's cheerful personality is definitely a valuable asset; she doesn't let anything faze her. _____

11. Although he seemed a truthful person, the young man's account of the incident was different than those of the other witnesses. _____

12. Laura inferred in her remarks that she and Ken were adverse to their daughter's plan to marry Philip. _____

13. Horace, I am not kidding when I say that you have flaunted the law once too often with your speeding. _____

14. Being as cereal companies are continuously advertising the healthiness of their products, one wonders whether all these assertions are true. _____

15. I wish that I could play the piano like Joan can; we stayed up until twelve midnight listening to her play. _____

Exercise 91 Diction

Underline all errors, colloquialisms, and trite expressions; then write the correct or preferred forms at the right.

Example: I recognized the distinctive green <u>stationary</u>
as Barbara's.   *stationery*

1. As Molly laid on the chaise lounge, she saw a peli-
   can with a fish in it's bill.   _____

2. Mr. Tompkins was all together outraged at the two
   youngsters who aggravated him constantly by
   stealing apples from his fruit stand.   _____

3. That fellow in the brown leather jacket has been
   setting here in the library pouring over the same
   book for hours.   _____

4. I feel that you have come to an inaccurate conclusion due to the fact that this data is incomplete.   _____

5. Lars told me that his parents immigrated from
   Denmark when he was just a kid of three.   _____

6. Mary Sue's new drapes are a delicate shade of
   peach, which compliments the colors in her sofa.   _____

7. Patricia has loaned me her satin shoes to wear to
   the dance; I'm glad that they are plenty big
   enough.   _____

8. Jim is a very unique individual whose been a good
   friend of mine for years.   _____

9. The Dolphins were in a punting situation, at fourth
   down with the ball on their own thirty-yard line.   _____

10. I cannot agree on your going way out to Rob's
    house in this terrible weather, David.   _____

11. The stature by Rodin is in the Louvre Museum in
    Paris.   _____

12. Shown in the photo are Mrs. Hunt, Mr. Shelby, and Signora Longino, who come from London, San Francisco, and Milan respectfully. _____

13. Danny is in bad shape with a case of flu; he has felt nauseous for two days. _____

14. Your planning to come home as soon as the game is over with, aren't you, Ben? _____

15. Most all the students who signed up for this class are here; Red Morris will be late because he has to come from clear across town. _____

16. Mr. Roland critiqued the magazine article about Abraham Lincoln, but personally, I don't think that he did a credible job. _____

17. We played our collection of compact discs for awhile, and then we ate popcorn, gossiped, and etc., before going to bed. _____

18. By dieting conscientiously, Katie has effected a real stunning transformation in her formally chubby figure. _____

19. At about twelve noon everyday I get hungry, and all I can think about is chocolate ice cream. _____

20. Many people believe that the man who was acquitted of the crime was equally as guilty as the man who was hung. _____

Exercise 92   Diction

Underline all errors and colloquialisms; then write the correct or preferred forms at the right.

Example: I would like to know <u>if</u> it's going to rain
today.   *whether*

1. It was extremely hard to orientate myself in the
   dark, and I was all ready feeling panicky about the
   others' having left me behind.   _____

2. The chairperson of the local historical society talked
   to the group about the adverse affects of air pollution on old buildings and possible solutions to the
   problem.   _____

3. You may think that it is alright to wear those kind
   of shoes with slacks, Meg, but I am very opposed
   to the idea.   _____

4. I don't remember who's suppose to pick up the
   dry cleaning, but there's no need for the both of us
   to go.   _____

5. The warden decided that Thomas was worthy of
   being made a trustee; two weeks later Thomas
   made a daring escape over the prison wall.   _____

6. Several pupils in my English class at the University
   were arguing between themselves about whether
   the word *data* is singular or plural.   _____

7. I cannot persuade Tim that although my views are
   different than his, mine are equally as valid.   _____

8. The man who owns that beautiful yacht has
   amassed a considerable fortune, due to hard work
   and perseverance.   _____

9. We tried to contact him yesterday, but I believe
   that I accidently dialed the wrong number.   _____

10. I felt badly at not having recognized Jane, but the
    reason is because she has changed a lot in the past
    ten years.   _____

11. Watching the boy closely, I saw that he walked like
    he was an old man; however, I should of realized
    that he had been hurt bad.   _____

12. Jerry didn't remain peeved for long because Hank
    offered a real sincere apology.   _____

13. The huge man's furious shouts literally took my
    breath away as he told us to get off of his
    property.   _____

14. Catherine walked in to our dorm room and, with a
    big smile, showed me her term paper with an $A+$
    on it.   _____

15. I am afraid that Dick has got himself in a fix, trying
    to go steady with three girls at one time.   _____

16. Many people who have emigrated to the United
    States have made significant contributions to their
    new communities and have been cordially excepted
    by their neighbors.   _____

17. A television commercial states that the famous
    magician David Copperfield vanished an automo-
    bile on one of his shows.   _____

18. Nan didn't have a reasonable alibi for missing class
    yesterday, and she was awfully embarrassed when
    Dr. King asked her to explain.   _____

19. Peggy has the allusion that she will one day be a
    big star; I expect that she is living in a fool's
    paradise.   _____

20. The lady who swindled that elderly couple out of
    their life savings is certainly a mean person.   _____

23

Building a Vocabulary

As you know from your own experience, one of your greatest needs for success-ful composition is to improve your vocabulary. One of the best ways to build a vocabulary, of course, is always to look up in a dictionary the meanings of unfamiliar words that you hear or read. This chapter on vocabulary will provide you with a minimal body of information concerning word formation and the derivations of various words comprising the English language. For a more inten-sified study of all aspects of this fascinating subject, including ways to strengthen your own vocabulary, consult and use frequently a book devoted exclusively to this purpose.

Learning the derivation of a word will fix in your mind the meaning and spelling of that word. Because the largest part of our English vocabulary comes from three main sources — the Old English, the Greek, and the Latin languages — a knowledge of commonly used prefixes, roots, and suffixes from these languages will prove useful.

A *prefix* is a short element — a syllable or syllables — that comes before the main part of the word, which is the *root*. A *suffix* is added to the end of the word. Thus the word *hypodermic* has *hypo-*, meaning "under," as its *prefix*; *derm*, mean-ing "skin," as its *root*; and *-ic*, meaning "having to do with," as its *suffix*. You see that the *prefix* and the *suffix* of a word modify the meaning of the *root*. The word *hypodermic*, then, when used as an adjective, means "having to do with some-thing under the skin."

There are actually more words of classical origin, that is, Greek and Latin, than of Old English in our language; however, we use Old English words much more frequently in every sentence that we write or speak. For instance, the Old English prefixes *un-* (not) and *for-* (from) are found in many of our words, such as *unfair* and *forbid*. The Old English root-word *hlaf* (loaf) gives us the word *lord*, a lord being a loafkeeper or warden (*hlaf-weard*). The root-word *god* (God) gives us *goodbye,* a contraction of *God be with ye.* Old English suffixes such as *-ish* (having the qualities of) and *-ly* (like) are seen in many words such as *foolish* and *courtly.*

If you combine the Greek root *tele,* meaning "at a distance," with *graph* (writing), *phone* (sound), *scope* (seeing), *pathy* (feeling), you have *telegraph* (writing at a distance), *telephone* (sound at a distance), *telescope* (seeing at a distance), *telepathy* (feeling at a distance).

The Latin root *duc* is seen in such words as *adduce, aqueduct, conduce, conduct, induce, produce, reduce, seduce, conductor, ducal,* and *ductile.* If you know that *duc* means "to lead," and if you know the meanings of the prefixes and suffixes combined with it, you can make out the meanings of most of these words.

Each prefix, root, and suffix that you learn may lead to a knowledge of many new words or give a clearer understanding of many you already know. Therefore, a list of some of the most common prefixes, roots, and suffixes is given below. Look up others in your dictionary, or, as suggested earlier, get a good vocabulary textbook and use it often.

■ 23a Prefixes

Prefixes Showing Number or Amount

BI– (*bis–*) two	(*bi*)annual, (*bis*)sextile
CENT– (*centi–*) hundred	(*cent*)enarian, (*centi*)pede
DEC– (*deca–*) ten	(*dec*)ade, (*Deca*)logue
HEMI– half	(*hemi*)sphere, (*hemi*)stich
MILLI– (*mille–*) thousand	(*milli*)on, (*mille*)nnium
MULTI– many, much	(*multi*)form, (*multi*)graph
MON– (*mono–*) one	(*mono*)gyny, (*mono*)tone
OCTA– (*octo–*) eight	(*octa*)ve, (*octo*)pus
PAN– all	(*pan*)acea, (*pan*)demonium, (*pan*)orama
PENTA– five	(*penta*)gon, (*Penta*)teuch
POLY– much, many	(*poly*)glot, (*poly*)chrome
PROT– (*proto–*) first	(*prot*)agonist, (*proto*)type
SEMI– half	(*semi*)circle, (*semi*)final
TRI– three	(*tri*)angle, (*tri*)ad
UNI– one	(*uni*)fy, (*uni*)cameral

Prefixes Showing Relationship in Place and Time

AB– (*a–, abs–*) from, away from	(*a*)vert, (*ab*)sent, (*abs*)tract
AD– (*ac–, af–, al–, ag–, an–, ap–, ar–, as–, at–*) to, at	(*ad*)mit, (*ac*)cede, (*af*)fect, (*al*)lude, (*ag*)gre-gate, (*an*)nounce, (*ap*)pear, (*ar*)rive, (*as*)sume, (*at*)tain
AMB– (*ambi–*) around, both	(*ambi*)dextrous, (*ambi*)guous
ANTE– (*ant–*) before	(*ante*)cedent, (*ante*)date
ANTI– (*ant–*) against	(*anti*)thesis, (*ant*)agonist
CATA– away, against, down	(*cata*)clysm, (*cata*)strophe
CIRCUM– around, about	(*circum*)scribe, (*circum*)stance
CON– (*com–, col–, cor–*) with, together, at the same time	(*con*)tract, (*com*)pete, (*col*)league, (*cor*)relate

CONTRA– (*counter–*) opposite, against   (*contra*)dict, (*counter*)mand
DE– from, away from, down   (*de*)pend, (*de*)form, (*de*)tract
DIA– through, across   (*dia*)gram, (*dia*)meter
DIS– (*di, dif–*) off, away from   (*dis*)tract, (*di*)verge, (*dif*)fuse
EN– (*em–, in–*) in, into   (*en*)counter, (*em*)brace, (*in*)duct
EPI– on, over, among, outside   (*epi*)dermis, (*epi*)demic
EX– (*e–, ec–, ef–*) out of, from   (*ex*)pel, (*e*)lect, (*ec*)centric, (*ef*)face
EXTRA– (*extro–*) outside, beyond   (*extra*)mural, (*extro*)vert
HYPO– under   (*hypo*)dermic, (*hypo*)crite
INTER– among, between, within   (*inter*)fere, (*inter*)rupt
INTRO– (*intra–*) within   (*intro*)spection, (*intra*)mural
OB– (*oc–, of–, op–*) against, to, before, toward   (*ob*)ject, (*oc*)casion, (*of*)fer, (*op*)press
PER– through, by   (*per*)ceiver, (*per*)ennial
PERI– around, about   (*peri*)meter, (*peri*)odical
POST– after   (*post*)script, (*post*)erity
PRE– before   (*pre*)cedent, (*pre*)decessor
PRO– before in time or position   (*pro*)logue, (*pro*)bate
RETRO– back, backward   (*retro*)gress, (*retro*)spect
SE– aside, apart   (*se*)clude, (*se*)duce
SUB– (*suc–, suf–, sug–, sum–, sup–, sus–*) under, below   (*sub*)scribe, (*suc*)cumb, (*suf*)fer, (*sug*)gest, (*sum*)mon, (*sup*)pose, (*sus*)pect
SUPER– (*sur–*) above, over   (*super*)sede, (*super*)b, (*sur*)pass
TRANS– (*tra–, traf–, tres–*) across   (*trans*)port, (*tra*)vesty, (*traf*)fic, (*tres*)pass
ULTRA– beyond   (*ultra*)marine, (*ultra*)modern

Prefixes Showing Negation

A– (*an–*) without   (*an*)onymous, (*a*)theist
IN– (*ig–, im–, il–, ir–*) not   (*in*)accurate, (*ig*)nore, (*im*)pair, (*il*)legal, (*ir*)responsible

NON– not   (*non*)essential, (*non*)entity
UN– not   (*un*)tidy, (*un*)happy

■ 23b Greek Roots

ARCH	chief, rule	(*arch*)bishop an(*archy*), mon(*archy*)
AUTO	self	(*auto*)graph, (*auto*)mobile, (*auto*)matic
BIO	life	(*bio*)logy, (*bio*)graphy, (*bio*)chemistry
CAU(S)T	burn	(*caust*)ic, holo(*caust*), (*caut*)erize
CHRON(O)	time	(*chron*)icle, (*chron*)ic, (*chrono*)logy
COSM(O)	order, arrangement	(*cosm*)os, (*cosm*)ic, (*cosmo*)graphy
CRIT	judge, discern	(*crit*)ic, (*crit*)erion
DEM(O)	people	(*demo*)crat, (*demo*)cracy, (*dem*)agogue
DERM	skin	epi(*dermis*), (*derm*)a, pachy(*derm*), (*derm*)ophobe
DYN(A)(M)	power	(*dynam*)ic, (*dynam*)o, (*dyn*)asty
GRAPH	write	auto(*graph*), (*graph*)ic, geo(*graphy*)
HIPPO	horse	(*hippo*)potamus, (*hippo*)drome
HYDR(O)	water	(*hydr*)ant, (*hydr*)a, (*hydro*)gen
LOG(Y), LOGUE	saying, science	(*log*)ic, bio(*logy*), eu(*logy*), dia(*logue*)

MET(E)R	measure	thermo(*meter*), speedo(*meter*), (*metr*)ic
MICRO	small	(*micro*)be, (*micro*)scope, (*micro*)cosm
MOR(O)	fool	(*moro*)n, sopho(*more*)
NYM	name	ano(*nym*)ous, pseudo(*nym*)
PATH	experience, suffer	a(*path*)y, sym(*path*)y, (*path*)os
PED	child	(*ped*)agogue, (*ped*)ant, (*ped*)iatrician
PHIL	love	(*phil*)anthropy, (*phil*)osophy, (*phil*)ander
PHON(O)	sound	(*phono*)graph, (*phon*)etic, (*phono*)gram
PSYCH(O)	mind, soul	(*psycho*)logy, (*psych*)ic, (*Psych*)e
SOPH	wisdom	philo(*sopher*), (*soph*)ist, (*soph*)istication
THEO	God	(*theo*)logy, (*theo*)sophy, (*theo*)cratic
THERM	heat	(*therm*)ostat, (*therm*)ometer, (*therm*)os

■ 23c Latin Roots

AM	love	(*am*)ity, (*am*)orist, (*am*)orous
ANIM	breath, soul, spirit	(*anim*)al, (*anim*)ate, un(*anim*)ous
AQU(A)	water	(*aqu*)educt, (*aqua*)tic, (*aqua*)rium
AUD	hear	(*aud*)itor, (*aud*)ience, (*aud*)itorium
CAPIT	head	(*capit*)al, (*capit*)ate, (*capit*)alize
CAP(T), CEP(T), CIP(T)	take	(*cap*)tive, pre(*cept*), pre(*cip*)itate
CED, CESS	go, yield	ante(*ced*)ent, con(*cede*), ex(*cess*)ive
CENT	hundred	(*cent*)ury, (*cent*)urion, per(*cent*)age
CER(N), CRI(M,T), CRE(M,T)	separate, judge, choose	dis(*cern*), (*crim*)inal, dis(*crete*)
CRED	believe, trust	(*cred*)it, in(*cred*)ible, (*cred*)ulity
CLAR	clear, bright	(*clar*)ity, (*clar*)ify, de(*clar*)ation
CORD	heart	dis(*cord*), con(*cord*), (*cord*)ial
CORP(OR)	body, substance	(*corpor*)al, (*corp*)se, (*corp*)ulent
DOM(IN)	tame, subdue	(*domin*)ant, (*domin*)ate, (*domin*)ion
DON	give	(*don*)or, (*don*)ate
DORM	sleep	(*dorm*)ant, (*dorm*)itory, (*dorm*)ient
DUC	lead	con(*duc*)t, (*duc*)tile, aque(*duc*)t
FER	bear	in(*fer*)ence, (*fer*)tile, re(*fer*)
FORT	strong	(*fort*)ress, (*fort*)e, (*fort*)itude
FRAG, FRING, FRACT	break	(*frag*)ile, in(*fring*)e, (*fract*)ure
GEN	beget, origin	en(*gen*)der, con(*gen*)ital, (*gen*)eration
JAC(T), JEC(T)	cast	e(*jac*)ulate, pro(*ject*), e(*ject*)
LATE	carry	col(*late*), vacil(*late*), re(*late*)
MI(SS,T)	send	dis(*miss*), (*miss*)ionary, re(*mit*)
NOMIN, NOMEN	name	(*nomin*)ate, (*nomen*)clature
NOV	new	(*nov*)el, (*nov*)ice, in(*nov*)ation
PED	foot	(*ped*)al, centi(*pede*), (*ped*)estrian
PLEN, PLET	full	(*plen*)ty, (*plen*)itude, re(*plete*)
PORT	bear	(*port*)er, de(*port*), im(*port*)ance
POTENT	able, powerful	(*potent*), (*potent*)ial, (*potent*)ate
SECT	cut	dis(*sect*), in(*sect*), (*sect*)ion

■ 23d Suffixes

Noun Suffixes

1. *Suffixes Denoting an Agent*

–ANT (*–ent*) one who, that which	ten(*ant*), ag(*ent*)
–AR (*–er*) one who	schol(*ar*), farm(*er*)
–ARD (*–art*) one who (often deprecative)	cow(*ard*), bragg(*art*)
–EER one who	privat(*eer*), auction(*eer*)
–ESS a woman who	waitr(*ess*), seamstr(*ess*)
–IER (*–yer*) one who	cash(*ier*), law(*yer*)
–IST one who	novel(*ist*), Commun(*ist*)
–OR one who, that which	act(*or*), tract(*or*)
–STER one who, that which	young(*ster*), road(*ster*)

2. *Suffix Denoting the Receiver of an Action*

–EE one who is the object of some action	appoint(*ee*), divorc(*ee*)

3. *Suffixes Denoting Smallness or Diminutiveness*

–CULE (*–cle*)	mole(*cule*), ventri(*cle*)
–ETTE	din(*ette*), cigar(*ette*)
–LET	ring(*let*), brace(*let*)
–LING	duck(*ling*), prince(*ling*)

4. *Suffixes Denoting Place*

–ARY indicating location or repository	diction(*ary*), api(*ary*)
–ERY place or establishment	bak(*ery*), nunn(*ery*)
–ORY (*–arium*, *–orium*) place for, concerned with	dormit(*ory*), audit(*orium*)

5. *Suffixes Denoting Act, State, Quality, or Condition*

–ACY denoting quality, state	accur(*acy*), delic(*acy*)
–AL pertaining to action	refus(*al*), deni(*al*)
–ANCE (*–ancy*) denoting action or state	brilli(*ance*), buoy(*ancy*)
–ATION denoting result	migr(*ation*), el(*ation*)
–DOM denoting a general condition	wis(*dom*), bore(*dom*)
–ENCE (*–ency*) state, quality of	abstin(*ence*), consist(*ency*)
–ERY denoting quality, action	fool(*ery*), prud(*ery*)
–HOOD state, quality	knight(*hood*), false(*hood*)
–ICE condition or quality	serv(*ice*), just(*ice*)
–ION (*–sion*) state or condition	un(*ion*), ten(*sion*)
–ISM denoting action, state, or condition	bapt(*ism*), plagiar(*ism*)
–ITY (*–ety*) action, state, or condition	joll(*ity*), gai(*ety*)
–MENT action or state resulting from	punish(*ment*), frag(*ment*)
–NESS quality, state of	good(*ness*), prepared(*ness*)
–OR denoting action, state, or quality	hon(*or*), lab(*or*)

–TH pertaining to condition, state, or action	warm(*th*), steal(*th*)
–URE denoting action, result, or instrument	legislat(*ure*), pleas(*ure*)

Adjective Suffixes

–ABLE (*–ible, –ile*) capable of being	lov(*able*), ed(*ible*), contract(*ile*)
–AC relating to, like	elegi(*ac*), cardi(*ac*)
–ACIOUS inclined to	pugn(*acious*), aud(*acious*)
–AL pertaining to	radic(*al*), cordi(*al*)
–AN pertaining to	sylv(*an*), urb(*an*)
–ANT (*–ent*) inclined to	pleas(*ant*), converg(*ent*)
–AR pertaining to	sol(*ar*), regul(*ar*)
–ARY pertaining to	contr(*ary*), revolution(*ary*)
–ATIVE inclined to	demonstr(*ative*), talk(*ative*)
–FUL full of	joy(*ful*), pain(*ful*)
–IC (*–ical*) pertaining to	volcan(*ic*), angel(*ical*)
–ISH like, relating to, being	devil(*ish*), boy(*ish*)
–IVE inclined to, having the nature of	elus(*ive*), nat(*ive*)
–LESS without, unable to be	piti(*less*), resist(*less*)
–OSE full of	bellic(*ose*), mor(*ose*)
–OUS full of	pi(*ous*), fam(*ous*)
–ULENT (*–olent*) full of	fraud(*ulent*), vi(*olent*)

Verb Suffixes

The following verb suffixes usually mean "to make" (to become, to increase, etc.).

–ATE	toler(*ate*), vener(*ate*)
–EN	madd(*en*), wid(*en*)
–FY	magni(*fy*), beauti(*fy*)
–IZE (*–ise*)	colon(*ize*), exerc(*ise*)

Exercise 93   Word Analysis: Prefixes

Break the following English words into their parts, and give the literal meaning of each part as derived from the source. Consult the list of prefixes and roots given on the previous pages. Use your dictionary if you find a part not given in these lists. Be able to use each word in a sentence.

Word	Prefix (and literal meaning)	Root (and literal meaning)	Meaning of whole word
descend	*de-, from,*	*scandere, to*	*to come or go down*
	down	*climb*	
1. abstain			
2. antipathy			
3. circumvent			
4. concoct			
5. diadem			
6. disable			
7. eject			

Word	Prefix (and literal meaning)	Root (and literal meaning)	Meaning of whole word
8. enclose	_____	_____	_____
	_____	_____	_____
9. extend	_____	_____	_____
	_____	_____	_____
10. extravagant	_____	_____	_____
	_____	_____	_____
11. forebear	_____	_____	_____
	_____	_____	_____
12. incredible	_____	_____	_____
	_____	_____	_____
13. intercept	_____	_____	_____
	_____	_____	_____
14. mistake	_____	_____	_____
	_____	_____	_____
15. monologue	_____	_____	_____
	_____	_____	_____
16. nonchalant	_____	_____	_____
	_____	_____	_____
17. obstacle	_____	_____	_____
	_____	_____	_____

Word	Prefix (and literal meaning)	Root (and literal meaning)	Meaning of whole word
18. octagon	_____	_____	_____
	_____	_____	_____
19. period	_____	_____	_____
	_____	_____	_____
20. polygamy	_____	_____	_____
	_____	_____	_____
21. postpone	_____	_____	_____
	_____	_____	_____
22. retroactive	_____	_____	_____
	_____	_____	_____
23. semisweet	_____	_____	_____
	_____	_____	_____
24. subject	_____	_____	_____
	_____	_____	_____
25. superstition	_____	_____	_____
	_____	_____	_____
26. transgress	_____	_____	_____
	_____	_____	_____
27. tricycle	_____	_____	_____
	_____	_____	_____

Word	Prefix (and literal meaning)	Root (and literal meaning)	Meaning of whole word
28. ultrasonic	_____	_____	_____
	_____	_____	_____
29. unaware	_____	_____	_____
	_____	_____	_____
30. unilateral	_____	_____	_____
	_____	_____	_____

Exercise 94   Word Analysis: Suffixes

Break the following English words into their parts and give the literal meaning of
each part as derived from its source. Consult the lists of suffixes and roots given on
previous pages. Use your dictionary if you find a part not given in the lists. Be able
to use each word in a sentence.

Word	Root (and literal meaning)	Suffix (and literal meaning)	Meaning of Whole Word
Example: *creative*	*creare, to*	*-ive, inclined to, having the*	*having imagination*
	create	*nature of*	*and artistic ability*
1. active			
2. annual			
3. bookish			
4. bracelet			
5. capable			
6. defendant			
7. drunkard			

Word	Root (and literal meaning)	Suffix (and literal meaning)	Meaning of Whole Word
8. edible	_____	_____	_____
	_____	_____	_____
9. employee	_____	_____	_____
	_____	_____	_____
10. falsehood	_____	_____	_____
	_____	_____	_____
11. fusion	_____	_____	_____
	_____	_____	_____
12. gladness	_____	_____	_____
	_____	_____	_____
13. heroism	_____	_____	_____
	_____	_____	_____
14. historic	_____	_____	_____
	_____	_____	_____
15. joyous	_____	_____	_____
	_____	_____	_____
16. kingdom	_____	_____	_____
	_____	_____	_____

Word	Root (and literal meaning)	Suffix (and literal meaning)	Meaning of Whole Word
17. lawyer	_____	_____	_____
	_____	_____	_____
18. lengthen	_____	_____	_____
	_____	_____	_____
19. malice	_____	_____	_____
	_____	_____	_____
20. maniac	_____	_____	_____
	_____	_____	_____
21. molecule	_____	_____	_____
	_____	_____	_____
22. painless	_____	_____	_____
	_____	_____	_____
23. penalize	_____	_____	_____
	_____	_____	_____
24. pestilent	_____	_____	_____
	_____	_____	_____
25. petrify	_____	_____	_____
	_____	_____	_____
26. quality	_____	_____	_____
	_____	_____	_____

Word	Root (and literal meaning)	Suffix (and literal meaning)	Meaning of Whole Word
27. sailor	_____	_____	_____
	_____	_____	_____
28. satisfy	_____	_____	_____
	_____	_____	_____
29. solitary	_____	_____	_____
	_____	_____	_____
30. youngster	_____	_____	_____
	_____	_____	_____

Exercise 95 | Word Analysis: Roots

For each root listed below write the meaning and at least three words containing the root. Do not use the same word with two roots. If the root given is not among the roots listed on the previous pages, look it up in your dictionary, which is also the best source for finding the words you need. Remember, however, that some words containing these roots will have prefixes.

Root	Meaning	Words Containing Root
facere	*to make, to do*	*facility, faculty, factory*
1. amare		
2. bio		
3. chron(o)		
4. craeft		
5. duc, duct		
6. fort		
7. gram, graph		
8. hemo		
9. mit, miss		
10. nym		
11. ortho		
12. path		
13. pend, pens		
14. plen, plet		
15. potent		
16. scrib, script		
17. spect		
18. stare, stat		
19. tele		
20. tort, tors		

Exercise 96   Vocabulary: Prefixes and Suffixes

A. Underline the prefix in each of the following words, give its meaning, and use the word in a sentence so as to show the meaning of the prefix.

Word	Meaning of Prefix	Sentence
<u>contra</u>dict	opposite, against	Jack contradicted me twice while I was telling what happened last night.
1. ambivalent		
2. congenial		
3. dismay		
4. enthrall		
5. excel		
6. intervene		
7. peripheral		
8. precede		
9. submarine		
10. transfer		

B. In the following list of words underline each suffix, give its meaning, and use the word in a sentence.

	Meaning of Suffix	Sentence
wis<u>dom</u>	general condition	I hope that Frank will acquire wisdom as he grows older.
1. baker		
2. cashier		
3. cooperative		
4. diplomacy		
5. jaundice		
6. laboratory		
7. library		
8. merchant		
9. merriment		
10. motherhood		

Exercise 97   Vocabulary: Greek and Latin Roots

A. Use the derivatives of *cred,* meaning "believe" or "trust," necessary to complete the following statements. (In this and the following exercises remember that these roots may be found in words containing prefixes. The lists of prefixes in Chapter 23 may suggest certain words to you, as in the word *diagram,* with the prefix *dia-,* meaning "across," and *gram,* the root, meaning "writing.")

1. If one's account of an incident is _____, then it is taken to be believable or reliable.

2. A brief statement of one's religious belief is called his _____.

3. A person's _____ entitle him to trust and confidence.

4. A card establishing a person's privilege to charge bills at designated places of business is known as a _____ card.

5. One who tends to believe too readily or who is easily convinced is said to be _____.

B. Use the derivatives of *extra,* meaning "outside, outside the scope of, beyond," necessary to complete the following statements.

1. Anything not according to the usual custom or regular plan, or in some way very unusual, may be described as _____.

2. The process called _____ takes place when a government turns over an alleged criminal or fugitive to the jurisdiction of another country or state.

3. Going beyond reasonable limits in conduct, speech, or the spending of money is the distinguishing quality of _____.

4. An _____ is a person whose interest is more in his environment and in other people than in himself.

5. One whose perception seems to occur apart from, or in addition to, the normal function of the senses is said to have _____ perception.

C. Use the derivatives of *met(e)r,* meaning "measure," necessary to complete the following statements.

1. Musicians frequently use a clockwork device that beats time at a predetermined rate to enable them to maintain a regular tempo; this device is a

   _____.

2. A unit of length or distance, equal to one thousand meters, or about five-eighths of a mile, is a _____.

3. In an automobile, the _____ is the instrument used for measuring the distance traveled.

4. When one allots, distributes, or apportions something, he is said to _____ it out.

5. A decimal system of weights and measures in which the gram, the meter, and the liter are the basic units of weight, length, and capacity is called the _____ system.

D. Use the derivatives of *nov,* meaning "new," necessary to complete the following statements.

1. In astronomy, a type of variable star that suddenly increases in brightness and intensity, later decreasing slowly in brightness, is known as a

   _____.

2. The word _____ is used to designate a person who is new to a particular occupation or activity.

3. _____ is an adjective used to describe something new, fresh, and unusual.

4. A _____ is an author who writes long fictional prose narratives with complex plots about human beings and their experiences.

5. Something representing newness, freshness, change, or innovation is a

   _____.

Spelling

Spelling is an important aspect of written communication. Instructors seldom have the opportunity, however, to spend adequate classroom time on the subject. The responsibility for the mastery of spelling, therefore, rests almost solely on the individual student.

Here are a few practical suggestions on how to approach the problem of spelling:

1. Always use the dictionary when you are in doubt about the spelling of a word.

2. If there is a rule applicable to the type of words that you misspell, learn that rule.

3. Employ any "tricks" that might assist you in remembering the spelling of particular words giving you trouble. If, for example, you confuse the meaning and hence the spelling of *statue* and *stature*, remember that the longer word refers to bodily "longness." Certain troublesome words can be spelled correctly if you will remember their prefixes (as in *dis/appoint*) or their suffixes (as in *cool/ly*). Also, it might help you to remember that there are only three *-ceed* words: *exceed, proceed,* and *succeed.*

4. Keep a list of the words that you misspell. In writing down these words, observe their syllabication and any peculiarities of construction. Try to "see" — that is, to have a mental picture of — these words.

5. Practice the correct pronunciation of troublesome words. Misspelling is often the result of mispronunciation.

Of the many rules governing spelling, four are particularly useful since they are widely applicable. Study these four rules carefully.

■ 24a Final e

Drop the final *e* before a suffix begnning with a vowel (*-ing, -ous,* etc.) but retain the final *e* before a suffix beginning with a consonant (*-ment, -ly,* etc.):

Final *e* dropped: come + ing = coming
                      fame + ous = famous
                      love + able = lovable
                      guide + ance = guidance

Final *e* retained: move + ment = movement
                      fate + ful = fateful
                      sole + ly = solely

Exceptions: Acknowledge, acknowledgment; abridge, abridgment; judge, judgment; dye, dyeing; singe, singeing; hoe, hoeing; mile, mileage; due, duly; awe, awful; whole, wholly. The final **e** is retained after **c** or **g** when the suffix begins with **a** or **o**: peace, peaceable; courage, courageous.

■ 24b Final Consonant

Double a final consonant before a suffix beginning with a vowel if (1) the word is of one syllable or is accented on the last syllable and (2) the final consonant is preceded by a single vowel:

Word of one syllable: stop + ed = stopped

Word in which the accent falls on the last syllable: occur + ence = occurrence

Word in which the accent does not fall on the last syllable: differ + ence = difference

■ 24c *ei* and *ie*

When **ei** and **ie** have the long **ee** sound (as in *keep*), use **i** before **e** except after **c**. (The word *lice* will aid you in remembering this rule; **i** follows **l** and all other consonants except **c**, while **e** follows **c**.)

ie	*ei* (after *c*)
chief	ceiling
field	receive
niece	deceive
siege	conceit

Exceptions *(grouped to form a sentence):*   Neither financier seized either species of weird leisure.

■ 24d Final y

In words ending in *y* preceded by a consonant, change the *y* to *i* before any suffix except one beginning with *i.*

Suffix beginning with a letter other than *i*:

fly + es = flies
ally + es = allies
easy + ly = easily
mercy + ful = merciful
study + ous = studious

Suffix beginning with *i*:

fly + ing = flying
study + ing = studying

■ 24e Spelling List

The following list is made up of approximately 480 frequently misspelled words. Since these are commonly used words, you should learn to spell all of them after you have mastered the words on your individual list.

absence	appreciate	camouflage
academic	appropriate	candidate
accelerate	arctic	captain
accept	argument	carburetor
accessible	arithmetic	carriage
accidentally	around	category
accommodate	arrangement	cavalry
accumulate	ascend	ceiling
accustomed	assassin	cemetery
acknowledge	association	certain
acknowledgment	athletics	changeable
acquaintance	attendance	characteristic
acquire	attractive	chauffeur
across	audience	choose
address	autumn	chosen
adolescent	auxiliary	clothes
advantage	awkward	colloquial
aggravate	bankruptcy	colonel
allege	barbarous	column
all right	becoming	coming
altogether	beginning	commission
always	believe	committee
amateur	beneficial	comparative
among	benefited	compel
amount	brilliant	compelled
analysis	Britain	competent
angel	broccoli	competition
anonymous	buoyant	complement
anxiety	bureau	completely
apology	business	compliment
apparatus	cafeteria	compulsory
apparent	caffeine	confident
appearance	calendar	congratulate

connoisseur
conqueror
conscience
conscientious
conscious
contemptible
continuous
controversy
convenient
coolly
council
counsel
courteous
criticism
curiosity
curriculum
dealt
deceit
decide
defendant
definite
dependent
descend
descent
describe
description
desert
desirable
despair
desperate
dessert
dictionary
dietitian (dietician)
difference
dilapidated
dining
diphtheria
disappear
disappoint
disastrous
discipline
discussion
disease
dissatisfied
dissipate
distribute
divine
division
dormitories
drudgery

dual
duchess
duel
dyeing
dying
ecstasy
efficiency
eighth
eligible
eliminate
embarrassed
eminent
emphasize
enthusiastic
environment
equipped
equivalent
erroneous
especially
exaggerate
excellent
except
exercise
exhaust
exhilaration
existence
exorbitant
expel
expelled
experience
explanation
extraordinary
familiar
fascinate
February
finally
financial
financier
flier
foregoing
forehead
foreign
foreword
forfeit
forgo
formally
formerly
forth
forty
fourth

fraternity
friend
fulfill
fundamental
furniture
futile
gauge
generally
genius
government
grammar
granddaughter
grandeur
grievance
guarantee
guerrilla
handkerchief
harass
having
height
hindrance
hitchhike
hoping
humorous
hygiene
hypocrisy
illusion
imaginary
imitation
immediately
incidentally
independenc
indispensable
inevitable
infinite
influential
ingenious
innocence
instance
instant
integrity
intellectual
intelligence
intentionally
interested
irrelevant
irresistible
its
it's
judgment

kindergarten
knowledge
laboratory
led
legitimate
leisure
library
likable
literature
livelihood
loose
lose
lovable
magazine
maintain
maintenance
maneuver
manual
manufacture
marriage
mathematics
meant
medicine
mediocre
miniature
mirror
mischievous
misspell
momentous
monotonous
morale
mortgage
murmur
muscle
mysterious
naive
naturally
necessary
nevertheless
nickel
niece
ninety
ninth
noticeable
notoriety
nowadays
nucleus
obedience
obstacle
occasion

occasionally
occurrence
o'clock
off
omission
omitted
operate
opinion
opportunity
optimism
organization
original
outrageous
overrun
paid
pamphlet
parallel
paralysis
paralyzed
parliament
particularly
partner
passed
past
pastime
perform
permanent
permissible
perseverance
persistent
personal
personnel
perspiration
persuade
physically
physician
picnicking
piece
pleasant
pneumonia
politician
politics
politicking
possession
possible
practically
precede
precedence
preference
preferred

prejudice
preparation
prevalent
principal
principle
privilege
probably
procedure
proceed
professor
prominent
pronunciation
propaganda
psychology
publicly
purchase
pursue
quantity
quarter
questionnaire
quiet
quite
quiz
quizzes
realize
really
recognize
recommend
referred
region
reign
rein
relevant
religious
remembrance
repetition
representative
resistance
respectfully
respectively
restaurant
rhetoric
rheumatism
rhythm
ridiculous
sacrifice
sacrilegious
salable
salary
sandwich

schedule
science
scissors
secretary
seize
sense
sentence
separate
sergeant
severely
sheriff
shining
shriek
siege
significant
silhouette
similar
sincerely
skiing
sophomore
source
speak
specimen
speech
stationary
stationery
statue
stature
statute

strength
strenuous
stretch
studying
superintendent
supersede
surprise
susceptible
syllable
symmetry
temperament
temperature
tendency
their
thorough
too
tournament
tragedy
transferred
tremendous
truly
Tuesday
twelfth
tying
tyranny
unanimous
undoubtedly
universally
unnecessary

until
unusual
usable
using
usually
vaccine
vacuum
valuable
vegetable
vengeance
vigilance
vigorous
village
villain
waive
wave
weather
Wednesday
weird
whether
wholly
who's
whose
wield
women
writing
written
yacht
yield

Exercise 98 Spelling

A. Combine the specified suffix with each of the following words, and write the correct form in the blank space.

Example: *drop + ed*   _____*dropped*_____

1. allot + ing   _____
2. apology + s   _____
3. benefit + ed   _____
4. bury + al   _____
5. confer + ed   _____
6. confident + ce   _____
7. defense + able   _____
8. desire + ous   _____
9. duty + ful   _____
10. dye + ing   _____
11. envy + ous   _____
12. eventual + ly   _____
13. forbid + en   _____
14. frequent + cy   _____
15. grieve + ance   _____
16. happy + ly   _____
17. pop + ed   _____
18. judge + ment   _____
19. lazy + ness   _____
20. lie + ing   _____
21. luster + ous   _____
22. marry + age   _____
23. merry + ment   _____
24. mile + age   _____

25. note + able   _____

26. notice + able   _____

27. pronounce + ation   _____

28. refer + al   _____

29. true + ly   _____

30. wise + dom   _____

B. Supply either *ei* or *ie* in each of the following words. Then write the correct form in the space provided.

Example: th_ei_r   ____*their*____

1. br__f   _____   11. l__sure   _____

2. c__ling   _____   12. l__utenant   _____

3. dec__t   _____   13. n__ther   _____

4. f__gn   _____   14. n__ce   _____

5. f__rce   _____   15. p__rce   _____

6. fr__ght   _____   16. rec__pt   _____

7. fr__nd   _____   17. rel__ve   _____

8. gr__ve   _____   18. s__ze   _____

9. h__fer   _____   19. s__ve   _____

10. h__ress   _____   20. w__rd   _____

Name _____   Score _____

Exercise 99   Spelling

If there is a misspelled word in any line of five words given below, underline it and write it correctly in the space at the right. If all five words are correctly spelled, write C in the blank.

Example: accumolate, *benefited, athletics, candidate, religious*   _***accumulate***_

1. lovable, mortgage, peice, politician, rhythm   _____

2. quarter, really, reconize, persuade, quite   _____

3. region, necessary, mirrow, pleasant, forty   _____

4. hygiene, handkerchief, disatisfied, pursue, pastime   _____

5. original, rhetoric, sacreligious, likable, interested _____

6. overrun, mischievous, privilege, parlament, height   _____

7. sandwich, precede, hinderance, exhaust, omission   _____

8. restaraunt, publicly, judgment, existence, forfeit   _____

9. permissible, reign, harrass, excellent, definite   _____

10. assassin, referred, monotonous, genius, brilliant   _____

11. ascend, bankruptcy, clothes, calander, choose   _____

12. camouflage, compell, address, repetition, conscious _____

13. category, quantity, livelihood, gauge, nickle   _____

14. beginning, compulsory, alledge, twelfth, until   _____

15. supersede, yacht, seperate, tendency, broccoli   _____

16. mathmatics, around, manual, relevant, probably   _____

17. auxiliary, column, comming, whether, usable   _____

18. surprise, temprature, yield, defendant, foreign   _____

19. muscle, perform, infinite, nineth, flier   _____

20. fascinate, nucleus, exhileration, dining, ecstasy   _____

Exercise 100 Spelling

Underline any word which is misspelled in the following sentences. Then write it correctly in the space at the right. If a sentence contains no misspelled word, write C in the blank. (There is more than one misspelled word in some of the sentences.)

Example: Kim said that he was <u>throughly</u> pleased at the outcome of his project for his physics class.

_____*thoroughly*_____

1. Virginia told us that her starting salery will be quite adequate.

_____

2. My great-aunt, who is ninty-four years old, has a keen mind and a likable personality.

_____

3. Father says that he is a fortunate man: he never has personel problems in his office.

_____

4. It was hard to have to forfiet the game, but we had no choice when the whole team came down with mumps.

_____

5. June showed great perserverance when she was learning to dive; many children would have given up in dispair.

_____

6. It appears that almost everyone has finally become concerned about polluting the enviroment.

_____

7. Some people, however, say that they care about pollution but are guilty of hypocricy in their actions.

_____

8. Judy's ancestors came from Great Britian, but I believe that the family has been in this country for three generations.

_____

9. Let me be the first to congradulate you on your exellent victory in the golf tournament, Jack.

_____

10. Jimmy always whistled loudly when he walked by the cemetary after dark.   _____

11. Well, I must say that these acommodations are splendid; I could grow accustomed to this luxury quite easily.   _____

12. Tina felt utterly desserted during that terrifying night; she began to shreik uncontrollably.   _____

13. This is the most lovable child I have ever known, but being his uncle, I am predjudiced.   _____

14. My parents, whose home is now rather dilapidated, have lived there for fourty years.   _____

15. The place should really be restored to it's former grandure, but the family is not dissatisfied with it as it is.   _____

16. The surprise party for Grace was a momentous ocassion, with paper hats, streamers, a huge birthday cake, and an outrageously funny banner draped accross the wall.   _____

17. The principal involved here is not money, Irene, but ethical behavior.   _____

18. Although the dense fog had finally disippated, it would have been disasterous for us to begin our trip so late in the afternoon.   _____

19. The fluffy white minature poodle siezed the rubber bone in his teeth and began gnawing it vigorously.   _____

20. Everyone in the class greatly admires Proffesor Wright; it has been a priviledge to learn about American literature from him.   _____

21. Her conscience was bothering her because she had not managed to fullfil the promise she had made to return the valuable necklace.   _____

22. The dutchess looked devine in her satin evening gown; her grandaughter, however, looked somewhat dowdy.   _____

23. Everyone was exausted after the five-mile hike, and
    no one was interested in attending the play for
    which we had reservations.   _____

24. Last Febuary I ordered some spring clothes from a
    catalog, and now that it is autumn and they still
    have not come, I believe that I will cancel the
    order.   _____

25. Harry shows no enthusiasm for atheletics, but his
    sister Beth is wholly dedicated to both tennis and
    basketball.   _____

Paragraph Tests **Paragraph Test 1**

Each of the following paragraphs contains twenty errors in grammar, punctuation, mechanics, diction, or spelling. Mark each error that you find with a check mark (√) as close to the error as possible or bracket any groups of words that need correction. Then, with these marks as guides, rewrite the paragraphs, eliminating all errors. If you find and correct all errors, your score for the paragraph will be *100*. Any error that you fail to correct counts off five points. If, in rewriting a paragraph, you eliminate existing errors but make others, each of these will count off five points.

Our cottage in the Appalachian Mountains is in a beautiful, secluded spot, it is one of a group of houses that many georgia people use as summer, vacation homes. Our first summer there we were on the lookout for black bears, because friends had told us they had been seen in our area. The bears don't look for trouble but are real ferocious when you arouse them, especially if a cub is with it's mother or father. We thought it would be fantastic to see one from a distance, but we weren't too enthused at the thought of meeting one face to face. Anyways, one morning before daylight we heard a loud noise outside the house where the kitchen stoop is at. We tried to use a flashlight to see whom or what was out there, but we should of known that plan wouldn't work. Then we heard a strange snorting sound and another noise like something being whacked with a two-by-four. We turned on the outside lights and saw a huge black bear, wrestling with our garbage can and eating its contents. While standing in the house watching the bear, a little gray kitten came and sat on a rock wall near the house and didn't hardly seem interested in what was going on. Feeling venturesome, I tried for a better view by going into the kitchen. Turning the light on and looking out the screen door, I saw the bear standing on his hind legs and peering into the room with his face about six inches from mine. He was around six feet tall and stood with his forepaws clawing at the screen. I almost jumped ten feet in the air and rushed hurriedly leaving the kitchen. I had seen enough of that bear. The holes from his claws continue to remain in our screen kitchen door.

Paragraph Test 2

One of my ancestors was the French Huguenot, Pierre Henri Morel. I don't know if it is true, but if so, the story of his departure from France and arrival in north America indicate that he was a very unique fellow. My Great-grandmother claims that the facts are these: Pierre Henri Morel was a wealthy eighteenth-century French landowner who wanted to leave his native country because he was a Protestant and was being persecuted for religious reasons. He sold all his property and purchased a ship, he then bought hundreds of pairs of leather shoes, filled his ship with them and sailed for America. After enduring a stormy passage across the Atlantic, Indians met him on the South Carolina coast. The Indians were friendly, which made Morel's idea appear to be as good if not better than he had thought it would be. His plan was to trade the shipload of shoes to the Indians for land. The Indians accepted the offer real quick, and Morel sure was relieved. He only settled in South Carolina for a short time, later moving down the coast to Savannah. There Morel married the daughter of another French Huguenot emigrant, the owner of Ossabaw Island, one of Georgias Golden Isles. Ossabaw, which was the location of Buckhead Plantation, remained in the Morel family until after the Civil War, when it was sold on the steps of the Chatham County Courthouse for the $128 in taxes that the impoverished family could not pay. It is now the property of the State of Georgia, but if a private individual owned it today, they probably would still be unable to pay the taxes.

Paragraph Test 3

When I was a boy of about ten I had two fox terriers from the same litter. Jock and Jabbo were almost identical in every way, including their strong dislike for one another. They followed me everyplace I went except school, my Mother had to lock them in the house to keep them from going to school. The antagonism among them was caused by sibling rivalry, I expect, because they were at their worst when I or members of my family were nearby. They snarled at each other, each one lunging and baring their teeth in a threatening way. One day, when I was playing ball with my friends across the street, Jock and Jabbo were aggravating us by being constantly underfoot. I shooed them away, making them mad—not with me, but with each other. Finally, the fight began in earnest, it was so fierce that all of we boys stopped playing ball to watch the battle. Jock had Jabbo by the throat and would not let go, and Jabbo had one of Jack's legs in his jaws. Both were uttering vicious savage growls, and after fighting for ten minutes or more, we were sure that neither of them were going to give up. We were all screaming, and the reason I was so frightened was because I thought that one of them would be killed. My father tried to pull them apart with a big stick but was unsuccessful. We were at our wits end when a neighbor came plodding across the street, carrying a large bucket. Without saying a word the woman dumped water from the bucket onto the dogs, then she turned silently and walked away. Instantly, each dog released his death grip, and the crisis was over. It was an adventure that us and the neighbors are still discussing to this day.

Paragraph Test 4

In the late fifties Louis Armstrong and his band, sponsered by a fraternity, played for a big dance on our campus. There were six topflight musicians in the group, everyone on campus had anticipated them coming for weeks in advance. Besides Louis Armstrong himself, the band included Barney Bigard on clarinet, Trummy Young on trombone, and the incomparable Teddy Wilson at the piano. I am not sure, but I believe that the other two were Sid Catlett on drums and John Simmons playing bass. Their style was a combination of traditional New Orleans jazz and Dixieland, blended with selections from the best of the Swing Era. After dancing a few numbers, it was obvious that this music was meant more for listening and watching the band than dancing. "Satchmo" was fascinating, when he first came onto the stage, he placed a large stack of neatly folded white handkerchiefs on top of the piano. After each number he wiped his face and brow with one of the handkerchiefs, discarding them later for a fresh one. The raspy sweetness of his trumpet solos were breathtaking, and I'll never forget his "Yellow Dog Blues", "Nobody Knows You When You're Down and Out," and "A Good Man Is Hard to Find." Barney Bigard another New Orleans native, had formally played with Duke Ellington, and was co-composer with Ellington of the famous song, *Mood Indigo.* His best solos that night were "Vine Street Blues" and "Steps Steps Up". Teddy Wilson at the piano defied description playing with fluid elegant improvisation that was always fresh and never repettitive. The other three were the skillful musicians to be expected of a Louis Armstrong band, which provided my friends and I with an unforgettable evening.

Paragraph Test 5

During the second half of the 20th century, the fabric of the american family changed dramaticly, primarily because of World War II and the demands, that the war made on women. From necessity women entered the work force in large numbers to fill jobs previously performed by men, women became the backbone of the countries war effort at home. Volunteers was needed as never before. They rolled bandages, conducted blood drives, and they worked in canteens. "Rosie the Riveter", and her fellow workers seemed perfectly at home on the assembly line. Women joined the armed services as WAVES, SPARS, and WACS—the female counterparts of the men who served in the Navy, Coast Guard, and the Army. Although service women were not permitted to bare arms or fight; they were able to perform many duties needed by the military and release men for combat. Meanwhile, women were being admitted to graduate and professional schools in greater numbers than ever before. The phrase 'working mother' became commonplace and with time, raised expectations often required not one but 2 incomes. Furthermore, many women found that they enjoyed this "brave new world" and were reluctant to relinquish their new found independence or to sacrifice stimulating careers. Of course there were women who had worked outside the home prior to 1941. However, from a sense of patriotism and duty, women in great numbers left their homes and joined the nations work force to be part of the war effort: the American family would never hardly be quite the same again.

Paragraph Test 6

Accept for the indians, the earliest backpackers in America were frontiersmen, who roamed the wilderness either looking for necessities such as food and water, or for sources of wealth such as fur and gold. For them backpacking was a way of survival or a means of achieving what one day would be called the "American Dream". Today, however many people enjoy backpacking as a recreational activity. Shouldering a pack and leaving behind the world of telephone, television and traffic promises an exhilarating experience. Testing one's stamina and skills are challenging and recapturing a sense of ones place in the natural world can be rewarding. Moreover, backpacking is an activity that can last any length of time, and can be enjoyed alone or with friends. Then too, a backpacking trip may be organized within a day or two. The backpacker and his friends has only to decide on there destination and then organize the all important kit, who's contents they must depend on throughout their trip. A map, a compass, a flashlight, along with first aid equipment, food and extra clothing can be rounded up without much difficulty. Once the backpackers' have left word of their whereabouts in a note on the refrigerator door or in a message on an answering machine, they can look forward to an adventure that will lift the spirit and nourish the soul. Their outing will enable them to return in a short time to the age of technology with the courage and independance of Natty Bumppo who did indeed belong to the age of the frontier.

Paragraph Test 7

If I was writing a history of my family, some of the darkest moments recorded would be those surrounding christmas trees. You would certainly think otherwise, nevertheless, selecting and putting up our trees has always been fraught with peril. For instance, one afternoon dangerously close to Christmas Eve, my Mother bought what she perceived to be a bargain: a glorious tree that was so full and tall that we could hardly get it into the house. Once we did my father immediately realized that we would have to hire a carpenter to build a stand for it. Another December, perhaps the very next one, we bought a tree earlier than we ever had before. We were pleased with its shape, and delighted that its size was manageable. We easily placed it in a stand, decorated it from top to bottom and then smugly sat back to bask in its soft light. Two or three days passed, and the truth could not be hidden: we had bought a tree cut so long ago that it was now shedding it's needles without provocation. Their was nothing to do but to undecorate it, take it down, and begin tree-shopping again. Our most recent Christmas tree offered still another challenge. When we brought it home, once again it seemed larger than it had in the great outdoors. To complicate matters, we had bought a new stand, one who's nuts and bolts worked more mysterious than our old stand. Our only recourse was to persuade two young neighbors to stop dunking basketballs and to help us get the tree into the house and sit it securely in the stand. Unfortunately, no one noticed the mud on our helpers sneakers, so only after removing several reddish, brown spots from the carpet were we able to discuss the question of where the lights and ornaments were stored. Perhaps those who cut their own trees have tails to tell more harrowing than these. I do'nt care to hear them, for my family's experiences, of which these are but three, are enough to tempt me to make the following suggestion: "Let's forget the tree next Christmas; let's simply drape a garland over the mirror in the hall and hang a wreath on the front door''.

Paragraph Test 8

In 1816, Thomas Jefferson wrote a letter in which he made the following observation "If a nation expects to be ignorant and free, in a state of civilization, it expects what never was and never will be". Therein lays one of the great arguments in support of public education. Such an education can offer all persons not only the opportunity to develop their potential as individuals, but also to become informed citizens capable of participating and contributing to their own governance. Only an informed electorate can vote responsibly for its leaders and ultimately its laws thus assuring its freedom. Being informed about candidates for political office, requires more then turning a dial, watching a political ad now and then or listening to a new's commentator explain and interpret what candidates have done or said. Being informed requires knowledge of the nations political history as well as it's economic and social history. How does the "checks and balances" of government work? What is "free enterprise?" What exactly are the "unalienable rights"? Being informed also requires an awareness of the political, economic, and social forces presently at work in the nation and throughout the world. What should be this nation's response to the abuse of human rights? How can a favorable balance of trade be achieved? How can we avoid playing havoc with the world's enviroment? It only is within such a broad context that voters can examine candidates past records and analyze their present views. The task of becoming a knowledgeable electorate was not an easy one in the eighteenth century; it is undoubtedly even more difficult in this last decade of the Twentieth Century. Isolation may have been a barrier in Jefferson's world, complexity magnifies the problem in this one. Nonetheless, the truth remains that every generation that would be free must find a way to escape the bonds of ignorance.

Sentence-Combining Exercise 1

A. Combine the following pairs of sentences, changing one of the two to a participial phrase. Punctuate each newly formed sentence correctly.

Example: I have finished studying for my test. Now I am going for a walk around the block.

Having finished studying for my test, I am now going for a walk around the block.

1. I drove slowly on the slippery pavement. I wanted to avoid a sudden skid.

2. Marian had always been an *A* student in history. She was shocked to find a *C* on her test paper.

3. I looked everywhere for my glasses. I was disgusted over the wasted time.

4. I walked two miles to the Millers' house. I grew so weary that I decided to take the bus home.

5. Hubert's term paper lay on the desk. He looked at it with pride.

6. Eric looked out the window. His pet rabbit was in the middle of the busy thoroughfare.

7. Mrs. Lovelace is noted for her lemon chiffon pie. She has made ten pies for the church bazaar.

8. I am trying my best to lose weight. I eat only green salads for lunch every day.

9. Harry nodded in approval. He was pleased with his daughter's tennis backhand.

10. Jack tried to talk above the noise of the children's quarrel. He was greatly frustrated.

B. Combine the following pairs of sentences, changing one of the two to a gerund phrase. Punctuate each newly formed sentence correctly.

Example: We thought that we could easily find a new house. It was much harder than we had thought.

Finding a new house was much harder than we had thought it would be.

1. Jamie is an only child. He is sometimes inconsiderate of other children.

2. Rosalie has been lying on the beach all afternoon. She will be badly sunburned.

3. Dot knows that she can have a job in her uncle's office. This knowledge makes her feel secure about the future.

4. It is necessary that we work together on this project. Its success depends on that.

5. I walked down the Champs Élysées. That walk was my idea of heaven.

6. Dr. Paine decided to retire at the end of the academic year. The decision was a difficult one.

7. Fred thought that he must get into the locked house. There lay his only chance.

8. I have to set my alarm clock thirty minutes ahead. This practice is the solution to my problem of poor class attendance.

9. David owns a fast-food restaurant. He says that he is sick of hamburgers.

10. Julia and Suzy are close friends. They have many common interests.

Sentence-Combining Exercise 2

A. Combine the following pairs of sentences, changing one of the two to an appositive phrase. Punctuate each newly formed sentence correctly.

Example: Mr. Harris caught a dozen fish yesterday. He is a good fisherman.

Mr. Harris, a good fisherman, caught a dozen fish yesterday.

1. Grace is my favorite neighbor. She baked me a wonderful chocolate cake for my birthday.

2. *Shake Hands Forever* is a mystery novel by Ruth Rendell. It has recently been dramatized for television.

3. I can't believe that Joan got up at five this morning. She is usually quite a sleepyhead.

4. My 1969 car is a real "clunker." It got us from Natchez to Mobile without trouble, however.

5. Our dessert tonight was a spectacular one. It was crêpes suzette.

6. Robbie was a meek-looking, silent boy. He shocked everyone when he suddenly kicked his sister in the shins.

7. My family has been happy to have Guillaume as a guest in our home this year. He is an exchange student from France.

8. Terry Lawrence has been our team's third baseman for the past two seasons. The manager has moved him to first base.

9. The author of this book was a master of suspense. His name is Sir Arthur Conan Doyle.

10. Madame Marcelle is a native of France. She designs chic dresses for a famous fashion house.

B. Combine the following pairs of sentences, changing one of the two to an absolute phrase. Punctuate each newly formed sentence correctly.

Example: The old movie finally ended with the expected kiss. We went sleepily upstairs to bed.

The old movie having finally ended with the expected kiss, we went sleepily upstairs to bed.

1. Alice had a headache. I could not ask her to baby-sit with Peter.

2. My automobile battery went dead this morning. I had to walk to a service station for help.

3. The road was six inches deep in water. Many drivers were afraid to continue their journeys.

4. Vicki's clothes were drenched. She shivered in the cold night air.

5. The mountain cabin had been built with two bedrooms. Floyd and Jodie often invited another couple up for a weekend.

6. The heavy snow had fallen sometime during the night. We were amazed when we awoke to a white world the next morning.

7. The ninety-mile-an-hour wind had vented its fury on the coastal houses. The inhabitants feared that they had lost everything in the storm.

8. My phone conversation with Aunt Henrietta had lasted forty-five minutes. My ears and my patience were growing weary.

9. The trained porpoise had performed all its tricks perfectly. The spectators called delightedly for an encore.

10. Our telephone has been out of order since yesterday. I failed to receive Mr. Schneider's important message until now.

Sentence-Combining Exercise 3

A. Combine the following pairs of sentences, making one of the two an adverbial clause. Be careful to avoid upside-down subordination in your formulation of the new sentence. Punctuate each new sentence correctly.

Example: Mary Sue had been thinking all day about the beautiful blue sofa. She drove to the furniture store to look at it again.

After Mary Sue had thought all day about the beautiful blue sofa, she drove to the furniture store to look at it again.

1. My brother runs with speed and stamina. His lack of coordination prevents his being a star at track.

2. Jane, are you going to Marineland with us tomorrow? Be ready by nine-thirty.

3. We must decide how many to invite to the wedding. That decision must be made before any other.

4. I worked late on Friday afternoon. I wanted to have Saturday free for the swimming party.

5. Jimmy and Gene walked through winding city streets. They had never ventured to this area before.

405

6. Fernanda is angry with Dexter. He was an hour late picking her up for the Little Theater production of *Cats*.

7. Mother's angel food cake is delicious. Mrs. Carson's cake is inferior to Mother's.

B. Combine the following pairs of sentences, making one of the two a noun clause. Punctuate each newly formed sentence correctly.

Example: To make an *A* in this course is possible, Karen. You can achieve that goal by studying consistently.

That you can make an A *in this course is possible, Karen, by studying consistently.*

1. To be a surgeon is his ultimate goal. I hope for his success.

2. My decision is to wait until tomorrow to call again. Then we can try to phone Miriam at her office.

3. Why did you scowl at Roger this morning at breakfast? I want to know the reason.

4. The girl was adamant. She would not give her reason for having stolen the loaf of bread.

5. Peggy's manner indicated her lack of interest in me. She clearly showed her boredom.

6. Rufus is hopeless with a computer. He does not understand its method of operation.

7. I am in doubt about the weather. It may rain, or it may snow.

C. Combine the following pairs of sentences, making one of the two an adjective clause. Punctuate each newly formed sentence correctly.

Example: Here is the recipe for extra-rich brownies. I described it to you recently.

Here is the recipe that I recently described to you for extra-rich brownies.

1. Kevin walked over to the weeping child and offered his help. Kevin is a sympathetic person.

2. We both saw that woman yesterday. She was buying tulip bulbs at the garden store.

3. My new car uses far too much gasoline. I may have to trade it in.

4. I am going to tell you an exciting piece of news. You will be amazed by it.

5. I remember vividly a certain day in my childhood. My parents gave me a shiny new red bicycle.

6. This book cost eighteen dollars at Brentano's. It is well worth the price, I think.

Sentence-Combining Exercise 4

Combine the following pairs of sentences, making one sentence a participial phrase, a gerund phrase, an infinitive phrase, an absolute phrase, or an appositive phrase. Punctuate each sentence correctly.

Example: Ted had often hiked in the mountains.
He looked forward to the trip to Linville Gorge.

Having often hiked in the mountains, Ted looked forward to the trip to Linville Gorge.

1. Suzanne had more luggage than she could easily carry.
She began looking for a luggage cart.

2. She struggled half the length of the airport with a suitcase, a garment bag, and a tennis racket.
Finally she spotted a long line of luggage carts at the foot of the escalator.

3. Technology may one day transform Wall Street's trading floor into a computer room.
Technology is a force that modifies even entrenched institutions.

4. Every spring my father and a friend of his take a week off from work.
They go fishing in a lake in the northern part of the state.

5. Alice Bernini had been artistic director of the theater for a decade.
   Sunday afternoon she was honored at a reception in Collier Hall.

6. Charles Kaiser is president of Friends of the Environment.
   He has proposed that this summer the group sponsor a day camp at Willow Woods.

7. The price of oil dropped with the spring thaw.
   I was able to buy gas at Simpson's for somewhat less than I had bought it in January.

8. All through college Arthur mused over the pot of gold at the end of every rainbow.
   He has now graduated and is busy chasing those rainbows.

9. Dawson searched for his appointment book in his briefcase.
   Then he remembered that he had left it on his desk at home.

10. In summer we frequently come to Chestnut Park.
    We play tennis here or watch a softball game.

11. Both newspapers had been read from cover to cover.
    Dad gathered them up and added them to the towering stack in the utility room.

12. The U.S. Department of Labor reports the unemployment rate each month.
    This rate invariably influences economic forecasters.

13. My friend Millie Morrison works as a clerk-typist in the Pentagon.
    Somewhat surprisingly, her favorite pastime is windsurfing.

14. I always buy a copy of the current issue of *The New York Times Book Review*.
    I read the reviews and see what titles are on the best-seller list.

15. The light had begun to fade.
    The artist stepped back to consider his canvas and then gathered up his paints and brushes.

16. On our way to Florida I saw huge live oaks festooned with Spanish moss.
    Spanish moss is an epiphytic plant common to the Southern coastal plain.

17. Yesterday the Bernsteins were overjoyed.
    They got a letter from their oldest son, who is backpacking in Europe.

18. I had never driven a car with a stick shift.
    I knew that I was in trouble when my sister's subcompact stalled on a hill.

19. Both the House and the Senate had finally passed the farm bill.
    It was sent to the White House for the President's signature.

20. I did not really understand Professor Sutton's question about levers and fulcrums.
    I certainly should not have tried to answer it.

Sentence-Combining Exercise 5

Combine the following pairs of sentences, making one either an adverbial clause, an adjective clause, a noun clause, or an elliptical clause. Punctuate each sentence correctly.

Example: Nell has a great deal to read for her history classes.
Only occasionally can she treat herself to a novel.

Because Nell has a great deal to read for her history classes, only occasionally can she treat herself to a novel.

1. The navy dress didn't look terribly attractive on the hanger.
   Nevertheless, with its brass buttons and its cerise belt, it was becoming to Judy.

2. The fact should have been obvious even to a novice cook.
   The chili wanted proper seasoning.

3. Every quarter I arrange my class schedule around *The Young and the Restless*.
   It continues to be my all-time favorite soap opera.

4. Maggie was looking for some sandals to wear with skirts and slacks.
   Instead she bought an irresistible pair of pink and white spectators.

5. The night I drove back alone from Danville I learned a lesson.
   I should keep an eye on my gas gauge.

6. Sophie was in her first year of high school.
   She became interested in gymnastics and began training for the team.

7. Michael had sautéed the onions and celery and browned the ground
   beef.
   Next he combined these ingredients with the tomatoes and spices.

8. Carlos and Bill have been lifelong friends.
   They grew up in the same neighborhood, went to the same schools, and
   sometimes dated the same girl.

9. My sister and brother-in-law have come to a conclusion.
   A location convenient to their work will be an important consideration
   when they buy a house.

10. On Saturday I thought that spring had actually arrived.
    Then overnight the temperature dropped well below freezing and proved
    me wrong.

11. I know the perfect gift for our friend Mason.
    It is a copy of *Glorious Chocolate: The Ultimate Chocolate Cookbook.*

12. On Sunday afternoon we were riding our bikes.
    We saw two art students sketching the view of the river from the north
    campus.

13. I did not believe my roommate's warning.
    The statistics course is extremely demanding.

14. The crowd seemed unusually late arriving at the stadium.
    However, we didn't see an empty seat by the time we had begun singing
    the national anthem.

15. Karl intended to watch Bela Lugosi in *Dracula.*
    He fell asleep on the couch long before the movie began.

16. The four of us plan to catch a late-afternoon train into the city.
    There we'll have dinner and then see a show.

17. Absolutely no one heard the doorbell.
    Mrs. Waller was listening to *Rigoletto* on WBCX, and Mr. Waller was engrossed in a basketball game on ESPN.

18. After rummaging through my backpack, I suddenly remembered the whereabouts of the film.
    I had left it in the glove compartment of the car.

19. The Canada geese have recently joined the ducks on our pond.
    Their arrival is a harbinger of cold weather.

20. Dien had always been fond of his mother's egg rolls.
    His grandmother had taught her daughter to make them when they still lived in Saigon.

Sentence-Combining Exercise 6

In the following exercise combine the ideas in the groups of sentences into one effective simple or complex sentence.

Example: Marcia spent three hours looking for her gold bracelet.
The bracelet was a family heirloom.
She finally gave up the search in despair.
Moments later her little brother came in from the playground with the bracelet on his arm.

Although Marcia had given up in despair after a three-hour search for her heirloom gold bracelet, her little brother came in moments later from the playground with the bracelet on his arm.

1. John Forrest has become a partner in his law firm.
He has been an associate member of the firm for three years.
He has proved effective in grasping legal points.
He is also good at arguing court cases.

2. We have selected new draperies for our family room.
They are made of a sheer fabric.
The color is sea-foam green.
The room is dark, and the pastel draperies will lighten it up.

3. I am reading an intriguing book.
It is about Navajo Indians.
The book gives a great deal of information about the traditions and religion of the Navajos.
Many of the religious customs are marked by poetic beauty and grandeur.

4. A walk on the beach provides interesting sights.
   There are beautiful shells of various shapes and colors.
   Occasionally one sees a school of tiny minnows in the oncoming surf.

5. My older brother has graduated from college.
   He is now attending our state medical college.
   He hopes to specialize in surgery as a hospital resident before going into
     practice.

6. Kay was a beautiful and fascinating person.
   She never seemed interested in me or my affairs.
   She made me feel inferior.

7. The old house creaked strangely.
   Footsteps came slowly down the hall and stopped outside my door.
   I held my breath when the door opened.
   To my relief it was my mother, coming to bring me an extra blanket.

8. Laurie admires Kurt's good looks.
   She is also drawn to Robert for his sense of humor.
   She plans, however, to marry Bill because she loves him.

9. The Hopkins's front yard is planted with boxwood, holly, and magnolia
     trees.
   The lawn is a velvety green.
   It is a well-landscaped yard.

10. I had pepperoni pizza for supper last night.
    I also had chocolate mousse for dessert.
    At midnight I awoke with a stomachache.

11. I was lying there, trying to think how to ease my pain.
    A friend of mine called me on the telephone.
    She asked me to go out with her for some Mexican food.

12. Mariana has been playing the violin since age four.
    She gave her first important concert at only seventeen.
    She was quite poised and confident.

13. There is a British comedy series called *To the Manor Born*.
    It concerns an impoverished widow, forced to sell her generations-old
       manor in order to pay her debts.
    She sells the manor to a rich man whom she dislikes at first.
    Eventually, the widow and the rich man get married.

14. Mother insisted that I not wear jeans and sneakers to Aunt Mary's.
    I put on a dress shirt and tie.
    At Aunt Mary's my two cousins were both dressed in jeans and
       sneakers.

15. I cannot meet you at eight A.M. as promised.
    I had unexpected overnight guests last night.
    I must give them their breakfast.

16. Gwen developed a toothache on the opening day of the volleyball
    tournament.
    She kept her toothache a secret.
    The coach would have disqualified her if she had known about the
    toothache.

17. You will easily find our house, Ned.
    It is at the end of a dead-end street.
    It is the only house with a red tile roof.

18. Bob has a coin collection.
    He left a rare coin on the front hall table.
    His little sister found the coin and used it to buy ice cream.

19. Last Tuesday Sylvia had a dinner party.
    That afternoon it began to sleet, and electric power went off.
    Sylvia could not cook the food for her party.
    She had to serve her guests fried chicken from a fast-food restaurant.

20. Caroline wanted to paint her bedroom.
    She rejected all advice on the best color to choose.
    She painted the room a bright hot pink.
    The pink walls were sickening.
    Disgusted, Caroline threw away the pink paint and asked advice of the
    man at the paint store.

Sentence-Combining Exercise 7

Combine the ideas in each of the following groups of sentences into one effective simple or complex sentence.

Example: I was striding along the sidewalk at my usual rapid pace.
My toe struck a rough place in the pavement.
I tripped and sprawled headlong onto the pavement.
A finger was broken and my wrist was sprained as a result of my fall.

As I strode along the sidewalk at my usual rapid pace, my toe struck a rough place, and I tripped and sprawled headlong onto the pavement, breaking a finger and spraining my wrist as a result.

1. The girl wore a pale green dress.
The color complemented her dark skin and hair.
She was charming.
She attracted a great deal of attention.

2. Every citizen of a democracy has rights that must be protected by the state.
Every right, however, implies responsibility.
As important as the protection of his rights is the citizen's fulfilling of his responsibilities.
Many citizens do not fulfill these responsibilities.

3. Our plane was scheduled to arrive in Atlanta at 9:45 P.M.
A heavy fog had delayed its departure from Dallas.
We finally arrived at our destination over three hours late.

423

4. The popular singer stepped onto the stage.
   He held up his hands for silence.
   He began his first number.
   The teen-age girls screamed so loudly that no one could hear his song.

5. I settled into my seat on the plane.
   I was sitting next to the window.
   A man of about eighty sat down beside me.
   He confided that this was his first plane trip.

6. Out in the orchard the boys picked apples all day.
   They used ladders to reach the highest fruits.
   It was backbreaking work.

7. Travis played football enthusiastically.
   He played as though his life depended on winning.
   In the game yesterday he was so alert that he made two interceptions.
   After one of the interceptions he scored a touchdown.

8. Today I picked up my photos of the Grand Canyon.
   I eagerly examined them after I got home.
   I was unhappy at the discovery that almost half the exposures were
      fuzzy and unrecognizable.

9. The elderly woman had misplaced her purse in the supermarket.
   She immediately assumed that it had been stolen.
   She was relieved when her husband walked up with the purse.

10. Rodney was bored with the lecture on astronomy.
    The auditorium was dark enough for him to slip out unnoticed.
    He quickly and quietly left the place.

11. Velcro was invented by George deMestral.
    He was a Swiss engineer.
    He conceived the idea after noticing that cockleburs stuck to his socks in
      the woods.
    He duplicated with nylon the tiny hooks of the cockleburs.

12. Roland spent several years in Europe.
    He spent most of that time in France.
    He now speaks French almost as fluently as a native.

13. The four-o'clock is a plant of the bougainvillea family.
    It has long-tubed yellow, red, or white blossoms.
    These blossoms generally open late in the afternoon.

14. The Marquis de Lafayette was a French general and statesman.
    He served as a volunteer in the Continental Army in the American
      Revolution.
    He served in America from 1777 to 1781.

15. The human heart is a hollow muscular organ.
    It receives blood from the veins.
    It then pumps blood through the arteries by alternate dilation and
      contraction.

16. My dog is of the Weimaraner breed.
    The name comes from the city of Weimar, Germany, where the breed
      was developed.
    He has a smooth gray coat and light green eyes.
    His name is Siegfried.

17. The Sphinx of Egypt is a tremendous and awe-inspiring statue.
    It is located at Giza, near Cairo.
    It has the body of a lion and the head of a man.

18. Gail and Perry were canoeing on the Colorado River.
    They came to some very rough rapids.
    Perry was thrown from the canoe and almost drowned.
    Gail's quick action and his life jacket saved him.

19. My mother is from New Orleans.
    She makes delicious traditional Louisiana dishes.
    My favorite is her jambalaya.
    It is a Creole stew made of rice, shrimp, crab, crayfish, and many vegetables and spices.

20. Margarita is a new friend from Mexico.
    She and her famiy have come to live in Jacksonville.
    Her father practiced medicine in Mexico.
    He now works as a laboratory technician in a hospital.

Sentence-Combining Exercise 8

In the following exercise combine the ideas in the groups of sentences into one effective simple or complex sentence.

Example: I had a history test and a chemistry test scheduled for today.
Last night I tried to study, but was interrupted by several phone calls.
Then my brother came in to borrow money.
Finally, after a frustrating evening I simply went to bed and hoped for the best.

Having both history and chemistry tests scheduled for today and having my study last night interrupted by phone calls and my brother's coming to borrow money, I finally went to bed frustrated and hoped for the best.

1. Dr. Rothberg is a pediatrician.
   He was my father's doctor.
   He was also my doctor.
   The doctor is a kind and gentle man, loved by all his patients and their parents.

2. Edwin Newman is the author of a book titled *Strictly Speaking.*
   He is a former television newscaster.
   Newman has always been a spokesman for clear, concise language.
   The book uses examples of poor usage to support Newman's opinions.

3. My new swim suit is red and white.
   It is one-piece.
   My sister likes it so much that she wishes it were hers.

429

4. My neighbor is a crossword puzzle fan.
   He loves difficult puzzles, like double-crostics and those in *The New York Times*.
   He was baffled, however, when he first encountered British crosswords, which are full of puns and other misleading clues.

5. On our return trip from a vacation in the mountains, we took a new, so-called scenic route.
   We had to inch slowly down a long series of hairpin curves.
   The new route also took us twenty miles out of our way.
   Father said that he would gladly forgo the scenery in the future.

6. I badly need a new car.
   The brakes on my present car need relining.
   The transmission makes strange noises.
   Worst of all, the air conditioner has broken down.

7. The slang word *limey* originated from the former practice of serving lime juice to the crews of British ships.
   Lime juice prevented scurvy in the men, who were referred to as "limeys."
   Nowadays the slang word is used to designate any Englishman.

8. We have a marine watercolor by Lamar Dodd.
   Dodd is a famous Georgia artist.
   The watercolor is in dark shades of gray and deep blue.
   It depicts an approaching thunderstorm.

9. The new house next door is unusual.
   It is square, with eight large rooms and a foyer grouped symmetrically around a square, glass-roofed atrium.
   The house has skylights instead of windows.

10. The Boyers have invited us for a week's visit to the beach.
    Their house faces the ocean.
    We all enjoy the swimming, sunbathing, and surf-fishing.

11. We visited the home of artist Claude Monet at Giverny, France.
    Monet belonged to the school of French Impressionism, a style of painting.
    Visiting Monet's home was like stepping into one of his familiar paintings that show masses of flower beds and the little Japanese bridge over a lily pool.

12. The planet Jupiter is named for the supreme god in Roman mythology.
    It is the largest planet in our solar system.
    It is more than three hundred times the size of Earth.

13. One wonders where Mrs. Pettibone comes by her various hair colors.
    The colors range from brassy orange to dusty pink to lavender-blue.
    They resemble nothing ever seen in nature.

14. The Parkers have seven children.
    The oldest child is fourteen years old, and the youngest is five months.
    One would expect conditions in that house to be noisy and untidy.
    The opposite is true: the house is quiet and neat.

15. The metamorphosis of a butterfly is an amazing phenomenon.
    The change from caterpillar to butterfly is a transformation that seems
      almost magical.
    It is not a unique occurrence, however, taking place also in other insects
      and in the change from tadpole to frog.

16. Today I had the pleasant experience of seeing a manatee at close
      quarters.
    The manatee is a large, gentle aquatic mammal.
    It ate lettuce directly from my hand.
    Manatees are on the endangered species list because the blades of motor
      boats maim and kill hundreds every year.

17. Trudy does many time-consuming things in preparation for study.
    She sharpens several pencils.
    She then carefully adjusts her lamp.
    Sometimes it takes her almost an hour to collect books, notes, and
      glasses before study actually begins.

18. Highly flavored Italian dishes are popular in the United States.
    Pastas like spaghetti, linguine, and lasagna are delicious.
    There are wonderful toppings and seasonings like oregano, pepperoni,
      tomato sauce and garlic.

19. My Shakespeare professor always celebrates Shakespeare's birthday in an unusual way.
He wears a jester's costume of cap and bells to his classes.
There he plays a mandolin and sings sixteenth-century ballads to the students.

20. Cruise lines advertise life aboard ship as "unstructured and carefree."
Actually, shipboard life is highly structured.
There are exercise and dancing classes in the morning, movies and bridge games in the afternoon, and nightclub entertainment in the evening.

Sentence-Combining Exercise 9

Combine the ideas in each of the following groups of sentences into one effective simple or complex sentence.

Example: In 1896 Adolph Simon Ochs bought a controlling interest in *The New York Times.*
He introduced the slogan "All the News That's Fit to Print."
He was responsible for making it a great newspaper.

Adolph Simon Ochs, who bought a controlling interest in The New York Times *in 1896, was responsible for introducing the slogan "All the News That's Fit to Print" and for making the* Times *a great newspaper.*

1. *The American Heritage Dictionary* defines a dragon as a "fabulous monster represented as a gigantic reptile."
   Through the centuries the creature has frequently appeared in Scandinavian and British literature.
   Usually it is fierce as well as fabulous.

2. A dragon may occasionally be depicted as a gentle soul.
   Perhaps the mildest of dragons is the one in Kenneth Grahame's story "The Reluctant Dragon."
   It refuses to do battle with St. George, the patron saint of England.

3. Certainly one of the fiercest dragons in all literature is the one that Beowulf mortally wounds.
   Beowulf was the "lord of the Geats."
   But the beast in turn is responsible for the old hero's death.

4. The settlers of the Appalachian Mountains brought their folk tales with them from Europe.
   They told and retold the stories.
   Gradually the tales' characters, settings, and language were modified to reflect the settlers' new world.

5. C. Auguste Dupin is a detective in three stories by Edgar Allan Poe.
   Dupin is often considered the prototype of similar characters in contemporary fiction.
   The three stories in which Dupin appears are "The Murders in the Rue Morgue," "The Mystery of Marie Rogêt," and "The Purloined Letter."

6. The Huang He River is the second longest river in China.
   It is also known as the Yellow River.
   Its name is derived from the color of the silt that it carries from Qinghai Province to the Yellow Sea.

7. The longest river in China is the Yangtze.
   It is the third longest river in the world.
   It also rises in Qinghai Province, but it empties at Shanghai into the East China Sea.

8. A group of students has been raising vegetables in water rather than in soil.
   This method of horticulture is known as hydroponics.
   The vegetables receive the necessary nutrients through an especially prepared solution of water and minerals.

9. On March 1, 1990, Dr. Antonia Coella Novello was confirmed as Surgeon General of the United States.
   She is the first woman to hold this position.
   She is also the first Hispanic American to be appointed to the position.

10. *Haiku* is a form of Japanese poetry.
    It first became popular in the sixteenth century.
    Contemporary poets continue to be interested in the form.

11. A *haiku* consists of seventeen syllables in three lines.
    The first and third lines have five syllables each.
    The middle line comprises seven syllables.
    Each *haiku* is built upon an image that conveys a spiritual truth.

12. "Laissez faire" is now a part of standard English.
    Originally it was a French expression.
    The phrase may be translated "let do" or "let act."
    It identifies a policy that supports economic activity without government intervention.

13. Thousands of acres of vegetation have been and are being destroyed in the great rain forest of the Amazon Basin.
    Environmentalists throughout the world are deeply concerned about the loss of the rain forest.
    They are also concerned about the extinction of species depending on it.

14. *Mystery!* is a popular program appearing on PBS on Thursday nights.
    It usually features dramatized versions of stories by authors of detective or espionage fiction.
    In 1990 it celebrated its tenth anniversary.

15. Maurice Sendak is a greatly admired illustrator of children's books.
    Of all his books, *Where the Wild Things Are* is probably the most widely read.
    He is the author of this story as well as its illustrator.

16. In 1963, *Where the Wild Things Are* received the Caldecott Medal for the best picture book published in the United States that year.
    It has remained popular with children and adults.
    In 1988, the twenty-fifth anniversary of the book was marked with the publication of a special edition.

17. Jonas E. Salk discovered the anti-polio vaccine.
    It is certainly one of the great achievements of the century.
    In an interview on television Dr. Salk observed that successful scientific research requires one "to think like nature."

18. *The Red Lantern* is an example of Peking opera.
    This form of musical drama is popular throughout China.
    In the 1965 version of *The Red Lantern* Chinese guerrillas are at war with Japanese invaders.

19. In *The Red Lantern,* Tieh-mei is the young heroine.
    She must deliver a secret code to the guerrillas in the "north hills."
    The musical drama concludes with her succeeding despite great
        difficulties.

20. Maria Tallchief has been one of America's great ballerinas.
    For many years she danced with the New York City Ballet.
    She is noted for several roles, one of which is in *The Firebird*.
    This ballet is based on themes from Russian folk literature.

Sentence-Combining Exercise 10

Combine the ideas in each of the following groups of sentences into one effective simple or complex sentence.

Example: Charles Schulz is a cartoonist.
He creates what is surely one of the most popular comic strips in the world.
Its title is *Peanuts*.

The cartoonist Charles Schulz is the creator of Peanuts, *surely one of the most popular comic strips in the world.*

1. The Mediterranean Sea is approximately twenty-three hundred miles long.
   It is an average of four to five hundred miles wide.
   It touches the shores of three continents.
   These are Europe, Africa, and Asia.

2. Charlie Chaplin was the author and director of *Modern Times*.
   He also starred in this film.
   The film considers the individual in industrialized society.
   This serious theme is treated with comedy characteristic of Chaplin.

3. A scene in *Modern Times* depicts Chaplin as a factory worker.
   He is tightening bolts on an assembly line.
   The scene may remind the viewer of a television episode starring Lucille Ball.
   She is working on an assembly line in a candy factory.

4. Mistletoe is a parasitic shrub.
   The Druids considered it a sacred plant with magical powers.
   The Druids were priests in the Celtic culture of early Britain.

5. According to Norse mythology, a twig of mistletoe killed Balder.
   Balder was the god of "light, peace, virtue, and wisdom."
   Hoder threw the twig.
   Hoder was the blind god of darkness.

6. William Morris was an Englishman of many interests.
   He was interested in creating handsome, well-made books.
   For this purpose he established the Kelmscott Press.

7. The *Kelmscott Chaucer* was the last book created under William Morris's supervision.
   This book is considered Kelmscott Press's finest publication.
   It took five years to produce.

8. Georgia O'Keeffe was an American artist.
   She was born in Sun Prairie, Wisconsin.
   She died in Taos, New Mexico.
   She spent much of her life in the Southwest.
   Her work reflects her association with this section of the United States.

9. Mithridates VI was a king of Pontus.
   He had numerous enemies.
   He is said to have created an immunity to poison by regularly consuming small amounts of a deadly brew.

10. A.E. Housman wrote a poem in which he alludes to Mithridates.
    The title of the poem is "Terence, This Is Stupid Stuff."
    The poet uses the allusion to support the notion that his melancholy poetry aids his friends to "train for ill."

11. Quebec is the largest province of Canada.
    It was once a possession of France.
    Then it came under British rule.
    It is not surprising that many of its citizens are bilingual.

12. The capital of this province is also named Quebec.
    It was established on the site of an Indian village.
    The name of this village was Stadacona.
    It is believed that its first European visitor was Jacques Cartier, a French navigator.

13. *Yellow Sweater* is an oil painting.
    It was painted by Amedeo Modigliani, an Italian artist.
    It hangs in the Solomon R. Guggenheim Museum.
    Modigliani's portraits are greatly admired and, according to critics, suggest "innocence and tragedy."

14. A statue of Mary Jane McLeod Bethune stands in Lincoln Park in Washington, D.C.
    It is a memorial to a teacher, the daughter of former slaves.
    She dedicated her life to the education of African-Americans.
    She was especially interested in the education of African-American women.

15. Aleksandr Pushkin is considered by many critics to be Russia's greatest poet.
    He wrote a long narrative poem entitled *Eugene Onegin*.
    He also was the author of *Boris Godunov*, a tragedy in blank verse.
    These and several of his other works served as bases for operas.

16. McDonald's opened the doors of its first restaurant in Russia on January 31, 1990.
    The restaurant is located in Pushkin Square in the heart of Moscow.
    According to a news account, McDonald's served thirty thousand Muscovites the day it opened.

17. The novel assigned for reading and discussion in English 101 is *Things Fall Apart*.
    It was written by Chinua Achebe, a Nigerian author.
    The novel examines European and African cultures and the tensions that arise when they conflict.
    Chinua Achebe is acclaimed by critics for his work.

18. Puerto Rico is one of a group of islands known as the Greater Antilles.
    Three other islands belonging to this group are Cuba, Jamaica, and
    Hispaniola.
    The Greater Antilles, in turn, is a part of an island chain recognized as
    the West Indies.

19. Puerto Rico is a commonwealth associated with the United States.
    It is represented in the U.S. Congress by a Resident Commissioner, who
    is elected for a four-year term.
    He can vote only in congressional committees.

20. Helen of Troy was very beautiful.
    She was the wife of Menelaos, the King of Sparta.
    Paris, son of the King of Troy, abducted her.
    His action precipitated the Trojan War.

Test on Lessons 1–7

A. In each of the following sentences underline the subject once and the verb twice; then circle the complement (or complements). In the first column at the right tell whether the verb is transitive active (**TA**), transitive passive (**TP**), or intransitive (**I**). In the second column tell whether the complement is a direct object (**DO**), an indirect object (**IO**), a predicate nominative (**PN**), a predicate adjective (**PA**), an objective complement (**OC**), or a retained object (**RO**). Note that not all sentences have complements.

1. In 1752 Benjamin Franklin performed his famous kite experiment. _____ _____

2. Classes do not begin until Monday. _____ _____

3. A colander is a very useful kitchen utensil. _____ _____

4. Mr. Potts painted my front door deep red. _____ _____

5. The mountain house has been closed for the winter. _____ _____

6. Will you order me a new calendar? _____ _____

7. Both Ruth and her roommate are engineers. _____ _____

8. May's house is tastefully decorated. _____ _____

9. We all became quite fond of our exchange student. _____ _____

10. I.B.M. gives university professors a special price on personal computers. _____ _____

11. Sam will bring you a piece of my birthday cake. _____ _____

12. The governor will appoint her judge. _____ _____

B. What part of speech is each of the following underlined words?

1. In in the first sentence above _____

2. not in the second sentence above _____

3. useful in the third sentence above _____

4. front in the fourth sentence above _____

5. winter in the fifth sentence above _____

6. <u>me</u> in the sixth sentence above   _____

7. <u>Both . . . and</u> in the seventh sentence above   _____

8. <u>tastefully</u> in the eighth sentence above   _____

9. <u>of</u> in the ninth sentence above   _____

10. <u>computers</u> in the tenth sentence above   _____

11. <u>birthday</u> in the eleventh sentence above   _____

12. <u>her</u> in the twelfth sentence above   _____

C. In each of the sentences below identify the *italicized* expression by writing one of the following numbers in the space at the right:

    1 if it is a *prepositional phrase*,   **6** if it is an *absolute phrase*,
    2 if it is a *participial phrase*,   **7** if it is a *noun clause*,
    3 if it is a *gerund phrase*,   **8** if it is an *adjective clause*,
    4 if it is an *infinitive phrase*,   **9** if it is an *adverbial clause*.
    5 if it is an *appositive phrase*,

1. The Vietnam War resulted in scars and wounds *to America's spirit.*   _____

2. Cleanth Brooks, *who is a literary scholar,* graduated from Vanderbilt University.   _____

3. Bernice Johnson Reagan is founder and director of Sweet Honey in the Rock, *a famous female vocal ensemble.*   _____

4. *When you go mountain climbing,* be sure you have the right equipment.   _____

5. There is a certain satisfaction in seeing all the pieces *coming together.*   _____

6. *To complete the task swiftly* is not one of Tim's abilities.   _____

7. *The game having ended,* the stadium was again silent.   _____

8. *Fighting crime* is one of America's major concerns.   _____

9. *That he accepted responsibility willingly* was particularly important to his supervisor.   _____

10. I do enjoy *watching people.*   _____

D. Underline the dependent clause (or clauses) in each of the following sentences. In the first column at the right tell whether the clause is a noun clause (**N**), an adjective clause (**Adj**), or an adverbial clause (**Adv**). In the second column tell how the noun clause is used (that is, whether it is a subject, direct object, etc.), or what the adjective or adverbial clause modifies.

1. While we were traveling abroad, my purse was stolen. _____ _____

2. My family is embroiled in a debate over who cooks the best Brunswick stew. _____ _____

3. After a natural disaster occurs, the country rallies to help rebuild the area. _____ _____

4. Shirley, I did not know that you liked Shakespeare, but I am glad that you do. _____ _____

5. The national monuments in Washington are beautiful when they are lighted at night. _____ _____

6. Ticks are a hazard for people who work in the woods. _____ _____

7. When the first national census was taken in 1790, the population of the United States was four million. _____ _____

8. That she did not like her professor was obvious to everyone in the class. _____ _____

9. Stan believes that seven years of bad luck will follow anyone who breaks a mirror. _____ _____

10. Chocolate milk shakes that are made with extra scoops of ice cream are delicious. _____ _____

E. In the following sentences insert all necessary commas and semicolons. Rewrite sentence fragments in such a way as to make complete sentences. If a sentence is correct, mark it **C**.

1. Wanda an assistant to the college president knows more about computers than anyone else on campus.

2. I think that Cliff is planning to attend the conference but I am not sure.

3. Because he has difficulty hearing he didn't know that his name had been called.

4. The enclosed policy replaces the one previously submitted I hope our new policy meets with your approval.

5. Can you give me Jennifer's new address or should I call her mother?

6. The clock having stopped during the night. I did not get up in time for church.

7. After Doris completes her bachelor's degree she is taking a year off to travel through Europe then she will enter medical school.

8. The keynote speaker at the Time Capsule Ceremony will be Carl E. Sanders a former governor of our state.

9.   While I am not an expert on laser technology I do
think that it will be the technology used in the 1990's.

10.   Chancellor Davis who is a frequent speaker noted for his
frankness, persuasiveness, and humor.

Test on Lessons 8–18

Correct all errors in the following sentences. Many sentences will have to be rewritten. In some cases a misplaced element may be circled and its correct position indicated by a caret (∧). Other errors may be crossed out and corrections written above the sentence. If a sentence is correct, write **C**.

1. After trying on at least a dozen pairs of shoes, not one of them fit.

2. Everyone agreed that Bert was talented: he was a poet, a musician, and he also was a skilled cabinetmaker.

3. Reed has not only gone fishing today, but also he is going tomorrow.

4. Talking and laughing among ourselves over lunch, time seemed to fly.

5. Having completed a weaving class at the Arts and Crafts Center, Winnie thought that she now knew enough about it to work on her own.

6. Dale is one of those peculiar readers who scans the last chapter of a book first.

7. The young woman stepped onto the escalator, which wasn't easy with a suitcase in one hand and a tote bag full of books in the other.

8. I can assure you that neither Jack nor I are the owner of the motorcycle in the driveway.

9. This morning the chemistry professor lectured at length on polymers, which he seemed to know more about than any one in the world.

10. We've needed library services in our neighborhood for a long time, so I am happy to hear that the cornerstone for a branch library will be laid next week.

11. Everyone standing on the corner had their own idea of what had happened just before the car and the truck collided.

12. Certainly Tam knows more about the Vietnamese language than me.

13. Whom does the *Wall Street Journal* think will finally succeed in taking over the conglomerate?

14. The small country was able to export a great deal of fruit, which helped its balance of trade.

15. Mitzi has been assigned to the fashion desk at the newspaper, even though she told the editor that she knows little about it.

16. He jumped from the taxi, strode hurriedly into the office building, and then he had to wait an eternity for an elevator.

17. Because we had neither peanut butter nor jelly caused my three-year-old nephew to have a terrible tantrum.

18. If I was you, I would buy some posters from the bookstore to brighten this room.

19. Having already seen all the magazines in the doctor's waiting room, my entertainment was watching the other patients.

20. Because the water was unusually choppy, the tourists sure didn't look forward to crossing the channel.

21. The handsome pieces of sculpture are the work of various artists in Brookgreen Gardens.

22. Last semester Emory wanted to have completed his foreign language requirement.

23. The cloisonné beads that Lynn received for Christmas are as pretty, if not prettier than, any I have ever seen.

24. The news on Channel 9 reported that it is her and not her husband who has been appointed Secretary of Labor.

25. Sometimes we think that happiness is when we can do exactly what we please.

26. We washed the car, and we waxed it, and then we polished it.

27. The jacket that I ordered from L.L. Bean is heavier than my friend.

28. The two Grinnell students who are skiing with us now want to go back to the lodge.

29. A large percentage of the houses in this subdivision has been built by the same construction company.

30. We were able to get everything into the back of the station wagon: a chair, a table, and an oval mirror that will look elegant in the dining room.

31. We were told that the judge setting on the bench for this term of court is from Raleigh.

32. Surely neither that large forsythia nor these camellias needs to be pruned.

33. Jamie can talk of nothing else since the music bug has bit him.

34. By noon the bikers had nearly ridden to Bald Mountain.

35. The moment I opened the front door I knew that it was Thanksgiving: the turkey, already in the oven, smelled divinely.

36. Sitting on the back porch, it was difficult for Margo to see the lake through the trees.

37. We had not met the principal speaker but did not dream that the woman in the tangerine suit was her.

38. Although I checked into the hotel last night, I only met the tour guide this morning at breakfast.

39. The reason none of us brought our umbrellas is because the meteorologist had predicted a sunny day.

40. Having been washed up during the storm, the beach was littered with seaweed.

41. We were twenty miles from home when Mary Louise said that she couldn't remember if she had turned off the oven.

42. Every morning my mother gets up at seven o'clock, and she puts the coffee on, and then she goes out to get the paper.

43. Year in and year out you can depend on the World Series' attracting the attention of millions of Americans.

44. For breakfast my sister often has a cup of coffee, piece of fruit, and an English muffin with orange marmalade.

45. Neither of the boxes are large enough to hold all these books that Father is sending to the book fair.

46. No one who knows Hank is surprised at him joining the Peace Corps.

47. Brian was real lucky to get both a ticket to the Super Bowl and a hotel reservation.

48. Practice as well as instruction are necessary if one is to master a computer program.

49. The Men's Garden Club heard Mr. Price-Jones discuss planning formal gardens on Saturday.

50. To get to Snowshoe from here, it seems to me that I should go up I-81 to Lexington and then go west on I-64.

Test on Lessons 19–24

A. In the following sentences insert all necessary punctuation marks and correct all errors of punctuation and mechanics.

1. All things considered William I wish that you would'nt leave for Columbus, until after lunch.

2. The man, who is wearing the Scottish tartan hat, is my sister's brother in law.

3. Before leaving for class Bud clean up your room, and eat some breakfast.

4. In his Sonnet 73 "That Time of Year" Shakespeare compares aging in human life with autumn with sunset and with a slowly dying fire.

5. No Bea you can't oh I knew that would happen carry four plates of food at one time.

6. When he saw that no one wanted to play checkers with him, Henry was annoyed, however he was soon his normal cheerful self again.

7. The dog said Barry is ready for his daily walk in the park.

8. Didn't you hear Monica say "This is the last straw?"

9. Reproduced in full color in this book   page 49   is The Gleaners by the French painter, Millet.

10. This is the procedure for submitting a manuscript   1
    Type your material on good-quality paper   2   Double-space
    your typing and   3   Mail the manuscript along with a
    self-addressed, stamped envelope to the publisher.

11. Wait" Emily cried excitedly. "You have forgotten your letter".

12. The news story read as follows   "Mr. Kennedy said, 'This
    incident   the robbery of his bank   has shocked me
    greatly.' "

13. To Charlie Foster seemed a threat to his friendship with
    Susan.

14. I thought you said that Senator Fielding would be here for
    our New Years Day banquet.

15. Nancys been wanting to go to Fran's and Richard's house
    to see the sofa that theyve recovered.

B. After each of the following groups of words indicate the level of usage of the italicized word(s), using the following abbreviations: **A** for archaic, **D** for dialectal, **I** for informal (colloquial), and **S** for slang. Use your dictionary for this test.

1. Whoever told you that Percy is a *jerk* is absolutely right.   _____

2. William Tell went to the *fletcher* to get some arrows.   _____

3. I believe that Steve's car was *totaled* in the accident last night.   _____

4. The man put the potatoes into his *poke* and walked away.   _____

5. Patrick thinks that Jim got the job because he has *pull* with the district manager.   _____

6. Bucky *psyched* himself up and was in a winning attitude just before his big tennis match.   _____

7. There is nothing better at a baseball game than a bag of hot roasted *goobers* and a cool soda.   _____

8. If you are still ailing on the day of the party—heaven *for-fend*—should we postpone it?   _____

9. Ernie walked to the pool, spread his beach towel, and put on his *shades* and tanning lotion before sunning himself.   _____

10. The *sting* operation that the police carried out last night ena-bled them to make nine arrests.   _____

C. The following section of the test is based on the Glossary of Faulty Diction. Underline all errors or colloquialisms and write the preferred forms above each sentence.

1. I am awfully sorry that I accidently spilled the maple syrup on your new slacks.

2. As far as talent, I am told that Shirley has lots of it.

3. Don't you think that anyone of these blouses will go real well with my beige skirt?

4. Father says that Dr. Bennett is notorious for the amount of his charitable works.

5. Alexander is appealingly childish in his trusting devotion to his friends.

6. The consensus of opinion was that the district attorney would persecute Warren's suit against Mr. Henson.

7. Janie is on a diet, and she has decided to forego sweets and eat only healthy foods.

8. Gary and myself are plenty worried about Nick; he flaunts the law when he drives too fast.

9. If you can loan me fifty dollars, George, I plan on repaying you with

interest.

10. I have never seen anyone so enthused about being in college as Louise;

she is literally walking on air.

11. There was a delay in the supermarket's opening this morning; the

reason is because the big freezer had broken down.

12. Dr. Prince inferred that he was not too impressed

with the book, but his daughter says that it is totally awesome.

13. Hopefully, the principle of our high school

will not take the position he has been offered in North Dakota.

14. I was only kidding around, Kelley, when I told you

that I had heard that you failed algebra.

15. Tommy couldn't hardly stand up after the Peachtree Road Race;

he said that he couldn't have gone a single step further.

D. Give the meaning of each of the following prefixes or roots; then write two words containing each prefix or root.

1. *umbra*   _____

    (1) _____   (2) _____

2. *de-*   _____

    (1) _____   (2) _____

3. *anti-*   _____

    (1) _____   (2) _____

4. *liber*   _____

    (1) _____   (2) _____

5. *inter-* _____

    (1) _____   (2) _____

6. *polis* _____

    (1) _____   (2) _____

7. *mono-* _____

    (1) _____   (2) _____

8. *ob-* _____

    (1) _____   (2) _____

9. *finis* _____

    (1) _____   (2) _____

10. *genus* _____

    (1) _____   (2) _____

E. If there is a misspelled word in any line of five words given below, write it correctly in the space at the right. If all five words are spelled correctly, write **C** in the space.

1. argument, compell, committee, athletics, perspiration   _____

2. physician, medicine, restaurant, flier, auxilary   _____

3. brocoli, completely, ridiculous, original, maneuver   _____

4. grandeur, naive, religious, sandwich, marriage   _____

5. disease, irrevelant, hindrance, sacrifice, yield   _____

6. silhouette, sheriff, yacht, repitition, integrity   _____

7. necessary, pursue, preceed, mortgage, grievance   _____

8. embarrassed, ninth, muscle, loveable, persuade   _____

9. nucleus, kindergarden, pneumonia, partner, friend   _____

10. hitchike, expel, February, forgo, exorbitant   _____

11. dilapidated, dissatisfied, column, benefitted, allege   _____

12. bureau, bankruptcy, quantity, nickel, assasin   _____

13. Britain, absence, fullfil, exhaust, permanent   _____

14. arctic, cavalry, publicly, predjudice, buoyant   _____

15. caffeine, changeable, comming, mediocre, diphtheria   _____

Achievement Test

A. In the following sentences identify the part of speech of each *italicized* word by writing one of the following numbers in the space at the right:

1 if it is a noun,	**5** if it is an adverb,
2 if it is a pronoun,	**6** if it is a preposition,
3 if it is a verb,	**7** if it is a conjunction,
4 if it is an adjective,	**8** if it is an interjection.

1. Sometime his frankness *is viewed* as harshness. _____

2. Movies reflect the ethics *and* customs of society. _____

3. The tobacco industry is using a *more* subtle type of advertisement than it formerly did. _____

4. The Christmas tree was covered *with* ornaments from around the world. _____

5. *Political* campaigns tend to become very negative. _____

6. Fountain pens *have become* popular again. _____

7. *Nearly* every radio station has a talk show. _____

8. The hail *storm* ruined the corn crop. _____

9. The BMW *car's* initials stand for Bavarian Motor Works. _____

10. The draperies were made in France *by* an interior designer. _____

11. The Navajo Indians made that *beautiful* blanket. _____

12. Children learn manners *from* their parents. _____

13. Baseball is *America's* favorite spectator sport. _____

14. *No!* I have told you once that I don't want to go shopping. _____

15. *Everyone* except Russ enjoyed the play. _____

16. We cannot come over tonight, *but* we will come tomorrow. _____

17. *In* 1867, the United States purchased Alaska from Russia. _____

18. Contact lenses must be kept *scrupulously* clean. _____

19. *Chess* matches sometimes take months to play. _____

20. The newlyweds spent their honeymoon in *Tahiti.* _____

21. Did you see *him* at the dance? _____

22. The world's largest diamond mines *are located* in South Africa.   _____

23. Where are you spending your *spring* holidays?   _____

24. Gourmet cooking consists of fancy *and* exotic dishes prepared by expensive chefs.   _____

25. Tracy concocted a wild *story* explaining his absence from our party.   _____

B. Each of the following sentences either contains an error of grammar or is correct. Indicate the error or the correctness by writing one of the following numbers in the space at the right:

    1 if the case of the pronoun is incorrect,
    2 if the subject and the verb do not agree,
    3 if a pronoun and its antecedent do not agree,
    4 if an adjective or adverb is used incorrectly,
    5 if the sentence is correct.

26. We appreciated your inviting both Hal and I to your open house.   _____

27. Lenore is the older of three children.   _____

28. A team of efficiency experts are expected here next week.   _____

29. You did very good on your final.   _____

30. Every cadet waited patiently for their uniform.   _____

31. Some of our friends is coming over for coffee.   _____

32. The highway department is using signs with more symbols than words.   _____

33. National Educational Television has real informative and challenging programs.   _____

34. As usual, the grand jury made their presentments in open court.   _____

35. A number of the English majors is making plans to attend the Shakespeare Festival.   _____

36. I am sure glad to hear that the game with Notre Dame is to be televised.   _____

37. Each of the dancers in the revue had their costume fitted this morning by Ms. Armstrong.   _____

38. The owner of the new fishing boat tied up at the dock is thought to be him.   _____

39. Which of your two tapes by the B-52's do you consider is the best? _____

40. Sally says that ten gallons are all that she needs to fill her gas tank. _____

41. Once the criteria for the scholarship in general business had been established, the departmental newsletter published it. _____

42. Skating as well as her and Louis did last night certainly must require hours of practice. _____

43. Appearing as handsomely as ever, James Bond miraculously escaped from the enemy once again. _____

44. Are either of you going out for flag football? _____

45. Did either Nan or Bob call to let us know who will meet our train in New Orleans? _____

46. The warm relationship between she and her cousin began when they were children in St. Paul. _____

47. When we move into the new office building, everyone will have their own parking space. _____

48. The family whom I think has lived longest in these apartments is the Markleys. _____

49. After Winter Weekend, thinking about lab reports and research papers was real hard. _____

50. Although Dr. Vincent explained the phenomenon carefully, few of us in Biology 101 understood it. _____

C. Each of the following sentences either contains an error in sentence structure or is correct. Indicate the error or correctness by writing one of the following numbers in the space at the right.

   1 if the sentence contains a *dangling modifier,*
   2 if the sentence contains a *misplaced modifier,*
   3 if the sentence contains *faulty reference of a pronoum,*
   4 if the sentence contains *faulty parallelism,*
   5 if the sentence is *correct.*

51. John was flattered but nervous about the invitation to dinner at the White House. _____

52. The number of houses built in the city during May is greater than April. _____

53. While coming down in the elevator this afternoon, it stopped between the first and second floors. _____

54. I've nearly addressed all the envelopes for Mr. Turner's letters to his clients. _____

55. The grass was beginning to come up, which improved the appearance of the recently completed houses. _____

56. Listening to the tape, the traffic doesn't seem quite as slow as it usually does. _____

57. This production of *The Death of a Salesman* is as fine, if not finer than, any I have ever seen. _____

58. To once and for all end our political argument, we have agreed to disagree. _____

59. Mr. Lloyd is a kind and patient man but who expects his employees to meet his high standards. _____

60. Gina not only made some chocolate chip cookies, but she also baked two loaves of banana bread. _____

61. We have heard only recently about his running for a seat in the General Assembly. _____

62. After searching through the desk drawers, there seemed to be nowhere else to look for his checkbook. _____

63. In History 201 we had a test covering the unification of Italy on Thursday. _____

64. The finance students were interested and enthusiastic about the investment banker's speech. _____

65. Although Agnes says that she enjoys her book club, she does have difficulty reading all of them. _____

66. Another quart of paint is needed to paint these chests properly. _____

67. Falling hundreds of feet into Tallulah Gorge, we saw the beautiful waterfalls. _____

68. Everyone who turned in their term papers late will automatically receive a reduced grade. _____

69. I think you are mistaken, Aunt Ida; Bob never has and never will smoke. _____

70. While fishing on the dock, a large flounder took my line. _____

71. Jerome only got two words out of his mouth before his father said, "No!" _____

72. At age five my grandmother taught me to make biscuits. _____

73. In walked Max, dripping wet, mad as a hornet, and the rain had ruined his new sport coat. _____

74. Either you must get up an hour earlier, Liz, or be late for work every day. _____

75. Unless first given an anesthetic, the extraction of a wisdom tooth can be quite painful. _____

D. Each of the following sentences contains an error in punctuation or mechanics or is correct. Indicate the error or the correctness by writing one of the following numbers in the space at the right:

    1 if a comma has been omitted,
    2 if a semicolon has been omitted,
    3 if an apostrophe has been omitted,
    4 if quotation marks have been omitted,
    5 if the sentence is correct.

76. The rain which I thought would never stop finally ended about midnight. _____

77. Mary Beths cat, Jupey, is a beautiful white Persian. _____

78. I can't remember when I lost my raincoat it may have been last night at the basketball game. _____

79. My friend Ellis is going water-skiing with us tomorrow. _____

80. You are early, said Nancy; I haven't had my breakfast yet. _____

81. Joining the crowd at the dolphin tank Richard was amazed at the skill and speed with which the trained dolphins performed. _____

82. Its not often that one has the chance to hear a really fine violinist play. _____

83. The man standing over there with Dr. Roberts is his only son Jeff. _____

84. My nephew Gary is graduating from Princeton today. _____

85. Dedham, Massachusetts is the home of the Bowens, our closest friends. _____

86. For Jimmy Bruce's arrival was a delightful surprise. _____

87. Disappointed, I gave up and started walking home I had
    been waiting for Jackie for a half-hour.   _____

88. Howell whom I had never suspected of discourtesy was
    shockingly rude in his behavior toward Mr. Crosby.   _____

89. "This horse, said Pat, may very well be a Kentucky Derby
    entry."   _____

90. When you are ready to leave, call my house I will be waiting
    at the front door for your arrival.   _____

91. I have just talked with Francesca who is planning a trip to
    Budapest next fall.   _____

92. Have you ever heard Edmond Hall's clarinet-solo recording
    of the New Orleans song Burgundy Street?   _____

93. Tommys plans are to meet Frank in St. Louis next Saturday.   _____

94. Melanie's sister whose name I can't recall is in two of my
    classes this semester.   _____

95. Lois and Eleanor had a misunderstanding about whose turn
    it was to load the dishwasher.   _____

96. To be honest I don't believe that either of those girls has
    done her share of the work lately.   _____

97. The late Sir Winston Churchill is a widely quoted speaker he
    is eminently quotable.   _____

98. Mrs. Andreotti's husband, Aldo, is a handsome interesting
    and intelligent man.   _____

99. Albert walked in the door, took off his coat, and shouted,
    "Honey, Im home!"   _____

100. Believing that he was alone in the deserted house Curtis
     started violently when he heard a low voice in the next
     room.   _____

Glossary of Grammatical Terms

Absolute phrase. A construction grammatically independent of the rest of the sentence. It is formed by use of a noun followed by a participle. It is not a subject and does not modify any word in the sentence.

The rain having ended, we decided to walk home.

Abstract noun. A noun that names a quality, condition, action, or idea; it cannot be perceived by one of the five physical senses.

kindness   truth   courtesy   dishonesty

Active voice. The form of a verb indicating that the subject of the sentence performs the action of the verb.

The dog *ate* its supper.

Mary *is going* to town.

Adjective. A word that modifies, describes, limits, or adds to the meaning of a noun, pronoun, or any other substantive.

Your late arrival caused trouble.

Ellen is *beautiful.*

Adjective clause. A dependent clause that modifies a noun, pronoun, or any other substantive.

The girl *whom you met* is a flight attendant.

The place *where I was born* is a thousand miles from here.

Adverb. A word that modifies or adds to the meaning of a verb, adjective, or other adverb. It may also modify or qualify a phrase or clause, adding to the meaning of the whole idea expressed in the sentence.

I finished the test *quickly.*

Trent is *truly* worthy of this award.

Luckily, we got to class on time.

Adverbial clause. A dependent clause that functions exactly as if it were an adverb. It modifies verbs, adjectives, adverbs, or the whole idea expressed in the sentence's independent clause.

When I was a child, I lived in Missouri.

After you have eaten lunch, I will help you wash dishes.

Because you are tired, I will drive home.

Don't leave here *until you have finished your work.*

Ambiguous modifier. A modifier carelessly placed between two sentence elements so that it may be taken to modify either element.

The boy who had been walking *slowly* came into our driveway.

Ambiguous pronoun reference.   Improper use of a pronoun that may grammatically refer to more than one word as its antecedent in a sentence.

> John told Fred that *he* should lose weight.

Antecedent.   The substantive to which a pronoun refers and with which it must agree in person, number, and gender.

> *Peter* told Sue that *he* would be late for dinner.

Apostrophe.   A mark of grammatical mechanics used to show possession, indicate omitted letters in contractions, or show plurals of letters or numerals.

> Ted's glove
>
> It's raining.
>
> Mind your *p*'s and *q*'s.

Appositive.   A word or phrase that explains, identifies, or renames the word it follows and refers to.

> William Faulkner, author of "The Bear," was a native Mississippian.

Archaic words.   Words that are out of date and no longer in general use.

> "*Oft* in the *stilly* night."

Articles.   Three words, classified as adjectives, that appear before nouns or certain other substantives. *A* and *an* are indefinite articles; *the* is a definite article.

Auxiliary verbs.   Verbs that help to form the various tenses of main verbs. The use of auxiliary verbs creates verb phrases and enables the writer to express time and time relationships much more precisely than by using simple present and past tenses. *Was, have,* and *will* are the auxiliary verbs in these examples:

> She *was going* with me.
>
> I *have finished* my work.
>
> Tom *will go* to New York.

Brackets.   Marks of grammatical mechanics used to enclose any interpolation or insertion added to material being quoted.

> "Four score and seven years ago [Lincoln began] our forefathers brought forth on this continent. . . ."

Broad pronoun reference.   Incorrect use of a pronoun to refer broadly to the whole idea of the preceding clause.

> She was late, **which** made me angry.

Capitalization.   The use of capital letters for the first word of a sentence, a line of traditional poetry, or a direct quotation. Capitals are also used for the first letter of proper nouns, days of the week, months, holidays, and historical periods.

Case.   The inflection of a noun or pronoun to show its relationship to another word or sentence element. Nouns change form only to show the possessive case. Pronouns have three forms to show case: nominative, objective, and possessive.

Clause.   A group of words containing a subject and a verb. The two types of clause are independent and dependent. Dependent clauses cannot stand alone as completed thoughts; independent clauses express complete thoughts.

Cliché.   An overused expression that has lost its original freshness.

dull thud	one fell swoop
bitter end	through thick and thin
having a ball	last but not least

Collective nouns.   Those nouns that name groups of persons, places, or things functioning as units.

jury   team   class   club   herd

Colloquialism.   Words or expressions (also referred to as informal diction) that are acceptable in the speech of the educated person but not in formal writing.

We have *lots* of apples on our trees this year.

Colon.   The mark of punctuation that introduces a formal list or an explanation or amplification of a statement. Also used after the formal salutation in a letter, between hour and minute numerals of time, between chapter and verse of Bible references, and between titles and subtitles of books.

Comma.   Punctuation mark used to indicate the smallest interruptions in thought or grammatical construction.

Comma splice.   Incorrect use of a comma as punctuation between two independent clauses not joined by a coordinating conjunction. A stronger separation must be shown through use of a semicolon or a period.

I saw the plane landing, it was a 747 jet.

I saw the plane landing; it was a 747 jet.

Common noun.   A noun that names a class of persons, places, things, or ideas.

woman	honesty
book	friendship
house	

Comparative degree.   The inflection of an adjective or adverb that compares two things, persons, or actions.

Peggy's camera is *better* than yours.

Marcia felt the disappointment *more keenly* than Harry did.

Comparison.   Indication of the extent to which one noun or verb has a particular quality in common with another noun or verb through use of the comparative degree of an adjective or adverb.

Complement.   A word, phrase, or clause that completes the action of the verb and the sense of the sentence. It may be a direct object, an indirect object, a predicate adjective, a predicate noun, an objective complement, or a retained object.

Complex sentence.   A sentence that contains one independent clause and one or more dependent clauses.

> I know what you are going to say.

Compound sentence.   A sentence that contains at least two independent clauses and no dependent clause.

> I will ride with you, and Patsy will stay at home.

Compound-complex sentence.   A sentence that contains at least two independent clauses and one or more dependent clauses.

> I was sorry that I could not attend the meeting, but my throat was sore.

Concrete noun.   A noun that names a person, place, or thing that can be perceived by one of the five physical senses.

> desk   chocolate   aroma   shout   rain

Conjugation.   The showing of all forms of a verb in all its tenses.

Conjunction.   A word used to join words or groups of words. Coordinating conjunctions (like *and* and *but*) join sentence elements of equal rank. Subordinating conjunctions introduce subordinate, or dependent, elements, joining them to the main part of the sentence.

Conjunctive adverb.   An adverb (sometimes called a transitional adverb) used to connect two independent clauses while modifying the sense of the sentence and showing the relationship between the two clauses.

> I had neglected to buy coffee yesterday; consequently, my breakfast today lacked a vital ingredient.

Connotation.   The associative meaning of a word or expression; connotation goes beyond the literal dictionary definition.

Coordinate elements.   Elements of equal rank within a sentence. They may be single words, phrases, or clauses, but they must have similar values as sentence parts.

Coordinating conjunction.   A conjunction that joins two sentence elements of equal rank. The coordinating conjunctions are *and, but, or, nor, for, yet* in the sense of *but*, and *so* in the sense of *therefore*. The correlative conjunctions *either . . . or* and *neither . . . nor* are also coordinating conjunctions.

Correlative conjunctions.   Coordinating conjunctions used in pairs, as shown in the entry on coordinating conjunctions.

> either . . . or   neither . . . nor
> both . . . and   not only . . . but also

Dangling modifier. A phrase or elliptical clause that does not modify any particular word in the sentence.

> *To be a good cook,* the kitchen must be conveniently arranged.

Dash. A mark of punctuation that indicates an abrupt shift or break in the thought of a sentence or sets off an informal or emphatic parenthesis. It is also used to set off an appositive or parenthetic element that is internally punctuated.

> I'm trying to be sympathetic, but — oh, Mack, you aren't even listening.

> The three of us — Jim, Susan, and Dot — are trying out for parts in the play.

Demonstrative adjective. An adjective that modifies a substantive by pointing it out.

> *this* picture   *these* glasses
> *that* woman   *those* apples

Demonstrative pronoun. A pronoun that points out persons, things, qualities, or ideas.

> *Those* are my friends.

> *These* are the problems.

> *That* is the question.

> My answer is *this.*

Dependent clause. A group of words that contains a subject and a verb but that cannot stand alone as a complete thought. It begins with a subordinating word. Dependent clauses function as grammatical units within a sentence; that is, as nouns, adjectives, and adverbs.

Dialectal words. Words whose usage is common to the speech of a particular group or geographical region.

> *branch* for creek

> *polecat* for skunk

> *poke* for sack or bag

Diction. One's style of writing or speaking in terms of word choice.

Direct object. A noun or other substantive that completes the verb and receives the action expressed in the verb.

> The child ate the *candy.*

> Carol hates *arithmetic.*

> Frank thought the *fine* excessive.

Elliptical clause or expression. A grammatically incomplete expression whose meaning is nevertheless clear; frequently a dependent clause from which subject and/or verb is omitted.

> *When a child,* I had a great many freckles.

Essential appositive.   An appositive that positively identifies that which it re-names, most frequently by use of a proper noun. Essential appositives are not set off by commas.

> The actress *Katharine Hepburn* has had a long and distinguished career.

Essential clause (modifier).   An adjective or adverbial clause that is necessary in a sentence because it identifies or points out a particular person or thing. An essential clause is not set off by commas.

> A child *who grows up in the country* learns a great deal about nature.

Euphemism.   An expression used to avoid the outright statement of a dis-agreeable, delicate, or painful idea, or to give dignity to something essen-tially lowly or undignified.

> The Jacobs family had a *blessed event* at their house last week.

> Mr. Thompson's present *financial embarrassment* is said to be the result of *uneven cash flow*.

> Sally received a *pink slip* in her pay envelope last week.

Excessive predication.   The use of too many independent clauses, strung to-gether with coordinating conjunctions. Proper subordination of less impor-tant ideas is the remedy for excessive predication.

> I went to a movie, and I ate two boxes of popcorn, and I later had a stomach ache.

Expletive.   An idiomatic introductory word, used to begin a sentence when the subject is deferred to a later position.

> *There* are too many cooks in this kitchen.

> *It* has been raining since Monday.

Gerund.   A verbal used as a noun. In its present tense it always ends in *-ing*. It may function as a sentence element in any way that a noun can.

> *Riding* a bicycle in the street can be risky.

Hyphen.   A mechanical mark that is used in compound numbers and other compound words formed from phrases. It is also used at the end of a line to indicate the division of a word continued on the next line.

> *thirty-four*   *ex-governor*
> *sister-in-law*   *sixteen-year-old* boy

Idiom.   The characteristic construction used to form sentences in a particular language; the pattern and sequence of words normal to that language.

Illogical comparison.   Comparison, usually through careless writing, of two things that do not have a point of similarity. In "My car is newer than Mark," *car* and *Mark* have no point in common to be compared. A logical comparison would state:

> My car is newer than Mark's.

Indefinite pronouns. Pronouns that do not point out a specific person, place, or thing, but only a general class. Many indefinite pronouns are concerned with indefinite quantity:

some   any   each   everyone   several

Independent clause. A group of words containing a subject and verb and expressing a complete thought. It may stand alone as a simple sentence, or it may be combined with other independent clauses or with dependent clauses to form a compound or complex sentence.

Indirect object. A word or words denoting the person or thing indirectly affected by the action of a transitive verb. It is the person or thing to which something is given or for which something is done. Words such as *give, offer, grant, lend* represent the idea of something done for the indirect object. The idea of taking something away can also have an indirect object, with the use of words like *deny, refuse,* and the like.

Infinitive. A verbal consisting of the simple form of a verb preceded by *to,* and used as a noun, adjective, or adverb.

> I want *to win.*
>
> I have work *to do.*
>
> You must leave now *to get* there on time.

Inflection. A change in the form of a word to indicate a change in its meaning or use. Nouns show inflection only in plural and possessive forms. Some pronouns are inflected to show case, number, and gender. Verbs are inflected to show person, number, voice, and mood. Most adjectives are inflected to show comparative and superlative degrees.

Informal diction. Words or expressions that are acceptable in the speech of the educated but not in formal writing. Also called colloquial diction.

Intensive pronouns. Pronouns combined with *-self* or *-selves* and used in conjunction with nouns and simple pronouns for emphasis.

> I *myself* will write the letter.
>
> Frank did the work *himself.*

Interjection. An exclamatory word thrown into a sentence or sometimes used alone. It is grammatically independent of the rest of the sentence.

> *Oh,* why are you doing that?
>
> *Goodness!* I am hot!

Interrogative adverb. An indefinite adverb that asks a question, namely *how, when, where,* or *why.*

> *How* are you going to pay for that car?
>
> *When* will you leave for the airport?
>
> *Where* does Dorothy live?
>
> *Why* did you call me at midnight?

Interrogative pronoun.   A pronoun that is part of a sentence asking a question.

> *What* is that noise?
>
> *Which* of the cakes do you prefer?

Intransitive verb.   A verb whose action is not directed toward a receiver.

> Mike *walked* around the block.
>
> The river *is overflowing*.
>
> You *are* foolish.

Irregular verb.   A verb that forms its past tense not by adding *-d* or *-ed*, but by a change in the vowel of the root verb.

> sing   sang   begin   began   choose   chose
> ride   rode   do   did

Italics.   A device of mechanics that uses a printing style sloping to the right in the manner of handwriting. Italics are used to emphasize a word or expression or to designate book, play, opera, magazine, newspaper, painting, sculpture, television show and ship titles. In typing or handwriting, italics are shown by underlining.

Jargon.   Vague, pretentious language so general in meaning that many words may be omitted without loss of the sense of a statement.

Levels of usage.   Divisions of usage within the categories of Standard and Substandard English. The following are usage labels usually applied by most dictionaries and grammarians: formal, informal, dialectal, slang, archaic, and obsolete.

Linking verb.   An intransitive verb that makes a statement not by expressing action but by indicating a state of being or a condition. It follows the subject and must be followed by a predicate noun or predicate adjective to complete the sense of the sentence. The verb *to be* in all its forms is the most common linking verb; however, any other verb that expresses a state of being and is followed by a noun identifying the subject or an adjective describing it is a linking verb. Some examples are *appear, become, look, seem, smell, sound, taste,* and *feel.*

Misplaced modifier.   A word or phrase that by its position in the sentence does not seem to modify the word it is intended to modify. A modifier should be as close as is logically possible to the word it modifies.

> The crystal chandelier brilliantly lit the huge banquet table that hung from the ceiling.
>
> *Correction:*
>
> The crystal chandelier that hung from the ceiling brilliantly lit the huge banquet table.

Mixed construction.   A shift in the original construction of a sentence, causing the sentence to be confused in its meaning and incorrect in its grammatical structure.

> Honesty *is when* someone is truthful in word and deed.

Modifier. A word, phrase, or other sentence element that describes, qualifies, or limits another element in the same sentence.

Mood. The form a verb may take to indicate whether it is used to make a statement, give a command, or express a condition contrary to fact. Moods of a verb are *indicative, imperative,* and *subjunctive.*

Nominative case. The case of a noun or pronoun that is the subject or the predicate noun of a sentence. Nouns in the nominative case are not inflected; personal pronouns have inflections for each of the three cases.

Nonessential appositive. An appositive that is not necessary in the identification of the word with which it is in apposition. It merely provides additional information as a method of renaming. Note that a nonessential appositive is set off by commas.

> P.D. James, *a mystery novelist,* is an Englishwoman.

Nonessential modifier. A modifier that is not necessary to the meaning of the sentence but simply provides additional description rather than identification. Nonessential modifiers are set off by commas.

> My father, *who is a lawyer,* often has to travel in connection with his practice.

Noun. The part of speech that names a person, place, thing, or idea.

Noun clause. A dependent clause that functions within the sentence as a noun.

> Tell me *what you want for breakfast.*

Number. Inflection of verbs, nouns, and pronouns indicating whether they are *singular* or *plural.*

tree	*trees*	he *loves*	they *love*
woman	*women*	*I*	*we*

Object. A sentence element that receives directly or indirectly the action of a verb, gerund, participle, or infinitive; or shows relationship as object of the preposition to some other element in the sentence.

Object of a preposition. The substantive that follows a preposition and shows a relationship between the object of the preposition and some other element in the sentence.

Objective case. The case of a noun or pronoun that receives the action of a verb, either directly or indirectly, or that refers to that receiver. The object of the preposition is also in the objective case.

Objective complement. A noun, pronoun, or adjective that completes the action of the verb and refers to the direct object.

> Henry VIII made Catherine of Aragon his *queen.*
>
> Todd considers Marilyn quite *intelligent.*

Parallelism.   The use of equal, or parallel, grammatical constructions within a sentence. Coordinate elements of equal rank should be expressed in parallel language.

> The girl was tall, slender, and beautiful.   (*Three adjectives are used.*)

> She is a woman who is conscientious and who is a splendid worker.   (*Two adjective clauses are used.*)

Parentheses.   A device of punctuation that encloses parenthetic information like brief explanation of a foregoing term or a figure repeated to ensure accuracy.

> Lincoln said (in the Gettysburg Address), "Four score and seven years ago. . . ."

> I am enclosing eight dollars ($8) to cover the cost of my order.

Parenthetical expressions.   Expressions that are not a part of the central statement of a sentence but are used as comments upon the statement. Parenthetical expressions are usually, but not always, enclosed by commas.

> He is, *as the saying goes,* a real football buff.

> What *do you suppose* can be done?

Participle.   A verb form that functions as an adjective while retaining some of the characteristics of a verb. It is called a *verbal.*

> *shining* light   *worn* coat   *known* danger.

Parts of speech.   The various elements that go to make up a sentence. There are eight parts of speech: noun, pronoun, adjective, verb, adverb, preposition, conjunction, and interjection.

Passive voice.   The inflection of a transitive verb showing that the subject of the sentence is the receiver of the verb's action.

> He *was taken* to jail.

Person.   The inflection of verbs and personal pronouns indicating the speaker (first person), the person spoken to (second person), or the person or thing spoken about (third person).

Personal pronouns.   Pronouns used in one of the three persons (*I; you; he, she, it*) and their plural forms as well.

Phrase.   A group of words generally without a subject and predicate, used as a single part of speech.

> *Living alone* has some advantages. (*gerund phrase, used as subject*)

> Marcia, *waving wildly,* tried to catch our attention. (*participial phrase, used to modify **Marcia***)

> I want *to go to Paris.* (*infinitive phrase, used as direct object*)

> His cousin, *a computer specialist,* lives in Nevada. (*appositive phrase, in apposition with **cousin***)

> We climbed *up the mountain.* (*prepositional phrase, used adverbially*)

Positive degree (of adjectives and adverbs).   The regular form of an adjective or an adverb.

Possessive case.   The inflection of a noun or pronoun, showing possession.

> *Janet's* last name is Rogers.
>
> *My* friend has moved away.
>
> The cat has lost *its* tongue.
>
> *Mine* is the only true story of the incident.

Predicate.   The part of the sentence that makes a statement about the subject. It always includes the sentence verb.

Predicate adjective.   The adjective in the predicate that describes or modifies the subject. It follows a linking verb.

> Charlotte is *friendly*.
>
> This soup smells *good*.
>
> Mr. Thomas appears *ill*.

Predicate noun or nominative.   The noun in the predicate that renames or identifies the subject. It follows a linking verb.

> That woman is a *lawyer*.
>
> Jim was *master* of ceremonies.

Prefix.   A short element (a syllable or syllables) that comes before the main part of the word (the root), adding to or modifying its meaning.

> *sub*marine   *centi*pede   *contra*dict

Preposition.   A part of speech that shows a relationship between its object (a substantive) and some other word or sentence element.

> She is a friend *of* the family.

Primer style.   The monotonous style of writing that reflects no relative importance of ideas and no emphasis. Primer style is found in writing that does not vary sentence structure through subordination or other rhetorical devices, but uses only simple sentences without variation.

Principal parts (of a verb).   The principal parts of a verb are *first-person singular, present tense; first-person singular, past tense;* and *past participle.* Knowledge of these three principal parts enables one to conjugate any verb.

Pronominal adjective.   An adjective that is the possessive form of a pronoun:

your hat, *their* intentions, *our* home, *my* watch

or a pronoun used to modify a substantive:

this house, *that* glove, *these* grapes, *those* books, *some* people, *any* students, *either* dress.

Pronoun.   A word used in place of a noun; it sometimes refers to a noun or other substantive already mentioned.

Pronoun-antecedent agreement.   The agreement that must exist between a pronoun and its antecedent in person and number.

> Each girl was told to bring *her* lunch with *her* for the outing.

Proper noun.   A noun that names a particular person, place, or thing. It always begins with a capital letter.

> Angela   Senator Smith   Christmas   Atlanta   Idaho

Quotation marks.   Punctuation marks used to enclose direct quotations, titles of short works, smaller units of books, and words from special vocabularies.

Redundancy.   Unnecessary repetition.

> *Repeat* that *again.*
>
> She *returned back* to her home.
>
> The coat that I bought is *blue in color.*

Reflexive pronouns.   Pronouns ending in -*self* or -*selves* and indicating that the subject acts upon itself.

> Jack bruised *himself* on the leg at the playground.
>
> Millie treated *herself* to a hot fudge sundae.

Relative pronoun.   A pronoun that is used to introduce a dependent adjective clause.

> The information *that* I gave you is correct.
>
> My uncle, *whom you met last year,* is coming for a visit.

Retained object.   A noun or other substantive remaining as the object when a verb that has both direct and indirect objects is put into the passive voice.

> President Rogers has been given a *vote* of confidence.   (*Vote* is the retained object.)

Root.   The central or main part of a word. A prefix may begin the word, and a suffix may end it, each one modifying the meaning of the root.

> peri*meter*, post*script*, *wis*dom, *false*hood

Run-together sentences.   Sentences without punctuation between independent clauses not joined by a coordinating conjunction.

> Mark ran quickly to the door he opened it and saw the burglar.

Semicolon.   Punctuation mark used to separate independent clauses not joined by a coordinating conjunction, coordinate elements internally punctuated with commas, and independent clauses joined by a coordinating conjunction but heavily punctuated internally.

Sentence.   A group of words combined into a pattern that expresses a complete thought.

Sentence fragment.   A part of a sentence written and punctuated as though it were a whole sentence (a complete thought), although some necessary element has been omitted.

> The baby crying.

Because I was tired.

When we arrived at the hotel.

Simple sentence.   A single independent clause that has one subject and one predicate. It may have more than one noun or pronoun as its subject and more than one verb in its predicate.

The dog ran across the street.

The dog ran across the street and barked at the cat.

The dog and the cat fought and made noise.

Squinting modifier.   Another name for ambiguous modifier, which is a modifier carelessly placed between two sentence elements so that it may be taken to modify either element.

The boys who were eating *noisily* complained that there was no dessert.

Subject.   The person, place, or thing being spoken or written about in a sentence.

Subject-verb agreement.   The agreement in person and number that each verb in a sentence must have with its subject. The verb is inflected as to person and number according to those of the clause's subject.

Subjunctive mood.   The mood used in a verb to express a wish or to state a condition contrary to fact. It is also used to express certain formal suggestions or proposals.

I wish that I *were* going with you.

If I *were* president, no one would go hungry.

I move that the nominations *be* closed.

Subordinate clause.   See **Dependent clause.**

Subordination.   In writing or speaking, the reflection that one sentence element is less important or worthy of emphasis than another. Dependent clauses, phrases, and single words may be used instead of full-fledged independent clauses to convey subordinate ideas.

Jenny Martin is my cousin, and she is a senior in high school, and she has just been awarded a scholarship to Tulane.   (*no subordination*)

My cousin Jenny Martin, who is a senior in high school, has just been awarded a scholarship to Tulane.   (*subordination through use of appositive phrase and dependent adjective clause*)

My cousin Jenny Martin, a senior in high school, has just been awarded a scholarship to Tulane.   (*subordination through use of two appositive phrases*)

Subordinating conjunctions.   Conjunctions that introduce dependent clauses, subordinating them in rank to the idea expressed in the independent clause.

Substantive.   A noun, pronoun, or any word or group of words that is used as a noun.

Suffix.   A word part that is added to the end of a word and modifies the meaning of the root.

> accur*acy*   law*yer*   young*ster*
> commun*ion*   altru*ism*

Superlative degree.   The inflection of an adjective or an adverb indicating the highest degree of quality, quantity, or manner. It is formed by adding -*est* as a suffix to the simple form of the adjective, or, with adverbs or adjectives of several syllables, by preceding the word with *most*.

> kindest   most agreeable   most thoughtfully
> poorest   least honorable   most nearly

Tense.   The form that a verb takes in order to express the time of an action or a state of being.

Tense sequence.   The logic that governs time relationships shown by the verbs in a sentence. If the action in one verb or verbal form occurs before or after the action in the main verb, these differences must be indicated by differences in the tenses.

Terminal marks.   The marks of punctuation that signal the end of a sentence. They are the *period*, the *question mark*, and the *exclamation mark*.

Transitional adverb.   The adverb, sometimes called conjunctive adverb, that introduces the second of two independent clauses, showing the relationship between the two clauses and frequently modifying the entire sense of the sentence. Sometimes the second adverb comes within the second clause.

Transitive verb.   A verb whose action is directed toward a receiver, which may be the object of the verb or (with a transitive verb in the passive voice) its subject.

> Bob Horner hit the ball.
>
> A home run was hit by Bob Horner.

Triteness.   The use of stale, hackneyed expressions that have lost their original freshness. See also **Cliché.**

Upside-down subordination.   The subordination of an important idea to a less important one through careless writing.

> When the house caught fire, I was reading the paper.

Vagueness.   The too-frequent use of abstract words instead of concrete ones.

> The fact that the plan was of a risky nature was known by everyone.
>
> *Correction:*
>
> Everyone knew that the plan was risky.

Verb.   A word used to state or to ask something, expressing action or a state of being. Every sentence must contain a verb.

Verbal.   A verb form made from a verb but performing the function of a noun, an adjective, or an adverb. The three verbal forms are the *gerund*, the *participle*, and the *infinitive*.

Verbal phrase.   A group of words that contains a verbal and all its modifiers and complements.

> *Your running too fast* has left you out of breath.

Voice.   The form of a verb that indicates whether the subject of the sentence performs the action or is the receiver of the action of the verb. If the subject performs the action, the verb is in the *active voice;* if the subject receives the action, the verb is in the *passive voice.*

> *The chorus sang* "America" at the end of the program. (*Chorus* is the subject; *sang* is the verb in the active voice.)

> "America" *was sung* by the chorus at the end of the program ("America" is the subject; *was sung* is the verb in the passive voice.)

Weak pronoun reference.   Faulty reference by a pronoun to a word that has been merely implied by the context.

> Mother made delicious grape jelly yesterday; I gathered *them* for her.

Wordiness.   Use of more words than are necessary to express an idea clearly and accurately. Excessive predication, redundancy, and certain abstractions are all forms of wordiness, also known as verbosity.

Index

"Taut and compelling. . . . Tightly written sequences."
—*West Coast Review of Books*

DEEP SIX

"Politics, advanced technology, romance, marine mysteries . . . The sheer speed and adroitness of this yarn will leave you gasping."
—*John Barkham Reviews*

"Cussler can keep anyone on the edge of their chair with his gripping descriptions of action . . ."
—*United Press International*

"The author of the bestselling *Raise the Titanic!* has another exciting, action-packed thriller. . . ."
—*Publishers Weekly*

DIRK PITT

is the consummate man of action who lives by the moment and for the moment . . . without regret. A graduate of the Air Force Academy, son of a United States Senator, and Special Projects Director for the U.S. National Underwater and Marine Agency (NUMA), he is cool, courageous, and resourceful—a man of complete honor at all times and of absolute ruthlessness whenever necessary. With a taste for fast cars, beautiful women, and tequila on the rocks with lime, he lives as passionately as he works. Pitt answers to no one but Admiral James Sandecker, the wily commander of NUMA, and trusts no one but the shrewd, street-smart Al Giordino, a friend since childhood and his partner in undersea adventure for twenty years.

A Literary Guild Featured Alternate Selection

Dirk Pitt® Adventures by Clive Cussler

CLIVE CUSSLER

DEEP SIX

POCKET BOOKS

New York   London   Toronto   Sydney   Tokyo   Singapore

POCKET BOOKS, a division of Simon & Schuster Inc.
1230 Avenue of the Americas, New York, NY 10020

ISBN: 0-671-70945-3

First Pocket Books printing June 1985

20   19   18

POCKET and colophon are registered trademarks of
Simon & Schuster Inc.

DIRK PITT is a registered trademark of Clive Cussler.

Cover art by Steven Stroud

Printed in the U.S.A.

To Tubby's Bar & Grill in Alhambra,
Rand's Roundup on Wilshire Boulevard,
The Black Knight in Costa Mesa,
and Shanners' Bar in Denver.
GONE BUT NOT FORGOTTEN

Prelude

The San Marino

July 15, 1966
The Pacific Ocean

The girl shaded the sun from her brown eyes and stared at a large petrel gliding above the ship's after cargo boom. She admired the bird's soaring grace for a few minutes, then, growing bored, she rose to a sitting position, revealing evenly spaced red bars across her tanned back, etched there by the slats of an ancient steamer chair.

She looked around for signs of the deck crew, but they were nowhere in sight, so she shyly shifted her breasts to a more comfortable position inside the scoop-necked bra of her bikini.

Her body was hot and sweaty from the humid tropical air. She moved her hand across her firm stomach and felt the sweat rising through the skin. She sat back in the chair again, soothed and relaxed, the throbbing beat of the old freighter's engines and the heavy warmth of the sun coaxing her into drowsiness.

The fear that churned inside her when she came on board had faded. She no longer lay awake to the pounding of her heart, or searched the crew's faces for expressions of suspicion, or waited for the captain to grimly inform her that she was under ship's arrest. She was slowly closing her mind to her crime and beginning to think about the future. She was relieved to find that guilt was a fleeting emotion after all.

Out of the corner of her eye she caught the white jacket of the

3

Oriental mess boy as he stepped from a companionway. He approached apprehensively, his eyes staring down at the deck, as if he was embarrassed to look at her nearly nude figure.

"Excuse me, Miss Wallace," he said. "Captain Masters respectfully requests you please dine with him and his officers tonight—if you are feeling better, that is."

Estelle Wallace was thankful her deepening tan covered her blush. She had feigned illness since embarking in San Francisco and had taken all her meals alone in her stateroom to avoid any conversation with the ship's officers. She decided she couldn't remain a recluse forever. The time had come to practice living a lie.

"Tell Captain Masters I feel much better. I'll be delighted to dine with him."

"He'll be glad to hear that," the mess boy said with a broad smile that revealed a large gap in the middle of his upper teeth. "I'll see the cook fixes you something special."

He turned and shuffled away with a gait that seemed to Estelle a trifle too obsequious, even for an Asian.

Secure in her decision, she idly stared up at the three-deck-high midship superstructure of the *San Marino*. The sky was remarkably blue above the black smoke curling from the single stack, contrasting starkly with the flaking white paint on the bulkheads.

"A stout ship," the captain had boasted when he led her to a stateroom. He reassuringly ticked off her history and statistics, as if Estelle were a frightened passenger on her first canoe ride down the rapids.

Built during 1943 to the standard Liberty ship design, the *San Marino* had carried military supplies across the Atlantic to England, making the round-trip crossing sixteen times. On one occasion, when she had strayed from the convoy she was struck by a torpedo, but she refused to sink and made it under her own power to Liverpool.

Since the war she had tramped the oceans of the world under the registry of Panama—one of thirty ships owned by the Manx Steamship Company of New York, plying in and out of backwater ports. Measuring 441 feet in length overall, with a raked stem and cruiser

4

stern, she plodded through the Pacific swells at eleven knots. With only a few more profitable years left in her, the *San Marino* would eventually end up as scrap.

Rust streaked her steel skin. She looked as sordid as a Bowery hooker, but in the eyes of Estelle Wallace she was virgin and beautiful.

Already Estelle's past was blurring. With each revolution of the worn engines, the gap widened between Estelle's drab life of self-denial and an eagerly sought fantasy.

The first step of Arta Casilighio's metamorphosis into Estelle Wallace was when she discovered a lost passport wedged under the seat of a Wilshire Boulevard bus during the Los Angeles evening rush hour. Without really knowing why, Arta slipped it into her purse and took it home.

Days later, she had still not returned the document to the bus driver or mailed it to the rightful owner. She studied the pages with their foreign stamps for hours at a time. She was intrigued by the face in the photo. Although more stylishly made up, it bore a startling resemblance to her own. Both women were about the same age—less than eight months separated their birthdays. The brown shade of their eyes matched, and except for a difference in hairstyles and a few shades of tint, they might have passed for sisters.

She began to make herself up to look like Estelle Wallace, an alter ego that could escape, mentally at least, to the exotic places of the world that were denied timid, mousy Arta Casilighio.

One evening after closing hours at the bank where she worked, she found her eyes locked on the stacks of newly printed currency delivered that afternoon from the Federal Reserve Bank in downtown Los Angeles. She had become so used to handling large sums of money during her four-year tenure that she was immune to the mere sight—a lassitude that afflicts all tellers sooner or later. Yet inexplicably, this time the piles of green-printed tender beguiled her. Subconsciously she began to picture it as belonging to her.

Arta went home that weekend and locked herself in her apartment to fortify her resolve and plan the crime she intended to commit, practicing every gesture, every motion until they came smoothly to her without hesitation. All Sunday night she lay awake until the alarm went off, bathed in cold sweat, but determined to see the act through.

The cash shipment arrived every Monday by armored car and usually totaled from six to eight hundred thousand dollars. It was then re-counted and held until distribution on Wednesday to the bank's branch offices, scattered throughout the Los Angeles basin. She had decided the time to make her move was on Monday evening, while she was putting her money drawer in the vault.

In the morning, after she showered and made up her face, Arta donned a pair of panty hose. She wound a roll of two-sided sticky tape around her legs from mid-calf to the top of her thighs, leaving the protective outer layer of the tape in place. This odd bit of handiwork was covered with a long skirt that came almost to her ankles, hiding the tape with inches to spare.

Next she took neatly trimmed packets of bond paper and slipped them into a large pouch-style purse. Each displayed a crisp new five-dollar bill on the outer sides and was bound with genuine blue and white Federal Reserve Bank wrappers. To the casual eye they would appear authentic.

Arta stood in front of a full-length mirror and repeated over and over, "Arta Casilighio no longer exists. You are now Estelle Wallace." The deception seemed to work. She felt her muscles relax, and her breathing became slower, shallower. Then she took a deep breath, threw back her shoulders and left for work.

In her anxiety to appear normal she inadvertently arrived at the bank ten minutes early, an astounding event to all who knew her well, but this was Monday morning and no one took notice. Once she settled behind her teller's counter every minute seemed an hour, every hour a lifetime. She felt strangely detached from the familiar surroundings, and yet any thought of forgetting the hazardous scheme was quickly suppressed. Mercifully, fear and panic remained dormant.

When six o'clock finally rolled around, and one of the assistant vice presidents closed and locked the massive front doors, she quickly balanced her cash box and slipped quietly off to the ladies' room, where in the privacy of a stall she unwound the tape's outer layer from around her legs and flushed it down the toilet. She then took the bogus money packets and fixed them to the tape, stamping her feet to make certain none would drop off as she walked.

Satisfied everything was ready, she came out and dawdled in the lobby until the other tellers had placed their cash drawers in the vault and left. Two minutes alone inside that great steel cubicle was all she needed and two minutes alone was what she got.

Swiftly she pulled up the skirt and with precise movements exchanged the phony packets for those containing genuine bills. When she stepped out of the vault and smiled a good evening to the assistant vice president as he nodded her out a side door, she couldn't believe she'd actually gotten away with it.

Seconds after entering her apartment, she shed the skirt, stripped the money packets from her legs and counted them. The tally came to $51,000.

Not nearly enough.

Disappointment burned within her. She would need at least twice that sum to escape the country and maintain a minimal level of comfort while increasing the lion's share through investments.

The ease of the operation had made her heady. Did she dare make another foray into the vault? she wondered. The Federal Reserve Bank money was already counted and wouldn't be distributed to the branch banks until Wednesday. Tomorrow was Tuesday. She still had another chance to strike again before the loss was discovered.

Why not?

The thought of ripping off the same bank twice in two days excited her. Perhaps Arta Casilighio lacked the guts for it, but Estelle Wallace required no coaxing at all.

That evening she bought a large old-fashioned suitcase at a secondhand store and made a false bottom in it. She packed the money along with her clothes and took a cab to the Los Angeles International Airport, where she stored the suitcase overnight in a locker and purchased a ticket to San Francisco on an early-evening Tuesday flight. Wrapping her unused Monday night ticket in a newspaper, she dropped it in a trash receptacle. With nothing remaining to be done, she went home and slept like a rock.

The second robbery went as smoothly as the first. Three hours after leaving the Beverly-Wilshire Bank for the last time, she was re-counting the money in a San Francisco hotel. The combined total came to $128,000. Not a staggering prize by inflationary standards, but more than ample for her needs.

The next step was relatively simple. She checked through the newspapers for ship departures and found the *San Marino*, a cargo freighter bound for Auckland, New Zealand, at six-thirty the following morning.

An hour before sailing time, she mounted the gangplank. The captain claimed he seldom took passengers, but kindly consented to take her on board for a mutually agreed fare—which Estelle suspected went into his wallet instead of the steamship company's coffers.

Estelle stepped across the threshold of the officers' dining saloon and paused uncertainly for a moment, facing the appraising stares of six men sitting in the room.

Her coppery-tinted hair fell past her shoulders and nearly matched her tan. She wore a long, sleek pink T-shirt dress that clung in all the right places. A white bone bracelet was her only accessory. To the officers rising to their feet the simple elegance of her appearance created a sensation.

Captain Irwin Masters, a tall man with graying hair, came over and took her arm. "Miss Wallace," he said, smiling warmly. "It's good to see you looking fit."

"I think the worst is over," she said.

"I don't mind admitting, I was beginning to worry. Not leaving your cabin for five days made me fear the worst. With no doctor on board, we would have been in a fix if you needed medical treatment."

"Thank you," she said softly.

He looked at her in mild surprise. "Thank me, for what?"

"For your concern." She gave his arm a gentle squeeze. "It's been a long time since anyone worried about me."

He nodded and winked. "That's what ship captains are for." Then he turned to the other officers. "Gentlemen, may I present Miss Estelle Wallace, who is gracing us with her lovely presence until we dock in Auckland."

The introductions were made. She was amused by the fact that most of the men were numbered. The first officer, the second officer—even a fourth. They all shook her hand as if it were made of delicate china—all except the engineering officer, a short ox-shouldered man with a Slavic accent. He stiffly bent over and kissed the tips of her fingers.

The first officer motioned at the mess boy, who was standing behind a small mahogany bar. "Miss Wallace, what's your pleasure?"

"Would it be possible to have a daiquiri? I'm in the mood for something sweet."

"Absolutely," the first officer replied. "The *San Marino* may not be a luxurious cruise liner, but we do run the finest cocktail bar in this latitude of the Pacific."

"Be honest," the captain admonished good-naturedly. "You neglected to mention we're probably the *only* ship in this latitude."

"A mere detail." The first officer shrugged. "Lee, one of your famous daiquiris for the young lady."

Estelle watched with interest as the mess boy expertly squeezed the lime and poured the ingredients. Every movement came with a flourish. The frothy drink tasted good, and she had to fight a desire to down it all at once.

"Lee," she said, "you're a marvel."

"He is that," said Masters. "We were lucky to sign him on."

Estelle took another sip of her drink. "You seem to have a number of Orientals in your crew."

"Replacements," Masters explained. "Ten of the crew jumped ship after we docked in San Francisco. Fortunately, Lee and nine of his fellow Koreans arrived from the maritime hiring hall before sailing time."

"All damned queer, if you ask me," the second officer grunted.

Masters shrugged. "Crew members jumping ship in port has been going on since Cro-Magnon man built the first raft. Nothing queer about it."

The second officer shook his head doubtfully. "One or two maybe, but not ten! The *San Marino* is a tight ship, and the captain here is a fair skipper. There was no reason for a mass exodus."

"The way of the sea." Masters sighed. "The Koreans are clean, hardworking seamen. I wouldn't trade them for half the cargo in our holds."

"That's a pretty stiff price," muttered the engineering officer.

"Is it improper," Estelle ventured, "to ask what cargo you're carrying?"

"Not at all," the very young fourth officer offered eagerly. "In San Francisco our holds were loaded with—"

"Titanium ingots," Captain Masters cut in.

"Eight million dollars' worth," added the first officer, eyeing the fourth sternly.

"Once again, please," Estelle said, handing her empty glass to the mess boy. She turned back to Masters. "I've heard of titanium, but I have no idea what it's used for."

"When properly processed in pure form, titanium becomes stronger and lighter than steel, an asset that puts it in great demand by builders of jet aircraft engines. It's also widely used in the manufacture of paints, rayon and plastics. I suspect you even have traces of it in your cosmetics."

The cook, an anemic-looking Oriental with a sparkling white apron leaned through a side door and nodded at Lee, who in turn tapped a glass with a mixing spoon.

"Dinner ready to be served," he said in his heavily accented English, while flashing his gap-toothed smile.

It was a fabulous meal, one Estelle promised herself never to forget. To be surrounded by six handsomely uniformed and attentive men was all that her female vanity could endure in one evening.

After a demitasse, Captain Masters excused himself and headed for the bridge. One by one, the other officers drifted off to their

duties, and Estelle took a tour of the deck with the engineering officer. He entertained her with tales of sea superstitions, eerie monsters of the deep and funny tidbits of scuttlebutt about the crew that
made her laugh.

At last they reached the door of her stateroom, and he gallantly
kissed her hand again. She accepted when he asked her to join him
for breakfast in the morning.

She entered the tiny cabin, clicked the lock on the door and
switched on the overhead light. Then she closed the curtain tightly
over the single porthole, pulled the suitcase from under the bed and
opened it.

The top tray contained her cosmetics and carelessly jumbled un-
derthings, and she removed it. Next came several neatly folded
blouses and skirts. These she also removed and set aside to later
steam out the wrinkles in the shower. Gently inserting a nail file
around the edges of the false bottom of the suitcase, she pried it up.
Then she sat back and sighed with relief. The money was still
there, stacked and bound in the Federal Reserve Bank wrappers.
She had hardly spent any of it.

She stood up and slipped her dress over her head—daringly, she
wore nothing beneath—and collapsed across the bed, hands behind
her head.

She closed her eyes and tried to picture the shocked expressions
on her supervisors' faces when they discovered the money and reliable little Arta Casilighio missing at the same time. She had fooled
them all!

She felt a strange, almost sexual, thrill at knowing the FBI
would post her on their list of most wanted criminals. The investigators would question all her friends and neighbors, search all her
old haunts, check a thousand and one banks for sudden large deposits of consecutively numbered bills—but they would come up
dry. Arta, alias Estelle, was not where they'd expect her to be.

She opened her eyes and stared at the now familiar walls of her
stateroom. Oddly the room began to slip away from her. Objects
were focusing and unfocusing into a blurry montage. Her bladder
signaled a trip to the bathroom, but her body refused to obey any

command to move. Every muscle seemed frozen. Then the door opened and Lee the mess boy entered with another Oriental crewman.

Lee wasn't smiling.

This can't be happening, she told herself. The mess boy wouldn't *dare* intrude on her privacy while she was lying naked on the bed. It had to be a crazy dream brought on by the lavish food and drink, a nightmare stoked by the fires of indigestion.

She felt detached from her body, as if she were watching the eerie scene from one corner of the stateroom. Lee gently carried her through the doorway, down the passageway and onto the deck.

Several of the Korean crewmen were there, their oval faces illuminated by bright overhead floodlights. They were hoisting large bundles and dropping them over the ship's railing. Abruptly, one of the bundles stared at her. It was the ashen face of the young fourth officer, eyes wide in a mixture of disbelief and terror. Then he too disappeared over the side.

Lee was leaning over her, doing something to her feet. She could feel nothing, only a lethargic numbness. He appeared to be attaching a length of rusty chain to her ankles.

Why would he do that? she wondered vaguely. She watched indifferently as she was lifted into the air. Then she was released and floated through the darkness.

Something struck her a great blow, knocking the breath from her lungs. A cool, yielding force closed over her. A relentless pressure enveloped her body and dragged her downward, squeezing her internal organs in a giant vise.

Her eardrums exploded, and in that instant of tearing pain, total clarity flooded her mind and she knew it was no dream. Her mouth opened to emit a hysterical scream.

No sound came. The increasing water density soon crushed her chest cavity. Her lifeless body drifted into the waiting arms of the abyss ten thousand feet below.

PART 1

The <u>Pilottown</u>

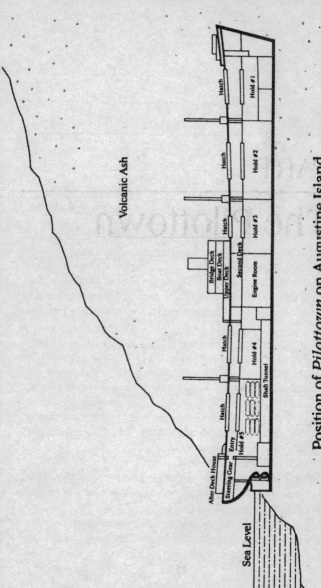

Position of *Pilottown* on Augustine Island

"Not even a good guess," Murphy came back. "No indication of struggle. No marks on the bodies, yet they bled like slaughtered pigs. Looks like whatever killed them struck everyone at the same time."

"Stand by."

Dover turned and surveyed the faces around him until he spotted the ship's surgeon, Lieutenant Commander Isaac Thayer.

Doc Thayer was the most popular man aboard the ship. An old-timer in the Coast Guard service, he had long ago given up the plush offices and high income of shore medicine for the rigors of sea rescue.

"What do you make of it, Doc?" Dover asked.

Thayer shrugged and smiled. "Looks as though I better make a house call."

Dover paced the bridge impatiently while Doc Thayer entered a second Zodiac and motored across the gap dividing the two vessels. Dover ordered the helmsman to position the *Catawba* to take the crab boat in tow. He was concentrating on the maneuver and didn't notice the radio operator standing at his elbow.

"A signal just in, sir, from a bush pilot airlifting supplies to a team of scientists on Augustine Island."

"Not now," Dover said brusquely.

"It's urgent, Captain," the radio operator persisted.

"Okay, read the guts of it."

" 'Scientific party all dead.' Then something unintelligible and what sounds like 'Save me.' "

Dover stared at him blankly. "That's all?"

"Yes, sir. I tried to raise him again, but there was no reply."

Dover didn't have to study a chart to know Augustine was an uninhabited volcanic island only thirty miles northeast of his present position. A sudden, sickening realization coursed through his mind. He snatched the microphone and shouted into the mouthpiece.

"Murphy! You there?"

Nothing.

"Murphy . . . Lawrence . . . do you read me?"

19

Again no answer.

He looked through the bridge window and saw Doc Thayer climb over the rail of the *Amie Marie*. Dover could move fast for a man of his mountainous proportions. He snatched a bullhorn and ran outside.

"Doc! Come back, get off that boat!" his amplified voice boomed over the water.

He was too late. Thayer had already ducked into a hatchway and was gone.

The men on the bridge stared at their captain, incomprehension written in their eyes. His facial muscles tensed and there was a look of desperation about him as he rushed back into the wheelhouse and clutched the microphone.

"Doc, this is Dover, can you hear me?"

Two minutes passed, two endless minutes while Dover tried to raise his men on the *Amie Marie*. Even the earsplitting scream of the *Catawba*'s siren failed to draw a response.

At last Thayer's voice came over the bridge with a strange icy calm.

"I regret to report that Ensign Murphy and Lieutenant Lawrence are dead. I can find no life signs. Whatever the cause it will strike me before I can escape. You must quarantine this boat. Do you understand, Amos?"

Dover found it impossible to grasp that he was suddenly about to lose his old friend. "Do not understand, but will comply."

"Good. I'll describe the symptoms as they come. Beginning to feel light-headed already. Pulse increasing to one fifty. May have contracted the cause by skin absorption. Pulse one seventy."

Thayer paused. His next words came haltingly.

"Growing nausea. Legs . . . can no longer . . . support. Intense burning sensation . . . in sinus region. Internal organs feel like they're exploding."

As one, everybody on the bridge of the *Catawba* leaned closer to the speaker, unable to comprehend that a man they all knew and respected was dying a short distance away.

"Pulse . . . over two hundred. Pain . . . excruciating. Blackness closing vision.'' There was an audible moan. "Tell . . . tell my wife . . .''

The speaker went silent.

You could smell the shock, see it in the widened eyes of the crew standing in stricken horror.

Dover stared numbly at the tomb named the *Amie Marie*, his hands clenched in helplessness and despair.

"What's happening?'' he murmured tonelessly. "What in God's name is killing everyone?''

2

"I SAY HANG THE BASTARD!"

"Oscar, mind your language in front of the girls."

"They've heard worse. It's insane. The scum murders four kids and some cretin of a judge throws the case out of court because the defendant was too stoned on drugs to understand his rights. God, can you believe it?"

Carolyn Lucas poured her husband's first cup of coffee for the day and whisked their two young daughters off to the school bus stop. He gestured menacingly at the TV as if it were the fault of the anchorman announcing the news that the killer roamed free.

Oscar Lucas had a way of talking with his hands that bore little resemblance to sign language for the deaf. He sat stoop-shouldered at the breakfast table, a position that camouflaged his lanky six-foot frame. His head was as bald as an egg except for a few graying strands around the temples, and his bushy brows hovered over a pair of oak-brown eyes. Not one to join the Washington, D.C., blue pinstripe brigade, he was dressed in slacks and sportcoat.

In his early forties, Lucas might have passed for a dentist or bookkeeper instead of the special agent in charge of the Presidential Protection Division of the Secret Service. During his twenty years as an agent he had fooled many people with his nice neighbor-next-door appearance, from the Presidents whose lives he guarded to the potential assassins he'd stonewalled before they had an opportunity to act. On the job he came off aggressive and

22

solemn, yet at home he was usually full of mischief and humor—except, of course, when he was influenced by the eight A.M. news.

Lucas took a final sip of coffee and rose from the table. He held open his coat—he was left-handed—and adjusted the high-ride hip holster holding a Smith and Wesson .357 Magnum Model 19 revolver with a 2½-inch barrel. The standard issue gun was provided by the Service when he had finished training and started out as a rookie agent in the Denver field office investigating counterfeiters and forgers. He had drawn it only twice in the line of duty, but had yet to pull the trigger outside a firing range.

Carolyn was unloading the dishwasher when he came up behind her, pulled away a cascade of blond hair and pecked her on the neck. "I'm off."

"Don't forget tonight is the pool party across the street at the Hardings'."

"I should be home in time. The boss isn't scheduled to leave the White House today."

She looked up at him and smiled. "You see that he doesn't."

"I'll inform the President first thing that my wife frowns on me working late."

She laughed and leaned her head briefly on his shoulder. "Six o'clock."

"You win," he said in mock weariness and stepped out the back door.

Lucas backed his leased government car, a plush Buick sedan, into the street and headed downtown. Before reaching the end of the block he called the Secret Service central command office over his car radio.

"Crown, this is Lucas. I'm en route to the White House."

"Have a nice trip," a metallic voice replied.

Already he began to sweat. He turned on the air conditioner. The summer heat in the nation's capital never seemed to slacken. The humidity was in the nineties and the flags along Embassy Row on Massachusetts Avenue hung limp and lifeless in the muggy air.

He slowed and stopped at the checkpoint gate on West Executive Avenue and paused for a few moments while a uniformed guard of the Service nodded and passed him through. Lucas parked the car and entered the west executive entrance on the lower level of the White House.

At the SS command post, code-named W-16, he stopped to chat with the men monitoring an array of electronic communication equipment. Then he took the stairs to his office on the second floor of the East Wing.

The first thing he did each morning after settling behind his desk was to check the President's schedule, along with advance reports by the agents in charge of planning security.

Lucas studied the folder containing future presidential "movements" a second time, consternation growing across his face. There had been an unexpected addition—a big one. He flung down the folder in irritation, swung around in his swivel chair and stared at the wall.

Most Presidents were creatures of habit, ran tight schedules and rigidly adhered to them. Clocks could be set by Nixon's comings and goings. Reagan and Carter seldom deviated from fixed plans. Not the new man in the Oval Office. He looked upon the Secret Service detail as a nuisance, and what was worse, he was unpredictable as hell.

To Lucas and his deputy agents it was a twenty-four-hour game trying to keep one step ahead of the "Man," guessing where he might suddenly decide to go and when, and what visitors he might invite without providing time for proper security measures. It was a game Lucas often lost.

In less than a minute he was down the stairs and in the West Wing confronting the second most powerful man in the executive branch, Chief of Staff Daniel Fawcett.

"Good morning, Oscar," Fawcett said, smiling benignly. "I thought you'd come charging in about now."

"There appears to be a new excursion in the schedule," Lucas said, his tone businesslike.

"Sorry about that. But a big vote is coming up on aid to the Eastern bloc countries and the President wants to work his charms on

Senator Larimer and Speaker of the House Moran to swing their support for his program.''

"So he's taking them for a boat ride."

"Why not? Every President since Herbert Hoover has used the presidential yacht for high-level conferences.''

"I'm not arguing the reason," Lucas replied firmly. "I'm protesting the timing."

Fawcett gave him an innocent look. "What's wrong with Friday evening?"

"You know damn well what's wrong. That's only two days away."

"So?"

"For a cruise down the Potomac with an overnight layover at Mount Vernon my advance team needs five days to plan security. A complete system of communications and alarms has to be installed on the grounds. The boat must be swept for explosives and listening devices, the shores checked out—and the Coast Guard requires lead time to provide a cutter on the river as an escort. We can't do a decent job in two days."

Fawcett was a feisty, eager individual with a sharp nose, a square red face and intense eyes; he always looked like a demolition expert eyeing a deserted building.

"Don't you think you're making this into an overkill, Oscar? Assassinations take place on crowded streets, or in theaters. Who ever heard of a head of state being attacked on a boat?"

"It can happen anywhere, anytime," Lucas said with an uncompromising look. "Have you forgotten the guy we stopped who was attempting to hijack a plane he intended to crash into *Air Force One?* The fact is, most assassination attempts take place when the President is away from his customary haunts.''

"The President is firm on the date," Fawcett said. "As long as you work for the President you'll do as you're ordered, same as me. If he wants to row a dinghy alone to Miami, that's his choice."

Fawcett had struck the wrong nerve. Lucas' face turned rigid and he moved until he was standing toe to toe with the White House Chief of Staff.

"First off, by order of Congress, I don't work for the President. I work for the Treasury Department. So he can't tell me to bug off and go his own way. My duty is to provide him with the best security with the least inconvenience to his private life. When he takes the elevator to his living quarters upstairs, my men and I remain below. But from the time he steps out on the first floor until he goes back up again, his ass belongs to the Secret Service."

Fawcett was perceptive about the personalities of the men who worked around the President. He realized he'd overstepped with Lucas and was wise enough to call off the war. He knew Lucas was dedicated to his job and loyal beyond any question to the man in the Oval Office. But there was no way they could be close friends—professional associates perhaps, reserved, but watchful of each other. Since they were not rivals for power, they would never be enemies.

"No need to get upset, Oscar. I stand reprimanded. I'll inform the President of your concern. But I doubt if he'll change his mind."

Lucas sighed. "We'll do our best with the time left. But he *must* be made to understand that it's imperative for him to cooperate with his security people."

"What can I say? You know better than I do that all politicians think they're immortal. To them power is more than an aphrodisiac—it's a drug high and alcoholic haze combined. Nothing excites them or inflates their ego like a mob of people cheering and clamoring to shake their hand. That's why they're all vulnerable to a killer standing in the right place at the right time."

"Tell me about it," said Lucas. "I've baby-sat four Presidents."

"And you haven't lost one," Fawcett added.

"I came close twice with Ford, once with Reagan."

"You can't predict behavior patterns accurately."

"Maybe not. But after all these years in the protection racket you develop a gut reaction. That's why I feel uneasy about this boat cruise."

Fawcett stiffened. "You think someone is out to *kill* him?"

26

"Someone is *always* out to kill him. We investigate twenty possible crazies a day and carry an active caseload of two thousand persons we consider dangerous or capable of assassination."

Fawcett put his hand on Lucas' shoulder. "Don't worry, Oscar. Friday's excursion won't be given to the press until the last minute. I promise you that much."

"I appreciate that, Dan."

"Besides, what can happen out on the Potomac?"

"Maybe nothing. Maybe the unexpected," Lucas answered, a strange vacancy in his voice. "It's the unexpected that gives me nightmares."

Megan Blair, the President's secretary, noticed Dan Fawcett standing in the doorway of her cubbyhole office and nodded at him over her typewriter. "Hi, Dan. I didn't see you."

"How's the Chief this morning?" he asked, his daily ritual of testing the water before entering the Oval Office.

"Tired," she answered. "The reception honoring the movie industry ran past one A.M."

Megan was a handsome woman in her early forties, with a bright small-town friendliness. She wore her black hair cropped short and was ten pounds on the skinny side. She was a dynamo who loved her job and her boss like nothing else in her life. She arrived early, left late and worked weekends. Unmarried, with only two casual affairs behind her, she relished her independent single life. Fawcett was always amazed that she could carry on a conversation and type at the same time.

"I'll tread lightly, and keep his appointments to a minimum so he can take it easy."

"You're too late. He's already in conference with Admiral Sandecker."

"Who?"

"Admiral James Sandecker. Director of the National Underwater and Marine Agency."

A look of annoyance crossed Fawcett's face. He took his role as the guardian of the President's time seriously and resented any intrusion on his territory. Any penetration of his protective ring was a threat to his power base. How in hell had Sandecker sneaked around him? he wondered.

Megan read his mood. "The President sent for the admiral," she explained. "I think he's expecting you to sit in on the meeting."

Pacified to a small degree, Fawcett nodded and walked into the Oval Office. The President was seated on a sofa studying several papers strewn on a large coffee table. A short, thin man with red hair and a matching Vandyke beard sat across from him.

The President looked up. "Dan, I'm glad you're here. You know Admiral Sandecker?"

"Yes."

Sandecker rose and shook his hand. The admiral's grip was firm and brief. He nodded wordlessly to Fawcett, curtly acknowledging his presence. It was not rudeness on Sandecker's part. He came across as a man who played straight ball, encasing himself in a cold, tensile shell, bowing to no one. He was hated and envied in Washington, but universally respected because he never chose sides and always delivered what was asked of him.

The President motioned Fawcett to the sofa, patting a cushion next to him. "Sit down, Dan. I've asked the admiral to brief me on a crisis that's developed in the waters off Alaska."

"I haven't heard of it."

"I'm not surprised," said the President. "The report only came to my attention an hour ago." He paused and pointed the tip of a pencil at an area circled in red on a large nautical chart. "Here, a hundred and eighty miles southwest of Anchorage in the Cook Inlet region, an undetermined poison is killing everything in the sea."

"Sounds like you're talking oil spill?"

"Far worse," replied Sandecker, leaning back on the couch. "What we have here is an unknown agent that causes death in humans and sea life less than one minute after contact."

"How is that *possible*?"

"Most poisonous compounds gain access to the body by ingestion or inhalation," Sandecker explained. "The stuff we're dealing with kills by skin absorption."

"It must be highly concentrated in a small area to be so potent."

"If you call a thousand square miles of open water *small.*"

The President looked puzzled. "I can't imagine a substance with such awesome potency."

Fawcett looked at the admiral. "What kind of statistics are we facing?"

"A Coast Guard cutter found a Kodiak fishing boat drifting with the crew dead. Two investigators and a doctor were sent onboard and died too. A team of geophysicists on an island thirty miles away were found dead by a bush pilot flying in supplies. *He* died while sending out a distress signal. A few hours later a Japanese fishing trawler reported seeing a school of nearly a hundred gray whales suddenly turn belly up. The trawler then disappeared. No trace was found. Crab beds, seal colonies—wiped out. That's only the beginning. There may be many more fatalities that we don't have word on yet."

"If the spread continues unchecked, what's the worst we can expect?"

"The virtual extinction of all marine life in the Gulf of Alaska. And if it enters the Japan Current and is carried south, it could poison every man, fish, animal and bird it touched along the West Coast as far south as Mexico. The human death toll could conceivably reach into the hundreds of thousands. Fishermen, swimmers, anyone who walked along a contaminated shoreline, anybody who ate contaminated fish—it's like a chain reaction. I don't even want to *think* what might happen if it evaporates into the atmosphere and falls with the rain over the inland states!"

Fawcett found it almost impossible to grasp the enormity of it. "Christ, what in hell *is* it?"

"Too early to tell," Sandecker replied. "The Environmental Protection Agency has a computerized mass data storage and retrieval system that contains detailed information on two hundred relevant characteristics of some eleven hundred chemical compounds. Within a few seconds they can determine the effects a hazardous substance can have when spilled, its trade name, formula, major producers, mode of transportation and threat to the environment. The Alaskan contamination doesn't fit any of the data in their computer files.''

"Surely they must have *some* idea?"

"No, sir. They don't. There is one *slim* possibility—but without autopsy reports it's strictly conjecture."

"I'd like to hear it," the President said.

Sandecker took a deep breath. "The three worst poisonous substances known to man are plutonium, Dioxin and a chemical warfare system. The first two don't fit the pattern. The third—at least in my mind—is a prime suspect."

The President stared at Sandecker, realization and shock on his face. "Nerve Agent S?" he said slowly.

Sandecker nodded silently.

"That's why the EPA wouldn't have a handle on it," the President mused. "The formula is ultrasecret."

Fawcett turned to the President. "I'm afraid I'm not familiar . . ."

"Nerve Agent S was an ungodly compound the scientists at the Rocky Mountain Arsenal developed about twenty years ago," the President explained. "I've read the report on the tests. It could kill within a few seconds of touching the skin. It seemed the ideal answer to an enemy wearing gas masks or protective gear. It clung to everything it touched. But its properties were too unstable—as dangerous to the troops dispersing it as to those on the receiving end. The Army gave up on it and buried it in the Nevada desert."

"I fail to see a connection between Nevada and Alaska," Fawcett said.

"During shipment by railroad from the arsenal outside Denver," Sandecker enlightened him, "a boxcar containing nearly a thousand gallons of Nerve Agent S vanished. It is still missing and unaccounted for."

"If the spill is indeed this nerve agent, once it's found, what is the process for eliminating it?"

Sandecker shrugged. "Unfortunately, the present state of the art in containment and cleanup technology and the physical-chemical characteristics of Nerve Agent S are such that once it enters the water very little *can* be done to ameliorate the penetration. Our only hope is to cut off the source before it releases enough poison to turn the ocean into a cesspool devoid of all life."

"Any lead on where it originates?" asked the President.

"In all probability a ship sunk between Kodiak Island and the Alaskan mainland," replied Sandecker. "Our next step is to backtrace the currents and draw up a search grid."

The President leaned over the coffee table and studied the red circle on the chart for a few moments. Then he gave Sandecker an appraising stare. "As director of NUMA, Admiral, you'll have the dirty job of neutralizing this thing. You have my authority to tap any agency or department of the government with the necessary expertise—the National Science Board, the Army and Coast Guard, the EPA, whoever." He paused thoughtfully, then asked, "Exactly how potent is Nerve Agent S in seawater?"

Sandecker looked tired, his face drawn. "One teaspoon will kill every living organism in four million gallons of seawater."

"Then we better *find* it," said the President, a touch of desperation in his voice. "And damned quick!"

3

DEEP BENEATH THE MURKY WATERS of the James River, off the shoreline of Newport News, Virginia, a pair of divers struggled against the current as they burrowed their way through the muck packed against the rotting hull of the shipwreck.

There was no sense of direction in the black dimensionless liquid. Visibility was measured in inches as they grimly clutched the pipe of an airlift that sucked up the thick ooze and spit it onto a barge seventy feet above in the sunlight. They labored almost by Braille, their only illumination coming from the feeble glimmer of underwater lights mounted on the edge of the crater they'd slowly excavated over the past several days. All they could see clearly were particles suspended in the water that drifted past their face masks like windswept rain.

It was hard for them to believe there was a world above, sky and clouds and trees bending in a summer breeze. In the nightmare of swirling mud and perpetual darkness it hardly seemed possible that five hundred yards away people and cars moved on the sidewalks and streets of the small city.

There are some people who say you can't sweat underwater, but you *can*. The divers could feel the sweat forcing its way through the pores of their skin against the protective constriction of their dry suits. They were beginning to experience the creeping grasp of weariness, yet they had only been on the bottom for eight minutes.

Inch by inch they worked their way into a gaping hole on the starboard bow of the hulk. The planking that framed the cavernlike opening was shattered and twisted as though a giant fist had rammed into the ship. They began to uncover artifacts: a shoe, the hinge from an old chest, brass calipers, tools, even a piece of cloth. It was an eerie sensation to touch man-made objects that no one had seen in 127 years.

One of the men paused to check their air gauges. He calculated they could work another ten minutes and still have a safe supply of breathable air to reach the surface.

They turned off the valve on the airlift, stopping the suction, while they waited for the river current to carry away the cloud of disturbed silt. Except for the exhaust of their breathing regulators, it became very still. A little more of the wreck became visible. The deck timbers were crushed and broken inward. Coils of rope trailed into the murklike mud-encrusted snakes. The interior of the hull seemed bleak and forbidding. They could almost sense the restless ghosts of the men who had gone down with the ship.

Suddenly they heard a strange humming—not the sound made by the outboard motor of a small boat, but heavier, like the distant drone of an aircraft engine. There was no way of telling its direction. They listened for a few moments as the sound grew louder, magnified by the density of the water. It was a surface sound and did not concern them, so they reactivated the airlift and turned back to their work.

No more than a minute later the end of the suction pipe struck something hard. Quickly they closed off the air valve again and excitedly brushed away the mud with their hands. Soon they realized they were touching, not wood, but an object that was harder, much harder, and covered with rust.

To the support crew on the barge over the wreck site time seemed to have reversed itself. They stood spellbound as an ancient PBY Catalina flying boat made a sweeping bank from the west, lined up on the river and kissed the water with the ungainly finesse of an inebriated goose. The sun glinted on the aquamarine paint covering the aluminum hull, and the letters NUMA grew larger as the lumbering seaplane taxied toward the barge. The engines shut down; the co-pilot emerged from a side hatch and threw a mooring line to one of the men on the barge.

Then a woman appeared and jumped lightly onto the battered wooden deck. She was slim, her elegant body covered by a narrow-falling tan overshirt, worn long and loose, held low on the hip by a thin sash, over tapering pants in green cotton. She wore moccasin-style boater shoes on her feet. In her mid-forties, she was about five foot seven; her hair was the color of aspen gold and her skin a copper tan. Her face was handsome, with high cheekbones, the face of a woman who fits no mold but her own.

She picked her way around a maze of cables and salvage equipment and stopped when she found herself surrounded by a gallery of male stares registering speculation mixed with undisguised fascination. She raised her sunglasses and stared back through plum-brown eyes.

"Which one of you is Dirk Pitt?" she demanded without preamble.

A rugged individual, shorter than she was, but with shoulders twice the width of his waist stepped forward and pointed into the river.

"You'll find him down there."

She turned and her eyes followed the protruding finger. A large orange buoy swayed in the rippling current, its cable angling into the dirty green depths. About thirty feet beyond, she could see the diver's bubbles boil to the surface.

"How soon before he comes up?"

"Another five minutes."

"I see," she said, pondering a moment. Then she asked, "Is Albert Giordino with him?"

"He's standing here talking to you."

Clad only in shabby sneakers, cutoff jeans and torn T-shirt, Giordino's tacky outfit was matched by his black, curly windblown hair and a two-week beard. He definitely did not fit her picture of NUMA's deputy director of special projects.

She seemed more amused than taken aback. "My name is Julie Mendoza, Environmental Protection Agency. I have an urgent matter to discuss with the two of you, but perhaps I should wait until Mr. Pitt surfaces.''

Giordino shrugged. ''Suit yourself.'' He broke into a friendly smile. ''We don't stock much in the way of creature comforts but we do have cold beer.''

''Love one, thank you.''

Giordino pulled a can of Coors from an ice bucket and handed it to her. ''What's an EPA man—ah—woman doing flying around in a NUMA plane?''

''A suggestion of Admiral Sandecker.''

Mendoza didn't offer more, so Giordino didn't press.

''What project is this?'' Mendoza asked.

''The *Cumberland*.''

''A Civil War ship, wasn't she?''

''Yes, historically very significant. She was a Union frigate sunk in 1862 by the Confederate ironclad *Merrimack*—or the *Virginia*, as she was known to the South.''

''As I recall, she went down before the *Merrimack* fought the *Monitor*, making her the first ship ever destroyed by one that was armored.''

''You know your history,'' said Giordino, properly impressed.

''And NUMA is going to raise her?''

Giordino shook his head. ''Too costly. We're only after the ram.''

''Ram?''

''A hell of a battle,'' Giordino explained. ''The crew of the *Cumberland* fought until the water came in their gun barrels, even though their cannon shot bounced off the Confederate's casemate like golf balls off a Brink's truck. In the end the *Merrimack* rammed the *Cumberland*, sending her to the bottom, flag still flying. But as the *Merrimack* backed away, her wedge-shaped ram caught inside the frigate and broke off. We're looking for that ram.''

''What possible value can an old hunk of iron have?''

''Maybe it doesn't put dollar signs in the eyes of people like treasure from a Spanish galleon, but historically it's priceless, a piece of America's naval heritage.''

Mendoza was about to ask another question, but her attention was diverted by two black rubber-helmeted heads that broke water beside the barge. The divers swam over, climbed a rusty ladder and shrugged off their heavy gear. Water streamed from their dry suits, gleaming in the sunlight.

The taller of the two pulled off his hood and ran his hands through a thick mane of ebony hair. His face was darkly tanned and the eyes were the most vivid green Mendoza had ever seen. He had the look of a man who smiled easily and often, who challenged life and accepted the wins and losses with equal indifference. When he stood at his full height he was three inches over six feet, and the lean, hard body under the dry suit strained at the seams. Mendoza knew without asking that this was Dirk Pitt.

He waved at the barge crew's approach. "We found it," he said with a wide grin.

Giordino slapped him on the back delightedly. "Nice going, pal.''

Everyone began asking the divers a barrage of questions, which they answered between swallows of beer. Finally Giordino remembered Mendoza and motioned her forward.

"This is Julie Mendoza of the EPA. She wants to have a chat with us.''

Dirk Pitt extended his hand, giving her an appraising stare. "Julie.''

"Mr. Pitt.''

"If you'll give me a minute to unsuit and dry off—''

"I'm afraid we're running late," she interrupted. "We can talk in the air. Admiral Sandecker thought the plane would be faster than a helicopter.''

"You've lost me.''

"I can't take the time to explain. We have to leave immediately. All I can say is that you've been ordered to a new project.''

There was a huskiness in her voice that intrigued Pitt, not masculine exactly, but a voice that would be at home in a Harold Robbins novel. "Why the mad rush?" he asked.

"Not here or now," she said, glancing around at the salvage crew tuned in to the conversation.

He turned to Giordino. "What do you think, Al?"

Giordino faked a bemused look. "Hard to say. The lady looks pretty determined. On the other hand, I've found a home here on the barge. I kind of hate to leave."

Mendoza flushed in anger, realizing the men were toying with her. "Please, minutes count."

"Mind telling us where we're going?"

"Langley Air Force Base, where a military jet is waiting to take us to Kodiak, Alaska."

She might as well have told them they were going to the moon. Pitt looked into her eyes, searching for something he wasn't sure he'd find. All he could read was her dead seriousness.

"I think, to be on the safe side, I'd better contact the admiral and confirm."

"You can do that on the way to Langley," she said, her tone unyielding. "I've seen to your personal affairs. Your clothes and whatever else you might need for a two-week operation have already been packed and loaded onboard." She paused and stared him squarely in the eye. "So much for small talk, Mr. Pitt. While we stand here, people are dying. You couldn't know that. But take my word for it. If you're half the man you're reported to be, you'll stop screwing around and get on the plane—now!"

"You really go for the jugular, don't you, lady?"

"If I have to."

There was an icy silence. Pitt took a deep breath, then blew it out. He faced Giordino.

"I hear Alaska is beautiful this time of year."

Giordino managed a faraway look. "Some great saloons in Skagway we should check out."

Pitt gestured to the other diver, who was peeling off his dry suit. "She's all yours, Charlie. Go ahead and bring up the *Merrimack*'s ram and get it over to the conservation lab."

"I'll see to it."

Pitt nodded, and then along with Giordino walked toward the Catalina, talking between themselves as if Julie Mendoza no longer existed.

"I hope she packed my fishing gear," said Giordino with a straight voice. "The salmon should be running."

"I've a mind to ride a caribou," Pitt carried on. "Heard tell they can outrun a dog sled."

As Mendoza followed them, the words of Admiral Sandecker came back to haunt her: "I don't envy you riding herd on those two devils, Pitt in particular. He could con a great white shark into becoming a vegetarian. So keep a sharp eye and your legs crossed."

4

JAMES SANDECKER WAS CONSIDERED a prime catch by the feminine circles of Washington society. A dedicated bachelor whose only mistress was his work, he seldom entered into a relationship with the opposite sex that lasted more than a few weeks. Sentiment and romance, the qualities women thrive on, were beyond him. In another life he might have been a hermit—or, some suggested, Ebenezer Scrooge.

In his late fifties and an exercise addict, he still cut a trim figure. He was short and muscular, and his red hair and beard had yet to show a trace of gray. He possessed an aloofness and coarse personality that appealed to women. Many cast out lures, but few ever put a hook in him.

Bonnie Cowan, an attorney for one of the city's most respected law firms, considered herself fortunate to have wrangled a dinner date with him. "You look pensive tonight, Jim," she said.

He did not look directly at her. His gaze drifted over the other diners seated amid the quiet decor of the Company Inkwell restaurant. "I was wondering how many people would dine out if there were no seafood."

She gave him a puzzled stare, then laughed. "After dealing with dull legal minds all day, I'll confess it's like inhaling mountain air to be with someone who wanders in aimless circles."

His stare returned over the table's candle and into her eyes. Bonnie Cowan was thirty-five years old, and unusually attractive. She had learned long ago that beauty was an asset in her career and never tried to disguise it. Her hair was fine, silken and fell below her shoulders. Her breasts were small but nicely proportioned, as were the legs that were amply displayed by a short skirt. She was also highly intelligent and could hold her own in any courtroom. Sandecker felt remiss at his inattentiveness.

"That's a damned pretty dress," he said, making a feeble attempt at looking attentive.

"Yes, I think the red material goes well with my blond hair."

"A nice match," he came back vaguely.

"You're hopeless, Jim Sandecker," she said, shaking her head. "You'd say the same thing if I were sitting here naked."

"Hmmmm?"

"For your information, the dress is brown, and so is my hair."

He shook his head as if to clear the cobwebs. "I'm sorry, but I warned you I'd be poor company."

"Your mind is seeing something a thousand miles away."

He reached across the table almost shyly and held her hand. "For the rest of the evening, I'll focus my thoughts entirely on you. I promise."

"Women are suckers for little boys who need mothering. And *you* are the most pathetic little boy I've ever seen."

"Mind your language, woman. Admirals do not take kindly to being referred to as pathetic little boys."

"All right, John Paul Jones, then how about a bite for a starving deckhand?"

"Anything to prevent a mutiny," he said, smiling for the first time that evening.

He recklessly ordered champagne and the most expensive seafood delicacies on the menu, as though it might be his last opportunity. He asked Bonnie about the cases she was involved with and masked his lack of interest as she relayed the latest gossip about the Supreme Court and legal maneuverings of Congress. They finished the entree and were attacking the pears poached in red wine when a man with the build of a Denver Bronco linebacker entered the foyer, stared around and, recognizing Sandecker, made his way over to the table.

He flashed a smile at Bonnie. "My apologies, ma'am, for the intrusion." Then he spoke softly into Sandecker's ear.

The admiral nodded and looked sadly across the table. "Please forgive me, but I must go."

"Government business?"

He nodded silently.

"Oh, well," she said resignedly. "At least I had you all to myself until dessert."

He came over and gave her a brotherly kiss on the cheek. "We'll do it again."

Then he paid the bill, asked the maître d' to call Bonnie a cab and left the restaurant.

The admiral's car rolled to a stop at the special tunnel entrance to the Kennedy Center for the Performing Arts. The door was opened by a sober-faced man wearing a formal black suit.

"If you will please follow me, sir."

"Secret Service?"

"Yes, sir."

Sandecker asked no more questions. He stepped out of the car and trailed the agent down a carpeted corridor to an elevator. When the doors parted, he was led along the tier level behind the box seats of the opera house to a small meeting room.

Daniel Fawcett, his expression the consistency of marble, simply waved an offhand greeting.

"Sorry to break up your date, Admiral."

"The message emphasized 'urgent.' "

"I've just received another report from Kodiak. The situation has worsened."

"Does the President know?"

"Not yet," answered Fawcett. "Best to wait until the intermission. If he suddenly left his box during the second act of *Rigoletto*, it might fuel too many suspicious minds."

A Kennedy Center staff member entered the room carrying a tray of coffee. Sandecker helped himself while Fawcett idly paced the floor. The admiral fought off an overwhelming desire to light a cigar.

After a wait of eight minutes, the President appeared. The audience applause at the end of the act was heard in the brief interval between the opening and closing of the door. He was dressed in black evening wear with a blue handkerchief nattily tucked in the breast pocket of his jacket.

"I wish I could say it was good seeing you again, Admiral, but every time we meet we're up to our butts in a crisis."

"Seems that way," Sandecker answered.

The President turned to Fawcett. "What's the bad news, Dan?"

"The captain of an auto ferry disregarded Coast Guard orders and took his ship on its normal run from Seward on the mainland to Kodiak. The ferry was found a few hours ago grounded on Marmot Island. All the passengers and crew were dead."

"Christ!" the President blurted. "What was the body count?"

"Three hundred and twelve."

"That tears it," said Sandecker. "All hell will break loose when the news media get the scent."

"Nothing we can do," Fawcett said helplessly. "Word is already coming over the wire services."

The President sank into a chair. He seemed a tall man on the TV screens. He carried himself like a tall man but he was only two inches over Sandecker. His hairline was recessed and graying, and his narrow face wore a set and solemn expression, a look rarely revealed to the public. He enjoyed tremendous popularity, helped immensely by a warm personality and an infectious smile that could melt the most hostile audience. His successful negotiations to merge Canada and the United States into one nation had served to establish an image that was immune to partisan criticism.

"We can't delay another minute," he said. "The entire Gulf of Alaska has got to be quarantined and everyone within twenty miles of the coast evacuated."

"I must disagree," Sandecker said quietly.

"I'd like to hear why."

"As far as we know the contamination has kept to open waters.

No trace has shown up on the mainland. Evacuation of the population would mean a time-consuming and massive operation. Alaskans are a tough breed, especially the fishermen tho live in the region. I doubt if they'd willingly leave under any circumstances, least of all when ordered to by the federal government."

"A hardheaded lot."

"Yes, but not *stupid*. The fishermen's associations have all agreed to restrict their vessels to port, and the canneries have begun burying all catches brought in during the past ten days."

"They'll need economic assistance."

"I expect so."

"What do you recommend?"

"The Coast Guard lacks the men and ships to patrol the entire gulf. The Navy will have to back them up."

"That," mused the President, "presents a problem. Throwing more men and ships in there increases the threat of a higher death toll."

"Not necessarily," said Sandecker. "The crew of the Coast Guard cutter that made the first discovery of the contamination received no ill effects, because the fishing boat had drifted out of the death area."

"What about the boarding crew, the doctor? They died."

"The contamination had already covered the decks, the railings, almost anything they touched on the exterior of the vessel. In the case of the ferry, its entire center section was open to accommodate automobiles. The passengers and crew had no protection. Modern naval ships are constructed to be buttoned up in case of radioactivity from nuclear attack. They can patrol the contaminated currents with a very small, acceptable degree of risk."

The President nodded his consent. "Okay, I'll order an assist from the Navy Department, but I'm not sold on dropping an evacuation plan. Stubborn Alaskans or not, there are still women and children to consider."

"My other suggestion, Mr. President, or request if you will, is a delay of forty-eight hours before you initiate the operation. That might give my response team time to find the source."

43

The President fell silent. He stared at Sandecker with deepening interest. "Who are the people in charge?"

"The on-scene coordinator and chairman of the Regional Emergency Response Team is Dr. Julie Mendoza, a senior biochemical engineer for the EPA."

"I'm not familiar with the name."

"She's recognized as the best in the country on assessment and control of hazardous contamination in water," Sandecker said without hesitation. "The underwater search for the shipwreck we believe contains the nerve agent will be headed by my special projects director, Dirk Pitt."

The President's eyes widened. "I know Mr. Pitt. He proved most helpful on the Canadian affair a few months ago."

You mean, saved your ass, Sandecker thought, before he continued. "We have nearly two hundred other pollution experts who have been called in to assist. Every expert in private industry has been tapped to provide the experience and technical data for a successful cleanup."

The President glanced at his watch. "I've got to cut this short," he said. "They won't start the third act without me. Anyway, you've got forty-eight hours, Admiral. Then I order an evacuation and declare the area a national disaster."

Fawcett accompanied the President back to his box. He seated himself slightly to the rear but close enough so they could converse in low tones while feigning interest in the performance on stage.

"Do you wish to cancel the cruise with Moran and Larimer?"

The President imperceptibly shook his head. "No. My economic recovery package for the Soviet satellite countries has top priority over any other business."

"I strongly advise against it. You're waging a hopeless battle for a lost cause."

"So you've informed me at least five times in the past week." The President held a program over his face to conceal a yawn. "How do the votes stack up?"

"A wave of nonpartisan, conservative support is gaining ground against you. We'll need fifteen votes in the House and five, maybe six, to pass the measure in the Senate."

"We've faced bigger odds."

"Yes," Fawcett muttered sadly. "But if we're defeated this time your administration may never see a second term."

5 _____

THE DAWN WAS CREEPING out of the east as a low, dark line began to rise above the horizon. Through the windows of the helicopter the black blur took on a symmetrical cone-shaped feature and soon became a mountain peak, surrounded by the sea. There was a three-quarter moon behind it. The light altered from ivory to indigo blue and then to an orange radiance as the sun rose, and the slopes could be seen mantled in snow.

Pitt glanced over at Giordino. He was asleep—a state he could slip in and out of like an old sweater. He had slept from the time they left Anchorage. Five minutes after transferring to the helicopter, he promptly drifted off again.

Pitt turned to Mendoza. She sat perched behind the pilot. The look on her face was that of a little girl eager to see a parade. Her gaze was fixed on the mountain. In the early light it seemed to Pitt her face had softened. Her expression was not so businesslike and the lines of her mouth held a tenderness that was not there before.

"Augustine Volcano," she said, unaware that Pitt's attention was focused on her and not out the window. "Named by Captain Cook in 1778. You wouldn't know to look at it but Augustine is the most active volcano in Alaska, having erupted six times in the last century."

Pitt regretfully turned away and stared below. The island seemed devoid of any human habitation. Long swirling flows of lava rock spilled down the mountain's sides until they met the sea. A small cloud drifted about the summit.

"Very picturesque," he said, yawning. "Might have possibilities as a ski resort."

"Don't bet on it." She laughed. "That cloud you see over the peak is steam. Augustine is a constant performer. The last eruption in 1987 surpassed Mount St. Helens in Washington. The fall of ash and pumice was measured as far away as Athens."

Pitt had to ask, "What's its status now?"

"Recent data confirm the heat around the summit is increasing, probably forecasting an impending explosion."

"Naturally, you can't say when."

"Naturally." She shrugged. "Volcanoes are unpredictable. Sometimes they become violent without the slightest warning; sometimes they take months to build up to a spectacular climax that never happens. They sputter, rumble a little and then go dormant. Those earth scientists I told you about who died from the nerve agent—they were on the island to study the impending activity."

"Where are we settling down?"

"About ten miles off the shore," she replied, "on the Coast Guard cutter *Catawba.*"

"The *Catawba,*" he repeated as if reminiscing.

"Yes, you know of her?"

"Set a copter on her flight pad myself a few years ago."

"Where was that?"

"North Atlantic, near Iceland." He was gazing beyond the island now. He sighed and massaged his temples. "A good friend and I were hunting for a ship imbedded in an iceberg."

"Did you find it?"

He nodded. "A burned-out hulk. Barely beat the Russians to it. Later we crashed in the surf on the Icelandic coast. My friend was killed."

She could see his mind was reliving the events. The expression on his face took on a faraway sadness. She changed the subject.

"We'll have to say goodbye—temporarily, I mean—when we land."

He shook off the past and stared at her. "You're leaving us?"

"You and Al will be staying on the *Catawba* to search for the nerve agent's location. I'm going to the island where the local response team has set up a data base.''

"And part of my job is to send water samples from the ship to your lab?''

"Yes, by measuring trace levels of the contamination we can direct you toward the surface.''

"Like following breadcrumbs.''

"That's one way of putting it.''

"After we find it, what then?''

"Once your salvage team brings up the drums containing the nerve agent, the Army will dispose of it by deep well injection, on an island near the Arctic Circle.''

"How deep is the well?''

"Four thousand feet.''

"All neat and tidy.''

The open-for-business look returned to her eyes. "It happens to be the most efficient method open to us.''

"You're optimistic.''

She looked at him questioningly. "What do you mean?''

"The salvage. It could take months.''

"We can't even afford weeks,'' she came back almost vehemently.

"You're treading in my territory now,'' Pitt said as if lecturing. "Divers can't risk working in water where one drop on their skin will kill them. The only reasonably safe way is to use submersibles—a damned slow and tedious process. And submersibles require highly trained crews, with specially constructed vessels as work platforms.''

"I've already explained,'' she said impatiently, "presidential authority gives us carte blanche on any equipment we need.''

"That's the easy part,'' Pitt continued. "Despite your water sample directions, finding a shipwreck is like looking for a coin in the middle of a football field in the dark with a candle. Then if we get lucky and make contact, we may find the hull broken in sections and the cargo scattered, or the drums too corroded to move.

Murphy's Law can hit us from every angle. No deep-sea recovery operation is ever cut and dried.''

Mendoza's face reddened. ''I'd like to point out—''

''Don't bother,'' Pitt cut her off. ''I'm the wrong guy for a gung-ho speech. I've heard them all before. You won't get a chorus of the Notre Dame fight song from me. And save your breath for the 'countless lives hang in the balance' routine. I'm aware of it. I don't have to be reminded every five minutes.''

She looked at him, annoyed with him for his arrogant charm, feeling that he was testing her somehow. ''Have you ever seen someone who came in contact with Nerve Agent S?''

''No.''

''It's not a pretty sight. They literally drown in their own blood as their internal membranes burst. Every body orifice bleeds like a river. Then the corpse turns black.''

''You're very descriptive.''

''It's all a game to you,'' she lashed out. ''It's not a game to me.''

He didn't reply. He simply nodded downward at the *Catawba* looming through the pilot's windshield. ''We're landing.''

The pilot noted that the ship had turned bow-on to the wind from the fluttered ensign on the halyards. He eased the helicopter over the stern, hovered a few moments and set down on the pad. The rotor blades had hardly swung to a stop when two figures dressed from head to toe in astronaut-looking suits approached while unfolding a circular plastic tube about five feet in diameter that looked like a huge umbilical cord. They secured it around the exit door and gave three knocks. Pitt undid the latches and swung the door inward. The men outside passed him cloth hoods with see-through lenses and gloves.

''Best put them on,'' commanded a muffled voice.

Pitt prodded Giordino awake and handed him a hood and pair of gloves.

''What in hell are these?'' Giordino mumbled, emerging from the cobwebs.

''Welcome gifts from the sanitation department.''

Two more crewmen appeared in the plastic tunnel and took their gear. Giordino, still half asleep, stumbled from the helicopter. Pitt hesitated and stared into Mendoza's eyes.

"What's my reward if I find your poison in forty-eight hours?"

"What do you want it to be?"

"Are you as hard as you pretend?"

"Harder, Mr. Pitt, much harder."

"Then you decide."

He gave her a rakish smile and was gone.

6

THE CARS THAT MADE UP the presidential motorcade were lined in a row beside the South Portico of the White House. As soon as the Secret Service detail was in position, Oscar Lucas spoke into a tiny microphone whose wire looped around the watch on his wrist and ran up the sleeve of his coat.

"Tell the Boss, we're ready."

Three minutes later the President, accompanied by Fawcett, walked briskly down the steps and entered the presidential limousine. Lucas joined them and the cars moved out through the southwest gate.

The President relaxed into the leather of the rear seat and idly stared out the window at the passing buildings. Fawcett sat with an open attaché case on his lap and made a series of notes inside the top folder. After a few minutes of silence, he sighed, snapped the case shut and set it on the floor.

"There it is, arguments from both sides of the fence, statistics, CIA projections, and the latest reports from your economic council on Communist bloc debts. Everything you should need to sell Larimer and Moran on your way of thinking."

"The American public doesn't think much of my plan, does it?" the President asked quietly.

"To be perfectly honest, no, sir," Fawcett replied. "The general feeling is to let the Reds stew in their own problems. Most Americans are cheering the fact that the Soviets and their satellites are facing starvation and financial ruin. They consider it proof positive that the Marxist system is a pathetic joke."

"It won't be a joke if the Kremlin leaders, backs against an economic wall, strike out in desperation and march through Europe."

"Your opposition in Congress feel the risk is offset by the very real threat of starvation, which will undermine Russia's capacity to maintain its military machine. And there are those who are banking on the eroding morale of the Russian people to crystallize in active resistance toward the ruling party."

The President shook his head. "The Kremlin is fanatical about its military buildup. They'll never slack off in spite of their economic dilemma. And the people will never rise up or stage mass demonstrations. The party's collar is too tight."

"The bottom line," said Fawcett, "is that both Larimer and Moran are dead set against taking the burden off Moscow."

The President's face twisted in disgust. "Larimer is a drunk and Moran is tainted with corruption."

"Still, there is no getting around the fact you have to sell them on your philosophy."

"I can't deny their opinions," the President admitted. "But I am convinced that if the United States saves the Eastern bloc nations from almost total disintegration, they will turn away from the Soviet Union and join with the West."

"There are many who see that as wishful thinking, Mr. President."

"The French and Germans see it my way."

"Sure, and why not? They're playing both ends of the field, relying on our NATO forces for security while expanding economic ties with the East."

"You're forgetting the many grass-roots American voters who are behind my aid plan too," said the President, his chin thrust forward at his words. "Even they realize its potential for defusing the threat of nuclear holocaust and pulling down the Iron Curtain for good."

Fawcett knew it was senseless to try to sway the President when he was in a crusading mood and passionately convinced he was right. There was a kind of virtue in killing your enemies with kindness, a truly civilized tactic that might move the conscience of reasonable people, but Fawcett remained pessimistic. He turned inward to his thoughts and remained silent as the limousine turned off M Street into the Washington Naval Yard and rolled to a stop on one of the long docks.

A dark-skinned man with the stony facial features of an American Indian approached as Lucas stepped from the car.

"Evening, George."

"Hello, Oscar. How's the golf game?"

"Sad shape," answered Lucas. "I haven't played in almost two weeks."

As Lucas spoke he looked into the piercing dark eyes of George Blackowl, the acting supervisor and advance agent for the President's movement. Blackowl was about Lucas' height, five years younger and carried about ten pounds of excess weight. A habitual gum chewer—his jaws worked constantly—he was half Sioux and was constantly kidded about his ancestors' role at the Little Big Horn.

"Safe to board?" asked Lucas.

"The boat has been swept for explosives and listening devices. The frogmen finished checking the hull about ten minutes ago, and the outboard chase boat is manned and ready to follow."

Lucas nodded. "A hundred-and-ten-foot Coast Guard cutter will be standing by when you reach Mount Vernon."

"Then I guess we're ready for the Boss."

Lucas paused for nearly a minute while he scanned the surrounding dock area. Detecting nothing suspicious, he opened the door for the President. Then the agents formed a security diamond around him. Blackowl walked ahead of the point man, who was directly in front of the President. Lucas, because he was left-handed and required ease of movement in case he had to draw his gun, walked the left point and slightly to the rear. Fawcett tailed several yards behind and out of the way.

At the boarding ramp Lucas and Blackowl stood aside to let the others pass.

"Okay, George, he's all yours."

"Lucky you," Blackowl said, smiling. "You get the weekend off."

"First time this month."

"Heading home from here?"

"Not yet. I have to run by the office and clear my desk first. There were a few hitches during the last trip to Los Angeles. I want to review the planning."

They turned in unison as another government limousine pulled up to the dock. Senator Marcus Larimer climbed out and strode toward the presidential yacht followed by an aide who dutifully carried an overnight bag.

Larimer wore a brown suit with a vest; he always wore a brown suit with a vest. It had been suggested by one of his fellow legislators that he was born in one. His hair was sandy colored and styled in the dry look. He was big and rough-cut, with the look of a hod carrier trying to crash a celebrity benefit.

He simply nodded to Blackowl and threw Lucas the standard politician's greeting: "Nice to see you, Oscar."

"You're looking healthy, Senator."

"Nothing a bottle of scotch won't cure," Larimer replied with a booming laugh. Then he swept up the ramp and disappeared into the main salon.

"Have fun," Lucas said sarcastically to Blackowl. "I don't envy you this trip."

A few minutes later, while driving through the naval-yard gate onto M Street, Lucas passed a compact Chevrolet carrying Congressman Alan Moran going in the opposite direction. Lucas didn't like the Speaker of the House. Not nearly as flamboyant as his predecessor, Moran was a Horatio Alger type who had succeeded not so much from intelligence or perception as from stowing away in the congressional power circles and supplying more favors than he begged. Once accused of masterminding an oil-leasing scheme on government lands, he had greased his way out of the impending scandal by calling in his political IOU's.

He looked neither right nor left as he drove by. His mind, Lucas deduced, was grinding on ways to pick the President's influential pocket.

Not quite an hour later, as the crew of the presidential yacht were preparing to cast off, Vice President Margolin came aboard with a garment bag draped over one shoulder. He hesitated a moment and then spied the President, seated alone in a deck chair near the stern, watching the sun begin to set over the city. A steward appeared and relieved Margolin of the garment bag.

The President looked up and stared as though not fully recognizing him.

"Vince?"

"Sorry I'm late," Margolin apologized. "But one of my aides misplaced your invitation and I only discovered it an hour ago."

"I wasn't sure you could make it," the President murmured obscurely.

"Perfect timing. Beth is visiting our son at Stanford and won't be home until Tuesday, and I had nothing on my schedule that couldn't be shoved ahead."

The President stood up, forcing a friendly smile. "Senator Larimer and Congressman Moran are on board too. They're in the dining salon." He tilted his head in their direction. "Why don't you say hello and rustle up a drink."

"A drink I could use."

Margolin bumped into Fawcett in the doorway and they exchanged a few words.

The President's face was a study in anger. As much as he and Margolin differed in style and appearance—the Vice President was tall and nicely proportioned, not a bit of fat on his body, with a handsome face, bright blue eyes and a warm, outgoing personality—they differed even more in their politics.

The President maintained a high level of personal popularity by his inspirational speeches. An idealist and a visionary, he was almost totally occupied with creating programs that would be of global benefit ten to fifty years in the future. Unfortunately, for the most part they were programs that did not fit in with the selfish realities of domestic politics.

Margolin, on the other hand, kept a low profile with the public and news media, aiming his energies more toward domestic issues. His stand on the President's Communist bloc aid program was that the money would be better spent at home.

The Vice President was a born politician. He had the Constitution in his blood. He had come up the hard way—through the ranks, beginning with his state legislature, then governor and later the Senate. Once entrenched in his office in the Russell Building, he surrounded himself with a powerhouse staff of advisers who possessed a flair for strategic compromise and innovative political concepts. While it was the President who proposed legislation, it was Margolin who orchestrated its passage through the maze of committees into law and policy, all too often making the White House staff appear like fumbling amateurs, a situation that did not sit well with the President and caused considerable internal backstabbing.

Margolin might have been the people's choice for the Presidency, but he was not the party's. Here his integrity and image as a "shaker and doer" worked against him. He too often refused to fall in line on partisan issues if he believed in a better path; he was a maverick who followed his own conscience.

The President watched Margolin disappear into the main salon, irritation and jealousy burning within him.

"What is Vince doing here?" Fawcett asked him nervously.

"Damned if I know," snapped the President. "He said he was invited."

Fawcett looked stricken. "Christ, somebody on the staff must have screwed up."

"Too late now. I can't tell him he's not wanted and to please leave."

Fawcett was still confused. "I don't understand."

"Neither do I, but we're stuck with him."

"He could blow it."

"I don't think so. Regardless of what we think about Vince, he's never made a statement that tarnished my image. That's more than a lot of Presidents could say about their VP's."

Fawcett resigned himself to the situation. "There aren't enough staterooms to go around. I'll give up mine and stay on shore."

"I appreciate that, Dan."

"I can stay on the boat until tonight and then bunk at a nearby motel."

"Perhaps, under the circumstances," the President said slowly, "it would be best if you remained behind. With Vince along, I don't want our guests to think we're ganging up on them."

"I'll leave the documents supporting your position in your stateroom, Mr. President."

"Thank you. I'll study them before dinner." Then the President paused. "By the way, any word on the Alaskan situation?"

"Only that the search for the nerve agent is under way."

The President's eyes reflected a disturbed look. He nodded and shook Fawcett's hand. "See you tomorrow."

Later Fawcett stood on the dock among the irritated Secret Service agents of the Vice President's detail. As he watched the aging white yacht cut into the Anacostia River before turning south toward the Potomac, a knot began to tighten in the pit of his stomach.

There had been no written invitations!

None of it made any sense.

Lucas was putting on his coat, about to leave his office, when the phone linked to the command post buzzed.

"Lucas."

"This is 'Love Boat,' " replied George Blackowl, giving the code name of the movement in progress.

The call was unexpected and like a father with a daughter on a date Lucas immediately feared the worst. "Go ahead," he said tersely.

"We have a situation. This is no emergency, I repeat, no emergency. But something's come up that isn't in the movement."

Lucas expelled a sigh of relief. "I'm listening."

" 'Shakespeare' is on the boat," said Blackowl, giving the code name for the Vice President.

"He's *where?*" Lucas gasped.

"Margolin showed up out of nowhere and came onboard as we were casting off. Dan Fawcett gave him his stateroom and went ashore. When I queried the President about the last-minute switch in passengers, he told me to let it ride. But I smell a screwup."

"Where's Rhinemann?"

"Right here with me on the yacht."

"Put him on."

There was a pause and then Hank Rhinemann, the supervisor in charge of the Vice President's security detail, came on. "Oscar, we've got an unscheduled movement."

"Understood. How did you lose him?"

"He came charging out of his office and said he had to attend an urgent meeting with the President on the yacht. He didn't tell me it was an overnight affair."

"He kept it from you?"

" 'Shakespeare' is tight-mouthed as hell. I should have known when I saw the garment bag. I'm sorry as hell, Oscar."

A wave of frustration swept Lucas. God, he thought, the leaders of the world's leading superpowers were like kids when it came to their own security.

"It's happened," said Lucas sharply. "So we'll make the best of it. Where is your detail?"

"Standing on the dock," answered Rhinemann.

"Send them down to Mount Vernon and back up Blackowl's people. I want that yacht cordoned off tighter than a bass drum."

"Will do."

"At the slightest hint of trouble, call me. I'm spending the night at the command post."

"You got a line on something?" Rhinemann asked.

"Nothing tangible," Lucas replied, his voice so hollow it seemed to come from a distant source. "But knowing that the President and the next three men in line for his office are all in the same place at the same time scares the hell out of me."

7

"WE'VE TURNED AGAINST THE CURRENT." Pitt's voice was quiet, almost casual, as he stared at the color video screen on the Klein hydroscan sonar that read the seafloor. "Increase speed about two knots."

Dressed in bleached Levi's, Irish knit turtleneck sweater and brown tennis shoes, his brushed hair laid back under a NUMA baseball cap, he looked cool and comfortable with a bored, indifferent air about him.

The wheel moved slowly under the helmsman's hands and the *Catawba* lazily shoved aside the three-foot swells as she swept back and forth over the sea like a lawn mower. Trailing behind the stern like a tin can tied to the tail of a dog, the sidescan sonar's sensor pinged the depths, sending a signal to the video display, which translated it into a detailed image of the bottom.

They took up the search for the nerve agent source in the southern end of Cook Inlet and discovered that the residual traces rose as they worked westward into Kamishak Bay. Water samples were taken every half-hour and ferried by helicopter to the chemical lab on Augustine Island. Amos Dover philosophically compared the project to a children's game of finding hidden candy with an unseen voice giving "warmer" or "colder" clues.

As the day wore on, the nervous tension that had been building up on the *Catawba* grew unbearable. The crew was unable to go on deck for a breath of air. Only the EPA chemists were allowed outside the exterior bulkheads, and they were protected by airtight encapsulating suits.

"Anything yet?" Dover asked, peering over Pitt's shoulder at the high-resolution screen.

"Nothing man-made," Pitt answered. "Bottom terrain is rugged, broken, mostly lava rock."

"Good clear picture."

Pitt nodded. "Yes, the detail is quite sharp."

"What's that dark smudge?"

"A school of fish. Maybe a pack of seals."

Dover turned and stared through the bridge windows at the volcanic peak on Augustine Island, now only a few miles away. "Better make a strike soon. We're coming close to shore."

"Lab to ship," Mendoza's feminine voice broke over the bridge speaker.

Dover picked up the communications phone. "Go ahead, lab."

"Steer zero-seven-zero degrees. Trace elements appear to be in higher concentrations in that direction."

Dover gave the nearby island an apprehensive eye. "If we hold that course for twenty minutes we'll park on your doorstep for supper."

"Come in as far as you can and take samples," Mendoza answered. "My indications are that you're practically on top of it."

Dover hung up without further discussion and called out, "What's the depth?"

The watch officer tapped a dial on the instrument console. "One hundred forty feet and rising."

"How far can you see on that thing?" Dover asked Pitt.

"We read the seabed six hundred meters on either side of our hull."

"Then we're cutting a swath nearly two thirds of a mile wide."

"Close enough," Pitt admitted.

"We should have detected the ship by now," Dover said irritably. "Maybe we missed it."

"No need to get uptight," Pitt said. He paused, leaned over the computer keyboard and fine-tuned the image. "Nothing in this world is more elusive than a shipwreck that isn't ready to be found. Deducing the murderer in an Agatha Christie novel is kindergarten stuff compared to finding a lost derelict under hundreds of square miles of water. Sometimes you get lucky early. Most of the time you don't."

"Very poetic," Dover said dryly.

Pitt stared at the overhead bulkhead for a long and considering moment. "What's the visibility under the water surface?"

"The water turns crystal fifty yards from shore. On the flood tide I've seen a hundred feet or better."

"I'd like to borrow your copter and take aerial photos of this area."

"Why bother?" Dover said curtly. "*Semper Paratus*, Always Ready, is not the Coast Guard's motto for laughs." He motioned through a doorway. "We have charts showing three thousand miles of Alaskan coastline in color and incredible detail, courtesy of satellite reconnaissance."

Pitt nodded for Giordino to take his place in front of the hydroscan as he rose and followed the *Catawba*'s skipper into a small compartment stacked with cabinets containing nautical charts. Dover checked the label inserts, pulled open a drawer and rummaged inside. Finally he extracted a large chart marked "Satellite Survey Number 2430A, South Shore of Augustine Island." Then he laid it on a table and spread it out.

"Is this what you have in mind?"

Pitt leaned over and studied the bird's-eye view of the sea off the volcanic island's coast. "Perfect. Got a magnifying glass?"

"In the shelf under the table."

Pitt found the thick, square lens and peered through it at the tiny shadows on the photo survey. Dover left and returned shortly with two mugs of coffee.

"Your chances are nil of spotting an anomaly in that geological nightmare on the seafloor. A ship could stay lost forever in there."

"I'm not looking at the seafloor."

Dover heard Pitt's words all right, but the meaning didn't register. Vague curiosity reflected in his eyes, but before he could ask the obvious question the speaker above the doorway crackled.

"Skipper, we've got breakers ahead." The watch officer's voice was tense. "The Fathometer reads thirty feet of water under the hull—and rising damned fast."

"All stop!" Dover ordered. A pause, then: "No, reverse engines until speed is zero."

"Tell him to have the sonar sensor pulled in before it drags bottom," Pitt said offhandedly. "Then I suggest we drop anchor."

Dover gave Pitt a strange look, but issued the command. The deck trembled beneath their feet as the twin screws reversed direction. After a few moments the vibration ceased.

"Speed zero," the watch officer notified them from the bridge. "Anchor away."

Dover acknowledged, then sat on a stool, cupped his hands around the coffee mug and looked directly at Pitt.

"Okay, what do you see?"

"I have the ship we're looking for," Pitt said, speaking slowly and distinctly. "There are no other possibilities. You were mistaken in one respect, Dover, but correct in another. Mother Nature seldom makes rock formations that run in a perfectly straight line for several hundred feet. Consequently, the outline of a ship *can* be detected against an irregular background. You were right, though, in saying our chances were nil of finding it on the seafloor."

"Get to the point," Dover said impatiently.

"The target is on shore."

"You mean grounded in the shallows?"

"I mean on shore, as in high and dry."

"You can't be serious?"

Pitt ignored the question and handed Dover the magnifying glass. "See for yourself." He took a pencil and circled a section of cliffs above the tideline.

Dover bent over and put his eye to the glass. "All I see is rock."

"Look closer. The projection from the lower part of the slope into the sea."

62

Dover's expression turned incredulous. "Oh, Jesus, it's the stern of a ship!"

"You can make out the fantail and the top half of the rudder."

"Yes, yes, and a piece of the after deckhouse." Dover's frustration was suddenly washed away by the mounting excitement of the discovery. "Incredible. She's buried bow-on into the shore, as though she were covered by an avalanche. Judging from the cruiser stern and the balanced rudder, I'd say she's an old Liberty ship." He looked up, a deepening interest in his eyes. "I wonder if she might be the *Pilottown?*"

"Sounds vaguely familiar."

"One of the most stubborn mysteries of the northern seas. The *Pilottown* tramped back and forth between Tokyo and the West Coast until ten years ago, when her crew reported her sinking in a storm. A search was launched and no trace of the ship was found. Two years later an Eskimo stumbled on the *Pilottown* caught in the ice about ninety miles above Nome. He went aboard but found the ship deserted, no sign of the crew or cargo. A month later, when he returned with his tribe to remove whatever they could find of value, it was gone again. Nearly two years passed, and she was reported drifting below the Bering Strait. The Coast Guard was sent out but couldn't locate her. The *Pilottown* wasn't sighted again for eight months. She was boarded by the crew of a fishing trawler. They found her in reasonably good shape. Then she disappeared for the last time."

"I seem to recall reading something . . ." Pitt paused. "Ah, yes, the 'Magic Ship.' "

"That's what the news media dubbed her," Dover acknowledged. "They described her disappearing act as a 'now you see it, now you don't' routine."

"They'll have a field day when it gets out she was drifting around for years with a cargo of nerve agent."

"No way of predicting the horror if the hull had been crushed in an ice pack or shattered on a rocky shore, creating an instant spill," Dover added.

"We've got to get in her cargo holds," said Pitt. "Contact Mendoza, give her the position of the wreck and tell her to airlift a team of chemists to the site. We'll approach from the water.''

Dover nodded. ''I'll see to the launch.''

''Throw in acetylene equipment in case we have to cut our way inside.''

Dover bent over the chart table and stared solemnly at the center of the marked circle. ''I never thought for a minute I'd stand on the deck of the Magic Ship.''

''If you're right,'' said Pitt, staring into his coffee mug, ''the *Pilottown* is about to give her last performance.''

8

THE SEA HAD BEEN CALM, but by the time the *Catawba*'s launch was a quarter-mile from the lonely, forbidding coast, a twenty-knot wind kicked up the water. The spray, tainted by the nerve agent, struck the cabin windows with the fury of driven sand. Yet where the derelict lay beached, the water looked reasonably peaceful, protected as it was by jagged pinnacles of rock that rose up a hundred yards offshore like solitary chimneys from burned-out houses.

Far above the turbulent waters Augustine Volcano seemed calm and serene in the late afternoon sun. It was one of the most beautifully sculptured mountains in the Pacific, rivaling the classic contour of Mount Fuji in Japan.

The powerful launch surfed for an instant on a whitecapped swell before diving over the crest. Pitt braced his feet, gripped a railing with both hands while his eyes studied the shore.

The wreck was heeled over at a twenty-degree angle and her stern section blanketed in brown rust. The rudder was canted in the full starboard position and two barnacle-encrusted blades of the propeller protruded from the black sand. The letters of her name and home port were too obscured to read.

Pitt, Giordino, Dover, the two EPA scientists and one of the *Catawba*'s junior officers all were garbed in white encapsulating suits to protect them from the plumes of deadly spray. They communicated by tiny transmitters inside their protective headgear. Attached to their waist belts were intricate filter systems designed to refine clean, breathable air.

The sea around them was carpeted with dead fish of every species. A pair of whales rolled lifelessly back and forth with the tide, united in rotting decay with porpoises, sea lions and spotted seals. Birds by the thousands floated amid the morbid debris. Nothing that had lived in the area had escaped.

Dover expertly threaded the launch between the threatening offshore barrier of projecting rock, the remnant of an ancient coastline. He slowed, waiting for a momentary lull in the surf, biding his time while carefully eyeing the depth. Then as a wave slammed onto the shore and its backwash spilled against the next one coming in, he aimed the bow at the small spit of sand formed around the base of the wreck and pushed the throttle forward. Like a horse bracing for the next hurdle at the Grand National, the launch rose up on the wave crest and rode it through the swirling foam until the keel dropped and scraped onto the spit.

"A neat bit of handiwork," Pitt complimented him.

"All in the timing," Dover said, a grin visible behind his helmet's face mask. "Of course, it helps if you land at low tide."

They tilted back their heads and stared up at the wreck towering above them. The faded name on the stern could be deciphered now. It read *Pilottown*.

"Almost a pity," Dover said reverently, "to write *finish* to an enigma."

"The sooner the better," Pitt said, his tone grim as he considered the mass death inside.

Within five minutes the equipment was unloaded, the launch securely moored to the *Pilottown*'s rudder, and the men laboriously climbing the steep slope on the port side of the stern. Pitt took the lead, followed by Giordino and the rest as Dover brought up the rear.

The incline was not made up of solid rock but rather a combination of cinder ash and mud with the consistency of loose gravel. Their boots struggled to find a foothold, but mostly they slid back two steps for every three they gained. The dust from the ash rose and clung to their suits, coating them a dark gray. Soon the sweat was seeping through their pores and the increasingly heavy rasp of their breathing became more audible over the earphones inside their helmets.

Pitt called a halt at a narrow ledge, not four feet wide and just long enough to hold all six men. Wearily Giordino sank to a sitting position and readjusted the straps that held the acetylene tank to his back. When he could finally pant a coherent sentence, he said, "How in hell did this old rust bucket jam herself in here?"

"She probably drifted into what was a shelving inlet before 1987," replied Pitt. "According to Mendoza, that was the year the volcano last erupted. The explosion gases must have melted the ice around the mantle, forming millions of gallons of water. The mudflow, along with the cloud of ash, poured down the mountain until it met the sea and buried the ship."

"Funny the stern wasn't spotted before now."

"Not so remarkable," Pitt answered. "So little is showing it was next to impossible to detect from the air, and beyond a mile from shore it blends into the rugged shoreline and becomes nearly invisible. Erosion caused by recent storms is the only reason she's uncovered now."

Dover stood up, pressing his weight against the steep embankment to maintain his balance. He unraveled a thin knotted nylon rope from his waist and unfolded a small grappling hook tied to the end.

He looked down at Pitt. "If you'll support my legs, I think I can heave the hook over the ship's railing."

Pitt grasped his left leg as Giordino edged over and held the right. The burly Coast Guardsman leaned back over the lip of the ledge, swung the hook in a widening arc and let it fly.

It sailed over the stern rails and caught.

The rest of the ascent took only a few minutes. Pulling themselves upward, hand over hand, they soon climbed onto the deck. Heavy layers of rust mingled with ash flaked away beneath their feet. What little they could see of the *Pilottown* looked a dirty, ugly mess.

"No sign of Mendoza," said Dover.

"Nearest flat ground to land a copter is a thousand yards away," Pitt replied. "She and her team will have to hike in."

Giordino walked over to the railing beside the corroded shaft of the jackstaff and stared at the water below. "The poison must be seeping through the hull during high tide."

"Probably stored in the after hold," said Dover.

"The cargo hatches are buried under tons of this lava crap," Giordino said in disgust. "We'll need a fleet of bulldozers to get through."

"You familiar with Liberty ships?" Pitt asked Dover.

"Should be. I've inspected enough of them over the years, looking for illegal cargo." He knelt down and began tracing a ship's outline in the rust. "Inside the aft deckhouse we should find a hatch to an escape trunk that leads to the tunnel holding the screw shaft. At the bottom is a small recess. We might be able to cut our way into the hold from there."

They all stood silent when Dover finished. They should all have felt a sense of accomplishment at having found the source of the nerve agent. But instead they experienced apprehension—a reaction, Pitt supposed, that stemmed from a letdown after the excitement of the search. Then also there was a hidden dread of what they might actually find behind the steel bulkheads of the *Pilottown*.

"Maybe . . . maybe we better wait for the lab people," one of the chemists stammered.

"They can catch up," Pitt said pleasantly, but with cold eyes.

Giordino silently took a prybar from the toolpack strapped on Pitt's back and attacked the steel door to the after deckhouse. To his surprise it creaked and moved. He put his muscle to it, the protesting hinges surrendered and the door sprung open. The interior was completely empty, no fittings, no gear, not even a scrap of trash.

"Looks as though the movers have been here," observed Pitt.

"Odd it was never in use," Dover mused.

"The escape trunk?"

"This way." Dover led them through another compartment that was also barren. He stopped at a round hatch in the center of the deck. Giordino moved forward, pried open the cover and stepped back. Dover aimed a flashlight down the yawning tunnel, the beam stabbing the darkness.

"So much for that idea," he said dejectedly. "The tunnel recess is blocked with debris."

"What's on the next deck below?"

"The steering gear compartment." Dover paused, his mind working. Then he thought aloud. "Just forward of the steering gear there's an after steering room. A holdover from the war years. It's possible, barely possible, it might have an access hatch to the hold."

They went aft then and returned to the first compartment. It felt strange to them to walk the decks of a ghost ship, wondering what happened to the crew that abandoned her. They found the hatch-way and climbed down the ladder to the steering gear compartment and made their way around the old, still oily machinery to the forward bulkhead. Dover scanned the steel plates with his flashlight. Suddenly the wavering beam stopped.

"Son of a bitch!" he grunted. "The hatch is here, but it's been welded shut."

"You're certain we're in the right spot?" Pitt asked.

"Absolutely," Dover answered. He rapped his gloved fist against the bulkhead. "On the other side is cargo hold number five—the most likely storage of the poison."

"What about the other holds?" asked one of the EPA men.

"Too far forward to leak into the sea."

"Okay, then let's do it," Pitt said impatiently.

Quickly they assembled the cutting torch and connected the oxygen-acetylene bottles. The flame from the tip of the torch hissed as Giordino adjusted the gas mixture. Blue flame shot out and assaulted the steel plate, turning it red, then a bright orange-white. A narrow gap appeared and lengthened, crackling and melting under the intense heat.

As Giordino was cutting an opening large enough to crawl

through, Julie Mendoza and her lab people appeared, packing nearly five hundred pounds of chemical analysis instruments.

"You found it," she stated straight from the shoulder.

"We can't be sure yet," Pitt cautioned.

"But our test samples show the water around this area reeks with Nerve Agent S," she protested.

"Disappointment comes easy," said Pitt. "I never count my chickens till the check clears the bank."

Further conversation broke off as Giordino stood back and snuffed out the cutting torch. He handed it to Dover and picked up his trusty prybar.

"Stand back," he ordered. "This thing is red hot and it's damned heavy."

He hooked one end of the bar into the jagged, glowing seam and shoved. Grudgingly, the steel plate twisted away from the bulkhead and crashed to the deck with a heavy clang and spray of molten metal.

A hush fell over the dark compartment as Pitt took a flashlight and leaned carefully through the opening, staying clear of the superheated edges. He probed the beam into the bowels of the darkened cargo hold, sweeping it around in a 180-degree arc.

It seemed a long time before he straightened and faced the bizarrely clad, faceless figures pressing against him.

"Well?" Mendoza demanded anxiously.

Pitt answered with one word: "Eureka!"

9

FOUR THOUSAND MILES and five hours ahead in a different time zone, the Soviet representative to the World Health Assembly worked late at his desk. There was nothing elaborate about his office in the Secretariat building of the United Nations; the furnishings were cheap and Spartan. Instead of the usual photographs of Russian leaders, living and dead, the only piece of wall decor was a small amateurish watercolor of a house in the country.

The light blinked and a soft chime emitted from his private phone line. He stared at it suspiciously for a long moment before picking up the receiver.

"This is Lugovoy."

"Who?"

"Aleksei Lugovoy."

"Is Willie dere?" asked a voice, heavy with the New York City accent that always grated on Lugovoy's ears.

"There is no Willie here," Lugovoy said brusquely. "You must have the wrong number." Then he abruptly hung up.

Lugovoy's face was expressionless, but a faint pallor was there that was missing before. He flexed his fists, inhaled deeply and eyed the phone, waiting.

The light blinked and the phone chimed again.

"Lugovoy."

"Youse sure Willie ain't dere?"

"Willie ain't here!" he replied, mimicking the caller's accent. He slammed the receiver onto the cradle.

Lugovoy sat shock-still for almost thirty seconds, hands tightly clasped together on the desk, head lowered, eyes staring into space. Nervously, he rubbed a hand over his bald head and adjusted the horn-rimmed glasses on his nose. Still lost in thought, he rose, dutifully turned out the lights and walked from the office.

He exited the elevator into the main lobby and strode past the stained-glass panel by Marc Chagall symbolizing man's struggle for peace. He ignored it, as he always had.

There were no cabs at the stand in front of the building, so he hailed one on First Avenue. He gave the driver his destination and sat stiffly in the back seat, too tense to relax.

Lugovoy was not worried that he might be followed. He was a respected psychologist, admired for his work in mental health among the underdeveloped countries. His papers on thought processes and mind response were widely studied. During his six months in New York with the United Nations he had kept his nose clean. He indulged in no espionage work and held no direct ties with the undercover people of the KGB. He was discreetly told by a friend with the embassy in Washington that the FBI had given him a low priority and only performed an occasional, almost perfunctory observation.

Lugovoy was not in the United States to steal secrets. His purpose went far beyond anything the American counterspy investigators ever dreamed. The phone call meant the plan that was conceived seven years earlier had been put into motion.

The cab pulled to a stop at West and Liberty streets in front of the Vista International Hotel. Lugovoy paid the driver and walked through the ornate lobby into the concourse outside. He paused and stared up at the awesome towers of the World Trade Center.

Lugovoy often wondered what he was doing here in this land of glass buildings, uncountable automobiles, people always rushing, restaurants and grocery stores in every block. It was not his kind of world.

He showed his identification to a guard standing by a private express elevator in the south tower and took it to the one hundredth floor. The doors parted and he entered the open lobby of the Bougainville Maritime Lines, Inc., whose offices covered the entire floor. His shoes sank into a thick white carpet. The walls were paneled in a gleaming hand-rubbed rosewood, and the room was richly decorated in Oriental antiques. Curio cases containing exquisite ceramic horses stood in the corners, and rare examples of Japanese-designed textiles hung from the ceiling.

An attractive woman with large dark eyes, a delicate oval Asian face and smooth amber skin smiled as he approached. "May I help you, sir?"

"My name is Lugovoy."

"Yes, Mr. Lugovoy," she said, pronouncing his name correctly. "Madame Bougainville is expecting you."

She spoke softly into an intercom and a tall raven-haired woman with Eurasian features appeared in a high-arched doorway.

"If you will please follow me, Mr. Lugovoy."

Lugovoy was impressed. Like many Russians he was naïve in Western business methods and wrongly assumed the office employees had stayed late for his benefit. He trailed the woman down a long corridor hung with paintings of cargo ships flying the Bougainville Maritime flag, their bows surging through turquoise seas. The guide knocked lightly on an arched door, opened it and stepped aside.

Lugovoy crossed the threshold and stiffened in astonishment. The room was vast—mosaic floor in blue and gold floral patterns, massive conference table supported by ten carved dragons that seemed to stretch into infinity. But it was the life-size terra-cotta warriors in armor and prancing horses standing in silent splendor under soft spotlights in alcoves that held him in awe.

He instantly recognized them as the tomb guardians of China's early emperor Ch'in Shih Huang Ti. The effect was dazzling. He marveled that they had somehow slipped through the Chinese government's fingers into private hands.

"Please come forward and sit down, Mr. Lugovoy."

He was so taken aback by the magnificence of the room that he failed to notice a frail Oriental woman sitting in a wheelchair. In

73

front of her was an ebony chair with gold silk cushions and a small table with a teapot and cups.

"Madame Bougainville," he said. "We meet at last."

The matriarch of the Bougainville shipping dynasty was eighty-nine years old and weighed about the same number of pounds. Her glistening gray hair was pulled back from her temples in a bun. Her face was strangely unlined, but her body looked ancient and frail. It was her eyes that absorbed Lugovoy. They were an intense blue and blazed with a ferocity that made him uncomfortable.

"You are prompt," she said simply. Her voice was soft and clear without the usual hesitation of advanced age.

"I came as soon as I received the coded telephone call."

"Are you prepared to conduct your brainwashing project?"

"Brainwashing is an ugly term. I prefer mind intervention."

"Academic terminology is irrelevant," she said indifferently.

"My staff has been assembled for months. With the proper facilities we can begin in two days."

"You'll begin tomorrow morning."

"So soon?"

"I've been informed by my grandson that ideal conditions have turned in our favor. The transfer will take place tonight."

Lugovoy instinctively looked at his watch. "You don't give me much time."

"The opportunity has to be snatched when it arrives," she said firmly. "I made a bargain with your government, and I am about to fulfill the first half of it. Everything depends on speed. You and your staff have ten days to finish your part of the project—"

"Ten days!" he gasped.

"Ten days," she repeated. "That is your deadline. Beyond that I will cast you adrift."

A shiver ran up Lugovoy's spine. He didn't need a detailed picture. It was plain that if something went wrong, he and his people would conveniently vanish—probably in the ocean.

A quiet muffled the huge boardroom. Then Madame Bougainville leaned forward in the wheelchair. "Would you like some tea?"

Lugovoy hated tea, but he nodded. "Yes, thank you."

"The finest blend of Chinese herbs. It costs over a hundred dollars a pound on the retail market."

He took the offered cup and made a polite sip before he set it on the table. "You've been informed, I assume, that my work is still in the research stage. My experiments have only been proven successful eleven times out of fifteen. I cannot guarantee perfect results within a set time limit."

"Smarter minds than yours have calculated how long White House advisers can stall the news media."

Lugovoy's eyebrows rose. "My understanding was that my subject was to be a minor American congressman whose temporary disappearance would go unnoticed."

"You were misled," she explained matter-of-factly. "Your General Secretary and President thought it best you should not know your subject's identity until we were ready."

"If I'd been given time to study his personality traits, I could have been better prepared."

"I shouldn't have to lecture on security requirements to a Russian," she said, her eyes burning into him. "Why do you think we've had no contact between us until tonight?"

Unsure of what to answer, Lugovoy took a long swallow of the tea. To his peasant taste it was like drinking watered-down perfume.

"I must know who my subject is," he said finally, mustering his courage and returning her stare.

Her answer burst like a bomb in the cavernous room, reverberated in Lugovoy's brain and left him stunned. He felt as though he'd been thrown into a bottomless pit with no hope of escape.

10

AFTER YEARS OF BUFFETING by storms at sea, the drums containing the nerve agent had broken the chains holding them to wooden cradles and now they lay scattered about the deck of the cargo hold. The one-ton standard shipping containers, as approved by the Department of Transportation, measured exactly 81½ inches in length by 30½ inches in diameter. They had concave ends and were silver in color. Neatly stenciled on the sides in green paint were the Army code letters "GS."

"I make the count twenty drums," said Pitt.

"That tallies with the inventory of the missing shipment," Mendoza said, the relief audible in her voice.

They stood in the hold's depths, now brightly lit by floodlights connected to a portable generator from the *Catawba*. Nearly a foot of water flooded the deck, and the sloshing sounds as they waded between the deadly containers echoed off the rusting sides of the hold.

An EPA chemist made a violent pointing motion with his gloved hand. "Here's the drum responsible for the leak!" he said excitedly. "The valve is broken off its threads."

"Satisfied, Mendoza?" Pitt asked her.

"You bet your sweet ass," she exclaimed happily. Pitt moved toward her until their faceplates were almost touching. "Have you given any thought to my reward?"

"Reward?"

"Our bargain," he said, trying to sound earnest. "I found your nerve agent thirty-six hours ahead of schedule."

"You're not going to hold me to a silly proposition?"

"I'd be foolish not to."

She was glad he couldn't see her face redden under the helmet. They were on an open radio frequency and every man in the room could hear what they were saying.

"You pick strange places to make a date."

"What I thought," Pitt continued, "was dinner in Anchorage, cocktails chilled by glacier ice, smoked salmon, elk Remington, baked Alaska. After that—"

"That's enough," she said, her embarrassment growing.

"Are you a party girl?"

"Only when the occasion demands," she replied, coming back on even keel. "And this is definitely not the occasion."

He threw up his arms and then let them drop dejectedly. "A sad day for Pitt, a lucky day for NUMA."

"Why NUMA?"

"The contamination is on dry land. No need for an underwater salvage job. My crew and I can pack up and head for home."

Her helmet nodded imperceptibly. "A neat sidestep, Mr. Pitt, dropping the problem straight into the Army's lap."

"Do they know?" he asked seriously.

"Alaskan Command was alerted seconds after you reported discovering the *Pilottown*. A chemical warfare disposal team is on its way from the mainland to remove the agent."

"The world applauds efficiency."

"It's not important to you, is it?"

"Of course it's important," Pitt said. "But my job is finished, and unless you have another spill and more dead bodies, I'm going home."

"Talk about a hard-nosed cynic."

"Say 'yes.' "

Thrust, parry, lunge. He caught her on an exposed flank. She felt trapped, impaled, and was annoyed with herself for enjoying it. She answered before she could form a negative thought. "Yes."

The men in the hold stopped their work amid enough poison to kill half the earth's population and clapped muted gloves together, cheering and whistling into their transmitters. She suddenly realized that her stock had shot up on the Dow Jones. Men admired a woman who could ramrod a dirty job and not be a bitch.

Later, Dover found Pitt thoughtfully studying a small open hatchway, shining his flashlight inside. The glow diminished into the darkness within, reflecting on dull sparkles on the oil-slicked water rippling from the cargo hold.

"Got something in mind?" Dover asked.

"Thought I'd do a little exploring," Pitt answered.

"You won't get far in there."

"Where does it lead?"

"Into the shaft tunnel, but it's flooded nearly to the roof. You'd need air tanks to get through."

Pitt swung his light up the forward bulkhead until it spotlighted a small hatch at the top of a ladder. "How about that one?"

"Should open into cargo hold four."

Pitt merely nodded and began scaling the rusty rungs of the ladder, closely followed by Dover. He muscled the dog latches securing the hatch, swung it open and clambered down into the next hold, again followed by Dover. A quick traverse of their lights told them it was bone empty.

"The ship must have been traveling in ballast," Pitt speculated out loud.

"It would appear so," said Dover.

"Now where?"

"Up one more ladder to the alleyway that runs between the fresh water tanks into the ship's storerooms."

Slowly they made their way through the bowels of the *Pilottown*, feeling like gravediggers probing a cemetery at midnight. Around every corner they half expected to find the skeletons of the crew. But there were no bones. The crew's living quarters should have looked like an anniversary sale at Macy's—clothes, personal belongings, everything that should have been strewn about by a crew hastily abandoning ship. Instead, the pitch-black interior of the *Pilottown* looked like the tunnels and chambers of a desert cavern. All that was missing were the bats.

The food lockers were bare. No dishes or cups lined the shelves of the crew mess. Even the toilets lacked paper. Fire extinguishers, door latches, furnishings, anything that could be unbolted or was of the slightest value was gone.

"Mighty peculiar," muttered Dover.

"My thought too," Pitt said. "She's been systematically stripped."

"Scavengers must have boarded and carried away everything during the years she was adrift."

"Scavengers leave a mess," Pitt disagreed. "Whoever was behind this job had a fetish for neatness."

It was an eerie trip. Their shadows flitted on the dark walls of the alleyways and followed alongside the silent and abandoned machinery. Pitt felt a longing to see the sky again.

"Incredible," mumbled Dover, still awed by what they'd found, or rather not found. "They even removed all the valves and gauges."

"If I was a gambling man," said Pitt thoughtfully, "I'd bet we've stumbled on an insurance scam."

"Wouldn't be the first ship that was posted missing for a Lloyd's of London payday," Dover said.

"You told me the crew claimed they abandoned the *Pilottown* in a storm. They abandoned her all right, but they left nothing but a barren, worthless shell."

"Easy enough to check out," said Dover. "Two ways to scuttle a ship at sea. Open the sea cocks and let her flood, or blow out the bottom with explosive charges."

"How would you do it?"

"Flooding through the sea cocks could take twenty-four hours or more. Time enough for a passing ship to investigate. I opt for the charges. Quick and dirty; put her on the seafloor in a matter of minutes."

"Something must have prevented the explosives from detonating."

"It's only a theory."

"Next question," Pitt persisted. "Where would you lay them?"

"Cargo holds, engine room, most any place against the hull plates so long as it was below the waterline."

"No sign of charges in the after holds," said Pitt. "That leaves the engine room and the forward cargo holds."

"We've come this far," Dover said. "We might as well finish the job."

"Faster if we split up. I'll search the engine room. You know your way around the ship better than I do—"

"The forward cargo holds it is," Dover said, anticipating him.

The big Coast Guardsman started up a companionway, whistling the Notre Dame fight song under his breath. His bearlike gait and hulking build, silhouetted by the wavering flashlight in his hand, grew smaller and finally faded.

Pitt began probing around the maze of steam pipes leading from the obsolete old steam reciprocating engines and boilers. The walkway gratings over the machinery were nearly eaten through by rust, and he treaded lightly. The engine room seemed to come alive in his imagination—creaks and moans, murmurings drifting out of the ventilators, whispering sounds.

He found a pair of sea cocks. Their handwheels were frozen in the closed position.

So much for the sea-cock theory, he thought.

An icy chill crept up the back of Pitt's neck and spread throughout his body, and he realized the batteries operating the heater in his suit were nearly drained. He switched off the light for a moment. The pure blackness nearly smothered him. He flicked it on again and quickly swept the beam around as if he expected to see a specter of the crew reaching out for him. Only there were no specters. Nothing except the dank metal walls and the worn machinery. He could have sworn he felt the grating shudder as if the engines looming above him were starting up.

Pitt shook his head to purge the phantoms in his mind and methodically began searching the sides of the hull, crawling between pumps and asbestos-covered pipes that led into the darkness and nowhere. He fell down a ladder into six feet of greasy water. He struggled back up, out of the seeming clutches of the dead and evil and ugly bilge, his suit now black with oil. Out of breath, he hung there a minute, making a conscious effort to relax.

It was then he noticed an object dimly outlined in the farthest reach of the light beam. A corroded aluminum canister about the size of a five-gallon gas can was wired to a beam welded on the inner hull plates. Pitt had set explosives on marine salvage projects and he quickly recognized the detonator unit attached to the bottom of the canister. An electrical wire trailed upward through the grating to the deck above.

Sweat was pouring from his body but he was shivering from the cold. He left the explosive charge where he found it and climbed back up the ladder. Then he began inspecting the engines and boilers.

There were no markings anywhere, no manufacturer's name, no inspector's stamped date. Wherever there had been a metal ID tag it was removed. Wherever there had been letters or numbers stamped into the metal, they were filed away. After probing endless nooks and crannies around the machinery, he got lucky when he felt a small protrusion through his gloved hand. It was a small metal plate partially hidden by grease under one of the boilers. He rubbed away the grime and aimed the light on the indented surface. It read:

PRESSURE	220 psi.
TEMPERATURE	450° F.
HEATING SURFACE	5,017 sq. ft.

MANUFACTURED BY THE
ALHAMBRA IRON AND BOILER COMPANY
CHARLESTON, SOUTH CAROLINA
SER. #38874

Pitt memorized the serial number and then made his way back to where he started. He wearily sank to the deck and tried to rest while suffering from the cold.

Dover returned in a little under an hour, carrying an explosive canister under one arm, as indifferently as if it were a jumbo can of peaches. Cursing fluently and often as he slipped on the oily deck, he stopped and sat down heavily next to Pitt.

"There's four more between here and the forepeak," Dover said tiredly.

"I found another one about forty feet aft," Pitt replied.

"Wonder why they didn't go off."

"The timer must have screwed up."

"Timer?"

"The crew had to jump ship before the bottom was blown out. Trace the wires leading from the canisters and you'll find they all meet at a timing device hidden somewhere on the deck above. When the crew realized something was wrong, it must have been too late to reboard the ship."

"Or they were too scared it would go up in their faces."

"There's that," Pitt agreed.

"So the old *Pilottown* began her legendary drift. A deserted ship in an empty sea."

"How is a ship officially identified?"

"What's on your mind?"

"Just curious."

Dover accepted that and stared up at the shadows of the engines. "Well, ID can be found most anywhere. Life jackets, lifeboats, on the bow and stern the name is often bead welded, outlining the painted letters. Then you have the builder's plates, one on the exterior of the superstructure, one in the engine room. And, oh, yeah, the ship's official number is burned into a beam around the outer base of the hatch covers."

"I'll wager a month's pay that if you could dig the ship from under the mountain you'd find the hatch number burned off and the builder's plate gone."

"That leaves one in the engine room."

"Missing too. I checked, along with all the manufacturer's markings."

"Sounds devious," said Dover quietly.

"You're damn right," Pitt replied abruptly. "There's more to the *Pilottown* than a marine insurance rip-off."

"I'm in no mood to solve mysteries now," Dover said, rising awkwardly to his feet. "I'm freezing, starved and tired as hell. I vote we head back."

Pitt looked and saw Dover was still clutching the canister of explosives. "Bringing that along?"

"Evidence."

"Don't drop it," Pitt said with a sarcastic edge in his voice.

They climbed from the engine room and hurried through the ship's storerooms, anxious to escape the damp blackness and reach daylight again. Suddenly Pitt stopped in his tracks. Dover, walking head down, bumped into him.

"Why'd you stop?"

"You feel it?"

Before Dover could answer, the deck beneath their feet trembled and the bulkheads creaked ominously. What sounded like the muffled roar of a distant explosion rumbled closer and closer, quickly followed by a tremendous shock wave. The *Pilottown* shuddered under the impact and her welded seams screeched as they split under enormous pressure. The shock flung the two men violently against the steel bulkheads. Pitt managed to remain on his feet, but Dover, unbalanced by his heavy burden, crashed like a tree to the deck, embracing the canister with his arms and cushioning its fall with his body. A grunt of pain passed his lips as he dislocated his shoulder and wrenched a knee. He dazedly struggled to a sitting position and looked up at Pitt.

"What in God's name was that?" he gasped.

"Augustine Volcano," Pitt said, almost clinically. "It must have erupted."

"Jesus, what next?"

Pitt helped the big man to his feet. He could feel Dover's arm tense through the heavy suit. "You hurt?"

"A little bent, but I don't think anything's broken."

"Can you make a run for it?"

"I'm all right," Dover lied through clenched teeth. "What about the evidence?"

"Forget it," Pitt said urgently. "Let's get the hell out of here."

Without another word they took off through the storerooms and into the narrow alleyway between the freshwater tanks. Pitt slung his arm around Dover's waist and half dragged, half carried him through the darkness.

Pitt thought the alleyway would never end. His breath began to come in gasps and his heart pounded against his ribs. He struggled to stay on his feet as the old *Pilottown* shook and swayed from the earth's tremors. They reached cargo hold number four and scrambled down the ladder. He lost his grip and Dover fell to the deck. The precious seconds lost manhandling Dover over to the opposite ladder seemed like years.

Pitt had barely set foot on the scaly rungs when there was a crack like thunder and something fell past him and struck the deck. He threw the light beam up. At that instant the hatch cover disintegrated and tons of rock and debris cascaded into the hold.

"Climb, damn it, climb!" he yelled at Dover. His chest heaved and the blood roared in his ears. With an inner strength he thrust Dover's 220 pounds up the ladder.

Suddenly a voice shouted. The light showed a figure leaning through the upper hatch, his hands grabbing Dover and pulling him through into the aft hold. Pitt instinctively knew it was Giordino. The burly little Italian had a keen sense of arriving at the right place at the right moment.

Then Pitt was at the top and crawling into the hold containing the nerve agent. The hatch cover was still intact, because the sloping ground above was not as dense near the stern section. When he reached the bottom of the ladder, willing hands were helping Dover toward the after deckhouse and temporary safety. Giordino gripped Pitt's arm.

"We took casualties during the quake," he said grimly.

"How bad?" asked Pitt.

"Four injured, mostly broken bones, and one dead."

Giordino hesitated and Pitt knew.

"Mendoza?"

"One of the drums crushed her legs," Giordino explained, his voice more solemn than Pitt had ever known it. "She suffered a compound fracture. A bone splinter pierced her suit." His words died.

"The nerve agent leaked onto her skin," Pitt finished, a sense of helplessness and shock flooding through him.

Giordino nodded. "We carried her outside."

Pitt found Julie Mendoza lying on the *Pilottown*'s stern deck. Overhead a great cloud of volcanic ash rose into a blue sky and fortuitously drifted to the northward and away from the ship.

She lay alone and off to one side. The uninjured people were attending to the living. Only the young officer from the *Catawba* stood beside her, and his entire body was arching convulsively as he was being violently sick into his air filter.

Someone had removed her helmet. Her hair flared out on the rusty deck and glinted orange under the setting sun. Her eyes were open and staring into nothingness, the jaw jutting and rigid in what must have been indescribable agony. The blood was hardening as it dried in sun-tinted copper rivers that had gushed from her gaping mouth, nose and ears. It had even seeped from around the edges of her eyes. What little facial skin still showed was already turning a bluish black.

Pitt's only emotion was cold rage. It swelled up inside him as he knelt down beside her and struck the deck repeatedly with his fist.

"It won't end here," he snarled bitterly. "I won't let it end here."

11

OSCAR LUCAS STARED MOODILY at his desktop. Everything depressed him: the acid tasting coffee in a cold cup, his cheaply furnished government office, the long hours on his job. For the first time since he became special agent in charge of the presidential detail, he found himself longing for retirement, cross-country skiing in Colorado, building a mountain retreat with his own hands.

He shook his head to clear the fantasies, sipped at a diet soft drink and studied the plans of the presidential yacht for perhaps the tenth time.

Built in 1919 for a wealthy Philadelphia businessman, the *Eagle* was purchased by the Department of Commerce in 1921 for presidential use. Since that time, thirteen Presidents had paced her decks.

Herbert Hoover tossed medicine balls while onboard. Roosevelt mixed martinis and discussed war strategy with Winston Churchill. Harry Truman played poker and the piano. John Kennedy celebrated his birthdays. Lyndon Johnson entertained the British Royal Family, and Richard Nixon hosted Leonid Brezhnev.

Designed with an old straight-up-and-down bow, the mahogany-trimmed yacht displaced a hundred tons and measured 110 feet in length with a beam of twenty feet. Her draft was five feet and she could slice the water at fourteen knots.

The *Eagle* was originally constructed with five master staterooms, four baths and a large glass-enclosed deckhouse, used as a combination dining and living room. A crew of thirteen Coast Guardsmen manned the yacht during a cruise, their quarters and galley located forward.

Lucas went through the files on the crew, rechecking their personal backgrounds, family histories, personality traits, the results of psychological interviews. He could find nothing that merited any suspicion.

He sat back and yawned. His watch read 9:20 P.M. The *Eagle* had been tied up at Mount Vernon for three hours. The President was a night owl and a late riser. He would keep up his guests, Lucas was certain, sitting around the deckhouse, thrashing out government affairs, with little thought given to sleep.

He twisted sideways and looked out the window. A falling mist was a welcome sight. The reduced visibility eliminated the chances of a sniper, the greatest danger to a President's life. Lucas persuaded himself that he was chasing ghosts. Every detail that could be covered was covered.

If there was a threat, its source and method eluded him.

The mist had not yet reached Mount Vernon. The summer night still sparkled clear and the lights from nearby streets and farms danced on the water. The river at this stretch widened to slightly over a mile, with trees and shrubs lining its sweeping banks. A hundred yards from the shoreline, a Coast Guard cutter stood at anchor, her bow pointing upriver, radar antenna in constant rotation.

The President was sitting in a lounge chair on the foredeck of the *Eagle*, earnestly promoting his Eastern European aid program to Marcus Larimer and Alan Moran. Suddenly he came to his feet and stepped to the railing, his head tilted, listening. A small herd of cows were mooing in a nearby pasture. He became momentarily absorbed; the problems of the nation vanished and a country boy surfaced. After several seconds he turned and sat down again.

"Sorry for the interruption," he said with a broad smile. "For a minute there I was tempted to find a bucket and squeeze us some fresh milk for breakfast."

"The news media would have a field day with a picture of you milking a cow in the dead of night." Larimer laughed.

"Better yet," said Moran sarcastically, "you could sell the milk to the Russians for a fat profit."

"Not as farfetched as it sounds," said Margolin, who was sitting off to one side. "Milk and butter have all but disappeared from Moscow state food stores."

"It's a fact, Mr. President," said Larimer seriously. "The average Russian is only two hundred calories a day from a starvation diet. The Poles and Hungarians are even worse off. Why, hell, our pigs eat better than they do."

"Exactly my point," said the President in a fervent voice. "We cannot turn our backs on starving women and children simply because they live under Communist domination. Their plight makes my aid plan all the more important to echo the humanitarian generosity of the American people. Think of the benefits such a program will bring in good will from the Third World countries. Think of how such an act could inspire future generations. The potential rewards are incalculable."

"I beg to differ," said Moran coldly. "In my mind what you propose is foolish, a sucker play. The billions of dollars they spend annually propping up their satellite countries have nearly wiped out their financial resources. I'll take bets the money they save by your proposed bailout plan would go directly into their military budget."

"Perhaps, but if their troubles continue unchecked the Soviets will become more dangerous to the U.S.," the President argued. "Historically, nations with deep economic problems have lashed out in foreign adventures."

"Like grabbing control of the Persian Gulf oil?" said Larimer.

"A gulf takeover is the threat they constantly dangle. But they know damned well the Western nations would intervene with force to keep the lifeblood of their economies flowing. No, Marcus, their sights are set on a far easier target. One that would open up their complete dominance of the Mediterranean."

Larimer's eyebrows raised. "Turkey?"

"Precisely," the President answered bluntly.

"But Turkey is a member of NATO," Moran protested.

"Yes, but would France go to war over Turkey? Would England or West Germany? Better yet, ask yourselves if we would send American boys to die there, any more than we would in Afghanistan? The truth is Turkey has few natural resources worth fighting over. Soviet armor could sweep across the country to the Bosporus in a few weeks, and the West would only protest with words."

"You're talking remote possibilities," said Moran, "not high probabilities."

"I agree," said Larimer. "In my opinion, further Soviet expansionism on the face of their faltering system is extremely remote."

The President raised a hand to protest. "But this is far different, Marcus. Any internal upheaval in Russia is certain to spill over her borders, particularly into Western Europe."

"I'm not an isolationist, Mr. President. God knows my record in the Senate shows otherwise. But I, for one, am getting damned sick and tired of the United States being constantly twisted in the wind by the whims of the Europeans. We've left more than our share of dead in their soil from two wars. I say if the Russians want to eat the rest of Europe, then let them choke on it, and good riddance."

Larimer sat back, satisfied. He had gotten the words off his chest that he didn't dare utter in public. Though the President fervently disagreed, he couldn't help wondering how many grass-roots Americans shared the same thoughts.

"Let's be realistic," he said quietly. "You know and I know we cannot desert our allies."

"Then what about our constituents," Moran jumped back in. "What do you call it when you take their tax dollars from a budget overburdened with deficit spending and use them to feed and support our enemies?"

"I call it the humane thing to do," the President replied wearily. He realized he was fighting a no-win war.

"Sorry, Mr. President," Larimer said, rising to his feet. "But I cannot with a clear conscience support your Eastern bloc aid plan. Now if you'll excuse me, I think I'll hit the sack.''

"Me too," Moran said, yawning. "I can hardly keep my eyes open."

"Are you settled in all right?" asked the President.

"Yes, thank you," replied Moran.

"If I haven't been seasick by now," said Larimer with a half grin, "I should keep my supper till morning."

They bid their good nights and disappeared together down the stairs to their staterooms. As soon as they were out of earshot, the President turned to Margolin.

"What do you think, Vince?"

"To be perfectly honest, sir, I think you're pissing up a rope."

"You're saying it's hopeless?"

"Let's look at another side to this," Margolin began. "Your plan calls for buying surplus grain and other agricultural products to give to the Communist world for prices lower than our farmers could receive on the export market. Yet, thanks to poor weather conditions during the last two years and the inflationary spiral in diesel fuel costs, farms are going bankrupt at the highest rate since 1934. . . . If you persist in handing out aid money, I respectfully suggest you do it here—not in Russia."

"Charity begins at home. Is that it?"

"What better place? Also, you must consider the fact that you're rapidly losing party support—and getting murdered in the polls."

The President shook his head. "I can't remain mute while millions of men, women and children die of starvation."

"A noble stand, but hardly practical."

The President's features became shrouded with sadness. "Don't you see," he said, staring out over the dark waters of the river, "if we can show that Marxism has failed, no guerrilla movement anywhere in the world will be justified in using it as a battle cry for revolution."

"Which brings us to the final argument," said Margolin. "The Russians don't *want* our help. As you know, I've met with Foreign Minister Gromyko. He told me in no uncertain terms that if Congress should pass your aid program, any food shipments will be stopped at the borders."

"Still, we must try."

Margolin sighed softly to himself. Any argument was a waste of time. The President could not be moved.

"If you're tired," the President said, "please don't hesitate to go to bed. You don't have to stay awake just to keep me company."

"I'm not really in the mood for sleep."

"How about another brandy then?"

"Sounds good."

The President pressed a call button beside his chair and a figure in the white coat of a steward appeared on deck.

"Yes, Mr. President? What is your pleasure?"

"Please bring the Vice President and me another brandy."

"Yes, sir."

The steward turned to bring the order, but the President held up his hand.

"One moment."

"Sir?"

"You're not Jack Klosner, the regular steward."

"No, Mr. President. I'm Seaman First Class Lee Tong. Seaman Klosner was relieved at ten o'clock. I'm on duty until tomorrow morning."

The President was one of the few politicians whose ego was attuned to people. He spoke as graciously to an eight-year-old boy as he did to an eighty-year-old woman. He genuinely enjoyed drawing strangers out, calling them by their Christian names as if he'd known them for years.

"Your family Chinese, Lee?"

"No, sir. Korean. They immigrated to America in nineteen fifty-two."

"Why did you join the Coast Guard?"

"A love of the sea, I guess."

"Do you enjoy catering to old bureaucrats like me?"

Seaman Tong hesitated, obviously uneasy. "Well . . . if I had my choice, I'd rather be serving on an icebreaker."

"I'm not sure I like coming in second to an icebreaker." The President laughed good-naturedly. "Remind me in the morning to put in a word to Commandant Collins for a transfer. We're old friends."

"Thank you, Mr. President," Seaman Tong mumbled excitedly. "I'll get your brandies right away."

Just before Tong turned away he flashed a wide smile that revealed a large gap in the middle of his upper teeth.

12 _____

A HEAVY FOG CREPT OVER the *Eagle*, smothering her hull in damp, eerie stillness. Gradually the red warning lights of a radio antenna on the opposite shore blurred and disappeared. Somewhere overhead a gull shrieked, but it was a muted, ghostly sound; impossible to tell where it came from. The teak decks soon bled moisture and took on a dull sheen under the mist-veiled floodlights standing above the pilings of the old creaking pier anchored to the bank.

A small army of Secret Service agents, stationed at strategic posts around the landscaped slope that gently rose toward George Washington's elegant colonial home, guarded the nearly invisible yacht. Voice contact was kept by shortwave miniature radios. So that both hands could be free at all times, the agents wore earpiece receivers, battery units on their belts and tiny microphones on their wrists.

Every hour the agents changed posts, moving on to the next prescheduled security area while their shift leader wandered the grounds checking the efficiency of the surveillance network.

In a motor home parked in the drive beside the old manor house, agent Blackowl sat scanning a row of television monitors. Another agent manned the communications equipment, while a third eyeballed a series of warning lights wired to an intricate system of alarms spaced around the yacht.

"You'd think the National Weather Service could give an accurate report ten miles from its forecast office," Blackowl groused as he sipped his fourth coffee of the night. "They said 'light mist.' If this is light mist, I'd like to know what in hell they call fog so thick you can dish it with a spoon?"

The agent in charge of radio communications turned and lifted the earphones on his headset. "The chase boat says they can't see beyond their bow. They request permission to come ashore and tie up."

"Can't say I blame them," said Blackowl. "Tell them affirmative." He stood and massaged the back of his neck. Then he patted the communications agent on the shoulder. "I'll take over the radio. You get some sleep."

"As advance agent, you should be bedded down yourself."

"I'm not tired. Besides, I can't see crap on the monitors anyway."

The agent looked up at a large digital clock on the wall. "Zero one fifty hours. Ten minutes till the next post change."

Blackowl nodded and slid into the vacated chair. He had no sooner settled the earphones on his head than a call came from the Coast Guard cutter anchored near the yacht.

"Control, this is River Watch."

"This is Control," Blackowl replied, recognizing the voice of the cutter's commander.

"We're experiencing a problem with our scanning equipment."

"What kind of problem?"

"A high-energy signal on the same frequency as our radar is fouling reception."

A look of concern crossed Blackowl's face. "Could someone be jamming you?"

"I don't think so. It looks like cross traffic. The signal comes and goes as if messages are being transmitted. I suspect that some neighborhood radio freak has plugged onto our frequency by accident."

"Do you read any contacts?"

"Boat traffic this time of night is nil," answered the commander. "The only blip we've seen on the oscilloscope in the last two hours was from a city sanitation tug pushing trash barges out to sea.''

"What time did it go by?"

"Didn't. The blip merged with the riverbank a few hundred yards upstream. The tug's skipper probably tied up to wait out the fog."

"Okay, River Watch, keep me assessed of your radar problem."

"Will do, Control. River Watch out."

Blackowl sat back and mentally calculated the potential hazards. With river traffic at a standstill, there was little danger of another ship colliding with the *Eagle*. The Coast Guard cutter's radar, though operating intermittently, *was* operating. And any assault from the river side was ruled out because the absence of visibility made it next to impossible to home in on the yacht. The fog, it seemed, was a blessing in disguise.

Blackowl glanced up at the clock. It read one minute before the post change. He quickly reread the security plan that listed the names of the agents, the areas they were scheduled to patrol and the times. He noted that agent Lyle Brock was due to stand post number seven, the yacht itself, while agent Karl Polaski was slated for post number six, which was the pier.

He pressed the transmit button and spoke into the tiny microphone attached to his headset. "Attention all stations. Time zero two hundred hours. Move to your next post. Repeat, move to the next post on your schedule." Then he changed frequencies and uttered the code name of the shift leader. "Cutty Sark, this is Control."

A veteran of fifteen years in the service, agent Ed McGrath answered almost immediately. "Cutty Sark here."

"Tell posts numbers six and seven to keep a sharp watch on the river."

"They won't see much in this slop."

"How bad is it around the dock area?"

"Let's just say you should have issued us white canes with red tips."

"Do the best you can," Blackowl said.

A light blinked and Blackowl cut transmission to McGrath and answered the incoming call.

"Control."

"This is River Watch, Control. Whoever is screwing up our radar signals seems to be transmitting continuously now."

"You read nothing?" asked Blackowl.

"The geographic display on the oscilloscope is forty percent blanked out. Instead of blips we receive a large wedge shape."

"Okay, River Watch, let me pass the word to the special agent in charge. Maybe he can track the interference and stop any further transmission."

Before he apprised Oscar Lucas at the White House of the radar problem, Blackowl turned and gazed curiously at the television monitors. They reflected no discernible image, only vague shadows wavering in wraithlike undulation.

Agent Karl Polaski refixed the molded earplug of his Motorola HT-220 radio receiver and wiped the dampness from his Bismarck mustache. Forty minutes into his watch on the pier, he felt damp and downright miserable. He wiped the moisture from his face and thought it odd that it felt oily.

His eyes wandered to the overhead floodlights. They gave out a dim yellowish halo, but the edges had a prismatic effect and displayed the colors of the rainbow. From where he stood, about midpoint on the thirty-foot dock, the *Eagle* was completely hidden by the oppressive mist. Not even her deck or mast lights were visible.

Polaski walked over the weatherworn boards, occasionally stopping and listening. But all he heard was the gentle lapping of the water around the pilings and the soft hum of the yacht's generators. He was only a few steps from the end of the pier when the *Eagle* finally materialized from the gray tentacles of the fog.

He called softly to agent Lyle Brock, who was manning post seven onboard the boat. "Hey, Lyle. Can you hear me?"

A voice replied slightly above a whisper. "What do you want?"

"How about a cup of coffee from the galley?"

"The next post change is in twenty minutes. You can get a cup when you come onboard and take my place."

"I can't wait twenty minutes," Polaski protested mildly. "I'm already soaked to the bones."

"Tough. You'll have to suffer."

Polaski knew that Brock couldn't leave the deck under any circumstances, but he goaded the other agent good-naturedly. "Wait till you want a favor from me."

"Speaking of favors, I forgot where I go from here."

Polaski gave a quizzical look at the figure in the shadows on the *Eagle*'s deck. "Look at your diagram, numb brain."

"It got soggy and I can't read it."

"Post eight is fifty yards down the bank."

"Thanks."

"If you want to know where post nine is it'll cost you a cup of coffee," Polaski said, grinning.

"Screw you. I remember that one."

Later, during the next post change, the agents merely waved as they passed each other, two indistinct forms in the mist.

Ed McGrath could not recall having seen fog this thick. He sniffed the air, trying to identify the strange aroma that hung everywhere, and finally wrote it off as a common oily smell. Somewhere in the mist he heard a dog bark. He paused, cocking one ear. It was not the baying of a hound in chase or the frightened yelps of a mutt, but the sharp yap of a dog alert to an unfamiliar presence. Not too far away, judging by the volume. Seventy-five, maybe a hundred, yards beyond the security perimeter, McGrath estimated.

A potential assassin would have to be sick or brain damaged or both, he thought, to stumble blindly around a strange countryside in weather such as this. Already, McGrath had tripped and fallen down, walked into an unseen tree branch and scratched his cheek, found himself lost three times, and almost got himself shot when he accidentally walked onto a guard post before he could radio his approach.

The barking stopped abruptly, and McGrath figured a cat or some wild animal had set the dog off. He reached a familiar bench beside a fork in a graveled path and made his way toward the riverbank below the yacht. He spoke into his lapel microphone.

"Post eight, coming up on you."

There was no reply.

McGrath stopped in his tracks. "Brock, this is McGrath, coming up on you."

Still nothing.

"Brock, do you read me?"

Post number eight was oddly quiet and McGrath began to feel uneasy. Moving very slowly, one step at a time, he cautiously closed on the guard area. He called faintly through the mist, his voice weirdly magnified by the heavy dampness. Silence was his only reply.

"Control, this is Cutty Sark."

"Go ahead, Cutty Sark," came back Blackowl's tired voice.

"We're missing a man on post eight."

Blackowl's tone sharpened considerably. "No sign of him?"

"None."

"Check the boat," Blackowl said without hesitation. "I'll meet you there after I inform headquarters."

McGrath signed off and hurried along the bank to the dock. "Post six, coming up on you."

"Aiken, post six. Come ahead."

McGrath groped his way onto the dock and found agent John Aiken's hulking figure under a floodlight. "Have you seen Brock?"

"You kidding?" answered Aiken. "I haven't seen shit since the fog hit."

McGrath dogtrotted along the dock, repeating the call-warning process. By the time he reached the *Eagle*, Polaski had come around from the opposite deck to meet him.

"I'm missing Brock," he said tersely.

Polaski shrugged. "Last I saw of him was about a half-hour ago when we changed posts."

"Okay, stand here by the dockside. I'm going to take a look below decks. And keep an eye peeled for Blackowl. He's on his way down from Control."

When Blackowl lurched out into the damp morning, the fog was thinning and he could see the faint glimmer of stars through the fading overcast above. He steered his way from post to post, breaking into a run along the pathway to the pier as the visibility improved. Fear smoldered in his stomach, a dread that something was terribly wrong. Agents did not desert their posts without warning, without reason.

When at last he leaped aboard the yacht, the fog had disappeared as if by magic. The ruby lights of the radio antenna across the river sparkled in the newly cleared air. He brushed by Polaski and found McGrath sitting alone in the deckhouse, staring trancelike into nothingness.

Blackowl froze.

McGrath's face was as pale as a white plaster death mask. He stared with such horror in his eyes that Blackowl immediately feared the worst.

"The President?" he demanded.

McGrath looked at him dully, his mouth moving but no words coming out.

"For Christ's sake, is the President safe?"

"Gone," McGrath finally muttered.

"What are you talking about?"

"The President, the Vice President, the crew, everybody, they're all gone."

"You're talking crazy!" Blackowl snapped.

"True . . . it's true," McGrath said lifelessly. "See for yourself."

Blackowl tore down the steps of the nearest companionway and ran to the President's stateroom. He threw open the door without knocking. It was deserted. The bed was still neatly made and there were no clothes in the closet, no toilet articles in the bathroom. His heart felt as if it were being squeezed between two blocks of ice.

As though in a nightmare, he rushed from stateroom to stateroom. Everywhere it was the same; even the crew's quarters lay in undisturbed emptiness.

The horror was real.

Everyone on the yacht had vanished as though they had never been born.

PART II

The Eagle

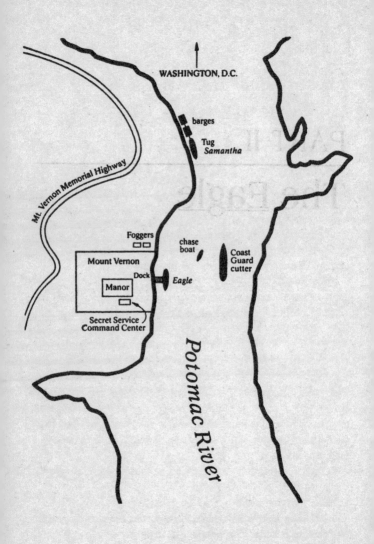

13

UNLIKE ACTORS IN MOTION PICTURES, who take forever to wake up and answer a ringing telephone in bed, Ben Greenwald, Director of the Secret Service, came instantly alert and snatched the receiver before the second ring.

"Greenwald."

"Greetings," said the familiar voice of Oscar Lucas. "Sorry to wake you, but I knew you were anxious to hear the score of the soccer game."

Greenwald tensed. Any Secret Service communication opening with the word "greetings" meant the beginning of an urgent, top-secret report on a critical or grave situation. The sentence that followed was meaningless; a caution in case the telephone line might not be secure—a real possibility, since the Kissinger State Department had allowed the Russians to build their new embassy on a rise overlooking the city, vastly increasing their telephone eavesdropping capacity.

"Okay," Greenwald said, trying to sound conversational. "Who won?"

"You lost your bet."

"Bet" was another key word indicating that the next statement was coming in coded double-talk.

103

"Jasper College, one," Lucas continued, "Drinkwater Tech, nothing. Three of the Jasper players were sidelined for injuries."

The dire news exploded in Greenwald's ears. Jasper College was the code for a presidential abduction. The reference to the sidelined players meant the next three men in succession were taken too. It was a code that in Greenwald's wildest dreams he never thought he would hear.

"There's no mistake?" he asked, dreading the answer.

"None," replied Lucas, his tone like the thin edge of broken glass.

"Who else in the office pool knows the score?"

"Only Blackowl, McGrath and myself."

"Keep it that way."

"To be on the safe side," said Lucas, "I initiated an immediate assessment of the second-string players and future rookies."

Greenwald instantly picked up on Lucas' drift. The wives and children of the missing parties were being located and protected, along with the men next in line for the Presidency.

He took a deep breath and quickly arranged his thoughts. Speed was essential. Even now, if the Soviets were behind the President's kidnapping to gain an edge for a pre-emptive nuclear strike, it was too late. On the other hand, with the top four men in American government effectively removed, it hinted at a plot to overthrow the government.

There was no time left to be shackled by security. "Amen," said Greenwald, signaling Lucas that he was dropping the double-talk.

"Understood."

A sudden terrifying thought swept Greenwald's mind. "The bag man?" he asked nervously.

"Gone with the rest."

Oh, dear God, Greenwald agonized to himself silently. Disaster was piling on top of disaster. "Bag man" was the irreverent nick-name for the field-grade officer at the President's side day and night who carried the briefcase containing codes called release messages that could unleash the nation's 10,000 strategic nuclear warheads on preselected targets inside Soviet Russia. The consequences of the ultrasecret codes falling into alien hands were beyond any conceivable horror.

"Alert the Chairman of the Joint Chiefs of Staff," he ordered. "Then send a detail to pick up the Secretaries of State and Defense, also the National Security Adviser, and rush them to the White House Situation Room."

"Anyone on the presidential staff?"

"Okay, bring in Dan Fawcett. But for now let's keep it a closed club. The fewer who know the 'Man' is missing until we can sort things out, the better."

"In that case," Lucas said, "it might be wise to hold the meeting someplace besides the Situation Room. The press constantly monitor the White House. They'd be on us like locusts if the heads of state suddenly converged there at this time of morning."

"Sound thinking," Greenwald replied. He paused a moment, then said, "Make it the Observatory."

"The Vice President's residence?"

"Press cars are almost never in evidence there."

"I'll have everyone on the premises as soon as possible."

"Oscar?"

"Yes."

"Very briefly, what happened?"

There was a slight hesitation and then Lucas said, "They all vanished from the presidential yacht."

"I see," said Greenwald heavily, but it was clear he didn't.

Greenwald wasted no more time on talk. He hung up and hurriedly dressed. On the drive to the Observatory his stomach twisted into knots, a delayed reaction to the catastrophic news. His vision blurred and he fought off an overwhelming urge to vomit.

He drove in a mental haze through the deserted streets of the capital. Except for an occasional delivery truck, traffic was nearly nonexistent and most of the traffic signals were simply blinking on a cautious yellow.

Too late he saw a city streetsweeper make a sudden U-turn from the right-hand gutter. His windshield was abruptly filled with the bulky white-painted vehicle. In the cab the driver jumped sideways at the protesting scream of tires, his eyes wide in the glare of Greenwald's headlights.

There was a metal-tearing crunch and the splash of flying glass. The hood bent double, flew up, and the steering wheel rammed into Greenwald's chest, crushing his rib cage.

Greenwald sat pinned to the seat as the water from the mangled radiator hissed and steamed over the car's engine. His eyes were open as though staring in vague indifference at the abstract cracks on the shattered windshield.

Oscar Lucas stood in front of the corner fireplace in the living room of the Vice President's mansion and described the presidential kidnapping. Every few seconds he glanced nervously at his watch, wondering what was keeping Greenwald. The five men seated around the room listened to him in undisguised astonishment.

Secretary of Defense Jesse Simmons clamped his teeth on the stem of an unlit meerschaum pipe. He was dressed casually in a summer sportcoat and slacks, as was Dan Fawcett and National Security Adviser Alan Mercier. Army General Clayton Metcalf was in uniform, while Douglas Oates, the Secretary of State, sat fastidiously groomed in a dark suit and necktie.

Lucas came to the end of his briefing and waited for the barrage of questions he was certain would be fired. Instead, there was a prolonged hush. They just sat there, numb and immobile.

Oates was the first to break the stunned silence. "Good Lord!" he gasped. "How could such a thing happen? How could everyone on the yacht simply evaporate into thin air?"

"We don't know," Lucas answered helplessly. "I haven't ordered an investigating team to the site yet for obvious security reasons. Ben Greenwald slammed a lid on the affair until you gentlemen could be informed. Outside this room, only three Secret Service personnel, including Greenwald, are privy to the facts."

"There has to be a logical explanation," said Mercier. The President's adviser on national security rose to his feet and paced the room. "Twenty people were not whisked away by supernatural powers or aliens from outer space. If, and I make that a questionable *if*, the President and the others are indeed missing from the *Eagle*, it has to be a highly organized conspiracy."

"I assure you, sir," said Lucas, staring directly into Mercier's eyes, "my deputy agent found the boat totally deserted."

"You say the fog was thick," Mercier continued.

"That's how Agent Blackowl described it."

"Could they have somehow penetrated your security network and driven away?"

Lucas shook his head. "Even if they managed to elude my security detail in the fog, their movement would have been detected by the sensitive alarm systems we installed around the estate."

"That leaves the river," observed Jesse Simmons. The Secretary of Defense was a taciturn man, given to telegramlike statements. A leathery tan face was evidence of his weekends as an avid water skier. "Suppose the *Eagle* was boarded from the water? Suppose they were forcibly removed to another boat?"

Oates gave Simmons a dubious stare. "You make it sound as if Blackbeard the Pirate was responsible."

"Agents were patrolling the dock and riverbank," Lucas explained. "No way passengers and crew could be subdued and carried off without a sound."

"Maybe they were drugged," suggested Dan Fawcett.

"A possibility," admitted Lucas.

"Let's look at this head-on," said Oates. "Rather than speculate on how the abduction occurred, I think we must concentrate on the reason and the force responsible before we can plan a response."

"I agree," said Simmons. He turned to Metcalf. "General, any evidence the Russians are behind this as a time cushion to launch a first strike?"

"If that was the case," answered Metcalf, "their strategic rocket forces would have taken us out an hour ago."

"They still might."

Metcalf gave a slight negative tilt to his head. "Nothing indicates they're in a state of readiness. Our Kremlin intelligence sources report no signs of increased activity in or around the eighty underground command posts in Moscow, and our satellite surveillance shows no troop buildup along the Eastern bloc border. Also, President Antonov is on a state visit to Paris."

"So much for World War Three," said Mercier with a look of relief.

"We're not out of shallow water yet," Fawcett said. "The officer carrying the codes designating nuclear strike sites is also gone."

"Not to worry on that score," said Metcalf, smiling for the first time. "As soon as Lucas here alerted me to the situation, I ordered the alphabetical code words changed."

"What's to stop whoever has them from using the old code words to break the new ones?"

"For what purpose?"

"Blackmail, or maybe an insane attempt to hit the Russians first."

"Can't be done," Metcalf replied simply. "There are too many built-in safeguards. Why hell, even the President couldn't launch our nuclear arsenal on his own, in a fit of madness. The order to start a war has to be transmitted through Secretary of Defense Simmons and the Joint Chiefs. If any of us knew for certain the order was invalid, we could countermand it."

"All right," said Simmons, "we temporarily shelve a Soviet conspiracy or an act of war. What are we left with?"

"Damned little," grunted Mercier.

Metcalf looked squarely at Oates. "As things stand, Mr. Secretary, you are the constitutionally designated successor."

"He's right," said Simmons. "Until the President, Margolin, Larimer and Moran are found alive, you're the acting President."

For several seconds there was no sound in the library. Oates's flamboyant and forceful facial exterior cracked ever so slightly, and he seemed to suddenly age five years. Then, just as suddenly, he regained control and his eyes took on a cold, visceral expression.

"The first thing we must do," he said in a level tone, "is to act as though nothing has happened."

Mercier tilted back and gazed unseeing at the high ceiling. "Granted we can't hold a press conference and announce to the world we've misplaced the nation's four ranking leaders. I don't care to think about the repercussions when the word leaks out. But we can't hide the facts from the press for more than a few hours."

"And we have to consider the likelihood the people responsible for the kidnapping will give us an ultimatum or make a ransom demand through the news media," Simmons added.

Metcalf looked doubtful. "My guess is that when contact is made it will come without a trumpet blast to Secretary Oates, and any demand will be for something besides money."

"I can't fault your thinking, General," said Oates. "But our top priority is still to conceal the facts and stall for as long as it takes to find the President."

Mercier had the look of an atheist buttonholed by a Hare Krishna at an airport. "Lincoln said it: 'You can't fool all the people all the time.' It won't be easy keeping the President and Vice President out of the public eye for more than a day, at most. And you can't simply erase Larimer and Moran; they're too highly visible around Washington. Then there is the *Eagle*'s crew to consider. What do you tell their families?"

"Jack Sutton!" Fawcett blurted as though he was having a revelation.

"Who?" Simmons demanded.

"The actor, the spitting image of the President who plays him in TV commercials and on comedy shows."

Oates sat up. "I think I see your point. The resemblance is remarkable, but we'd never get away with it, not on a face-to-face basis. Sutton's voice is a far from perfect imitation, and anyone who is in close daily contact with the President would see through the deception."

"Yes, but from thirty feet his own wife couldn't tell the difference."

"Where is this leading?" Metcalf asked Fawcett.

The White House Chief of Staff took his cue. "Press Secretary Thompson can hand out a press release saying the President is taking a working vacation on his New Mexico farm to study congressional reaction to his Eastern aid program. The White House press corps will be kept on the sidelines—a situation that's not uncommon when the President isn't in the mood to answer questions. All they'd see from a roped-off distance would be him—in this case, Sutton the actor—entering the helicopter for the flight to Andrews Air Force Base for departure in *Air Force One*. They could follow on a later plane, of course, but be denied entry onto the farm itself."

"Why not have a phony Vice President go with Sutton?" Mercier suggested.

"Both men can't fly on the same plane," Lucas reminded him.

"Okay, send him on a plane leaving at night," Mercier persisted. "Not much news coverage is given to Margolin's movements. No one would notice a stand-in."

"Or care," added Oates, alluding to the public apathy toward vice presidents.

"I can handle the details from the White House end," offered Fawcett.

"Two down," said Simmons. "Now what about Larimer and Moran?"

"This is an odd-numbered year," Mercier said, warming up to the scheme. "Congress recesses for the entire month of August—only two days away. Our one slice of luck. Why not invent a mutual fishing trip or a junket to some out-of-the-way resort?"

Simmons shook his head. "Scratch the fishing trip."

"Why?"

Simmons gave a tight smile. "Because it's known all over Capitol Hill that Moran and Larimer relate like syrup and vinegar."

"No matter. A fishing hole conference to discuss foreign relations sounds logical," said Oates. "I'll write up the memorandum from the State Department end."

"What do you tell their office staffs?"

110

"This is Saturday; we've got two days' grace to iron out the bugs."

Simmons began making notes on a pad. "Four down. That leaves the *Eagle*'s crew."

"I think I can come up with a convenient cover," offered Metcalf. "I'll work through the Coast Guard Commandant. The crew's families can be told the yacht was ordered on an unscheduled cruise for a top-secret military meeting. No further details need be given."

Oates stared around the room at his companions. "If there are no further questions—"

"Who else do we let in on the hoax?" queried Fawcett.

"A poor choice of words, Dan," said Oates. "Let's call it a 'distraction.' "

"It goes without saying," said Metcalf, "that Emmett of the FBI will have to handle the domestic end of the investigation. And, of course, Brogan of CIA must be called in to check out the international conspiracy angle."

"You've just touched on an ungodly thought, General," said Simmons.

"Sir?"

"Suppose the President and the rest have already been spirited out of the country?"

Simmons' speculation brought no immediate response. It was a grim possibility none of them had dared consider. With the President beyond reach of their vast internal resources, their investigative effectiveness would be cut by 80 percent.

"They could also be dead," Oates said in a controlled voice. "But we'll operate on the premise they're alive and held somewhere in the United States."

"Lucas and I will brief Emmett and Brogan," Fawcett volunteered.

There was a knock on the door. A Secret Service agent entered, walked over to Lucas and spoke softly in his ear. Lucas' eyebrows arched upward and he paled slightly. Then the agent retreated from the room, closing the door behind him.

Oates stared at Lucas questioningly. "A new development, Oscar?"

"Ben Greenwald," Lucas answered vacantly. "He was killed thirty minutes ago. His car struck a city maintenance vehicle."

Oates wasted no words of sympathy. "With the powers temporarily vested in me, I name you as the new Director of the Secret Service."

Lucas visibly recoiled. "No, please, I don't think I can—"

"Doesn't make sense to select somebody else," Oates interrupted him. "Like it or not, Oscar, you're the only man who can be named for the job."

"Somehow it doesn't seem right to be promoted for losing the men I'm sworn to protect," said Lucas dejectedly.

"Blame me," said Fawcett. "I forced the yacht cruise on you before your people were fully prepared."

"There's no time for self-recrimination," Oates said sharply. "We each have our jobs cut out for us. I suggest we get to work."

"When should we meet again?" Simmons asked.

Oates looked at his watch. "Four hours from now," he replied. "The White House Situation Room."

"We're flirting with exposure if everyone shows up at the same time," said Fawcett.

"There's an underground utility tunnel running from the basement of the Treasury building beneath the street to the White House," Lucas explained. "Perhaps some of you gentlemen could enter unseen from that direction."

"Good idea," Metcalf agreed. "We can arrive at the Treasury building in unmarked government cars, cross under the street through the tunnel and take the elevator to the Situation Room."

"That settles it then," Oates said, rising from his chair. "If any of you ever dreamed of going on the stage, this is your big chance. And I don't have to tell you, if the show's a flop, we just may bring down the whole country along with the curtain."

14

AFTER THE BRISK AIR OF ALASKA, the hot, humid atmosphere of South Carolina felt like the inside of a sauna. Pitt made a phone call and then rented a car at the Charleston airport. He drove south on Highway 52 toward the city and took the turnoff for the sprawling naval base. About a mile after turning right on Spruill Avenue, he came to a large red brick building with an ancient rusting sign perched on the roof advertising the Alhambra Iron and Boiler Company.

He parked the car and walked under a high iron archway with the date 1861 suspended on a panel. The reception area took him by surprise. The furnishings were ultramodern. Chrome was everywhere. He felt as though he'd walked onto a photo layout from *Architectural Digest*.

A sweet young thing looked up, pursed an ever so small smile and said, "Can ah help you, sir?"

Pitt stared into the mossy green magnolia eyes and imagined her as a former homecoming queen. "I called from the airport and set an appointment with Mr. Hunley. My name is Pitt."

The recognition was automatic and the smile didn't alter so much as a millimeter. "Yes, he's expecting you. Please come this way."

She led him into an office decorated entirely in brown tones. Pitt was suddenly overwhelmed with the sensation of drowning in oatmeal. A rotund, smiling little man rose from behind an enormous kidney-shaped desk and extended his hand.

"Mr. Pitt. I'm Charlie Hunley."

113

"Mr. Hunley," Pitt said, shaking hands. "Thank you for seeing me."

"Not at all. Your phone call ticked my curiosity. You're the first person to ask about our boiler making capacity in, golly, must be forty years."

"You're out of the business?"

"Heavens, yes. Gave it up during the summer of fifty-one. End of an era, you might say. My great-granddaddy rolled armor plate for the Confederate ironclad fleet. After World War Two, my daddy figured the time had come for a change. He retooled the plant and started fabricating metal furniture. As things turned out, it was a shrewd decision."

"Did you, by chance, save any of your old production records?" Pitt asked.

"Unlike you Yankees, who throw out everything," Hunley said with a sly smile, "we Southern boys hold onto everything, including our women."

Pitt laughed politely and didn't bother asking how his California upbringing had qualified him as a Yankee.

"After your call," Hunley continued, "I ran a search in our file storage room. You didn't give me a date, but since we only supplied forty water-tube boilers with the specifications you mentioned for Liberty ships, I found the invoice listing the serial number in question in fifteen minutes. Unfortunately, I can't tell you what you don't already know."

"Was the boiler shipped to the company that supplied the engines or direct to the shipyard for installation?"

Hunley picked up the yellowing paper from his desk and studied it for a moment. "It says here we shipped to the Georgia Shipbuilding Corporation in Savannah on June fourteenth, 1943." Hunley picked up another piece of paper. "Here's a report from one of our men who inspected the boilers after they were installed in the ship and connected to the engines. All that is mentioned of any interest is the name of the ship."

"Yes, I have that," said Pitt. "It was the *Pilottown*."

A strange expression of puzzlement crossed Hunley's face as he restudied the inspector's report. "We must be talking about two different ships."

Pitt looked at him. "Could there be a mistake?"

"Not unless you wrote down the wrong serial number."

"I was careful," Pitt replied firmly.

"Then I don't know what to tell you," said Hunley, passing the paper across the desk. "But according to the inspection report, boiler number 38874 went into a Liberty ship called the *San Marino.*"

15

CONGRESSWOMAN LOREN SMITH was waiting on the concourse when Pitt's flight from Charleston arrived at Washington's National Airport. She waved to get his attention, and he smiled. The gesture was unnecessary. She was an easy woman to spot.

Loren stood tall, slightly over five foot eight. Her cinnamon hair was long but layered around the face, which accented her prominent cheekbones and deep violet eyes. She was dressed in a pink cotton-knit tunic-style dress with scoop neck and long sleeves that were rolled up. For an elegant touch, she wore a Chinese-patterned sash around her waist.

She possessed an air of breezy sophistication, yet underneath one could sense a tomboyish daring. A representative elected from the state of Colorado, Loren was serving her second term. She loved her job; it was her life. Feminine and softspoken, she could be an unleashed tiger on the floor of Congress when she tackled an issue. Her colleagues respected her for her shrewdness as well as her beauty. She was a private woman, shunning the parties and dinners unless they were politically necessary. Her only outside activity was an "on again, off again" affair with Pitt.

She approached him and kissed him lightly on the mouth. "Welcome home, voyager."

He put his arm around her and they set off toward the baggage claim. "Thank you for meeting me."

"I borrowed one of your cars. I hope you don't mind."

"Depends," he said. "Which one?"

"My favorite, the blue Talbot-Lago."

"The coupé with the Saoutchik coachwork? You have expensive taste. That's a $200,000 car."

"Oh, dear, I hope it doesn't get dented in the parking lot."

Pitt gave her a solemn look. "If it does, the sovereign state of Colorado will have a vacant seat in Congress."

She clutched his arm and laughed. "You think more of your cars than you do your women."

"Cars never nag and complain."

"I can think of a few other things they never do," she said with a girlish smile.

They threaded their way through the crowded terminal and waited at the baggage claim. Finally the conveyor belt hummed into motion and Pitt retrieved his two suitcases. They passed outside into a gray, sticky morning and found the blue 1948 Talbot-Lago sitting peacefully under the watchful eye of an airport security guard. Pitt relaxed in the passenger's seat as Loren slipped behind the wheel. The rakish car was a right-hand drive, and it always struck Pitt odd to sit and stare out the left side of the windshield at the approaching traffic with nothing to do.

"Did you call Perlmutter?" he asked.

"About an hour before you landed," she answered. "He was quite agreeable, for someone who was jolted out of a sound sleep. He said he'd go through his library for data on the ships you asked about."

"If anyone knows ships, it's St. Julien Perlmutter."

"He sounds like a character over the phone."

"An understatement. Wait till you meet him."

Pitt watched the passing scenery for a few moments without speaking. He stared at the Potomac River as Loren drove north along the George Washington Memorial Parkway and cut over the Francis Scott Key Bridge to Georgetown.

Pitt was not fond of Georgetown; "Phonyville," he called it. The drab brick town houses looked like they had all been popped from the same biscuit mold. Loren steered the Talbot onto N

Street. Parked cars jammed the curbs, trash lay in the gutters, little of the sidewalk shrubbery was trimmed, and yet it was perhaps four blocks of the most overpriced real estate in the country. Tiny houses, Pitt mused, filled with gigantic egos generously coated with megadoses of forged veneer.

Loren squeezed into a vacant parking space and turned off the ignition. They locked the car and walked between two vine-encrusted homes to a carriage house in the rear. Before Pitt could lift a bronze knocker shaped like a ship's anchor, the door was thrown open by a great monster of a man who mashed the scales at nearly four hundred pounds. His sky-blue eyes twinkled and his crimson face was mostly hidden under a thick forest of gray hair and beard. Except for his small tulip nose, he looked like Santa Claus gone to seed.

"Dirk," he fairly boomed. "Where've you been hiding?"

St. Julien Perlmutter was dressed in purple silk pajamas under a red and gold paisley robe. He encompassed Pitt with his chunky arms and lifted him off the doorstep in a bear hug, without a hint of strain. Loren's eyes widened in astonishment. She'd never met Perlmutter in person and wasn't prepared.

"You kiss me, Julien," said Pitt sternly, "and I'll kick you in the crotch."

Perlmutter gave a belly laugh and released Pitt's 180 pounds. "Come in, come in. I've made breakfast. You must be starved after your travels."

Pitt introduced Loren. Perlmutter kissed her hand with a Continental flourish and then led them into a huge combination living room, bedroom and study. Shelves supporting the weight of thousands of books sagged from floor to ceiling on every wall. There were books on tables, books on chairs. They were even stacked on a king-size water bed that rippled in an alcove.

Perlmutter possessed what was acknowledged by experts as the finest collection of historical ship literature ever assembled. At least twenty marine museums were constantly angling to have it donated to their libraries after a lifetime of excess calories sent him to a mortuary.

He motioned Pitt and Loren to sit at a hatch-cover table laid with an elegant silver and china service bearing the emblem of a French transatlantic steamship line.

"It's all so lovely," said Loren admiringly.

"From the famous French liner *Normandie*," Perlmutter explained. "Found it all in a warehouse where it had been packed away since before the ship burned and rolled over in New York harbor."

He served them a German breakfast, beginning with schnapps, thin-sliced Westphalian ham garnished with pickles and accompanied by pumpernickel bread. For a side dish he'd whipped up potato dumplings with a prune-butter filling.

"Tastes marvelous," said Loren. "I love eating something besides eggs and bacon for a change."

"I'm addicted to German cooking." Perlmutter laughed, patting his ample stomach. "Lots more substance than that candy-ass French fare, which is nothing but an exotic way to prepare garbage."

"Did you find any information on the *San Marino* and the *Pilottown?*" asked Pitt, turning the conversation to the subject on his mind.

"Yes, as a matter of fact, I did." Perlmutter hefted his bulk from the table and soon returned with a large dusty volume on Liberty ships. He donned a pair of reading glasses and turned to a marked page.

"Here we are. The *San Marino*, launched by the Georgia Shipbuilding Corporation, July of 1943. Hull number 2356, classed as a cargo carrier. Sailed Atlantic convoys until the end of the war. Damaged by submarine torpedo from the U-573. Reached Liverpool under her own power and was repaired. Sold after the war to the Bristol Steamship Company of Bristol, England. Sold 1956 to the Manx Steamship Company of New York, Panamanian registry. Vanished with all hands, north Pacific, 1966.

"So that was the end of her."

"Maybe, maybe not," said Perlmutter. "There's a postscript. I found a report in another reference source. About three years after the ship was posted missing, a Mr. Rodney Dewhurst, who was a marine insurance underwriter for the Lloyd's office in Singapore, noticed a ship moored in the harbor that struck him as vaguely familiar. There was an unusual design to the cargo booms, one he'd seen on only one other Liberty-class ship. He managed to talk his way onboard and after a brief search smelled a rat. Unfortunately, it was a holiday and it took him several hours to round up the harbor authorities and convince them to arrest the ship in port and hold it for an investigation. By the time they reached the dock, the vessel was long gone, steaming somewhere out to sea. A check of custom records showed her to be the *Belle Chasse*, Korean registry, owned by the Sosan Trading Company of Inchon, Korea. Her next destination was Seattle. Dewhurst cabled an alert to the Seattle Harbor Police, but the *Belle Chasse* never arrived."

"Why was Dewhurst suspicious of her?" Pitt asked.

"He had inspected the *San Marino* before underwriting the insurance on her and was dead certain she and the *Belle Chasse* were one and the same."

"Surely the *Belle Chasse* turned up in another port?" Loren asked.

Perlmutter shook his head. "She faded from the records until two years later, when she was reported scrapped in Pusan, Korea." He paused and looked across the table. "Does any of this help you?"

Pitt took another swallow of the schnapps. "That's the problem. I don't know." He went on to briefly relate the discovery of the *Pilottown*, but omitted any mention of the nerve gas cargo. He described finding the serial number on the ship's boiler and running a check on it in Charleston.

"So the old *Pilottown*'s been tracked down at last." Perlmutter sighed wistfully. "She wanders the sea no more."

"But her discovery opened a new can of worms," Pitt said. "Why was she carrying a boiler that was recorded by the manufacturer as installed in the *San Marino*? It doesn't add up. Both ships were probably constructed on adjoining slipways and launched about the same time. The on-site inspector must have been confused. He simply wrote up the boiler as placed in the wrong hull."

"I hate to spoil your black mood," said Perlmutter, "but you may be wrong."

"Isn't there a connection between the two ships?"

Perlmutter gave Pitt a scholarly gaze over the tops of his glasses. "Yes, but not what you think." He turned to the book again and began reading aloud. "The Liberty ship *Bart Pulver*, later the *Rosthena* and *Pilottown*, launched by Astoria Iron and Steel Company, Portland, Oregon, in November of 1942—"

"She was built on the West Coast?" Pitt interrupted in surprise.

"About twenty-five hundred miles from Savannah, as the crow flies," Perlmutter replied indirectly, "and nine months earlier than the *San Marino*." He turned to Loren. "Would you like some coffee, dear lady?"

Loren stood up. "You two keep talking. I'll get it."

"It's espresso."

"I know how to operate the machine."

Perlmutter looked at Pitt and gave a jolly wink. "She's a winner."

Pitt nodded and continued. "It's not logical a Charleston boilermaker would ship across the country to Oregon with a Savannah shipyard only ninety miles away."

"Not logical at all," Perlmutter agreed.

"What else do you have on the *Pilottown?*"

Perlmutter read on. "Hull number 793, also classed as a cargo carrier. Sold after the war to the Kassandra Phosphate Company Limited of Athens. Greek registry. Ran aground with a cargo of phosphates off Jamaica, June of 1954. Refloated four months later. Sold 1962 to the Sosan Trading Company—"

"Inchon, Korea," Pitt finished. "Our first connection."

Loren returned with a tray of small cups and passed the espresso coffee around the table.

"This is indeed a treat," said Perlmutter gallantly. "I've never been waited on by a member of Congress before."

"I hope I didn't make it too strong," Loren said, testing the brew and making a face.

"A little mud on the bottom sharpens a woolly mind,' Perlmutter reassured her philosophically.

"Getting back to the *Pilottown*," Pitt said. "What happened to her after 1962?"

"No other entry is shown until 1979, when she's listed as sunk during a storm in the northern Pacific with all hands. After that she became something of a cause célèbre by reappearing on a number of occasions along the Alaskan coast."

"Then she went missing in the same area of the sea as the *San Marino*," said Pitt thoughtfully. "Another possible tie-in."

"You're grabbing at bubbles," said Loren. "I can't see where any of this is taking you."

"I'm with her." Perlmutter nodded. "There's no concrete pattern."

"I think there is," Pitt said confidently. "What began as a cheap insurance fraud is unraveling into a cover-up of far greater proportions."

"Why your interest in this?" Perlmutter asked, staring Pitt in the eyes.

Pitt's gaze was distant. "I can't tell you."

"A classified government investigation maybe?"

"I'm on my own in this one, but it's related to a 'most secret' project."

Perlmutter gave in good-naturedly. "Okay, old friend, no more prying questions." He helped himself to another dumpling. "If you suspect the ship buried under the volcano is the *San Marino* and not the *Pilottown*, where do you go from here?"

"Inchon, Korea. The Sosan Trading Company might hold the key."

"Don't waste your time. The trading company is most certainly a false front, a name on a registry certificate. As is the case with most shipping companies, all trace of ownership ends at an obscure post office box. If I were you, I'd give it up as a lost cause."

"You'd never make a football coach," Pitt said with a laugh.

"Your half-time locker-room speech would discourage your team into throwing away a twenty-point lead."

"Another glass of schnapps, if you please?" said Perlmutter in a grumbling tone, holding out his glass as Pitt poured. "Tell you what I'll do. Two of my corresponding friends on nautical research are Koreans. I'll have them check out Sosan Trading for you."

"And the Pusan shipyards for any records covering the scrapping of the *Belle Chasse.*"

"All right, I'll throw that in too."

"I'm grateful for your help."

"No guarantees."

"I don't expect any."

"What's your next move?"

"Send out press releases."

Loren looked up, puzzled. "Send what?"

"Press releases," Pitt answered casually, "to announce the discovery of both the *San Marino* and the *Pilottown* and describe NUMA's plans for inspecting the wrecks."

"When did you dream up that foolish stunt?" Loren asked.

"About ten seconds ago."

Perlmutter gave Pitt the stare of a psychiatrist about to commit a hopeless mental case. "I fail to see the purpose."

"No one in the world is immune from curiosity," Pitt exclaimed with a devious glint in his green eyes. "Somebody from the parent company that owned those ships will step from behind the shroud of corporate anonymity to check the story. And when they do, I'll have their ass."

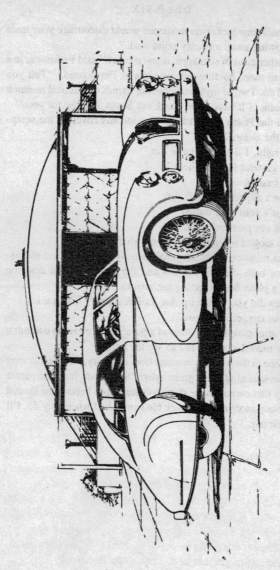

Dirk Pitt's 1948, Talbot-Lago with coachwork by Saoutchik.

16

When Oates entered the White House Situation Room, the men seated around the conference table came to their feet. It was a sign of respect for the man who now shouldered the vast problems of the nation's uncertain future. The responsibility for the far-reaching decisions of the next few days, and perhaps longer, would be his alone. There were some in the room who had mistrusted his cold aloofness, his cultivated holy image. They now cast off personal dislike and rallied to his side.

He took the chair at the head of the table. He motioned to the others to sit and turned to Sam Emmett, the gruff-spoken chief of the FBI, and Martin Brogan, the urbane, intellectual director of the CIA.

"Have you gentlemen been fully briefed?"

Emmett nodded toward Fawcett, seated at the table's other end. "Dan has described the situation."

"Either of you got anything on this?"

Brogan shook his head slowly. "Off the top of my head I can't recall hearing any indications or rumors from our intelligence sources pointing to an operation of this magnitude. But that doesn't mean we don't have something that was misinterpreted."

"I'm in pretty much the same boat as Martin," said Emmett. "It's beyond comprehension that a presidential abduction could slip through the Bureau's fingers without even a vague clue."

Oates's next question was put to Brogan. "Do we have any intelligence that might lead us to suspect the Russians?"

"Soviet President Antonov doesn't consider our President half the threat he did Reagan. He'd be risking a massive confrontation if it ever leaked to the American public his government was involved. You could compare it to striking a hornet's nest with a stick. I can't see what, if any, gains the Russians would net."

"What's your gut reaction, Sam?" Oates asked Emmett. "Could this be terrorist-inspired?"

"Too elaborate. This operation took an immense amount of planning and money. The ingenuity is incredible. It goes far beyond the capabilities of any terrorist organization."

"Any theories?" asked Oates, addressing the table.

"I can think of at least four Arab leaders who might have a motive for blackmailing the U.S.," said General Metcalf. "And Qaddafi of Libya heads the list."

"They certainly have the financial resources," said Defense Secretary Simmons.

"But hardly the sophistication," Brogan added.

Alan Mercier, the National Security Adviser, motioned with his hand to speak. "In my estimation the conspiracy is of domestic origin rather than foreign."

"What's your reasoning?" Oates asked.

"Our land and space listening systems monitor every telephone and radio transmission around the world, and it's no secret to everyone present that our new tenth-generation computers can break any code the Russians or our Allies devise. It stands to reason that an intricate operation of this size would require a flow of international message traffic leading up to the act and a report of success afterwards." Mercier paused to make his point. "Our analysts have not intercepted a foreign communication that suggests the slightest connection with the disappearance."

Simmons sucked noisily on his pipe. "I think Alan makes a good case."

"Okay," Oates said, "foreign blackmail rates a low score. So what are we looking at from the domestic angle?"

Dan Fawcett, who had previously been silent, spoke up. "It

may sound farfetched, but we can't eliminate a corporate plot to overthrow the government."

Oates leaned back and straightened his shoulders. "Maybe not as farfetched as we think. The President went after the financial institutions and the multinational conglomerates with a vengeance. His tax programs took a hell of a bite out of their profits. They're pumping money into the opposition party's campaign coffers faster than their banks can print the checks."

"I warned him about grandstanding on the issue of helping the poor by taxing the rich," Fawcett said. "But he refused to listen. He alienated the nation's businessmen, as well as the working middle class. Politicians just can't seem to get it into their heads that a vast number of American families with a working wife are in a fifty-percent tax bracket."

"The President has powerful enemies," Mercier conceded. "However, it's inconceivable to me that any corporate empire could steal away the President and congressional leaders without its leaking to a law-enforcement agency."

"I agree," Emmett said. "Too many people had to be in on it. Somebody would have gotten cold feet and spilled the scheme."

"I think we'd better call a halt to speculation," said Oates. "Let's get back on the track. The first step is to launch a massive investigation while keeping up a business-as-usual front. Use whatever cover story you feel is plausible. If at all possible, don't even let your key people in on this."

"What about a central command post during the investigation?" Emmett asked.

"We'll continue to gather here every eight hours to assess incoming evidence and coordinate efforts between your respective investigative agencies."

Simmons pushed forward in his chair. "I have a problem. I'm scheduled to fly to Cairo this afternoon to confer with Egypt's Minister of Defense."

"By all means go," Oates replied. "Keep up normal appearances. General Metcalf can cover for you at the Pentagon."

Emmett shifted in his chair. "I'm supposed to speak before a law class at Princeton tomorrow morning."

Oates pondered a moment. "Claim you have the flu and can't make it." He turned to Lucas. "Oscar, if you'll forgive me for saying so, you're the most expendable. Substitute for Sam. Certainly no one would suspect a presidential kidnapping if the new Director of the Secret Service can take time out to give a speech."

Lucas nodded. "I'll be there."

"Good." Oates looked around the table. "Everybody plan on being back here at two o'clock. Maybe we'll know something by then."

"I've already sent a crack lab team over to the yacht," Emmett volunteered. "With luck they'll turn up some solid leads."

"Let's pray they do." Oates's shoulders sagged and he appeared to stare through the tabletop. "My God," he muttered quietly. "Is this any way to run a government?"

17

BLACKOWL STOOD ON THE DOCK and watched as a team of FBI agents swarmed over the *Eagle*. They were an efficient lot, he observed. Each man was a specialist in his particular field of scientific detection. They went about their job of scrutinizing the yacht from bilge to radio mast with a minimum of conversation.

A constant parade of them crossed the dock to vans parked along the shore, removing furniture, carpeting, anything that wasn't screwed down and a considerable amount that was. Each item was carefully wrapped in a plastic covering and inventoried.

More agents arrived, expanding the search for a mile around the first President's estate, examining every square inch of ground, the trees and shrubbery. In the water beside the yacht, divers scoured the muddy bottom.

The agent in charge noticed Blackowl rubbernecking beside the loading ramp and came over. "You got permission to be in the area?" he asked.

Blackowl showed his ID without answering.

"What brings the Secret Service to Mount Vernon on a weekend?"

"Practice mission," Blackowl replied conversationally. "How about the FBI?"

"Same thing. The Director must have thought we were getting lazy, so he dreamed up a top-priority exercise."

"Looking for anything in particular?" Blackowl asked, feigning indifferent interest.

"Whatever we can determine about the last people who were onboard—identification through fingerprints, where they came from. You know."

Before Blackowl could reply, Ed McGrath stepped onto the dock from the gravel path. His forehead was glistening in sweat and his face was flushed. Blackowl guessed he had been running.

"Excuse me, George," he panted between intakes of breath. "You got a minute?"

"Sure." Blackowl waved to the FBI agent. "Nice talking with you."

"Same to you."

As soon as they were out of earshot, Blackowl asked softly, "What's going down, Ed?"

"The FBI guys found something you should see."

"Where?"

"About a hundred and fifty yards upriver, hidden away in trees. I'll show you."

McGrath led him along a path that bordered the river. When it curved toward the outer estate buildings, they stayed in a straight line across a manicured lawn. Then they climbed a rail fence into the unkempt undergrowth on the other side. Working their way into a dense thicket, they suddenly came upon two FBI investigators who were hunkered down studying two large tanks connected to what looked like electrical generators.

"What in hell are these things?" Blackowl demanded without a greeting.

One of the men looked up. "They're foggers."

Blackowl stared, puzzled. Then his eyes widened. "Foggers!" he blurted out. "Machines that make fog!"

"Yeah, that's right. Fog generators. The Navy used to mount them on destroyers during World War Two for making smoke-screens."

"Christ!" Blackowl gasped. "So that's how it was done!"

18

OFFICIAL WASHINGTON TURNS INTO a ghost town over the weekends. The machinery of government grinds to a halt at five o'clock Friday evening and hibernates until Monday morning, when it fires to life again with the obstinacy of a cold engine. Once the cleaning crews have come and gone, the huge buildings are as dead as mausoleums. What is most surprising, the phone systems are shut down.

Only the tourists are out in force, crawling over the Mall, throwing Frisbees and swarming around the Capitol, climbing the endless staircases and staring slack-jawed at the underside of the dome.

Some were peering through the iron fence around the White House around noontime when the President came out, quick stepped across the lawn and gave a jaunty wave before entering a helicopter. He was followed by a small entourage of aides and Secret Service agents. Few of the elite press corps were present. Most were home watching baseball on TV or roaming a golf course.

Fawcett and Lucas stood on the South Portico and watched until the ungainly craft lifted over E Street and dissolved to a speck as it beat its way toward Andrews Air Force Base.

"That was fast work," Fawcett said quietly. "You made the switch in less than five hours."

"My Los Angeles office tracked down Sutton and crammed him

into the cockpit of a Navy F-20 fighter forty minutes after they were alerted."

"What about Margolin?"

"One of my agents is a reasonable facsimile. He'll be onboard an executive jet for New Mexico as soon as it's dusk."

"Can your people be trusted not to leak this charade?"

Lucas shot Fawcett a sharp look. "They're trained to keep quiet. If there's a leak it will come from the presidential staff."

Fawcett smiled faintly. He knew he was on shaky footing. The looseness of the White House staff was open territory for the press corps. "They can't spill what they didn't know," he said. "Only now will they be waking up to the fact that the man in the helicopter with them isn't the President."

"They'll be well guarded at the farm," Lucas said. "Once they arrive no one gets off the property, and I've seen to it all communications are monitored."

"If a correspondent figures the game, Watergate will seem as tame as an Easter-egg hunt."

"How are the wives taking it?"

"Cooperating a hundred percent," Fawcett answered. "The First Lady and Mrs. Margolin have volunteered to stay shut up in their bedrooms claiming to have a virus."

"What now?" Lucas asked. "What else can we do?"

"We wait," Fawcett replied, his voice wooden. "We stick it out until we find the President."

"Looks to me like you're overloading the circuits," said Don Miller, Emmett's deputy director of the FBI.

Emmett didn't look up at Miller's negative remark. Within minutes after he had returned to the Bureau's headquarters at Pennsylvania Avenue and Tenth Street he set into motion an All Bureaus Alert, followed by a standby for Emergency Action of the Highest Priority to every office in the fifty states and all agents on assignments overseas. Next came orders to pull files, records and descriptions on every criminal or terrorist who specialized in abduction.

His cover story to the Bureau's six thousand agents was that the Secret Service had come on evidence of a planned abduction attempt on Secretary of State Oates and other as yet unnamed officials on high government levels.

"It may be a heavy conspiracy," Emmett said finally, his tone vague. "We can't take the chance the Secret Service is wrong."

"They've been wrong before," Miller said.

"Not on this one."

Miller gave Emmett a curious look. "You've given out damned little information to work with. Why the great secrecy?"

Emmett didn't answer, so Miller dropped the subject. He passed three file folders across the desk. "Here's the latest data on PLO kidnapping operations, the Mexican Zapata Brigade's hostage activities, and one I'm in the dark about."

Emmett gave him a cold stare. "Can you be more explicit?"

"I doubt if there's a connection, but since they acted strange—"

"Who are you talking about?" Emmett demanded, picking up the file and opening the cover.

"A Soviet representative to the United Nations, name of Aleksei Lugovoy—"

"A prominent psychologist," Emmett noted as he read.

"Yes, he and several of his staff members on the World Health Assembly have gone missing."

Emmett looked up. "We've lost them?"

Miller nodded. "Our United Nations surveillance agents report that the Russians left the building Friday night—"

"This is only Saturday morning," Emmett interrupted. "You're talking a few hours ago. What's so suspicious about that?"

"They went to great lengths to shake our shadows. The special agent in charge of the New York bureau checked it out and discovered none of the Russians returned to their apartments or hotels. Collectively they dropped from sight."

"Anything on Lugovoy?"

"All indications are he's straight. He appears to steer clear of the Soviet mission's KGB agents."

"And his staff?"

"None of them have been observed engaging in espionage activities either."

Emmett looked thoughtful for several moments. Ordinarily he might have brushed the report aside or at most ordered a routine follow-up. But he had a nagging doubt. The disappearance of the President and Lugovoy on the same night could be a mere coincidence. "I'd like your opinion, Don," he said at last.

"Hard to second-guess this one," Miller replied. "They may all show up at the United Nations on Monday as though nothing had happened. On the other hand, I'd have to suggest that the squeaky clean image Lugovoy and his staff have projected may be a screen."

"For what purpose?"

Miller shrugged. "I haven't a clue."

Emmett closed the file. "Have the New York bureau stay on this. I want priority-one updates whenever they're available."

"The more I think about it," Miller said, "the more it intrigues me."

"How so?"

"What vital secrets could a bunch of Soviet psychologists want to steal?"

19

SUCCESSFUL SHIPPING LINE MAGNATES travel through the glittering waters of the international jet set in grand fashion. From exotic yachts to private airliners, from magnificent villas to resplendent hotel suites, they roam the world in an unending pursuit of power and wealth.

Min Koryo Bougainville cared nothing for a freewheeling lifestyle. She spent her waking hours in her office and her nights in small but elegant quarters on the floor above. She was frugal in most matters, her only weakness being a fondness for Chinese antiques.

When she was twelve, her father sold her to a Frenchman who operated a small shipping line consisting of three tramp steamers that plied the coastal ports between Pusan and Hong Kong. The line prospered and Min Koryo bore René Bougainville three sons. Then the war came and the Japanese overran China and Korea. René was killed in a bombing raid and the three sons were lost somewhere in the South Pacific, after being forced into the Imperial Japanese Army. Only Min Koryo and one grandson, Lee Tong, survived.

After Japan surrendered, she raised and salvaged one of her husband's ships which had been sunk in Pusan harbor. Slowly she built up the Bougainville fleet, buying old surplus cargo ships, never paying more than their scrap value. Profits were few and far between, but she hung on until Lee Tong finished his master's degree at the University of Pennsylvania's Wharton School of Business and began running the day-to-day operation. Then, almost magically, the Bougainville Maritime Lines grew into one of the world's largest fleet of ships. When their armada totaled 138 cargo ships and tankers, Lee Tong moved the principal offices to New York. In a ritual going back thirty years, he sat dutifully near her bedside in the evening discussing the current dealings of their far-flung financial empire.

Lee Tong wore the misleading look of a jolly Oriental peasant. His round brown face split in a perpetual smile that seemed chiseled in ivory. If the Justice Department and half the federal law-enforcement agencies had wanted to close the book on a backlog of unsolved maritime crimes, they would have hung him from the nearest streetlight, but, oddly, none had a file on him. He skirted in the shadow of his grandmother; he was not even listed as a director or an employee of Bougainville Maritime. Yet it was he, the anonymous member of the family, who handled the dirty-tricks department and built the base of the company.

Too systematic to place his faith in hired hands, he preferred to direct the highly profitable illicit operations from the front rank. His act often ran on blood. Lee Tong was not above murder to achieve a profit. He was equally at home during a business luncheon at the "21" Club or at a waterfront throat cutting.

He sat a respectful distance from Min Koryo's bedside, a long silver cigarette holder planted between his uneven teeth. She disliked his smoking habit, but he clung to it, not so much as a pleasure but as a small measure of independence.

"By tomorrow the FBI will know how the President disappeared," said Min Koryo.

"I doubt it," Lee Tong said confidently. "The chemical analysis people are good, but not that good. I say closer to three days. And then a week to find the ship."

"Enough time so no loose threads can be traced to us?"

"Enough time, *aunumi,*" said Lee Tong, addressing her in the Korean term for mother. "Rest assured, all threads lead to the grave."

Min Koryo nodded. The inference was crystal clear: The

handpicked team of seven men who had aided Lee Tong in the abduction had been murdered by his own hand.

"Still no news from Washington?" she asked.

"Not a word. The White House is acting as though nothing happened. In fact, they're using a double for the President."

She looked at him. "How did you learn that?"

"The six o'clock news. The TV cameras showed the President boarding *Air Force One* for a flight to his farm in New Mexico."

"And the others?"

"They appear to have stand-ins too."

Min Koryo sipped at a cup of tea. "Seems odd that we must depend on Secretary of State Oates and the President's Cabinet to provide a successful masquerade until Lugovoy is ready."

"The only road open to them," said Lee Tong. "They won't dare make any kind of an announcement until they know what happened to the President."

Min Koryo stared at the tea leaves in the bottom of her cup. "Still, I must believe we may have taken too large a bite."

Lee Tong nodded at her meaning. "I understand, *aunumi*. The congressmen just happened to be fish in the same net."

"But not Margolin. It was your scheme to misguide him onto the yacht."

"True, but Aleksei Lugovoy has stated his experiments have proven successful eleven out of fifteen times. Not exactly a perfect ratio. If he fails with the President, he has an extra guinea pig to produce the required result."

"You mean *three* guinea pigs."

"If you include Larimer and Moran in the rank of succession, yes."

"And if Lugovoy succeeds in each case?" asked Min Koryo.

"So much the better," answered Lee Tong. "Our influence would reach further than we originally dared hope. But I sometimes wonder, *aunumi*, if the financial rewards are worth risking imprisonment and the loss of our business."

"Do not forget, Grandson, the Americans killed my husband, your father and his two brothers during the war."

"Revenge makes for a poor gambling game."

"All the more reason to protect our interests and guard against double-dealing by the Russians. President Antonov will do everything in his power to keep from paying our fee."

"Should they be stupid enough to betray us at this crucial stage, they'd lose the whole project."

"They don't think that way," said Min Koryo gravely. "The Communist mind thrives on mistrust. Integrity is beyond their comprehension. They're driven to take the devious path. And that, my grandson, is their Achilles' heel."

"What are you thinking?"

"We continue to play the role of their honest but gullible partner." She paused, thinking.

"And when Lugovoy's project is finished?" Lee Tong prompted her.

She looked up and a crafty smile cut across her aging face. Her eyes gleamed with a cunning look. "Then we'll pull the rug from under them."

20

ALL IDENTIFICATION AND WRISTWATCHES were taken from the Russians when the Bougainvilles' men transferred them from the Staten Island ferry in midchannel. They were blindfolded, and padded radio headsets were placed over their ears that emitted soothing chamber music. Minutes later they were airborne, lifted from the dark harbor waters by a jet-engined seaplane.

The flight seemed long and wearisome, terminating at last on what Lugovoy judged by the smooth landing was a lake. After a drive of twenty minutes, the disoriented Russians were led across a metal walkway and into an elevator. Only when they stepped out of the elevator and were led across a carpeted corridor to their bedrooms were the blindfolds and the earphones removed.

Lugovoy was profoundly impressed by the facilities provided by the Bougainvilles. The electronics and laboratory equipment went far beyond any he'd seen in the Soviet Union. Every piece of the several hundred items he had requested was present and installed. Nor had any creature comforts for his staff been overlooked. They were assigned individual sleeping quarters with private bathrooms, while at the end of the central corridor stretched an elegant dining room that was serviced by an excellent Korean chef and two waiters.

Furnishings, including kitchen freezers and ovens, office fixtures and the data control room were tastefully color-coordinated, with walls and carpeting in cool blues and greens. The design and execution of every detail was as exotic as it was complex.

And yet the self-contained habitat also served as a luxurious prison. Lugovoy's staff was not permitted to come and go. The elevator doors were closed at all times and there were no outer controls. He made a compartment-to-compartment search but detected no windows or visible crack of an exterior exit. No sounds filtered in from the outside.

Further investigation was cut short by the arrival of his subjects. They were semi-conscious from the effects of sedation and oblivious to their surroundings. All four had been prepared and laid inside separate cubicles called cocoons. The padded insides were seamless, with rounded corners, giving no reference point for the eye to dwell on. Dim illumination came by reflection from an indirect light, tinting the cocoon monochrome gray. Specially constructed walls shielded all sound and electrical current that could interfere with or enhance brain activity.

Lugovoy sat at a console with two of his assistants and studied the row of color video monitors that revealed the subjects lying in their cocoons. Most remained in a trancelike state of limbo. One, however, was raised to a near level of consciousness, vulnerable to suggestion and mentally disoriented. Drugs were injected that numbed his muscle control, effectively paralyzing any body movement. His head was covered by a plastic skull cap.

Lugovoy still found it difficult to grasp the power he held. He trembled inwardly at knowing he was embarking on one of the great experiments of the century. What he did in the next days could affect the world as radically as the development of atomic energy.

"Dr. Lugovoy?"

Lugovoy's concentration was interrupted by the strange voice, and he turned, surprised, to see a stocky man with rugged Slavic features and shaggy black hair who seemingly stepped out of a wall.

"Who are you?" he blurted.

The stranger spoke very softly as though he didn't wish to be overheard. "Suvorov, Paul Suvorov, foreign security."

Lugovoy paled. "My God, you're KGB? How did you get here?"

"Pure luck," Suvorov muttered sarcastically. "You were assigned to my security section for observation from the day you set foot in New York. After your suspicious visit to the Bougainville Maritime offices, I took over your surveillance myself. I was present on the ferryboat when you were contacted by the men who brought you here. Because of the darkness I had no difficulty mingling with your staff and being included for the trip to wherever it is we are. Since our arrival I've kept to my room."

"Do you have any idea what you've stuck your nose into?" Lugovoy said, his face flushing with anger.

"Not yet," Suvorov said, unperturbed. "But it is my duty to find out."

"This operation originates from the highest level. It is of no concern to the KGB."

"I'll be the judge—"

"You'll be crap in Siberian frost," Lugovoy hissed, "if you interfere with my work here."

Suvorov appeared mildly amused at Lugovoy's irritated tone. It slowly began to dawn on him that he might have overstepped his authority. "Perhaps I could be of help to you."

"How?"

"You may have need of my special skills."

"I don't require the services of an assassin."

"I was thinking more of escape."

"There is no reason to escape."

Suvorov was becoming increasingly annoyed. "You must try to understand my position."

Lugovoy was in command now. "There are more important problems to occupy my mind than your bureaucratic interference."

"Like what?" Suvorov swept his hand around the room. "Just what is going on here?"

Lugovoy stared at him consideringly for a long moment before yielding to vanity. "A mind-intervention project."

Suvorov's eyebrows rose. "Mind intervention?"

141

"Brain control if you prefer."

Suvorov faced the video monitor and nodded at the image. "Is that the reason for the small helmet?"

"On the subject's head?"

"The same."

"A microelectronic integrated circuit module containing a hundred and ten probes, measuring internal body functions ranging from common pulse to hormone secretions. It also intercepts data flowing through the subject's brain and transmits it to the computers here in this room. The brain's talk, so to speak, is then translated into a comprehensible language."

"I see no electrode terminals."

"From a bygone era," answered Lugovoy. "Everything we wish to record can be telemetered through the atmosphere. We no longer rely on the unnecessary bulk of wires and terminals."

"You can actually understand what he's thinking?" asked Suvorov incredulously.

Lugovoy nodded. "The brain speaks a language of its own, and what it says reveals the inner thoughts of its landlord. Night and day, the brain speaks incessantly, providing us with a vivid look into the working mind, how a man thinks and why. The impressions are subliminal, so lightning-quick that only a computer designed to operate in picoseconds can memorize and decipher them."

"I had no idea brain science had evolved to such a high level."

"After we establish and chart his brain rhythms," Lugovoy continued, "we can forecast his intentions and physical movements. We can tell when he is about to say or do something in error. And most important, we can intervene in time to stop him. In less than the blink of an eye the computer can erase his mistaken intent and rephrase his thought."

Suvorov was awed. "A religious capitalist would accuse you of breaching man's soul."

"Like you, I am a loyal member of the Communist Party, Comrade Suvorov. I do not believe in the salvation of souls. However, in this case we can't tolerate a drastic conversion. There'll be no disruption of his fundamental thought processes. No change in speech patterns or mannerisms."

"A form of controlled brainwashing."

"This is not a crude brainwashing," Lugovoy replied indignantly. "Our sophistication goes far beyond anything the Chinese invented. They still believe in destroying a subject's ego in order to re-educate him. Their experiments in drugs and hypnosis have met with little success. Hypnosis is too vague, too slippery to have lasting value. And drugs have proved dangerous by accidentally producing a sudden shift in personality and behavior. When I finish with the subject here, he will re-enter reality and return to his personal lifestyle as though he'd never left it. All I intend to do is alter his political perspective."

"Who is the subject?"

"Don't you know? Don't you recognize him?"

Suvorov studied the video display. Gradually his eyes widened and he moved two steps closer to the screen, his face taut, his mouth working mechanically. "The President?" His voice was an unbelieving whisper. "Is that really the President of the United States?"

"In the flesh."

"How . . . where . . . ?"

"A gift from our hosts," Lugovoy explained vaguely.

"He'll suffer no side effects?" Suvorov asked in a haze.

"None."

"Will he remember any of this?"

"He will recall only going to bed when he wakes up ten days from now."

"You can do this thing, really do it?" Suvorov questioned with a security man's persistence.

"Yes," Lugovoy said with a confident gleam behind his eyes. "And much more."

21

A MAD FLAPPING OF WINGS broke the early morning stillness as two pheasants broke toward the sky. Soviet President Georgi Antonov snapped the over-and-under Purdey shotgun to his shoulder and pulled the two triggers in quick succession. The twin blasts echoed through the mist-dampened forest. One of the birds suddenly stopped flying and fell to the ground.

Vladimir Polevoi, head of the Committee for State Security, waited an instant until he was sure Antonov had missed the second pheasant before he brought it down with one shot.

Antonov fixed his KGB director with a hard-eyed stare. "Showing up your boss again, Vladimir?"

Polevoi read Antonov's mock anger correctly. "Your shot was difficult, Comrade President. Mine was quite easy."

"You should have joined the Foreign Ministry instead of the Secret Police," Antonov said, laughing. "Your diplomacy ranks with Gromyko's." He paused and looked around the forest. "Where is our French host?"

"President L'Estrange is seventy meters to our left." Polevoi's statement was punctuated by a volley of gunshots somewhere out of sight beyond the undergrowth.

"Good," grunted Antonov. "We can have a few minutes of conversation." He held out the Purdey to Polevoi, who replaced the empty shells and clicked the safety switch.

Polevoi moved in close and spoke in a low tone. "I would caution about speaking too freely. French intelligence has listening probes everywhere."

"Secrets seldom last long these days," Antonov said with a sigh.

Polevoi cracked a knowing smile. "Yes, our operatives recorded the meeting between L'Estrange and his Finance Minister last night."

"Any revelations I should know about?"

"Nothing of value. Most of their conversation centered on persuading you to accept the American President's financial assistance program."

"If they're stupid enough to believe I would not take advantage of the President's naïve generosity, they're also stupid enough to think I agreed to fly here to discuss it."

"Rest assured, the French are completely unaware of the true nature of your visit."

"Any late word from New York?"

"Only that Huckleberry Finn exceeded our projections." Polevoi's Russian tongue pronounced Huckleberry as Gulkleberry.

"And all goes well?"

"The trip is under way."

"So the old bitch accomplished what we thought was impossible."

"The mystery is how she managed it."

Antonov stared at him. "We don't know?"

"No, sir. She refused to take us into her confidence. Her son shielded her operation like the Kremlin wall. So far we haven't been able to penetrate her security."

"The Chinese whore," Antonov snarled. "Who does she think she's dealing with, empty-headed schoolboys?"

"I believe her ancestry is Korean," said Polevoi.

"No difference." Antonov stopped and sat down heavily on a fallen log. "Where is the experiment taking place?"

Polevoi shook his head. "We don't know that either."

"Have you no communication with Comrade Lugovoy?"

"He and his staff departed lower Manhattan Island on the Staten

Island ferry late Friday night. They never stepped ashore at the landing. We lost all contact."

"I want to know where they are," Antonov said evenly. "I want .o know the exact location of the experiment."

"I have our best agents working on it."

"We can't allow her to keep us wandering in the dark, especially when there is one billion American dollars' worth of our gold reserves at stake."

Polevoi gave the Communist Party Chairman a crafty look. "Do you intend to pay her fee?"

"Does the Volga melt in January?" Antonov replied with a broad grin.

"She won't be an easy prey to outfox."

The sound of feet tramping through the underbrush could be heard. Antonov's eyes flickered to the groundkeepers who were approaching with the downed pheasants and then back to Polevoi.

"Just find Lugovoy," he said softly, "and the rest will take care of itself."

Four miles away in a sound truck two men sat in front of a sophisticated microwave receiving set. Beside them two reel-to-reel tape decks were recording Antonov and Polevoi's conversation in the woods.

The men were electronic surveillance specialists with the SDECE, France's intelligence service. Both could interpret six languages, including Russian. In unison they lifted their earphones and exchanged curious looks.

"What in hell do you suppose that was all about?" said one.

The second man gave a Gallic shrug. "Who can say? Probably some kind of Russian double-talk."

"I wonder if an analyst can make anything important out of it?"

"Important or not, we'll never know."

The first man paused, held an earphone to his ear for a few moments and then set it down again. "They're talking with President L'Estrange now. That's all we're going to get."

"Okay, let's close down shop and get the recordings to Paris. I've got a date at six o'clock."

22

THE SUN WAS TWO HOURS ABOVE the eastern edge of the city when Sandecker drove through a back gate of Washington's National Airport. He stopped the car beside a seemingly deserted hangar standing in a weed-covered part of the field far beyond the airlines' maintenance area. He walked to a side door whose weathered wood had long since shed its paint and pressed a small button opposite a large rusting padlock. After a few seconds the door silently swung open.

The cavernous interior was painted a glossy white, which brightly reflected the sun's rays through huge skylights in the curved roof, and had the look of a transportation museum. The polished concrete floor held four long orderly rows of antique and classic automobiles. Most gleamed as elegantly as the day their coachmakers added the finishing touch. A few were in various stages of restoration. Sandecker lingered by a majestic 1921 Rolls-Royce Silver Ghost with coachwork by Park-Ward and a massive red 1925 Isotta-Fraschini with a torpedo body by Sala.

The two centerpieces were an old Ford trimotor aircraft known to aviation enthusiasts as the "tin goose" and an early-twentieth-century railroad Pullman car with the words MANHATTAN LIMITED painted in gilded letters on its steel side.

Sandecker made his way up a circular iron stairway to a glass-enclosed apartment that spanned the upper level across one end of the hangar. The living room was decorated in marine antiques. One wall was lined with shelves supporting delicately crafted ship models in glass cases.

He found Pitt standing in front of a stove studying a strange-looking mixture in a frying pan. Pitt wore a pair of khaki hiking shorts, tattered tennis shoes and a T-shirt with the words RAISE THE LUSITANIA across the front.

"You're just in time to eat, Admiral."

"What have you got there?" asked Sandecker, eyeing the mixture with suspicion.

"Nothing fancy. A spicy Mexican omelet."

"I'll settle for a cup of coffee and half a grapefruit."

Pitt served as they sat down at a kitchen table and poured the coffee. Sandecker frowned and waved a newspaper in the air. "You made page two."

"I hope I do as well in other papers."

"What do you expect to prove?" Sandecker demanded. "Holding a press conference and claiming you found the *San Marino*, which you didn't, and the *Pilottown*, which is supposed to be top secret. Have you lost your gray matter?"

Pitt paused between bites of the omelet. "I made no mention of the nerve agent."

"Fortunately the Army quietly buried it yesterday."

"No harm done. Now that the *Pilottown* is empty, she's just another rusting shipwreck."

"The President won't see it that way. If he wasn't in New Mexico, we'd both be picking our asses out of a White House carpet by now."

Sandecker was interrupted by a buzzing noise. Pitt rose from the table and pushed a switch on a small panel.

"Somebody at the door?" inquired Sandecker.

Pitt nodded.

"This is a Florida grapefruit." Sandecker grumbled, spitting out a seed.

"So?"

"I prefer Texas."

"I'll make a note," said Pitt with a grin.

"Getting back to your cockamamie story," Sandecker said, squeezing out the last drops of juice in a spoon, "I'd like to know your reasoning."

Pitt told him.

"Why not let the Justice Department handle it?" Sandecker asked. "That's what they're paid for."

Pitt's eyes hardened and he pointed his fork menacingly. "Because the Justice people will never be called in to investigate. The government isn't about to admit over three hundred deaths were caused by a stolen nerve agent that isn't supposed to exist. Lawsuits and damaging publicity would go on for years. They want to whitewash the whole mess into oblivion. The Augustine Volcano eruption was timely. Later today the President's press secretary will hand out a bogus cover-up blaming sulphuric gas clouds for the deaths."

Sandecker looked at him sternly for a moment. Then he asked, "Who told you that?"

"I did," came a feminine voice from the doorway.

Loren's face was wrapped in a disarming smile. She had been out jogging and was dressed in brief red satin shorts with a matching tank top and headband. The Virginia humidity had brought out the sweat and she was still a little breathless. She dried her face with a small towel that was tucked in her waistband.

Pitt made the introductions. "Admiral James Sandecker, Congresswoman Loren Smith."

"We've sat across from each other during Maritime Committee meetings," said Loren, extending her hand.

Sandecker didn't need clairvoyance to read Pitt and Loren's relationship. "Now I see why you've always looked kindly on my NUMA budget proposals."

If Loren felt any embarrassment at his insinuation, she didn't show it. "Dirk is a very persuasive lobbyist," she said sweetly.

"Like some coffee?" asked Pitt.

"No, thanks. I'm too thirsty for coffee." She went over to the refrigerator and poured herself a glass of buttermilk.

"You know the subject of Press Secretary Thompson's news release?" Sandecker prompted her.

Loren nodded. "My press aide and his wife are chummy with the Sonny Thompsons. They all had dinner together last night. Thompson mentioned that the White House was laying the Alaskan tragedy to rest, but that was all. He didn't slip the details."

Sandecker turned to Pitt. "If you persist in this vendetta, you'll be stepping on a lot of toes."

"I won't give it up," Pitt said gravely.

Sandecker looked at Loren. "And you, Congresswoman Smith?"

"Loren."

"Loren," he obliged. "May I ask what your interest is in this?"

She hesitated for a fraction of a second and then said, "Let's just say congressional curiosity about a possible government scandal."

"You haven't told her the true purpose behind your Alaskan fishing expedition?" Sandecker asked Pitt.

"No."

"I think you should tell her."

"Do I have your official permission?"

The admiral nodded. "A friend in Congress will come in handy before your hunt is over."

"And you, Admiral, where do you stand?" Pitt asked him.

Sandecker stared hard across the table at Pitt, examining every feature of the craggy face as though he were seeing it for the first time, wondering what manner of man would step far beyond normal bounds for no personal gain. He read only a fierce determination. It was an expression he had seen many times in the years he'd known Pitt.

"I'll back you until the President orders your ass shot," he said at last. "Then you're on your own."

Pitt held back an audible sigh of relief. It was going to be all right. Better than all right.

Min Koryo looked down at the newspaper on her desk. "What do you make of this?"

Lee Tong leaned over her shoulder and read the opening sentences of the article aloud. " 'It was announced yesterday by Dirk Pitt, Special Projects Director for NUMA, that two ships missing for over twenty years have been found. The *San Marino* and the *Pilottown*, both Liberty-class vessels built during World War Two, were discovered on the seafloor in the North Pacific off Alaska.' "

"A bluff!" Min Koryo snapped. "Someone in Washington, probably from the Justice Department, had nothing better to do, so they sent up a trial balloon. They're on a fishing expedition, nothing more."

"I think you're only half right, *aunumi*," Lee Tong said thoughtfully. "I suspect that while NUMA was searching for the source behind the deaths in Alaskan waters, they stumbled on the ship containing the nerve agent."

"And this press release is a scheme to ferret out the true owners of that ship," Min Koryo added.

Lee Tong nodded. "The government is gambling we will make an inquiry that can be traced."

Min Koryo sighed. "A pity the ship wasn't sunk as planned."

Lee Tong came around and sank into a chair in front of the desk. "Bad luck," he said, thinking back. "After the explosives failed to detonate, the storm hit, and I was unable to reboard the ship."

"You can't be faulted for nature's whims," Min Koryo said impassively. "The true blame lies with the Russians. If they hadn't backed out of their bargain to buy Nerve Agent S, there would have been no need to scuttle the ship."

"They were afraid the agent was too unstable to transport across Siberia to their chemical warfare arsenal in the Urals."

"What's puzzling is how did NUMA tie the two ships together?"

"I can't say, *aunumi*. We were careful to strip every piece of identification."

"No matter," Min Koryo said. "The fact remains, the article in the newspaper is a ploy. We must remain silent and do nothing to jeopardize our anonymity."

"What about the man who made the announcement?" Lee Tong asked. "This Dirk Pitt?"

A long, cold, brooding look came over Min Koryo's narrow face. "Investigate his motives and observe his movements. See where he fits in the picture. If he appears to be a danger to us, arrange his funeral."

The gray of evening softened the harsh outlines of Los Angeles, and the lights came on, pimpling the sides of the buildings. The noise of the street traffic rose and seeped through the old-fashioned sash window. The tracks were warped and jammed under a dozen coats of paint. It hadn't been opened in thirty years. Outside, an air conditioner rattled in its brackets.

The man sat in an aging wooden swivel chair and stared unseeing through the grime filming the glass. He stared through eyes that had seen the worst the city had to give. They were hard, stark eyes, still clear and undimmed after sixty years. He sat in shirtsleeves, the well-worn leather of a holster slung over his left shoulder. The butt of a .45 automatic protruded from it. He was large-boned and stocky. The muscles had softened over the years, but he could still lift a two-hundred-pound man off the sidewalk and imbed him in a brick wall.

The chair creaked as he swung around and leaned over a desk that was battle-scarred with uncountable cigarette burns. He picked up a folded newspaper and read the article on the ship discoveries for perhaps the tenth time. Pulling open a drawer, he searched out a dog-eared folder and stared at the cover for a long while. Long ago he had memorized every word on the papers inside. Along with the newspaper he slipped it inside a worn leather briefcase.

He rose and stepped over to a washbowl hung in one corner of the room and rinsed his face with cold water. Then he donned a coat and a battered fedora, turned off the light and left the office.

As he stood in the hallway waiting for the elevator, he was surrounded by the smells of the aging building. The mold and rot seemed stronger with each passing day. Thirty-five years at the same stand was a long time, he mused, too long.

His thoughts were interrupted by the clatter of the elevator door. An operator who looked to be in his seventies gave him a yellow-toothed grin. "Callin' it quits for the night?" he asked.

"No, I'm taking the red-eye flight to Washington."

"New case?"

"An old one."

There were no more questions and they rode the rest of the way in silence. As he stepped into the lobby he nodded at the operator. "See you in a couple of days, Joe."

Then he passed through the main door and melted into the night.

23

TO MOST, HIS NAME WAS HIRAM YAEGER. To a select few he was known as Pinocchio because he could stick his nose into a vast number of computer networks and sift over their software. His playground was the tenth-floor communications and information network of NUMA.

Sandecker hired him to collect and store every scrap of data ever written on the oceans, scientific or historical, fact or theory. Yaeger tackled the job with a fierce dedication, and within five years had accumulated a huge computer library of knowledge about the sea.

Yaeger worked erratic hours, sometimes coming in with the morning sun and working straight through until the following dawn. He seldom showed up for departmental meetings, but Sandecker left him alone because there was none better, and because Yaeger had an uncanny ability to pry out secret access codes to a great number of worldwide computer networks.

Always dressed in Levi's jacket and pants, he wore his long blond hair in a bun. A scraggly beard combined with his probing eyes gave him the appearance of a desert prospector peering over the next hill for Eldorado.

He sat at a computer terminal stuck away in a far corner of NUMA's electronic maze. Pitt stood off to one side watching with interest the green block letters on a display screen.

"That's all we're going to comb from the Maritime Administration's mass storage system."

"Nothing new there," Pitt agreed.

"What now?"

"Can you tap the Coast Guard headquarters documents?"

Yaeger gave a wolfish grin. "Can Aunt Jemima make pancakes?"

He consulted a thick black notebook for a minute, found the insertion he was looking for and punched the number into a pushbutton telephone connected to a modem link. The Coast Guard computer system answered and accepted Yaeger's access code, and the green block letters swept across the display: "PLEASE STATE YOUR REQUEST."

Yaeger gave Pitt a questioning look.

"Ask for an abstract of title on the *Pilottown*," Pitt ordered.

Yaeger nodded and sent the request into the terminal. The answer flashed back and Pitt studied it closely, noting all the transactions of the vessel from the time she was built, who owned it as long as it was a documented vessel flying the United States flag, and the mortgages against it. The probe was redundant. The *Pilottown* had been removed from documentation when it was sold to an alien, in this case the Kassandra Phosphate Company of Athens, Greece.

"Anything promising?" Yaeger inquired.

"Another dry hole," Pitt grunted.

"How about Lloyd's of London? They'll have it in their register."

"Okay, give it a shot."

Yaeger logged out of the Coast Guard system, checked his book again and routed the terminal to the computer bank of the great maritime insurance company. The data printed out at 400 characters a second. This time the history of the *Pilottown* was revealed in greater detail. And yet little of it appeared useful. Then an item at the bottom of the display screen caught Pitt's attention.

"I think we might have something."

"Looks pretty much like the same stuff to me," said Yaeger.

"The line after Sosan Trading Company."

"Where they're listed as operators? So what? That showed up before."

"As owners, not operators. There's a difference."

"What does it prove?"

Pitt straightened, and his eyes took on a reflective look. "The reason owners register their vessel with what is called a 'country of convenience' is to save costly licenses, taxes and restrictive operating regulations. Another reason is they become lost to any kind of investigation. So they set up a dummy front and carry the company headquarters address as a post office box, in this case, Inchon, Korea. Now, if they contract with an operator to arrange cargoes and crews for the ship, the transfer of money from one to the other must take place. Banking facilities must be used. And banks keep records."

"All right, but say I'm a parent outfit. Why let my shady shipping line be run by some sleazy second party if we leave traceable banking links? I fail to see the advantage."

"An insurance scam," Pitt answered. "The operator does the dirty work while the owners collect. For example, take the case of a Greek tanker several years ago. A tramp called the *Trikeri*. It departed Surabaja, Indonesia, with its oil tanks filled to the brim. After reaching Capetown, South Africa, it slipped onto an offshore pipeline and removed all but a few thousand gallons. A week later it mysteriously sank off West Africa. An insurance claim was filed on the ship and a full cargo of oil. Investigators were dead certain the sinking was intentional, but they couldn't prove it. The *Trikeri*'s operator took the heat and quietly went out of business. The registered owners collected the insurance payoff and then siphoned it off through a corporate maze to the power at the top."

"This happen often?"

"More than anyone knows," Pitt replied.

"You want to dig into the Sosan Trading Company's bank account?"

Pitt knew better than to ask Yaeger if he could do it. He simply said, "Yes."

Yaeger logged out of the Lloyd's computer network and walked over to a file cabinet. He returned with a large bookkeeping ledger.

"Bank security codes," he said without elaboration.

Yaeger set to work and homed in on Sosan Trading's bank in two minutes. "Got it!" he exclaimed. "An obscure Inchon branch of a big bank headquartered in Seoul. Account was closed six years ago."

"Are the statements still on file?"

Without answering, Yaeger stabbed the terminal's keys and then sat back, arms folded, and eyed the printouts. The data blinked on with the account number and a request for the monthly statements desired. He looked up at Pitt expectantly.

"March through September 1976," Pitt directed.

The bank's computer system in Korea obliged.

"Most curious," Yaeger said, digesting the data. "Only twelve transactions over a span of seven years. Sosan Trading must have cleared their overhead and payroll with cash."

"Where did the deposits originate?" Pitt asked.

"Appears to be a bank in Bern, Switzerland."

"One step closer."

"Yes, but here it gets tricky," said Yaeger. "Swiss bank security codes are more complex. And if this shipping outfit is as cagey as they appear, they probably juggle bank accounts like a vaudeville act."

"I'll get the coffee while you start digging."

Yaeger looked pensively at Pitt for a moment. "You never give up, do you?"

"No."

Yaeger was surprised at the sudden coldness in Pitt's tone. He shrugged. "Okay, pal, but this isn't going to be a walkover. It may take all night and turn up zilch. I'll have to keep sending different number combinations until I strike the right codes."

"You got something better to do?"

"No, but while you're getting the coffee, I'd appreciate it if you scare up some donuts."

The bank in Bern, Switzerland, proved discouraging. Any trail to Sosan Trading's parent company ended there. They spot-checked six other Swiss banks, hoping they might get lucky, like a treasure hunter who finds the shipwreck chart he's searching for hidden away in the wrong drawer of an archive. But they turned up nothing of value. Groping through the account records of every banking house in Europe presented a staggering problem. There were over six thousand of them.

"Looks pretty dismal," said Yaeger after five hours of staring at the display screen.

"I agree," said Pitt.

"Shall I keep punching away?"

"If you don't mind."

Yaeger raised his arms and stretched. "This is how I get my kicks. You look like you've had it, though. Why don't you shove off and get some sleep? If I stumble on anything, I'll give you a call."

Pitt gratefully left Yaeger at NUMA headquarters and drove across the river to the airport. He stopped the Talbot-Lago in front of his hangar door, slipped a small transmitter from his coat pocket and pressed a preset code. In sequence the security alarm systems closed down and the massive door lifted to a height of seven feet. He parked the car inside and reversed the process. Then wearily he climbed the stairway, entered the living room and turned on the lights.

A man was sitting in Pitt's favorite reading chair, his hands folded on a briefcase that rested on his lap. There was a patient look about him, almost deadly, with only the tiniest hint of an indifferent smile. He wore an old-fashioned fedora hat and his custom-tailored coat, specially cut to conceal a lethal bulge, was unbuttoned just enough to reveal the butt of a .45 automatic.

For a moment they stared at each other, neither speaking, like fighters sizing up their opponents.

At last Pitt broke the silence. "I guess the appropriate thing to say is, Who the hell are you?"

The thin smile broadened into a set grin. "I'm a private investigator, Mr. Pitt. My name is Casio, Sal Casio."

24

"YOU HAVE ANY PROBLEM ENTERING?"

"Your security system is good—not great, but good enough to discourage most burglars and juvenile vandals."

"That mean I flunked the test?"

"Not entirely. I'd grade you a C-plus."

Pitt moved very slowly to an antique oak icebox he'd rebuilt into a liquor cabinet and eased open the door. "Would you like a drink, Mr. Casio?"

"A shot of Jack Daniel's on ice, thanks."

"A lucky guess. I happen to have a bottle."

"I peeked," said Casio. "Oh, and by the way, I took the liberty of removing the clip from the gun."

"Gun?" Pitt asked innocently.

"The .32-caliber Mauser automatic, serial number 922374, cleverly taped behind the half-gallon bottle of gin."

Pitt gave Casio a long look indeed. "How long did it take?"

"To make a search?"

Pitt nodded silently as he opened the refrigerator door for the ice.

"About forty-five minutes."

"And you found the other two guns I squirreled away."

"Three actually."

"You're very thorough."

"Nothing that is hidden in a house can't be found. And some of us are more talented at probing than others. It's simply a matter of technique." There was nothing boastful in Casio's tone. He spoke as though merely stating an accepted truth.

Pitt poured the drink and brought it into the living room on a tray. Casio took the glass with his right hand. Then suddenly Pitt dropped the tray, exposing a small vest-pocket .25-caliber automatic aimed at Casio's forehead.

Casio's only reaction was a thin smile. "Very good," he said approvingly. "So there were a total of five."

"Inside an empty milk carton," Pitt explained.

"Nicely done, Mr. Pitt. A clever touch, waiting until my gun hand was holding a glass. That shows you were thinking. I'll have to mark you up to a B-minus."

Pitt clicked on the safety and lowered the gun. "If you came here to kill me, Mr. Casio, you could have blown me away when I stepped through the door. What's on your mind?"

Casio nodded down at his briefcase. "May I?"

"Go ahead."

He set the drink down, opened the case and pulled out a bulging cardboard folder that was held together with rubber bands. "A case I've worked on since 1966."

"A long time. You must be a stubborn man."

"I hate to let go of it," Casio admitted. "It's like walking away from a jigsaw puzzle before it's completed, or putting down a good book. Sooner or later every investigator gets on a case that has him staring at the ceiling nights, the case he can never solve. This one has a personal tie, Mr. Pitt. It began twenty-three years ago when a girl, a bank teller by the name of Arta Casilighio, stole $128,000 from a bank in Los Angeles."

"How can that concern me?"

"She was last seen boarding a ship called the *San Marino*."

"Okay, so you read the press story about the shipwreck discovery."

"Yes."

"And you think this girl disappeared with the *San Marino?*"

"I'm certain of it."

"Then your case is solved. The thief is dead and the money gone forever."

"Not that simple," said Casio, staring into his glass. "There's no doubt Arta Casilighio is dead, but the money is not *gone forever*. Arta took freshly printed currency from the Federal Reserve Bank. All serial numbers were recorded, so it was an easy matter to account for the missing bills." Casio paused to look over his glass into Pitt's eyes. "Two years ago the missing money finally turned up."

Sudden interest flared in Pitt's eyes. He sat down in a chair facing Casio. "All of it?" he asked cautiously.

Casio nodded. "It appeared in dribbles and spurts. Five thousand in Frankfurt, a thousand in Cairo, all in foreign banks. None came to light in the United States, except one hundred-dollar bill."

"Then Arta didn't die on the *San Marino*."

"She vanished with the ship all right. The FBI connected her to a stolen passport belonging to an Estelle Wallace. With that lead they were able to follow her as far as San Francisco. Then they lost her. I kept digging and finally ran down a drifter who sometimes drove a cab when he needed booze money. He remembered hauling her to the boarding ramp of the *San Marino*."

"Can you trust the memory of a lush?"

Casio smiled confidently. "Arta gave him a crisp new hundred-dollar bill for the fare. He couldn't make change so she told him to keep it. Believe me, it took little effort for him to recall the event."

"If stolen Federal Reserve currency is in FBI jurisdiction, where do you fit in the picture? Why the dogged pursuit of a criminal whose trail is ice cold?"

"Before I shortened my name for business reasons, it was Casilighio. Arta was my daughter."

There was an uncomfortable silence. From outside the windows overlooking the river came the rumble of a jetliner taking off. Pitt stood up and went into the kitchen, where he poured a cup of coffee from a cold pot and placed it in a microwave oven. "Care for another drink, Mr. Casio?"

Casio shook his head.

"So the bottom line is that you think there's something queer about your daughter's disappearance?"

"She and the ship never made port, but the money she stole turns up in a manner that suggests it's being laundered a little at a time. Doesn't that suggest a queer circumstance to you, Mr. Pitt?"

"I can't deny you make a good case." The microwave beeped and Pitt retrieved a steaming cup. "But I'm not sure what you want from me."

"I have some questions."

Pitt sat down, his interest going beyond mere curiosity. "Don't expect detailed answers."

"I understand."

"Fire away."

"Where did you find the *San Marino?* I mean in what part of the Pacific Ocean?"

"Near the southern coast of Alaska," Pitt replied vaguely.

"A bit far off the track for a ship steaming from San Francisco to New Zealand, wouldn't you say?"

"Way off the track," Pitt agreed.

"As far as two thousand miles?"

"And then some." Pitt took a swallow of coffee and made a face. It was strong enough to use as brick mortar. He looked up. "Before we continue it's going to cost you."

Casio gave him a reappraising eye. "Somehow you never struck me as the type who'd extend a greasy palm."

"I'd like to have the names of the banks in Europe that passed the stolen money."

"Any particular reason?" Casio asked, not bothering to conceal his puzzlement.

"None I can tell you about."

"You're not very cooperative."

Pitt started to reply, but the phone on an end table rang loudly. "Hello."

"Dirk, this is Yaeger. You still awake."

"Thank you for calling. How is Sally? Is she out of intensive care yet?"

"Can't talk, huh?"

"Not too well."

"But you can listen."

"No problem."

"Bad news. I'm not getting anywhere. I'd stand a better chance of throwing a deck of cards in the air and catching a straight flush."

"Maybe I can knock down the odds. Hold on a minute." Pitt turned to Casio. "About that list of banks."

Casio slowly rose, poured himself another shot of Jack Daniel's and stood with his back to Pitt.

"A trade-off, Mr. Pitt. The bank list for what you know about the *San Marino.*"

"Most of my information is government classified."

"I don't give a damn if it's stenciled on the inside of the President's jockey shorts. Either we deal or I pack up and hike."

"How do you know I won't lie?"

"My list could be phony."

"Then we'll just have to trust each other," said Pitt with a loose grin.

"The hell we will," grunted Casio. "But neither of us has any choice."

He took a sheet of paper from the folder and handed it to Pitt, who in turn read off the names over the phone to Yaeger.

"Now what?" Casio demanded.

"Now I tell you what happened to the *San Marino.* And by breakfast I may also be able to tell you who killed your daughter."

25

FIFTEEN MINUTES AFTER SUNRISE, the photoelectric controllers in all of Washington's streetlights closed off their circuits. One by one, separated by no more than a few seconds, the yellow and red rays of the high-pressure sodium lamps faded and died, to wait through the daylight hours until fifteen minutes before sunset, when their light-sensitive controllers would boost them to life again.

Beneath the dimming glow of the streetlights, Sam Emmett could hear the vibration from the early-morning traffic as he walked hurriedly through the utility tunnel. There was no Marine Corps or Secret Service escort. He came alone, as did the others. The only person he'd met since leaving his car under the Treasury building was the White House guard stationed at the basement door. At the head of the hallway leading to the Situation Room, Emmett was greeted by Alan Mercier.

"You're the last," Mercier informed him.

Emmett checked his watch and noted he was five minutes early. "Everyone?" he questioned.

"Except for Simmons in Egypt and Lucas, who's giving your speech at Princeton, they're all present."

As he entered, Oates motioned him to a chair beside his, while Dan Fawcett, General Metcalf, CIA chief Martin Brogan and Mercier gathered around the conference table.

"I'm sorry for moving the scheduled meeting up by four hours," Oates began, "but Sam informed me that his investigators

164

have determined how the kidnapping took place." Without further explanation he nodded to the FBI Director.

Emmett passed out folders to each of the men at the table, then rose, moved to a blackboard and took a piece of chalk. Quickly and to precise scale he drew in the river, the grounds of Mount Vernon and the presidential yacht tied to the dock. Then he filled in the detail and labeled specific areas. The completed drawing had a realism about it that suggested a talent for architectural design.

Satisfied finally that each piece of the scene was in its correct place, he turned and faced his audience. "We'll walk through the event chronologically," he explained. "I'll briefly summarize while you gentlemen study the details shown in the report. Some of what I'm about to describe is based on fact and hard evidence. Some is conjecture. We have to fill in the blanks as best we can."

Emmett wrote in a time on the upper left corner of the blackboard.

"1825: The *Eagle* arrives at Mount Vernon, where the Secret Service has installed its security network and the surveillance begins.

"2015: The President and his guests sit down to dinner. In the same hour, officers and the crew began their meal in the messroom. The only men on duty were the chef, one assistant and the dining-room steward. This fact is important because we feel that it was during dinner that the President, his party, and the ship's crew were drugged."

"Drugged or poisoned?" Oates said, looking up.

"Nothing so drastic as poison," Emmett answered. "A mild drug that induced a gradual state of drowsiness was probably administered in their food by either the chef or the steward who served the table."

"Sounds practical," said Brogan. "It wouldn't do to have bodies dropping all over the decks."

Emmett paused to gather his thoughts. "The Secret Service agent whose post was onboard the yacht the hour before midnight reported the President and Vice President Margolin were the last to retire. Time: 2310."

"That's too early for the President," said Dan Fawcett. "I've seldom known him to be in bed before two in the morning."

"0025: A light mist drifts in from the northeast. Followed at 0135 by a heavy fog caused by two Navy surplus fogging generators concealed in the trees one hundred and sixty yards upriver from the *Eagle.*"

"They could blanket the entire area?" Oates asked.

"Under the right atmospheric conditions—in this case, no wind—the units left on site by the kidnappers can cover two square acres."

Fawcett looked lost. "My God, this operation must have taken an army."

Emmett shook his head. "Our projections figure it took as few as seven and certainly no more than ten men."

"Surely the Secret Service scouted the woods surrounding Mount Vernon before the President's arrival," said Fawcett. "How did they miss the foggers?"

"The units weren't in place prior to 1700 the night of the abduction," replied Emmett.

"How could the equipment operators see what they were doing in the dark?" Fawcett pressed. "Why weren't their movements and the sound of the generators overheard?"

"Infrared night visual gear would answer your first question. And the noise made by the equipment was muffled by the mooing of cattle."

Brogan gave a thoughtful twist of his head. "Who would have ever thought of that?"

"Somebody did," said Emmett. "They left the tape recorder and an amplifier behind with the foggers."

"It says here the only thing the security people noticed was an oily aroma to the fog."

Emmett nodded. "The fogger heats a deodorized kerosene type of fuel to a high pressure and blows it out a nozzle in very fine droplets, producing the fog."

"Let's move on to the next event," said Oates.

"0150: The small chase boat moors to the dock because of limited visibility. Three minutes later the Coast Guard cutter notifies agent George Blackowl at the Secret Service command post that a high-intensity signal is jamming their radar reception. They also apprised agent Blackowl that before their equipment went blind the only contact on their oscilloscope was a city sanitation tugboat and its trash barges that tied up to the bank to wait out the fog.''

Metcalf looked up. ''Tied up how far away?''

''Two hundred yards upriver.''

''Then the tug was above the artificial fog.''

''A crucial point,'' Emmett acknowledged, ''which we'll come to later.''

He turned to the blackboard and wrote in another time sequence. The room fell quiet. The men seated around the long table sat in rocklike stillness waiting for Emmett to reveal the final solution to the presidential abduction.

''0200: The agents moved to their new guard posts. Agent Lyle Brock took up station onboard the *Eagle* after agent Karl Polaski relieved him on the pier entrance. What is most important is that during this time the *Eagle* was hidden from his sight. He later walked to the boarding gangway of the yacht and talked to someone he thought was Brock. Brock by now was either unconscious or dead. Polaski did not notice anything suspicious except that Brock appeared to have forgotten his next post.''

''Polaski couldn't tell he was talking with a stranger?'' questioned Oates.

''They conversed from at least ten feet away from each other in low tones so they wouldn't disturb anyone on the yacht. When the 0300 post change came around, Brock simply melted into the fog. Agent Polaski states that he was never able to see more than a vague figure. It wasn't until 0348 that agent Edward McGrath discovered that Brock was not at his scheduled post. McGrath then notified Blackowl, who met him on the *Eagle* four minutes later. The yacht was searched and found empty, except for Polaski who had moved onboard to replace Brock.''

Emmett placed the chalk back in the tray and wiped his hands together. ''The rest is cut and dried. Who was alerted and when . . . the results of a fruitless search on the river and around the grounds of Mount Vernon . . . the roadblocks that failed to produce the missing men . . . and so on.''

"What was the disposition of the tugboat and trash barges after the alert?'' Metcalf questioned cannily.

"The barges were found moored to the riverbank,'' Emmett answered him. ''The tug was gone.''

"So much for facts,'' said Oates. ''The prize question is How were almost twenty men spirited off the yacht under the noses of an army of Secret Service agents and passed undetected through the most advanced security alarm system that money can buy?''

"Your answer is, Mr. Secretary, they weren't.''

Oates's eyebrows raised. ''How was it done?''

Emmett noticed a smug expression on Metcalf's face. ''I think the general has figured it out.''

"I wish someone would tell me,'' said Fawcett.

Emmett took a deep breath before he spoke. ''The yacht that agents Blackowl and McGrath found deserted is not the same yacht that carried the President and his party to Mount Vernon.''

"Son of a bitch!'' gasped Mercier.

"That's hard to swallow,'' said Oates skeptically.

Emmett picked up the chalk again and began diagramming. ''About fifteen minutes after the fogging generators began laying a dense cloud over the river and Mount Vernon, the abduction team transmitted on the Coast Guard's radar frequency and knocked it out of commission. Upriver the sanitation tugboat—except in this instance it was not a river tug but a yacht identical in every detail to the *Eagle*—cast off from the barges, which we found to be empty, and slowly cruised downstream. Its radar, of course, was operating on a different frequency from the Coast Guard's.''

Emmett drew in the path of the approaching yacht. ''When it was fifty yards from the Mount Vernon pier and the stern of the *Eagle*, it shut down its engines and drifted with the current, which was running about one knot. Then the abductors—''

"What I'd like to know, is how they got onboard in the first place,'' Mercier interrupted.

Emmett made a shrugging gesture with his hands. "We don't know. Our best guess at the moment is that they killed the galley crew earlier in the day and took their places, using counterfeit Coast Guard identification and orders."

"Please continue your findings," Oates persisted.

"Then the abductors on the yacht," Emmett repeated, "untied the mooring lines, allowing the *Eagle* to drift silently from the pier to make room for its double. Polaski heard nothing from his post near the bank, because any strange sounds were covered by the hum of the engine-room generators. Then, once the bogus yacht was tied to the pier its crew, probably no more than two men, rowed a small dinghy to the *Eagle* and escaped with the others downriver. One remained, however, to impersonate agent Brock. By the time Polaski conversed with Brock's impersonator, the switch had already been made. At the next post change, the man calling himself Brock slipped off and joined the men operating the foggers. Together they drove off and swung on the highway toward Alexandria. We know that much by footprints and tire tracks."

Everyone but Emmett focused his attention on the blackboard, as if trying to visualize the scene. The incredible timing, the ease with which presidential security was breached, the smoothness of the entire operation, staggered everyone.

"I can't help but admire the execution," General Metcalf said. "They must have taken a long time to plan this thing."

"Our estimate is three years," said Emmett.

"Where could they possibly have found an identical boat?" Fawcett muttered to no one in particular.

"My investigating team considered that. They traced the old boating records and found that the original builder constructed the *Eagle* and a sister ship named the *Samantha* at the same time. The last registered owner of the *Samantha* was a stockbroker in Baltimore. He sold it about three years ago to a guy named Dunn. That's all he could tell us. It was an under-the-table cash transaction to beat a profit tax. He never saw Dunn or the yacht again. The *Samantha* was never registered or licensed under the new owner. They both dropped from sight."

"Was it identical in every respect to the *Eagle?*" Brogan asked.

"A creative job of deception. Every stick of furniture, bulkhead decor, paint and equipment is a perfect match."

Fawcett nervously tapped a pencil on the table. "How did you catch on?"

"Every time you enter and leave a room, you leave particles of your presence behind. Hair, dandruff, lint, fingerprints—they can all be detected. My lab people couldn't find one tiny hint that the President or the others had ever been on board."

Oates straightened in his chair. "The Bureau has done a magnificent job, Sam. We're all grateful."

Emmett gave a curt nod and sat down.

"The yacht transfer brings up a new angle," Oates continued. "As gruesome as it sounds, we have to consider the possibility they were all assassinated."

"We've got to find the yacht," Mercier said grimly.

Emmett looked at him. "I've already ordered a surface and air search."

"You won't find it that way," Metcalf interjected. "We're dealing with damned smart people. They're not about to leave it lying around where it can be found."

Fawcett poised his pencil in midair. "Are you saying the yacht was destroyed?"

"That may well be the case," Metcalf said, apprehension forming in his eyes. "If so, we have to be prepared to find corpses."

Oates leaned on his elbows and rubbed his face with his hands and wished he was anyplace but in that room at that moment. "We're going to have to spread our trust," he said finally. "The best man I can think of for an underwater search is Jim Sandecker over at NUMA."

"I concur," said Fawcett. "His special project team has just wrapped up a ticklish job off Alaska, where they found the ship responsible for widespread contamination."

"Will you brief him, Sam?" Oates asked Emmett.

"I'll go directly from here to his office."

"Well, I guess that's it for now," Oates said, exhaustion creeping into his voice. "Good or bad, we have a lead. Only God knows what we'll have after we find the *Eagle.*" He hesitated, staring up at the blackboard. Then he said, "I don't envy the first man who steps inside."

DEEP SIX

I'll go anyway if you open the office.
I will," Pitt said, a trace now. Uncertain, or uncertain if one
put into fancies. "Could or bad, we have a clue. Only God knows
what we'll have after we find the night." He hesitated, then go
in the Atocha said. "Then he said, "I don't carry the first man who
some fancy.

26 _____

EVERY MORNING, including Saturdays and Sundays,
Admiral Sandecker jogged the six miles from his Watergate apartment to the NUMA headquarters building. He had just stepped out
of the bathroom shower adjoining his office when his secretary's
voice came over a speaker above the sink: "Admiral, Mr. Emmett
is here to see you."

Sandecker was vigorously toweling his hair and he was not sure
he heard the name right. "Sam Emmett, as in FBI?"

"Yes, sir. He asked to see you immediately. He says it's extremely urgent."

Sandecker saw his face turn incredulous in the mirror. The esteemed Director of the FBI did not make office calls at eight in the
morning. The Washington bureaucratic game had rules. Everyone
from the President on down abided by them. Emmett's unannounced visit could only mean a dire emergency.

"Send him right in."

He barely had time to throw on a terry-cloth robe, his skin still
dripping, when Emmett strode through the door.

"Jim, we've got a hell of a problem." Emmett didn't bother
with a preliminary handshake. He quickly laid his briefcase on
Sandecker's desk, opened it and handed the admiral a folder. "Sit
down and look this over, and then we'll discuss it."

Sandecker was not a man to be shoved and ordered around, but
he could read the tension in Emmett's eyes, and he did as he was
asked without comment.

172

Sandecker studied the contents of the folder for nearly ten minutes without speaking. Emmett sat on the other side of the desk and looked for an expression of shock or anger. There was none. Sandecker remained enigmatic. At last he closed the folder and said simply, "How can I help?"

"Find the *Eagle*."

"You think they sank her?"

"An air and surface search has turned up nothing."

"All right, I'll get my best people on it." Sandecker made a movement toward his intercom. Emmett raised his hand in a negative gesture.

"I don't have to describe the chaos if this leaks out."

"I've never lied to my staff before."

"You'll have to keep them in the dark on this one."

Sandecker gave a curt nod and spoke into the intercom. "Sylvia, please get Pitt on the phone."

"Pitt?" Emmett inquired in an official tone.

"My special projects director. He'll head up the search."

"You'll tell him only what's necessary?" It was more an order than a request.

A yellow caution light glimmered in Sandecker's eyes. "That will be at my discretion."

Emmett started to say something but was interrupted by the intercom.

"Admiral?"

"Yes, Sylvia."

"Mr. Pitt's line is busy."

"Keep trying until he answers," Sandecker said gruffly. "Better yet, call the operator and cut in on his line. Tell her this is a government priority."

"Will you be able to mount a full-scale search operation by evening?" asked Emmett.

Sandecker's lips parted in an all-devouring grin. "If I know Pitt, he'll have a crew scanning the depths of the Potomac River before lunch."

* * *

Pitt was speaking to Hiram Yaeger when the operator broke in. He cut the conversation short and then dialed the admiral's private line. After listening without doing any talking for several moments, he replaced the receiver in its cradle.

"Well," asked Casio expectantly.

"The money was exchanged, never deposited," Pitt said, looking miserably down at the floor. "That's all. That's all there is. No thread left to pick up."

There was only a flicker of disappointment in Casio's face. He'd been there before. He let out a long sigh and stared at his watch. He struck Pitt as a man drained of emotional display.

"I appreciate your help," he said quietly. He snapped his briefcase shut and stood up. "I'd better go now. If I don't lag, I can catch the next flight back to L.A."

"I'm sorry I couldn't provide an answer."

Casio shook Pitt's hand in a tight grip. "Nobody scores one hundred percent every time. Those responsible for the death of my daughter and your friend have made a mistake. Somewhere, sometime, they overlooked a detail. I'm glad to have you on my side, Mr. Pitt. It's been a lonely job until now."

Pitt was genuinely moved. "I'll keep digging from my end."

"I couldn't ask for more." Casio nodded and then walked down the stairs. Pitt watched him shuffle across the hangar floor, a proud, hardened old man, battling his own private windmill.

27

THE PRESIDENT SAT UPRIGHT in a black leather-cushioned chrome chair, his body held firmly in place by nylon belts. His eyes stared off in the distance, unfocused and vacant. Wireless sensor scans were taped onto his chest and forehead, transmitting the physical signatures of eight different life functions to a computer network.

The operating room was small, no more than a hundred square feet, and crammed with electronic monitoring equipment. Lugovoy and four members of his surgical team were quietly and efficiently preparing for the delicate operation. Paul Suvorov stood in the only empty corner, looking uncomfortable in a green sterile gown. He watched as one of Lugovoy's technicians, a woman, pressed a small needle into one side of the President's neck and then the other.

"Odd place for an anesthetic," Suvorov remarked.

"For the actual penetration we'll use a local," Lugovoy replied while staring at an image-intensified X ray on a video display. "However, a tiny dose of Amytal into the carotid arteries puts the left and right hemispheres of the brain in a drowsy state. This procedure is to eliminate any conscious memory of the operation."

"Shouldn't you shave his head?" Suvorov asked, gesturing toward the President's hair, which protruded through an opening of a metal helmet encasing his skull.

"We must ignore normal surgical procedures," Lugovoy patiently answered. "For obvious reasons, we cannot alter his appearance in any form."

"Who will direct the operation?"

"Who do you think?"

"I'm asking you, comrade."

"I will."

Suvorov looked puzzled. "I've studied your file and the file of every member of the staff. I can almost repeat their contents by heart. Your field is psychology, most of the others are electronic technicians and one is a biochemist. None of you has surgical qualifications."

"Because we don't require them." He dismissed Suvorov and scrutinized the TV display again. Then he nodded. "We can begin now. Set the laser in place."

A technician pressed his face against the rubber eyepiece of a microscope attached to an argon laser. The machine tied into a computer and displayed a set of coordinates in orange numbers across the bottom of the microscope's position fixer. When the numbers read only zeros the placement was exact.

The man at the laser nodded. "Position set."

"Commence," Lugovoy directed.

A wisp of smoke, so faint that only the laser operator could see it in the microscope, signaled the contact of the imperceptibly thin blue-green beam with the President's skull.

It was a strange scene. Everyone stood with his back to the patient, watching the monitors. The images were magnified until the beam could be seen as a weblike filament strand. With a precision far above human dexterity, the computer guided the laser in cutting a minute hole one thirtieth of a millimeter in the bone, penetrating only to the membrane covering the brain and its fluid. Suvorov moved closer in rapt fascination.

"What happens next?" he asked hoarsely.

Lugovoy motioned him over to an electron microscope. "See for yourself."

Suvorov peered through the twin lenses. "All I make out is a dark speck."

176

"Adjust the focus to your eyes."

Suvorov did so and the speck became a chip—an integrated circuit.

"A microminiaturized implant that can transplant and receive brain signals. We're going to place it in his cerebral cortex, where the brain's thought processes originate."

"What does the implant use for an energy source?"

"The brain itself produces ten watts of electricity," Lugovoy explained. "The President's brainwaves can be telemetered to a control unit thousands of miles away, translated and any required commands returned. You might say it's like changing TV channels with a remote control box."

Suvorov stepped back from the microscope and stared at Lugovoy. "The possibilities are even more overwhelming than I thought," he murmured. "We'll be able to learn every secret of the United States government."

"We'll also be able to manipulate his days and nights for as long as he lives," Lugovoy continued. "And through the computer, direct his personality so that neither he nor anyone close to him will notice."

A technician stepped behind him. "We're ready to position the implant."

He nodded. "Proceed."

A robotlike machine was moved in place of the laser. The incredibly diminutive implant was taken from under the microscope and exactingly fitted into the end of a single slim wire protruding from a mechanical arm. It was then aligned with the opening in the President's skull.

"Beginning penetration . . . now," droned the voice of the man seated at a console.

As with the viewer on the laser, he studied a series of numbers on a display screen. The entire procedure was preprogrammed. No human hand was lifted. Led by the computer, the robot delicately eased the wire through the protective membrane into the soft folds of the brain. After six minutes the display screen flashed, "MARK."

Lugovoy's eyes never left the color X-ray monitor. "Release and withdraw the probe."

"Released and withdrawing," a voice echoed.

After the wire was removed it was replaced with a miniature tubelike instrument containing a small plug with three hairs and their roots, removed from one of the Russian staff whose head growth closely resembled the President's. The plug was then inserted into the tiny hole neatly cut by the laser beam. When the robot unit was pulled back, Lugovoy approached and studied the results with a large magnifying glass.

"What little scabbing that transpires should flake away in a few days," he remarked. Satisfied, he straightened and viewed the computer-directed screens.

"The implant is operational," announced his female assistant.

Lugovoy massaged his hands in a pleased gesture. "Good, we can begin the second penetration."

"You're going to place another implant?" Suvorov asked.

"No, inject a small amount of RNA into the hippocampus."

"Could you enlighten me in layman terms?"

Lugovoy reached over the shoulder of the man sitting at the computer console and twisted a knob. The image of the President's brain enlarged until it covered the entire screen of the X-ray monitor.

"There," he said, tapping the glass screen. "The sea-horse-shaped ridge running under the horns of the lateral ventricles, a vital section of the brain's limbic system. It's called the hippocampus. It's here where new memories are received and dispersed. By injecting RNA—ribonucleic acid, which transmits genetic instructions—from one subject, one who's been programmed with certain thoughts, we can accomplish what we term a 'memory transfer.' "

Suvorov had been furiously storing what he saw and heard in his mind, but he was falling behind. He could not absorb it all. Now he stared down at the President, eyes uncertain.

"You can actually inject the memory of one man into another's brain?"

"Exactly," Lugovoy said nonchalantly. "What do you think happens in the mental hospitals where the KGB sends enemies of the state. Not all are re-educated to become good party lovers. Many are used for important psychological experiments. For example, the RNA we are about to administer into the President's hippocampus comes from an artist who insisted on creating illustrations depicting our leaders in awkward and uncomplimentary poses. . . . I can't recall his name."

"Belkaya?"

"Yes, Oskar Belkaya. A sociological misfit. His paintings were either masterpieces of modern art or nightmarish abstractions, depending on your taste. After your fellow state security agents arrested him at his studio, he was secretly taken to a remote sanitarium outside of Kiev. There he was placed in a cocoon, like the ones we have here, for two years. With new memory storage techniques, discovered through biochemistry, his memory was erased and indoctrinated with political concepts we wish the President to implement within his government."

"But can't you accomplish the same thing with the control implant?"

"The implant, with its computerized network, is extremely complex and liable to breakdown. The memory transfer acts as a backup system. Also, our experiments have shown that the control process operates more efficiently when the subject creates the thought himself, and the implant then commands a positive or negative response."

"Very impressive," Suvorov said earnestly. "And that's the end of it?"

"Not entirely. As an added safety margin, one of my staff, a highly skilled hypnotist, will put the President in a trance and wipe out any subconscious sensations he might have absorbed while under our care. He'll also be primed with a story of where he's been for ten days in vivid detail."

"As the Americans are fond of saying, you have all the bases covered."

Lugovoy shook his head. "The human brain is a magical uni-

179

verse we will never fully understand. We may think we've finally harnessed its three and a half pounds of grayish-pink jelly, but its capricious nature is as unpredictable as the weather."

"What you're saying is that the President might not react the way you want him to."

"It's possible," Lugovoy said seriously. "It's also possible for his brain to break the bonds of reality, despite our control, and make him do something that will have terrible consequences for us all."

28

SANDECKER STOPPED HIS CAR in the parking lot of a small yacht marina forty miles below Washington. He climbed from under the wheel and stood looking out over the Potomac River. The sky sparkled in a clear blue as the dull green water rolled eastward toward Chesapeake Bay. He walked down a sagging stairway to a floating dock. Tied up at the end was a tired old clamming boat, its rusting tongs hanging from a deck boom like the claws of some freakish animal.

The hull was worn from years of hard use and most of the paint was gone. Her diesel engine chugged out little puffs of exhaust that leaped from the tip of the stack and dissolved into a soft breeze. Her name, barely discernible over the stern transom, read *Hoki Jamoki*.

Sandecker glanced at his watch. It showed twenty minutes to noon. He nodded in approval. Only three hours after he'd briefed Pitt, the search for the *Eagle* was on. He jumped on deck and greeted the two engineers connecting the sonar sensor to the recorder cable, then entered the wheelhouse. He found Pitt scrutinizing a large satellite photograph through a magnifying glass.

"Is this the best you can do?" Sandecker asked.

Pitt looked up and grinned humorously. "You mean the boat?"

"I do."

"Not up to your spit and polish naval standards, but she'll serve nicely."

"None of our research vessels were available?"

181

"They were, but I chose this old tub for two reasons. One, she's a damn good little workboat; and two, if somebody really snatched a government boat with a party of VIP's on board and deep-sixed her, they'll expect a major underwater search effort and will be watching for it. This way, we'll be in and out before they're wise."

Sandecker had told him only that a boat belonging to the naval yard had been stolen from the pier at Mount Vernon and presumed sunk. Little else. "Who said anything about VIP's being on-board?"

"Army and Navy helicopters are as thick as locusts overhead, and you can walk across the river on the Coast Guard ships crowding the water. There's more to this search project than you've let on, Admiral. A hell of a lot more."

Sandecker didn't reply. He could only admit to himself that Pitt was thinking four jumps ahead. His silence, he knew, only heightened Pitt's suspicions. Sidestepping the issue, he asked, "You see something that caused you to begin looking this far below Mount Vernon?"

"Enough to save us four days and twenty-five miles," Pitt answered. "I figured the boat would be spotted by one of our space cameras, but which one? Military spy satellites don't orbit over Washington, and space weather pictures won't enhance to pinpoint small detail."

"Where did you get that one?" Sandecker asked, motioning toward the photograph.

"From a friend at the Department of Interior. One of their geological survey satellites flew 590 miles overhead and shot an infrared portrait of Chesapeake Bay and the adjoining rivers. Time: four-forty the morning of the boat's disappearance. If you look through the glass at the blowup of this section of the Potomac, the only boat that can be seen downriver from Mount Vernon is cruising a mile below this dock."

Sandecker peered at the tiny white dot on the photograph. The enhancement was incredibly sharp. He could detect every piece of gear on the decks and the figures of two people. He stared into Pitt's eyes.

"No way of proving that's the boat we're after," he said flatly.

"I didn't fall off a pumpkin truck, Admiral. That's the presidential yacht *Eagle*."

"I won't run you around the horn," Sandecker spoke quietly, "but I can't tell you any more than I already have."

Pitt gave a noncommittal shrug and said nothing.

"So where do you think it is?"

Pitt's green eyes deepened. He gave Sandecker a sly stare and picked up a pair of dividers. "I looked up the *Eagle*'s specifications. Her top speed was fourteen knots. Now, the space photo was taken at four-forty. Daylight was an hour and a half away. The crew who pirated the yacht couldn't risk being seen, so they put her on the bottom under cover of darkness. Taking all that into consideration, she could have traveled only twenty-one miles before sunup."

"That still takes in a lot of water."

"I think we can slice it some."

"By staying in the channel?"

"Yes, sir, deep water. If I was running the show, I'd sink her deep to prevent accidental discovery."

"What's the average depth of your search grid?"

"Thirty to forty feet."

"Not enough."

"True, but according to the depth soundings on the navigation charts, there are several holes that drop over a hundred."

Sandecker paused and gazed out the wheelhouse window as Al Giordino marched along the dock carrying a pair of air tanks on his beefy shoulders. He turned back to Pitt and observed him thoughtfully.

"If you dive on it," Sandecker said coldly, "you're not to enter. Our job is strictly to discover and identify, nothing else."

"What's down there that we can't see?"

"Don't ask."

Pitt smiled wryly. "Humor me. I'm fickle."

"The hell you are," grunted Sandecker. "What do you think is in the yacht?"

"Make that *who.*"

"Does it matter?" Sandecker asked guardedly. "It's probably empty."

"You're jerking me around, Admiral. I'm sure of it. After we find the yacht, what then?"

"The FBI takes over."

"So we do our little act and step aside."

"That's what the orders say."

"I say screw them."

"Them?"

"The powers who play petty secret games."

"Believe me, this project isn't petty."

A hard look crossed Pitt's face. "We'll make that judgment when we find the yacht, won't we?"

"Take my word for it," said Sandecker, "you don't want to see what might be inside the wreck."

Almost as the words came out, Sandecker knew he'd waved a flag in front of a bull elephant. Once Pitt dropped beneath the river's surface, the thin leash of command was broken.

29

SIX HOURS LATER and twelve miles downriver, target number seventeen crept across the recording screen of the Klein High Resolution Sonar. It lay in 109 feet of water between Persimmon and Mathias points directly opposite Popes Creek and two miles above the Potomac River Bridge.

"Dimensions?" Pitt asked the sonor operator.

"Approximately thirty-six meters long by seven meters wide."

"What kind of size are we looking for?" asked Giordino.

"The *Eagle* has an overall length of a hundred and ten feet with a twenty-foot beam," Pitt replied.

"That matches," Giordino said, mentally juggling meters to feet.

"I think we've got her," Pitt said as he examined the configurations revealed by the sidescan sonar. "Let's make another pass—this time about twenty meters to starboard—and throw out a buoy."

Sandecker, who was standing outside on the after deck keeping an eye on the sensor cable, leaned into the wheelhouse. "Got something?"

Pitt nodded. "A prime contact."

"Going to check it out?"

"After we drop a buoy, Al and I'll go down for a look."

Sandecker stared at the weathered deck and said nothing. Then he turned and walked back to the stern, where he helped Giordino hoist a fifty-pound lead weight attached to a bright orange buoy onto the *Hoki Jamoki*'s bulwark.

Pitt took the helm and brought the boat about. When the target began to raise on the depth sounder, he shouted, "Now!"

The buoy was thrown overboard as the boat slowed. One of the engineers moved to the bow and lowered the anchor. The *Hoki Jamoki* drifted to a stop with her stern pointed downstream.

"Too bad you didn't include an underwater TV camera," said Sandecker as he helped Pitt into his dive gear. "You could have saved yourself a trip."

"A wasted effort," Pitt said. "Visibility is measured in inches down there."

"The current is running about two knots," Sandecker judged.

"When we begin our ascent to the surface, it will carry us astern. Better throw out a hundred-yard lifeline on a floating buoy to pull us aboard."

Giordino tightened his weight belt and flashed a jaunty grin. "Ready when you are."

Sandecker gripped Pitt on the shoulder. "Mind what I said about entering the wreck."

"I'll try not to look too hard," Pitt said flatly.

Before the admiral could reply, Pitt adjusted his face mask over his eyes and dropped backwards into the river.

The water closed over him and the sun diffused into a greenish orange blur. The current pulled at his body and he had to swim on a diagonal course against it until he found the buoy. He reached out and clutched the line and stared downward. Less than three feet away the white nylon braid faded into the opaque murk.

Using the line as a guide and a support, Pitt slipped into the depths of the Potomac. Tiny filaments of vegetation and fine particles of sediment swept past his face mask. He switched on his dive light, but the dim beam only added a few inches to his field of vision. He paused to work his jaws and equalize the growing pressure within his ear canals.

The density increased as he dove deeper. Then suddenly, as if he'd passed through a door, the water temperature dropped by ten degrees and visibility stretched to almost ten feet. The colder layer acted as a cushion pushing against the warm current above. The bottom appeared and Pitt discerned the shadowy outline of a boat off to his right. He turned and gestured to Giordino, who gave an affirmative nod of his head.

As though growing out of a fog, the superstructure of the *Eagle* slowly took on shape. She lay like a lifeless animal, alone in haunted silence and watery gloom.

Pitt swam around one side of the hull while Giordino kicked around the other. The yacht was sitting perfectly upright with no indication of list. Except for a thin coating of algae that was forming on her white paint, she looked as pristine as when she rode the surface.

They met at the stern, and Pitt wrote on his message board, "Any damage?"

Giordino wrote back, "None."

Then they slowly worked their way over the decks, past the darkened windows of the staterooms and up to the bridge. There was nothing to suggest death or tragedy. They probed their lights through the bridge windows into the black interior, but all they saw was eerie desolation. Pitt noted that the engine-room telegraph read ALL STOP.

He hesitated for a brief moment and wrote a new message on his board: "I'm going in."

Giordino's eyes glistened under the face-mask lens and he scrawled back, "I'm with you."

Out of habit they checked their air gauges. There was enough time left for another twelve minutes of diving. Pitt tried the door to the wheelhouse. His heart squeezed within his chest. Even with Giordino at his side, the apprehension was oppressive. The latch turned and he pushed the door open. Taking a deep breath, Pitt swam inside.

The brass gave off a dull gleam under the dive lights. Pitt was curious at the barren look about the room. Nothing was out of place. The floor was clean of any spilled debris. It reminded him of the *Pilottown*.

Seeing nothing of interest, they threaded their way down a stairway into the lounge area of the deckhouse. In the fluid darkness the large enclosure seemed to yawn into infinity. Everywhere was the same strange neatness. Giordino aimed his light upward. The overhead beams and mahogany paneling had a stark, naked appearance. Then Pitt realized what was wrong. The ceiling should have been littered with objects that float. Everything that might have drifted to the surface and washed ashore must have been removed.

Accompanied by the gurgle of their escaping air bubbles, they glided through the passageway separating the staterooms. The same neat look was everywhere; even the beds and mattresses had been stripped. Their lights darted amid the furniture securely bolted to the carpeted deck. Pitt checked the bathrooms as Giordino probed the closets. By the time they reached the crew's quarters, they only had seven minutes of air left. Communicating briefly with hand signals, they divided up, Giordino searching the galley and storerooms while Pitt took the engine room.

He found the hatch cover over the engine room locked and bolted. Without a second of lost motion, he quickly removed his dive knife from its leg sheath and pried out the pins in the hinges. The hatch cover, released from its mountings and thrust upward by its buoyancy, sailed past him.

And so did a bloated corpse that burst through the open hatch like a jack-in-the-box.

30 _____

PITT REELED BACKWARD into a bulkhead and watched numbly as an unearthly parade of floating debris and bodies erupted from the engine room. They drifted up to the ceiling, where they hung in grotesque postures like trapped balloons. Though the internal gases had begun to expand, the flesh had not yet started to decompose. Sightless eyes bulged beneath strands of hair that wavered from the disturbance in the water.

Pitt struggled to fight off the grip of shock and revulsion, hardening his mind for the repugnant job he could not leave undone. With creeping nausea merged with cold fear he snaked through the hatch into the engine room.

His eyes were met with a charnel house of death. Bedding, clothing from half-open suitcases, pillows and cushions, anything buoyant enough to float, mingled between a crush of bodies. The scene was a nightmare that could never be imagined or remotely duplicated by a Hollywood horror film.

Most of the corpses wore white Coast Guard uniforms that added to their ghostly appearance. Several had on ordinary work clothes. None showed signs of injury or wounds.

He spent two minutes, no more, in there, cringing when a lifeless hand brushed across his arm or a white expressionless face drifted inches in front of his face mask. He could have sworn they were all staring at him, begging for something that was not his to give. One was dressed differently from the others, in a knit sweater covered by a stylish raincoat. Pitt swiftly rifled through the dead man's pockets.

Pitt had seen enough to be permanently etched in his mind for a lifetime. He hurriedly kicked up the ladder and out of the engine room. Once free of the morbid scene below, he hesitated to read his air gauge. The needle indicated a hundred pounds, an ample supply to reach the sun again if he didn't linger. He found Giordino rummaging through a cavernous food locker and made an upward gesture with his thumb. Giordino nodded and led the way through a passageway to the outside deck.

A great wave of relief swept over Pitt as the yacht receded into the murk. There wasn't time to search for the buoy line so they ascended with the bubbles that flowed from their air regulators' exhaust valves. The water slowly transformed from an almost brown-black to a leaden green. At last they broke the surface and found themselves fifty yards downstream from the *Hoki Jamoki*.

Sandecker and the boat's crew of engineers spotted them immediately and quickly began hauling on the lifeline. Sandecker cupped his hands to his mouth and shouted, "Hang on, we'll pull you in."

Pitt waved, thankful he could lie back and relax. He felt too drained to do anything but lazily float against the current and watch the trees lining the banks slip past. A few minutes later he and Giordino were lifted onto the deck of the old clamming boat.

"Is it the *Eagle?*" Sandecker asked, unable to mask his curiosity.

Pitt hesitated in answering until he'd removed his air tank. "Yes," he said finally, "it's the *Eagle.*"

Sandecker could not bring himself to ask the question that was gripping his mind. He sidestepped it. "Find anything you want to talk about?"

"The outside is undamaged. She's sitting upright, her keel resting in about two feet of silt."

"No sign of life?"

"Not from the exterior."

190

It was obvious that Pitt wasn't going to volunteer any information unless asked. His healthy tan seemed strangely paled.

"Could you see inside?" Sandecker demanded.

"Too dark to make out anything."

"All right, dammit, let's have it straight."

"Now that you've asked so pleasantly," Pitt said stonily, "there's more dead bodies in the yacht than a cemetery. They were stacked in the engine room from deck to overhead. I counted twenty-one of them."

"Christ!" Sandecker rasped, suddenly taken aback. "Could you recognize any of them?"

"Thirteen were crewmen. The rest looked to be civilians."

"Eight civilians?" Sandecker seemed stunned.

"As near as I could judge by their clothing. They weren't in any condition to interrogate."

"Eight civilians," Sandecker repeated. "And none of them looked remotely familiar to you?"

"I'm not sure their own mothers could identify them," said Pitt. "Why? Was I supposed to know somebody?"

Sandecker shook his head. "I can't say."

Pitt couldn't recall seeing the admiral so distraught. The iron armor had fallen away. The penetrating, intelligent eyes seemed stricken. Pitt watched for a reaction as he spoke.

"If I had to venture an opinion, I'd say someone snuffed the candle on half the Chinese embassy."

"Chinese?" The eyes suddenly turned as sharp as ice picks. "What are you saying?"

"Seven of the eight civilians were from eastern Asia."

"Could you be in error?" Sandecker asked, regaining a foothold. "With little or no visibility—"

"Visibility was ten feet. And, I'm well aware of the difference between the eye folds of a Caucasian and an Oriental."

"Thank God," Sandecker said, exhaling a deep breath.

"I'd be much obliged if you would inform me just what in hell you expected Al and me to find down there."

Sandecker's eyes softened. "I owe you an explanation," he

said, "but I can't give you one. There are events occurring around us that we have no need to know."

"I have my own project," said Pitt, his voice turning cold. "I'm not interested in this one."

"Yes, Julie Mendoza. I understand."

Pitt pulled something from under the sleeve of his wet suit. "Here, I almost forgot. I took this from one of the bodies."

"What is it?"

Pitt held up a soggy leather billfold. On the inside was a waterproof ID card with a man's photograph. Opposite was a badge in the shape of a shield. "A Secret Service agent's identification," Pitt answered. "His name was Brock, Lyle Brock."

Sandecker took the billfold without comment. He glanced at his watch. "I've got to contact Sam Emmett at FBI. This is his problem now."

"You can't drop it that easily, Admiral. We both know NUMA will be called on to raise the *Eagle*."

"You're right, of course," Sandecker said wearily. "You're relieved of that project. You do what you have to do. I'll have Giordino handle the salvage." He turned and stepped into the wheelhouse to use the ship-to-shore phone.

Pitt stood looking for a long time at the dark forbidding water of the river, reliving the terrible scene below. A line from an old seaman's poem ran through his head: "A ghostly ship, with a ghostly crew, with no place to go."

Then as though closing a curtain, he turned his thoughts back to the *Pilottown*.

On the east bank of the river, concealed in a thicket of ash trees, a man dressed in Vietnam leaf camouflage fatigues pressed his eye to the viewfinder of a video camera. The warm sun and the heavy humidity caused sweat to trickle down his face. He ignored the discomfort and kept taping, zooming in the telephoto lens until Pitt's upper body filled the miniature viewing screen. Then he panned along the entire length of the clamming boat, holding for a few seconds on each member of the crew.

A half-hour after the divers climbed out of the water, a small fleet of Coast Guard boats descended around the *Hoki Jamoki*. A derrick on one of the vessels lifted a large red-banded buoy with a flashing light over the side and dropped it beside the wreck of the *Eagle*.

When the battery of his recording unit died, the hidden cameraman neatly packed away his equipment and slipped into the approaching dusk.

31 _____

PITT WAS CONTEMPLATING A MENU when the maître d' of Positano Restaurant on Fairmont Avenue steered Loren to his table. She moved with an athletic grace, nodding and exchanging a few words with the Capitol crowd eating lunch amid the restaurant's murals and wine racks.

Pitt looked up and their eyes met. She returned his appraising stare with an even smile. Then he rose and pulled back her chair.

"Damn, you look ugly today," he said.

She laughed. "You continue to mystify me."

"How so?"

"One minute you're a gentleman, and the next a slob."

"I was told women crave variety."

Her eyes, clear and soft, were amused. "I do give you credit, though. You're the only man I know who doesn't kiss my fanny."

Pitt's face broke into his infectious grin. "That's because I don't need any political favors."

She made a face and opened a menu. "I don't have time to be made fun of. I have to get back to my office and respond to a ton of constituents' mail. What looks good?"

"I thought I'd try the *zuppa di pesce.*"

"My scale said I was up a pound this morning. I think I'll just have a salad."

The waiter approached.

"A drink?" Pitt asked.

"You order."

"Two Sazerac cocktails on the rocks, and please ask the bartender to pour rye instead of bourbon."

"Very good, sir," the waiter acknowledged.

Loren laid her napkin in her lap. "I've phoned for two days. Where've you been?"

"The admiral sent me on an emergency salvage job."

"Was she pretty?" she asked, playing the age-old game.

"A coroner might think so. But drowned bodies never turned me on."

"Sorry," she said and went sober and quiet until the drinks were brought. They stirred the ice around the glasses and then sipped the reddish contents.

"One of my aides ran across something that might help you," she said finally.

"What is it?"

She pulled several stapled sheets of typewritten paper from her attaché case and passed them to Pitt. Then she began explaining in a soft undertone.

"Not much meat, I'm afraid, but there's an interesting report on the CIA's phantom navy."

"Didn't know they had one," Pitt said, scanning the pages.

"Since 1963 they have accumulated a small fleet of ships that few people inside the government know about. And the few who are aware of the fleet won't admit it exists. Besides surveillance, its primary function is to carry out clandestine operations involving the transporting of men and supplies for the infiltration of agents or guerrillas into unfriendly countries. Originally it was put together to harass Castro after his takeover of Cuba. Several years later, when it became apparent that Castro was too strong to topple, their activities were curtailed, partly because the Cubans threatened to retaliate against American fishing vessels. From that time on the CIA navy expanded its sphere of operations from Central America to the fighting in Vietnam to Africa and the Middle East. Do you follow?"

"I'm with you, but I have no idea where it's leading."

"Just be patient," she said. "Several years ago an attack cargo transport called the *Hobson* was a part of the Navy's reserve mothball fleet at Philadelphia. She was decommissioned and sold to a commercial shipping company, a cover for the CIA. They spared no expense in rebuilding her to outwardly resemble a common cargo carrier, while her interior was filled with concealed armament, including a new missile system, highly sophisticated communications and listening gear, and a facility for launching fast patrol and landing boats through swinging bow doors.

"She was manned and ready on station during Iran's disastrous invasion of Kuwait and Saudi Arabia in 1985. Flying the maritime flag of Panama, she secretly sank two Soviet spy ships in the Persian Gulf. The Russians could never prove who did it, because none of our Navy ships were within range. They still think the missiles that destroyed their ships came from the Saudi shore."

"And you found out about all this?"

"I have my sources," she informed him.

"Does the *Hobson* have anything to do with the *Pilottown?*"

"Indirectly," Loren answered.

"Go on."

"Three years ago, the *Hobson* vanished with all hands off the Pacific Coast of Mexico."

"So?"

"So three months later the CIA found her again."

"Sounds familiar," Pitt mused.

"My thought too." Loren nodded. "A replay of the *San Marino* and the *Belle Chasse.*"

"Where was the *Hobson* discovered?"

Before Loren could answer, the waiter set their plates on the table. The *zuppa di pesce,* an Italian bouillabaisse, looked sensational.

As soon as the waiter walked out of earshot he nodded to her. "Go on."

"I don't know how the CIA tracked the ship down, but they came on her sitting in a dry dock in Sydney, Australia, where she was undergoing a major face-lift."

"They find who she was registered to?"

"She flew the Philippine flag under the registry of Samar Exporters. A bogus firm that was incorporated only a few weeks earlier in Manila. Her new name was *Buras.*"

"*Buras,*" Pitt echoed. "Must be the name of a person. How's your salad?"

"The dressing is very tasty. And yours?"

"Excellent," he answered. "An act of sheer stupidity on the part of the pirates to steal a ship belonging to the CIA."

"A case of a mugger rolling a drunk and finding out the drunk was an undercover detective."

"What happened next in Sydney?"

"Nothing. The CIA, working with the Australian branch of the British Secret Service, tried to apprehend the owners of the *Buras* but were never able to find them."

"No leads, no witnesses?"

"The small Korean crew living onboard had been recruited in Singapore. They knew little and could only give a description of the captain, who had vanished."

Pitt took a swallow of water and examined a page of the report. "Not much of an ID. Korean, medium height, one hundred sixty-five pounds, black hair, gap in front teeth. That narrows it down to about five or ten million men," he said sarcastically "Well, at least now I don't feel so bad. If the CIA can't pin a make on whoever is sailing around the world hijacking ships, I sure as hell can't."

"Has St. Julien Perlmutter called you?"

Pitt shook his head. "Haven't heard a word. Probably lost heart and deserted the cause."

"I have to desert the cause too," Loren said gently. "But only for a little while."

Pitt looked at her sternly a moment, then relaxed and laughed. "How did a nice girl ever become a politician?"

She wrinkled her nose. "Chauvinist."

"Seriously, where will you be?"

"A short fact-finding junket on a Russian cruise ship sailing the Caribbean."

"Of course," Pitt said. "I'd forgotten you chair the committee for merchant marine transport."

Loren nodded and patted her mouth with her napkin. "The last cruise ship to fly the Stars and Stripes was taken out of service in 1984. To many people this is a national disgrace. The President feels strongly that we should be represented in ocean commerce as well as naval defense. He's asking Congress for a budget outlay of ninety million dollars to restore the S.S. *United States*, which has been laid up at Norfolk for twenty years, and put her back in service to compete with the foreign cruise lines."

"And you're going to study the Russian method of lavishing their passengers with vodka and caviar?"

"That," she said, looking suddenly official, "and the economics of their government-operated cruise ship."

"When do you sail?"

"Day after tomorrow. I fly to Miami and board the *Leonid Andreyev*. I'll be back in five days. What will you do?"

"The admiral has given me time off to pursue the *Pilottown* investigation."

"Does any of this information help you?"

"Every bit helps," he said, straining to focus on a thought that was a distant shadow on the horizon. Then he looked at her. "Have you heard anything through the congressional grapevine?"

"You mean gossip? Like who's screwing who?"

"Something heavier. Rumors of a missing party high in government or a foreign diplomat."

Loren shook her head. "No, nothing quite so sinister. The Capitol scene is pretty dull while Congress is in recess. Why? You know of a scandal brewing I don't?"

"Just asking," Pitt said noncommittally.

Her hand crept across the table and clasped his. "I have no idea where all this is taking you, but please be careful. Fu Manchu might get wise you're on his scent and lay in ambush."

Pitt turned and laughed. "I haven't read Sax Rohmer since I was a kid. Fu Manchu, the yellow peril. What made you think of him?"

She gave a little shrug. ''I don't really know. A mental association with an old Peter Sellers movie, the Sosan Trading Company and the Korean crew of the *Buras*, I guess.''

A faraway look came over Pitt's eyes and then they widened. The thought on the horizon crystallized. He hailed the waiter and paid the bill with a credit card.

''I've got to make a couple of phone calls,'' he explained briefly. He kissed her lightly on the lips and hurried onto the crowded sidewalk.

32

PITT QUICKLY DROVE to the NUMA building and closed himself in his office. He assembled his priorities for several moments and dialed Los Angeles on his private phone line. On the fifth ring a girl answered who couldn't pronounce her r's.

"Casio and Associates Investigatahs."

"I'd like to speak to Mr. Casio, please."

"Who shall I say is calling?"

"My name is Pitt."

"He's with a client. Can you call back?"

"No!" Pitt growled menacingly. "I'm calling from Washington and it's urgent."

Suitably intimidated, the receptionist replied, "One moment."

Casio came on the line almost immediately. "Mr. Pitt. Good to hear from you."

"Sorry to interrupt your meeting," said Pitt, "but I need a few answers."

"I'll do my best."

"What do you know about the crew of the *San Marino?*"

"Not much. I ran a make on the officers, but nothing unusual turned up. They were all professional merchant mariners. The captain, as I recall, had a very respectable record."

"No ties to any kind of organized crime?"

"Nothing that came to light in the computers of the National Crime Information Center."

"How about the rest of the crew?"

"Not much there. Only a few had maritime union records."

"Nationality?" Pitt asked.

"Nationality?" Casio repeated, thought a moment, then said, "A mixture. A few Greek, a few Americans, several Koreans."

"Koreans?" Pitt came back, suddenly alert. "There were Koreans onboard?"

"Yeah, that's right. Now that you mention it, as I remember, a group of about ten signed on just before the *San Marino* sailed."

"Would it be possible to trace the ships and companies they served prior to the *San Marino?*"

"You're going back a long time, but the files should be available."

"Could you throw in the history of the *Pilottown's* crew as well?"

"Don't see why not."

"I'd appreciate it."

"What are you after exactly?" Casio asked.

"Should be obvious to you."

"A link between the crew and our unknown parent company, is that it?"

"Close enough."

"You're going back before the ship disappeared," said Casio thoughtfully.

"The most practical way to take over a ship is by the crew."

"I thought mutiny went out with the *Bounty.*"

"The modern term is hijacking."

"You've got a good hunch going," said Casio. "I'll see what I can do."

"Thank you, Mr. Casio."

"We've danced enough to know each other. Call me Sal."

"Okay, Sal, and make it Dirk."

"I'll do that," Casio said seriously. "Goodbye."

After he hung up, Pitt leaned back and put his feet on the desk. He felt good, optimistic that a vague instinct was about to pay off. Now he was about to try another long shot, one that was so crazy he almost felt foolish for pursuing it. He copied a number out of the National University Directory and called it.

"University of Pennsylvania, Department of Anthropology."

"May I speak to Dr. Grace Perth?"

"Just a sec."

"Thank you."

Pitt waited for nearly two minutes before a motherly voice said, "Hello."

"Dr. Perth?"

"Speaking."

"My name is Dirk Pitt and I'm with the National Underwater and Marine Agency. Have you got a moment to answer a couple of academic questions for me?"

"What do you wish to know, Mr. Pitt?" Dr. Perth asked sweetly.

Pitt tried to picture her in his mind. His initial image was that of a prim, white-haired lady in a tweed suit. He erased it as a stereotype.

"If we take a male between the ages of thirty and forty, of medium height and weight, who was a native of Peking, China, and another male of the same description from Seoul, South Korea, how could we tell them apart?"

"You're not doing a number on me, are you, Mr. Pitt?"

Pitt laughed. "No, Doctor, I'm quite serious," he assured her.

"Hmmm, Chinese versus Korean," she muttered while thinking. "By and large, people of Korean ancestry tend to be more classic, or extreme, Mongoloid. Chinese features, on the other hand, lean more generally to Asian. But I wouldn't want to make my living guessing which was which, because the overlap is so great. It would be far simpler to judge them by their clothes or behavior, or the way they cut their hair—in short, their cultural characteristics."

"I thought they might have certain facial features that could separate them, such as you find between Chinese and Japanese."

"Well now, here the genetic spread is more obvious. If your Oriental male has a fairly dense beard growth, you'd have a rather strong indication that he's Japanese. But in the case of China and Korea, you're dealing with two racial groups that have intermixed for centuries, so much so that the individual variations would tend to blur out any distinction.''

"You make it sound hopeless."

"Awfully difficult, maybe, but not hopeless," Dr. Perth said. "A series of laboratory tests could raise your probability factor."

"My interest is strictly from a visual view."

"Are your subjects living?"

"No, drowning victims."

"A pity. With the living individual there are little traits of facial expressions that are culturally acquired and can be detected by someone who has had a lot of experience with both races. A pretty good guess may be made on that basis alone."

"No such luck."

"Perhaps if you could define their facial characteristics to me."

Pitt dreaded the thought, but he closed his eyes and began describing the lifeless heads he'd seen on the *Eagle*. At first the vision was vague, but soon it focused with clarity and he found himself dissecting each detail with the callous objectivity of a surgeon narrating a heart transplant into a tape recorder. At one point he suddenly broke off.

"Yes, Mr. Pitt, please go on," said Dr. Perth.

"I just remembered something that escaped me," Pitt said. "Two of the bodies did in fact have thick facial hair. One had a mustache while another sprouted a goatee."

"Interesting."

"So they weren't Korean or Chinese?"

"Not necessarily."

"What else could they be but Japanese?"

"You're leaping before you look, Mr. Pitt," she said, as if lecturing a student. "The features you've described to me suggest a heavy tendency toward the classic Mongoloid."

"But the facial hair?"

"You must consider history. The Japanese have been invading and marauding Korea since the sixteenth century. And for thirty-five years, from 1910 until 1945, Korea was a colony of Japan, so there was a great blending of their particular genetic variations."

Pitt hesitated before he put the next question to Dr. Perth. Then he chose his words carefully. "If you were to stick your neck out and give an opinion on the race of the men I've described, what would you say?"

Grace Perth came back with all flags flying. "Looking at it from a percentage factor, I'd say your test group's ancestry was ten percent Japanese, thirty percent Chinese and sixty percent Korean."

"Sounds like you've constructed the genetic makeup of your average Korean."

"You read it anyway you wish to see it, Mr. Pitt. I've gone as far as I can go."

"Thank you, Dr. Perth," Pitt said, suddenly exultant. "Thank you very much."

33

"So that's Dirk Pitt," Min Koryo said. She sat in her wheelchair peering over a breakfast tray at a large TV screen in her office wall.

Lee Tong sat beside her watching the videotape of the *Hoki Jamoki* anchored over the presidential yacht. "What puzzles me," he said quietly, "is how he discovered the wreck so quickly. It's as though he knew exactly where to search."

Min Koryo set her chin in frail hands and bowed her graying head, eyes locked on the screen, the thin blue veins in her temples pulsing in concentration. Her face slowly tightened in anger. She looked like an Egyptian mummy whose skin had somehow bleached white and remained smooth.

"Pitt and NUMA." She hissed in exasperation. "What are those wily bastards up to? First the *San Marino* and *Pilottown* publicity hoax, and now this."

"It can only be coincidence," Lee Tong suggested. "There is no direct link between the freighters and the yacht."

"Better an informer." Her voice cut like a whip. "We've been sold out."

"Not a valid conclusion, *aunumi*," said Lee Tong, amused at her sudden outburst. "Only you and I knew the facts. Everyone else is dead."

"Nothing is ever immune to failure. Only fools think they're perfect."

Lee Tong was in no mood for his grandmother's Oriental philos-

205

ophy. "Do not concern yourself unnecessarily," he said acidly. "A government investigating team would have eventually stumbled onto the yacht anyway. We could not make the President's transfer in broad daylight without running the danger of being seen and stopped. And since the yacht wasn't reported after sunrise, simple mathematics suggested that it was still somewhere on or below the river between Washington and Chesapeake Bay."

"A conclusion Mr. Pitt apparently had no trouble arriving at."

"It changes nothing," said Lee Tong. "Time is still on our side. Once Lugovoy is satisfied at his results, all that remains for us is to oversee the gold shipment. After that, President Antonov can have the President. But we keep Margolin, Larimer and Moran for insurance and future bargaining power. Trust me, *aunumi*, the tricky part is past. The Bougainville corporate fortress is secure."

"Maybe so, but the hounds are getting too close."

"We're matching ourselves against highly trained and intelligent people who possess the finest technology in the world. They may come within reach, but they'll never fully grasp our involvement."

Mollified somewhat, Min Koryo sighed and sipped at her ever present teacup. "Have you talked to Lugovoy in the past eight hours?"

"Yes. He claims he's encountered no setbacks and can complete the project in five more days."

"Five days," she said pensively. "I think it is time we made the final arrangements with Antonov for payment. Has our ship arrived?"

"The *Venice* docked at Odessa two days ago."

"Who is ship's master?"

"Captain James Mangyai, a trusted employee of the company," Lee Tong answered.

Min Koryo nodded approvingly. "And a good seaman. He hired on with me almost twenty years ago."

"He has his orders to cast off and set sail the minute the last crate of gold is loaded aboard."

"Good. Now we'll see what kind of stalling tactics Antonov will try. To begin with, he'll no doubt demand to hold up payment until Lugovoy's experiment is a proven success. This we will not do. In the meantime, he'll have an army of KGB agents combing the American countryside, looking for the President and our laboratory facilities."

"No Russian or American will figure out where we have Lugovoy and his staff hidden," Lee Tong said firmly.

"They found the yacht," Min Koryo reminded him.

Before Lee Tong could reply, the video screen turned to snow as the tape played out. He set the control for rewind. "Do you wish to view it again?" he asked.

"Yes, I want to examine the diving crew more closely."

When the recorder automatically switched off, Lee Tong pressed the "play" button and the picture returned to life.

Min Koryo watched it impassively for a minute and then said, "What is the latest status report on the wreck site?"

"A NUMA salvage crew is bringing up the bodies and preparing to raise the yacht."

"Who is the man with the red beard talking with Pitt?"

Lee Tong enlarged the scene until both men filled the screen. "That's Admiral James Sandecker, Director of NUMA."

"Your man was not seen filming Pitt's movements?"

"No, he's one of the best in the business. An ex-FBI agent. He was contracted for the job through one of our subsidiary corporations and told that Pitt is suspected of selling NUMA equipment to outside sources."

"What do we know about Pitt?"

"I have a complete dossier flying in from Washington. It should be here within the hour."

Min Koryo's mouth tightened as she moved closer to the TV. "How could he know so much? NUMA is an oceanographic agency. They don't employ secret agents. Why is he coming after us?"

"It'll pay us to find out."

"Move in closer," she ordered.

Lee Tong again enlarged the image, moving past Sandecker's

shoulder until it seemed as though Pitt was talking to the camera. Then he froze the picture.

Min Koryo placed a pair of square-lensed glasses over her narrow nose and stared at the weathered but handsome face that stared back. Her dark eyes flashed briefly. "Goodbye, Mr. Pitt."

Then she reached over and pushed the "off" switch, and the screen went black.

The smoke from Suvorov's cigarette hung heavily in the air of the dining room as he and Lugovoy shared a bottle of 1966 Croft Vintage Port. Suvorov looked at the red liquid in his glass and scowled.

"All these Mongolians ever serve us is beer and wine. What I wouldn't give for a bottle of good vodka."

Lugovoy selected a cigar out of a box that was held by one of the Korean waiters. "You have no culture, Suvorov. This happens to be an excellent port."

"American decadence has not rubbed off on me," Suvorov said arrogantly.

"Call it what you will, but you rarely see Americans defecting to Russia because of *our* disciplined lifestyle," Lugovoy retorted sarcastically.

"You're beginning to talk like them, drink like them; next you'll want to murder and rape in the streets like them. At least I know where my loyalties lie."

Lugovoy studied the cigar thoughtfully. "So do I. What I accomplish here will have grave effects on our nation's policy toward the United States. It is of far greater importance than your KGB's petty theft of industrial secrets."

Suvorov appeared too mellowed by the wine to respond angrily to the psychologist's remarks. "Your actions will be reported to our superiors."

"I've told you endlessly. This project is underwritten by President Antonov himself."

"I don't believe you."

Lugovoy lit the cigarette and blew a puff of smoke toward the ceiling. "Your opinion is irrelevant."

"We must find a means to contact the outside." Suvorov's voice rose.

"You're crazy," Lugovoy said seriously. "I'm telling you, no! I'm ordering you not to interfere. Can't you use your eyes, your brain? Look around you. All this was in preparation for years. Every detail has been carefully planned to carry out this operation. Without Madame Bougainville's organization, none of this would have been possible."

"We are her prisoners," Suvorov protested.

"What's the difference, so long as our government benefits?"

"We should be masters of the situation," Suvorov insisted. "We must get the President out of here and into the hands of our own people so he can be interrogated. The secrets you can pry from his mind are beyond comprehension."

Lugovoy shook his head in exasperation. He did not know what else to say. Trying to reason with a mind scored by patriotic fervor was like trying to teach calculus to a drunk. He knew that when it was all over Suvorov would write up a report depicting him as unreliable and a potential threat to Soviet security. Yet he laughed inwardly. If the experiment succeeded, President Antonov might be of a mood to name him Hero of the Soviet Union.

He stood up, stretched and yawned. "I think I'll catch a few hours' sleep. We'll begin programming the President's responses first thing in the morning."

"What time is it now?" Suvorov inquired dully. "I've lost all track of day and night in this tomb."

"Five minutes to midnight."

Suvorov yawned and sprawled on a couch. "You go ahead to bed. I'm going to have another drink. A good Russian never leaves the room before the bottle is empty."

"Good night," said Lugovoy. He turned and entered the hallway.

Suvorov waved halfheartedly and pretended he was on the verge of dozing off. But he studied the second hand of his watch for three minutes. Then he rose swiftly, crossed the room and noiselessly made his way down the hallway to where it made a ninety-degree turn toward the sealed elevator. He stopped and pressed his body to the wall and glanced around the edge of the corner.

Lugovoy was standing there patiently smoking his cigar. In less than ten seconds the elevator door silently opened and Lugovoy stepped inside. The time was exactly twelve o'clock. Every twelve hours, Suvorov noted, the project's psychologist escaped the laboratory, returning twenty to thirty minutes later.

He left and walked past the monitoring room. Two of the staff members were intently examining the President's brain rhythms and life signs. One of them looked up at Suvorov and nodded, smiling slightly.

"Going smoothly?" Suvorov asked, making conversation.

"Like a prima ballerina's debut," answered the technician.

Suvorov entered and looked up at the TV monitors. "What's happening with the others?" he inquired, nodding toward the images of Margolin, Larimer and Moran in their sealed cocoons.

"Sedated and fed heavy liquid concentrations of protein and carbohydrates intravenously."

"Until it's their time for programming," Suvorov added.

"Can't say. You'll have to ask Dr. Lugovoy that question."

Suvorov watched one of the screens as an attendant in a laboratory coat lifted a panel on Senator Larimer's cocoon and inserted a hypodermic needle into one arm.

"What's he doing?" Suvorov asked, pointing.

The technician looked up. "We have to administer a sedative every eight hours or the subject will regain consciousness."

"I see," said Suvorov quietly. Suddenly it all became clear in his mind as the details of his escape plan fell into place. He felt good, better than he had in days. To celebrate, he returned to the dining room and opened another bottle of port. Then he took a small notebook from his pocket and scribbled furiously on its pages.

34

OSCAR LUCAS PARKED HIS CAR in a VIP slot at the Walter Reed Army Medical School and hurried through a side entrance. He jogged around a maze of corridors, finally stopping at a double door guarded by a Marine sergeant whose face had a Mount Rushmore solemnity about it. The sergeant carefully screened his identification and directed him into the hospital wing where sensitive and highly secret autopsies were held. Lucas quickly found the door marked LABORATORY. AUTHORIZED PERSONNEL ONLY and entered.

"I hope I haven't kept you waiting," he said.

"No, Oscar," said Alan Mercier. "I only walked in a minute ago myself."

Lucas nodded and looked around the glass-enclosed room. There were five men besides himself: General Metcalf, Sam Emmett, Martin Brogan, Mercier and a short chesty man with rimless glasses introduced as Colonel Thomas Thornburg, who carried the heavy title of Director of Comparative Forensics and Clinical Pathology.

"Now that everyone is here," said Colonel Thornburg in a strange alto voice, "I can show you gentlemen our results."

He went over to a large window and peered at a huge circular machine on the other side of the glass. It looked like a finned turbine attached by a shaft to a generator. Half of the turbine disappeared into the concrete floor. Inside its inner diameter was a

211

cylindrical opening, while just outside lay a corpse on a translucent tray.

"A spatial analyzer probe, or SAP as it's affectionately called by my staff of researchers who developed it. What it does essentially is explore the body electronically through enhanced X rays while revealing precise moving pictures of every millimeter of tissue and bone."

"A kind of CAT scanner," ventured Brogan.

"Their basic function is the same, yes," answered Thornburg. "But that's like comparing a propeller aircraft to a supersonic jet. The CAT scanner takes several seconds to display a single cross section of the body. The SAP will deliver twenty-five thousand in less time. The findings are then automatically fed into the computer, which analyzes the cause of death. I've oversimplified the process, of course, but that's a nuts-and-bolts description."

"I assume your data banks hold nutritional and metabolic disorders associated with all known poisons and infectious diseases?" Emmett asked: "The same information as our computer records at the Bureau?"

Thornburg nodded. "Except that our data are more extensive because we occasionally deal with living tissue."

"In a pathology lab?" asked Lucas.

"We also examine the living. Quite often we receive field agents from our intelligence agencies—and from our allies too—who have been injected by a poisonous material or artificially infected by a contagious disease and are still alive. With SAP we can analyze the cause and come up with an antidote. We've saved a few, but most arrive too late."

"You can do an entire analysis and determine a cause in a few seconds?" General Metcalf asked incredulously.

"Actually in microseconds," Thornburg corrected him. "Instead of gutting the corpse and going through an elaborate series of tests, we can now do it in the wink of an eye with one elaborate piece of equipment, which, I might add, cost the taxpayer something in the neighborhood of thirty million dollars."

"What did you find on the bodies from the river?"

As if cued, Thornburg smiled and patted the shoulder of a technician who was sitting at a massive panel of lights and buttons. "I'll show you."

All eyes instinctively turned to the naked body lying on the tray. Slowly it began moving toward the turbine and disappeared into the center cylinder. Then the turbine began to revolve at sixty revolutions a minute. The X-ray guns encircling the corpse fired in sequence as a battery of cameras received the images from a fluorescent screen, enhanced them and fed the results into the computer bank. Before any of the men in the lab control room turned around, the cause of the corpse's demise flashed out in green letters across the center of a display screen. Most of the wording was in anatomical terminology, giving description of the internal organs, the amount of toxicity present and its chemical code. At the bottom were the words "Conium maculatum."

"What in hell is Conium maculatum?" wondered Lucas out loud.

"A member of the parsley family," said Thornburg, "more commonly known as hemlock."

"Rather an old-fashioned means of execution," Metcalf remarked.

"Yes, hemlock was very popular during classical times. Best remembered as the drink given to Socrates. Seldom used these days, but still easy to come by and quite lethal. A large enough dose will paralyze the respiratory organs."

"How was it administered?" Sam Emmett inquired.

"According to SAP, the poison was ingested by this particular victim along with peppermint ice cream."

"Death for dessert," Mercier muttered philosophically.

"Of the Coast Guard crewmen we identified," Thornburg continued, "eight took the hemlock with the ice cream, four with coffee, and one with a diet soft drink."

"SAP could tell all that from bodies immersed in water for five days?" asked Lucas.

"Decay starts immediately at death," explained Thornburg, "and travels outward from the intestines and other organs contain-

213

ing body bacteria. The process develops rapidly in the presence of air. But when the body is underwater, where the oxygen content is low, decay proceeds very slowly. The preservation factor that worked in our favor was the confinement of the bodies. A drowning victim, for example, will float to the surface after a few days as the decomposition gases begin to expand, thereby hastening decay from air exposure. The bodies you brought in, however, had been totally submerged until an hour before we began the autopsies.''

"The chef was a busy man,'' noted Metcalf.

Lucas shook his head. "Not the chef, but the dining-room steward. He's the only crewman unaccounted for.''

"An impostor,'' said Brogan. "The real steward was probably murdered and his corpse hidden.''

"What about the others?'' queried Emmett.

"The Asians?''

"Were they poisoned too?''

"Yes, but in a different manner. They were all shot.''

"Shot, poisoned, which is it?''

"They were killed by fragmenting darts loaded with a highly lethal venom that comes from the dorsal spines of the stonefish.''

"No amateurs, these guys,'' commented Emmett.

Thornburg nodded in agreement. "The method was very professional, especially the means of penetration. I removed a similar dart two years ago from a Soviet agent brought in by Mr. Brogan's people. As I recall, the poison was injected by a bio-inoculator.''

"I'm not familiar with it,'' said Lucas.

"An electrically operated handgun,'' said Brogan, giving Thornburg an icy stare. "Totally silent, used on occasion by our resident agents.''

"A little loose with your arsenal, aren't you, Martin?'' Mercier goaded him good-naturedly.

"The unit in question was probably stolen from the manufacturer,'' Brogan said defensively.

"Has an ID been made on any of the Asian bodies?'' Lucas asked.

"They have no records in FBI files,'' admitted Emmett.

"Nor with the CIA and Interpol," Brogan added. "None of the intelligence services of friendly Asian countries have anything on them either."

Mercier stared idly at the corpse moving out from the interior of the spatial analyzer probe. "It appears, gentlemen, that every time we open a door we walk into an empty room."

35 _____

"WHAT KIND OF MONSTERS are we dealing with?" Douglas Oates growled after listening to General Metcalf's report on the autopsies. His face wore a chalky pallor and his voice was cold with fury. "Twenty-one murders. And for what purpose? Where is the motive? Is the President dead or alive? If this is a grand extortion scheme, why haven't we received a ransom demand?"

Metcalf, Dan Fawcett and Secretary of Defense Jesse Simmons sat in silence in front of Oates's desk.

"We can't sit on this thing much longer," Oates continued. "Any minute now the news media will become suspicious and stampede into an investigation. Already they're grousing because no presidential interviews have been granted. Press Secretary Thompson has run out of excuses."

"Why not have the President face the press?" Fawcett suggested.

Oates looked dubious. "That actor—what's his name—Sutton? He would never get away with it."

"Not up close on a podium under a battery of lights, but in a setting under shadows at a distance of a hundred feet . . . Well, it might work."

"You got something in mind?" Oates asked.

"We stage a photo opportunity to enhance the President's image. It's done all the time."

"Like Carter playing softball and Reagan chopping wood," said

Oates thoughtfully. "I think I see a down-home scene on the President's farm."

"Complete with crowing roosters and bleating sheep," allowed Fawcett.

"And Vice President Margolin? Our double for him can't be faked in shadows at a hundred feet."

"A few references by Sutton and a friendly wave by the double at a distance should suffice," Fawcett answered, becoming more enthusiastic over his brainstorm.

Simmons gazed steadily at Fawcett. "How soon can you have everyone ready?"

"First thing in the morning. Dawn, as a matter of fact. Reporters are night owls. They hang around waiting for late news to break. They're not at their best before sunup."

Oates looked at Metcalf and Simmons. "Well, what do you think?"

"We've got to throw the reporters a bone before they become bored and start snooping," answered Simmons. "I vote yes."

Metcalf nodded. "The only stalling tactic we've got."

Fawcett came to his feet and peered at his watch. "If I leave for Andrews Air Force Base now, I should arrive at the farm in four hours. Plenty of time to arrange the details with Thompson and make an announcement to the press corps."

Fawcett's hand froze on the doorknob as Oates's voice cut across the room like a bayonet.

"Don't bungle it, Dan. For God's sake, don't bungle it."

36 _____

VLADIMIR POLEVOI CAUGHT UP with Antonov as the Soviet leader strolled beneath the outer Kremlin wall with his bodyguards. They were moving past the burial area where heroes of the Soviet Union were interred. The weather was unusually warm and Antonov carried his coat over one arm.

"Taking advantage of the fine summer day?" Polevoi asked conversationally as he approached.

Antonov turned. He was young for a Russian head of state, sixty-two, and he walked with a brisk step. "Too pleasant to waste behind a desk," he said with a curt nod.

They walked for a while in silence as Polevoi waited for a sign or a word that Antonov was ready to talk business. Antonov paused before the small structure marking Stalin's gravesite.

"You know him?" he asked.

Polevoi shook his head. "I was too far down the party ladder for him to notice me."

Antonov's expression went stern and he muttered tensely. "You were fortunate." Then he stepped on, dabbing a handkerchief at the perspiration forming on the back of his neck.

Polevoi could see his chief was in no mood for small talk, so he came to the point. "We may have a break on the Huckleberry Finn Project."

"We could use one," Antonov said grudgingly.

"One of our agents in New York who is in charge of security for our United Nations workers has turned up missing."

218

"How does that concern Huckleberry Finn?"

"He disappeared while following Dr. Lugovoy."

"Any possibility he defected?"

"I don't think so."

Antonov stopped in midstep and gave Polevoi a hard stare. "We'd have a disaster in the making if he went over to the Americans."

"I personally vouch for Paul Suvorov," said Polevoi firmly. "I'd stake my reputation on his loyalty."

"The name is familiar."

"He is the son of Viktor Suvorov, the agriculture specialist."

Antonov seemed appeased. "Viktor is a dedicated party member."

"So is his son," said Polevoi. "If anything, he's overzealous."

"What do you think happened to him?"

"I suspect he somehow passed himself off as one of Lugovoy's staff of psychologists and was taken along with them by Madame Bougainville's men."

"Then we have a security man on the inside."

"An assumption. We have no proof."

"Did he know anything?"

"He was aware of nothing," Polevoi said unequivocally. "His involvement is purely coincidental."

"A mistake to have Dr. Lugovoy watched."

Polevoi took a deep breath. "The FBI keeps a tight collar on our United Nations delegates. If we had allowed Dr. Lugovoy and his team of psychologists to roam freely about New York without our security agents observing their actions, the Americans would have become suspicious."

"So they watch us while we watch ours."

"In the last seven months, three of our people have asked for political asylum. We can't be too careful."

Antonov threw up his hands in a vague gesture. "I accept your argument."

"If Suvorov is indeed with Lugovoy, he will no doubt attempt to make contact and disclose the location of the laboratory facility."

"Yes, but if Suvorov, in his ignorance, makes a stupid move, there is no predicting how that old bitch Bougainville will react."

"She might raise the ante."

"Or worse, sell the President and the others to the highest bidder."

"I can't see that," said Polevoi thoughtfully. "Without Dr. Lugovoy, the project isn't possible."

Antonov made a thin smile. "Excuse my cautious nature, Comrade Polevoi, but I tend to look on the dark side. That way I'm seldom taken by surprise."

"The completion of Lugovoy's experiment is only three days away. We should be thinking of how to handle the payment."

"What are your proposals?"

"Not to pay her, of course."

"How?"

"There are any number of ways. Switching the gold bars after her representative has examined them. Substituting lead that is painted gold or bars of lesser purity."

"And the old bitch would smell out every one of them."

"Still, we must try."

"How will it be transferred?" Antonov asked.

"One of Madame Bougainville's ships is already docked at Odessa, waiting to load the gold on board."

"Then we'll do what she least expects."

"Which is?" Polevoi asked expectantly.

"We hold up our end of the bargain," said Antonov slowly.

"You mean pay?" Polevoi asked incredulously.

"Down to the last troy ounce."

Polevoi was stunned. "I'm sorry, Comrade President, but it was my understanding—"

"I've changed my mind," Antonov said sharply. "I have a better solution."

Polevoi waited several moments in silence, but it was apparent Antonov wasn't going to confide in him. He slowly dropped back, finally coming to a halt.

Surrounded by his entourage, Antonov kept walking, his mind

rapidly altering course and dwelling on other matters of state concern.

Suvorov pressed the switch to his night-light and checked the time on his watch. It read 4:04. Not too bad, he thought. He had programmed his mind to awaken at four in the morning and he'd only missed by four minutes.

Unable to suppress a yawn, he quickly pulled on a shirt and pair of pants, not bothering with socks or shoes. Stepping into the bathroom, he splashed his face with cold water, then moved across the small bedroom and cracked the door.

The brightly lit corridor was empty. Except for two psychologists monitoring the subjects, everyone else was asleep. As he walked the carpet in his bare feet, he began measuring the interior dimensions of the facilities and jotting them down in the notebook. Between the four outer walls he arrived at 168 feet in length by 33 feet in width. The ceiling was nearly ten feet high.

He came to the door of the medical supply room and gently eased open the door. It was never locked, because Lugovoy saw no reason for anyone to steal anything. He stepped inside, closed the door and turned on the light. Moving swiftly, Suvorov found the small bottles containing sedative solutions. He set them in a row on the sink and sucked out their contents with a syringe, emptying the fluid down the drain. Then he refilled the bottles with water and neatly rearranged them on the shelf.

He returned unseen to his sleeping quarters and slipped into bed once again and stared at the ceiling.

He was pleased with himself. His moves had gone undetected with no sign of the slightest suspicion. Now all he had to do was wait for the right moment.

37

IT WAS A SHADOWY DREAM. The kind he could never remember when he woke up. He was searching for someone in the bowels of a deserted ship. Dust and gloom obscured his vision. Like the dive on the *Eagle:* green river algae and russet silt.

His quarry drifted in front of him, blurred, always beyond reach. He hesitated and tried to focus through the gloom, but the form taunted him, beckoning him closer.

Then a high-pitched ringing sound went off in his ear and he floated out of the dream and groped for the telephone.

"Dirk?" came a cheery voice from a throat he wanted to throttle.

"Yes."

"Got some news for you."

"Huh?"

"You asleep? This is St. Julien."

"Perlmutter?"

"Wake up. I found something."

Then Pitt switched on the bed light and sat up. "Okay, I'm listening."

"I've received a written report from my friends in Korea. They went through Korean shipyard records. Guess what? The *Belle Chasse* was never scrapped."

Pitt threw back the covers and dropped his feet on the floor. "Go on."

"Sorry I took so long getting back to you, but this is the most

222

incredible maritime puzzle I've ever seen. For thirty years somebody has been playing musical chairs with ships like you wouldn't believe.''

"Try me."

"First, let me ask you a question," said Perlmutter. "The name on the stern of the ship you found in Alaska?"

"The *Pilottown?*"

"Were the painted letters framed by welded beading?"

Pitt thought back. "As I recall it was faded paint. The raised edges must have been ground away."

Perlmutter uttered a heavy sigh of relief over the phone. "I was hoping you'd say that."

"Why?"

"Your suspicions are confirmed. The *San Marino*, the *Belle Chasse* and the *Pilottown* are indeed one and the same ship."

"Damn!" Pitt said, suddenly excited. "How'd you make the link?"

"By discovering what happened to the genuine *Pilottown,*" said Perlmutter with a dramatic inflection. "My sources found no record of a *Belle Chasse* being scrapped in the shipyards of Pusan. So I played a hunch and asked them to check out any other yards along the coast. They turned up a lead in the port of Inchon. Shipyard foremen are interesting guys. They never forget a ship, especially one they've junked. They act hard-nosed about it, but deep down they're sad to see a tired old vessel pulled into their dock for the last time. Anyway, one old retired foreman talked for hours about the good old days. A real gold mine of ship lore."

"What did he say?" Pitt asked impatiently.

"He recalled in great detail when he was in charge of the crew who converted the *San Marino* from a cargo transport into an ore carrier renamed the *Belle Chasse.*"

"But the shipyard records?"

"Obviously falsified by the shipyard owners, who, by the way, happened to be our old friends the Sosan Trading Company. The foreman also remembered breaking up the original *Pilottown.* It looks like Sosan Trading, or the shady outfit behind it, hijacked the

San Marino and its cargo and killed the crew. Then they modified the cargo holds to carry ore, documented it under a different name and sent it tramping around the seas."

"Where does the *Pilottown* come in?" asked Pitt.

"She was a legitimate purchase by Sosan Trading. You may be interested to know the International Maritime Crime Center has her listed with ten suspected customs violations. A hell of a high number. It's thought she smuggled everything from plutonium to Libya, rebel arms to Argentina, secret American technology to Russia, you name it. She sailed under a smart bunch of operators. The violations were never proven. On five occasions she was known to have left port with clandestine cargo but was never caught unloading it. When her hull and engines finally wore out, she was conveniently scrapped and all records destroyed."

"But why claim her as sunk if it was really the *San Marino*, alias the *Belle Chasse*, they scuttled?"

"Because questions might be raised regarding the *Belle Chasse*'s pedigree. The *Pilottown* had solid documentation, so they claimed it was she that sank in 1979, along with a nonexistent cargo, and demanded a fat settlement from the insurance companies."

Pitt glanced down at his toes and wiggled them. "Did the old foreman talk about other ship conversions for Sosan Trading?"

"He mentioned two, a tanker and a container ship," Perlmutter answered. "But they were both refits and not conversions. Their new names were the *Boothville* and the *Venice*."

"What were their former names?"

"According to my friend's report, the foreman claimed that all previous identification had been removed."

"Looks like somebody built themselves a fleet out of hijacked ships."

"A cheap and dirty way of doing business."

"Anything new on the parent company?" Pitt asked.

"Still a closed door," Perlmutter replied. "The foreman did say, however, some big shot used to show up to inspect the ships when they were completed and ready to sail."

Pitt stood up. "What else?"

"That's about it."

"There has to be something, a physical description, a name, something."

"Wait a minute while I check through the report again."

Pitt could hear the rustle of papers and Perlmutter mumbling to himself. "Okay, here it is. 'The VIP always arrived in a big black limousine.' No make mentioned. 'He was tall for a Korean—' "

"Korean?"

"That's what it says," replied Perlmutter. " 'And he spoke Korean with an American accent.' "

The shadowed figure in Pitt's dream moved a step closer. "St. Julien, you do good work."

"Sorry I couldn't take it all the way."

"You bought us a first down."

"Nail the bastard, Dirk."

"I intend to."

"If you need me, I'm more than willing."

"Thank you, St. Julien."

Pitt walked to the closet, threw on a brief kimono and knotted the sash. Then he padded into the kitchen, treated himself to a glass of guava juice laced with dark rum and dialed a number on the phone.

After several rings an indifferent voice answered: "Yeah?"

"Hiram, crank up your computer. I've got a new problem for you."

38

THE TENSION WAS LIKE A TWISTING KNOT in the pit of Suvorov's stomach. For most of the evening he had sat in the monitoring room making small talk with the two psychologists who manned the telemetry equipment, telling jokes and bringing them coffee from the kitchen. They failed to notice that Suvorov's eyes seldom strayed from the digital clock on one wall.

Lugovoy entered the room at 11:20 P.M. and made his routine examination of the analogous data on the President. At 11:38 he turned to Suvorov. "Join me in a glass of port, Captain?"

"Not tonight," Suvorov said, making a pained face. "I have a heavy case of indigestion. I'll settle for a glass of milk later."

"As you wish," Lugovoy said agreeably. "See you at breakfast."

Ten minutes after Lugovoy left, Suvorov noticed a small movement on one of the TV monitors. It was almost imperceptible at first, but then it was caught by one of the psychologists.

"What in hell!" he gasped.

"Something wrong?" asked the other.

"Senator Larimer—he's waking up."

"Can't be."

"I don't see anything," said Suvorov, moving closer.

"His alpha activity is a clear nine-to-ten-cycle-per-second set of waves that shouldn't be there if he was in his programmed sleep stage."

"Vice President Margolin's waves are increasing too."

226

"We'd better call Dr. Lugovoy—"

The words hardly escaped his mouth when Suvorov cut him down with a savage judo chop to the base of the skull. In almost the same gesture, Suvorov swung a crosscut with the palm of the other hand into the throat of the second psychologist, crushing the man's windpipe.

Even before his victims hit the floor, Suvorov coldly gazed at the clock. The blinking red numbers displayed 11:49—eleven minutes before Lugovoy was scheduled to exit the laboratory in the elevator. Suvorov had practiced his movements many times, allowing no more than two minutes for unpredictable delays.

He stepped over the lifeless bodies and ran from the monitor room into the chamber containing the subjects in their soundproofed cocoons. He unlatched the top of the third one, threw back the cover and peered inside.

Senator Marcus Larimer stared back at him. "What is this place? Who the hell are you?" the senator mumbled.

"A friend," answered Suvorov, lifting Larimer out of the cocoon and half carrying, half dragging him to a chair.

"What's going on?"

"Be quiet and trust me."

Suvorov took a syringe from his pocket and injected Larimer with a stimulant. He repeated the process with Vice President Margolin, who looked around dazedly and offered no resistance. They were naked, and Suvorov brusquely threw them blankets.

"Wrap yourselves in these," he ordered.

Congressman Alan Moran had not yet awakened. Suvorov lifted him out of the cocoon and laid him on the floor. Then he turned and walked over to the unit enclosing the President. The American leader was still unconscious. The latch mechanism was different from the other cocoons, and Suvorov wasted precious seconds trying to pry open the cover. His fingers seemed to lose all feeling and he fought to control them. He began to sense the first prickle of fear.

His watch read 11:57. He was beyond his timetable; his two-minute reserve evaporated. Panic was replacing fear. He reached down and snatched a Colt Woodsman .22-caliber automatic from a holster strapped to his right calf. He screwed on a four-inch suppressor; and for a brief instant he was not himself, a man outside himself, a man whose only code of duty and unleashed emotion blinded his perception. He aimed the gun at the President's forehead on the other side of the transparent cover.

Through the mist of his drugged mind, Margolin recognized what Suvorov was about to do. He staggered across the cocoon chamber and lurched into the Russian agent, grabbing for the gun. Suvorov just sidestepped and pushed him against the wall. Somehow Margolin remained on his feet. His vision was blurred and distorted, and a wave of sudden nausea threatened to gag him. He flung himself forward in another attempt to save the President's life.

Suvorov smashed the barrel of the gun against Margolin's temple and the Vice President dropped limply in a heap, blood streaming down the side of his face. For a moment Suvorov stood rooted. His well-rehearsed plan was cracking and crumbling apart. Time had run out.

His last fleeting hope lay in salvaging the pieces. He forgot the President, kicked Margolin out of the way and shoved Larimer through the door. Heaving the still unconscious Moran over his shoulder, he herded the uncomprehending senator down the corridor to the elevator. They stumbled around the final corner just as the concealed doors parted and Lugovoy was about to step inside.

"Stop right where you are, Doctor."

Lugovoy whirled and stared dumbly. The Colt was held rock-steady in Suvorov's hand. The eyes of the KGB agent blazed with a contemptuous disdain.

"You fool!" Lugovoy blurted as the full realization of what was happening struck him. "You bloody fool!"

"Shut up!" Suvorov snapped. "And step back out of the way."

"You don't know what you're doing."

"I'm only doing my duty as a good Russian."

"You're ruining years of planning," Lugovoy said angrily. "President Antonov will have you shot."

"No more of your lies, Doctor. Your insane project has placed our government in extreme jeopardy. It is you who will be executed. It is you who is the traitor."

"Wrong," Lugovoy said in near shock. "Can't you see the truth?"

"I see you working for the Koreans. Most likely the South Koreans who have bought you off."

"For God's sake, listen to me."

"A good Communist has no God but the party," said Suvorov, roughly elbowing Lugovoy aside and shoving the unprotesting Americans into the elevator. "I have no more time to argue."

A wave of despair swept Lugovoy. "Please, you can't do this," he pleaded.

Suvorov did not reply. He turned and glared malevolently as the elevator doors closed and blocked him from view.

39 _____

As the elevator rose, Suvorov reversed the gun and smashed out the overhead light with the butt. Moran moaned and went through the motions of coming to, rubbing his eyes and shaking his head to clear the fog. Larimer became sick and vomited in a corner, his breath coming in great croaking heaves.

The elevator eased to a smooth stop and the doors automatically opened to a smothering rush of warm air. The only light came from three dim yellow bulbs that hung suspended on a wire like ailing glowworms. The air was dank and heavy and smelled of diesel oil and rotting vegetation.

Two men stood about ten feet away, engaged in conversation, waiting for Lugovoy to make his scheduled progress report. They turned and peered questioningly into the darkened elevator. One of them held an attaché case. The only other detail Suvorov noted before he shot them each twice in the chest was the Oriental fold of their eyes.

He slung his free arm under Moran's waist and hauled him across what seemed like a rusting iron floor. He kicked Larimer ahead of him as he would a remorseful dog that had run away from home. The senator reeled like a drunk, too sick to speak, too stunned to resist. Suvorov pushed the gun inside his belt and took Larimer's arm, guiding him. The skin under his hand felt goose-fleshed and clammy. Suvorov hoped the old legislator's heart wasn't about to give out.

Suvorov cursed as he stumbled over a large chain. Then he

stopped and peered down an enclosed ramp that stretched into the dark. He felt as if he were inside a sauna; his clothes were turning damp with sweat and his hair was plastered down his forehead and temples. He tripped and almost fell, regaining his balance just before he was about to sprawl on the cross slats of the ramp.

Moran's dead weight was becoming increasingly burdensome, and Suvorov realized his strength was ebbing. He doubted whether he could lug the congressman another fifty yards.

At last they left the tunnel-like ramp and staggered out into the night. He looked up and was vastly relieved to see a diamond-clear sky carpeted with stars. Beneath his feet the ground felt like a graveled road and there were no lights to be seen anywhere. In the shadows off to his left he dimly recognized the outline of a car. Pulling Larimer into a ditch beside the road, he gratefully dropped Moran like a bag of sand and cautiously circled around, approaching the car from the rear.

He froze into immobility, rigid against the shadowless landscape, and listened. The engine was running and music was playing on the radio. The windows were tightly rolled up and Suvorov rightly assumed the air conditioner was on.

Silent as a cat, he crouched and moved in closer, keeping low and out of any reflection in the sideview mirror on the door. The inside was too dark to make out more than one vague form behind the wheel. If there were others, Suvorov's only ally was the element of surprise.

The car was a stretch-bodied limousine, and to Suvorov it seemed as long as a city block. From the raised letters on the rear of the trunk, he identified it as a Cadillac. He'd never driven one and hoped he would have no trouble finding the right switches and controls.

His groping fingers found the door handle. He took a deep breath and tore open the door. The interior light flicked on and the man in the front seat twisted his head around, his mouth opening to shout. Suvorov shot him twice, the silver-tip hollow-point bullets tearing through the rib cage under the armpit.

Almost before the blood began to spurt, Suvorov jerked the driver's body out of the car and rolled it away from the wheels. Then he roughly crowded Larimer and Moran into the back seat. Both men had lost their blankets, but they were too deeply gripped by shock to even notice or care. No longer the power brokers of Capitol Hill, they were as helpless as children lost in the forest.

Suvorov dropped the shift lever into drive and jammed the accelerator to the floor mat so fiercely, the rear tires spun and sprayed gravel for fifty yards before finally gaining traction. Only then did Suvorov's fumbling hand find the headlight switch and pull it on. He sagged in relief at discovering the big car was hurtling down the precise middle of a rutted country road.

As he threw the heavy, softly sprung limousine over three miles of choppy washboard, he began to take stock of his surroundings. Cypress trees bordering the road had great tentacles of moss hanging from their limbs. This and the heavy atmosphere suggested they were somewhere in the Southern United States. He spotted a narrow paved crossroad ahead and slid to a stop in a swirling cloud of dust. On the corner stood a deserted building, more of a shack actually, with a decrepit sign illuminated by the headlights: GLOVER CULPEPPER. GAS & GROCERIES. Apparently Glover had packed up and moved on many years before.

The intersection had no marker, so he mentally flipped a coin and turned left. The cypress gave way to groves of pine and soon he began passing an occasional farmhouse. Traffic was scarce at this hour of morning. Only one car and a pickup truck passed him, both going in the opposite direction. He came to a wider road and spotted a bent sign on a leaning post designating it as State Highway 700. The number meant nothing to him, so he made another left turn and continued on.

Throughout the drive, Suvorov's mind remained cold and rigidly alert. Larimer and Moran sat silently watchful, blindly putting their faith in the man at the wheel.

Suvorov relaxed and eased his foot from the gas pedal. No following headlights showed in the rearview mirror, and as long as he maintained the posted speed limit his chances of being stopped by a local sheriff were remote. He wondered what state he was in.

Georgia, Alabama, Louisiana? It could be any one of a dozen. He watched for some clue as the roadside became more heavily populated; darkened buildings and houses squatted under increasing numbers of overhead floodlights.

After another half-hour he came to a bridge spanning a waterway called the Stono River. He'd never heard of it. From the high point of the bridge, the lights of a large city blinked in the distance. Off to his right the lights suddenly halted and the entire horizon went pure black. A seaport, he swiftly calculated. Then the headlights fell on a large black-and-white directional sign. The top line read CHARLESTON 5 MILES.

"Charleston!" Suvorov said aloud in a sudden burst of jubilation, sifting through his knowledge of American geography. "I'm in Charleston, South Carolina."

Two miles further he found an all-night drugstore with a public telephone. Keeping a wary eye on Larimer and Moran, he dialed the long-distance operator and made a collect call.

233

40

A LONE CLOUD WAS DRIFTING overhead, scattering a few drops of moisture when Pitt slipped the Talbot beside the passenger departure doors of Washington's Dulles International Airport. The morning sun roasted the capital city, and the rain steamed and evaporated almost as soon as it struck the ground. He lifted Loren's suitcase out of the car and passed it to a waiting porter.

Loren unwound her long legs from the cramped sports car, demurely keeping her knees together, and climbed out.

The porter stapled the luggage claim check to the flight ticket and Pitt handed it to her.

"I'll park the car and baby-sit you until boarding time."

"No need," she said, standing close. "I've some pending legislation to scan. You head back to the office."

He nodded at the briefcase clamped in her left hand. "Your crutch. You'd be lost without it."

"I've noticed you never carry one."

"Not the type."

"Afraid you might be taken for a business executive?"

"This is Washington; you mean bureaucrat."

"You are one, you know. The government pays your salary, same as me."

Pitt laughed. "We all carry a curse."

She set the briefcase on the ground and pressed her hands against his chest. "I'll miss you."

He circled his arms around her waist and gave a gentle squeeze.

"Beware of dashing Russian officers, bugged staterooms and vodka hangovers."

"I will," she said, smiling. "You'll be here when I return?"

"Your flight and arrival time are duly memorized."

She tilted her head up and kissed him. He seemed to want to say something more, but finally he released her and stood back. She slowly entered the terminal through the automatic sliding glass doors. A few steps into the lobby she turned to wave, but the blue Talbot was pulling away.

On the President's farm, thirty miles south of Raton, New Mexico, members of the White House press corps were spaced along a barbed-wire fence, their cameras trained on an adjoining field of alfalfa. It was seven in the morning, Mountain Daylight-Saving Time, and they were drinking black coffee and complaining about the early hour, the high-plains heat, the watery scrambled eggs and burned bacon catered by a highway truck stop, and any other discontents, real or imagined.

Presidential Press Secretary Jacob (Sonny) Thompson walked brightly through the dusty press camp prepping the bleary-eyed correspondents like a high school cheerleader and assuring them of great unrehearsed homespun pictures of the President working the soil.

The press secretary's charm was artfully contrived—bright white teeth capped with precision, long sleek black hair, tinted gray at the temples, dark eyes with the tightened look of cosmetic surgery. No second chin. No visible sign of a potbelly. He moved and gestured with a bouncy enthusiasm that didn't sit well with journalists, whose major physical activities consisted of pounding typewriters, punching word processors and lifting cigarettes.

The clothes didn't hurt the image either. The tailored seersucker suit with the blue silk shirt and matching tie. Black Gucci moccasins coated lightly with New Mexico dust. A classy, breezy guy who was no dummy. He never showed anger, never let the correspondents' needles slip under his fingernails. Bob Finkel of the Baltimore *Sun* slyly suggested that an undercover investigation revealed that Thompson had graduated with honors from the Joseph Goebbels School of Propaganda.

He stopped at the CNN television motor home. Curtis Mayo, the White House correspondent network newscaster, sagged in a director's chair looking generally miserable.

"Got your crew set up, Curt?" Thompson asked jovially.

Mayo leaned back, pushed a baseball cap to the rear of a head forested with billowy silver hair and gazed up through orange-tinted glasses. "I don't see anything worth capturing for posterity."

Sarcasm ran off Thompson like rainwater down a spout. "In five minutes the President is going to step from his house, walk to the barn and start up a tractor."

"Bravo," Mayo grunted. "What does he do for an encore?"

Mayo's voice had a resonance to it that made a symphonic kettledrum sound like a bongo: deep, booming, with every word enunciated with the sharpness of a bayonet.

"He is going to drive back and forth across the field with a mower and cut the grass."

"That's alfalfa, city slicker."

"Whatever," Thompson acknowledged with a good-natured shrug. "Anyway, I thought it would be a good chance to roll tape on him in the rural environment he loves best."

Mayo leveled his gaze into Thompson's eyes, searching for a flicker of deception. "What's going down, Sonny?"

"Sorry?"

"Why the hide-and-seek? The President hasn't put in an appearance for over a week."

Thompson stared back, his nut-brown eyes unreadable. "He's been extremely busy, catching up on his homework away from the pressures of Washington."

Mayo wasn't satisfied. "I've never known a President to go this long without facing the cameras."

"Nothing devious about it," said Thompson. "At the moment, he has nothing of national interest to say."

"Has he been sick or something?"

"Far from it. He's as fit as one of his champion bulls. You'll see."

236

Thompson saw through the verbal ambush and moved on along the fence, priming the other news people, slapping backs and shaking hands. Mayo watched him with interest for a few moments before he reluctantly rose out of the chair and assembled his crew.

Norm Mitchell, a loose, ambling scarecrow, set up his video camera on a tripod, aiming it toward the back porch of the President's farmhouse, while the beefy sound man, whose name was Rocky Montrose, connected the recording equipment on a small folding table. Mayo stood with one booted foot on a strand of barbed wire, holding a microphone.

"Where do you want to stand for your commentary?" asked Mitchell.

"I'll stay off camera," answered Mayo. "How far do you make it to the house and barn?"

Mitchell sighted through a pocket range finder. "About a hundred and ten yards from here to the house. Maybe ninety to the barn."

"How close can you bring him in?"

Mitchell leaned over the camera's eyepiece and lengthened the zoom lens, using the rear screen door for a reference. "I can frame him with a couple of feet to spare."

"I want a tight close-up."

"That means a two-X converter to double the range."

"Put it on."

Mitchell gave him a questioning look. "I can't promise you sharp detail. At that distance, we'll be giving up resolution and depth of field."

"No problem," said Mayo. "We're not going for air time."

Montrose looked up from his audio gear. "Then you don't need me."

"Roll sound anyway and record my comments."

Suddenly the battalion of news correspondents came alive as someone shouted, "Here he comes!"

Fifty cameras went into action as the screen door swung open and the President stepped onto the porch. He was dressed in cowboy boots and a cotton shirt tucked into a pair of faded Levi's. Vice President Margolin followed him over the threshold, a large

Stetson hat pulled low over his forehead. They paused for a minute in conversation, the President gesturing animatedly while Margolin appeared to listen thoughtfully.

"Go tight on the Vice President," Mayo ordered.

"Have him," Mitchell responded.

The sun was climbing toward the middle of the sky and the heat waves were rising over the reddish earth. The President's farm swept away in all directions, mostly fields of hay and alfalfa, with a few pastures for his small herd of breeding cattle. The crops were a vivid green in contrast to the barren areas, and watered by huge circular sprinkling systems. Except for a string of cottonwoods bordering an irrigation ditch, the land unfolded in flat solitude.

How could a man who had spent most of his life in such desolation drive himself to influence billions of people? Mayo wondered. The more he saw of the strange egomania of politicians the more he came to despise them. He turned and spat at a colony of red ants, missing their tunnel entrance by only a few inches. Then he cleared his throat and began describing the scene into the microphone.

Margolin turned and went back into the house. The President, acting as though the press corps were still back in Washington, hiked to the barn without turning in their direction. The exhaust of a diesel engine was soon heard and he reappeared seated on a green John Deere tractor, Model 2640, that was hooked to a hay mower. There was a canopy and the President sat out in the open, a small transistor radio clipped to his belt and earphones clamped to his head. The correspondents began yelling questions at him, but it was obvious he couldn't hear them above the rap of the exhaust and music from the local FM station.

He wrapped a red handkerchief over the lower part of his face, bandit style, to keep from breathing dust and exhaust fumes. Then he let down the mower's sliding blades and started cutting the field, driving back and forth in long rows, working away from the people crowding the fence.

After about twenty minutes the correspondents slowly packed away their equipment and returned to the air-conditioned comfort of their trailers and motor homes.

"That's it," announced Mitchell. "No more tape, unless you want me to reload."

"Forget it." Mayo wrapped the cord around the microphone and handed it to Montrose. "Let's get out of this heat and see what we've got."

They tramped into the cool of the motor home. Mitchell removed the cassette holding the three-quarter-inch videotape from the camera, inserted it into the playback recorder and rewound it. When he was ready to roll from the beginning, Mayo pulled up a chair and parked himself less than two feet from the monitor.

"What are we looking for?" asked Montrose.

Mayo's concentration didn't waver from the images moving before his screen. "Would you say that's the Vice President?"

"Of course," said Mitchell. "Who else could it be?"

"You're taking what you see for granted. Look closer."

Mitchell leaned in. "The cowboy hat is covering his eyes, but the mouth and chin match. The build fits too. Looks like him to me."

"Anything odd about his mannerisms?"

"The guy is standing there with his hands in his pockets," said Montrose dumbly. "What are we supposed to read in that?"

"Nothing unusual about him at all?" Mayo persisted.

"Don't notice a thing," said Mitchell.

"All right, forget him," said Mayo as Margolin turned and went back into the house. "Now look at the President."

"If that ain't him," muttered Montrose acidly, "then he's got an identical twin brother."

Mayo brushed off the remark and sat quietly as the camera followed the President across the barnyard, revealing the slow, recognizable gait known to millions of television viewers. He disappeared into the dark of the barn, and two minutes later emerged on the tractor.

Mayo snapped erect. "Stop the tape!" he shouted.

Startled, Mitchell pressed a button on the recorder and the image froze.

"The hands!" Mayo said excitedly. "The hands on the steering wheel!"

239

"So he's got ten fingers," mumbled Mitchell, his expression sour. "So what?"

"The President wears only a wedding band. Look again. No ring on the middle finger of the left hand, but on the index finger you see a good-sized sparkler. And the pinkie on the right—"

"I see what you mean," Montrose interrupted. "A flat blue stone in a silver setting, probably an amethyst."

"Doesn't the President usually sport a Timex watch with an Indian silver band inlaid with turquoise?" observed Mitchell, becoming swept along.

"I think you're right," Mayo recalled.

"The detail is fuzzy, but I'd say that's one of those big Rolex chronometers on his wrist."

Mayo pounded a fist on his knee. "That clinches it. The President is known never to buy or wear anything of foreign manufacture."

"Hold on," Montrose said slowly. "This is crazy. We're talking about the President of the United States as if he wasn't real."

"Oh, he's flesh and bone all right," said Mayo, "but the body sitting on that tractor belongs to someone else."

"If you're right, you've got a live bomb in your hands," said Montrose.

Mitchell's enthusiasm began to dim. "We may be digging for clams in Kansas. Seems to me the evidence is damned shaky. You can't go on the air, Curt, and claim some clown is impersonating the President unless you have documented proof."

"Nobody knows that better than me," Mayo admitted. "But I'm not about to let this story slip through my hands."

"You're launching a quiet investigation then?"

"I'd turn in my press card if I didn't have the guts to see it through." He looked at his watch. "If I leave now, I should be in Washington by noon."

Montrose crouched in front of the TV screen. His face had the look of a child who found his tooth still in the glass of water the next morning. "It makes you wonder," he said in a hurt tone, "how many times one of our Presidents used a double to fool the public."

41

VLADIMIR POLEVOI GLANCED UP from his desk as his chief deputy and number-two man of the world's largest intelligence-gathering organization, Sergei Iranov, walked purposefully into the room. "You look as if you've got a hot stake up your ass this morning, Sergei."

"He's escaped," Iranov said tersely.

"Who are you talking about?"

"Paul Suvorov. He's managed to break out of Bougainville's hidden laboratory."

Sudden anger flushed Polevoi's face. "Damn, not now!"

"He called our New York covert action center from a public telephone in Charleston, South Carolina, and asked for instructions."

Polevoi rose and furiously paced the carpet. "Why didn't he call the FBI and ask them for instructions too? Better yet, he could have taken out an advertisement in *USA Today*."

"Fortunately his superior immediately sent a coded message to us reporting the incident."

"At least someone is thinking."

"There's more," said Iranov. "Suvorov took Senator Larimer and Congressman Moran with him."

Polevoi halted and spun around. "The idiot! He's queered everything!"

"He is not entirely to blame."

"How do you draw that conclusion?" Polevoi asked cynically.

241

"Suvorov is one of our five top agents in the United States. He is not a stupid man. He was not briefed on Lugovoy's project and it's logical to assume it was entirely beyond his comprehension. He undoubtedly treated it with great suspicion and acted accordingly."

"In other words, he did what he was trained to do."

"In my opinion, yes."

Polevoi gave an indifferent shrug. "If only he'd concentrated on simply giving us the location of the laboratory. Then our people could have moved in and removed the Huckleberry Finn operation from Bougainville's control."

"As things are now, Madame Bougainville may be angry enough to cancel the experiment."

"And lose a billion dollars in gold? I doubt that very much. She still has the President and Vice President in her greedy hands. Moran and Larimer are no great loss to her."

"Nor to us," Iranov stated. "The Bougainvilles were our smokescreen in case the American intelligence agencies scuttled Huckleberry Finn. Now, with two abducted congressmen in our hands, it might be considered an act of war, or at very least a grave crisis. It would be best if we simply eliminated Moran and Larimer."

Polevoi shook his head. "Not yet. Their knowledge of the inner workings of the United States military establishment can be of incalculable benefit to us."

"A hazardous game."

"Not if we're careful and quickly dispose of them when and if the net tightens."

"Then our first priority is to keep them from discovery by the FBI."

"Has Suvorov found a safe place to hide?"

"Not known," Iranov answered. "He was only told by New York to report every hour until they reviewed the situation and received orders from us in Moscow."

"Who heads our undercover operations in New York?"

"His name is Basil Kobylin."

"Advise him of Suvorov's predicament," said Polevoi, "omitting, of course, any reference pertaining to Huckleberry Finn. His orders are to hide Suvorov and his captives in a secure place until we can plan their escape from U.S. soil."

"Not an easy matter to arrange." Iranov helped himself to a chair and sat down. "The Americans are searching under every rock for their missing heads of state. All airfields are closely watched, and our submarines can't come within five hundred miles of their coastline without detection by their underwater warning line."

"There is always Cuba."

Iranov looked doubtful. "The waters are too closely guarded by the U.S. Navy and Coast Guard against drug traffic. I advise against any escape by boat in that direction."

Polevoi gazed out the windows of his office overlooking Dzerzhinsky Square. The late-morning sun was fighting a losing battle to brighten the drab buildings of the city. A tight smile slowly crossed his lips.

"Can we get them safely to Miami?"

"Florida?"

"Yes."

Iranov stared into space. "There is the danger of roadblocks, but I think that could be overcome."

"Good," said Polevoi, suddenly relaxing. "See to it."

Less than three hours after the escape, Lee Tong Bougainville stepped out of the laboratory's elevator and faced Lugovoy. It was a few minutes before three in the morning, but he looked as if he had never slept.

"My men are dead," Lee Tong said without a trace of emotion. "I hold you responsible."

"I didn't know it would happen." Lugovoy spoke in a quiet but steady voice.

"How could you not know?"

"You assured me this facility was escape-proof. I didn't think he would actually make an attempt."

243

"Who is he?"

"Paul Suvorov, a KGB agent, who your men picked off the Staten Island ferry by mistake."

"But you knew."

"He didn't make his presence known until after we arrived."

"And yet you said nothing."

"That's true," Lugovoy admitted. "I was afraid. When this experiment is finished I must return to Russia. Believe me, it doesn't pay to antagonize our state security people."

The built-in fear of the man behind you. Bougainville could see it in the eyes of every Russian he met. They feared foreigners, their neighbors, any man in uniform. They'd lived with it for so long it became an emotion as common as anger or happiness. He did not find it in himself to pity Lugovoy. Instead, he despised him for willingly living under such a depressing system.

"Did this Suvorov cause any damage to the experiment?"

"No," Lugovoy answered. "The Vice President has a slight concussion, but he is back under sedation. The President was untouched."

"Nothing delayed?"

"Everything is proceeding on schedule."

"And you expect to finish in three more days?"

Lugovoy nodded.

"I'm moving your deadline up."

Lugovoy acted as though he hadn't heard correctly. Then the truth broke through to him. "Oh, God, no!" he gasped. "I need every minute. As it is, my staff and I are cramming into ten days what should take thirty. You're eliminating all our safeguards. We must have more time for the President's brain to stabilize."

"That is President Antonov's concern, not mine or my grandmother's. We fulfilled our part of the bargain. By allowing a KGB man in here, you jeopardized the entire project."

"I swear I had nothing to do with Suvorov's breakout."

"Your story," Bougainville said coldly. "I choose to believe his presence was planned, likely on President Antonov's orders. Certainly by now Suvorov has informed his superiors and every

Soviet agent in the States is converging on us. We will have to move the facility.''

That was the final shattering blow. Lugovoy looked as if he was about to gag. ''Impossible!'' he howled like an injured dog. ''Absolutely no way can we move the President and all this equipment to another site and still meet your ridiculous deadline.''

Bougainville glared at Lugovoy through narrow slits of eyes. When he spoke again, his voice was rock calm. ''Not to worry, Doctor. No upheaval is necessary.''

42

WHEN PITT WALKED INTO HIS NUMA office, he found Hiram Yaeger asleep on the couch. With his sloppy clothes, long knotted hair and beard, the computer expert looked like a derelict wino. Pitt reached down and gently shook him by the shoulder. An eyelid slowly raised, then Yaeger stirred, grunted and pushed himself to a sitting position.

"Hard night?" Pitt inquired.

Yaeger scratched his head with both hands and yawned. "You have any Celestial Seasonings Red Zinger Tea?"

"Only yesterday's warmed-over coffee."

Yaeger clicked his lips sourly. "The caffeine will kill you."

"Caffeine, pollution, booze, women—what's the difference?"

"By the way, I got it."

"Got what?"

"I nailed it, your cagey shipping company."

"Jesus!" Pitt said, coming alive. "Where?"

"Right in our own backyard," Yaeger said with a great grin. "New York."

"How did you do it?"

"Your hunch about Korean involvement was the key, but not the answer. I attacked it from that angle, probing all the shipping and export lines that were based in Korea or sailed under their registry. There were over fifty of them, but none led to the trail of banks we checked earlier. With nowhere else to go, I let the computer fly on its own. My ego is shattered. It proved a better sleuth than I am. The kicker was in the name. Not Korean, but French.''

"French."

"Based in the World Trade Center in lower Manhattan, their fleet of legitimate ships flies the flag of the Somali Republic. How does that grab you?''

"Go on."

"A first-rate company, no rust-bucket operation, rated lily-white by *Fortune*, *Forbes* and Dun and Bradstreet. So damned pure that their annual report comes accompanied with harp music. Scratch the surface deep enough though, and you find more phony front men and dummy subsidiary companies than gays in San Francisco. Documentary ship fraud, bogus insurance claims, chartering phantom ships with nonexistent cargoes, substitution of worthless cargoes for ones of great value. And always beyond the jurisdiction of the private outfits and governments they screw.''

"What's their name?"

"Bougainville Maritime," answered Yaeger. "Ever heard of it?''

"Min Koryo Bougainville—the 'Steel Lotus'?" said Pitt, impressed. "Who hasn't? She's right up there with the celebrity British and Greek shipping tycoons.''

"She is your Korean connection."

"Your data are conclusive? No chance of error?"

"Solid stuff," Yaeger replied adamantly. "Take my word for it. Everything triple-checks. Once I tuned in on Bougainville as the source, it became a simple chore of working backwards. It all came together; bank accounts, letters of credit—you wouldn't believe how the banks turn their backs on these frauds. The old broad reminds me of one of those East Indian statues with twenty arms, sitting there with a holy look on her face while the hands are making obscene gestures.''

"You did it," Pitt said enthusiastically. "You actually pinned Sosan Trading, the *San Marino* and *Pilottown* on the Bougainville shipping empire.''

"Like a stake through the heart."

"How far back did you go?"

"I can give you the old girl's biography almost to when she spit out the tit. A tough old bird. Started from scratch and a lot of guts after World War Two. Slowly added old tramp ships to her fleet, crewed by Koreans who were glad to work for a bowl of rice and pennies a day. With practically no overhead, she cut-rate her freight costs and built a thriving business. About twenty-five years ago, when her grandson joined the company, things really took off. A slippery customer, that one. Keeps in the background. Except for school records, his data file is almost blank. Min Koryo Bougainville built the foundation for maritime crime that spanned thirty nations. When her grandson—Lee Tong is his name—came along, he honed and smoothed the piracy and fraud part of the organization to a fine art. I had the whole mess printed out. There's a hard copy on your desk."

Pitt turned and for the first time noticed a five-inch-thick sheaf of computer printout paper on his desk. He sat down and briefly scanned the notched pages. The incredible reach of the Bougainvilles was mind-boggling. The only criminal activity they appeared to shy away from was prostitution.

After several minutes he looked up and nodded. "A super job, Hiram," he said sincerely. "Thank you."

Yeager nodded toward the printouts. "I wouldn't let that out of my sight if I were you."

"Any chance of us getting caught?"

"A foregone conclusion. Our illegal taps have been recorded on the bank's computer log and printed out on a daily form. If a smart supervisor scans the list, he'll wonder why an American oceanographic agency is snooping in his biggest depositor's records. His next step would be to rig the computer's communications line with a tracing device."

"The bank would most certainly notify old Min Koryo," said Pitt thoughtfully. Then he looked up. "Once they identify NUMA as the tap, can Bougainville's own computer network probe ours to see what we've gleaned from their data banks?"

"Our network is as vulnerable as any other. They won't learn much, though. Not since I removed the magnetic storage disks."

"When do you think they'll smoke us out?"

"I'd be surprised if they haven't pegged us already."

"Can you stay one jump ahead of them?"

Yaeger gave Pitt an inquiring stare. "What sneaky plan are you about to uncork?"

"Go back to your keyboard and screw them up but good. Re-enter the network and alter the data, foul up the Bougainville day-to-day operations, erase legitimate bank records, insert absurd instructions into their programs. Let them feel the heat from somebody else for a change."

"But we'll lose vital evidence for a federal investigation."

"So what?" Pitt declared. "It was obtained illegally. It can't be used anyway."

"Now wait a minute. We can be stepping into big trouble."

"Worse than that, we might get killed," Pitt said with a faint smile.

An expression blossomed on Yaeger's face, one that wasn't there before. It was sudden misgiving. The game had ceased to be fun and was taking on darker dimensions. It had never dawned on him that the search could turn ugly and he might be murdered.

Pitt read the apprehension in Yaeger's eyes. "You can quit now and take a vacation," he said. "I wouldn't blame you."

Yaeger seemed to waver for a moment. Then he shook his head. "No, I'll stick with it. These people should be put away."

"Come down hard on them. Jam the works in all aspects of their shipping company—outside investments, subsidiary businesses, real estate dealings, everything they touch."

"It's my ass, but I'll do it. Just keep the admiral out of my hair for a few more nights."

"Keep a lookout for any information relating to a ship called the *Eagle.*"

"The presidential yacht?"

"Just a ship called the *Eagle.*"

"Anything else?"

Pitt nodded grimly. "I'll see that security is increased around your computer processing center."

"Mind if I stay here and use your couch. I've developed this sudden aversion to sleeping alone in my apartment."

"My office is yours."

Yaeger stood up and stretched. Then he nodded at the data sheets again. "What are you going to do with it?"

Pitt stared down at the first breach ever in the Bougainville criminal structure. The pace of his personal investigation was gaining momentum, pieces falling into his hands to be fitted in the overall picture, jagged edges meshing together. The scope was far beyond anything he'd imagined in the beginning.

"You know," he said pensively, "I don't have the vaguest idea."

43 _____

WHEN SENATOR LARIMER AWOKE in the rear seat of the limousine, the eastern sky was beginning to turn orange. He slapped at the mosquito whose buzzing had interrupted his sleep. Moran stirred in his corner of the seat, his squinting eyes unfocused, his mind still unaware of his surroundings. Suddenly a door was opened and a bundle of clothes was thrown in Larimer's lap.

"Put these on," Suvorov ordered brusquely.

"You never told me who you are," Larimer said, his tongue moving in slow motion.

"My name is Paul."

"No surname?"

"Just Paul."

"You FBI?"

"No."

"CIA?"

"It doesn't matter," Suvorov said. "Get dressed."

"When will we arrive in Washington?"

"Soon," Suvorov lied.

"Where did you get these clothes? How do you know they'll fit?"

Suvorov was losing his patience with the inquisitive American. He shrugged off an impulse to crack the senator in the jaw with the gun.

"I stole them off a clothesline," he said. "Beggars can't be particular. At least they're washed."

251

"I can't wear a stranger's shirt and pants," Larimer protested indignantly.

"If you wish to return to Washington in the nude, it is no concern of mine."

Suvorov slammed the door, moved to the driver's side of the car and edged behind the wheel. He drove out of a picturesque residential community called Plantation Estates and cut onto Highway 7. The early-morning traffic was starting to thicken as they crossed over the Ashley River bridge to Highway 26, where he turned north.

He was grateful that Larimer went silent. Moran was climbing from his semi-conscious state and mumbling incoherently. The headlights reflected off a green sign with white letters: AIRPORT NEXT RIGHT. He took the off ramp and came to the gate of the Charleston Municipal Airport. Across the main landing strip the brightening sky revealed a row of jet fighters belonging to the Air National Guard.

Following the directions given over the phone, he skirted the airport searching for a narrow cutoff. He found it and drove over a dirt road until he came to a pole holding a wind sock that hung limp in the dank atmosphere.

He stopped and got out, checked his watch and waited. Less than two minutes later the steady beat of a helicopter's rotor could be heard approaching from behind a row of trees. The blinking navigation lights popped into view and a teardrop blue-and-white shape hovered for a few moments and then sat down beside the limousine.

The door behind the pilot's seat swung outward and a man in white coveralls stepped to the ground and walked up to the limousine.

"You Suvorov?" he asked.

"I'm Paul Suvorov."

"Okay, let's get the baggage inside before we attract unwanted attention."

Together they led Larimer and Moran into the passenger compartment of the copter and belted them in. Suvorov noted that the

letters on the side of the fuselage read SUMTER AIRBORNE AMBU-
LANCE.

"This thing going to the capital?" asked Larimer with a spark of
his old haughtiness.

"Sir, it'll take you anyplace you want," said the pilot agreeably.

Suvorov eased into the empty co-pilot's seat and buckled the
harness. "I wasn't told our destination," he said.

"Russia, eventually," the pilot said with a smile that was anything but humorous. "First thing is to find where you came from."

"Came from?"

"My orders are to fly you around the back country until you
identify the facility in which you and those two windbags in the
back have spent the last eight days. When we accomplish that mission, I'm to fly you to another departure area."

"All right," said Suvorov. "I'll do my best."

The pilot didn't offer his name and Suvorov knew better than to
ask. The man was undoubtedly one of the estimated five thousand
Soviet-paid "charges" stationed around the United States, experts
in specialized occupations, all waiting for a call instructing them to
surface, a call that might never come.

The helicopter rose fifty feet in the air and then banked off toward Charleston Bay. "Okay, which way?" asked the pilot.

"I can't be sure. It was dark and I was lost."

"Can you give me a landmark?"

"About five miles from Charleston; I crossed a river."

"From what direction?"

"West, yes, the dawn was breaking ahead of me."

"Must be Stono River."

"Stono, that's it."

"Then you were traveling on State Highway 700."

"I turned onto it about half an hour before the bridge."

The sun had heaved itself above the horizon and was filtering
through the blue summer haze that hung over Charleston. The helicopter climbed to nine hundred feet and flew southwestward until
the highway unreeled beyond the cockpit windows. The pilot

pointed downward and Suvorov nodded. They followed the out-bound traffic as the South Carolina coastal plain spread beneath them. Here and there a few cultivated fields lay enclosed on all sides by forests of long-leafed pines. They passed over a farmer standing in a tobacco field who waved his hat at them.

"See anything familiar?" the pilot asked.

Suvorov shook his head helplessly. "The road I turned off of might be anywhere."

"What direction were you facing when you met the highway?"

"I made a left turn so I must have been heading south."

"This area is called Wadmalaw Island. I'll start a circular search pattern. Let me know if you spot something."

An hour slipped by, and then two. The scene below transformed into a maze of creeks and small rivers snaking through bottomland and swamps. One road looked the same as another from the air. Thin ribbons of reddish-brown dirt or potholed asphalt slicing through dense overgrowth like lines on the palm of a hand. Suvorov became more confused as time wore on, and the pilot lost his patience.

"We'll have to knock off the search," he said, "or I won't have enough fuel to make Savannah."

"Savannah is in the state of Georgia," Suvorov said, as though reciting in a school class.

The pilot smiled. "Yeah, you got it."

"Our departure point for the Soviet Union?"

"Only a fuel stop." Then the pilot clammed up.

Suvorov saw it was impossible to draw any information out of the man, so he turned his attention back to the ground.

Suddenly he pointed excitedly over the instrument panel. "There!" he shouted above the engine's roar. "The small inter-section to the left."

"Recognize it?"

"I think so. Drop lower. I want to read the sign on that shabby building sitting on the corner."

The pilot obliged and lowered the helicopter until it hovered thirty feet over the bisecting roadways. "Is that what you want?" he asked. " 'Glover Culpepper—gas and groceries'?"

"We're close," said Suvorov. "Fly up the road that leads toward that river to the north."

"The Intracoastal Waterway."

"A canal?"

"A shallow canal that provides an almost continuous inshore water passage from the North Atlantic States to Florida and the Gulf of Mexico. Used mostly by small pleasure boats and tugs."

The helicopter beat over the tops of trees, whipping leaves and bending branches with the wash from its rotor blades. Suddenly, at the edge of a wide marshy creek, the road ended. Suvorov stared through the windshield.

"The laboratory, it must be around here."

"I don't see anything," the pilot said, banking the craft and studying the ground.

"Set us down!" Suvorov demanded nervously. "Over there, a hundred meters from the road in that glade."

The pilot nodded and gently eased the helicopter's landing skids into the soft grassy earth, sending up a swirl of dead and moldy leaves. He set the engine on idle with the blades slowly turning and opened the door. Suvorov leaped out and ran stumbling through the underbrush back to the road. After a few minutes of frantic searching he stopped at the bank of the creek and looked around in exasperation.

"What's the problem?" asked the pilot as he approached.

"Not here," Suvorov said dazedly. "A warehouse with an elevator that dropped down to a laboratory. It's gone."

"Buildings can't vanish in six hours," said the pilot. He was beginning to look bored. "You must be on the wrong road."

"No, no, this has to be the right one."

"I only see trees and swamp"—he hesitated and pointed—"and that decrepit old houseboat on the other side of the creek."

"A boat!" Suvorov said as though having a revelation. "It must have been a boat."

The pilot gazed down into the muddy water of the creek. "The bottom here is only three or four feet deep. Impossible to bring a vessel the size of a warehouse, requiring an elevator, in here from the waterway.''

Suvorov threw up his hands in bewilderment. "We must keep searching.''

"Sorry,'' the pilot said firmly. "We haven't the time or the fuel to continue. To keep our appointment we've got to leave now.''

He turned without waiting for a reply and walked back to the helicopter. Slowly Suvorov followed him, looking for all the world like a man deep in a trance.

As the helicopter lifted above the trees and swung toward Savannah, a gunnysack curtain in the window of the houseboat was pulled aside to reveal an old Chinaman peering through an expensive pair of Celestron 11 x 80 binoculars.

Satisfied he had read the aircraft's identification number on the fuselage correctly, he laid down the glasses and dialed a number on a portable telephone scrambling unit and spoke in rapid Chinese.

44

"GOT A MINUTE, DAN?" Curtis Mayo asked as Dan Fawcett got out of his car in the private street beside the White House.

"You'll have to catch me on the run," Fawcett replied without looking in Mayo's direction. "I'm late for a meeting."

"Another heavy situation in the Situation Room?"

Fawcett sucked in his breath. Then, as calmly as his trembling fingers would permit, he locked the car door and picked up his attaché case.

"Care to comment?" Mayo asked.

Fawcett marched off toward the security gate. "I shot an arrow in the air . . ."

"It fell to earth, I know not where," Mayo finished, keeping step. "Longfellow. Want to see my arrow?"

"Not particularly."

"This one is going to land on the six o'clock news."

Fawcett slowed his pace. "Just what are you after?"

Mayo took a large tape cassette from his pocket and handed it to Fawcett. "You might like to view this before air time."

"Why are you doing this?"

"Call it professional courtesy."

"Now *that's* news."

Mayo smiled. "Like I said, view the tape."

"Save me the trouble. What's on it?"

"A folksy scene of the President playing farmer. Only it isn't the President."

Fawcett drew up and stared at Mayo. "You're full of crap."

"Can I quote you?"

"Don't get cute," Fawcett snapped. "I'm in no mood for a slanted interview."

"Okay, straight question," said Mayo. "Who is impersonating the President and Vice President in New Mexico?"

"Nobody."

"I've got proof that says otherwise. Enough to use it as a news item. I release this and every muckraker between here and Seattle will crawl over the White House like an army of killer ants."

"Do that and you'll have a dozen eggs on your face when the President stands as close to you as I am and denies it."

"Not if I find out what sort of mischief he's been up to while a double played hide-and-seek down on the farm."

"I won't wish you luck, because the whole idea is outlandish."

"Level with me, Dan. Something big is going down."

"Trust me, Curt. Nothing off limits is happening. The President will be back in a couple of days. You can ask him yourself."

"What about the sudden burst of secret Cabinet meetings at all hours?"

"No comment."

"It's true, isn't it?"

"Who's your source for that little gem?"

"Somebody who's seen a lot of unmarked cars entering the subbasement of the Treasury Department in the dead of night."

"So the Treasury people are burning the midnight oil."

"No lights go on in the building. My guess is they're sneaking into the White House through the utility tunnel and congregating in the Situation Room."

"Think what you like, but you're dead wrong. That's all I have to say on the subject."

"I'm not going to drop it," Mayo said defiantly.

"Suit yourself," Fawcett replied indifferently. "It's your funeral."

Mayo dropped back and watched as Fawcett walked through the security gate. The presidential adviser had put up a good front, he thought, but that's all it was, a front. Any doubts Mayo might have entertained about sinister maneuvers emanating behind the walls of the nation's executive branch were swept away.

He was more determined than ever to damn well find out what was going on.

Fawcett slid the cassette in a videotape recorder and sat down in front of the TV screen. He ran the tape three times, examining every detail until he knew what Mayo had caught.

Wearily he picked up a phone and asked for a secure line to the State Department. After a few moments the voice of Doug Oates answered through the earpiece.

"Yes, Dan, what is it?"

"We have a new development."

"News of the President?"

"No, sir. I've just had a talk with Curtis Mayo of CNN News. He's onto us."

There was a taut pause. "What can we do?"

"Nothing," said Fawcett somberly, "absolutely nothing."

Sam Emmett left the FBI building in downtown Washington and drove over to CIA headquarters in Langley, Virginia. A summer shower passed overhead, moistening the forested grounds of the intelligence complex and leaving behind the sweet smell of dampened greenery.

Martin Brogan was standing outside his office when Emmett walked through the anteroom door. The tall ex-college professor offered an outstretched hand. "Thank you for taking time from your busy schedule to drive over."

Emmett smiled as he took his hand. Brogan was one of the few men around the President he genuinely admired. "Not at all. I'm not a desk man. I jump at any excuse to get off my butt and move around."

They entered Brogan's office and sat down. "Coffee or a drink?" Brogan asked.

"Nothing, thanks." Emmett opened his briefcase and laid a bound report on the CIA Director's desk. "This spells out the Bureau's findings until an hour ago on the President's disappearance."

Brogan handed him a similarly bound report. "Likewise from Central Intelligence. Damned little to add since our last meeting, I'm sorry to say."

"You're not alone. We're miles from a breakthrough too."

Brogan paused to light a ropelike Toscanini cigar. It seemed oddly out of place with his Brooks Brothers suit and vest. Together the men began reading. After nearly ten minutes of quiet, Brogan's expression softened from deep concentration to curious interest, and he tapped a page of Emmett's report.

"This section about a missing Soviet psychologist."

"I thought that would interest you."

"He and his entire United Nations staff vanished the same night as the *Eagle*'s hijacking?"

"Yes, to date none of them have turned up. Could be merely an intriguing coincidence, but I felt it shouldn't be ignored."

"The first thought that crossed my mind is that this"—Brogan glanced at the report again—"Lugovoy, Dr. Aleksei Lugovoy, may have been assigned by the KGB to use his psychological knowledge to pry national secrets from the abducted men."

"A theory we can't afford to dismiss."

"The name," Brogan said vacantly. "It strikes a chord."

"You've heard it before?"

Suddenly Brogan's brows raised and his eyes widened ever so slightly and he reached for his intercom. "Send up the latest file from the French Internal Security Agency."

"You think you've got something?"

"A recorded conversation between President Antonov and his KGB chief Vladimir Polevoi. I believe Lugovoy was mentioned."

"From French intelligence?" Emmett asked.

"Antonov was on a state visit. Our friendly rivals in Paris are quietly cooperative about passing along information they don't consider sensitive to their national interests."

In less than a minute, Brogan's private secretary knocked on the door and gave him a transcription of the secret tape recording. He quickly consumed its contents.

"This is most encouraging," he said. "Read between the lines and you can invent all sorts of Machiavellian schemes. According to Polevoi, the UN psychologist disappeared off the Staten Island ferry in New York and all contact was severed."

"The KGB lost several sheep from their herd at one time?" Emmett asked in mild astonishment. "That's a new twist. They must be getting sloppy."

"Polevoi's own statement." Brogan held out the transcript papers. "See for yourself."

Emmett read the typed print and reread it. When he looked up, a trace of triumph brightened his eyes. "So the Russians *are* behind the abduction."

Brogan nodded in agreement. "From all appearances, but they can't be in it alone. Not if they're ignorant of Lugovoy's whereabouts. Another source is working with them, someone here in the United States with the power to dictate the operation."

"You?" Emmett asked wolfishly.

Brogan laughed. "No, and you?"

Emmett shook his head. "If the KGB, the CIA and the FBI are all kept in the dark, then who's dealing the cards?"

"The person they refer to as the 'old bitch' and 'Chinese whore.'"

"No gentlemen these Communists."

"The code word for their operation must be Huckleberry Finn."

Emmett stretched out his legs, crossing them at the ankles, and sagged comfortably in his chair. "Huckleberry Finn," he repeated, enunciating every syllable. "Our counterpart in Moscow has a dark sense of humor. But what's important, he's unwittingly given us an eye to shove a sharp stick into."

No one paid any attention to the two men seated comfortably in a pickup truck parked in a loading zone by the NUMA building. A cheap plastic removable sign adhered to the passenger's door advertised GUS MOORE'S PLUMBING. Behind the cab in the truck's bed, several lengths of copper pipe and an assortment of tools lay in casual disorder. The men's coveralls were stained with dirt and grease, and neither had shaved in three or four days. The only odd thing about their appearance was their eyes. They never shifted from the entrance to NUMA's headquarters.

The driver tensed and made a directional movement with a nod of his head. "I think this is him coming."

The other man raised a pair of binoculars wrapped in a brown paper bag with the bottom torn out and gazed at a figure emerging from the revolving glass doors. Then he laid the glasses in his lap and examined a face in a large eleven-by-fourteen-inch glossy photograph.

"Confirmed."

The driver checked a row of numbers on a small black transmitter. "Counting one hundred forty seconds from . . . now." He punctuated his words by pushing a toggle switch to the "on" position.

"Okay," his partner said. "Let's get the hell away."

Pitt reached the bottom of the broad stone steps as the plumber's truck drove past in front of him. He stood a moment to let another car by and began walking through the parking lot. He was seventy yards from the Talbot-Lago when he turned at the honking of a horn.

Al Giordino drew up alongside in a Ford Bronco four-wheel drive. His curly black hair was shaggy and uncombed and a heavy growth covered his chin. He looked as if he hadn't slept in a week.

"Sneaking home early?" he said.

"I was until you caught me," Pitt replied, grinning.

"Lucky you, sitting around with nothing to do."

"You wrap the *Eagle* salvage?" Pitt asked.

Giordino gave a tired nod. "Towed her up the river and pushed her into dry dock about three hours ago. You can smell her death stink a mile away.''

"At least you didn't have to remove the bodies.''

"No, a Navy diving team was stuck with that ugly chore.''

"Take a week off. You've earned it.''

Giordino spread his Roman smile. "Thanks, boss. I needed that." Then his expression turned solemn. "Anything new on the *Pilottown?*''

"We're zeroing in—''

Pitt never finished the sentence. A thunderous explosion tore the air. A ball of flame erupted between the densely packed cars and jagged metal debris burst in all directions. A tire and wheel, the chrome spokes flashing in the sun, flew in a high arc and landed with a loud crunch in the middle of Giordino's hood. Bouncing inches over Pitt's head, it then rolled through a landscaped parkway before coming to rest in a cluster of rosebushes. The rumble from the blast echoed across the city for several seconds before it finally faded and died.

"God!" Giordino rasped in bewildered awe. "What was that?''

Pitt took off running, dodging between the tightly parked cars, until he slowed and halted in front of a scrambled mass of metal that smoldered and coughed up a cloud of dense black smoke. The asphalt underneath was gouged and melting from the heat, turning into a heavy sludge. The tangled wreck was nearly unrecognizable as a car.

Giordino ran up behind him. "Jesus, whose was it?''

"Mine," said Pitt, his features twisted in bitterness as he stared at the remains of the once beautiful Talbot-Lago.

PART III

The Leonid Andreyev

45

LOREN WAS GREETED by Captain Yakov Pokofsky when she boarded the *Leonid Andreyev*. Pokofsky was a charming man with thick silver hair and eyes as round and black as caviar. Though he acted polite and diplomatic, Loren sensed he wasn't actually thrilled at having an American politician snooping about his ship, asking questions about its management. After the usual niceties, the first officer led her to a celebrity suite filled with enough flowers for a state funeral. The Russians, she mused, knew how to accommodate a visiting VIP.

In the evening, when the last of the passengers had boarded and settled down in their staterooms, the crew cast off the mooring lines and the cruise ship steamed out of Biscayne Bay through the channel into the Atlantic. The lights of the hotels on Miami Beach glittered under a tropical breeze and slowly closed together in a thin glowing line as the *Leonid Andreyev*'s twin screws thrust her further from shore.

Loren stripped off her clothes and took a shower. When she stepped out and toweled, she struck an exaggerated model's pose in front of a full-length mirror. The body was holding up quite well, considering thirty-seven years of use. Jogging and ballet classes four hours a week kept the centrifugal forces at bay. She pinched her tummy and sadly noted that slightly more than an inch

267

of flesh protruded between her thumb and forefinger. The lavish food on the cruise ship wasn't going to do her weight any good. She steeled her mind to lay off the alcohol and desserts.

She slipped on a mauvé silk damask jacket over a black lace and taffeta skirt. Loosening the businesslike knot at the top of her head, she let her hair down so that it spilled over her shoulders. Satisfied with the effect, she felt in the mood for a stroll around the deck before dinner at the captain's table.

The air was so warm she dispensed with a sweater. On the aft end of the sun deck she found a vacant deck chair and relaxed, raising her knees and clasping her hands around her calves. For the next half-hour she let her mind wander as she watched the half-moon's reflection dash across the dark swells. Then the exterior deck lights abruptly went out from bow to stern.

Loren didn't notice the helicopter until it was almost over the fantail of the ship. It had arrived at wavetop level, flying without navigation lights. Several crew members appeared from the shadows and quickly laid a roof over the boat-deck swimming pool. Then a ship's officer signaled with a flashlight and the helicopter descended lightly onto the improvised landing pad.

Loren rose to her feet and stared over the railing. Her vantage point was one deck above and forty feet distant from the closed-over swimming pool. The area was dimly lit by the partial moon, enabling her to observe most of the action. She glanced around, looking for other passengers, but saw only five or six who were standing fifty feet further away.

Three men left the aircraft. Two of them, it appeared to Loren, were treated roughly. The ship's officer placed the flashlight under his arm so he could have both hands free to brusquely shove one of the men into an open hatchway. For a brief instant the unaimed beam caught and held on a paper-white face, eyes bulging in fear. Loren saw the facial details clearly. Her hands gripped the deck rail and her heart felt locked in ice.

Then the copter rose into the night and turned sharply back toward shore. The cover over the pool was quickly removed and the crew melted away. In a few seconds the ship's lights came back on.

Everything happened so fast, Loren wondered for a moment if she had actually witnessed the landing and takeoff.

But there was no mistaking the frightened creature she saw on the pool deck below. She was positive it was the Speaker of the House, Congressman Alan Moran.

On the bridge Captain Pokofsky peered at the radarscope. He was of medium height and portly. A cigarette dangled from one corner of his mouth. He straightened and smoothed the jacket of his white dress uniform.

"At least they waited until we were beyond the twelve-mile limit," he said in a guttural voice.

"Any sign they were followed?" asked the officer of the watch.

"No aerial contacts and no craft approaching by sea," answered Pokofsky. "A smooth operation."

"Like the others," the watch officer said with a cocky smile.

Pokofsky did not return the smile. "I'm not fond of taking deliveries on short notice under moonlit skies."

"This one must be a high priority."

"Aren't they all?" Pokofsky said caustically.

The watch officer decided to remain quiet. He'd served with Pokofsky long enough to recognize when the captain was in one of his moods.

Pokofsky checked the radar again and swept his eyes across the black sea ahead. "See that our guests are escorted to my cabin," he ordered before turning and leaving the bridge.

Five minutes later the ship's second officer knocked on the captain's door, opened it and ushered in a man wearing a rumpled business suit.

"I'm Captain Pokofsky," he said, rising from a leather reading chair.

"Paul Suvorov."

"KGB or GRU?"*

---

* Soviet Military Intelligence.

"KGB."

Pokofsky gestured toward a sofa. "Do you mind informing me of the purpose behind your unscheduled arrival?"

Suvorov gratefully sat down and took the measure of Pokofsky. He was uncomfortable with what he read. The captain was clearly a hardened seaman and not the type to be intimidated by state security credentials. Suvorov wisely chose to tread lightly.

"Not at all. I was instructed to smuggle two men out of the country."

"Where are they now?"

"I took the liberty of having your first officer lock them in the brig."

"Are they Soviet defectors?"

"No, they're American."

Pokofsky's brows raised. "Are you saying you've kidnapped American citizens?"

"Yes," said Suvorov with an icy calm. "Two of the most important leaders in the United States government."

"I'm not sure I heard you correctly."

"Their names do not matter. One is a congressman, the other a senator."

Pokofsky's eyes burned with sudden belligerence. "Do you have any idea of the jeopardy you've placed my ship in?"

"We're in international waters," Suvorov said placidly. "What can happen?"

"Wars have started for less," Pokofsky said sharply. "If the Americans are alerted, international waters or not, they wouldn't hesitate for one instant to send their Navy and Coast Guard to stop and board this vessel."

Suvorov came to his feet and stared directly into Pokofsky's eyes. "Your precious ship is in no danger, Captain."

Pokofsky stared back. "What are you saying?"

"The ocean is a big dumping ground," Suvorov said steadily. "If the situation requires, my friends in the brig will simply be committed to the deep."

46

TALK AROUND THE CAPTAIN'S TABLE was dull and inane, as could be expected. Loren's dining companions bored her with long-drawn-out descriptions of their previous travels. Pokofsky had heard such travelogues a thousand times before. He smiled politely and listened with feigned courtesy. When asked, he told how he had joined the Russian Navy at seventeen, worked up through the officers' ranks until he commanded a troop transport, and after twenty years' service transferred to the Soviet state-subsidized passenger line.

He described the *Leonid Andreyev* as a 14,000-ton vessel, built in Finland, with a capacity of 478 passengers with two crew members for every three of them. The modern white-hulled liner had indoor and outdoor swimming pools, five cocktail bars, two nightclubs, ten shops featuring Russian merchandise and liquor, a movie and stage theater, and a well-stocked library. She cruised from Miami on ten-day sailings during the summer months to several resort islands in the West Indies.

During a lull in the conversation, Loren casually mentioned the helicopter landing. Captain Pokofsky lit a cigarette with a wooden match and waved out the flame.

"You Americans and your affluence," he said easily. "Two wealthy Texans missed the boat in Miami and hired a helicopter to fly them to the *Andreyev*. Very few of my countrymen can afford such luxury."

"Not many of mine can either," Loren assured him. The captain was not only congenial and charming, she thought, he was an accomplished liar as well. She dropped the subject and nibbled on her salad.

Before dessert, Loren excused herself and went to her suite on the sun deck. She kicked off her shoes, removed and hung up her skirt and jacket, and sprawled on the soft king-size bed. She ran the picture of Alan Moran's terrified face through her mind, telling herself it must have been someone who resembled the congressman, and perhaps the beam of the flashlight outlined similar features. Reason dictated that it was merely a trick of imagination.

Then Pitt's inquiry at the restaurant returned to her. He'd asked if she had heard any rumors of a missing party high in government. Now her gut instinct said she was right.

She laid out a ship's directory and deck diagram on the bed and flattened out the creases. To look for Moran in a floating city with 230 staterooms, quarters for a crew of over 300, cargo holds and engine room, all spread over eleven decks nearly 500 feet in length was a lost cause. She also had to consider that she was a representative of the American government on Russian property. Obtain permission from Captain Pokofsky to search every nook and cranny of his ship? She'd stand a better chance of persuading him to give up vodka for Kentucky bourbon.

She decided the logical move would be to establish Alan Moran's whereabouts. If he was at home in Washington watching TV, she could forget the whole madness and get a good night's sleep. She put her dress back on and went to the communications room. Thankfully it wasn't crowded and she didn't have to wait in line.

A pretty Russian girl in a trim uniform asked Loren where she wished to call.

"Washington, D.C.," she replied. "Person to person to a Ms. Sally Lindemann. I'll write out the number."

"If you will please wait in booth five, I'll arrange your satellite transmission," the communications girl said in near flawless English.

Loren sat patiently, hoping her secretary was at home. She was.

A sleepy voice answered the operator and acknowledged her name was Sally Lindemann.

"That you, boss?" Sally asked when Loren was put through. "I bet you're dancing up a storm under Caribbean stars with some handsome playboy. Am I right?"

"You're not even close."

"I should have known this was a business call."

"Sally, I need you to contact someone."

"One sec." There was a pause. When Sally's voice came on again, it glowed with efficiency. "I've got a pad and pencil. Who do I contact and what do I say?"

"The congressman who opposed and shot down my Rocky Mountain water project."

"You mean old prune-face Mo—"

"He's the one," Loren cut her off. "I want you to talk to him, face to face if possible. Start with his home. If he's out, ask his wife where he can be reached. If she balks, tell her it's a matter of congressional urgency. Say whatever it takes but get to him."

"When I find him, then what?"

"Nothing," said Loren. "Say it was a mistake."

There were a few seconds' silence. Then Sally said carefully, "You drunk, boss?"

Loren laughed, knowing the puzzlement that must be running through Sally's mind.

"Dead sober."

"Can this wait until morning?"

"I have to know his location as quickly as possible."

"My alarm clock reads after midnight," Sally protested.

"Now!" Loren said sharply. "Call me the second you see his face and hear his voice."

She hung up and walked back toward her suite. The moon was directly overhead and she lingered a few minutes on deck, wishing Pitt were standing there beside her.

Loren had just finished putting on her morning face when she heard a knock at the door.

"Who's there?"

"Steward."

She went to the door and opened it. Her cabin steward raised his hand in a casual salute. He peered self-consciously at the cleavage revealed by her loosely knotted dressing gown.

"An emergency call for you from the mainland, Congresswoman Smith," he said in a heavy Slavic accent. "They're holding it for you in the communications room."

She thanked him and hurriedly dressed. A new girl directed her to a booth and the waiting call. Sally's voice came through the earpiece as if she were in the next booth.

"Good morning, boss," she said tiredly.

"Any luck?"

"Moran's wife said he went fishing with Senator Marcus Larimer," Sally snapped out before Loren thought to stop her. "She claimed they went to a place called Goose Lake, a private reserve for the good ole boys a few miles below the Quantico Marine Corps reservation. So I hopped in my car and drove down. After bluffing my way past an outdoorsy type guarding the gate, I checked every cottage, boathouse and dock. No congressman, no senator. Then back to the capital. I called and woke up three of Moran's aides. Don't ever look for favors from his office. They backed up the fishing story. As a double-check, I tried a couple of Larimer's staff too. Same bull. In fact, nobody has seen either of them in over a week. Sorry I failed you, boss, but it looks like a smoke screen to me."

Loren felt a cold chill run through her. The second man she saw manhandled from the helicopter, could he have been Marcus Larimer?

"Shall I stay on the hunt?" asked Sally.

"Yes, please," Loren answered.

"Do my best," Sally declared. "Oh, I almost forgot. Have you heard the latest news?"

"How could I at ten in the morning on a boat in the middle of the ocean?"

"Concerns your friend Dirk Pitt."

"Something happen to Dirk?" Loren asked anxiously.

"Persons unknown blew up his car. Lucky for him he wasn't inside at the time. Close, though. Walking toward it when he stopped to talk to a friend. According to District police, another couple of minutes and they'd have swept him up with a broom."

Everything caught up and jammed behind Loren's eyes. It was all happening too fast for her to accept. The mad events splashed behind her eyes in a complexity of color, like scraps making up a backwoods bed quilt. The seams were pulling apart in all directions. She grasped the only thread that seemed to hold.

"Sal, listen carefully. Call Dirk and tell him I need—" Suddenly a shrill buzzing sound flooded her eardrum. "Can you hear me, Sal?"

The only reply to Loren's question was the interference. She swung around to complain to the communications girl, but she was gone. Instead, there were two stewards, or rather two wrestlers in stewards' uniforms, and the first officer. He opened the door to her booth and bowed curtly.

"Will you please come with me, Congresswoman Smith. The captain would like to talk to you."

47

THE PILOT SET THE HELICOPTER on the ground at a small airport on the Isle of Palms near Charleston. He went through the standard shutdown procedure, running the engine at low RPM's until it cooled down. Then he climbed out, lined up one of the rotor blades and tied it to the tail boom.

His back and arms ached from the long hours in the air, and he did stretching exercises as he walked to a small office next to the landing pad. He unlocked the door and stepped inside.

A stranger sat in the tiny lobby area casually reading a newspaper. To the pilot he looked to be either Chinese or Japanese. The newspaper was lowered, revealing a shotgun with a pistol grip and twin sawed-off barrels that ended barely four inches in front of the shells.

"What do you want?" asked the pilot stupidly.

"Information?"

"You're in the wrong place," said the pilot, instinctively raising his hands. "We're a helicopter ambulance service, not a library."

"Very witty," said the Oriental. "You also carry passengers."

"Who told you that?"

"Paul Suvorov. One of your Russian friends."

"Never heard of the guy."

"How odd. He sat next to you in the co-pilot's seat for most of yesterday."

"What do you want?" the pilot repeated, the fear beginning to crawl up his spine.

The Oriental smiled wickedly. "You have ten seconds to tell me the precise destination where you flew Suvorov and two other men. If at the end of that time you feel stubborn, I shall blow away one of your knees. Ten seconds later you can bid goodbye to your sex life." He enforced his request by releasing the safety on the shotgun. "Countdown begins . . . now."

Three minutes later the Oriental stepped from the building and locked the door. Then he walked to a car parked nearby, climbed behind the wheel and drove toward a sandy road leading to Charleston.

The car was barely out of sight when a torrent of orange flame gushed through the thin roof of the pilot's office and spiraled into the white overcast sky.

Pitt spent the day dodging reporters and police detectives. He hid in a quiet pub called the Devil's Fork on Rhode Island Avenue and sat in a cushiony leather seat in a quiet corner staring pensively at a half-eaten Monte Cristo sandwich and a third Manhattan, a drink he seldom ordered.

A pert blond waitress in a micro-skirt and mesh stockings stopped by his table. "You're the most pitiful person in the place," she said with a motherly smile. "Lose your best girl or your wife?"

"Worse," said Pitt sadly. "My car."

She laid a look on him reserved for Martians and weirdos, shrugged and continued her rounds of the other tables.

Pitt sat there idly stirring the Manhattan with a cherry, scowling at nothing. Somewhere along the line he had lost his grip on things. Events were controlling him. Knowing who tried to kill him provided little satisfaction. Only the Bougainville hierarchy had the motive. He was getting too close. No brilliance required in solving that mystery.

He was angry at himself for playing adolescent computer games with their financial operation while they ran in a tougher league. Pitt felt like a prospector who'd discovered a safe full of currency in the middle of the Antarctic and no place to spend it. His only leverage was that he knew more than they thought he knew.

The enigma that nagged him was Bougainville's unlikely involvement with the *Eagle*. He knew of no motive for the sinking and murders. The only tie, and a slim one at that, was the overabundance of Korean bodies.

No matter; that was the FBI's problem, and he was glad to be rid of it.

The time had come, he decided, to get rolling, and the first step was to marshal his forces. No brilliance required in that decision either.

He rose and walked over to the bar. "Can I borrow your phone, Cabot?"

The bartender, a pixie-faced Irishman, name of Sean Cabot, gave Pitt a doleful glare. "Local or long distance?"

"Long distance, but don't cry in your cash register. I'll use a credit card."

Cabot nodded indifferently and set a telephone on the end of the bar away from the other customers. "Too bad about your car, Dirk. I saw her once. She was a beauty."

"Thanks. Buy yourself a drink and put it on my tab."

Cabot filled a glass with ginger ale from the dispenser and held it aloft. "To a Good Samaritan and a bon vivant."

Pitt didn't feel like a Good Samaritan and even less like a bon vivant as he punched out the numbers on the phone. He gave his credit card number to the operator and waited for a voice to answer.

"Casio and Associates Investigatahs."

"This is Dirk Pitt. Is Sal in?"

"One moment, sah."

Things were looking up. He'd been accepted into the receptionist's club.

"Dirk?" came Casio's voice. "I've been calling your office all morning. I think I've got something."

"Yes?"

"A hunt through maritime union files paid dividends. Six of the Korean seamen who signed on the *San Marino* had prior crew tickets. Mostly with foreign shipping lines. But all six had one thing in common. At one time or another they sailed for Bougainville Maritime. Ever hear of it?"

"It figures," said Pitt. Then he proceeded to tell Casio what he found during the computer search.

"Damn!" Casio exclaimed incredulously. "Everything fits."

"The maritime union, what did their records show on the Korean crew after the *San Marino* hijacking?"

"Nothing, they dropped from sight."

"If Bougainville history ran true to form, they were murdered."

Casio fell silent, and Pitt guessed what was running through the investigator's mind.

"I owe you," Casio said finally. "You've helped me zero in on Arta's killer. But it's my show. I'll take it alone from here."

"Don't give me the vengeance is mine martyr routine," Pitt said abruptly. "Besides, you still don't know who was directly responsible."

"Min Koryo Bougainville," said Casio, spitting out the name. "Who else could it be?"

"The old girl might have given the orders," said Pitt, "but she didn't dirty her hands. It's no secret she's been in a wheelchair for ten years. No interviews or pictures of her have been published since Nixon was President. For all we know, Min Koryo Bougainville is a senile, bedridden vegetable. Hell, she may even be dead. No way she scattered bodies over the seascape alone."

"You're talking a corporate hit squad."

"Can you think of a more efficient way to eliminate the competition?"

"Now you're insinuating she's a member of the Mafia," grunted Casio.

"The Mafia only kill informers and each other. The evil beauty of Min Koryo's setup is that by murdering crews in wholesale lots and stealing vessels from other shipping lines, she built her assets with almost no overhead. And to do it she has to have someone organize and orchestrate the crimes. Don't let your hate blind you to hard-core reality, Sal. You haven't got the resources to take on Bougainville alone."

"And you do?"

"Takes two to start an army."

There was another silence, and Pitt thought the connection might have been broken.

"You still there, Sal?"

"I'm here," Casio finally said in a thoughtful voice. "What do you want me to do?"

"Fly to New York and pay a visit to Bougainville Maritime."

"You mean toss their office?"

"I thought the term was 'breaking and entering.' "

"A cop and a judge use different dictionaries."

"Just employ your talents to see what you can find of interest that doesn't show up in the computers."

"I'll bug the place while I'm at it."

"You're the expert," said Pitt. "Our advantage is that you'll be coming from a direction they won't suspect. Me, I've already been marked."

"Marked?" asked Casio. "How?"

"They tried to kill me."

"Christ!" muttered Casio. "How?"

"Car bomb."

"The bastards!" he rasped. "I'll leave for New York this afternoon."

Pitt pushed the telephone across the bar and returned to his booth. He felt better after talking to Casio, and he finished the sandwich. He was contemplating his fourth Manhattan when Giordino walked up to the table.

"A private party?" he asked.

"No," Pitt said. "A hate-the-world, feel-sorry-for-yourself, down-in-the-dumps party."

"I'll join it anyway," Giordino said, sliding into the booth. "The admiral's concerned about you."

"Tell him I'll pay for the damage to the parking lot."

"Be serious. The old guy is madder than a stepped-on rattler. Raised hell with the Justice Department all morning, demanding they launch an all-out investigation to find out who was behind the bombing. To him, an attack on you is an attack on NUMA."

"The FBI nosing around my apartment and office?"

Giordino nodded. "No less than six of them."

"And reporters?"

"I lost count. What did you expect? The blast that disintegrated your car thrust your name in the limelight. Instant celebrity. First bomb explosion the city's had in four years. Like it or not, old friend, you've become the eye of the storm."

Pitt felt a mild elation at having scared the Bougainville interests enough for them to attempt his removal. They must somehow have learned he was nipping at their flanks, digging deeper into their secrets with each bite. But why the overreaction?

The fake announcement of his discovery of both the *San Marino* and the *Pilottown* no doubt alerted them. Yet it shouldn't have thrown them into a panic. Min Koryo wasn't the panicky type—point demonstrated by the fact she did not respond to the doctored story.

How then did they realize he was so close?

Bougainville couldn't have tied him to the computer penetration and planned his death in such short order. Then the revelation struck him. The notion had been there all the time, but he had pushed it aside, failing to pursue it because it did not fit a pattern. Now it burst like a flare.

Bougainville had linked him to the *Eagle*.

Pitt was so engrossed in thought he didn't hear Giordino telling him he had a phone call.

"Your mind must be a million miles away," said Giordino, pointing toward Cabot the bartender, who was holding up the bar phone.

Pitt walked over to the bar and spoke in the mouthpiece. "Hello."

Sally Lindemann's voice bubbled excitedly over the wire. "Oh, thank heavens I've finally tracked you down. I've been trying to reach you all day."

"What's wrong?" Pitt demanded. "Is Loren all right?"

"I think so, and then maybe not," said Sally, becoming flustered. "I just don't know."

"Take your time and spell it out," Pitt said gently.

"Congresswoman Smith called me in the middle of the night

281

from the *Leonid Andreyev* and told me to find the whereabouts of Speaker of the House Alan Moran. She never gave me a reason. When I asked her what to say when I contacted him, she said to tell him it was a mistake. Make sense to you?''

''Did you find Moran?''

''Not exactly. He and Senator Marcus Larimer were supposed to be fishing together at a place called Goose Lake. I went there but nobody else knew anything about them.''

''What else did Loren say?''

''Her last words to me were 'Call Dirk and tell him I need—' Then we were cut off. I tried several times to reach her again, but there was no answer.''

''Did you tell the ship's operator it was an emergency?''

''Of course. They claimed my message was passed on to her stateroom, but she made no attempt to reply. This is the damnedest thing. Not like Congresswoman Smith at all. Sound crazy?''

Pitt was silent, thinking it out. ''Yes,'' he said at last, ''just crazy enough to make sense. Do you have the *Leonid Andreyev*'s schedule?''

''One moment.'' Sally went off the line for nearly a minute. ''Okay, what do you want to know?''

''When does it make the next port?''

''Let's see, it arrives in San Salvador in the Bahamas at ten A.M. tomorrow and departs the same evening at eight P.M. for Kingston, Jamaica.''

''Thank you, Sally.''

''What's all this about?'' Sally asked. ''I wish you'd tell me.''

''Keep trying to reach Loren. Contact the ship every two hours.''

''You'll call if you find out anything,'' Sally said suspiciously.

''I'll call,'' Pitt promised.

He returned to the table and sat down.

''What was that all about?'' Giordino inquired.

''My travel agent,'' Pitt answered, pretending to be nonchalant. ''I've booked us for a cruise in the Caribbean.''

48

CURTIS MAYO SAT AT A DESK amid the studio mock-up of a busy newsroom and peered at the television monitor slightly to his right and below camera number two. He was ten minutes into the evening news and waited for his cue after a commercial advertising a bathroom disinfectant. The thirty-second spot wound down on a New York fashion model, who probably never cleaned a toilet bowl in her life, smiling demurely with the product caressing her cheek.

The floor director moved into Mayo's eye range, counted down the last three seconds and waved. The red light on the camera blinked on and Mayo stared into the lens, beginning the B segment of his news program.

"At the President's farm in New Mexico there have been rumors that the nation's chief executive and the Vice President are using look-alike stand-ins."

As Mayo continued his story line the engineer in the control booth cut to the tape of the President driving the tractor.

"These scenes of the President cutting alfalfa on his farm, when viewed close up, suggest to some that it is not him. Certain famous mannerisms seem exaggerated, different rings are seen on the fingers, the wristwatch is not the one he usually wears, and there appears to be a casual habit of scratching the chin that has not been noted before.

"John Sutton, the actor who bears a striking resemblance and who often imitates the President on TV shows and commercials, could not be found by reporters in Hollywood for comment. Which raises the question Why would our nation's leaders require doubles? Is it a secret security procedure, or a deception for darker motives? Could it be the pressures of the job are such that they have to be in two places at the same time? We can only speculate.''

Mayo let the story dangle on a thread of suspicion. The engineer in the booth switched back to the studio camera, and Mayo went into the next story.

"In Miami today, police claimed a breakthrough in a string of drug-related murders. . . .''

After the program, Mayo smiled in grim delight when informed of the hundreds of calls flooding the network news offices asking for more information on the President's double story. The same reaction, if not far heavier, had to be pouring into White House phone lines. In a spiteful sort of glee, he wondered how the presidential press secretary was taking it.

In New Mexico, Sonny Thompson stared blankly at the TV set long after Mayo left the air. He sat collapsed in his chair, his flesh the consistency of blubber. He envisioned his carefully nurtured world slamming to a rapid end. His peers in the news media were about to crucify him on a cross of sensationalism. When he was proven an accomplice to a conspiracy to deceive the American public, no newspaper or TV network would ever hire him after his looming White House departure.

John Sutton stood in back of him with a drink in one hand. "The vultures are circling," he said.

"In giant flocks," Thompson muttered.

"What happens now?"

"That's for others to decide."

"I'm not going to jail like Liddy, Colson and those other guys," Sutton said nastily.

"Nobody's going to jail," Thompson said wearily. "This isn't Watergate. The Justice Department is working with us."

"No way I'm going to take a fall for a bunch of politicians."

284

Sutton's eyes began to take on a greedy gleam. "A guy could make thousands, maybe a few million out of this."

Thompson looked at him. "How?"

"Interviews, articles, and there's book rights royalties—the possibilities for making a bundle are endless."

"And you think you're going to walk out of here and tell all."

"Why not?" said Sutton. "Who's going to stop me?"

It was Thompson's turn to smile. "You haven't been told the reasons behind your employment. You have no idea how vital your little act is to our country's interests."

"So who cares?" Sutton said indifferently.

"You may not believe it, Mr. Sutton, but there are many decent people in our government who are genuinely concerned about its welfare. They will never allow you to endanger it by speaking your piece for profit."

"How can those egomaniacs who run the fun house in Washington hurt me? Slap my hand? Draft me into a volunteer army at age sixty-two? Turn me over to the Internal Revenue Service? No sweat on that score. I get audited every year anyway."

"Nothing so mundane," said Thompson. "You will simply be taken out."

"What do you mean, taken out?" demanded Sutton.

"Perhaps I should have said 'disappear,' " Thompson replied, delighting in the realization that grew in Sutton's eyes. "It goes without saying your body will never be recovered."

49

FAWCETT FELT NO ENTHUSIASM for the day ahead.
As he scraped the beard from his chin, he occasionally glanced at
the stack of newspapers spilling off the bathroom sink. Mayo's
story made front page news across every morning edition in the nation. Suddenly the press began to ask why the President hadn't
been reachable for ten days. Half the editorial columns demanded
he step forward and make a statement. The other half asked the
question "Where is the real President?"

Wiping the remaining lather away with a towel and slapping his
face with a mild after-shave lotion, Fawcett decided his best approach was to play the Washington enigma game and remain silent. He would cover his personal territory, slide artfully into the
background and gracefully permit Secretary Oates to carry the
brunt of the media onslaught.

Time had slipped from days to a few hours. Soon only minutes
would be left. The inner sanctum could stall no longer.

Fawcett couldn't begin to predict the complications that would
arise from the announcement of the abduction. No crime against
the government had ever approached this magnitude.

His only conviction was that the great perpetuating bureaucracy
would continue to somehow function. The power elite were the
ones who were swept in and swept out by the whim of the voters.
But the institution endured.

He was determined to do everything within his shrinking realm of influence to make the next President's transition as painless as possible. With luck, he might even save his job.

He put on a dark suit, left the house and drove to his office, dreading every mile. Oscar Lucas and Alan Mercier were waiting for him as he entered the West Wing.

"Looks grim" was all Lucas said.

"Someone has to make a statement," said Mercier, whose face looked like it belonged in a coffin.

"Anybody I know draw the short straw?" asked Fawcett.

"Doug Oates thought you'd be the best man to hold a press conference and announce the kidnapping."

"What about the rest of the Cabinet?" Fawcett asked incredulously.

"They concurred."

"Screw Oates!" Fawcett said coarsely. "The whole idea is stupid. He's only trying to save his own ass. I don't have the credentials to drop the bombshell. As far as the grass-roots voters are concerned, I'm a nonentity. Not one out of a thousand can recall my name or give my position in the administration. You know exactly what would happen. The public would immediately sense their nation's leaders are floundering in a sinking boat, shrinking behind closed doors to save their political hides, and when it was over, any respect the United States ever had would be wiped out. No, I'm sorry. Oates is the logical choice to make the announcement."

"But you see," Mercier said patiently, "if Oates is forced to take the heat and plead ignorance to a lot of embarrassing questions, it might seem he had something to do with the abduction. As next in line for the Presidency, he has the most to gain. Every muckraker in the country will scream 'conspiracy.' Remember the public backlash when former Secretary of State Alexander Haig said he had everything under control right after Reagan was shot by Hinckley? Warranted or not, his image as a power seeker mushroomed. The public didn't like the idea of him running the country. His base of influence eroded until he finally resigned."

"You're comparing catsup to mustard," Fawcett said. "I'm

telling you, the people will be incensed if I stand up and state the President, Vice President and the two majority leaders in Congress have mysteriously vanished and are presumed dead. Hell, no one would believe me.''

''We can't sidestep the main issue,'' Mercier said firmly. ''Douglas Oates has to go into the White House as pure as the driven snow. He can't do a decent job of picking up the pieces if he's surrounded by doubt and malicious rumor.''

''Oates is not a politician. He's never expressed the slightest interest in attaining the Presidency.''

''He has no choice,'' Mercier said. ''He must serve in the interim until the next elections.''

''Can I have the Cabinet standing behind me for support during the press conference?''

''No, they won't agree to that.''

''So I'm to be run out of town on a rail,'' said Fawcett bitterly. ''Is that the mutual decision?''

''You're overstating your case,'' said Mercier mildly. ''You won't be tarred and feathered. Your job is secure. Doug Oates wants you to remain as White House Chief of Staff.''

''And ask me to resign six months later.''

''We can't guarantee the future.''

''All right,'' Fawcett said, his voice trembling in anger. He pushed past Mercier and Lucas. ''Go back and tell Oates he's got his human sacrifice.''

He never turned back but strode down the hallway and went directly to his office, where he paced the floor, fuming in rage. The bureaucracy, he cursed to himself, its wheels were about to rumble over him. He was so furious he did not even notice the President's secretary, Megan Blair, enter the room.

''Mercy, I've never seen you so agitated,'' she said.

Fawcett turned and managed a smile. ''Just complaining to the walls.''

''I do that too, especially when my visiting niece drives me mad with her disco recordings. Blasts that awful music all over the house.''

288

"Can I help you with anything?" he asked impatiently.

"Speaking of complaining," she said testily, "why wasn't I told the President had returned from his farm?"

"Must have slipped my mind—" He stopped and gazed at her queerly. "What did you say?"

"The President's back and no one on your staff warned me."

Fawcett's expression turned to abject disbelief. "He's in New Mexico."

"Certainly not," Megan Blair said adamantly. "He's sitting at his desk this very moment. He chewed me out for coming in late."

Megan was not a woman who could lie easily. Fawcett looked deeply into her eyes and saw she was telling the truth.

She stared back at him, her head tilted questioningly. "Are you all right?" she asked.

Fawcett didn't answer. He ran from his office and down the hallway, meeting Lucas and Mercier, who were still conferring in hushed tones. They looked up startled as Fawcett frantically pounded around them.

"Follow me!" he shouted over one shoulder, arms flinging.

They stood stone-still for a moment, blinking in utter confusion. Then Lucas reacted and dashed after Fawcett, with Mercier bringing up the rear.

Fawcett burst into the Oval Office and stopped dead, his face going white.

The President of the United States looked up and smiled. "Good morning, Dan. Ready to go over my appointment schedule?"

Less than a mile away, in a secure room on the top floor of the Russian embassy, Aleksei Lugovoy sat in front of a large monitor and read the deciphered brainwaves of the President. The display screen showed the thoughts in English while a nearby printer produced paper copies translated into Russian.

He sipped a cup of thick black coffee, then stood up, keeping his eyes on the green letters, the heavy bunched eyebrows raised in controlled conceit.

From a distance, the President's brain transmitted its every thought, speech pattern, and even the words spoken by others nearby as they were received and committed to memory.

The second stage of the Huckleberry Finn Project was a success.

Lugovoy decided to wait a few more days before he entered the final and most critical stage, the issuing of commands. If all went well, he knew with a sinking certainty, his revered project would be taken over by the men in the Kremlin. And then Chairman of the Party Antonov and not the President would direct policy for the United States.

50

THE MOLTEN SUN SLIPPED BELOW the western edge of the Aegean Sea as the ship cleared the Dardanelles and headed through the maze of Greek islands. The surface rolled under gentle two-foot swells and a hot breeze set in from the African coast to the south. Soon the orange faded from the sky and the sea lost its blue and they melted together into a solid curtain of black. The moon had not yet risen; the only light came from the stars and the sweeping beam of the navigation beacon on the island of Lesbos.

Captain James Mangyai, master of the 540-foot bulk freighter *Venice,* stood on the bridge and kept a close watch over the bow. He gave a cursory glance to the radar display and stared out the window again, relieved that the sea was empty of other shipping.

Since departing the Russian port of Odessa in the Black Sea, six hundred nautical miles behind, he had been extremely restless. Now he began to breathe easier. There were few tricks the Russians would dare attempt in Greek waters.

The *Venice* was in ballast—her only cargo was the gold shipment transferred from the Soviet government to Madame Bougainville—and her hull rode high in the water. Her destination was Genoa, where the gold was to be secretly unloaded and shipped to Lucerne, Switzerland, for storage.

Captain Mangyai heard footsteps behind him on the teak deck

and recognized his first officer, Kim Chao, in the reflection on the window.

"How does it look to you, Mr. Chao?" he said without turning.

Chao read over the hour-by-hour meteorological report from the automated data system. "Calm sailing for the next twelve hours," he said in an unhurried voice. "Extended forecast looks good too. We're fortunate. The southerly winds are usually much stronger this time of year."

"We'll need a smooth sea if we're to dock in Genoa under Madame Bougainville's schedule."

"Why the hurry?" asked Chao. "Another twelve hours of sailing won't matter."

"It matters to our employer," said Mangyai dryly. "She doesn't wish our cargo in transit any longer than necessary."

"The chief engineer is making more wind than a typhoon. He claims he can't keep up this speed for the whole voyage without burning up the engines."

"He always sees black clouds."

"You haven't left the bridge since Odessa, Captain. Let me spell you."

Mangyai nodded gratefully. "I could use a short rest. But first I should look in on our passenger."

He turned over the bridge watch to Chao and walked down three decks to a heavy steel door at the end of an alleyway amidships. He pressed a transmit button on a speaker bolted to the bulkhead.

"Mr. Hong, this is Captain Mangyai."

He was answered by the gentle creak of the massive door as it was pulled open. A small moon-faced man with thick-lensed spectacles peered cautiously around the edge. "Ah, yes, Captain. Please come in."

"Can I get you anything, Mr. Hong?"

"No, I'm quite comfortable, thank you."

Hong's idea of comfort was considerably different from Mangyai's. The only suggestion of human habitation was a suitcase neatly stowed under a canvas folding cot, one blanket, a small electric burner with a pot of tea, and a desk hanging from a bulkhead, its surface hidden under a pile of chemical analysis equipment. The rest of the compartment was packed with wooden crates and gold bars. The gold was stacked thirty high and ten deep in several rows. Some bars were scattered on the deck next to the open crates, the unsanded sides stenciled with the disclosure:

HANDLE WITH CARE
MERCURY IN GLASS
SUZAKA CHEMICAL COMPANY LIMITED
KYOTO, JAPAN

"How are you coming?" Mangyai asked.

"I should have it all examined and crated by the time we reach port."

"How many gilded lead bars did the Russians slip in?"

"None," said Hong, shaking his head. "The count tallies, and every bar I've checked so far is pure."

"Strange they were so accommodating. The shipment arrived at the preset hour. Their dockworkers loaded it onboard without incident. And we were cleared to depart without the usual administrative hassle. I've never experienced such efficiency in any of my previous dealings with Soviet port authorities."

"Perhaps Madame Bougainville has great influence in the Kremlin."

"Perhaps," said Mangyai skeptically. He looked curiously at the piles of gleaming yellow metal. "I wonder what was behind the transaction?"

"I'm not about to ask," said Hong, carefully wrapping a bar in wadding and placing it in a crate.

Before Mangyai could answer, a voice came over the speaker. "Captain, are you in there?"

He walked over and cracked the heavy door. The ship's communications officer was standing outside in the alleyway.

"Yes, what is it?"

"I thought you should know, Captain, someone is jamming our communications."

"You know this for a fact?"

"Yes, sir," said the young officer. "I managed to get a fix on it. The source is less than three miles off our port bow."

Mangyai excused himself to Hong and hurried to the bridge. First Officer Chao was calmly sitting in a high swivel chair studying the instruments on the ship's computerized control panel.

"Do you have any ship contacts in, Mr. Chao?" asked Mangyai.

If Chao was surprised at the captain's sudden reappearance, he didn't show it. "Nothing visual, nothing on radar, sir."

"What is our depth?"

Chao checked the reading on the depth sounder. "Fifty meters, or about a hundred and sixty feet."

The awful truth struck Mangyai's mind like a hammer. He leaned over the chart table and plotted their course. The keel of the *Venice* was passing over the Tzonston Bank, one of many areas in the middle of the Aegean where the seabed rose to within a hundred feet of the surface. Deep enough for a ship's safe passage, but shallow enough for a routine salvage operation.

"Steer for deep water!" he shouted.

Chao stared at the captain, hesitating in bewilderment. "Sir?"

Mangyai opened his mouth to repeat the order but the words froze in his throat. At that instant, two sound-tracking torpedoes homed in on the freighter's engine room and exploded with devastating effect. Her bottom torn in gaping holes, the sea rushed into her innards. The *Venice* shuddered and entered her death throes.

She took only eight minutes to die, going down by the stern and disappearing beneath the indifferent swells forever.

The *Venice* was hardly gone when a submarine surfaced

nearby and began playing her searchlight on the fragmented floating wreckage. The pitifully few survivors, clinging to the flotsam, were coldly machine-gunned until their shredded bodies sank out of sight. Boats were sent out, guided by the darting shaft of light. After searching for several hours until all the debris was pulled aboard, they returned to their ship.

Then the light was killed and the sub returned to the darkness.

51 _____

THE PRESIDENT SAT AT THE CENTER of the oval mahogany conference table in the White House Cabinet Room. There
were eleven men seated there besides himself. A bemused expression shone in his eyes as he surveyed the somber faces around the
table.

"I know you gentlemen are curious about where I've been for
the last ten days, and about the status of Vince Margolin, Al Moran
and Marcus Larimer. Let me put this fear to rest. Our temporary
disappearance was an event planned by me."

"You alone?" Douglas Oates put to him.

"Not entirely. President Antonov of the Soviet Union was also
involved."

For several moments, stunned and disbelieving, the President's
top advisers stared at him.

"You held a secret meeting with Antonov without the knowledge of anyone in this room?" Oates said. His face paled in dismay.

"Yes," the President admitted. "A face-to-face talk minus outside interference and preconceived notions, without the international news media second-guessing every word and unbound by
policy. Just our top four people against his." He paused and his
eyes swept the men before him. "An unorthodox way of negotiat-
ing, but one I believe the electorate will accept when they see the
results."

"Would you mind telling us how and where this talk was held, Mr. President?" asked Dan Fawcett.

"After the exchange of yachts, we transferred to a civilian helicopter and flew to a small airport outside of Baltimore. From there we took a private airliner belonging to an old friend of mine and crossed the Atlantic to an abandoned airstrip deep in the desert east of Atar, Mauritania. Antonov and his people were waiting when we arrived."

"I thought . . . rather it was reported," Jesse Simmons said hesitatingly, "that Antonov was in Paris last week."

"Georgi stopped over in Paris for a brief conference with President L'Estrange before continuing to Atar." He turned and looked at Fawcett. "By the way, Dan, that was a brilliant masquerade."

"We came within a hair of getting caught."

"For the time being, I'll deny the rumors of a double as too absurd to comment on. Everything will be explained to the press, but not before I'm ready."

Sam Emmett placed his elbows on the table and leaned toward the President. "Were you informed, sir, that the *Eagle* was sunk and its crew drowned?"

The President stared quizzically for a few moments. Then his eyes sharpened and he shook his head. "No, I wasn't aware of it. I'd appreciate a full report, Sam, as soon as possible."

Emmett nodded. "It will be on your desk when we adjourn."

Oates struggled to keep his emotions in rein. That a high-level meeting of such enormous consequences to world foreign policy had taken place behind the back of the State Department was unthinkable. It was without precedent in anyone's memory.

"I think we'd all be interested in knowing what you and Georgi Antonov discussed," he said stiffly.

"A very productive give-and-take," answered the President. "The most pressing item on the agenda was disarmament. Antonov and I hammered out an agreement to halt all missile production and start up a dismantling program. We arrived at a complicated formula that in simple terms means they break down a nuclear missile and we match them on a one-for-one basis with on-site inspection teams overseeing the operation.''

"France and England will never buy such a proposal," said Oates. "Their nuclear arsenals are independent from ours.''

"We will begin with the long-range warheads and work down," the President said, undaunted. "Europe will eventually follow.''

General Clayton Metcalf shook his head. "On the face of it, I'd have to say the proposal sounds incredibly naïve.''

"It's a beginning," said the President adamantly. "I believe Antonov is sincere in his offer, and I intend to show good faith by pursuing the dismantling program.''

"I'll reserve judgment until I've had a chance to study the formula," said Simmons.

"Fair enough.''

"What else did you discuss?'' asked Fawcett.

"A trade agreement," answered the President. "Briefly explained, if we allow the Russians to transport their agricultural purchases in their own merchant ships, Antonov promised to pay our farmers top world prices and, most important, not to buy from any other nation unless we fail to provide the goods as ordered. In other words, American farmers are now the exclusive suppliers of Soviet imported farm products.''

"Antonov bought your package?'' Oates asked incredulously. "I can't believe the old bear capable of giving away an exclusive license to any nation.''

"I have his assurance in writing.''

"It sounds great," said Martin Brogan. "But I'd like someone to explain how Russia can afford to make wholesale agricultural purchases. Their East bloc satellites have defaulted on massive loans to the West. The Soviet economy is in disastrous shape. They can't even pay their armed forces and government workers in anything but scrip good only for food and clothing. What are they going to use for money? Our farmers aren't about to go in hock for Communists. They need immediate payment to clear their own yearly debts.''

"There is a way out," the President said.

"Your East bloc bailout theory?" said Fawcett, anticipating him.

The President nodded. "Antonov agreed in principle to accept my economic assistance plan."

"If you'll excuse me, Mr. President," said Oates, his hands clutched to keep them from visibly trembling, "your plan solves nothing. What you're proposing is that we give billions of dollars in financial aid to the Communist nations so they can turn around and buy from our own farming community. I see that as a 'rob Peter to pay Paul' sucker game, with our taxpayers footing the bill."

"I'm with Doug," said Brogan. "What's in it for us?"

The President looked around the table, his face set in determination. "I made up my mind that this is the only way to show the world once and for all that, in spite of her monstrous military machine, Russia's system of government is a failure not to be envied or copied. If we do this thing, no country in the world can ever again accuse us of imperialist aggression, and no Soviet propaganda or disinformation campaigns against us will be taken seriously. Think of it, the United States helped its enemies back on their feet after World War Two. And now we can do the same for a nation that has made a crusade out of condemning our democratic principles. I devoutly believe no greater opportunity will be laid on our doorstep to set humanity on a straight course into the future."

"Frankly speaking, Mr. President," said General Metcalf in a stern voice, "your grand design will change nothing. As soon as their economy has recovered, the Kremlin leaders will return to their old belligerent ways. They're not about to give up the military expansion and political strategies of seventy years out of gratitude for American generosity."

"The general is right," Brogan said. "Our latest satellite surveillance photos show that even as we sit here the Russians are installing a string of their latest SS-Thirty multiple-warhead missiles along the northeast coast of Siberia, and each warhead is targeted at a city in the U.S."

"They will be dismantled," the President said, his tone set in concrete. "As long as we are aware of their existence, Antonov cannot sidestep his commitment."

Oates was mad and he didn't care who knew it. "All this talk is a waste of time." He almost spat the words at the President. "None of your giveaway schemes can be put into motion without congressional approval. And that, sir, isn't damned likely."

"The Secretary is quite correct," said Fawcett. "Congress still has to appropriate the money, and considering their present mood against Soviet troop incursions along the Iranian and Turkish borders, passage of your programs will most certainly die and be buried in committee."

The men around the table felt uneasy, all of them realizing that the President's administration would never function from a granite base of cohesion again. Differences would arise that had been held in check before. From now on, reverence for teamwork was gone and the line holding personal likes and dislikes broken. Respect for the President and his office had melted away. They saw only a man like themselves, with more faults than they cared to acknowledge. The realization laid a cloud upon the room and they looked to see if the President recognized it too.

He sat there, a strange expression of wickedness spreading across his face, his lips drawn back in cold anticipation of a triumph yet to come.

"I do not need Congress," he said cryptically. "They will have no voice in my policies."

During the short walk from the Cabinet Room to the South Portico, Douglas Oates made up his mind to submit his resignation as Secretary of State. The President's rude act of freezing him out of the negotiations with Antonov was an insult he refused to forgive. There was no turning back as the decision was reached and cemented. He smelled catastrophe in the air, and he wanted no part of it.

He was standing on the steps awaiting his official car when Brogan and Emmett approached.

"Can we have a word with you, Doug?" Emmett asked.

"I'm not in a mood for conversation," Oates grumbled.

"This is critical," Brogan said. "Please hear us out."

His car was not yet in sight on the drive, so Oates shrugged wearily. "I'm listening."

Brogan looked around him and then said softly, "Sam and I think the President is being manipulated."

Oates shot him a sarcastic stare. "Manipulated, hell. He's fallen off his track, and I for one refuse to be a party to his madness. There's more to the sinking of the *Eagle* than he let on, and he never did explain the whereabouts of Margolin, Larimer and Moran. I'm sorry, gentlemen; you two can be the first to know. As soon as I get back to the State Department, I'm clearing out my desk and calling a press conference to announce my resignation. Then I'm taking the next plane out of Washington."

"We suspected what was on your mind," Emmett said. "That's why we wanted to catch you before you went off the deep end."

"What exactly are you trying to tell me?"

Emmett looked at Brogan for help and then shrugged. "The idea is difficult to put across, but Martin and I believe the President is under some sort of . . . well . . . mind control."

Oates wasn't sure he heard right. But logic told him the directors of the CIA and FBI were not men to make light of a serious allegation.

"Controlled by whom?"

"We think the Russians," answered Brogan. "But we haven't accumulated all the evidence yet."

"We realize this sounds like science fiction," Emmett explained, "but it appears very real."

"My God, was the President under this influence as you suggest, when he flew to Mauritania for his talks with Antonov?"

Brogan and Emmett exchanged knowing looks. Then Brogan said, "There isn't a plane in flight anywhere in the world the Agency doesn't know about. I'll stake my job that our data will show no trace of an aircraft flying on a course from Maryland to Mauritania and return."

Oates's eyes widened. "The meeting with Antonov . . ."

Emmett shook his head slowly. "It never happened."

"Then everything—the disarmament, the agricultural trade agreements—was a lie," said Oates, his voice cracking slightly.

"A fact which is heightened by his vague denial of the *Eagle* murders," added Brogan.

"Why did he conceive such a crazy nightmare?" Oates asked dazedly.

"It really doesn't matter why he came up with it," said Emmett. "The programs probably were not even his idea. What matters is how his behavior is guided. Who is motivating his thought patterns, and from where?"

"Can we find out?"

"Yes," said Emmett. "That's why we wanted to catch you before you cut bait."

"What can I do?"

"Stay," Brogan replied. "The President is not fit for office. With Margolin, Moran and Larimer still missing, you remain the next man in line."

"The President must be held in check until we can finish our investigation," said Emmett. "With you at the helm, we keep a measure of control in the event he must be removed from office."

Oates straightened and took a deep breath. "Lord, this is beginning to sound like a conspiracy to assassinate the President."

"In the end," Brogan said grimly, "it may well come to that."

52

LUGOVOY TURNED FROM HIS NOTES and stared at his staff neurologist, who sat at the console monitoring the telemetric signals.

"Condition?"

"Subject has entered a relaxed state. Brain rhythms indicate normal sleep patterns." The neurologist looked up and smiled. "He doesn't know it, but he's snoring."

"I imagine his wife knows it."

"My guess is she sleeps in another bedroom. They haven't had sex since he returned."

"Body functions?"

"All reading normal."

Lugovoy yawned and read the time. "Twelve minutes after one A.M."

"You should get some sleep, Doctor. The President's internal clock wakes him between six and six-fifteen every morning."

"This is not an easy project," Lugovoy groused. "The President requires two hours' less sleep than I do. I detest early risers." He paused and scanned the polysomnography screen that monitored the President's physiological parameters accompanying his sleep. "It appears he's dreaming."

"Be interesting to see what the President of the United States dreams about."

303

"We'll get a rough idea as soon as his brain cell activity goes from coordinated thought patterns to disjointed abstractions."

"Are you into dream interpretations, Doctor?"

"I leave that to the Freudians," Lugovoy replied. "I am one of the few who believe dreams are meaningless. It's merely a situation where the brain, freed from the discipline of daytime thinking, goes on holiday. Like a city dog who lives in an apartment and is unleashed in the country, running in no particular direction, enjoying the new and different smells."

"There are many who would disagree."

"Dreams are not my specialty, so I cannot argue from a purely scientific base. However, I put it to you that if they *do* have a message, why are most of the senses usually missing?"

"You're referring to the absence of smell and taste?"

Lugovoy nodded. "Sounds are also seldom recorded. The same with touch and pain. Dreams are primarily visual sensations. So my own opinion, backed up by little personal research, is that a dream about a one-eyed goat who spits fire is simply that: a dream about a one-eyed goat who spits fire."

"Dream theory is the cornerstone of all psychoanalytic behavior. With your esteemed reputation, you'd shatter quite a few established icons with your goat opinion. Think how many of our psychiatrist comrades would be out of a job if it became known that dreams are meaningless."

"Uncontrolled dreams are quickly forgotten," Lugovoy continued. "But the demands and instructions we transmit to the President's brain cells while he is asleep will not be received as dreams. They are injected thoughts that can be recalled and acted upon by outside stimuli."

"When should I begin programming his implant unit?"

"Transmit the instructions shortly before he wakes up, and repeat them when he sits down at his desk." Lugovoy yawned again. "I'm going to bed. Ring my room if there is a sudden change."

The neurologist nodded. "Rest well."

Lugovoy stared briefly at the monitoring system before he left the room. "I wonder what his mind is envisioning?"

The neurologist waved casually at the data printer. "It should be there."

"No matter," said Lugovoy. "It can wait till morning." Then he turned and walked to his room.

His curiosity needled, the neurologist picked up the top printout sheet containing the President's interpreted brainwaves and glanced at the wording.

"Green hills of summer," he muttered to himself as he read. *"A city between two rivers with many Byzantine-style churches topped by hundreds of cupolas. One called St. Sophia. A river barge filled with sugar beets. The Catacombs of St. Anthony.* If I didn't know better, I'd say he was dreaming about the city of Kiev."

He stood beside a pathway on a hill overlooking a wide river, gazing at the ship traffic and holding an artist's brush. On the tree-covered slope below him he could see a large stone pedestal beneath a figure draped in robes and holding a tall cross as though it were a staff. An easel with a canvas stood slightly off to his right. The painting was nearly finished. The landscape before his eyes was perfectly mirrored in the exacting brush strokes, down to the stippled leaves in the trees. The only difference, if one looked close enough, was the stone monument.

Instead of a long flowing beard of some forgotten saint, the head was an exact likeness of Soviet President Georgi Antonov.

Suddenly the scene changed. Now he found himself being dragged out of a small cottage by four men. The cottage walls were carved with Gothic designs and it was painted a garish blue. The faces of his abductors were indistinct, yet he could smell their unwashed sweat. They were pulling him toward a car. He experienced no fear but rather blind rage and lashed out with his feet. His assailants began beating him, but the pain felt distant as though the agony belonged to someone else.

In the doorway of the cottage he could see the figure of a young woman. Her blond hair was raised in a knot atop her head and she wore a full blouse and a peasant skirt. Her arms were upraised and she seemed to be pleading, but he could not make out the words.

Then he was thrown on the rear floor of the car and the door slammed shut.

53

THE PURSER LOOKED AT the two tourists weaving up
the boarding ramp in frank amusement. They were an outlandish
pair. The female was dressed in a loose-fitting, ankle-length
sundress, and to the Russian purser's creative eye, she could have
passed for a rainbowed sack of Ukrainian potatoes. He couldn't
quite make out her face because it was partially obscured by a
wide-brimmed straw hat, tied around the chin by a silk scarf, but he
imagined if it was revealed it would break his watch crystal.

The man who appeared to be her husband was drunk. He reeled
onto the deck smelling of cheap bourbon, and laughed constantly.
Dressed in a loud flowered skirt and white duck pants, he leered at
his ugly wife and whispered gibberish in her ear. He noticed the
purser and raised his arm in a comical salute.

"Hi-ho, Captain," he said with a slack grin.

"I am not the captain. My name is Peter Kolodno. I am the
purser. How can I help you?"

"I'm Charlie Gruber and this is my wife, Zelda. We bought
tickets here in San Salvador."

He handed a packet to the purser, who studied them carefully for
a few moments.

"Welcome aboard the *Leonid Andreyev*," said the purser officially. "I regret that we do not have our usual hospitality festivities
to greet new passengers, but you've joined us rather late in the
cruise."

"We were sailing on a windjammer when the dumb helmsman

307

ran us onto a reef," the man called Gruber babbled. "My little woman and I near drowned. Couldn't see going back home to Sioux Falls early. So we're finishing our vacation on your boat. Besides, my wife turns on to Greeks."

"This is a Russian ship," the purser explained patiently.

"No kidding?"

"Yes, sir, the *Leonid Andreyev*'s home port is Sevastopol."

"You don't say. Where is that?"

"The Black Sea," the purser said, maintaining an air of politeness.

"Sounds polluted."

The purser was at a loss as to how America ever became a superpower with citizens such as these. He checked his passenger list and then nodded. "Your cabin is number thirty-four, on the Gorki deck. I'll have a steward show you the way."

"You're all right, pal," Gruber said, shaking his hand.

As the steward led the Grubers to their cabin, the purser looked down at his palm. Charlie Gruber had tipped him a twenty-five-cent piece.

As soon as the steward deposited their luggage and closed the door, Giordino threw off his wig and rubbed the lip gloss from his mouth. "God, Zelda Gruber! How am I ever going to live this one down?"

"I still say you should have taped a couple of grapefruit to your chest," Pitt said, laughing.

"I prefer the flat look. That way I don't stand out."

"Probably a good thing. There's not enough room in here for the four of us."

Giordino waved his arms around the small confines of the windowless cabin. "Talk about a discount excursion. I've been in bigger phone booths. Feel the vibration? We must be next to the engine."

"I requested the cheap accommodations so we could be on a lower deck," Pitt explained. "We're less visible down here, and closer to the working areas of the ship."

"You think Loren might be locked up somewhere below?"

"If she saw something or someone she wasn't supposed to, the Russians wouldn't keep her where she might contact other passengers."

"On the other hand, this could be a false alarm."

"We'll soon know," Pitt said.

"How shall we work it?" Giordino asked.

"I'll wander the crew's quarters. You check the passenger list in the purser's office for Loren's cabin. Then see if she's in it."

Giordino grinned impishly. "What shall I wear?"

"Go as yourself. Zelda we'll keep in reserve."

A minute after eight P.M. the *Leonid Andreyev* eased away from the dock. The engines beat softly as the bow came around. The sandy arms of San Salvador's harbor slid past as the ship entered the sea and sailed into a fiery sunset.

The lights flashed on and sparkled across the water like fireworks as the ship came alive with laughter and the music of two different orchestras. Passengers changed from shorts and slacks to suits and gowns, and lingered in the main dining room or perched in one of the several cocktail lounges.

Al Giordino, dressed in a formal tux, strutted along the corridor outside the penthouse suites as though he owned them. Stopping at a door, he looked around. A steward was approaching behind him with a tray.

Giordino stepped across to an opposite door marked MASSAGE ROOM and knocked.

"The masseuse goes off duty at six o'clock, sir," said the steward.

Giordino smiled. "I thought I'd make an appointment for tomorrow."

"I'll be glad to take care of that for you, sir. What time would be convenient?"

"How about noon?"

"I'll see to it," said the steward, his arm beginning to sag under the weight of the tray. "Your name and cabin?"

"O'Callaghan, cabin twenty-two, the Tolstoy deck," Giordino said. "Thank you. I appreciate it."

Then he turned and walked back to the passenger lift. He pushed the "down" button so it would ring and then glanced along the corridor. The steward balanced the tray and knocked lightly on a door two suites beyond Loren's. Giordino couldn't see who responded, but he heard a woman's voice invite the steward inside.

Without wasting a second, Giordino rushed to Loren's suite, crudely forced in the door with a well-aimed kick near the lock and entered. The rooms were dark and he switched on the lights. Everything was pin neat and luxurious with no hint of an occupant.

He didn't find Loren's clothes in the closet. He didn't find any luggage or evidence that she had ever been there. He combed every square foot carefully and slowly, room by room. He peered under the furniture and behind the drapes. He ran his hands over the carpets and under chair cushions. He even checked the bathtub and shower for pubic hairs.

Nothing.

But not quite nothing. A woman's presence lingers in a room after she leaves it. Giordino sniffed the air. A very slight whiff of perfume caught his nostrils. He couldn't have distinguished Chanel No. 5 from bath cologne, but this aroma had the delicate fragrance of a flower. He tried to identify it, yet it hung just beyond his reach.

He rubbed soap on the wooden splinter that broke off when he kicked in the door and pressed it into place. A poor glue job, he thought, but enough to hold for a few openings in case the suite was checked again by the crew before the ship docked back in Miami.

Then he snapped the lock, turned off the light and left.

Pitt suffered hunger pangs as he dropped down a tunnel ladder toward the engine room. He hadn't eaten since Washington, and the growls from his stomach seemed to echo inside the narrow steel access tube. He wished he was seated in the dining room putting away the delicacies from the gourmet menu. Suddenly he brushed away all thought of food as he detected voices rising from the compartment below.

He crouched against the ladder and gazed past his feet. A man's shoulder showed no more than four feet below him. Then the top of a head with stringy, unkempt blond hair moved into view. The crewman said a few words in Russian to someone else. There was a muffled reply followed by the sound of footsteps on a metal grating. After three minutes, the head moved away and Pitt heard the thin clap of a locker door closing. Then footsteps again and silence.

Pitt swung around the ladder, inserted his feet and calves through a rung and hung upside down, his eyes peering under the lip of the tunnel.

He found himself with an inverted view of the engine room crew's locker room. It was temporarily vacant. Quickly he climbed down and went through the lockers until he found a pair of grease-stained coveralls that were a reasonable fit. He also took a cap that was two sizes too large and pulled it over his forehead. Now he was ready to wander the working areas.

His next problem was that he only knew about twenty words of Russian, and most of them had to do with ordering dinner in a restaurant.

Nearly a half-hour passed before Pitt meandered into the main crew's quarters in the bow section of the ship. Occasionally he passed a cook from one of the kitchens, a porter pushing a cart loaded with liquor for the cocktail bars, or a cabin maid coming off duty. None gave him a second look except an officer who threw a distasteful glance at his grimy attire.

By a fortunate accident, he stumbled on the crew's laundry room. A round-face girl looked up at him across a counter and asked him something in Russian.

He shrugged and replied, "Nyet."

Bundles of washed uniforms lay neatly stacked on a long table. It occurred to him that the laundry-room girl had asked him which bundle was his. He studied them for a few moments and finally pointed to one containing three neatly folded white coveralls like the dirty pair he wore. By changing into clean ones he could have the run of the entire ship, pretending to be a crewman from the engine room on a maintenance assignment.

The girl laid the bundle on the counter and asked him another question.

His mind raced to dredge up something from his limited Russian vocabulary. Finally he mumbled, *"Yest' li u vas sosiski."*

The girl gave him an odd look indeed but handed him the bundle, making him sign for it, which he did in an illegible scrawl. Pitt was relieved to see that her eyes reflected curiosity rather than suspicion.

It was only after he found an empty cabin and switched coveralls that it dawned on him that he'd asked the laundry girl for frankfurters.

After pausing at a bulletin board to remove a diagram showing the compartments on the decks of the *Leonid Andreyev*, he calmly spent the next five hours browsing around the lower hull of the ship. Detecting no clue to Loren's presence, he returned to his cabin and found Giordino had thoughtfully ordered him a meal.

"Anything?" Giordino asked, pouring two glasses from a bottle of Russian champagne.

"Not a trace," said Pitt wearily. "We celebrating?"

"Allow me a little class in this dungeon."

"You search her suite?"

Giordino nodded. "What kind of perfume does Loren wear?"

Pitt stared at the bubbles rising from the glass for a moment. "A French name; I can't recall it. Why do you ask?"

"Have an aroma like a flower?"

"Lilac . . . no, honeysuckle. Yes, honeysuckle."

"Her suite was wiped clean. The Russians made it look like she'd never been there, but I could still smell her scent."

Pitt drained the champagne glass and poured another without speaking.

"We have to face the possibility they killed her," Giordino said matter-of-factly.

"Then why hide her clothes and luggage? They can't claim she fell overboard with all her belongings."

"The crew could have stored them below and are waiting for an opportune moment, like rough weather, to announce the tragic news. Sorry, Dirk," Giordino added, no apology in his voice. "We've got to look at every angle, good or bad."

"Loren is alive and onboard this ship somewhere," Pitt said steadfastly. "And maybe Moran and Larimer too."

"You're taking a lot for granted."

"Loren is a smart girl. She didn't ask Sally Lindemann to locate Speaker of the House Moran unless she had a damn good reason. Sally claims Moran and Senator Larimer have both mysteriously dropped from sight. Now Loren is missing too. What impression do you get?"

"You make a good sales pitch, but what's behind it?"

Pitt shrugged negatively. "I flatly don't know. Only a crazy idea this might somehow mix with Bougainville Maritime and the loss of the *Eagle.*"

Giordino was silent, thinking it over. "Yes," he said slowly, "a crazy idea, but one that makes a lot of circumstantial sense. Where do you want me to start?"

"Put on your Zelda getup and walk past every cabin on the ship. If Loren or the others are held prisoner inside, there will be a security guard posted outside the door."

"And that's the giveaway," said Giordino. "Where will you be?"

Pitt laid out the diagram of the ship on his bunk. "Some of the crew are quartered in the stern. I'll scrounge there." He folded up the diagram and shoved it in the pocket of the coveralls. "We'd best get started. There isn't much time."

"At least we have until the day after tomorrow, when the *Leonid Andreyev* docks in Jamaica."

"No such luxury," said Pitt. "Study a nautical chart of the Caribbean and you'll see that about this time tomorrow afternoon we'll be cruising within sight of the Cuban coast."

Giordino nodded in understanding. "A golden opportunity to

transfer Loren and others off the ship where they can't be touched.''

"The nasty part is they may not stay on Cuban soil any longer than it takes to put them on a plane for Moscow."

Giordino considered that for a moment and then went over to his suitcase, removed the mangy wig and slipped it over his curly head. Then he peered in a mirror and made a hideous face.

"Well, Zelda," he said sourly, "let's go walk the decks and see who we can pick up."

54

THE PRESIDENT WENT ON NATIONAL TELEVISION that same evening to reveal his meeting and accord with President Antonov of the Soviet Union. In his twenty-three-minute address, he briefly outlined his programs to aid the Communist countries. He also stated his intention to abolish the barriers and restrictions on purchases of American high technology by the Russians. Never once was Congress mentioned. He spoke of the Eastern bloc trade agreements as though they were already budgeted and set in motion. He closed by promising that his next task would be to throw his energies behind a war to reduce the national crime rate.

The ensuing uproar in government circles swept all other news before it. Curtis Mayo and other network commentators broadcast scathing attacks on the President for overstepping the limits of his authority. Specters of an imperial Presidency were raised.

Congressional leaders who had remained in Washington during the recess launched a telephone campaign encouraging their fellow lawmakers who were vacationing or campaigning in their home states to return to the capital to meet in emergency session. House and Senate members, acting without the counsel of their majority leaders, Moran and Larimer, who could not be reached, solidly closed ranks against the President in a bipartisan flood.

Dan Fawcett burst into the Oval Office the next morning, anguish written on his face. "Good God, Mr. President, you can't do this!"

315

The President looked up calmly. "You're referring to my talk last night?"

"Yes, sir, I am," Fawcett said emotionally. "You as good as went on record as saying you were proceeding with your aid programs without congressional approval."

"Is that what it sounded like?"

"It did."

"Good," said the President, thumping his hand on the desk. "Because that's exactly what I intend to do."

Fawcett was astonished. "Not under the Constitution. Executive privilege does not extend that far—"

"God damn it, don't try and tell me how to run the Presidency," the President shouted, suddenly furious. "I'm through begging and compromising with those conceited hypocrites on the Hill. The only way I'm going to get anything done, by God, is to put on the gloves and start swinging."

"You're setting out on a dangerous course. They'll band together to freeze out every issue you put before them."

"No, they won't!" the President shouted, rising to his feet and coming around the desk to face Fawcett. "Congress will not have a chance to upset my plans."

Fawcett could only look at him in shock and horror. "You can't stop them. They're gathering now, flying in from every state to hold an emergency session to block you."

"If they think that," the President said in a morbid voice Fawcett scarcely recognized, "they're in for a big surprise."

The early-morning traffic was spreading thin when three military convoys flowed into the city from different directions. One Army Special Counterterrorist Detachment from Fort Belvoir moved north along Anacostia Freeway while another from Fort Meade came down the Baltimore and Washington Parkway to the south. At the same moment, a Critical Operation Force attached to the Marine Corps base at Quantico advanced over the Rochambeau Bridge from the west.

As the long lines of five-ton personnel carriers converged on the

Federal Center, a flight of tilt-rotored assault transports settled onto the grass of the mall in front of the Capitol reflecting pool and disgorged their cargo of crack Marine field troops from Camp Lejeune, North Carolina. The two-thousand-man task force was made up of United Emergency Response teams that were on twenty-four-hour alert.

As they deployed around the federal buildings, they quickly cleared everyone out of the Capitol chambers, the House and Senate offices. Then they took up their positions and sealed off all entrances.

At first the bewildered lawmakers and their aides thought it was a building evacuation due to a terrorist bomb threat. The only other explanation was an unannounced military exercise. When they learned the entire seat of American government was shut down by order of the President, they stood shocked and outraged, conferring in heated indignation in small groups on the grounds east of the Capitol building. Lyndon Johnson had once threatened to lock out Congress, but no one could believe it was actually happening.

Arguments and demands went unheard by the purposeful-looking men dressed in field camouflage and holding M-20 automatic rifles and riot guns. One senator, nationally recognized for his liberal stands, tried to break through the cordon and was dragged back to the street by two grim-faced Marines.

The troops did not surround or close the executive departments or independent agencies. For most of the federal offices it was business as usual. The streets were kept open and traffic directed in an efficient manner local citizens found downright enjoyable.

The press and television media poured onto the Capitol grounds. The grass was nearly buried under a blanket of cables and electronic equipment. Interviews before cameras became so hectic and crowded the senators and congressmen had to stand in line to voice their objections to the President's unprecedented action.

Surprisingly, reaction from most Americans across the country was one of amusement rather than distaste. They sat in front of their television screens and viewed the event as if it were a circus. The consensus was that the President was throwing a temporary scare into Congress and would order the troops removed in a day or two.

At the State Department, Oates huddled with Emmett, Brogan and Mercier. The atmosphere was heavy with a sense of indecision and suspense.

"The President's a damned fool if he thinks he's more important than the constitutional government," said Oates.

Emmett stared steadily at Mercier. "I can't see why you didn't suspect what was going on."

"He shut me out completely," said Mercier, his expression sheepish. "He never offered the slightest clue of what was on his mind."

"Surely Jesse Simmons and General Metcalf weren't a party to it," Oates wondered aloud.

Brogan shook his head. "My Pentagon sources say Jesse Simmons flatly refused."

"Why didn't he warn us?" asked Emmett.

"After Simmons told the President in no uncertain terms that he was off base, the roof fell in. A military security guard detail escorted him home, where he was placed under house arrest."

"Jesus," muttered Oates in exasperation. "It gets worse by the minute."

"What about General Metcalf?" asked Mercier.

"I'm sure he voiced his objections," Brogan answered. "But Clayton Metcalf is a spit-and-polish soldier who's duty-bound to carry out the orders of his commander in chief. He and the President are old, close friends. Metcalf undoubtedly feels his loyalty is to the man who appointed him to be Chief of Staff, and not Congress."

Oates's fingers swept an imaginary dust speck off the desktop. "The President disappears for ten days and after his return falls off the deep end."

"Huckleberry Finn," Brogan said slowly.

"Judging from the President's behavioral patterns over the past twenty-four hours," Mercier said thoughtfully, "the evidence looks pretty conclusive."

"Has Dr. Lugovoy surfaced yet?" Oates asked.

Emmett shook his head. "He's still missing."

"We've obtained reports from our people inside Russia on the doctor," Brogan elucidated. "His specialty for the last fifteen years has been mind transfer. Soviet intelligence ministries have provided enormous funding for the research. Hundreds of Jews and other dissidents who vanished inside KGB-operated mental institutions were his guinea pigs. And he claims to have made a breakthrough in thought interpretation and control."

"Do we have such a project in progress?" Oates inquired.

Brogan nodded. "Ours is code-named 'Fathom,' which is working along the same lines."

Oates held his head in his hands for a moment, then turned to Emmett. "You still haven't a lead on Vince Margolin, Larimer and Moran?"

Emmett looked embarrassed. "I regret to say their whereabouts is still unknown."

"Do you think Lugovoy has performed the mind-transfer experiment on them too?"

"I don't believe so," Emmett answered. "If I were in the Russians' shoes, I'd keep them in reserve in the event the President doesn't respond to instructions as programmed."

"His mind could slip out of their grasp and react unpredictably," Brogan added. "Fooling around with the brain is not an exact science. There's no way of telling what he'll do next."

"Congress isn't waiting to find out," said Mercier. "They're out hustling for a place to convene so they can start impeachment proceedings."

"The President knows that, and he isn't stupid," Oates responded. "Every time the House and Senate members gather for a session, he'll send in troops to break it up. With the armed forces behind him, it's a no-win situation."

"Considering the President is literally being told what to do by an unfriendly foreign power, Metcalf and the other Joint Chiefs can't continue giving him their support," said Mercier.

"Metcalf refuses to act until we produce absolute proof of mind control," Emmett added. "But I suspect he's only waiting for a ripe excuse to throw his lot in with Congress."

Brogan looked concerned. "Let's hope he doesn't make his move too late."

"So the situation boils down to the four of us devising a way to neutralize the President," Oates mused.

"Have you driven past the White House today?" Mercier asked.

Oates shook his head. "No. Why?"

"Looks like an armed camp. The military is crawling over every inch of the grounds. Word has it the President can't be reached by anybody. I doubt even you, Mr. Secretary, could walk past the front door."

Brogan thought a moment. "Dan Fawcett is still on the inside."

"I talked to him over the phone," Mercier said. "He presented his opposition to the President's actions a bit too strongly. I gather he's now persona non grata in the Oval Office."

"We need someone who has the President's trust."

"Oscar Lucas," Emmett said.

"Good thinking," Oates snapped, looking up. "As head of the Secret Service, he's got the run of the place."

"Someone will have to brief Dan and Oscar face to face," Emmett advised.

"I'll handle it," Brogan volunteered.

"You have a plan?" asked Oates.

"Not off the top of my head, but my people will come up with something."

"Better be good," said Emmett seriously, "if we're to avoid the worst fear of our Founding Fathers."

"And what was that?" asked Oates.

"The unthinkable," replied Emmett. "A dictator in the White House."

55 _____

LOREN WAS SWEATING. She had never sweated so much in her life. Her evening gown was damp and plastered against her body like a second skin. The little windowless cell felt like a sauna and it was an effort just to breathe. A toilet and a bunk were her only creature comforts, and a dim bulb attached to the ceiling in a small cage glowed continuously. The ventilators, she was certain, were turned off to increase her discomfort.

When she was brought to the ship's brig, she had seen no sign of the man she thought might be Alan Moran. No food or water had been given to her since the crew locked her up, and hunger pangs were gnawing at her stomach. No one had even visited her, and she began to wonder if Captain Pokofsky meant to keep her in solitary confinement until she wasted away.

At last she decided to abandon her attempt at vanity and removed her clinging dress. She began to do stretching exercises to pass the time.

Suddenly she heard the muted sound of footsteps outside in the passageway. Muffled voices spoke in a brief conversation, and then the door was unlatched and swung open.

Loren snatched her dress off the bunk and held it in front of her, shrinking back into a corner of the cell.

A man ducked his head as he passed through the small doorway. He was turned out in a cheap business suit that looked to her several decades out of fashion.

"Congresswoman Smith, please forgive the condition I was forced to put you in."

"No, I don't think I will," she said defiantly. "Who are you?"

"My name is Paul Suvorov. I represent the Soviet government."

Contempt flooded into Loren's voice. "Is this an example of the way Communists treat visiting American VIP's?"

"Not under ordinary circumstances, but you gave us no choice."

"Please explain," she demanded, glaring at him.

He gave her an uncertain look. "I believe you know."

"Why don't you refresh my memory."

He paused to light a cigarette, carelessly tossing the match in the toilet. "The other evening when the helicopter arrived, Captain Pokofsky's first officer observed you standing very close to the landing area."

"So were several other passengers," Loren snapped icily.

"Yes, but they were too far away to see a familiar face."

"And you think I wasn't."

"Why can't you be reasonable, Congresswoman. Surely you can't deny you recognized your own colleagues."

"I don't know what you mean."

"Congressman Alan Moran and Senator Marcus Larimer," he said, closely watching her reaction.

Loren's eyes widened and suddenly she began to shiver in spite of the stifling heat. For the first time since she was made a prisoner, indignation was replaced by despair.

"Moran and Larimer, they're both here too?"

He nodded. "In the next cell."

"This must be an insane joke," she said, stunned.

"No joke," Suvorov said, smiling. "They are guests of the KGB, same as you."

Loren shook her head, unbelieving. Life didn't happen this way, she told herself, except in nightmares. She felt reality drifting slowly from her grasp.

"I have diplomatic immunity," she said. "I demand to be released."

"You carry no influence, not here on board the *Leonid Andreyev*," said Suvorov in a cold, disinterested voice.

"When my government hears of this—"

"They won't," he interrupted. "When the ship leaves Jamaica on its return voyage to Miami, Captain Pokofsky will announce with deep regret and sympathy that Congresswoman Loren Smith was lost overboard and presumed drowned."

A numbing hopelessness seized Loren. "What will happen to Moran and Larimer?"

"I'm taking them to Russia."

"But you're going to kill me," she said, more as a statement than a question.

"They represent senior members of your government. Their knowledge will prove quite useful once they're persuaded to provide it. You, I'm sorry to say, are not worth the risk."

Loren almost said, As a member of the House Armed Services Committee, I know as much as they do, but she recognized the trap in time and remained silent.

Suvorov's eyes narrowed. He reached over and tore the dress from in front of her and casually tossed it outside the doorway. "Very nice," he said. "Perhaps if we were to negotiate, I might find a reason to take you with me to Moscow."

"The most pathetic trick in the world," Loren spat contemptuously. "You're not even original."

He took a step forward, his hand lashing out and slapping her on the face. She staggered back against the steel bulkhead and sagged to her knees, staring up at him, her eyes blazing with fear and loathing.

He grasped her by the hair and tilted her head back. The conversational politeness disappeared from his voice. "I always wondered what it would be like to screw a high-ranking capitalist bitch."

Loren's answer was to swiftly reach out and grab him in the groin, squeezing with all her might.

Suvorov gasped in agony and swung his fist, connecting with her left cheekbone just below the eye. Loren fell sideways into the corner while Suvorov clutched himself and paced the tiny cubicle like a mad animal until the stabbing ache subsided. Then he brutally picked her up and threw her onto the bunk.

He leaned over her and ripped off her underclothes. "You rotten bitch!" he snarled. "I'm going to make you wish for a quick death."

Tears of agony coursed from Loren's eyes as she teetered on the verge of unconsciousness. Vaguely, through the mist of pain, she could see Suvorov slowly take off his belt and wrap it around his hand, leaving the buckle free and swinging. She tried to tense her body for the coming blow as his arm lifted upward, but she was too weak.

Suddenly Suvorov seemed to grow a third arm. It snaked over his right shoulder and then locked around his neck. The belt dropped to the deck and his body stiffened.

Shock swept across Suvorov's face, the shock of disbelief, then horror at the full realization of what was happening, and the torment as his windpipe was slowly and mercilessly crushed and his breathing choked off. He struggled against the relentless pressure, throwing himself around the cell, but the arm remained. In a sudden flash of certainty, he knew he would never live to feel the pressure ease. The terror and the lack of oxygen contorted his face and turned it reddish-blue. His starving lungs struggled for air and his arms flailed in frantic madness.

Loren tried to raise her hands over her face to shut out the horrible sight, but they refused to respond. She could only sit frozen and watch in morbid fascination as the life seeped out of Suvorov; watch his violent thrashings subside until finally the eyes bulged from their sockets and he went limp. He hung there several seconds, supported by the ghostly arm until it pulled away from his neck and he fell on the deck in a heap.

Another figure loomed in Suvorov's place, standing inside the cell's doorway, and Loren found herself staring into a friendly face with deep green eyes and a faint crooked grin.

"Just between you and me," said Pitt, "I've never believed that rot about getting there is half the fun."

56

NOON, A BRILLIANT AZURE SKY with small cottonball clouds nudged by a gentle westerly breeze, found the *Leonid Andreyev* passing within eighteen miles of Cabo Maisí, the easternmost tip of Cuba. Many of the passengers sunbathing around the swimming pools took no notice of the palm-lined coastline on the horizon. To them it was just another one of the hundred islands they had passed since leaving Florida.

On the bridge, Captain Pokofsky stood with binoculars to his eyes. He was observing a small powerboat that was circling from the land on his starboard quarter. She was old, her bow nearly straight up and down, and her hull was painted black. The topsides were varnished mahogany, and the name *Pilar* was lettered in gold across her transom. She looked an immaculately kept museum piece. On the ensign staff at her stern she flew the American stars and stripes in the inverted position of distress.

Pokofsky walked over to the automated ship's control console and pressed the "slow speed" switch. Almost immediately he could feel the engines reduce revolutions. Then, waiting a few minutes until the ship had slowed to a crawl, he leaned over and pressed the lever for "all stop."

He was about to walk out on the bridge wing when his first officer came hurrying up the companionway from the deck below.

"Captain," he said, catching his breath. "I've just come from the brig area. The prisoners are gone."

Pokofsky straightened. "Gone? You mean escaped?"

"Yes, sir. I was on a routine inspection when I found the two security guards unconscious and locked up in one of the cells. The KGB agent is dead."

"Paul Suvorov was killed?"

The first officer nodded. "From all appearances, he was strangled."

"Why didn't you call me immediately over the ship's phone?"

"I thought it best to tell you in person."

"You're right, of course," Pokofsky admitted. "This couldn't have come at a worse time. Our Cuban security people are arriving to transport the prisoners to shore."

"If you can stall them, I'm confident a search effort will quickly turn up the Americans."

Pokofsky stared through the doorway at the closing boat. "They'll wait," he said confidently. "Our captives are too important to leave onboard."

"There is one other thing, sir," said the first officer. "The Americans must have received help."

"They didn't break out by themselves?" Pokofsky asked in surprise.

"Not possible. Two old men in a weakened condition and one woman could never have overpowered two security people and murdered a professional KGB man."

"Damn!" Pokofsky cursed. He rammed a fist into a palm in exasperation, compounded equally by anxiety and anger. "This complicates matters."

"Could the CIA have sneaked onboard?"

"I hardly think so. If the United States government remotely suspected their government leaders were held on the *Leonid Andreyev*, their Navy would be converging on us like mad bears. See for yourself; no ships, no aircraft, and the Guantánamo Bay naval station is only forty miles away."

"Then who?" asked the first officer. "Certainly none of our crew."

"It can only be a passenger," Pokofsky surmised. He fell silent, thinking. Utter stillness fell on the bridge. At last he looked up and began issuing orders. "Collect every available officer and form five-man search parties. Divide up the ship in sections from keel to sun deck. Alert the security guards and enlist the stewards. If questioned by the passengers, make up a believable pretext for entering their cabins. Changing the bed linen, repairing plumbing, inspecting fire equipment, any story that fits the situation. Say or do nothing that will cause suspicion among the passengers or set them to asking embarrassing questions. Be as subtle as possible and refrain from violence, but recapture the Smith woman and the two men quickly."

"What about Suvorov's body?"

Pokofsky didn't hesitate. "Arrange a fitting tribute to our comrade from the KGB," he said sarcastically. "As soon as it's dark, throw him overboard with the garbage."

"Yes, sir," the first officer acknowledged with a smile and hurried away.

Pokofsky picked up a bullhorn from a bulkhead rack and stepped out on the bridge wing. The small pleasure boat was drifting about fifty yards away.

"Are you in distress?" he asked, his voice booming over the water.

A man with a squat body and the skin tone of an old wallet cupped his hands to his mouth and shouted back. "We have people who are quite ill. I suspect ptomaine poisoning. May we come aboard and use your medical facilities?"

"By all means," Pokofsky replied. "Come alongside. I'll drop the gangway."

Pitt watched the mini-drama with interest, seeing through the sham. Two men and a woman struggled up the metal stairway, clutching their midriffs and pretending they were in the throes of abdominal agony. He rated them two stars for their performance.

After a suitable length of time for pseudodoctoring, he reasoned, Loren, Moran and Larimer would have taken their places in the pleasure boat. He also knew full well the captain would not resume the cruise until the ship was scoured and the congressmen apprehended.

He left the railing and mingled with the other passengers, who soon returned to their deck chairs and tables around the swimming pools and cocktail bars. He took the elevator down to his deck. As the doors opened and he stepped out into the passageway, he rubbed shoulders with a steward who was entering.

Pitt idly noticed the steward was Asian, probably Mongolian if he was serving on a Russian ship. He brushed past and continued to his cabin.

The steward stared at Pitt curiously. Then his expression turned to blank astonishment as he watched Pitt walk away. He was still standing there gawking when the door closed and the elevator rose without him.

Pitt rounded the corner of the passageway and spied a ship's officer with several crewmen waiting outside a cabin three down and across from his. None of them displayed their usual shipboard conviviality. Their expressions looked deadly earnest. He fished in his pocket for the cabin key while watching out of the corner of one eye. In a few moments, a stewardess came out and said a few words in Russian to the officer and shook her head. Then they moved toward the next cabin and knocked.

Pitt quickly entered and closed the door. The tiny enclosure looked like a scene out of a Marx Brothers movie. Loren was perched on the upper pullman bunk while Moran and Larimer shared the lower. All three were ravenously attacking a tray of hors d'oeuvres that Giordino had smuggled from the dining-room buffet table.

Giordino, seated on a small chair, half in the bathroom, threw an offhand wave. "See anything interesting?"

"The Cuban connection arrived," Pitt answered. "They're drifting alongside, standing by to exchange passengers."

"The bastards will have a long wait," said Giordino.

"Try four minutes. That's how long before we'll all be chained and tossed on a boat bound for Havana."

"They can't help but find us," Larimer uttered in a hollow

328

voice. Pitt had seen many such washed-out men—the waxen skin, the eyes that once blazed with authority now empty, the vagrant thoughts. Despite his age and long years of self-indulgent living amid the political arena, Larimer was still a powerfully built man. But the heart and circulation were no longer up to the stress and dangers of staying alive in a hostile situation. Pitt didn't require an internship to recognize a man who was in dire need of medical treatment.

"A Russian search party is just across the hall," Pitt explained.

"We can't let them imprison us again," Moran shouted, springing to his feet and looking around wildly. "We must run!"

"You wouldn't make the elevator," snapped Pitt, grabbing him by the arm as he would a child throwing a tantrum. He didn't much care for Moran. The Speaker of the House struck him as an oily weasel.

"There's no place to hide," said Loren, her voice not quite steady.

Pitt didn't answer her but brushed past Giordino and went into the bathroom. He pulled back the shower curtain and turned on the hot water. Less than a minute later clouds of steam billowed into the cramped quarters.

"Okay," Pitt directed, "everybody in the shower."

Nobody moved. They all stared at him, standing wraithlike in the mist-filled doorway, as though he was from another earth.

"Move!" he said sharply. "They'll be here any second."

Giordino shook his head in bewilderment. "How are you going to get three people in that stall shower? It's hardly big enough for one."

"Get your wig on. You're going in too."

"The four of us?" Loren muttered incredulously.

"Either that or a free trip to Moscow. Besides, college kids cram entire fraternities in phone booths all the time."

Giordino slipped the wig over his head as Pitt re-entered the bathroom and turned the water to lukewarm. He placed a trembling Moran in a squatting position between Giordino's legs. Larimer pressed his heavy body against the far corner of the stall as Loren climbed on Giordino's back. At last they were jammed awkwardly into the stall, drenched by the flow from the shower head. Pitt was in the act of turning on the hot water in the sink to increase the steam cloud when he heard a knock on the door.

He hurried over and opened it so there was no suspicious hesitation. The ship's first officer bowed slightly and smiled.

"Mr. Gruber, is it? Very sorry to bother you, but we're making a routine inspection of the fire sprinklers. Do you mind if we enter?"

"Why, sure," Pitt said obligingly. "No problem with me, but my wife's in the shower."

The officer nodded to the stewardess who eased past Pitt and made a show of checking the overhead sprinkler heads. Then she pointed to the bathroom door. "May I?"

"Go on in," said Pitt good-naturedly. "She won't mind."

The stewardess opened the door and was enveloped in a cloud of steam. Pitt went over and leaned in the bathroom. "Hey, luv, our steward lady wants to check the fire sprinkler. All right with you?"

As the cloud began dissipating through the door, the stewardess saw a huge stringy mop of hair and a pair of heavy browed eyes peeking around the shower curtain.

"All right by me," came Loren's voice. "And could you bring us a couple of extra towels when you think of it?"

The stewardess simply nodded and said, "I'll be back with the towels shortly."

Pitt casually munched on a canapé and offered one to the first officer, who gave a polite shake of his head.

"Does my heart good to see you people so interested in the safety of the passengers," said Pitt.

"Merely doing our duty," said the first officer, looking curiously at the half-eaten stack of hors d'oeuvres. "I see you also enjoy our shipboard cuisine."

"My wife and I love appetizers," said Pitt. "We'd rather eat these than a main course."

The stewardess came out of the bathroom and said something to the first officer. The only word Pitt made out was *"nyet."*

"Sorry to have troubled you," said the first officer courteously.

"Any time," replied Pitt.

As soon as the door lock clicked, Pitt rushed to the bathroom. "Everybody stay just as you are," he ordered. "Don't move." Then he reclined on a bunk and stuffed his mouth with caviar on thin toast.

Two minutes later the door suddenly popped open and the stewardess burst through like a bulldozer, her eyes darting around the cabin.

"Can I help you?" Pitt mumbled with a full mouth.

"I brought the towels," she said.

"Just throw them on the bathroom sink," Pitt said indifferently.

She did precisely that and left the cabin, throwing Pitt a smile that was genuine and devoid of any suspicion.

He waited another two minutes, then opened the door a crack and peered into the passageway. The search crew was entering a cabin near the end of the passageway. He returned to the bathroom, reached in and turned off the water.

Whoever coined the phrase They look like drowned rats must have had the poor souls huddled together in that pocket-sized shower in mind. Their fingertips were beginning to shrivel and all their clothing was soaked through.

Giordino came out first and hurled his sopping wig in the sink. Loren climbed off his back and immediately began drying her hair. Pitt helped Moran to his feet and half carried Larimer to a bunk.

"A wise move," said Pitt to Loren, kissing her on the nape of the neck. "Asking for more towels."

"It struck me as the thing to do."

"Are we safe now?" asked Moran. "Will they be back?"

"We won't be in the clear till we're off the ship," said Pitt. "And we can count on their paying an encore visit. When they come up dry on this search, they'll redouble their efforts for a second."

"Got any more brilliant escape tricks up your sleeve, Houdini?" asked Giordino.

"Yes," Pitt replied, sure as the devil. "As a matter of fact, I do."

331

57

THE SECOND ENGINEER MOVED ALONG a catwalk between the massive fuel tanks that towered two decks above him. He was running a routine maintenance check for any trace of leakage in the pipes that transferred the oil to the boilers that provided steam for the *Leonid Andreyev*'s 27,000-horsepower turbines.

He whistled to himself, his only accompaniment coming from the hum of the turbo-generators beyond the forward bulkhead. Every so often he wiped a rag around a pipe fitting or valve, nodding in satisfaction when it came away clean.

Suddenly he stopped and cocked an ear. The sound of metal striking against metal came from a narrow walkway leading off to his right. Curious, he walked slowly, quietly along the dimly lit access. At the end, where the walkway turned and passed between the fuel tanks and the inner plates of the hull, he paused and peered into the gloom.

A figure in a steward's uniform appeared to be attaching something to the side of the fuel tank. The second engineer approached, stepping softly, until he was only ten feet away.

"What are you doing here?" he demanded.

The steward slowly turned and straightened. The engineer could see he was Oriental. The white uniform was soiled with grime, and a seaman's duffel bag lay open behind him on the walkway. The steward flashed a wide smile and made no effort to reply.

The engineer moved a few steps closer. "You're not supposed to be here. This area is off limits to the passenger service crew."

Still no answer.

Then the engineer noticed a strange misshapen lump pressed against the side of the fuel tank. Two strands of copper wire ran from it to a clock mechanism beside the duffel bag.

"A bomb!" he blurted in shock. "You're planting a damn bomb!"

He swung around and began running wildly down the walkway, shouting. He'd taken no more than five steps when the narrow steel confines echoed with a noise like twin handclaps in quick succession, and the hollow-point bullets from a silenced automatic tore into the back of his head.

The obligatory toasts were voiced and the glasses of iced vodka downed and quickly refilled. Pokofsky did the honors from the liquor cabinet in his cabin, avoiding the cold, piercing gaze of the man seated on a leather sofa.

Geidar Ombrikov, chief of the KGB residency in Havana, was not in a congenial mood. "Your report won't sit well with my superiors," he said. "An agent lost under your command will be considered a clear case of negligence."

"This is a cruise ship," Pokofsky said, his face reddening in resentment. "She was designed and placed in service for the purpose of bringing in hard Western currency for the Soviet treasury. We are not a floating headquarters for the Committee for State Security."

"Then how do you explain the ten agents our foreign directorate assigned onboard your vessel to monitor the conversations of the passengers?"

"I try not to think about it."

"You should," Ombrikov said in a threatening tone.

"I have enough to keep me busy running this ship," Pokofsky said quickly. "There aren't enough hours in my day to include intelligence gathering too."

"Still, you should have taken better precautions. If the American politicians escape and tell their story, the horrendous repercussions will have a disastrous effect on our foreign relations."

Pokofsky set his vodka on the liquor cabinet without touching it. "There is no place they can hide for long on this ship. They will be back in our hands inside the hour."

"I do hope so," said Ombrikov acidly. "Their Navy will begin to wonder why a Soviet cruise liner is drifting around off their precious Cuban base and send out a patrol."

"They wouldn't dare board the *Leonid Andreyev*."

"No, but my small pleasure boat is flying the United States flag. They won't hesitate to come aboard for an inspection."

"She's an interesting old boat," Pokofsky said, trying to change the subject. "Where did you find her?"

"A personal loan from our friend Castro," Ombrikov replied. "She used to belong to the author Ernest Hemingway."

"Yes, I've read four of his books—"

Pokofsky was interrupted by the sudden appearance of his first officer, who entered without knocking.

"My apologies for breaking in, Captain, but may I have a word in private with you?"

Pokofsky excused himself and stepped outside his cabin.

"What is it?"

"We failed to find them," the officer announced uneasily.

Pokofsky paused for some moments, lit a cigarette in defiance of his own regulations and gave his first officer a look of disapproval. "Then I suggest you search the ship again, more carefully this time. And take a closer look at the passengers wandering the decks. They may be hiding in the crowd."

His first officer nodded and hurried off. Pokofsky returned to his cabin.

"Problems?" Ombrikov asked.

Before Pokofsky could answer he felt a slight shudder run through the ship. He stood there curious for perhaps half a minute, tensed and alert, but nothing more seemed to happen.

The suddenly the *Leonid Andreyev* was rocked by a violent explosion that heeled her far over to starboard, flinging people off their feet and sending a convulsive shock wave throughout the ship. A great sheet of fire erupted from the port side of the hull, raining fiery steel debris and oil over the exposed decks. The blast reverberated over the water until it finally died away, leaving an unearthly silence in its wake and a solid column of black smoke that mushroomed into the sky.

What none of the seven hundred passengers and crew knew, what many of them would never come to learn, was that deep amidship the fuel tanks had detonated, blowing a gaping hole half above and half below the waterline, spraying a torrent of burning oil over the superstructure in blue and green flames, scarring the victims and blazing across the teak decks with the speed of a brushfire.

Almost instantly, the *Leonid Andreyev* was transformed from a luxurious cruise liner into a sinking fiery pyre.

Pitt stirred and wondered dully what had happened. For a full minute as the shock wore off he remained prone on the deck, where he'd been thrown by the force of the concussion, trying to orient himself. Slowly he rose to his hands and knees, then hoisted his aching body erect by grabbing the inner doorknob. Bruised but still functioning, nothing broken or out of joint, he turned to examine the others.

Giordino was partly crouched, partly lying across the threshold of the shower stall. The last thing he remembered was sitting in the cabin. He wore a surprised look in his eyes, but he appeared unhurt. Moran and Loren had fallen out of the bunks and were lying in the middle of the deck. They were both dazed and would carry a gang of black and blue marks for a week or two, but were otherwise uninjured.

Larimer was huddled in the far corner of the cabin. Pitt went over and gently lifted his head. There was an ugly welt rising above the senator's left temple and a trickle of blood dripped from a cut lip. He was unconscious but breathing easily. Pitt eased a pillow from the lower bunk under his head.

Giordino was the first to speak. "How is he?"

"Just knocked out," Pitt replied.

"What happened?" Loren murmured dazedly.

"An explosion," said Pitt. "Somewhere forward, probably in the engine room."

"The boilers?" Giordino speculated.

"Modern boilers are safety-designed not to blow."

"God," said Loren, "my ears are still ringing."

A strange expression came over Giordino's face. He took a coin out of his pocket and rolled it across the hard-carpeted deck. Instead of losing its momentum and circling until falling on one side, it maintained its speed across the cabin as though propelled by an unseen hand and clinked into the far bulkhead.

"The ship's listing," Giordino announced flatly.

Pitt went over and cracked the door. Already the passageway was filling with passengers stumbling out of their cabins and wandering aimlessly in bewilderment. "So much for plan B."

Loren gave him a quizzical look. "Plan B?"

"My idea to steal the boat from Cuba. I don't think we're going to find seats."

"What are you talking about?" Moran demanded. He rose unsteadily to his feet, holding on to a bunk chain for support. "A trick. It's a cheap trick to flush us out."

"Damned expensive trick if you ask me," Giordino said nastily. "The explosion must have seriously damaged the ship. She's obviously taking on water."

"Will we sink?" Moran asked anxiously.

Pitt ignored him and peered around the edge of the door again. Most of the passengers acted calm, but a few were beginning to shout and cry. As he watched, the passageway become clogged with people stupidly carrying armfuls of personal belongings and hastily packed suitcases. Then Pitt caught the smell of burning paint, quickly followed by the sight of a smoky wisp. He slammed the door and began tearing the blankets off the bunks and throwing them to Giordino.

"Hurry, soak these and any towels you can find in the shower!"

Giordino took one look at Pitt's dead-serious expression and did as he was told. Loren knelt and tried to lift Larimer's head and shoulders from the deck. The senator moaned and opened his eyes, looking up at Loren as if trying to recognize her. Moran cringed against the bulkhead, muttering to himself.

Pitt rudely pushed Loren aside and lifted Larimer to his feet, slinging one arm around his shoulder. Giordino came out of the bathroom and distributed the wet blankets and towels.

"All right, Al, you help me with the senator. Loren, you hold on to Congressman Moran and stick close behind me." He broke off and looked at everyone. "Okay, here we go."

He yanked open the door and was engulfed by a rolling wall of smoke that came out of nowhere.

Almost before the explosion faded, Captain Pokofsky shook off stunned disbelief and rushed to the bridge. The young watch officer was pounding desperately on the automated ship console in agonized frustration.

"Close all watertight doors and actuate the fire control system!" Pokofsky shouted.

"I can't!" the watch officer cried helplessly. "We've lost all power!"

"What about the auxiliary generators?"

"They're out too." The watch officer's face was wrapped in undisguised shock. "The ship's phones are dead. The damage-control computer is down. Nothing responds. We can't give a general alarm."

Pokofsky ran out on the bridge wing and stared aft. His once beautiful ship was vomiting fire and smoke from her entire midsection. A few moments before there was music and relaxed gaiety. Now the entire scene was one of horror. The open swimming pool and lounge decks had been turned into a crematorium. The two hundred people stretched under the sun were almost instantly incinerated by the tidal fall of fiery oil. Some had saved themselves by leaping into the pools, only to die after surfacing for air when the heat seared their lungs, and many had climbed the railings and thrown themselves overboard, their skin and brief clothing ablaze.

Pokofsky stood sick and stunned at the sight of the carnage. It was a moment in time borrowed from hell. He knew in his heart that his ship was lost. There was no stopping the holocaust, and the list was increasing as the sea poured into the *Leonid Andreyev*'s bowels. He returned to the bridge.

"Pass the word to abandon ship," he said to the watch officer. "The port boats are burning. Load what women and children you can into the starboard boats still intact."

As the watch officer hurried off, the chief engineer, Erik Kazinkin, appeared, out of breath from his climb from below. His eyebrows and half his hair were singed away. The soles of his shoes were smoldering but he appeared not to notice. His mind was numb to the pain.

"Give me a report," Pokofsky ordered in a quiet tone. "What caused the explosion?"

"The fuel tank blew," answered Kazinkin. "God knows why. Took out the power generating room and the auxiliary generator compartment as well. Boiler rooms two and three are flooded. We managed to manually close the watertight doors to the engine rooms, but she's taking on water at an alarming rate. And without power to operate the pumps . . ." He shrugged defeatedly without continuing.

All options to save the *Leonid Andreyev* had evaporated. The only morbid question was whether she would become a burned-out derelict or sink first? Few would survive the next hour, Pokofsky accepted with dread certainty. Many would burn and many would drown, unable to enter the pitifully few lifeboats that were still able to be launched.

"Bring your men up from below," said Pokofsky. "We're abandoning the ship."

"Thank you, Captain," said the chief engineer. He held out his hand. "Good luck to you."

They parted and Pokofsky headed for the communications room one deck below. The officer in charge looked up from the radio as the captain suddenly strode through the doorway.

"Send out the distress call," Pokofsky ordered.

"I took the responsibility, sir, of sending out Mayday signals immediately after the explosion."

Pokofsky placed a hand on the officer's shoulder. "I commend your initiative." Then he asked calmly, "Have you managed to transmit without problem?"

"Yes, sir. When the power supply went off, I switched to the emergency batteries. The first response came from a Korean container ship only ten miles to the southwest."

"Thank God someone is close. Any other replies?"

"The United States Navy at Guantánamo Bay is responding with rescue ships and helicopters. The only other vessel within fifty miles is a Norwegian cruise ship."

"Too late for her," said Pokofsky thoughtfully. "We'll have to pin our hopes on the Koreans and American Navy."

With the soaked blanket over his head, Pitt had to feel his way along the passageway and up the smoke-filled staircase. Three, four times he and Giordino tripped over the bodies of passengers who had succumbed to asphyxiation.

Larimer made a game effort of trying to keep in step, while Loren and Moran stumbled along behind, their hands clutching the belted trousers of Pitt and Giordino.

"How far?" Loren gasped.

"We have to climb four decks before we break out on the open promenade area," Pitt panted in reply.

At the second landing they ran into a solid wall of people. The staircase became so packed with passengers struggling to escape the smoke it became impossible to take another step. The crew acted with coolness, attempting to direct the human flow to the boat deck, but calm gave way to the inevitable contagion of panic, and they were trampled under the screaming, terror-driven mass of thrashing bodies.

"To the left!" Giordino shouted in Pitt's ear. "The passageway leads to another staircase toward the stern."

Relying on a deep trust in his little friend, Pitt veered down the passageway, pulling Larimer along. The senator finally managed to get his footing on the smooth surface and began carrying his own weight. To their vast relief the smoke decreased and the frightened tidal wave of people thinned. When at last they reached the aft staircase they found it practically empty. By not following the herd instinct, Giordino had led them to temporary safety.

They emerged in the clear on the deck aft of the observation lounge. After a few moments to ease their coughing spasms and cleanse their aching lungs with clean air, they looked in awe over the doomed ship.

The *Leonid Andreyev* was listing twenty degrees to port. Thousands of gallons of oil had spilled out into the sea and ignited. The water around the jagged opening caused by the blast was a mass of fire. The entire midsection of the ship was a blazing torch. The tremendous heat was turning steel plates red hot and warping them into twisted, grotesque shapes. White paint was blistering black, teak decks were nearly burned through and the glass in the portholes popped like gunshots.

The flames spread with incredible speed as the ocean breeze fanned them toward the bridge. Already the communications room was consumed and the officer in charge burned to death at his radio. Fire and swirling smoke shot upward through the companionways and ventilating ducts. The *Leonid Andreyev*, like all modern cruise liners, was designed and constructed to be fireproof, but no precise planning or visionary foresight could have predicted the devastating results of a fuel tank explosion that showered the ship like a flamethrower.

An immense billowing cloud of oily smoke reached hundreds of feet above, flattening in the upper air currents, stretching over the ship like a pall. The base of the cloud was a solid torrent of flame that twisted and surged in a violent storm of orange and yellow. While below, in the deeper reaches of the hull, the flames were an acetylene blue-white, fed into molten temperatures by the intake of air through the shattered plates, creating the effect of a blast furnace.

Though many of the passengers were able to fight their way up the stairways, over a hundred lay dead below, some trapped and burned in their cabins, others overtaken by smoke inhalation during their attempt to escape topside. The ones who made it were being driven by the flames toward the stern and away from the lifeboats.

All efforts by the crew to maintain order were engulfed by the chaos. The passengers were finally left to fend for themselves and no one knew which way to turn. All port lifeboats were ablaze, and only three were lowered on the starboard side before the fire drove the crew back. As it was, one boat was beginning to burn by the time it hit the sea.

Now people began jumping into the water like migrating lemmings. The drop was nearly fifty feet, and a number of those who had life jackets made the mistake of inflating them before plummeting over the side and broke their necks on impact. Women stood spellbound with terror, too frightened to leap. Men cursed in desperation. In the water the swimmers struck out for the few lifeboats, but the crews who manned them started up the engines and sailed beyond reach for fear of being swamped by overloading.

In the middle of the frenzied drama, the container ship arrived. The captain eased his vessel within a hundred yards of the *Leonid Andreyev* and put his boats over as fast as they could be lowered. A few minutes later, U.S. Navy sea rescue helicopters appeared and began plucking survivors from the sea.

58

LOREN GAZED IN ABSTRACT FASCINATION at the sheet of advancing fire. "Shouldn't we jump or something?" she asked in a vague tone.

Pitt didn't answer immediately. He studied the slanting deck and judged the list to be about forty degrees. "No call to rush things," he said with expressionless calm. "The flames won't reach us for another ten minutes. The further the ship heels to port, the shorter the distance to jump. In the meantime, I suggest we start heaving deck chairs overboard so those poor souls in the water have something to hang on to until they're picked up."

Surprisingly, Larimer was the first to react. He began sweeping up the wooden deck chairs in his massive arms and dropping them over the railings. He actually had the look on his face of a man who was enjoying himself. Moran stood huddled against a bulwark, silent, noncommittal, frozen in fear.

"Take care you don't hit a swimmer on the head," Pitt said to Larimer.

"I wouldn't dare," the senator replied with an exhausted smile. "They might be a constituent and I'd lose their vote."

After all the chairs in sight had gone over the side, Pitt stood for two or three seconds and took stock. The blast from the heat was not yet unbearable. The fire wouldn't kill those packed on the stern deck, at least not for a few more minutes. He shouldered his way through the dense throng to the port railing again. The waves rolled only twenty feet below.

342

He shouted to Giordino, "Let's help these people over the side." Then he turned and cupped his hands to his mouth.

"There's no more time to lose!" he yelled at the top of his lungs to make himself heard over the din of the frightened crowd and the roar of the holocaust. "Swim for it or die!"

Several men took the hint and, clutching the hands of their protesting wives, straddled the railing and slipped out of sight below. Next came three teenage girls who showed no hesitation but dove cleanly into the blue-green swells.

"Swim to a deck chair and use it for a float," Giordino instructed everyone repeatedly.

Pitt separated families into a group and while Loren cheered the children, he directed their parents to jump and latch onto a floating deck chair. Then he held the children over the side by the hands as far as he could reach and let them drop, holding his breath until the mother and father had them safely in tow.

The great curtain of flame crept closer and breathing became more difficult. The heat felt as though they were standing in front of an open furnace. A rough head count told Pitt only thirty people were left, but it would be a close race.

A great hulking fat man stopped and refused to move. "The water's full of sharks!" he screamed hysterically. "We're better off here, waiting for the helicopters."

"They can't hover over the ship because of air turbulence from the heat," Pitt explained patiently. "You can burn to a cinder or take your chances in the water. Which is it? Be quick, you're holding up the others."

Giordino took two paces, tensed his powerful muscles and lifted the fat procrastinator off his feet. There was no animosity, no expression of meanness in Giordino's unblinking eyes as he carried the man to the side and unceremoniously dumped him overboard.

"Send me a postcard," Giordino shouted after him.

The diverting action seemed to motivate the few passengers who hung back. One after the other, with Pitt assisting the elderly couples to take the plunge, they departed the burning ship.

When the last of them was finally gone, Pitt looked around at Loren. "Your turn," he said.

"Not without my colleagues," she said with a feminine resolve.

Pitt stared below to make certain the water was clear. Larimer was so weak he could barely lift his legs over the rail. Giordino gave him a hand as Loren jumped arm in arm with Moran. Pitt watched anxiously until they all cleared the side and swam away, admiring Loren's endurance as she shouted words of encouragement to Larimer while towing Moran by the collar.

"Better give her a hand," Pitt said to Giordino.

His friend didn't have to be urged. He was gone before another word passed between them.

Pitt took one last look at the *Leonid Andreyev*. The air around shimmered from the blasting heat waves as flames shot from her every opening. The list was passing fifty degrees and her end was only minutes away. Already her starboard propeller was clear of the water and steam was hissing in white tortured clouds around her waterline.

As he was poised to leap, Pitt abruptly went rigid in astonishment. At the outer edge of his peripheral vision he saw an arm snake out of a cabin porthole forty feet away. Without hesitation, he picked up one of the still soggy blankets from the deck, threw it over his head and covered the distance in seven strides. A voice inside the cabin was screaming for help. He peered in and saw a woman's face, eyes wide in terror.

"Oh, my God, please help us?"

"How many are you?"

"Myself and two children."

"Pass out the kids."

The face disappeared and quickly a boy about six years of age was thrust through the narrow port. Pitt set him between his legs, keeping the blanket suspended above the two of them like a tent. Next came a little girl no more than three. Incredibly she was sound asleep.

"Give me your hand," Pitt ordered, knowing in his heart it was hopeless.

"I can't get through!" the woman cried. "The opening is too small."

"Do you have water in the bathroom?"

"There's no pressure."

"Strip naked!" Pitt shouted in desperation. "Use your cosmetics. Smear your body with facial creams."

The woman nodded in understanding and disappeared inside. Pitt turned and, clutching a child under each arm, rushed to the rail. With great relief he spied Giordino treading water, looking up.

"Al," Pitt called. "Catch."

If Giordino was surprised to see Pitt collar two more children he didn't show it. He reached up and gathered them in as effortlessly as if they were footballs.

"Jump!" he yelled to Pitt. "She's going over."

Without lingering to answer, Pitt raced back to the cabin port. He realized with only a small corner of his mind that saving the mother was a sheer act of desperation. He passed beyond conscious thought; his movements seemed those of another man, a total stranger.

The air was so hot and dry his perspiration evaporated before it seeped from his pores. The heat rose from the deck and penetrated the soles of his shoes. He stumbled and nearly fell as a heavy shudder ran through the doomed ship, and she gave a sudden lurch as the deck dropped on an increasing angle to port. She was in her final death agony before capsizing and sinking to the sea bottom.

Pitt found himself kneeling against the slanting cabin wall, reaching through the port. A pair of hands clasped his wrists and he pulled. The woman's shoulders and breasts squeezed past the opening. He gave another heave and then her hips scraped through.

The flames were running up and licking at his back. The deck was dropping away beneath his feet. He held the woman around the waist and leaped off the edge of the cabin as the *Leonid Andreyev* rolled over, her propellers twisting out of the water and arching toward the sun.

They were sucked under by the fierce rush of water, swirled

around like dolls in a maelstrom. Pitt lashed out with his free hand and feet and struggled upward, seeing the glimmering surface turn from green to blue with agonizing slowness.

The blood pounded in his ears and his lungs felt as though they were filled with angry wasps. The thin veil of blackness began to tint his vision. He felt the woman go limp under his arm, her body creating an unwelcome drag against his progress. He used up the last particles of oxygen, and a pyrotechnic display flared inside his head. One burst became a bright orange ball that expanded until it exploded in a wavering flash.

He broke through the surface, his upturned face directed at the afternoon sun. Thankfully he inhaled deep waves of air, enough to ease the blackness, the pounding and the sting in his lungs. Then he quickly circled the woman's abdomen and squeezed hard several times, forcing the salt water from her throat. She convulsed and began retching, followed by a coughing spell. Only when her breathing returned to near normal and she groaned did he look around for the others.

Giordino was swimming in Pitt's direction, pushing one of the deck chairs in front of him. The two children were sitting on top, immune to the tragedy around them, gaily laughing at Giordino's repertory of funny faces.

"I was beginning to wonder if you were going to turn up," he said.

"Bad pennies usually do," said Pitt, keeping the children's mother afloat until she recovered enough to hang on to the deck chair.

"I'll take care of them," said Giordino. "You better help Loren. I think the senator's bought it."

His arms felt as if they were encased in lead and he was numb with exhaustion, but Pitt carved the water with swift even strokes until he reached the floating jetsam that supported Loren and Larimer.

Gray-faced, her eyes filled with sadness, Loren grimly held the senator's head above water. Pitt saw with sinking heart she needn't have bothered; Larimer would never sit in the Senate again. His skin was mottled and turning a dusky purple. He was game to the end, but the half-century of living in the fast lane had called in the inevitable IOU's. His heart had gone far beyond its limits and finally quit in protest.

Gently, Pitt pried Loren's hands from the senator's body, and pushed him away. She looked at him blankly as if to object, then turned away, unable to watch as Larimer slowly drifted off, gently pushed by the rolling sea.

"He deserves a state funeral," she said, her voice a husky whisper.

"No matter," said Pitt, "as long as they know he went out a man."

Loren seemed to accept that. She leaned her head on Pitt's shoulder, the tears intermingling with the salt water on her cheeks.

Pitt twisted and looked around. "Where's Moran?"

"He was picked up by a Navy helicopter."

"He deserted you?" Pitt asked incredulously.

"The crewman shouted that he only had room for one more."

"So the illustrious Speaker of the House left a woman to support a dying man while he saved himself."

Pitt's dislike for Moran burned with a cold flame. He became obsessed with the idea of ramming his fist into the little ferret's face.

Captain Pokofsky sat in the cabin of the powerboat, his hands clasped over his ears to shut out the terrible cries of the people drowning in the water and the screams of those suffering the agony of their burns. He could not bring himself to look upon the indescribable horror or watch the *Leonid Andreyev* plunge out of sight to the seabed two thousand fathoms below. He was a living dead man.

He looked up at Geidar Ombrikov through glazed and listless eyes. "Why did you save me? Why didn't you let me die with my ship?"

Ombrikov could plainly see Pokofsky was suffering from severe shock, but he felt no pity for the man. Death was an element the

KGB agent was trained to accept. His duty came before all consideration of compassion.

"I've no time for rituals of the sea," he said coldly. "The noble captain standing on the bridge saluting the flag as his ship sinks under him is so much garbage. State Security needs you, Pokofsky, and I need you to identify the American legislators."

"They're probably dead," Pokofsky muttered distantly.

"Then we'll have to prove it," Ombrikov snapped ruthlessly. "My superiors won't accept less than positive identification of their bodies. Nor can we overlook the possibility they may still be alive out there in the water."

Pokofsky placed his hands over his face and shuddered. "I can't—"

Before the words were out of his mouth, Ombrikov roughly dragged him to his feet and shoved him out on the open deck. "Damn you!" he shouted. "Look for them!"

Pokofsky clenched his jaws and stared at the appalling reality of the floating wreckage and hundreds of struggling men, women and children. He choked off a sound deep inside him, his face blanched.

"No!" he shouted. He leaped over the side so quickly, suddenly, neither Ombrikov nor his crew could stop him. He hit the water swimming and dove deep until the white of his uniform was lost to view on the surface.

The boats from the container ship hauled in the survivors as fast as they could reach them, quickly filling to capacity and unloading their human cargo before returning to the center of the flotsam to continue the rescue. The sea was filled with debris of all kinds, dead bodies of all ages, and those still fighting to live. Fortunately the water was warm and none suffered from exposure, nor did the threat of sharks ever materialize.

One boat jockeyed close to Giordino, who helped lift the mother and her two children onboard. Then he scrambled over the freeboard and motioned for the helmsman to steer toward Pitt and Loren. They were among the last few to be fished out.

As the boat slipped alongside, Pitt raised his hand in greeting to the short, stocky figure that leaned over the side.

"Hello," Pitt said, grinning widely. "Are we ever glad to see you."

"Happy to be of service," replied the steward Pitt had passed earlier at the elevator. He was also grinning, baring a set of large upper teeth parted by a wide gap.

He reached down, grasped Loren by the wrists and pulled her effortlessly out of the water and into the boat. Pitt stretched out his hand, but the steward ignored it.

"Sorry," he said, "we have no more room."

"What—what are you talking about?" Pitt demanded. "The boat is half empty."

"You are not welcome aboard my vessel."

"You damned well don't even own it."

"Oh, but I do."

Pitt stared at the steward in sheer incredulity, then slowly turned and took one long comprehensive look across the water at the container ship. The name of the starboard bow was *Chalmette*, but the lettering on the sides of the containers stacked on the main deck read "Bougainville." Pitt felt as though he'd been kicked in the stomach.

"Our confrontation is a lucky circumstance for me, Mr. Pitt, but I fear a misfortune for yourself."

Pitt stared at the steward. "You know me?"

The grin turned into an expression of hate and contempt. "Only too well. Your meddling has cost Bougainville Maritime dearly."

"Tell me who are you?" asked Pitt, stalling for time and desperately glancing in the sky for a Navy recovery helicopter.

"I don't think I'll give you the satisfaction," the steward said with all the warmth of a frozen food locker.

Unable to hear the conversation, Loren pulled at the steward's arm. "Why don't you bring him onboard? What are you waiting for?"

He turned and savagely backhanded her across the cheek, sending her stumbling backward, falling across two survivors who sat in stunned surprise.

Giordino, who was standing in the stern of the boat, started forward. A seaman produced an automatic shotgun from under a seat and rammed the wooden shoulder stock into his stomach. Giordino's jaw dropped open; he gasped for breath and lost his footing, dropping partially over the side of the boat, arms trailing in the water.

The steward's lips tightened and the smooth yellow features bore no readable expression. Only his eyes shone with evil. "Thank you for being so cooperative, Mr. Pitt. Thank you for so thoughtfully coming to me."

"Get screwed!" Pitt snapped in defiance.

The steward raised an oar over his head. "Bon voyage, Dirk Pitt."

The oar swung downward and clipped Pitt on the right side of his chest, driving him under the water. The wind was crushed from his lungs and a stabbing pain swept over his rib cage. He resurfaced and lifted his left arm above his head to ward off the next inevitable blow. His move came too late. The oar in the hands of the steward mashed Pitt's extended arm down and struck the top of his head.

The blue sky turned to black as consciousness left him, and slowly Pitt drifted under the lifeboat and sank out of sight.

59 _____

THE PRESIDENT'S WIFE ENTERED his second-floor study, kissed him good night and went off to bed. He sat in a soft highback embroidered chair and studied a pile of statistics on the latest economic forecasts. Using a large yellow legal pad, he scribbled a prodigious amount of notes. Some he saved, some he tore up and discarded before they were completed. After nearly three hours, he removed his glasses and closed his tired eyes for a few moments.

When he opened them again, he was no longer in his White House study, but in a small gray room with a high ceiling and no windows.

He rubbed his eyes and looked once more, blinking in the monotone light.

He was still in the gray room, only now he found himself seated in a hard wooden chair, his ankles strapped to square carved legs and his hands to the armrests.

A violent fear coursed through him, and he cried for his wife and the Secret Service guards, but the voice was not his. It had a different tonal quality, deeper, more coarse.

Soon a door that was recessed into one wall swung inward and a small man with a thin, intelligent face entered. His eyes had a dark, bemused look, and he carried a syringe in one hand.

"How are we today, Mr. President?" he asked politely.

Strangely, the words were foreign, but the President understood them perfectly. Then he heard himself shouting repeatedly, "I am

351

Oskar Belkaya, I am not the President of the United States, I am Oskar—'' He broke off as the intruder plunged the needle into his arm.

The bemused expression never left the little man's face; it might have been glued there. He nodded toward the doorway and another man wearing a drab prison uniform came in and set a cassette recorder on a Spartan metal table that was bolted to the floor. He wired the recorder to four small eyelets on the table's surface and left.

"So you won't knock your new lesson on the floor, Mr. President," said the thin man. "I hope you find it interesting." Then he switched on the recorder and left the room.

The President struggled to shake off the bewildering terror of the nightmare. Yet it all seemed too real to be dream fantasy. He could smell his own sweat, feel the hurt as the straps chafed his skin, hear the walls echo with his cries of frustration. His head sagged to his chest and he began to sob uncontrollably as the recorded message droned over and over. When at last he sufficiently recovered, he rasied his head as if lifting a ponderous weight and looked around.

He was seated in his White House study.

Secretary Oates took Dan Fawcett's call on his private line. "What's the situation over there?" he asked without wasting words.

"Critical," Fawcett replied. "Armed guards everywhere. I haven't seen this many troops since I was with the Fifth Marine Regiment in Korea."

"And the President?"

"Spitting out directives like a Gatling gun. He won't listen to advice from his aides any longer, myself included. He's getting increasingly harder to reach. Two weeks ago, he'd give full attention to opposing viewpoints or objective comments. No more. You agree with him or you're out the door. Megan Blair and I are the only ones still with access to his office, and my days are numbered. I'm bailing out before the roof caves in."

"Stay put," said Oates. "It's best for all concerned if you and

Oscar Lucas remain close to the President. You're the only open line of communications any of us have into the White House."

"Won't work."

"Why?"

"I told you, even if I stick around, I'll be closed out. My name is rapidly climbing to the top of the President's shit list."

"Then get back in his good graces," Oates ordered. "Crawl up his butt and support whatever he says. Play yes-man and relay up-to-the-minute reports on every course of action he takes."

There was a long pause. "Okay, I'll do my best to keep you informed."

"And alert Oscar Lucas to stand by. We're going to need him."

"Can I ask what's going on?"

"Not yet," Oates replied tersely.

Fawcett didn't press him. He switched tack. "You want to hear the President's latest brainstorm?"

"Bad?"

"Very bad," admitted Fawcett. "He's talking about withdrawing our military forces from the NATO alliance."

Oates clutched the phone until his knuckles turned ivory. "He's got to be stopped," he said grimly.

Fawcett's voice sounded far away. "The President and I go back a long way together, but in the best interests of the country, I must agree."

"Stay in touch."

Oates put down the phone, turned in his desk chair and gazed out the window, lost in thought. The afternoon sky had turned an ominous gray, and a light rain began to fall on Washington's streets, their slickened surfaces reflecting the federal buildings in eerie distortions.

In the end he would have to take over the reins of government, Oates thought bitterly. He was well aware that every President in the last thirty years had been vilified and debased by events beyond his control. Eisenhower was the last chief executive who left the White House as venerated as when he came in. No matter how saintly or intellectually brilliant the next President, he would be stoned by an unmovable bureaucracy and increasingly hostile news media; and Oates harbored no desire to be a target of the rock throwers.

He was pulled out of his reverie by the muted buzz of his intercom. "Mr. Brogan and another gentleman to see you."

"Send them in," Oates directed. He rose and came around his desk as Brogan entered. They shook hands briefly and Brogan introduced the man standing beside him as Dr. Raymond Edgely.

Oates correctly pegged Edgely as an academician. The old-fashioned crew cut and bow tie suggested someone who seldom strayed from a university campus. Edgely was slender, wore a scraggly barbed-wire beard, and his bristly dark eyebrows were untrimmed and brushed upward in a Mephistopheles set and blow.

"Dr. Edgely is the director of Fathom," Brogan explained, "the Agency's special study into mind-control techniques at Greeley University in Colorado."

Oates gestured for them to sit on a sofa and took a chair across a marble coffee table. "I've just received a call from Dan Fawcett. The President intends to withdraw our troops from NATO."

"Another piece of evidence to bolster our case," said Brogan. "Only the Russians would profit from such a move."

Oates turned to Edgely. "Has Martin explained our suspicions regarding the President's behavior to you?"

"Yes, Mr. Brogan has filled me in."

"And how does the situation strike you? Can the President be mentally forced to become an involuntary traitor?"

"I grant the President's actions demonstrate a dramatic personality change, but unless we can put him through a series of tests, there is no way of being certain of brain alteration or exterior domination."

"He will never consent to an examination," said Brogan.

"That presents a problem," Edgely said.

"Suppose you tell us, Doctor," Oates asked, "how the President's mind transfer was performed?"

"If that is indeed what we are faced with," replied Edgely, "the first step is to isolate the subject in a womblike chamber for a given length of time, removed from all sensorial influences. During this sequence his brain patterns are studied, analyzed and deciphered into a language that can be programmed and translated by computer. The next step is to design an implant, in this instance a microchip, with the desired data and then insert it by psychosurgery into the subject's brain.''

"You make it sound as elementary as a tonsillectomy," said Oates.

Edgely laughed. "I've condensed and oversimplified, of course, but in reality the procedures are incredibly delicate and involved.''

"After the microchip is imbedded into the brain, what then?''

"I should have mentioned that a section of the implant is a tiny transmitter/receiver which operates off the electrical impulses of the brain and is capable of sending thought patterns and other bodily functions to a central computer and monitoring post located as far away as Hong Kong.''

"Or Moscow," added Brogan.

"And not the Soviet embassy here in Washington, as you suggested earlier?'' Oates asked, looking at Brogan.

"I think I can answer that," Edgely volunteered. "The communication technology is certainly available to relay data from a subject via satellite to Russia, but if I were in Dr. Lugovoy's shoes, I'd set up my monitoring station nearby so I could observe the results of the President's actions at firsthand. This would also allow me a faster response time to redirect my command signals to his mind during unexpected political events.''

"Can Lugovoy lose control over the President?" asked Brogan.

"If the President ceases to think and act for himself, he breaks the ties to his normal world. Then he may tend to stray from Lugovoy's instructions and carry them to extremes.''

"Is this why he's instigated so many radical programs in such haste?''

"I can't say," Edgely answered. "For all I know he is responding precisely to Lugovoy's commands. I do suspect, however, that it goes far deeper.''

355

"In what manner?"

"The reports supplied by Mr. Brogan's operatives in Russia show that Lugovoy has attempted experiments with political prisoners, transferring the fluid from their hippocampuses—a structure in the brain's limbic system that holds our memories—to those of other subjects."

"A memory injection," Oates murmured wonderingly. "So there really is a Dr. Frankenstein."

"Memory transfer is a tricky business," Edgely continued. "There is no predicting with any certainty the end results."

"Do you think Lugovoy performed this experiment on the President?"

"I hate to say yes, but if he runs true to form, he might very well have programmed some poor Russian prisoner for months, even years, with thoughts promoting Soviet policy, and then transplanted the hippocampal fluid into the President's brain as a backup to the implant."

"Under the proper care," Oates asked, "could the President return to normal?"

"You mean put his mind back as it was before?"

"Something like that."

Edgely shook his head. "Any known treatment will not reverse the damage. The President will always be haunted by the memory of someone else."

"Couldn't you extract his hippocampal fluid as well?"

"I catch your meaning, but by removing the foreign thought patterns, we'd be erasing the President's own memories." Edgely paused. "No, I'm sorry to say, the President's behavior patterns have been irrevocably altered."

"Then he should be removed from office . . . permanently."

"That would be my recommendation," answered Edgely without hesitation.

Oates sat back in his chair and clasped his hands behind his head. "Thank you, Doctor. You've reinforced our resolve."

"From what I've heard, no one gets through the White House gates."

"If the Russians could abduct him," said Brogan, "I see no reason why we can't do the same. But first we have to disconnect him from Lugovoy."

"May I make a suggestion?"

"Please."

"There is an excellent opportunity to turn this situation around to our advantage."

"How?"

"Rather than cut off his brain signals, why not tune in on the frequency?"

"For what purpose?"

"So my staff and I can feed the transmissions into our own monitoring equipment. If our computers can receive enough data, say within a forty-eight-hour period, we can take the place of the President's brain."

"A substitution to feed the Russians false information," said Brogan, rising to Edgely's inspiration.

"Exactly!" Edgely exclaimed. "Because they have every reason to believe the validity of the data they receive from the President, Soviet intelligence can be led down whichever garden path you choose."

"I like the idea," said Oates. "But the stickler is whether we can afford the forty-eight hours. There's no telling what the President might attempt within that time frame."

"The risk is worth it," Brogan stated flatly.

There was a knock on the door and Oates's secretary leaned her head into the room. "Sorry to interrupt, Mr. Secretary, but Mr. Brogan has an urgent call."

Brogan got up quickly, lifted the phone on Oates's desk and pressed the winking button. "Brogan."

He stood there listening for close to a full minute without speaking. Then he hung up and faced Oates.

"Speaker of the House Alan Moran just turned up alive at our Guantánamo Bay naval base in Cuba," he said slowly.

"Margolin?"

"No report."

"Larimer?"

"Senator Larimer is dead."

"Oh, good God!" Oates moaned. "That means Moran could be our next President. I can't think of a more unscrupulous or ill-equipped man for the job!"

"A Fagin poised at the White House gate," commented Brogan. "Not a pleasant thought."

60

PITT WAS CERTAIN HE WAS DEAD. There was no reason why he shouldn't be dead. And yet he saw no blinding light at the end of a tunnel, no faces of friends and relatives who died before him. He felt as though he were dozing in his own bed at home. And Loren was there, her hair cascading on the pillow, her body pressed against his, her arms encircling his neck, holding tightly, refusing to let him drift away. Her face seemed to glow, and her violet eyes looked straight into his. He wondered if she was dead too.

Suddenly she released her hold and began to blur, moving away, diminishing ever smaller until she vanished altogether. A dim light filtered through his closed eyelids and he heard voices in the distance. Slowly, with an effort as great as lifting a pair of hundred-pound weights, he opened his eyes. At first he thought he was gazing at a flat white surface. Then as his mind crept past the veil of unconsciousness he realized he really was gazing at a flat white surface.

It was a ceiling.

A strange voice said, "He's coming around."

"Takes more than three cracked ribs, a brain concussion and a gallon of seawater to do this character in." There was no mistaking this laconic voice.

"My worst fears," Pitt managed to mutter. "I've gone to hell and met the devil."

359

"See how he talks about his best and only friend," said Al Giordino to a doctor in naval uniform.

"He's in good physical shape," said the doctor. "He should mend pretty quickly."

"Pardon the mundane question," said Pitt, "but where am I?"

"Welcome to the U.S. Naval Hospital at Guantánamo Bay, Cuba," the doctor answered. "You and Mr. Giordino were fished out of the water by one of our recovery craft."

Pitt focused his eyes on Giordino. "Are you all right?"

"He has a bruise the size of a cantaloupe on his abdomen, but he'll survive," the doctor said, smiling. "By the way, I understand he saved your life."

Pitt cleared the mist from his mind and tried to recall. "The steward from the *Leonid Andreyev* was playing baseball with my head."

"Pounded you under the boat with an oar," Giordino explained. "I slipped over the side, swam underwater until I grabbed your arm, and dragged you to the surface. The steward would have beat on me too except for the timely arrival of a Navy helicopter whose paramedics jumped into the water and helped sling us onboard."

"And Loren?"

Giordino averted his gaze. "She's listed as missing."

"Missing, hell!" Pitt snarled. He grimaced from the sudden pain in his chest as he rose to his elbows. "We both know she was alive and sitting in the lifeboat."

A solemn look clouded Giordino's face. "Her name didn't appear on a list of survivors given out by the ship's captain."

"A Bougainville ship!" Pitt blurted as his memory came flooding back. "The Oriental steward who tried to brain us pointed toward the—"

"*Chalmette,*" Giordino prompted.

"Yes, the *Chalmette,* and said it belonged to him. He also spoke my name."

"Stewards are supposed to remember passengers' names. He knew you as Charlie Gruber in cabin thirty-four."

"No, he rightly accused me of meddling in Bougainville affairs, and his last words were 'Bon voyage, Dirk Pitt.' "

Giordino gave a puzzled shrug. "Beats hell out of me how he knew you. But why would a Bougainville man work as a steward on a Russian cruise ship?"

"I can't begin to guess."

"And lie about Loren's rescue?"

Pitt merely gave an imperceptible shake of his head.

"Then she's being held prisoner by the Bougainvilles," said Giordino as if suddenly enlightened. "But for what reason?"

"You keep asking questions I can't answer," Pitt said irritably. "Where is the *Chalmette* now?"

"Headed toward Miami to land the survivors."

"How long have I been unconscious?"

"About thirty-two hours," replied the doctor.

"Still time," said Pitt. "The *Chalmette* won't reach the Florida coast for several hours yet."

He raised himself to a sitting position and swung his legs over the side of the bed. The room began to seesaw back and forth.

The doctor moved forward and steadied him by both arms. "I hope you don't think you're rushing off somewhere."

"I intend to be standing on the dock when the *Chalmette* arrives in Miami," Pitt said implacably.

A stern medical-profession look grew on the doctor's face. "You're staying in this bed for the next four days. You can't travel around with those fractured ribs, and we don't know how serious your concussion is."

"Sorry, Doc," Giordino said, "but you've both been overruled."

Pitt stared at him stonily. "Who's to stop me?"

"Admiral Sandecker, for one. Secretary of State Doug Oates for another," Giordino answered as detachedly as though he were reading aloud the stock market quotes for the day. "Orders came down for you to fly to Washington the minute you came around. We may be in big trouble. I have a hunch we dipped into the wrong

361

cookie jar when we discovered Congressman Moran and Senator Larimer imprisoned on a Soviet vessel."

"They can wait until I search the *Chalmette* for Loren."

"My job. You go to the capital while I go to Miami and play customs inspector. It's all been arranged."

Pacified to a small degree, Pitt relaxed on the bed. "What about Moran?"

"He couldn't wait to cut out," Giordino said angrily. "He demanded the Navy drop everything and fly him home the minute he was brought ashore. I had a minor confrontation with him in the hospital corridor after his routine examination. Came within a millimeter of cramming his hook nose down his gullet. The bastard didn't demonstrate the slightest concern about Loren, and he seemed downright delighted when I told him of Larimer's death."

"He has a talent for deserting those who help him," Pitt said disgustedly.

An orderly rolled in a wheelchair and together with Giordino eased Pitt into it. A groan escaped his lips as a piercing pain ripped through his chest.

"You're leaving against my express wishes," said the doctor. "I want that understood. There is no guarantee you won't have complications if you overtax yourself."

"I release you from all responsibility, Doc," Pitt said, smiling. "I won't tell a soul I was your patient. Your medical reputation is secure."

Giordino laid a pile of Navy-issue clothing and a small paper sack in Pitt's lap. "Here's some presentable clothes and the stuff from your pockets. You can dress on the plane to save time."

Pitt opened the sack and fingered a vinyl pouch inside. Satisfied the contents were secure and dry, he looked up at Giordino and shook hands. "Good hunting, friend."

Giordino patted him on the shoulder. "Don't worry. I'll find her. You go to Washington and give 'em hell."

No one could have suffered from a Rip Van Winkle syndrome and awakened more surprised than Alan Moran. He remembered going to sleep on the presidential yacht almost two weeks earlier, and his next conscious sensation was being dragged into a limousine somewhere in the river country of South Carolina. The imprisonment and escape from the burning Russian cruise ship seemed a distorted blur. Only when he returned to Washington and found both Congress and the Supreme Court evicted from their hallowed halls did he come back on track and retrieve his mantle of political power.

With the government in emotional and political shambles, he saw his chance to fulfill his deep, unfathomable ambition to become President. Not having the popular support to take the office by election, he was determined now to grab it by default. With Margolin missing, Larimer out of the way, and the President laid open for impeachment, there was little to stop him.

Moran held court in the middle of Jackson Square across Pennsylvania Avenue from the White House and answered questions fired by a battery of correspondents. He was the man of the hour and was enjoying every second of the attention.

"Can you tell us where you've been the last two weeks?" asked Ray Marsh of the New York *Times*.

"Be glad to," Moran replied gracefully. "Senate Majority Leader Marcus Larimer and I went on a fishing holiday in the Caribbean, partly to try our luck at snagging a record marlin, mostly to discuss the issues facing our great nation."

"Initial reports state that Senator Larimer died during the *Leonid Andreyev* tragedy."

"I'm deeply saddened to say that is true," Moran said, abruptly becoming solemn. "The senator and I were trolling only five or six miles away from the Russian cruise ship when we heard and observed an explosion that covered her in fire and smoke. We immediately ordered our skipper to change course for the disaster area. When we arrived, the *Leonid Andreyev* was ablaze from stem to stern. Hundreds of frightened passengers were tumbling into the sea, many with their clothes in flames."

Moran paused for effect and then enunciated in a vivid descriptive tone. "I leaped into the water, followed by the senator, to help those who were badly injured or unable to swim. We struggled for what seemed like hours, keeping women and children afloat until we could lift them into our fishing boat. I lost track of Senator Larimer. When I looked for him, he was floating facedown, an apparent victim of a heart attack due to overexertion. You can quote me as saying he died a real hero.''

"How many people do you reckon you saved?" This from Joe Stark of the United Press.

"I lost count," answered Moran, serenely pitching out the lies. "Our small vessel became dangerously overloaded with burned and half-drowned victims. So, rather than become the straw that might capsize it, so to speak, I remained in the water so one more pitiful creature could cheat death. Luckily for me, I was picked up by the Navy, which, I must add, performed magnificently.''

"Were you aware that Congresswoman Loren Smith was traveling on the *Leonid Andreyev?*" asked Marion Tournier of the Associated Press Radio Network.

"Not at the time," replied Moran, changing back to his solemn demeanor again. "Regretfully, I've only just been informed that she's reported as missing."

Curtis Mayo signaled his cameramen and edged closer to Moran. "Congressman, what is your feeling regarding the President's unprecedented closing of Congress?"

"Deeply mortified that such an arrogant deed could take place in our government. It's obvious the President has taken leave of his senses. With one terrible blow, he has swept our nation from a democracy into a fascist state. I fully intend to see that he is removed from office—the sooner, the better."

"How do you propose to do it?" Mayo pushed him. "Every time the members of the House convene to launch impeachment proceedings, the President sends in troops to disband them."

"The story will be different this time," Moran said confidently. "Tomorrow morning at ten o'clock, members of Congress will hold a joint session in Lisner Auditorium at George Washington University. And in order to meet without interference or disruption by the President's unauthorized and immoral use of the military, we intend to confront force with force. I have conferred with my House and Senate colleagues from the neighboring states of Maryland and Virginia who have prevailed upon their governors to protect our constitutional right to assemble by providing troops from their National Guard units."

"Will they have orders to shoot?" asked Mayo, smelling newsworthy blood.

"If attacked," Moran replied coldly, "the answer is an absolute yes."

"And so Civil War Two erupts," said Oates wearily as he switched off the TV set and turned to face Emmett, Mercier and Brogan.

"Moran is as daft as the President," Emmett said, shaking his head in disgust.

"I pity the American public for being forced to accept such miserable leadership material," Mercier grumbled.

"How do you read the upcoming confrontation at Lisner Auditorium?" Oates asked Emmett.

"The special forces of Army and Marines patrolling Capitol Hill are highly trained professionals. They can be counted on to stand firm and not attempt anything stupid. The National Guard is the real danger. All it takes is one weekend warrior to panic and fire off a round. Then we'll witness another Kent State bloodbath, except much worse. This time the Guard will have their fire returned by deadly marksmen."

"The situation won't be helped if a few congressmen fall in the crossfire," added Mercier.

"The President has to be isolated. The timetable must be moved up," said Oates.

Mercier looked unsold. "That means cutting back Dr. Edgely's evaluation of the President's brain signals."

"Preventing wholesale slaughter must take priority over a plan to mislead the Russians," said Oates.

Brogan gazed at the ceiling thoughtfully. "I think we might steal our chicken and pluck it too."

Oates smiled. "I hear the gears meshing in your head, Martin. What wild Machiavellian scheme has the CIA got up its sleeve now?"

"A way to give Edgely an advantage," answered Brogan with a foxlike grin. "A little something borrowed from *The Twilight Zone.*"

61

A LIMOUSINE WAS WAITING at Andrews Air Force Base when Pitt slowly eased his way down the boarding stairs from a Navy passenger jet. Admiral Sandecker was sitting in the car, hidden by the tinted windows.

He opened the door and helped Pitt inside. "How was the flight?"

"Mercifully, it was smooth."

"Do you have any luggage?"

"I'm wearing it," said Pitt. He winced and clenched his teeth as he slipped into the seat beside the admiral.

"You in much pain?"

"A little stiff. They don't tape cracked ribs like they did in the old days. Just let them heal on their own."

"Sorry I insisted on your return in such haste, but things in Washington are boiling up a storm, and Doug Oates is hoping you possess information that might clear up a few entanglements."

"I understand," Pitt said. "Has there been any news of Loren?"

"Nothing, I'm afraid."

"She's alive," said Pitt, staring out the window.

"I don't doubt it," Sandecker concurred. "Probably an oversight her name isn't on the survivor list. Maybe she requested anonymity to avoid the press."

"Loren had no reason to hide."

"She'll turn up," Sandecker said. "Now, suppose you tell me

367

how you managed to be present at the worst maritime tragedy in fifty years."

Pitt marveled at how the admiral could twist a conversation in another direction with the abruptness of leaping from a sauna into the snow.

"In the brief time we had together on the *Leonid Andreyev*," Pitt began, "Loren told me she was strolling on the deck on the first night of the cruise when the lights around the exterior of the ship went out, followed by the landing of a helicopter. Three passengers were taken off, two of them roughly handled. Loren thought she recognized one of them in the dim light as Alan Moran. Not certain whether her eyes were playing tricks, she called her aide Sally Lindemann over ship-to-shore phone and asked her to locate Moran's whereabouts. Sally turned up false trails covered over by vague reports and no Moran. She also discovered he and Marcus Larimer were supposed to be together. She then related the negative results to Loren, who told her to contact me. But the call was cut off. The Russians had monitored her calls and learned she'd accidentally stumbled into the middle of a delicate operation."

"So they made her a prisoner along with her congressional pals, who were on a one-way trip to Moscow."

"Except that Loren was more risk than asset. She was to be conveniently lost overboard."

"And after Lindemann contacted you?" Sandecker probed.

"Al Giordino and I drew up a plan and flew south, catching up with the ship in San Salvador and boarding there."

"Over two hundred people died on the *Leonid Andreyev*. You're lucky to be alive."

"Yes," Pitt said meditatively. "It was a near thing."

He went quiet, his mind's eye seeing only a face—the face of the steward who stood in the lifeboat leering down at him with the look of a man who enjoyed his work: a murderer without a shred of remorse.

"In case you're interested," said Sandecker, breaking the spell, "we're going direct to a meeting with Secretary Oates at the State Department."

"Make a detour by the Washington *Post*," Pitt said abruptly.

Sandecker gave him a negative look. "We can't spare the time to buy a newspaper."

"If Oates wants to hear what I've got, he'll damn well have to wait."

Sandecker made a sour expression and gave in. "Ten minutes is all you get. I'll call Oates and say your plane was delayed."

Pitt had met the Secretary of State previously, during the North American Treaty affair. The neatly trimmed hair was slate-colored, and the brown eyes moved with practiced ease as they read Pitt. Oates wore a five-hundred-dollar gray tailored suit and highly polished black custom shoes. There was a no-nonsense aggressiveness about him, and he moved well, almost like a track and field athlete.

"Mr. Pitt, how nice to see you again."

"Good to see you, Mr. Secretary."

Oates wrung Pitt's hand, then turned to the other men in the conference room and went through the introductions. The inner sanctum had turned out. Brogan of the CIA, Emmett of the FBI, National Security's Alan Mercier, whom Pitt also knew, and Dan Fawcett representing the White House. Admiral Sandecker remained at Pitt's side, keeping a wary eye on his friend.

"Please sit down," Oates said, waving them all to a chair.

Sam Emmett turned toward Pitt and regarded him with interest, noting the drawn lines in his face. "I've taken the liberty of pulling your packet, Mr. Pitt, and I must confess your service with the government reads like a novel." He paused to scan the dossier. "Directly responsible for saving innumerable lives during the Vixen operation. Instrumental in obtaining the Canadian merger treaty. Heading the project to raise the *Titanic*, with subsequent discovery of a rare element for the Sicilian project. You have an uncanny knack for getting around."

"I believe the word is 'ubiquitous,' " Oates injected.

"You were in the Air Force before joining NUMA," Emmett continued. "Rank of major. Excellent record in Vietnam." He hesitated, a strange inquisitive look growing on his face. "I see here you received a commendation for destroying one of our own aircraft."

"Perhaps I should explain that," Sandecker said, "since I was on the aircraft Dirk shot down."

"I realize we're pressed for time, but I'd be interested to hear that tale," said Oates.

Sandecker nodded agreeably. "My staff and I were flying on a twin turboprop transport from Saigon to a small coastal port north of Da Nang. Unknown to us, the field we were supposed to land on was overrun by North Vietnamese regulars. Our radio malfunctioned and my pilot was unable to receive the warning. Dirk was flying nearby, returning to his base from a bombing mission. The local commander directed him to intercept and alert us by whatever means available." Sandecker looked over at Pitt and smiled. "I have to say he tried everything short of a neon sign. He played charades from his cockpit, fired several bursts from his guns across our nose, but nothing penetrated our thick skulls. When we were on our final landing approach, coming in from the sea toward the airstrip, in what has to be a rare exhibition of precision aerial marksmanship, he shot out both our engines, forcing my pilot to ditch our plane in the water only one mile from shore. Dirk then flew cover, strafing enemy boats putting out from the beach, until everyone was taken aboard a Navy patrol vessel. After learning that he saved me from certain imprisonment and possible death, we became good friends. Several years later, when President Ford asked me to launch NUMA, I persuaded Dirk to join me."

Oates looked at Pitt through bemused eyes. "You lead an interesting life. I envy you."

Before Pitt could reply, Alan Mercier said, "I'm sure Mr. Pitt is curious why we asked him here."

"I'm well aware of the reason," Pitt said.

He looked from man to man. They all looked like they hadn't slept in a month. At last he addressed himself directly to Oates. "I know who was responsible for the theft and subsequent spill of Nerve Agent S into the Gulf of Alaska." He spoke slowly and distinctly. "I know who committed nearly thirty murders while hijacking the presidential yacht and its passengers. I know the identities of those passengers and why they were abducted. And lastly, I know who sabotaged the *Leonid Andreyev*, killing two hundred men, women and children. There is no speculation or guesswork on my part. The facts and evidence are rock solid."

The room took on an almost deathly stillness. No one made even the slightest attempt to speak. Pitt's statement had stunned them to the soles of their feet. Emmett had a distraught expression on his face. Fawcett clasped his hands to conceal his nervousness. Oates appeared dazed.

Brogan was the first to question Pitt. "I must assume, Mr. Pitt, you're alluding to the Russians?"

"No, sir, I am not."

"No chance you're mistaken?" asked Mercier.

"None."

"If not the Russians," asked Emmett in a cautious voice, "then who?"

"The head of the Bougainville Maritime empire, Min Koryo, and her grandson, Lee Tong."

"I happen to know Lee Tong Bougainville personally," said Emmett. "He is a respected business executive who donates heavily to political campaigns."

"So does the Mafia and every charlatan who's out to milk the government money machine," said Pitt icily. He laid a photograph on the table. "I borrowed this from the morgue file of the Washington *Post*. Do you recognize this man, Mr. Emmett, the one coming through the door in the picture?"

Emmett picked up the photograph and examined it. "Lee Tong Bougainville," he said. "Not a good likeness, but one of the few photos I've ever seen of him. He avoids publicity like herpes. You're making a grave error, Mr. Pitt, in accusing him of any crime."

"No error," Pitt said firmly. "This man tried to kill me. I have reason to believe he is accountable for the explosion that burned and sank the *Leonid Andreyev*, and the kidnapping of Congresswoman Loren Smith.''

"Congresswoman Smith's kidnapping is pure conjecture on your part.''

"Didn't Congressman Moran explain what occurred onboard the ship?'' Pitt asked.

"He refuses to be questioned by us,'' Mercier answered. "All we know is what he told the press.''

Emmett was becoming angry. He saw Pitt's revelations as an indictment of FBI fumbling. He leaned across the table with fire in his eyes. "Do you honestly expect us to believe your ridiculous fairy tales?'' he demanded in a cracking voice.

"I don't much care what you believe,'' Pitt replied, pinning the FBI director with his stare.

"Can you say how you collared the Bougainvilles?'' asked Oates.

"My involvement stems from the death of a friend by Nerve Agent S. I began a hunt for the responsible parties, I admit, purely for revenge. As my investigations gradually centered on Bougainville Maritime, other avenues of their illicit organization suddenly unfolded.''

"And you can prove your accusations?''

"Of course,'' Pitt answered. "Computer data describing their hijacking activities, drug business and smuggling operations is in a safe at NUMA.''

Brogan held up a hand. "Wait one moment. You stated the Bougainvilles were also behind the hijacking of the *Eagle?*''

"I did.''

"And you know who was abducted?''

"I do.''

"Not possible,'' Brogan stated flatly.

"Shall I name names, gentlemen?'' said Pitt. "Let's begin with the President, then Vice President Margolin, Senator Larimer and House Speaker Moran. I was with Larimer when he died. Margolin is still alive and held somewhere by the Bougainvilles. Moran is now here in Washington, no doubt conspiring to become the next messiah. The President sits in the White House immune to the political disaster he's causing, while his brain is wired to the apron strings of a Soviet psychologist whose name is Dr. Aleksei Lugovoy.''

If Oates and the others sat stunned before, they were absolutely petrified now. Brogan looked as if he'd just consumed a bottle of Tabasco sauce.

"You couldn't know all that!" he gasped.

"Quite obviously, I do," said Pitt calmly.

"My God, how?" demanded Oates.

"A few hours prior to the holocaust on the *Leonid Andreyev*, I killed a KGB agent by the name of Paul Suvorov. He was carrying a notebook, which I borrowed. The pages describe his movements after the President was abducted from the *Eagle.*"

Pitt took the tobacco pouch from under his shirt, opened it, and casually tossed the notebook on the table.

It lay there for several moments until Oates finally reached over and pulled it toward him slowly, as if it might bite his hand. Then he thumbed through the pages.

"That's odd," he said after a lapse. "The writing is in English. I would have expected some sort of Russian worded code."

"Not so strange," said Brogan. "A good operative will write in the language of the country he's assigned to. What is unusual is that this Suvorov took notes at all. I can only assume he was keeping an eye on Lugovoy, and the mind-control project was too technical for him to commit to memory, so he recorded his observations."

"Mr. Pitt," Fawcett demanded. "Do you have enough evidence for the Justice Department to indict Min Koryo Bougainville?"

"Indict yes, convict no," Pitt answered. "The government will never put an eighty-six-year-old woman as rich and powerful as Min Koryo behind bars. And if she thought her chances were on the down side, she'd skip the country and move her operations elsewhere."

"Considering her crimes," Fawcett mused, "extradition shouldn't be too tough to negotiate."

"Min Koryo has strong ties with the North Koreans," said Pitt. "She goes there and you'll never see her stand trial."

Emmett considered that and said stonily, "I think we can take over at this point." Then he turned to Sandecker as if dismissing Pitt. "Admiral, can you arrange to have Mr. Pitt available for further questioning, and supply us with the computer data he's accumulated on the Bougainvilles?"

"You can bank on full cooperation from NUMA," Sandecker said. Then he added caustically, "Always glad to help the FBI off a reef."

"That's settled," said Oates, stepping in as referee. "Mr. Pitt, do you have any idea where they might be holding Vice President Margolin?"

"No, sir. I don't think Suvorov did either. According to his notes, after he escaped from Lugovoy's laboratory, he flew over the area in a helicopter but failed to pinpoint the location or building. The only reference he mentions is a river south of Charleston, South Carolina."

Oates looked from Emmett to Brogan to Mercier. "Well, gentlemen, we have a starting point."

"I think we owe a round of thanks to Mr. Pitt," said Fawcett.

"Yes, indeed," said Mercier. "You've been most helpful."

Christ! Pitt thought to himself. They're beginning to sound like the Chamber of Commerce expressing their gratitude to a street cleaner who followed a parade.

"That's all there is?" he asked.

"For the moment," replied Oates.

"What about Loren Smith and Vince Margolin?"

"We'll see to their safety," said Emmett coldly.

Pitt awkwardly struggled to his feet. Sandecker came over and took his arm. Then Pitt placed his hands on the table and leaned toward Emmett, his stare enough to wither cactus.

"You better," he said with a voice like steel. "You damned well better."

62

As the *Chalmette* STEAMED TOWARD Florida, communications became hectic. Frantic inquiries flooded the ship's radio room, and the Koreans found it impossible to comply. They finally gave up and supplied only the names of the survivors onboard. All entreaties by the news media demanding detailed information on the *Leonid Andreyev*'s sinking went unanswered.

Friends and relatives of the passengers, frantic with anxiety, began collecting at the Russian cruise line offices. Here and there around the country flags were flown at half-mast. The tragedy was a subject of conversation in every home. Newspapers and television networks temporarily swept the President's closing of Congress out of the limelight and devoted special editions and newscasts to covering the disaster.

The Navy began airlifting the people whom their rescue operation had pulled from the water, flying them to naval air stations and hospitals nearest their homes. These were the first to be interviewed, and their conflicting stories blamed the explosion on everything from a floating mine of World War Two, to a cargo of weapons and munitions being smuggled by the Russians into Central America.

The Soviet diplomatic missions across the United States reacted badly by accusing the U.S. Navy of carelessly launching a missile at the *Leonid Andreyev*: a charge that had good play in the Eastern bloc countries but was generally shrugged off elsewhere as a crude propaganda ploy.

The excitement rose to a crescendo over a human interest story not seen since the sinking of the *Andrea Doria* in 1956. The continued silence from the *Chalmette* infuriated the reporters and correspondents. There was a mad rush to charter boats, airplanes and helicopters to meet the ship as she neared the coast. Fueled by the Korean captain's silence, speculation ran rampant as the tension built. Investigations into the cause were being demanded by every politician who could contrive an interview.

The *Chalmette* remained obstinate to the end. As she entered the main channel, she was surrounded by a wolf pack of buzzing aircraft and circling pleasure yachts and fishing boats crawling with reporters blasting questions through bullhorns. To their utter frustration, the Korean seamen simply waved and shouted back in their native tongue.

Slowly approaching the docking terminal at Dodge Island in the Port of Miami, the *Chalmette* was greeted by a massive crowd of over a hundred thousand people surging against a police cordon blocking the entrance to the pier. A hundred video and film cameras recorded the scene as the giant container ship's mooring lines were dropped over rusting bollards, gangways were rolled against the hull, and the survivors stood at the railings, astounded at the turnout.

Some appeared overjoyed to see dry land once again, others displayed solemn grief for husbands or wives, sons or daughters, they would never see again. A great hush suddenly fell on the mass of spectators. It was later described by an anchorman on the evening TV news as "the silence one experiences at the lowering of a coffin into the ground."

Unnoticed in the drama, a host of FBI agents dressed in the uniforms of immigration officials and customs inspectors swarmed aboard the ship, confirming the identities of the surviving passengers and crewmen of the *Leonid Andreyev,* interrogating each on the whereabouts of Congresswoman Smith, and searching every foot of the ship for any sign of her.

Al Giordino questioned the people whose faces he recalled seeing in the lifeboat. None of them could remember what happened to Loren or the Oriental steward after climbing aboard the *Chalmette*. One woman thought she saw them led away by the ship's captain, but she couldn't be sure. To many of those who had narrowly escaped death, their minds conveniently blanked out much of the catastrophe.

The captain and his crew claimed to know nothing. Photos of Loren provoked no recognition. Interpreters interrogated them in Korean, but their stories were the same. They never saw her. Six hours of in-depth search turned up nothing. At last the reporters were allowed to scramble onboard. The crew were acknowledged heroes of the sea. The image harvested by Bougainville Maritime and their courageous employees, who braved a sea of blazing oil to save four hundred souls, was a public relations windfall, and Min Koryo made the most of it.

It was dark and raining when Giordino wearily made his way across the now emptied dock and entered the customs office of the terminal. He sat at a desk for a long time staring out into the rain-soaked murk, his dark eyes mere shadows on his face.

He turned and looked at the telephone as though it was the enemy. Hyping his courage by a drink of brandy from a half-pint bottle in his coat pocket and lighting a cigar he had stolen from Admiral Sandecker, he dialed a number and let it ring, almost hoping no one would answer. Then a voice came on.

Giordino moistened his lips with his tongue and said, "Forgive me, Dirk. We were too late. She was gone."

The helicopter came in from the south and flashed on its landing lights. The pilot settled his craft into position, and then lowered it onto the roof of the World Trade Center in lower Manhattan. The side door dropped open and Lee Tong stepped out. He swiftly walked over to a privately guarded entrance and took an elevator down to his grandmother's living quarters.

He bent down and kissed her lightly on the forehead. "How was your day, *aunumi?*"

"Disastrous," she said tiredly. "Someone is sabotaging our bank records, shipping transactions, every piece of business that goes through a computer. What was once a study in efficient management procedures is now a mess."

Lee Tong's eyes narrowed. "Who can be doing it?"

"Every trail leads to NUMA."

"Dirk Pitt."

"He's the prime suspect."

"No more," said Lee Tong reassuringly. "Pitt is dead."

She looked up, her aged eyes questioning. "You know that for a fact?"

He nodded. "Pitt was onboard the *Leonid Andreyev*. An opportune stroke of luck. I watched him die."

"Your Caribbean mission was only half favorable. Moran lives."

"Yes, but Pitt is out of our hair and the *Leonid Andreyev* evens the score for the *Venice* and the gold."

Min Koryo suddenly lashed out at him. "That slimy scum Antonov tricked us out of one billion dollars in gold and cost us a good ship and crew, and you say the score is even?"

Lee Tong had never seen his grandmother so furious. "I'm enraged too, *aunumi*, but we're hardly in a position to declare war on the Soviet Union."

She leaned forward, her hands clasped so tightly around the armrests of her wheelchair that the knuckles showed through the delicate skin. "The Russians don't know what it's like to have terrorists striking at their throats. I want you to mount bombing attacks against their merchant fleet, especially their oil tankers."

Lee Tong put his arm around her shoulder as he would a hurt child. "The Hebrew eye-for-an-eye proverb may satisfy the vindictive soul, but it never adds to the bank account. Do not blind yourself with anger."

"What do you expect?" she snapped. "Antonov has the President and the gold where his Navy can salvage it. We allowed Lugovoy and his staff to leave with the President. Years of planning and millions of dollars wasted, and for what?"

"We have not lost our bargaining power," said Lee Tong.

"Vice President Margolin is still secure at the laboratory. And we have an unexpected bonus in Congresswoman Loren Smith."

"You abducted her?" she asked in surprise.

"She was also onboard the cruise ship. After the sinking, I arranged to have her flown off the *Chalmette* to the laboratory."

"She might prove useful," Min Koryo conceded.

"Don't be disheartened, *aunumi*," said Lee Tong. "We are still in the game. Antonov and his KGB bedfellow Polevoi badly underestimated the Americans' pathological devotion to individual rights. Instructing the President to close Congress to increase his powers was a stupid blunder. He will be impeached and thrown out of Washington within the week."

"Not so long as he has the backing of the Pentagon."

Lee Tong inserted a cigarette in the long silver holder. "The Joint Chiefs are sitting on the fence. They can't keep the House from meeting forever. Once they've voted for impeachment, the generals and admirals won't waste any time in swinging their support to Congress and the new chief executive."

"Which will be Alan Moran," Min Koryo said, as if she had a bad taste in her mouth.

"Unless we release Vincent Margolin."

"And cut our own throat. We'd be better off making him disappear for good or arrange to have his body found floating in the Potomac River."

"Listen, *aunumi*," said Lee Tong, his black eyes glinting. "We have two options. One, the laboratory is in perfect working order. Lugovoy's data is still in the computer disks. His mind-control techniques are ours for the taking. We can hire other scientists to program Margolin's brain. This time it will not be the Russians who control the White House, but Bougainville Maritime."

"But if Moran is sworn in as President before the brain-control transfer is accomplished, Margolin will be of no use to us."

"Option two," said Lee Tong. "Strike a deal with Moran to eliminate Margolin and pave his way to the White House."

"Can he be bought?"

"Moran is a shrewd manipulator. His political power base is

379

mortared with underhanded financial dealings. Believe me, *aunumi*, Alan Moran will pay any price for the Presidency."

Min Koryo looked at her grandson with great respect. He possessed an almost mystical grasp of the abstract. She smiled faintly. Nothing excited her merchant blood more than reversing a failure into a success. "Strike your bargain," she said.

"I'm happy you agree."

"You must move the laboratory facility to a safe place," she said, her mind beginning to shift gears. "At least until we know where we stand. Government investigators will soon fit the pieces together and concentrate their search on the Eastern Seaboard."

"My thoughts also," said Lee Tong. "I took the liberty of ordering one of our tugs to move it out of South Carolina waters to our private receiving dock."

Min Koryo nodded. "An excellent choice."

"And a practical one," he replied.

"How do we handle the congresswoman?" Min Koryo asked.

"If she talks to the press she might bring up a number of embarrassing questions for Moran to answer about his presence onboard the *Leonid Andreyev*. He'd be smart to pay for her silence also."

"Yes, he lied himself into a hole on that one."

"Or we can run her through the mind-control experiment and send her back to Washington. A servant in Congress could prove a great asset."

"But if Moran included her in the deal?"

"Then we sink the laboratory along with Margolin and Loren Smith in a hundred fathoms of water."

Unknown to Lee Tong and Min Koryo, their conversation was transmitted to the roof of a nearby apartment building where a secondary reception dish relayed the radio frequency signals to a voice-activated tape recorder in a dusty, vacant office several blocks away on Hudson Street.

The turn-of-the-century brick building was due to be demolished, and although most of the offices were empty, a few tenants were taking their sweet time about relocating.

Sal Casio had the tenth floor all to himself. He squatted in this particular site because the janitorial crew never bothered to step off the elevator, and the window had a direct line of sight to the secondary receiver. A cot, a sleeping bag and a small electric burner were all he needed to get by, and except for the receiver/recorder, his only other piece of furniture was an old faded and torn lobby chair that he'd salvaged out of a back-alley trash bin.

He turned the lock with his master key and entered, carrying a paper sack containing a corned beef sandwich and three bottles of Herman Joseph beer. The office was hot and stuffy, so he opened a window and stared at the lights across the river in New Jersey.

Casio performed the tedious job of surveillance automatically, welcoming the isolation that gave him a chance to let his mind run loose. He recalled the happy times of his marriage, the growing-up years with his daughter, and he began to feel mellowed. His long quest for retribution had finally threaded the needle and was drawing to a close. All that was left, he mused, was to write the Bougainville epilogue.

He looked down at the recorder while taking a bite out of the sandwich and noted the tape had rolled during his trip to the delicatessen. Morning would be soon enough to rewind and listen to it, he decided. Also, if he was playing back the recording when voices activated the system again, the previous conversation would be erased.

Casio had no way of guessing the critical content on the tape. The decision to wait was dictated by routine procedure, but the delay was to prove terribly costly.

"May I talk to you, General?"

About to leave for the day, Metcalf was in the act of snapping closed his briefcase. His eyes narrowed in apprehension at recognizing Alan Mercier, who was standing in the doorway.

"Of course, please come in and sit down."

The President's National Security Adviser moved toward the desk but remained standing. "I have some news you aren't going to like."

Metcalf sighed. "Bad news seems to be the order of the day lately. What is it?"

Mercier handed him an unmarked binder holding several sheets of typewritten paper and spoke in a soft, hurried voice. "Orders direct from the President. All American forces in Europe must be pulled out by Christmas. He's given you twenty days to draw up a plan for total withdrawal from NATO."

Metcalf slumped into his chair like a man struck with a hammer. "It's not possible!" he mumbled. "I can't believe the President would issue such orders!"

"I was as shocked as you are when he dropped the bomb on me," said Mercier. "Oates and I tried to reason with him, but it was useless. He's demanding everything be removed—Pershing and cruise missiles, all equipment, supply depots, our whole organization."

Metcalf was bewildered. "But what about our Western alliances?"

Mercier made a helpless gesture with his hands. "His outlook, one I've never heard him voice before, is to let Europe police Europe."

"But good God!" Metcalf snapped in sudden anger. "He's handing the entire continent to the Russians on a gold tray."

"I won't argue with you."

"I'll be damned if I'll comply."

"What will you do?"

"Go direct to the White House and resign," Metcalf said adamantly.

"Before you act hastily, I suggest you meet with Sam Emmett."

"Why?"

"There is something you should know," Mercier said in a low tone, "and Sam is in a better position to explain it than me."

63

THE PRESIDENT WAS SITTING at a writing table in his pajamas and bathrobe when Fawcett walked into the bedroom.

"Well, did you speak with Moran?"

Fawcett's face was grim. "He refused to listen to any of your proposals."

"Is that it?"

"He said you were finished as President, and nothing you could say was of any consequence. Then he threw in a few insults."

"I want to hear them," the President demanded sharply.

Fawcett sighed uncomfortably. "He said your behavior was that of a madman and that you belonged in the psycho ward. He compared you with Benedict Arnold and claimed he would see your administration wiped from the history books. After he ran through several more irrelevant slurs, he suggested you do the country a great service by committing suicide, thereby saving the taxpayers a long-drawn-out investigation and expensive trial."

The President's face became a mask of rage. "That sniveling little bastard thinks he's going to put me in a courtroom?"

"It's no secret, Moran is pulling out all stops to take your place."

"His feet are too small to fill my shoes," the President said through tight lips. "And his head is too big to fit the job."

"To hear him tell it, his right hand is already raised to take the oath of office," Fawcett said. "The proposed impeachment proceeding is only the first step in a blueprint for a transition from you to him."

"Alan Moran will never occupy the White House," the President said, his voice flat and hard.

"No congressional session, no impeachment," said Fawcett. "But you can't keep them corralled indefinitely."

"They can't meet until I give the word."

"What about tomorrow morning at Lisner Auditorium?"

"The troops will break that up in short order."

"Suppose the Virginia and Maryland National Guardsmen stand their ground?"

"For how long against veteran soldiers and Marines?"

"Long enough for a great many to die," said Fawcett.

"So what?" the President scoffed coldly. "The longer I keep Congress in disarray, the more I can accomplish. A few deaths are a small price to pay."

Fawcett looked at him uneasily. This was not the same man who solemnly swore during his campaign for the Presidency that no American boy would be ordered to fight and die under his administration. It was all he could do to act out his role of friend and adviser. After a moment he shook his head. "I hope you're not being overly destructive."

"Getting cold feet, Dan?"

Fawcett felt trapped in a corner, but before he could reply Lucas entered the room carrying a tray with cups and a teapot.

"Anyone care for some herbal tea?" he asked.

The President nodded. "Thank you, Oscar. That was very thoughtful of you."

"Dan?"

"Thanks, I could use some."

Lucas poured and passed out the cups, keeping one for himself. Fawcett drained his almost immediately.

"Could be warmer," he complained.

"Sorry," said Lucas. "It cooled on the way up from the kitchen."

"Tastes fine to me," the President said, between sips. "I don't care for liquid so hot it burns your tongue." He paused and set the cup on the writing desk. "Now then, where were we?"

"Discussing your new policies," Fawcett said, deftly sidestepping out of the corner. "Western Europe is in an uproar over your decision to withdraw American forces from NATO. The joke circulating around Embassy Row is that Antonov is planning a coming-out party at the Savoy Hotel in London."

"I don't appreciate the humor," the President said coldly. "President Antonov has given me his personal assurances that he will stay in his own yard."

"I seem to remember Hitler telling Neville Chamberlain the same thing."

The President looked as if he was going to make an angry retort, but suddenly he yawned and shook his head, fighting off a creeping drowsiness. "No matter what anyone thinks," he said slowly, "I've diffused the nuclear threat and that's all that matters."

Fawcett took the cue and yawned contagiously. "If you don't need me any more tonight, Mr. President, I think I'll head for home and a soft bed."

"Same here," said Lucas. "My wife and kids are beginning to wonder if I still exist."

"Of course. I'm sorry for keeping you so late." The President moved over to the bed, kicked off his slippers and removed his robe. "Turn on the TV, will you, Oscar? I'd like to catch a few minutes of the twenty-four-hour cable news." Then he turned to Fawcett. "Dan, first thing in the morning, schedule a meeting with General Metcalf. I want him to brief me on his troop movements."

"I'll take care of it," Fawcett assured him. "Good night."

In the elevator going down to the first floor Fawcett looked at his watch. "Two hours should do it."

"He'll sleep like the dead and wake up sicker than a dog," said Lucas.

"By the way, how did you manage it? I didn't see you slip anything into his tea, and yet you poured all three cups from the same pot."

"An old magician's trick," Lucas said, laughing. "The teapot had two interior compartments."

The elevator doors opened and they met Emmett, who was standing off to one side. "Any problems?" he asked.

Fawcett shook his head. "As smooth as glass. The President went down like a baby."

Lucas looked at him, his eyes cautious. "Now comes the hard part—fooling the Russians."

"He's sleeping unusually soundly tonight," said Lugovoy.

The monitoring psychologist who drew the early-morning shift nodded. "A good sign. Less chance for Comrade Belkaya to penetrate the President's dreams."

Lugovoy studied the display screen that recorded the President's body functions. "Temperature up one degree. Congestion forming in the nasal passages. Appears as though our subject is coming down with either a summer cold or the flu."

"Fascinating, we know he's been attacked by a virus before he feels it."

"I don't think it's serious," Lugovoy said. "But you better keep a tight watch in case it develops into something that could jeopardize the project—"

Abruptly the green data filling the dozen screens encompassing the console faded into distorted lines and vanished into blackness.

The monitoring psychologist tensed. "What in hell—"

Then, as quickly as the display data were wiped clean, they returned in bright, clear readings. Lugovoy quickly checked the circuit warning lights. They all read normal.

"What do you suppose that was?"

Lugovoy looked thoughtful. "Possibly a temporary failure in the implant transmitter."

"No indication of a malfunction."

"An electrical interference, perhaps?"

"Of course. An atmospheric disturbance of some kind. That would explain it. The symptoms match. What else could it be?"

Lugovoy passed a weary hand across his face and stared at the monitors. "Nothing," he said somberly. "Nothing of any concern."

General Metcalf sat in his military residence and swirled the brandy around in his glass as he closed the cover of the report in his lap. He looked up sadly and stared at Emmett, who was sitting across the room.

"A tragic crime," he said slowly. "The President had every chance for achieving greatness. No finer man ever sat in the White House."

"The facts are all there," said Emmett, gesturing at the report. "Thanks to the Russians, he's mentally unfit to continue in office."

"I must agree, but it's no easy thing. He and I have been friends for nearly forty years."

"Will you call off the troops and allow Congress to meet at Lisner Auditorium tomorrow?" Emmett pressed.

Metcalf sipped the brandy and gave a weary nod to his head. "I'll issue orders for their withdrawal first thing in the morning. You can inform the House and Senate leaders they can hold session in the Capitol building."

"Can I ask a favor?"

"Of course."

"Is it possible to remove the Marine guard from around the White House by midnight?"

"I don't see why not," said Metcalf. "Any particular reason?"

"A deception, General," Emmett replied. "One you will find most intriguing."

64

SANDECKER STOOD IN THE CHART ROOM of NUMA and peered through a magnification enhancer at an aerial photo of Johns Island, South Carolina. He straightened and looked at Giordino and Pitt, who were standing on the opposite side of the table. "Beats me," he said after a short silence. "If Suvorov pinpointed his landmarks correctly, I can't understand why he didn't find Bougainville's lab facility from a helicopter."

Pitt consulted the Soviet agent's notebook. "He used an old abandoned gas station for his base point," he said, pointing to a tiny structure on the photograph, "which can be distinguished here."

"Emmett or Brogan know you made a copy before we left Guantánamo Bay?" asked Giordino, nodding toward the notebook.

Pitt smiled. "What do you think?"

"I won't tell if you won't."

"If Suvorov escaped the lab at night," said Sandecker, "it's conceivable he got his bearings crossed."

"A good undercover operative is a trained observer," Pitt explained. "He was precise in his description of landmarks. I doubt he lost his sense of direction."

"Emmett has two hundred agents crawling over the area," Sandecker said. "As of fifteen minutes ago, they came up empty-handed."

"Then where?" Giordino asked in a general sense. "No structure the size Suvorov recorded shows on the aerial survey. A few

388

old houseboats, some scattered small homes, a couple of decrepit sheds, nothing on the order of a warehouse.''

"An underground facility?" Sandecker speculated.

Giordino considered the point. "Suvorov did say he took the elevator up to break out.''

"On the other hand, he mentions walking down a ramp to a gravel road.''

"A ramp might suggest a boat,'' Giordino ventured.

Sandecker looked doubtful. "No good. The only water near the spot where Suvorov puts the lab is a creek with a depth of no more than two or three feet. Far too shallow to float a vessel large enough to require an elevator.''

"There is another possibility," said Pitt.

"Which is?''

"A barge.''

Giordino looked across the table at Sandecker. "I think Dirk may have something.''

Pitt stepped over to a telephone, dialed a number and switched the call to a speaker.

"Data Department," came a groggy voice.

"Yaeger, you awake?''

"Oh, God, it's you, Pitt. Why do you always have to call after midnight?''

"Listen, I need information on a particular type of vessel. Can your computers come up with a projection of its class if I supply the dimensions?''

"Is this a game?''

"Believe you me, this is no game," Sandecker growled.

"Admiral!" Yaeger muttered, coming alert. "I'll get right on it. What are your dimensions?''

Pitt thumbed to the correct page in the notebook and read them off into the speaker phone. "A hundred sixty-eight feet in length at inside perpendiculars by thirty-three feet in the beam. The approximate height is ten feet.''

"Not much to go on," Yaeger grumbled.

"Try," Sandecker replied sternly.

"Hold on. I'm moving to the keyboard."

Giordino smiled at the admiral. "Care to make a wager?"

"Name it."

"A bottle of Chivas Regal against a box of your cigars Dirk's right."

"No bet," said Sandecker. "My specially rolled cigars cost far more than a bottle of scotch."

Yaeger could be heard clearing his throat. "Here it is." There was a slight pause. "Sorry, not enough data. Those figures are a rough match for any one of a hundred different craft."

Pitt thought a moment. "Suppose the height was the same from bow to stern."

"You talking a flat superstructure?"

"Yes."

"Hold on," said Yaeger. "Okay, you've lowered the numbers. Your mystery vessel looks like a barge."

"Eureka," exclaimed Giordino.

"Don't cash in your coupons yet," Yaeger cautioned. "The dimensions don't fit any known barge in existence."

"Damn!" Sandecker blurted. "So near, yet—"

"Wait," Pitt cut in. "Suvorov gave us interior measurements." He leaned over the speaker phone. "Yaeger, add two feet all around and run it through again."

"You're getting warmer," Yaeger's voice rasped over the speaker. "Try this on for size—no pun intended—one hundred and ninety-five by thirty-five by twelve feet."

"Beam and height correspond," said Pitt, "but your length is way off."

"You gave me interior length between perpendicular bulkheads. I'm giving you overall length including a raked bow of twenty-five feet."

"He's right," said Sandecker. "We didn't allow for the scoop of the forward end."

Yaeger continued. "What we've got is a dry cargo barge, steel construction, two hundred and eighty to three hundred tons—self-enclosed compartments for carrying grain, lumber and so forth.

Probably manufactured by the Nashville Bridge Company, Nashville, Tennessee.''

"The draft?" Pitt pushed.

"Empty or loaded?"

"Empty."

"Eighteen inches."

"Thanks, pal. You've done it again."

"Done what?"

"Go back to sleep."

Pitt switched off the speaker and turned to Sandecker. "The smoke clears."

Sandecker fairly beamed. "Clever, clever people, the Bougainvilles."

Pitt nodded. "I have to agree. The last place anyone would look for an expensively equipped laboratory is inside a rusty old river barge moored in a swamp."

"She also has the advantage of being movable," said Sandecker. The admiral referred to any vessel, scow or aircraft carrier in the feminine gender. "A tug can transport and dock her anywhere the water depth is over a foot and a half."

Pitt stared at the aerial photo pensively. "The next test is to determine where the Bougainvilles hid it again."

"The creek where she was tied leads into the Stono River," Sandecker noted.

"And the Stono River is part of the Intracoastal Waterway," Pitt added. "They can slip it into any one of ten thousand rivers, streams, bays and sounds from Boston to Key West."

"No way of second-guessing the destination," Giordino murmured dejectedly.

"They won't keep it in South Carolina waters," Pitt said. "Too obvious. The catch, as I see it, boils down to north or south, and a distance of six, maybe eight hundred miles."

"A staggering job," Sandecker said in a soft voice, "untangling her from the other barges plying the eastern waterways. They're thicker than leaves in a New England October."

"Still, it's more than we had to go on before," Pitt said hopefully.

Sandecker turned from the photo. "Better give Emmett a call and steer him onto our discovery. Someone in his army of investigators may get lucky and stumble on the right barge."

The admiral's words were empty of feeling. He didn't want to say what was on his mind.

If Lee Tong Bougainville suspected government investigators were breathing down his neck, his only option would be to kill the Vice President and Loren, and dispose of their bodies to cover his tracks.

65

"THE PATIENT WILL LIVE to fight another day," said Dr. Harold Gwynne, the President's physician, cheerfully. He was a cherubic little man with a balding head and friendly blue eyes. "A common case of the flu bug. Stay in bed for a couple of days until the fever subsides. I'll give you an antibiotic and something to relieve the nausea."

"I can't stay on my back," the President protested weakly. "Too much work to do."

There was little fight in his words. The chills from a 103-degree fever sandbagged him, and he was constantly on the verge of vomiting. His throat was sore, his nose stuffed up and he felt rotten from scalp to toenails.

"Relax and take it easy," Gwynne ordered. "The world can turn without you for a few hours." He jabbed a needle into the President's arm and then held a glass of water for him to wash down a pill.

Dan Fawcett entered the bedroom. "About through, Doc?" he inquired.

Gwynne nodded. "Keep him off his feet. I'll check back around two o'clock this afternoon." He smiled warmly, closed his black bag and stepped through the door.

"General Metcalf is waiting," Fawcett said to the President.

The President pushed a third pillow behind his back and struggled to a sitting position, massaging his temples as the room began to spin.

Metcalf was ushered in, resplendent in a uniform decorated by eight rows of colorful ribbons. There was a briskness about the general that was not present at their last meeting.

The President looked at him, his face pallid, his eyes drooping and watery. He began to hack uncontrollably.

Metcalf came over to the bed. "Is there anything I can get you, sir?" he asked solicitously.

The President shook his head and waved him away. "I'll survive," he said at last. "What's the situation, Clayton?"

The President never called his Joint Chiefs by rank, preferring to lower them a couple of notches down their pedestal by addressing them with their Christian names.

Metcalf shifted in his chair uncomfortably. "The streets are quiet at the moment, but there were one or two isolated incidents of sniping. One soldier was killed and two Marines wounded."

"Were the guilty parties apprehended?"

"Yes, sir," Metcalf answered.

"A couple of criminal radicals, no doubt."

Metcalf stared at his feet. "Not exactly. One was the son of Congressman Jacob Whitman of South Dakota and the other the son of Postmaster General Kenneth Potter. Both were under seventeen years of age."

The President's face looked stricken for an instant and then it quickly hardened. "Are your troops deployed at Lisner Auditorium?"

"One company of Marines is stationed on the grounds around the building."

"Hardly seems enough manpower," said the President. "The Maryland and Virginia Guard units combined will outnumber them five to one."

"The Guard will never come within rifle shot of the auditorium," said Metcalf knowingly. "Our plan is to defuse their effectiveness by stopping them before they arrive in the city."

"A sound strategy," the President said, his eyes briefly gleaming.

"I have a special news report," said Fawcett, who was kneeling

394

in front of the television set. He turned up the volume and stood aside so the picture could be seen from the bed.

Curtis Mayo was standing beside a highway blocked by armed soldiers. In the background a line of tracks stretched across the road, the muzzles of their guns pointing ominously at a convoy of personnel carriers.

"The Virginia National Guard troops that Speaker of the House Alan Moran was relying on to protect a meeting of Congress on the George Washington University campus this morning have been turned back outside the nation's capital by armored units of the Army special forces. I understand the same situation exists with the Maryland Guard northeast of the city. So far there has been no threat of fighting. Both state Guard units appeared subdued, if not in numbers, by superior equipment. Outside Lisner Auditorium, a company of Marines, under the command of Colonel Ward Clarke, a Vietnam Medal of Honor holder, is turning away members of Congress, refusing them entrance to hold a session. And so once again the President has thwarted House and Senate members while he continues his controversial foreign affairs programs without their approval. This is Curtis Mayo, CNN news, on a highway thirty miles south of Washington."

"Seen enough?" asked Fawcett, turning off the set.

"Yes, yes," the President rasped happily. "That ought to keep that egomaniac Moran floundering without a rudder for a while."

Metcalf rose to his feet. "If you won't need me any further, Mr. President, I should be getting back to the Pentagon. Conditions are pretty unsettled with our division commanders in Europe. They don't exactly share your views on pulling back their forces to the States."

"In the long haul they'll come to accept the risks of a temporary military imbalance in order to dilute the dreaded specter of nuclear conflict." The President shook Metcalf's hand. "Nice piece of work, Clayton. Thank you for keeping Congress paralyzed."

Metcalf walked along the corridor for fifty feet until it emptied into the vast interior of a barren warehouselike structure.

The stage set that contained an exact replica of the President's White House bedroom sat in the middle of the Washington Navy Yard's old brick ordnance building, which had gone virtually unused since World War Two.

Every detail of the deception was carefully planned and executed. A sound technician operated a stereo recorder whose tape played the muted sounds of street traffic at a precise volume. The lighting outside the bedroom windows matched the sky exactly, with an occasional shadowed effect to simulate a passing cloud. The filters over the lamps were set to emit changing yellow-orange rays to duplicate the day's movement of the sun. Even the plumbing in the adjacent bathroom worked with the familiar sounds of the original, but emptying its contents into a septic tank rather than the Washington city sewer system. The huge concrete floor was heavily populated with Marine guards and Secret Service agents, while overhead, amid great wooden rafters, men stood on catwalks manning the overhead lighting system.

Metcalf stepped across a network of electrical cables and entered a large mobile trailer parked against the far wall. Oates and Brogan were waiting and invited him into a walnut-paneled office.

"Coffee?" Brogan asked, holding up a glass urn.

Metcalf nodded gratefully, reached for a steaming cup and sank into a chair. "My God, for a minute there I could have sworn I was in the White House."

"Martin's people did an amazing job," said Oates. "He flew in a crew from a Hollywood studio and constructed the entire set in nine hours."

"Did you have a problem moving the President?"

"The easy part," replied Brogan. "We transferred him in the same moving van as the furniture. Strange as it might sound, the toughest hurdle was the paint."

"How so?"

"We had to cover the walls with a material that didn't have the smell of new paint. Fortunately, our chemists at the agency lab came up with a chalky substance they could tint that left no aroma."

"The news program was an ingenious touch," commented Metcalf.

"It cost us," Oates explained. "We had to make a deal with Curtis Mayo to give him the exclusive story in return for his cooperation in broadcasting the phony news report. He also agreed to hold off a network investigation until the situation cools."

"How long can you continue to deceive the President?"

"For as long as it takes," answered Brogan.

"For what purpose?"

"To study the President's brain patterns."

Metcalf threw Brogan a very dubious look indeed. "You haven't convinced me. Stealing back the President's mind from the Russians who stole it in the first place is stretching my gullibility past the breaking point."

Brogan and Oates exchanged looks and smiled. "Would you like to see for yourself?" Oates asked.

Metcalf put down the coffee. "I wouldn't miss it for a fifth star."

"Through here," Oates said, opening a door and gesturing for Metcalf to enter.

The entire midsection and one end of the mobile trailer was filled with exotic electronic and computer hardware. The monitoring data center was a generation ahead of Lugovoy's equipment onboard the Bougainville laboratory.

Dr. Raymond Edgely noticed their appearance and came over. Oates introduced him to General Metcalf.

"So you're the mysterious genius who heads up Fathom," Metcalf said. "I'm honored to meet you."

"Thank you, General," Edgely said. "Secretary Oates tells me you have some suspicions about the project."

Metcalf looked around the busy complex, studying the scientists who were engrossed in the digital readings on the monitors. "I admit I'm puzzled by all this."

"Basically, it's quite simple," Edgely said. "My staff and I are intercepting and accumulating data on the President's brain rhythms in preparation for switching control from his cerebral implant to our own unit, which you see before you."

Metcalf's skepticism melted away. "Then this is all true. The Russians really are dominating his thoughts."

"Of course. It was their instructions to close down Congress and the Supreme Court so he could instigate projects beneficial to the Communist bloc without legislative roadblocks. The order to withdraw our troops from NATO is a perfect example. Exactly what the Soviet military wants for Christmas."

"And you people can actually take the place of the President's mind?"

Edgely nodded. "Do you have any messages you wish sent to the Kremlin? Some misleading information perhaps?"

Metcalf brightened like a searchlight. "I think my intelligence people can write some interesting science fiction that should spur them to draw all the wrong conclusions."

"When do you expect to release the President from Lugovoy's command?" Brogan asked.

"I think we can make the transfer in another eight hours," answered Edgely.

"Then we'll get out of the way and leave you to your work," Oates said.

They left the data acquisition room and returned to the outer office, where they found Sam Emmett waiting. Oates could see that the expression on his face spelled trouble.

"I've just come from Capitol Hill," Emmett said. "They're acting like animals in a zoo who haven't been fed. Debate over impeachment is raging in Congress. The President's party is making a show of loyalty, but that's all it is—a show. There is no support on a broad front. Desertions come in wholesale lots."

"What about committee?" asked Oates.

"The opposition party rammed through a floor vote to bypass a committee investigation to save time."

"A guess as to when they'll decide?"

"The House may vote on impeachment this afternoon."

"The odds?"

"Five to one in favor."

"The Senate?"

"Not in the cards. A straw vote indicates the Senate will vote to convict with considerably more than the necessary two-thirds majority."

"They're not wasting any time."

"Considering the President's recent actions, the impeachment proceedings are looked upon as a national emergency."

"Any show of support for Vince Margolin?"

"Of course, but no one can stand behind him if he doesn't put in an appearance. Sixty seconds after the President is swept from office, someone has to take the oath as successor. The rumor mills have him hiding out until the last minute so he won't be associated with the President's crazy policies."

"What about Moran?"

"This is where it gets sticky. He's claiming he has proof that Margolin committed suicide and that I am covering up the fact."

"Anybody believe him?"

"Doesn't matter if he's believed. The news media are jumping on his statements like ants on honey. His news conferences are getting massive attention, and he's demanding Secret Service protection. His aides have already drafted a transition plan and named his inner circle of advisers. Shall I go on?"

"The picture is clear," Oates said resignedly. "Alan Moran will be the next President of the United States."

"We can't allow it," Emmett said coldly.

The others stared at him. "Unless we can produce Vince Margolin by tomorrow," asked Brogan, "how can we prevent it?"

"Any way possible," said Emmett. He produced a folder from an attaché case. "I'd like you gentlemen to take a look at this."

Oates opened the folder and studied the contents without comment, and then passed it on to Brogan, who in turn handed it to Metcalf. When they finished they gazed at Emmett as if silently nominating him to speak first.

"What you gentlemen read in the report is true," he said simply.

"Why hasn't this come out before?" Oates demanded.

"Because there was never a reason to order an in-depth investigation into the man before," answered Emmett. "The FBI is not in the habit of revealing skeletons in our legislators' closets unless there is solid evidence of criminal activity in their backgrounds. Dirt on divorces, petty misdemeanors, sexual perversions or traffic violations we file in a vault and look the other way. Moran's file showed him to be clean, too clean for someone who clawed his way to the top without benefit of education, average intelligence, a penchant for hard work, wealth or important contacts. Nothing about his character indicated aggressiveness or talent. As you can see the results aren't exactly a recommendation for a Pope."

Metcalf scanned the report again. "This stock brokerage firm in Chicago, what is it called? Ah, yes, Blackfox and Churchill."

"A front to launder Moran's bribery and payoff operation. The names came off tombstones in a Fargo, North Dakota, cemetery. Bogus stock transactions are conducted to hide bribe money from shady special-interest groups, defense contractors, state and city officials seeking federal funding and not caring how they get it, underworld payments for favors. Speaker of the House Moran makes the Bougainvilles look like Boy Scouts."

"We've got to go public with this," Brogan said adamantly.

"I wouldn't push it," cautioned Oates. "Moran would go to any length to deny it, claiming it was a frame-up to keep him from leading the country to reconciliation and unity. I can see him pleading for the American tradition of fair play while he's hanging from the cross. And by the time the Justice Department can make things tough for him, he will have been sworn in as President. Let's face it, you can't put the country through two impeachment proceedings in the same year."

Metcalf nodded his head in agreement. "Coming on the heels of the President's insane policies and Moran's ravings about the Vice President's presumed death, the upheaval may prove more than the public can accept. A complete loss of confidence in the federal system could ignite a voters' revolt during the next election."

"Or worse," Emmett added. "More and more people are refusing to pay taxes on the rationale they don't like where their tax dollars are spent. And you can't blame them for not wanting to support a government managed by inept leaders and rip-off artists. You get five million people out there who tear up their tax forms come next April fifteenth, and the federal machinery as we know it will cease to function."

The four men sat in the trailer office like frozen figures in a painting. The fantasy of their conjecture was not implausible. Nothing like this had ever happened before. The prospects of surviving the storm unscathed seemed remote.

At last Brogan said, "We're lost without Vince Margolin."

"That fellow Pitt over at NUMA gave us our first tangible lead," said Brogan.

"So what have you got?" asked Metcalf.

"Pitt deduced that the mind control laboratory where Margolin is held is inside a river barge."

"A what?" Metcalf asked as if he hadn't heard right.

"River barge," Emmett repeated. "Moored God knows where along the inland water route."

"Are you searching?"

"With every available agent Martin and I can spare from both our agencies."

"If you give me a few more details and come up with a quick plan to coordinate our efforts, I'll throw in whatever forces the Defense Department can muster in the search areas."

"That would certainly help, General," said Oates. "Thank you."

The phone rang and Oates picked it up. After listening silently for a moment, he set it down. "Crap!"

Emmett had never heard Oates use such an expletive before. "Who was that?"

"One of my aides reporting from the House of Representatives."

"What did he say?"

"Moran just railroaded through passage of the impeachment vote."

"Then nothing stands between him and the Presidency except trial by the Senate," Brogan said.

"He's moved up the timetable by a good ten hours," said Metcalf.

"If we can't produce the Vice President by this time tomorrow," Emmett said, "we can kiss the United States goodbye."

66

GIORDINO FOUND PITT IN HIS HANGAR, sitting comfortably in the back seat of an immense open touring car, his feet propped sideways on a rear door. Giordino couldn't help admiring the classic lines of the tourer. Italian built in 1925, with coachwork by Cesare Sala, the red torpedo-bodied Isotta-Fraschini sported long, flared fenders, a disappearing top and a coiled cobra on the radiator cap.

Pitt was contemplating a blackboard mounted on a tripod about ten feet from the car. A large nautical chart depicting the entire inland water route was tacked to the outer frame. Across the board he had written several notations and what appeared to Giordino as a list of ships.

"I've just come from the admiral's office," Giordino said.

"What's the latest?" Pitt asked, his eyes never leaving the blackboard.

"The Joint Chiefs of Staff have thrown the armed forces into the hunt. Combined with agents from the FBI and CIA, they should be able to cover every inch of shoreline by tomorrow evening."

"On the ground, by the sea and in the air," Pitt murmured uninterestedly. "From Maine to Florida."

"Why the sour grapes?"

"A damned waste of time. The barge isn't there," Pitt said, flipping a piece of chalk in the air.

Giordino shot him a quizzical look. "What are you babbling about? The barge has to be in there somewhere."

403

"Not necessarily."

"You saying they're searching in the wrong place?"

"If you were the Bougainvilles, you'd expect an exhaustive, whole-hog hunt, right?"

"Elementary reasoning," Giordino said loftily. "Me, I'd be more inclined to camouflage the barge under a grove of trees, hide it inside an enclosed waterfront warehouse, or alter the exterior to look like a giant chicken coop or whatever. Seems to me concealment is the logical way to go."

Pitt laughed. "Your chicken coop brainstorm, now that's class."

"You got a better idea?"

Pitt stepped out of the Isotta, went to the blackboard and folded over the inland waterway chart, revealing another chart showing the coastline along the Gulf of Mexico. "As it happens, yes, I do." He tapped his finger on a spot circled in red ink. "The barge holding Margolin and Loren captive is somewhere around here."

Giordino moved closer and examined the marked area. Then he looked at Pitt with an expression usually reserved for people who held signs announcing the end of the world.

"New Orleans?"

"Below New Orleans," Pitt corrected. "I judge it to be moored there now."

Giordino shook his head. "I think your brakes went out. You're telling me Bougainville towed a barge from Charleston, around the tip of Florida and across the gulf to the Mississippi River, almost seventeen hundred miles in less than four days? Sorry, pal, the tug isn't built that can push a barge that fast."

"Granted," Pitt allowed. "But suppose they cut off seven hundred miles?"

"How?" inquired Giordino, his voice a combination of doubt and sarcasm. "By installing wheels and driving it cross-country?"

"No joke," Pitt said seriously. "By towing it through the recently opened Florida Cross State Canal from Jacksonville on the Atlantic to Crystal River on the Gulf of Mexico, shortcutting the entire southern half of the state."

The revelation sparked Giordino. He peered at the chart again, studying the scale. Then, using his thumb and forefinger as a pair of dividers, he roughly measured the reduced distance between Charleston and New Orleans. When he finally turned and looked at Pitt, he wore a sheepish smile.

"It works." Then the smile quickly faded. "So what does it prove?"

"The Bougainvilles must have a heavily guarded dock facility and terminal where they unload their illegal cargoes. It probably sits on the banks of the river somewhere between New Orleans and the entrance to the gulf."

"The Mississippi Delta?" Giordino showed his puzzlement. "How'd you pull that little number out of the hat?"

"Take a look," Pitt said, pointing to the list of ships on the blackboard and then reading them off. "The *Pilottown*, *Belle Chasse*, *Buras*, *Venice*, *Boothville*, *Chalmette*—all ships under foreign registry but at one time owned by Bougainville Maritime."

"I fail to make the connection."

"Take another look at the chart. Every one of those ships is named after a town along the river delta."

"A symbolic cipher?"

"The only mistake the Bougainvilles ever let slip, using a code to designate their area of covert operations."

Giordino peered closer. "By God, it fits like a girl in tight shorts."

Pitt rapped the chart with his knuckles. "I'll bet my Isotta-Fraschini against your Bronco that's where we'll find Loren."

"You're on."

"Run over to the NUMA air terminal and sign out a Lear jet. I'll contact the admiral and explain why we're flying to New Orleans."

Giordino was already heading toward the door. "I'll have the plane checked out and ready for takeoff when you get there," he called over his shoulder.

Pitt hurried up the stairs to his apartment and threw some clothes in an overnight bag. He opened a gun cabinet and took out an old

Colt Thompson submachine serial number 8545, and two loaded drums of .45-caliber cartridges and laid them in a violin case. Then he picked up the phone and called Sandecker's office.

He identified himself to Sandecker's private secretary and was put through. "Admiral?"

"Dirk?"

"I think I've got the barge area fixed."

"Where?"

"The Mississippi River Delta. Al and I are leaving for there now."

"What makes you think it's in the delta?"

"Half guess, half deduction, but it's the best lead we've got."

Sandecker hesitated before replying. "You'd better hold up," he said quietly.

"Hold up? What are you talking about?"

"Alan Moran is demanding the search be called off."

Pitt was stunned. "What in hell for?"

"He says it's a waste of time and taxpayers' money to continue, because Vince Margolin is dead."

"Moran is full of crap."

"He has the clothes Margolin was wearing the night they all disappeared to back up his claim."

"We still have Loren to think about."

"Moran says she's dead too."

Pitt felt like he was sinking in quicksand. "He's a damned liar!"

"Maybe so, but if he's right about Margolin, you're defaming the next President of the United States."

"The day that little creep takes the oath is the day I turn in my citizenship."

"You probably won't be alone," Sandecker said sourly. "But your personal feelings don't alter the situation."

Pitt stood unbudging. "I'll call you from Louisiana."

"I was hoping you'd say that. Stay in close contact. I'll do everything I can to help from this end."

"Thanks, you old fraud."

"Get your ass in gear and tell Giordino to stop swiping my cigars."

Pitt grinned and hung up. He finished packing and hurried from the hangar. Three minutes after he drove off, his phone began to ring.

Two hundred miles away an ashen-faced Sal Casio despairingly waited in vain for an answer.

67 _____

TEN MINUTES AFTER TWELVE NOON, Alan Moran walked through the main corridor of the Capitol, down a narrow staircase and opened the door to an out-of-the-way office he kept for privacy. Most men in his position were constantly surrounded by a hive of aides, but Moran preferred to travel a solitary trail, unhindered by inane conversation.

He always wore the wary look of an antelope scanning the African plain for predators. He had the expressionless eyes of a man whose only love was power, power attained by whatever means, at whatever cost. To achieve his prestigious position in Congress, Moran had carefully nurtured a billboard image. In his public life he oozed a religious fervor, the personification of the friendly shy man with a warm sense of humor, the appeal of the neighbor next door, ever ready to lend his lawn mower, and the past of a man born underprivileged, self-made.

His private life couldn't have been more at odds. He was a closet atheist who looked on his constituents and the general public as ignorant rabble whose chronic complaints led to an open license to twist and control for his own advantage. Never married, with no close friends, he lived frugally like a penitent monk in a small rented apartment. Every dollar over and above subsistence level went into his secret corporation in Chicago, where it was added to funds obtained through illegal contributions, bribes and other corrupt investments. Then it was spread and sown to increase his power base until there were few men and women with top positions in business and government who weren't tied to his coattails by political favors and influence.

Douglas Oates, Sam Emmett, Martin Brogan, Alan Mercier and Jesse Simmons, who was recently released from house arrest, were seated in Moran's office as he entered. They all rose as he took his place behind a desk. There was an air of smugness about him that was obvious to his visitors. He had summoned them to his private territory and they had no choice but to respond.

"Thank you for meeting with me, gentlemen," he said with a false smile. "I assume you know the purpose."

"To discuss your possible succession to the Presidency," Oates replied.

"There is no *possible* about it," Moran rejoined waspishly. "The Senate is scheduled to begin the trial at seven o'clock this evening. As next in line to the executive office, I feel it is my sworn duty to take the oath immediately afterward and assume the responsibility for healing the wounds caused by the President's harmful delusions."

"Aren't you jumping the gun?" asked Simmons.

"Not if it means stopping the President from any more outrageous actions."

Oates looked dubious. "Some people might interpret your undue reaction, at least until Vince Margolin is proven dead, as an improper attempt to usurp power, especially when considering your part in motivating the President's ouster."

Moran glared at Oates and shifted his stare to Emmett. "You have the Vice President's clothing that was found in the river."

"My FBI lab has identified the clothing as belonging to Margolin," acknowledged Emmett. "But it shows no indication of being immersed in water for two weeks."

"Most likely it washed onshore and dried out."

"You say the fisherman who came to your office with the evidence stated he snagged it in the middle of the Potomac River."

"You're the Director of the FBI," snapped Moran angrily. "You figure it out. I'm not on trial here."

"Perhaps it would be in the best interests of everyone present," Oates said quietly, "to continue the search for Margolin."

"I'm in total agreement," said Brogan. "We can't write him off until we find his body."

"Questions will most certainly arise," added Mercier. "For example, how did he die?"

"Obviously he drowned," Moran answered. "Probably when the *Eagle* sank."

"Also," Mercier continued, "you never satisfactorily explained when and how you and Marcus Larimer disembarked from the *Eagle* and traveled to an as-yet-undisclosed resort for your Caribbean fishing trip."

"I'll be happy to answer any questions before a congressional investigating committee," said Moran. "Certainly not here and now in front of people who are in opposition to me."

"You must understand, in spite of his mistakes, our loyalties lie with the President," said Oates.

"I don't doubt it for a minute," said Moran. "That's why I summoned you here this morning. Ten minutes after the Senate votes, I will be sworn in as President. My first official act will be to announce either your resignations or firings; you have your choice. As of midnight tonight, none of you will be working for the United States government."

The narrow paved road snaked through the high hills that dropped steeply into the Black Sea. In the rear seat of a Cadillac Seville stretch limousine, Vladimir Polevoi sat reading the latest report from Aleksei Lugovoy. Every once in a while he looked up and gazed at the dawn sun creeping past the horizon.

The limousine turned heads wherever it rolled. Custom built with inlaid wood cabinets, color TV, electric divider, liquor bar and overhead stereo console, it had been ordered purchased by Polevoi and transported to Moscow under the guise of studying its mechanical technology. Shortly after its arrival he'd commandeered it as his own.

The long car climbed around the forested edge of a craggy cliff until the road ended at a huge wooden door hinged to a high brick wall. A uniformed officer saluted the KGB chief and pressed a switch. The door silently swung open to a vast garden that blazed with flowers, and the car was driven in and parked beside a spreading one-story house, constructed in a Western contemporary design.

Polevoi walked up circular stone steps and entered a foyer, where he was greeted by President Antonov's secretary and escorted to a table and chairs on a terrace overlooking the sea.

After a few moments Antonov appeared, followed by a pretty servant girl carrying a huge plate of smoked salmon, caviar and iced vodka. Antonov seemed in a happy mood and casually sat on the iron railing around the terrace.

"You have a beautiful new dacha," said Polevoi.

"Thank you. I had it designed by a firm of French architects. They didn't charge me a ruble. It won't pass critical inspection by a state building committee, of course. Too bourgeois. But what the hell. Times are changing." Then he switched the subject abruptly. "What news of events in Washington?"

"The President will be removed from office," answered Polevoi.

"When?"

"By this time tomorrow."

"No doubt of this."

"None."

Antonov picked up his vodka glass and emptied it, and the girl immediately refilled it. Polevoi suspected the girl did more than simply pour vodka for the head of the Soviet Union.

"Did we miscalculate, Vladimir?" Antonov asked. "Did we expect to accomplish too much too quickly?"

"Nobody can second-guess the Americans. They don't behave in predictable ways."

"Who will be the new President?"

"Alan Moran, Speaker of the House of Representatives."

"Can we work with him?"

"My sources say he has a devious mind, but can be swayed."

411

Antonov stared at a tiny fishing boat far below on the water. "If given the choice, I'd prefer Moran over Vice President Margolin."

"Most definitely," Polevoi agreed. "Margolin is a dedicated enemy of our Communist society, and an adamant believer in expanding the American military machine beyond our own."

"Anything our people can do, discreetly, of course, to assist Moran into the White House?"

Polevoi shook his head. "Very little worth the risk of exposure and adverse propaganda."

"Where is Margolin?"

"Still in the hands of the Bougainvilles."

"Any chance that that old Oriental bitch will release him in time to cut out Moran?"

Polevoi shrugged helplessly. "Who can predict her schemes with any accuracy?"

"If you were her, Vladimir, what would you do?"

Polevoi paused thoughtfully, then said, "I'd strike a deal with Moran to dispose of Margolin."

"Has Moran the guts to accept?"

"If one man who was being held prisoner in an extremely vulnerable situation stood between you and leadership of a superpower, how would you play it?"

Antonov broke into a loud laugh that frightened a nearby bird into flight. "You read through me like glass, old friend. I see your point. I wouldn't hesitate to remove him."

"The American news media report that Moran is claiming Margolin committed suicide by drowning."

"So your theory is on firm ground," said Antonov. "Maybe the old Steel Lotus will end up doing us a favor after all."

"At least our deal with her didn't cost anything."

"Speaking of cost, what is the status of the gold?"

"Admiral Borchavski has begun salvage operations. He expects to raise every bar within three weeks."

"That's good news," said Antonov. "And what of Dr. Lugovoy? Can he continue his project after the President is cast from office?"

"He can," Polevoi replied. "Locked inside the President's head is a vast treasure store of United States secrets. Lugovoy has yet to tap it."

"Then keep the project going. Provide Lugovoy with an extensive list of delicate political and military subjects we wish explored. All American leaders who leave office are consulted for their experience, regardless of inept handling of their administrations. The capitalist masses have short memories. The knowledge the President now possesses and has yet to learn from briefings by his successors can be of great benefit to us in the future. This time we shall practice patience and probe slowly. The President's brain may turn out to be a goose that lays golden intelligence eggs for decades to come."

Polevoi raised his glass. "A toast to the best secret agent we ever recruited."

Antonov smiled. "Long may he produce."

Across half a world, Raymond Edgely sat at a console and read the data that unrolled from a paper recorder. He raised his glasses and rubbed his reddened eyes. Despite his seeming tiredness, there was a tightly contained nervous energy about him. His competitive juices were stirred. The opportunity to beat his most esteemed counterpart in a game of psychological intrigue drove him beyond any thought of sleep.

Dr. Harry Greenberg, a respected psychiatric researcher in his own right, lit a curved-stem clay pipe. After stoking the stained yellow bowl to life, he pointed the mouthpiece at the recorder.

"No sense in waiting any longer, Ray. I'm satisfied we have the necessary data to make the switch."

"I hate to rush in before I'm certain we can fool Aleksei."

"Do it," Greenberg urged. "Stop screwing around and go for it."

Edgely looked around at his ten-member team of psychologists. They stared back at him expectantly. Then he nodded. "Okay, everybody stand by to transfer thought communication from the President's implant to our central computer."

413

Greenberg walked around the room, briefly talking to everyone, double-checking the procedures. Three sat at the computer console, their hands poised over the buttons. The rest studied the display screens and monitored the data.

Edgely nervously wiped his palms on a handkerchief. Greenberg stood slightly off to one side and behind him.

"We don't want to break in during a thought pattern or in the middle of Lugovoy's instructions," Greenberg cautioned.

"I'm aware of that," Edgely said without taking his eyes from the brainwave translator display. "Our computer transmission also has to match his heart rate and other life functions exactly."

The programmer punched in the command and waited. They all waited, watching the empty screen that would reveal success or failure. The minutes ticked by, nobody speaking, the only sounds coming from the soft hum of the electronic hardware as the computer poised for the precise millisecond to take command. Then suddenly the display screen read: "COMMUNICATIONS TRANSFER ACCOMPLISHED."

They all expelled a collective sigh of relief and began talking again, and shaking hands with the enthusiasm of a NASA flight control center after a successful rocket launch.

"Think Aleksei will fall for it?" Edgely asked.

"Don't worry. No suspicion will ever cross his mind. Aleksei Lugovoy's ego will never allow him to believe somebody pulled the wool over his eyes." Greenberg paused to expel a smoke ring. "He'll swallow everything we hand him and send it off to Moscow as if he was God's gift to espionage."

"I hope so," said Edgely, dabbing at his sweating forehead. "The next step is to get the President over to Walter Reed Hospital and remove the implant."

"First things first," said Greenberg, producing a bottle of champagne as a staff member passed out glasses. The cork was popped and the wine poured. Greenberg held up his glass.

"To Doc Edgely," he said, grinning, "who just set the KGB back ten years."

414

PART IV

The <u>Stonewall</u> <u>Jackson</u>

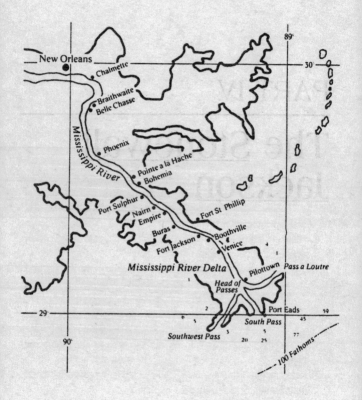

68

PITT DOZED MOST OF THE FLIGHT while Giordino manned the controls. The afternoon sun blazed from a clear sky as they dropped down over the blue-green waters of Lake Pontchartrain and lined up on the small airport that poked out from the New Orleans shore. The aquamarine-colored NUMA jet touched down on the asphalt landing strip and rolled to a stop near a helicopter with DELTA OIL LTD. painted on the side.

Nearby, a man in a seersucker suit stepped from a parked car and walked over. He removed his sunglasses and held out his hand as Pitt climbed from the Lear jet's cabin.

"Mr. Pitt?" he inquired, white teeth gleaming in a tanned face.

"I'm Pitt."

"Clyde Griffin, FBI, special agent in charge of the Louisiana field office."

Giordino stepped to the ground and Pitt made the introductions.

"What can we do for you, Mr. Griffin?"

"Director Emmett asked me to state officially that the Bureau cannot provide official assistance on your hunt."

"I don't recall asking for any," said Pitt.

"I said no 'official assistance,' Mr. Pitt." The white teeth locked in a broad smile. "Unofficially, this is Sunday. The Director suggested that what field agents do on their day off is their busi-

417

ness. I have eight men at my disposal who feel what you're doing is more important than their golf game."

"Emmett gave his blessing?"

"Strictly off the record, he strongly insinuated that if we don't find the Vice President pretty damned quick, he'll put a boot up my ass so far I'll never sit down at the piano again."

"My kind of guy," said Giordino.

"Were you briefed on what we're looking for?" Pitt asked.

Griffin nodded. "A river barge. We've already checked out about two hundred between here and Baton Rouge."

"You searched north. I figure it to be south."

Griffin stared down at the ground doubtfully. "Most all the incoming freighters and tankers unload at the city docks. Then the cargo is transferred north by towboat. Few barges ply the delta waters south except those carrying trash and garbage to be dumped in the ocean."

"All the more reason to look in that direction."

Griffin made an inviting gesture toward the helicopter. "My men are waiting in cars along the river front. We can direct them from the air."

"Delta Oil make a good cover?" Pitt asked.

"Oil company whirlybirds are a common sight around these parts," answered Griffin. "They're heavily used to carry men and supplies to offshore rigs in the gulf and pipe construction throughout the bayous. Nobody gives them a second glance."

Pitt excused himself and returned inside the NUMA plane, reappearing a minute later with the violin case. Then he entered the helicopter and was introduced to the pilot, a thin blond, dreamy-eyed woman who spoke in a slow, deep drawl. Pitt wouldn't have taken her for an FBI agent, which she was, nor did she fit her name. "Slats" Hogan.

"Y'all play the violin when ya fly?" Hogan asked curiously.

"Soothes my fear of height," Pitt replied, smiling.

"We get all kinds," Hogan muttered.

They fastened their seat belts and Hogan lifted the craft into the air and made a pass over the heart of the city before turning south.

A tiny green streetcar crept along St. Charles Avenue, the tracks glinting as they reflected the sun through the trees. Pitt could easily make out the massive white roof of the Superdome, the largest sports structure of its kind in the world. The tightly packed houses and narrow streets of the French Quarter, the green grass of Jackson Square and the spires of the St. Louis Cathedral slipped past off to their right. And then they broke over the muddy brown-green waters of the Mississippi River.

"There it is," announced Hogan. "Old Man River, too thick to drink and too thin to plow."

"Spend any time on it?" Griffin asked Pitt.

"I conducted a historical survey a few years ago on a pair of Confederate Civil War wrecks about sixty miles further down river in Plaquemines Parish."

"I know this great little restaurant in the parish—"

"So do I. The name is Tom's. Excellent gulf oysters on the half-shell. Be sure and ask for Tom's mama's special chili pepper juice. Fantastic on the oysters."

"You get around."

"I try."

"Got any idea where the barge might be hidden?"

"Keep an eye open for a dock and warehouse that appear rundown and little used, but well protected with heavy security—excessive number of guards, high fencing, perhaps dogs. The barge, rusted and in disrepair, will be stashed nearby. My guess is somewhere between Chalmette and Pilottown."

"You can only reach Pilottown by boat," said Griffin. "The delta highway ends ten miles above at a town called Venice."

"I stand corrected."

They went silent for a minute while the river below flowed along at almost four knots between the great levees that shielded the land from flood. Small farms with cows grazing in pastures and orange groves spread across the narrow strips of solid ground bordering the levees, before sliding away into marshland. They flew over

Port Sulphur, with its great piers entrenched along the west bank. Small mountains of yellow sulphur rose fifty feet over the flat, poisoned ground.

The next half-hour produced the first of three false alarms. A few miles below Port Sulphur they spotted an abandoned cannery with two barges tied up beside it. Griffin radioed his team of agents, who were chasing the helicopter from the road on the west bank. A quick search proved the building to be empty, and the barges contained only bilge water and silt.

They continued south, flying over the vast marshes and meandering bayous toward the gulf, spotting several grazing deer, a number of alligators sunning themselves in the mud and a small herd of goats that looked up at their passing with indifferent curiosity.

A huge freighter churned upriver, thrusting its blunt bow against the current. The flag of registry on its stern flapped red with a gold star and hammer and sickle.

"Russian," Pitt observed.

"The Soviets own a fair percentage of the five thousand ships that steam into New Orleans every year," said Griffin.

"Want to see what's on that barge?" Hogan asked, pointing. "There, tied up behind that dredge on the east bank."

Griffin nodded. "We'll check this one out ourselves."

Hogan nodded her blond mane. "I'll set you down on the levee."

She expertly dropped the tires of the helicopter onto the crushed-shell road that ran along the top of the levee. Three minutes later Griffin ran across a creaking ramp to the barge. Another three minutes and he was back strapping himself in his seat.

"No luck?" asked Pitt.

"A bummer. The old tub is half filled with oil. Must be used as a refilling station for the dredge."

Pitt looked at his watch. Two-thirty. Time was sifting away. A few more hours and Moran would be sworn in as President. He said, "Let's keep the show moving."

"Ah hear y'all talkin'," Hogan said as she brought the craft up and over the river in one quick bank that had Giordino feeling his stomach to see if it was still in place.

Eight more miles and they drew another blank after spying a barge moored suspiciously under a marine maintenance repair shed. A quick search by the ground team showed it was a derelict.

They pushed on past the fishing towns of Empire and Buras. Then suddenly, after dipping around a bend, they saw a sight straight out of the golden years of the river, a spectacular and picturesque vision almost forgotten. Long white hull, wide beam, with a plume of steam drifting over her decks, a sidewheel paddle steamer sat with her flat nose nudged into the west embankment.

"Shades of Mark Twain," said Giordino.

"She's a beauty," Pitt said as he admired the gingerbread carvings on the many-storied superstructure.

"The *Stonewall Jackson*," Griffin explained. "She's been an attraction on the river for seventy years."

The steamer's landing stages were lowered on the bank in front of an old brick fortress constructed in the shape of a pentagon. A sea of parked cars and a crowd of people wandered the parade ground and brick ramparts. In the center of a nearby field a cloud of blue smoke billowed above two opposing lines of men who seemingly stood shooting at each other.

"What's the celebration?" asked Giordino.

"A War Between the States re-enactment," Hogan replied.

"Run that by me again."

"A staging of a historic battle," Pitt explained. "As a hobby, men form brigades and regiments based on actual fighting units from the Civil War. They dress in authentic woven uniforms and shoot blanks out of exact-replica or original guns. I witnessed a re-enactment at Gettysburg. They're quite spectacular, almost like the real thing."

"Too bad we can't stop and watch the action," Griffin said.

"Plaquemines Parish is a storehouse of history," said Hogan. "The star-shaped structure where they're staging the mock battle is called Fort Jackson. Fort St. Philip, what little is left of it, is directly across the river. This is the area where Admiral Farragut ran the forts and captured New Orleans for the Yankees in 1862."

It required no imagination at all to see and hear in their minds the thundering clashes of cannon fire between Union gunboats and Confederate batteries. But the curve in the river where Admiral Farragut and his fleet forced their passage over a century past was now quiet. The water rolled silently between the scrub-lined shores, having long ago covered the bones of the ships that sank during the battle.

Hogan suddenly stiffened in her seat and peered over the instrument panel through the cockpit window. Not more than two miles away, a ship with her bow aimed downriver was tied alongside an old wooden dock whose pilings ran under a large metal warehouse. Behind the stern of the ship lay a barge and a towboat.

"This could be it," she said.

"Can you read the name on the ship?" Pitt asked from the rear passenger's seat.

Hogan momentarily took her left hand off the collective pitch control lever to shield her eyes. "Looks like . . . no, that's a town we just passed."

"Which town?"

"Buras."

"Could be it. Hell," Pitt said with triumph in his voice, "this *is* it."

"No crew members about on the ship," Griffin observed. "You've got your high fence about the place, but I don't see any sign of guards or dogs. Looks pretty quiet to me."

"Don't bet on it," Pitt said. "Keep flying downriver, Slats, until we're out of sight. Then swing back below the west levee and rendezvous with your people in the chase cars."

Hogan continued her course for five minutes and then came around in a great half-circle to the north and landed on a high school football field. Two cars crammed with FBI agents were waiting when the helicopter touched down.

Griffin twisted in his seat to face Pitt. "I'll take my team and enter through the front gate that opens onto the loading dock. You and Giordino remain with Hogan and act as aerial observers. Should be a routine operation.''

"Routine operation," Pitt replied acidly. "Walk up to the gate, flash your shiny FBI badge and watch everybody cringe. Never happen. These people kill like you and I swat mosquitoes. Driving up in the open is an invitation to get your head blown off. You'd be smart to wait and call up reinforcements.''

Griffin's face showed he was not one to be told how to run his business. He ignored Pitt and gave instructions to Hogan.

"Give us two minutes to reach the gate before you take off and circle the warehouse. Open a frequency with our field communications office and inform them of the situation. And tell them to relay our reports to Bureau headquarters in Washington.''

He stepped to the ground and got in the lead car. They drove around the high school gymnasium onto the almost invisible road that led to the Bougainville docking facility and disappeared over the levee.

Hogan raised the helicopter into the air and went on the radio. Pitt moved to the co-pilot's seat and watched as Griffin and his men approached a high chain-link fence enclosing the pier and warehouse. With a mounting uneasiness he observed Griffin leave the car and stand at the gate, but no one appeared to confront him.

"Something's happening," said Hogan. "The towboat and barge are moving.''

She was right. The towboat began to slip away from the pier, pushing the barge with its blunt snout. The helmsman expertly maneuvered the two craft into the main stream and turned toward the gulf.

Pitt grabbed a spare microphone/headset. "Griffin!" he snapped, "the barge is being moved from the area. Forget the ship and warehouse. Return to the road and take up the chase.''

"I read you," Griffin's voice acknowledged.

Abruptly, doors flew open on the ship and the crew scrambled across the decks, tearing canvas covers off two hidden gun emplacements on the foredeck and stern. The trap was sprung.

"Griffin!" Pitt shouted into the microphone. "Get out. For God's sake, get out."

The warning came too late. Griffin leaped into the lead car, which roared off toward the safety of the levee as 20-millimeter Oerlikon machine guns began rapping out a deadly hail. Bullets tore into the wildly careening car, shattering windows, shredding the thin metal like cardboard and ripping through the flesh and bones of those inside. The rear car coasted to a stop, bodies spilling out onto the ground, some lying still, some trying to crawl for cover. Griffin and his men made it over the top of the levee, but all of them were badly wounded.

Pitt had whipped open the violin case, stuck the barrel of the Thompson out the side window and sprayed the bow gun of the *Buras.* Hogan instantly realized what he was up to and banked the helicopter to give him a better angle of fire. Men fell around the deck, never knowing where the deadly barrage came from. The gunners on the stern were more alert. They swung their Oerlikon from Griffin and his agents and began spewing its shells into the sky. Hogan made a game effort to dodge the fire that missed not by feet but inches. She kicked the helicopter around the ship as though it had a charmed life as the one-sided gun duel clattered over the river.

Then the trajectory from the *Buras* swayed through the air and hammered into the helicopter. Pitt threw up an arm to protect his eyes as the windshield disintegrated and blew into the cockpit. Steel-nosed bullets punctured the thin aluminum fuselage and wreaked havoc with the engine.

"Ah can't see," Hogan announced in a surprisingly calm voice. Her face ran crimson from several cuts, most of the blood streaming from a scalp wound into her eyes, blinding her.

Except for a few deep scratches on his arm, Pitt was untouched. He passed the machine gun to Giordino, who was wrapping a sleeve torn from his shirt around a shell gash on his right calf. The helicopter was losing power and dipping sharply toward the middle of the river. Pitt reached out and took the controls from Hogan and banked away from a sudden murderous fire that erupted from the towboat. A dozen men appeared from the pilothouse and a hatch on top of the barge and wildly threw automatic weapons fire at the battered helicopter.

Oil was streaming out of the engine, and the rotor blades were madly vibrating. Pitt reduced the collective pitch to keep the rotor speed from falling too quickly. He saw the instrument panel break into fragments from a storm of bullets. He was fighting a hopeless battle; he couldn't hold on to the sky much longer. The forward motion dropped off and he was losing lateral control.

On the ground behind the levee, Griffin sat on his knees in helpless rage, holding a shattered wrist, watching the helicopter struggle like a great mortally wounded bird. The fuselage was so riddled by holes he couldn't believe anybody onboard was still alive. He watched the craft slowly die, dragging a long trail of smoke as it faltered and limped upriver, barely clearing a grove of trees along the bank and disappearing from sight.

69

SANDECKER SAT IN EMMETT'S PRIVATE OFFICE at FBI headquarters and chewed idly on a cigar stub, his thoughts depleted. Brogan nervously juggled a half-empty cup of coffee that had long since turned cold.

General Metcalf walked in and sat down. "You all look like pallbearers," he said with forced cheerfulness.

"Isn't that what we are?" said Brogan. "As soon as the Senate convicts, all that's left to do is hold the wake."

"I've just come from the Senate reception room," Metcalf said. "Secretary Oates is buttonholing members of the President's party, trying to persuade them to hold off."

"What are his chances?" asked Sandecker.

"Nil. The Senate is only going through the formality of a trial. Four hours from now, it will all be over."

Brogan shook his head disgustedly. "I hear Moran has Chief Justice O'Brien standing by to administer the oath."

"The oily bastard won't waste a second," Emmett muttered.

"Any word from Louisiana?" Metcalf asked.

Emmett gave the general a negative look. "Not for an hour. The last report from my agent in charge of the field office said he was making a sweep of a promising dock site."

"Any concrete reason to believe Margolin is hidden in the delta?"

"Only a stab in the dark by my special projects director," replied Sandecker.

Metcalf looked at Emmett. "What are you doing about the Bougainvilles?"

"I've assigned nearly fifty agents to the case."

"Can you make an arrest?"

"A waste of time. Min Koryo and Lee Tong would be back on the streets in an hour."

"Surely there must be enough evidence."

"Nothing the Attorney General can sink his teeth into. Most of their illegal operations are managed outside our borders in Third World nations that aren't overly friendly toward the United States—"

The phone buzzed.

"Emmett."

"Agent Goodman in communications, sir."

"What is it, Goodman?"

"I have contact with agent Griffin in Louisiana."

"About time," Emmett snapped impatiently. "Put me through."

"Hold on." There was a pause broken by an audible click, and then Emmett heard the sound of labored breathing. He switched on the speaker amplifer so the others could hear.

"Griffin, this is Sam Emmett, can you hear me?"

"Yes, sir, very clearly." The words seemed uttered in pain. "We ran . . . ran into trouble."

"What happened?"

"We spotted a Bougainville cargo ship tied to a pier beside a barge and towboat about seventy miles below New Orleans. Before my team and I could gain entry for a search, we were fired upon by heavy weapons mounted on the ship. Everyone was hit . . . I have two killed and seven wounded, including myself. It was a massacre." The voice choked and went quiet for a few moments. When it came back on the line the tone was noticeably weaker. "Sorry for not making contact sooner, but our communications gear was shot out and I had to walk two miles before I could find a telephone."

Emmett's face took on a compassionate look. The thought of a badly wounded man trailing blood for two miles in the scorching heat of summer stirred his normally rock-hard emotions.

Sandecker moved closer to the speaker. "What of Pitt and Giordino?"

"The NUMA people and one of my agents were flying surveillance in our helicopter," Griffin answered. "They got the hell shot out of them and crashed somewhere upriver. I doubt there were any survivors."

Sandecker stepped back, his expression gone lifeless.

Emmett leaned over the speaker. "Griffin?"

His only reply was a vague muttering.

"Griffin, listen to me. Can you go on?"

"Yes, sir . . . I'll try."

"The barge, what is the situation with the barge?"

"Tug . . . tug pushed it away."

"Pushed it where?"

"Downriver . . . last seen going toward Head of Passes."

"Head of Passes?"

"The bottom end of the Mississippi where the river splits into three main channels to the sea," answered Sandecker. "South Pass, Southwest Pass, and Pass a Loutre. Most major shipping uses the first two."

"Griffin, how long since the barge left your area?"

There was no answer, no buzzing of a broken connection, no sound at all.

"I think he's passed out," said Metcalf.

"Help is on the way. Do you understand, Griffin?"

Still no reply.

"Why move the barge out to sea?" Brogan wondered aloud.

"No reason I can think of," said Sandecker.

Emmett's phone buzzed on his interoffice line.

"There's an urgent call for Admiral Sandecker," said Don Miller, his deputy director.

Emmett looked up. "A call for you, Admiral. If you wish, you can take it in the outer office."

Sandecker thanked him and stepped into the anteroom, where

Emmett's private secretary showed him to a telephone at an empty desk.

He punched the blinking white button. "This is Admiral Sandecker."

"One moment, sir," came the familiar voice of the NUMA headquarters' chief operator.

"Hello?"

"Sandecker here. Who's this?"

"You're a tough nut to crack, Admiral. If I hadn't said my call concerned Dirk Pitt, your secretary would never have arranged our connection."

"Who is this?" Sandecker demanded again.

"My name is Sal Casio. I'm working on the Bougainville case with Dirk."

Ten minutes later, when Sandecker walked back into Emmett's office, he appeared stunned and shaken. Brogan instantly sensed something was wrong.

"What is it?" he asked. "You look like you've rubbed shoulders with a banshee."

"The barge," Sandecker murmured quietly. "The Bougainvilles have struck a deal with Moran. They're taking it out into the open sea to be scuttled."

"What are you saying?"

"Loren Smith and Vince Margolin are sentenced to die so Alan Moran can be President. The barge is to be their tomb in a hundred fathoms of water."

70

"ANY SIGN OF PURSUIT?" the river pilot asked, synchronizing the control levers of the helm console with the finesse of a conductor leading an orchestra.

Lee Tong stepped back from the large open window at the rear of the pilothouse and lowered the binoculars. "Nothing except a strange cloud of black smoke about two or three miles astern."

"Probably an oil fire."

"Seems to be following."

"An illusion. The river has a habit of doing weird things to the eyes. What looks to be a mile away is four. Lights where no lights are supposed to be. Ships approaching in a channel that fade away as you get closer. Yes, the river can fool you when she gets playful."

Lee Tong gazed up the channel again. He had learned to tune out the pilot's never-ending commentary on the Mississippi, but he admired his skill and experience.

Captain Kim Pujon was a longtime professional river pilot for Bougainville Maritime Lines, but he still retained his Asian superstitious nature. He seldom took his eyes off the channel and the barge ahead as he expertly balanced the speeds of the four engines generating 12,000 horsepower and delicately guided the towboat's four forward rudders and six backing rudders. Under his feet the huge diesels pounded over at full power, driving the barge through the water at nearly sixteen miles an hour, straining the cables that held the two vessels together.

They hurtled past an inbound Swedish oil tanker, and Lee Tong braced himself as the barge and towboat swept up and over the wash. "How much further to deep water?"

"Our hull passed from fresh to salt about ten miles back. We should cross the coastal shallows in another fifty minutes."

"Keep your eyes open for a research ship with a red hull and flying the British blue ensign."

"We're boarding a Royal Navy ship after we scuttle?" Pujon asked in surprise.

"A former Norwegian merchantman," explained Lee Tong. "I purchased her seven years ago and refitted her out as a research and survey vessel—a handy disguise to fool customs authorities and the Coast Guard."

"Let us hope it fools whoever chases after us."

Lee Tong grunted. "Why not? Any American search force will be told we were picked up and are under lock and key by the finest English accent money can buy. Before the research ship docks in New Orleans, you, I and our crew will be long gone."

Pujon pointed. "The Port Eads light coming up. We'll be in open water soon."

Lee Tong nodded in grim satisfaction. "If they couldn't stop us by now, they're too late, far too late."

General Metcalf, laying his long and distinguished career on the line, ignored Moran's threats and ordered a military alert throughout the Gulf Coast states. At Eglin Air Force Base and Hurlburt Field in Florida, tactical fighter wings and special operations gunships scrambled and thundered west while attack squadrons rose from Corpus Christi Naval Air Station in Texas and swept toward the east.

He and Sandecker raced by car to the Pentagon to direct the rescue operation from the war room. Once the vast machine was set into motion, they could do little but listen to reports and stare at an enormous satellite photomap thrown on the screen by a rear projector.

Metcalf failed to conceal his apprehension. He stood uneasily rubbing his palms together, peering at the lights on the map indicating the progress of the air strike as the planes converged on a circle lit in red.

"How soon before the first planes arrive?" asked Sandecker.

"Ten, no more than twelve minutes."

"Surface craft?"

"Not less than an hour," replied Metcalf bitterly. "We were caught short. No naval craft are in the immediate area except a nuclear sub sixty miles out in the gulf."

"Coast Guard?"

"There's an armed rescue-response cutter off Grand Island. It might make it in time."

Sandecker studied the photomap. "Doubtful. It's thirty miles away."

Metcalf wiped his hands with a handkerchief. "The situation looks grim," he said. "Except for scare tactics the air mission is useless. We can't send in planes to strike the towboat without endangering the barge. One is practically on top of the other."

"Bougainville would quickly scuttle the barge in any case."

"If only we had a surface craft in the area. At least we might attempt a boarding."

"And rescue Smith and Margolin alive."

Metcalf sank into a chair. "We might pull it off yet. A Navy special warfare SEAL attachment is due to arrive by helicopter in a few minutes."

"After what happened to those FBI agents, they could be going to a slaughter."

"Our last hope," Metcalf said helplessly. "If they can't save them, nobody can."

The first aircraft to arrive on the scene was not a screaming jet fighter but a Navy four-engined reconnaissance plane that had been diverted from weather patrol. The pilot, a boyish-faced man in his middle twenties, tapped his co-pilot on the arm and pointed down to his left.

"A towboat pushing one barge. She must be what all the fuss is about."

"What do we do now?" asked the co-pilot, a narrow-jawed slightly older man with bushy red hair.

"Notify base with the cheery news. Unless, of course, you want to keep it a secret."

Less than a minute after the sighting report was given, a gruff voice came over the radio. "Who is the aircraft commander?"

"I am."

"I am, who?"

"You go first."

"This is General Clayton Metcalf of the Joint Chiefs."

The pilot smiled and made a circular motion around the side of his head with an index finger. "Are you crazy or is this a gag?"

"My sanity is not an issue here, and no, this is not a gag. Your name and rank, please."

"You won't believe it?"

"I'll be the judge."

"Lieutenant Ulysses S. Grant."

"Why should I doubt you?" Metcalf laughed. "There was a great third baseman by that name."

"My father," Grant said in awe. "You remember him?"

"They don't hand out four stars for bad memories," said Metcalf. "Do you have television equipment onboard, Lieutenant?"

"Yes . . . yes, sir," Grant stammered as he realized who he was really talking to. "We tape storms close-on for the meteorologists."

"I'll have my communications officer give your video operator the frequency for satellite transmission to the Pentagon. Keep your camera trained on the towboat."

Grant turned to his co-pilot. "My God, what do you make of that?"

433

71

THE TOWBOAT SURGED PAST THE LOOKOUT at the South Pass pilot station, the last outpost of the muddy Mississippi, and swept into the open sea.

Captain Pujon said, "Thirty miles to deep water."

Lee Tong nodded as his eyes studied the circling weather plane. Then he picked up his binoculars and scanned the sea. The only ship in sight was his counterfeit research vessel approaching from the east about eight miles off the port bow.

"We've beaten them," he said confidently.

"They can still blow us out of the water from the air."

"And risk sinking the barge? I don't think so. They want the Vice President alive."

"How can they know he's onboard?"

"They don't, at least not for certain. One more reason they won't attack what might be an innocent towboat unloading a trash barge at sea."

A crewman scrambled up the steps to the pilothouse and stepped through the door. "Sir," he said, pointing, "an aircraft coming up astern."

Lee Tong swung the binoculars in the direction of the crewman's outstretched arm. A U.S. Navy helicopter was beating its way toward the towboat only fifteen feet above the waves.

He frowned and said, "Alert the men."

The crewman threw a salute and hurried off.

"A gunship?" Pujon asked uneasily. "It could hover and blast us to bits without scratching the barge."

"Fortunately no. She's an assault transport. Probably carrying a team of Navy SEALS. They mean to assault the towboat."

Lieutenant Homer Dodds stuck his head out the side jump door of the chopper and peered down. The two vessels looked peaceful enough, he thought as a crewman stepped from the pilothouse and waved a greeting. Nothing unusual or suspicious. The armament he had been warned about was not visible.

He spoke into a microphone. "Have you established radio contact?"

"We've hailed on every marine frequency in the book and they don't answer," replied the pilot from the cockpit.

"Okay, drop us over the barge."

"Roger."

Dodds picked up a bullhorn and spoke into the mouthpiece. "Ahoy, the towboat. This is the U.S. Navy. Reduce speed and slow to a stop. We are coming aboard."

Below, the crewman cupped hands to his ears and shook his head, signaling he couldn't hear above the exhaust whine of the helicopter's turbines. Dodds repeated the message and the crewman made an inviting wave of his arm. By now Dodds was close enough to see he was an Oriental.

The speed of the towboat and barge dropped off, and they began to roll in the swells. The pilot of the helicopter played the wind and hovered over the flat deck of the barge in preparation for Dodds's assault team to jump the final three or four feet.

Dodds turned and took a final look at his men. They were lean and hard, and probably the toughest, raunchiest, meanest bunch of multipurpose killers in the Navy. They were the only group of men Dodds ever commanded who genuinely liked combat. They were eager, their weapons at the ready and prepared for anything. Except, perhaps, for total surprise.

The copter was only ten feet above the barge when trapdoors

were sprung on the towboat, hatch covers thrown back and twenty crewmen opened up with Steyr-Mannlicher AUG assault carbines.

The .223-caliber shells flew into the SEALS from all directions; smoke and the grunts of men being hit erupted simultaneously. Dodds and his men reacted savagely, cutting down any towboat crewman who exposed himself, but bullets sprayed into their cramped compartment as if concentrated out of a firehose and turned it into a slaughter den. There was no escape. They were as helpless as if their backs were against the wall of a dead-end alley.

The noise of the concentrated firepower drowned out the sound of the helicopter's exhaust. The pilot was hit in the first burst, which exploded the canopy, hurling bits of metal and Plexiglas throughout the cockpit. The chopper shuddered and veered sharply around on its axis. The co-pilot wrestled with the controls but they had lost all response.

The Air Force fighters arrived and instantly appraised the situation. Their squadron leader gave hurried instructions and dived, skimming low over the stern of the towboat in an attempt to draw fire away from the battered and smoking helicopter. But the ploy didn't work. They were ignored by Lee Tong's gunners. With growing frustration at the orders not to attack, their passes became ever lower until one pilot clipped off the towboat's radar antenna.

Too badly mauled to remain in the air any longer, the crippled chopper and its pitiful cargo of dead and wounded finally gave up the struggle to remain airborne and fell into the sea beside the barge.

Sandecker and Metcalf sat in shock as the video camera on board the weather plane recorded the drama. The war room became deadly quiet and nobody spoke as they watched and waited for the camera to reveal signs of survivors. Six heads were all they could count in the blue of the sea.

"The end of the game," Metcalf said with chilly finality.

Sandecker didn't answer. He turned away from the screen and sat heavily in a chair beside the long conference table, the pepper-and-vinegar spirit gone out of him.

Metcalf listened without reaction to the voices of the pilots over the speakers. Their anger at not being able to pound the towboat turned vehement. Not told of the people held captive inside the barge, they voiced their anger at the high command, unaware their heated words were heard and recorded at the Pentagon a thousand miles away.

A shadow of a smile touched Sandecker's face. He could not help but sympathize with them.

Then a friendly voice cut in. "Lieutenant Grant calling. Is it okay to call you direct, General?"

"It's all right, son," said Metcalf quietly. "Go ahead."

"I have two ships approaching the area, sir. Stand by for a picture of the first one."

With a new shred of hope, their eyes locked on the screen. At first the image was small and indistinct. Then the weather plane's cameraman zoomed in on a red-hulled vessel.

"From up here I'd judge her to be a survey ship," reported Grant.

A gust of wind caught the flag on the ensign staff and stretched out its blue colors.

"British," announced Metcalf dejectedly. "We don't dare ask foreign nationals to die for our sake."

"You're right, of course. I've never known an oceanographic scientist to carry an automatic rifle."

Metcalf turned and said, "Grant?"

"Sir?"

"Contact the British research vessel and request they pick up survivors from the helicopter."

Before Grant could acknowledge, the video image distorted and the screen went black.

"We've lost your picture, Grant."

"One moment, General. My crewman manning the camera informs me the battery pack on the recorder went dead. He'll have it replaced in a minute."

"What's the situation with the towboat?"

"She and the barge are under way again, only more slowly than before."

Metcalf turned to Sandecker. "Luck just isn't on our side, is it, Jim?"

"No, Clayton. We've had none at all." He hesitated. "Unless, of course, the second ship is an armed Coast Guard cutter."

"Grant?" Metcalf boomed.

"Won't be long, sir."

"Never mind that. What type vessel is the second ship you reported? Coast Guard or Navy?"

"Neither. Strictly civilian."

Metcalf dissolved in defeat, but a spark stirred within Sandecker. He leaned over the microphone.

"Grant, this is Admiral James Sandecker. Can you describe her?"

"She's nothing like you'd expect to see on the ocean."

"What's her nationality?"

"Nationality?"

"Her flag, man. What flag is she flying?"

"You won't believe me."

"Spit it out."

"Well, Admiral, I was born and raised in Montana, but I've read enough history books to recognize a Confederate States flag when I see one."

72

OUT OF A WORLD ALL BUT VANISHED, her brass steam whistle splitting the air, the seawater frothing white beneath her churning paddle wheels, and spewing black smoke from her towering twin stacks, the *Stonewall Jackson* pitched toward the towboat with the awkward grace of a pregnant Southern belle hoisting her hooped skirts while crossing a mud puddle.

Shrieking gulls rode the wind above a giant stern flag displaying the crossed bars and stars of the Confederacy, while on the roof of the texas deck, a man furiously pounded out the old South's national hymn, "Dixie," on the keyboard of an old-fashioned steam calliope. The sight of the old riverboat charging across the sea stirred the souls of the men flying above. They knew they were witnessing an adventure none would see again.

In the ornate pilothouse, Pitt and Giordino stared at the barge and towboat that loomed closer with every revolution of the thirty-foot paddle wheels.

"The man was right," Giordino shouted above the steam whistle and calliope.

"What man?" Pitt asked loudly.

"The one who said, 'Save your Confederate money; the South will rise again.'"

"Lucky for us it has," Pitt said, smiling.

"We're gaining." This from a wiry little man who twisted the six-foot helm with both hands.

"They've lost speed," Pitt concurred.

"If the boilers don't blow, and the sweet old darlin' holds together in these damned waves . . ." The man at the wheel paused in midsentence, made an imperceptible turn of his big white-bearded head and let fly a spurt of tobacco juice with deadly accuracy into a brass cuspidor before continuing. "We ought to overtake 'em in the next two miles."

Captain Melvin Belcheron had skippered the *Stonewall Jackson* for thirty of his sixty-two years. He knew every buoy, bend, sandbar and riverbank light from St. Louis to New Orleans by heart. But this was the first time he'd ever taken his boat into the open sea.

The "sweet old darlin' " was built in 1915 at Columbus, Kentucky, on the Ohio River. Her like was the last to stoke the fires of imagination during the golden years of steamboating, and her like would never be seen again. The smell of burning coal, the swish of the steam engine, and the rhythmic splash of the paddle wheels would soon belong only in the history books.

Her shallow wooden hull was long and beamy, measuring 270 feet by forty-four. Her horizontal noncondensing engines ran at about forty revolutions per minute. She was rated at slightly over one thousand tons, yet despite her bulk, she walked the water with a draft of just thirty-two inches.

Down below on the main deck, four men, sweat-streaked and blackened with soot, furiously shoveled coal into the furnaces under four high-pressure boilers. When the pressure began to creep into the red, the chief engineer, a crusty old Scot by the name of McGeen, hung his hat over the steam gauge.

McGeen was the first man to vote for pursuit after Pitt crash-landed the helicopter in shallow water near Fort Jackson, waded ashore with Giordino and Hogan, and described the situation. At first there was undisguised disbelief, but after seeing their wounds, the bullet-riddled aircraft, and then hearing a deputy sheriff describe the dead and injured FBI agents a few miles downriver, McGeen stoked up his boilers, Belcheron rounded up his deck crew and forty men from the Sixth Louisiana Regiment tramped onboard hooting and hollering and dragging along two ancient field cannon.

"Pour on the coal, boys," McGeen pressed his black gang. He looked like the devil with his trimmed goatee and brushed-up eyebrows in the flickering glare of the open furnace doors. "If we mean to save the Vice President, we've got to have more steam."

The *Stonewall Jackson* thrashed after the towboat and barge, almost as if sensing the urgency of her mission. When new, her top speed was rated at fifteen miles an hour, but in the past forty years she was never called on to provide more than twelve.* She thrust downriver with the current at fourteen, then fifteen . . . sixteen . . . eighteen miles an hour. When she burst from the South Pass Channel, she was driving through the water at twenty, smoke and sparks exploding through the flared capitals atop her stacks.

The men of the Sixth Louisiana Regiment—the dentists, plumbers, accountants who marched and refought battles of the Civil War as a hobby—grunted and sweated in the nondescript woolen gray and butternut uniforms that once clothed the Army of the Confederate States of America. Under the command of a major, they heaved huge cotton bales into place as breastworks. The two Napoleon twelve-pounder cannon from Fort Jackson were wheeled into position on the bow, their smoothbore barrels loaded with ball bearings scrounged from McGeen's engine-room supply locker.

Pitt stared down at the growing fortress of wired bales. Cotton against steel, he mused, single-shot muskets against automatic rifles.

It was going to be an interesting fight.

Lieutenant Grant tore his eyes from the incredible sight under his wings and radioed the ship flying the British flag.

"This is Air Force Weather Recon zero-four-zero calling oceanographic research vessel. Do you read?"

"Righto, Yank. Hear you clearly," came back a cheery voice

---

* Speed on inland waterways is rated in miles per hour, never in knots.

fresh off a cricket field. "This is Her Majesty's Ship *Pathfinder*. What can we do for you, zero-four-zero?"

"A chopper went into the drink about three miles west of you. Can you effect a rescue of survivors, *Pathfinder?*"

"We bloody well better. Can't allow the poor chaps to drown, can we?"

"I'll circle the crash sector, *Pathfinder*. Home in on me."

"Jolly good. We're on our way. Out."

Grant took up a position over the struggling men in the water. The gulf current was warm, so there was no fear of their succumbing to exposure, but any bleeding wounds were certain to attract sharks.

"You don't carry much influence," said his co-pilot.

"What do you mean?" asked Grant.

"The Limey ship isn't responding. She's turned away."

Grant leaned forward and banked the plane to see out the opposite cockpit window. His co-pilot was right. The *Pathfinder*'s bow had come around on a course away from the helicopter's survivors and was aimed toward the *Stonewall Jackson*.

"*Pathfinder*, this is zero-four-zero," Grant called. "What is your problem? Repeat. What is your problem?"

There was no reply.

"Unless I'm suffering one hell of a hallucination," Metcalf said, staring in wonder at the video transmission, "that old relic from *Tom Sawyer* intends to attack the towboat."

"She's giving every indication," Sandecker agreed.

"Where do you suppose she came from?"

Sandecker stood with his arms crossed in front of him, his face radiating an elated expression. "Pitt," he muttered under his breath, "you wily, irrepressible son of a bitch."

"You say something?"

"Just speculating to myself."

"What can they possibly hope to accomplish?"

"I think they mean to ram and board."

"Insanity, sheer insanity," snorted Metcalf gloomily. "The gunners on the towboat will cut them to pieces."

Suddenly Sandecker tensed, seeing something in the background on the screen. Metcalf didn't catch it; no one else watching caught it either.

The admiral grasped Metcalf by the arm. "The British vessel!"

Metcalf looked up, startled. "What about it?"

"Good God, man, see for yourself. She's going to run down the steamboat."

Metcalf saw the distance between the two ships rapidly narrowing, saw the wake of the *Pathfinder* turn to foam as she surged ahead at full speed.

"Grant!" he bellowed.

"Here, sir."

"The Limey ship, why isn't she headed toward the men in the water?"

"I can't say, General. Her skipper acknowledged my request for rescue, but chased after the old paddleboat instead. I haven't been able to raise him again. He appears to be ignoring my transmissions."

"Take them out!" Sandecker demanded. "Call in an air strike and take the bastards out!"

Metcalf hesitated, torn by indecision. "But she's flying the British flag, for Christ's sake."

"I'll stake my rank she's a Bougainville ship, and the flag is a decoy."

"You can't know that."

"Maybe. But I do know that if she crushes the steamboat into firewood, our last chance to save Vince Margolin is gone."

73

IN THE PILOTHOUSE of the towboat a burst of fire from the SEALS had shattered the inner workings of the command console, fouling the rudder controls. Captain Pujon had no option but to reduce speed and steer by jockeying the throttle levers.

Lee Tong did not spare him a glance. He was busy issuing orders over the radio to the commander of the *Pathfinder,* while keeping a wary eye on the wallowing steamboat.

Finally he turned to Pujon. "Can't you regain our top speed?"

"Eight miles is the best I can do if we want to maintain a straight course."

"How far?" he asked for the tenth time that hour.

"According to the depth sounder, the bottom's beginning to drop off. Another two miles should do it."

"Two miles," Lee Tong repeated thoughtfully. "Time to set the detonators."

"I'll alert you by blowing the airhorn when we come over a hundred fathoms," said Pujon.

Lee Tong stared across the dark sea, stained by the runoff from the Mississippi River. The masquerading research ship was only a few hundred yards away from slicing through the brittle side of the *Stonewall Jackson.* He could hear the haunting wail of the calliope drifting with the wind. He shook his head in disbelief, wondering who was responsible for the old riverboat's sudden appearance.

He was about to leave the pilothouse and cross over to the barge when he noticed one of the milling aircraft overhead abruptly slide out of formation and dive toward the sea.

A ghost-white F/A 21 Navy strike aircraft leveled off two hundred feet above the wave tops and unleashed two anti-ship missiles. Lee Tong watched in numbed horror as the laser-controlled warheads skimmed across the water and slammed into the red-hulled decoy ship, stopping her dead in her tracks with a blast that turned the entire upper works into a grotesque tangle of shattered steel. Then came a second, even stronger explosion that enveloped the ship in a ball of flame. For an instant she seemed to hang suspended as if locked in time.

Lee Tong stood tensed in despair as the broken vessel slowly rolled over and died, falling to the floor of the gulf and sealing all hope of his escape.

Fiery fragments of the *Pathfinder* rained down around the *Stonewall Jackson*, igniting several small fires that were quickly extinguished by the crew. The sea surface over the sunken ship turned black with oily bubbles as a hissing cloud of steam and smoke spiraled into the sky.

"Christ in heaven!" Captain Belcheron gasped in astonishment. "Will you look at that. Those Navy boys mean business."

"Somebody is watching over us," Pitt commented thankfully. His eyes returned to the barge. His face was expressionless; but for the swaying of his body to compensate for the roll of the boat, he might have been sculpted from solid teak. The gap had closed to three quarters of a mile, and he could make out the tiny figure of a man scrambling across the bow of the towboat onto the barge before disappearing down a deck hatch.

An enormous man with the stout build of an Oliver Hardy barreled up the ladder from the texas deck and came through the door. He wore the gray uniform and gold braid of a Confederate major. The shirt under the unbuttoned coat was damp with perspiration, and he was panting from exertion. He stood there a moment, wiping his forehead with a sleeve, catching his breath.

At last he said, "Doggone, I don't know if I'd rather die by a bullet in the head, by drowning or a heart attack."

Leroy Laroche operated a travel agency by day, functioned as a loving husband and father by night, and acted as commander of the Sixth Louisiana Regiment of the Confederate States Army on weekends. He was popular among his men and was re-elected every year to lead the regiment in battlefield re-enactments around the country. The fact that he was about to engage in the real thing didn't seem to faze him.

"Lucky for us you had those cotton bales on board," he said to the captain.

Belcheron smiled. "We keep them on deck as historic examples of the sweet old darlin's maritime heritage."

Pitt looked at Laroche. "Your men in position, Major?"

"Loaded, primed full of Dixie beer and rarin' to fight," Laroche replied.

"What sort of weapons do they own?"

"Fifty-eight-caliber Springfield muskets, which most rebels carried late in the war. Shoots a minié ball five hundred yards."

"How fast can they fire?"

"Most of my boys can get off three rounds a minute, a few can do four. But I'm putting the best shots on the barricade while the others load."

"And the cannon? Do they actually fire?"

"You bet. They can hit a tree with a can of cement at half a mile."

"Can of cement?"

"Cheaper to make than real cannon shot."

Pitt considered that and grinned. "Good luck, Major. Tell your men to keep their heads down. Muzzle loaders take more time to aim than machine guns."

"I reckon they know how to duck," said Laroche. "When do you want us to open fire?"

"I leave that to you."

"Excuse me, Major," Giordino cut in. "Did any of your men happen to carry a spare weapon?"

Laroche unsnapped the leather holster on his belt and passed

Giordino a large pistol. "A Le Mat revolver," he said. "Shoots nine forty-two-caliber shells through a rifled barrel. But if you'll notice, there's a big smoothbore barrel underneath that holds a charge of buckshot. Take good care of it. My great-granddaddy carried it from Bull Run to Appomattox."

Giordino was genuinely impressed. "I don't want to leave you unarmed."

Laroche pulled his saber from its scabbard. "This will do me just fine. Well, I best get back to my men."

After the big jovial major left the pilothouse, Pitt bent down and opened the violin case, lifted out the Thompson and inserted a full drum. He held his side with one hand and cautiously straightened, his lips pressed tight from the pain that speared his chest.

"You be all right up here?" he asked Belcheron.

"Don't pay no mind to me," the captain answered. He nodded at a cast-iron potbellied stove. "I'll have my own armor when the fireworks start."

"Thank God for that," exclaimed Metcalf.

"What is it?" Sandecker asked.

Metcalf held up a paper. "A reply from the British Admiralty in London. The only *Pathfinder* on duty with the Royal Navy is a missile destroyer. They have no research ship by that name, nor is there any in the gulf area." He gave Sandecker a thankful look.

"You called a good play, Jim."

"We had a bit of luck after all."

"The poor bastards on that steamboat are the ones who need it now."

"Any more we can do? Anything we've overlooked?"

Metcalf shook his head. "Not from this end. The Coast Guard cutter is only fifteen minutes away and the nuclear sub is not far behind."

"Neither will arrive in time."

"Perhaps the people on the steamboat can somehow stall the tugboat until . . ." Metcalf didn't finish.

"You don't really believe in miracles, do you, Clayton?"

"No, I guess I don't."

74

A MAELSTROM OF AUTOMATIC WEAPONS FIRE lashed into the *Stonewall Jackson* as Lee Tong's crew opened up at three hundred yards. Bullets hummed and whistled, splintering the gleaming white wood and gingerbread carvings on the rails and deck cabins, clanging and ricocheting off the ship's bronze bell. The huge unglazed window in the pilothouse disintegrated into silvery fragments. Inside, Captain Belcheron was stunned by a shell that grazed the top of his head and turned his white hair red. His vision blurred and went double, but he hung on to the spokes of the great wheel with savage determination while hawking tobacco juice out the broken window.

The calliope player, protected by a forest of brass plumbing, began playing "Yellow Rose of Texas," which fell on several flat tones as holes suddenly appeared in his steam whistles.

On the main deck, Major Laroche and his regiment, along with Pitt and Giordino, crouched out of sight. The cotton bales made strong defensive works, and no bullets penetrated. The open boiler area behind the main staircase caught the worst of it. Two of McGeen's stokers were hit and the overhead tubing was penetrated, allowing steam to escape in scalding streams. McGeen took his hat off the pressure gauge. It was pegged in the red. He expelled a long sigh. A miracle nothing had burst, he thought. The rivets were straining on the boilers. He quickly began spinning relief valves to let off the immense pressure in preparation for the coming collision.

The *Stonewall Jackson*'s paddle wheels were still driving her at twenty miles an hour. If she had to die, she was not going to end up like her former sisters, rotting away in some forgotten bayou or broken up for wharf wood. She was going out a legend and ending her life on the water in style.

Brushing aside the waves that pounded her bow, shrugging off the frightful torrent of lead that shredded her flimsy superstructure, she forged ahead.

Lee Tong watched in bitter fascination as the steamboat came on steadily. He stood in an open hatch on the barge and poured a stream of bullets at her, hoping to hit a vital part and slow her down. But he might as well have been shooting air pellets at a rampaging elephant.

He set aside his Steyr-Mannlicher carbine and raised the binoculars. None of the crew was visible behind the barricade of cotton bales. Even the sieved pilothouse looked deserted. The gold letters of the smashed nameplate were visible, but all he could make out was the name JACKSON.

The flat bow was pointed square for the towboat's port side. It was a stupid, futile gesture, he reasoned, a stalling technique, nothing more. In spite of its superior size, the wooden paddle steamer could not expect to damage the towboat's steel hull.

He retrieved the Steyr-Mannlicher, inserted another ammo clip and concentrated his fire into the pilothouse in an attempt to damage the helm.

Sandecker and Metcalf watched too.

They sat captivated by the hopeless, irresistible magnificence of it all. Radio contact was attempted with the steamboat, but there was no response. Captain Belcheron had been too busy to answer, and the old river rat didn't think he had anything worth saying anyway.

Metcalf called Lieutenant Grant. "Spiral in closer," he ordered.

Grant acknowledged and made a series of tight banks over the vessels below. The detail of the towboat was quite sharp. They could pick out nearly thirty men blasting away across the water. The steamboat, however, was obscured by the smoke shooting from her stacks and great clouds of exhaust steam spurting out of the "scape pipes" aft of the pilothouse.

"She'll bash herself to bits when she strikes," said Sandecker.

"It's glorious but meaningless," Metcalf muttered.

"Give them credit. They're doing more than we can."

Metcalf nodded slowly. "Yes, we can't take that away from them."

Sandecker came out of his chair and pointed. "Look there, on the steamboat where the wind has blown the smoke off to the side."

"What is it?"

"Isn't that a pair of cannon?"

Metcalf came alert. "By God, you're right. They look like old monuments from a town park."

At two hundred yards Laroche raised his sword and yelled, "Batteries one and two, train and prime your guns."

"Battery one primed and aimed," shouted back a man in antique wire spectacles.

"Battery two ready, Major."

"Then fire!"

The lanyards were jerked and the two antique cannon belched their loads of ballbearing grapeshot from their muzzles in earsplitting claps. The first shot actually penetrated the side of the towboat, crashing into the galley and mangling the ovens. The second soared into the pilothouse, taking off Captain Pujon's head and carrying away the wheel. Dazed by the unexpected barrage, Lee Tong's men slackened their fire for several seconds, recovered and opened up with renewed ferocity, concentrating on the narrow slits between the cotton bales where the cannon barrels protruded.

Now the smoothbores were run back while the artillery men quickly rammed home the sponges and began reloading. Bullets whined over their heads and shoulders, and one man was struck in

450

the neck. But in less than a minute the old Napoleons were ready to blast again.

"Aim for the cables!" Pitt shouted. "Cut the barge away!"

Laroche nodded and relayed Pitt's orders. The guns were run out and the next broadside swept the towboat's bow, causing an explosion of coiled rope and cable, but the tenacious grip on the barge remained unbroken.

Coldly, almost contemptuous of the deadly blitz that swept the *Stonewall Jackson,* the make-believe soldiers lined up the sights on their single-shot muskets and waited for the command to fire.

Only two hundred yards separated the vessels when Laroche raised his sword again. "Firing rank, take aim. Okay, boys, give 'em hell. Fire!"

The front of the steamboat exploded in a tremendous torrent of fire and smoke. The towboat was raked with a seemingly solid wall of minié bullets. The effect was devastating. Glass dissolved in every port and window, paint chips flew off the bulkheads and bodies began falling, deluging the decks with blood.

Before Lee Tong's gunners could recover, Pitt stitched the towboat from bow to stern with a steady stream of fire from the Thompson. Giordino hunched against the cotton barricade, waiting for the range to close to fire the revolver, watching in rapt interest as the second and third ranks ran through the dozen cumbersome procedures of rearming a muzzle-loading musket.

The Confederates laid down a killing fire. Volley after volley followed in succession, almost every other shot striking flesh and bone. The smoke and shattering sounds were punctuated by the cries of the wounded. Laroche, swept away by the carnage and commotion, thundered and swore at the top of his lungs, prodding his sharpshooters to aim true, exhorting the loaders to move more rapidly.

One minute passed, two, then three, as the fighting reached a savage pitch. Fire broke out on the *Jackson* and flames soared up her wooden sides. In the pilothouse, Captain Belcheron yanked on the whistle cord and shouted into the voice tube leading to McGeen in the engine area. The riflemen ceased their fire and everyone braced themselves for the approaching collision.

A strange, unearthly silence fell over the steamboat as the crack of the guns faded and the haunting wail of the calliope died away. She was like a boxer who had taken a fearful beating from a far stronger adversary and could take no more, but had somehow reached deep into her exhausted reserves for one last knockout punch.

She struck the towboat square amidships with a rumbling crunch that knocked over the cotton-bale barricade, crushing back her bow by six feet as planks and beams gave way like laths. Both stacks fell forward, throwing sparks and smoke over the battle that rapidly resumed its intensity. Guns fired at point-blank range. The support ropes burned through and the landing stages dropped onto the towboat's decks like great claws gripping the two vessels fast together.

"Fix bayonets!" Laroche boomed.

Someone broke out the regiment's battle flag and began waving it wildly in the air. Muskets were reloaded and bayonets attached. The calliope player had returned to his post and was pounding out "Dixie" once again. Pitt was amazed that no one showed any sign of fear. Instead, there was a general feeling of uncontrolled delirium. He couldn't help thinking he'd somehow crossed a time barrier into the past.

Laroche whipped off his officer's hat, hung it on the tip of his sword and raised it into the air. "Sixth Louisiana!" he cried. "Go git 'em!"

Screaming the rebel yell like demons emerging from the center of the earth, the men in gray stormed onboard the towboat. Laroche was struck in the chin and one knee, but hobbled and pressed on. Pitt laid down a covering fire until the last cartridge poured from the Thompson. Then he laid the gun on a cotton bale and charged after Giordino, who hopped across a landing stage, favoring his injured leg and firing the revolver like a wild man. McGeen and his boiler crew followed, wielding their shovels like clubs.

Bougainville's men bore no resemblance to their attackers. They were hired killers, ruthless men who offered no mercy nor expected it, but they were not prepared for the incredible onslaught of the Southerners and made the mistake of leaping from the protected steel bulkheads and meeting the surge head-on.

The *Stonewall Jackson* was wreathed in fire. The artillery men fired one last volley at the towboat, aiming forward of the men fighting amidships, their shot sweeping away the cables attached to the barge. Shoved sideways by the continued momentum of the steamboat, the two steel vessels jackknifed around her crushed bow.

The Sixth Louisiana overran the decks, lunging with their bayonets, but keeping up a deadly rate of fire. There were a score of individual hand-to-hand struggles, the five-foot Springfield musket and two-foot bayonet making a nasty close-in weapon. None of the weekend soldiers paused; they fought with a strange kind of recklessness, too caught up in the unimaginable din and excitement to be afraid.

Giordino didn't feel the blow. He was steadily advancing into the crew's quarters, firing at any Oriental face that showed itself when suddenly he was flat on his face, a bullet breaking the calf bone of his good leg.

Pitt lifted Giordino under the arms and dragged him into an empty passageway. "You're not armor-plated, you know."

"Where in hell have you been?" Giordino's voice tensed as the pain increased.

"Staying out of the way," Pitt replied. "I'm not armed."

Giordino handed him the Le Mat revolver. "Take this. I'm through for the day anyway."

Pitt gave his friend a half-smile. "Sorry to leave you, but I've got to get inside the barge."

Giordino opened his mouth to make an offhand reply, but Pitt was already gone. Ten seconds and he was snaking through the debris on the towboat's bow. He was almost too late. A head and pair of shoulders raised from a hatch and fired off a burst. Pitt felt the passing bullets fan his hair and cheek. He dropped to the railing and rolled over the side into the sea.

Further aft, the Bougainville crew grimly hung on, obstinately giving way until they were finally overwhelmed by gray uniforms. The shouting and the gunfire slackened and went silent. The Confederate battle flag was run up the towboat's radio mast and the fight was over.

The amateur soldiers of the Sixth Louisiana Regiment had handled themselves well. Surprisingly, none had been killed in the melee. Eighteen were wounded, only two seriously. Laroche staggered from the midst of his cheering men and sagged to the deck beside Giordino. He reached over and the two bleeding men solemnly shook hands.

"Congratulations, Major," Giordino said. "You just made the playoffs."

A big grin spread across Laroche's bloodied face. "By God, we whipped 'em good, didn't we?"

Lee Tong emptied his weapon at the figure on the bow of the towboat, observing it fall into the water. Then he slumped against the edge of the hatch and watched the Confederate battle flag flutter in the gulf breeze.

With a kind of detachment, he accepted the unexpected disaster which had overtaken his carefully conceived operation. His crew was either dead or prisoner, and his escape ship was destroyed. Yet he was not ready to oblige his unknown opponents by surrendering. He was determined to carry out his grandmother's bargain with Moran and take his chances on escaping later.

He dropped down the side ladder of the elevator shaft into the laboratory quarters and ran along the main corridor until he came to the door of the chamber that held the isolation cocoons. He entered and peered through the insulated plastic lid at the body within the first one. Vince Margolin stared back, his body too numb to respond, his mind too drugged to comprehend.

Lee Tong moved to the next cocoon and looked down at the serene, sleeping face of Loren Smith. She was heavily sedated and in a deep state of unconsciousness. Her death would be a waste, he thought. But she could not be allowed to live and testify. He leaned over and opened the cover and stroked her hair, staring at her through half-open eyes.

He had killed countless men, their features forgotten less than seconds after their death. But the faces of the women lingered. He remembered the first, so many years ago on a tramp steamer in the middle of the Pacific Ocean: her haunting expression of bewilderment as her chained nude body was dropped over the side.

"Nice place you have here," came a voice from the doorway, "but your elevator is out of order."

Lee Tong spun around and gaped at the man who stood wet and dripping, pointing a strange antique revolver at his chest.

"You!" he gasped.

Pitt's face—tired, haggard and dark with beard stubble—lit up in a smile. "Lee Tong Bougainville. What a coincidence."

"You're alive!"

"A trite observation."

"And responsible for all this: those mad men in the old uniforms, the riverboat . . ."

"The best I could arrange on the spur of the moment," Pitt said apologetically.

Lee Tong's moment of utter confusion passed and he slowly curled his finger around the trigger of the Steyr-Mannlicher that hung loosely in one hand, muzzle aimed at the carpeted deck.

"Why have you pursued my grandmother and me, Mr. Pitt?" he demanded, stalling. "Why have you set out to wreck Bougainville Maritime?"

"That's like Hitler asking why the Allies invaded Europe. In my case, you were responsible for the death of a friend."

"Who?"

"It doesn't matter," said Pitt indifferently. "You never met her."

Lee Tong swung up the barrel of his carbine and pulled the trigger.

Pitt was faster, but Giordino had used up the last cartridge and the revolver's hammer fell on an empty cylinder. He stiffened, expecting the impact of a bullet.

It never came.

Lee Tong had forgotten to insert a new clip after firing his final round at Pitt on the towboat. He lowered the carbine, his lips stretched into an inscrutable smile. "It seems we have a standoff, Mr. Pitt."

"Only temporary," said Pitt, recocking the hammer and keeping the revolver raised and aimed. "My people will be coming aboard any minute now."

Lee Tong sighed and relaxed. "Then I can do little else but surrender and wait for arrest."

"You'll never stand trial."

The smile turned into a sneer. "That's not for you to decide. Besides, you're hardly in a position to—"

Suddenly he flipped the carbine around, gripping the barrel and raising it as a club. The rifle butt was on a vicious downswing when Pitt squeezed the trigger and blasted Lee Tong in the throat with the barrel loaded with buckshot. The carbine poised in midair and then fell from his hand as he stumbled backward until striking the wall and dropping heavily to the deck.

Pitt left him where he lay and threw off the cover over Loren's cocoon. He gently lifted her out and carried her to the open elevator. He checked the circuit breakers and found them on, but there was still no response from the lift motors when he pressed the "up" button.

He had no way of knowing the generators that provided electricity to the barge had run out of fuel and shut down, leaving only the emergency battery power to illuminate the overhead lighting. Scrounging through a supply locker, he found a rope, which he tied under Loren's arms. Then he pulled himself through the elevator roof's trapdoor and scaled the shaft ladder to the top deck of the barge.

Slowly, gently, he eased Loren's body upward until she lay on the rusting deck. Winded, he took a minute to catch his breath and look around. The *Stonewall Jackson* was still burning fiercely, but the flames were being fought with firehoses from the towboat. About two miles to the west a white Coast Guard cutter was driving through the light swells toward their position, while to the south he could just make out the sail tower of a nuclear submarine.

Taking a short length of the rope, Pitt tied Loren loosely to a cleat so she wouldn't roll into the sea, then he returned below. When he entered the isolation chamber again, Lee Tong was gone. A trail of blood led up the corridor and ended at an open hatch to a storage deck below. He saw no reason to waste time on a dying murderer and turned to rescue the Vice President.

Before he took two steps, a tremendous blast lifted him off his feet and hurled him face downward twenty feet away. The impact from the concussion drove the breath from his lungs and the ringing in his ears prevented him from hearing the sea rush in through a gaping hole torn in the hull of the barge.

Pitt awkwardly raised himself to his hands and knees and tried to orient himself. Then slowly, as the haze before his eyes melted away, he realized what had happened and what was coming. Lee Tong had detonated an explosive charge before he died and already the water was flowing across a corridor deck.

Pitt pushed himself to his feet and reeled drunkenly into the isolation chamber again. The Vice President looked up at him and tried to say something, but before he could utter a sound, Pitt had hoisted him over a shoulder and was lurching toward the elevator.

The water was surging around Pitt's knees now, splashing up the walls. He knew only seconds were left before the barge began its dive to the seabed. By the time he reached the open elevator, the sea was up to his chest and he half walked, half swam inside. It was too late to repeat the rope lift procedure. Furiously he manhandled Margolin through the ceiling trapdoor, clasped him under the chest and began climbing the iron ladder to the tiny square patch of blue sky that seemed miles away.

He remembered then that he had tied Loren to the upper deck to keep her from rolling into the sea. The sickening thought coursed through him that she would be pulled to her death when the barge sank.

Beyond fear lies desperation, and beyond that a raging drive to survive that cuts across the boundaries of suffering and exhaustion.

Some men yield to hopelessness, some try to sidestep its existence, while a very few accept and face it head-on.

Watching the froth tenaciously dog his rise up the elevator shaft, Pitt fought with every shred of his will to save the lives of Margolin and Loren. His arms felt as if they were tearing from their sockets. White spots burst before his eyes and the strain on his cracked ribs passed from mere pain to grinding agony.

His grip loosened on flakes of rust and he almost fell backward into the water boiling at his heels. It would have been so easy to surrender, to let go and drop into oblivion and release the torture that racked his body. But he hung on. Rung by rung, he struggled upward, Margolin's dead weight becoming heavier with each step.

His ears regained a partial sense of hearing and picked up a strange thumping sound, which Pitt wrote off as blood pounding in his head. The sea rose above his feet now, and the barge shuddered; it was about to go under.

A nightmare world closed in on him. A black shape loomed above, and then his hand reached out and clasped another hand.

Accounting

The Liftonic QW-607

75

HOUSE SPEAKER ALAN MORAN, his face wreathed in a confident smile, circulated around the East Room of the White House conversing with his aides and inner circle of advisers while awaiting final word of the trial taking place on the floor of the Senate.

He greeted a small group of party leaders and then turned and excused himself as Secretary of State Douglas Oates and Defense Secretary Jesse Simmons entered the room. Moran came over and held out his hand, which Oates ignored.

Moran shrugged off the snub. He could well afford to. "Well, it seems you're not of a mind to praise Caesar, but you haven't a prayer of burying him either."

"You've just reminded me of an old gangster movie I saw when I was a boy," Oates said icily. "The title fits you perfectly."

"Oh, really? What movie was that?"

"Little Caesar."

Moran's smile turned into a sinister glare. "Have you come with your resignation?"

Oates pulled an envelope partway out of his inside breast pocket. "I have it right here."

"Keep it!" Moran snarled. "I won't give you the satisfaction of bowing out gracefully. Ten minutes after I take the oath I'm holding a press conference. Besides assuring the nation of a smooth succession, I intend to announce that you and the rest of the President's Cabinet planned a conspiracy to set up a dictatorship, and my first order as chief executive is to fire the whole rotten lot of you."

"We expected no less. Integrity was never one of your character traits."

"There was no conspiracy and you know it," Simmons said angrily. "The President was the victim of a Soviet plot to control the White House."

"No matter," Moran replied nastily. "By the time the truth comes out, the damage to your precious reputations will have been done. You'll never work in Washington again."

Before Oates and Simmons could retort, an aide rushed up and spoke softly in Moran's ear. He dismissed his enemies with a snide look and turned away. Then he stepped to the center of the room and raised his hands for silence.

"Ladies and gentlemen," he announced. "I've just been informed that the Senate has voted for conviction by the required two-thirds. Our beleaguered President is no longer in office and the Vice Presidency is vacant. The time has come for us to put our house in order and begin anew."

As if on cue, Chief Justice Nelson O'Brien rose from a chair, smoothed his black robes and cleared his throat. Everyone crowded around Moran as his secretary held what was dubiously touted as his family Bible.

Just then Sam Emmett and Dan Fawcett came through the doorway and paused. Then they spied Oates and Simmons and approached.

"Any word?" Oates asked anxiously.

Emmett shook his head. "None. General Metcalf ordered a communications blackout. I haven't been able to reach him at the Pentagon to find out why."

"Then it's all over."

No one replied as they all turned in unison and stood in powerless frustration as Moran raised his right hand to take the oath of office as President, his left hand on the Bible.

"Repeat after me," Chief Justice O'Brien intoned like a drum roll. "I, Alan Robert Moran, do solemnly swear . . ."

". . . that I will faithfully execute the office of the President of the United States," O'Brien droned on.

Suddenly the room behind Oates went quiet. The prompting of the oath by the Chief Justice went unanswered by Moran. Curious, Oates turned around and looked at the crowd. They were all staring in frozen wonder at Vice President Vincent Margolin, who walked through the doorway preceded by Oscar Lucas and flanked by General Metcalf and Admiral Sandecker.

Moran's upraised arm slowly fell and his face turned ashen. The silence smothered the room like an insulating cloud as Margolin stepped up to the Chief Justice, the stunned audience parting for him. He gave Moran a frigid look and then smiled at the rest.

"Thank you for the rehearsal," he said warmly. "But I think I can take over from here."

76

August 13, 1989
New York City

SAL CASIO WAS WAITING in the vast lobby of the World Trade Center when Pitt came slowly through the entrance. Casio looked at him in stark appraisal. He couldn't remember when he'd seen any man so near the edge of physical collapse.

Pitt moved with the tired shuffle of a man who had endured too much. He wore a borrowed foul-weather jacket two sizes too small. His right arm hung slack while his left was pressed against his chest, as if holding it together, and his face was etched in a strange blending of suffering and triumph. The eyes burned with a sinister glow that Casio recognized as the fires of revenge.

"I'm glad you could make it," Casio said without referring to Pitt's haggard appearance.

"It's your show," said Pitt. "I'm only along for the ride."

"Only fitting and proper we be together at the finish."

"I appreciate the courtesy. Thank you."

Casio turned and guided Pitt over to a private elevator. Pulling a small push-button transmitter from his pocket, he punched the correct code and the doors opened. Inside was an unconscious guard who was bound with laundry cord. Casio stepped over him and opened a polished brass door to a circuit panel with the words LIFTONIC ELEVATOR QW-607 engraved on it. He made an adjustment in the settings and then pushed the button that read "100."

The elevator rose like a rocket and Pitt's ears popped three times before it slowed and the doors finally opened onto the richly furnished anteroom of Bougainville Maritime Lines Inc.

Before he stepped out, Casio paused and reprogrammed the elevator circuitry with his transmitter. Then he turned and stepped out onto the thick carpet.

"We're here to speak with Min Koryo," Casio announced mundanely.

The woman eyed them suspiciously, particularly Pitt, and opened a leather-bound journal. "I see nothing in Madame Bougainville's schedule that shows any appointments this evening."

Casio's face furrowed into his best hurt look. "Are you sure?" he asked, leaning over the desk and peering at the appointment book.

She pointed at the blank page. "Nothing is written in—"

Casio chopped her across the nape of the neck with the edge of his palm, and she fell forward, head and shoulders striking the desktop. Then he reached inside her blouse and extracted a vestpocket .25-caliber automatic pistol.

"Never know it to look at her," he explained, "but she's a security guard."

Casio tossed the gun to Pitt and took off down a corridor hung with paintings of the Bougainville Maritime fleet. Pitt recognized the *Pilottown*, and his weary expression hardened. He followed the brawny private investigator up an intricately carved rosewood circular staircase to the living quarters above. At the top of the landing Casio met another ravishing Asian woman who was leaving a bathroom. She was wearing silk lounging pajamas with a kimono top.

Her eyes widened and in a lightning reflex she lashed out with one foot at Casio's groin. He anticipated the thrust and shifted his weight ever so slightly, catching the blow on the side of his thigh. Then she flashed into the classic judo position and hurled several rapid cuts at his head.

She would have done more damage to an oak tree. Casio shook off her attack, crouched and sprung like an offensive back coming off the line. She spun to her left in an impressive display of feline grace but was knocked off balance by his shoulder. Then Casio straightened and smashed through her defense with a vicious left hook that nearly tore off her head. Her feet left the floor and she flew into a five-foot-high Sung Dynasty vase, breaking it into dust.

"You certainly have a way with women," Pitt remarked casually.

"Lucky for us there's still a few things we can do better than they can."

Casio motioned toward a large double door carved with dragons and quietly opened it. Min Koryo was propped up in her spacious bed, browsing through a pile of audit reports. For a moment the two men stood mute and unmoving, waiting for her to look up and acknowledge their intrusion. She looked so pathetic, so fragile, that any other trespassers might have wavered. But not Pitt and Casio.

Finally she lifted her reading glasses and gazed at them, showing no apprehension or fright. Her eyes were fixed in frank curiosity.

"Who are you?" she asked simply.

"My name is Sal Casio. I'm a private investigator."

"And the other man?"

Pitt stepped from the shadows and stood under the glow from the spotlights above the bed. "I believe you know me."

There was a faint flicker of surprise in her voice, but nothing else. "Mr. Dirk Pitt."

"Yes."

"Why have you come?"

"You are a slimy parasite who sucked the life out of untold innocent people to build your filthy empire. You're responsible for the death of a personal friend of mine and also for that of Sal's daughter. You tried to kill me, and you ask why I'm here?"

"You are mistaken, Mr. Pitt. I am guilty of nothing so criminal. My hands are unstained."

"A play on words. You live in your museum of Oriental arti-

466

facts, shielded from the outside world, while your grandson did your dirty work for you."

"You say I am the cause of your friend's death?"

"She was killed by the nerve agent you stole from the government and left on the *Pilottown.*"

"I'm sorry for your loss," she said gently. The politeness and sympathy were without a trace of irony. "And you, Mr. Casio. How am I to blame for your daughter?"

"She was murdered along with the crew of the same ship, only then it was called the *San Marino.*"

"Yes, I recall," said Min Koryo, dropping all pretense. "The girl with the stolen money."

Pitt stared into the old woman's face, examining it. The blue eyes were bright and glistening, and the skin was smooth, with only a bare hint of aging lines. She must have truly been a beautiful woman once. But beneath the veneer Pitt detected ugliness, a cesspool locked in ice. There was a black malignity inside her that filled him with contempt.

"I suppose you've smashed so many lives," he said, "you've become immune to human suffering. The mystery is how you got away with it for so long."

"You have come to arrest me?" she asked.

"No," Casio answered stonily. "To kill you."

The piercing eyes blazed briefly. "My security people will come through the door any second."

"We've already eliminated the guard at the receptionist's desk and the one outside your door. As to others"—Casio paused and pointed a finger at a TV camera mounted above her bed—"I've reprogrammed the tapes. Your guards at the monitors are watching whatever occurred in your bedroom a week ago last night."

"My grandson will hunt you both down, and your punishment will not be quick."

"Lee Tong is dead," Pitt informed her, relishing every syllable.

The face altered. Now the blood flowed out of it and it became a pale yellow. But not with the emotions of shock and hurt, Pitt thought. She was waiting, waiting for something. Then the flicker of expectancy vanished as quickly as it had come.

"I do not believe you," she said at last.

"He sank with the laboratory barge after I shot him."

Casio moved around to the side of the bed. "You must come with us now."

"May I ask where you're taking me?" The voice was still soft and gracious. The blue eyes remained set.

They didn't notice her right hand move beneath the covers.

Pitt never really accounted for the instinctive move that saved his life. Maybe it was the sudden realization that the TV camera was not exactly shaped like a camera. Maybe it was the complete absence of fear in Min Koryo, or the aura that she was in firm command, but as the beam of light stabbed out from above her bed, he pitched himself to the floor.

Pitt rolled to his side, tugging the automatic from his coat. Out of the corner of his eye he saw the laser beam sweep the room, cutting through furniture, scorching the draperies and wallpaper with a needle-thin spear of energy. The gun was in his hands, blasting away at the electron amplifier. At his fourth shot, the beam blinked out.

Casio was still standing. He reached out toward Pitt and then stumbled and fell. The laser had cut through his stomach as neatly as a surgeon's scalpel. He twisted over on his back and stared up. Casio was seconds away from death. Pitt wanted to say something, but he couldn't get the words out.

The case-hardened old investigator raised his head; his voice came in a rasping whisper. "The elevator . . . code four-one-one-six." And then his eyes went sightless and his breathing ceased.

Pitt took the transmitter from Casio's pocket, rose and trained the automatic just ten inches from Min Koryo's heart. Her face was locked in a fearless smile. Then Pitt lowered the gun and reached under the covers and silently lifted her out of the bed into her wheelchair.

She made no move to resist, spoke no words of defiance. She sat, wizened and mute, as Pitt pushed her into the corridor and onto a small lift that lowered them to the office floor. When they reached the reception lobby, she noted the unconscious security guard and looked up at him.

"What now, Mr. Pitt?"

"The final curtain for Bougainville Maritime," he said. "Tomorrow your rotten business will be no more. Your Oriental art objects will be given away to museums. A new tenant will come in and redecorate your offices and living quarters. In fact, your entire fleet of ships will be sold off. From now on the name of Bougainville will be nothing but a distant memory in newspaper microfilm files. No friends or relatives will mourn you, and I'll personally see that you're buried in a potter's field with no marker."

At last he had broken through and her face revealed a searing hate. "And *your* future, Mr. Pitt?"

He grinned. "I'm going to rebuild the car you blew up."

She weakly lifted herself from the wheelchair and spat at him. Pitt made no move to wipe away the spittle. He simply stood there and grinned wickedly, looked down and saw the evil viciousness erupt as she cursed him in Korean.

Pitt pressed the code numbers Casio had given him into the transmitter and watched as the doors to Liftonic QW-607 opened.

But there was no elevator, only an empty shaft.

"*Bon voyage,* you diabolic old crone."

Then he shoved the wheelchair into the vacant opening and stood listening as it clattered like a pebble down a well, echoing off the sides of the shaft until there was the faint sound of impact a hundred stories below.

Loren was sitting on a bench in the concourse as he came through the main door of the Trade Center. She came toward him and they met and embraced. They clung together without saying anything for a few moments.

She could feel the fatigue and the pain in him. And she sensed something more. A strange inner peace that she had never known was there. She kissed him lightly several times. Then she took his arm and led him to a waiting taxi.

"Sal Casio?" she asked.

"With his daughter."

"And Min Koryo Bougainville?"

"In hell."

She caught the distant look in his eyes. "You need rest. I'd better check you into a hospital."

Suddenly the old devilish look flashed on his face. "I had something else in mind."

"What?"

"The next week in a suite in the best hotel in Manhattan. Champagne, gourmet dinners sent up by room service, you making love to me."

A coquettish expression gleamed in her eyes. "Why do I have to do all the work?"

"Obviously I'm in no condition to take command."

She held on to him comfortingly. "I suppose it's the least I can do after you saved my life."

"*Semper Paratus,*" he said.

"*Semper* what?"

"The Coast Guard motto. Always Ready. If their rescue helicopter hadn't arrived over the barge when it did, we'd both be lying on the bottom of the Gulf of Mexico."

They reached the taxi and Loren held on to Pitt as he stiffly entered and sank into the seat. She eased in beside him and kissed his hand while the driver sat patiently looking out his windshield.

"Where to?" the driver asked.

"The Helmsley Palace Hotel," Pitt answered.

Loren looked at him. "You're getting a suite at the Helmsley?" she said.

"A penthouse suite," he corrected her.

"And who's going to pay for this opulent interlude?"

Pitt looked down at her in mock astonishment. "Why, the government, of course. Who else?"

New York Times bestselling author

CLIVE CUSSLER

THE SEA HUNTERS

True Adventures with Famous Shipwrecks

With the same wonderful storytelling that Clive Cussler brings to his novels, he describes his searches for such ships as the *Cumberland*, *Florida*, HMS *Pathfinder*, *Merrimack*, the *Hunley* submarine, *Richmond*, and the Lost Locomotive of Kiowa Creek. It's a must read for all who are fascinated by nonfiction accounts of the sea, great ships and those who sailed on them.

Available in paperback
from
Pocket Books

1219-01